PILGRIM HYMNAL

THE PILGRIM PRESS

01   00   99   98   34   33   32   31

Library of Congress Catalog Card Number: M 58-1015

Designed by Burton L. Stratton

Printed in the United States of America

ISBN 0-8298-0107-3 (red binding)
ISBN 0-8298-0460-9 (blue binding)
ISBN 0-8298-0454-4 (red spiral organist binding)

The Pilgrim Press, Cleveland, Ohio

Preface

THE HYMNBOOK has a central place in the worship of the church. The psalmist invites us to "sing to the Lord a new song." St. Paul urges the churches to praise God "in psalms and hymns and spiritual songs." The Reformation began in a burst of congregational singing. In our worship the people have always taken an active and significant part, and a zeal for corporate worship has featured every period of renewal within Protestantism. Our hymnbook, therefore, bears testimony to our concern that worship should be first and foremost an act of prayer and praise to God, understood and entered into by the whole company of the faithful.

This is especially true for those of us who stand within the Protestant tradition. By our hymns we mark the changing yet recurring accents of the Christian year; we balance and deepen our devotional life; we convey to members of each congregation the meanings of the gospel and voice the corporate claims and loyalties of our faith.

Every generation responds to the call of Christ in its own distinctive way. There is need for periodic revision of our hymnals, none of which can contain, in any case, more than a fraction of the great store of texts and tunes available for congregational worship gathered over the centuries.

This book was first conceived as a revision of the *Pilgrim Hymnal* of 1931, but the recent developments in hymnody, in church life, and in world history have made it necessary to plan our work in larger terms. Although making wide use of that hymnal, the present volume draws more heavily on the best hymnody of the Church Universal, while at the same time making fuller use of our particular heritage: the *Genevan Psalters*, the Bay Psalm Book, Isaac Watts — all the richness of the Reformed and Free Church traditions. Elements have also been incorporated from older musical and liturgical sources which have been long neglected and surrendered by default. Finally, looking to the future, the hymnal has benefited from the broadening and enriching impetus of the ecumenical movement.

The hymns in this book have been selected and arranged by a committee appointed by The Pilgrim Press. This committee has met at regu-

v

PREFACE

lar and frequent intervals during the past four and one-half years. By
means of questionnaires, seminars, interim reports, and correspondence
we have obtained the counsel of our church people across the land re-
garding their usage and preference in the singing of hymns. Careful re-
search has been done to guarantee the integrity of texts and tunes. We
have profited from the help of church musicians, pastors, and many
other interested individuals. Every hymn considered was brought be-
fore the full committee and a common decision made as to its omission
or inclusion. All this has helped to insure the representative and responsible character of the committee's work.

It is a pleasure to record here our special gratitude to our music editors,
Dr. and Mrs. Hugh Porter, who have shared their learning and experience with us, and have brought wise counsel and sensitive judgment to
our task. To our executive secretary, the Reverend Albert C. Ronander,
and to Mrs. Arthur A. Morrison, we are deeply grateful. They have
borne the burden of detailed responsibilities with imagination, vigor, and
thoroughness. To Dr. Ruth E. Messenger for invaluable critical and
scholarly assistance, and to Dr. Charles L. Atkins for help in preparing
the topical index; and to the many others who have given freely of their
knowledge, experience, and insight, we give our thanks.

As this new hymnbook enters into the hearts and minds of our fellow
church members, we pray that it will bring fresh strength and inspiration
to our common worship — as it has for us. It has been a privilege to
serve the church in the preparation of this hymnal and we offer it to
you now with our prayer that by the means provided herein, God may
be rightly praised and loved, according to the power of the Spirit that
worketh in us, through Jesus Christ our Lord.

THE HYMNAL COMMITTEE

James W. Lenhart, *Chairman*

Charles A. Butts	Roger Hazelton
Ross Cannon	Fred Hoskins
Truman B. Douglass	Elden H. Mills
Frederic E. Fox	Oliver Powell

Preface to the Music

ONE WOULD like to think that every tune in a hymnal could fit a statement of Ralph Vaughan Williams' that "the only correct music is that which is beautiful and noble." But an editor learns in working on a hymnal how many factors influence the final choice of words and music, how many differing demands and tastes of congregations have to be satisfied, how mighty a force "association" is in the hymns we know and love to sing. At the same time he becomes more aware of the vast riches in hymnody and of the scant use made of these treasures by ministers, church musicians, and congregations. He knows that the substitution of a new hymnal for an old one can contribute to the enrichment of corporate worship only if those responsible for its use will explore its contents with an open, receptive mind, seeking to find not only their "old favorites" but also to discover and learn to appreciate fine tunes hitherto unfamiliar to them.

Henry Ward Beecher in *The Plymouth Collection of Hymns and Tunes*, 1855, wrote: "We do not think that Congregational Singing will ever prevail with power, until *Pastors of Churches* appreciate its importance, and universally labor to secure it. . . . the pastor should . . . be the animating center of the music, encouraging the people to take part in it, ..." Only by continuously exploring a hymnal can one realize fully its inexhaustible resources. We cannot urge too strongly that in churches where a new hymnal is introduced there be times set aside regularly for the members to practice new hymns along with the old. Choirs, also, by making use of fine hymns as anthems and responses — particularly those that may be unfamiliar and may seem at first somewhat difficult — can do much to improve and strengthen congregational singing.

With the increase of musical knowledge and training among ministers, church musicians, and laymen, it is natural that the hymnbook of today contain a larger variety of the great tunes of every age of the church than it has in the past. In high school and college choirs, students are becoming familiar with and devoted to great sacred choral literature. The church can ill afford to let the music used in its services be of a quality inferior to that heard in schools and concert halls, for as Henry Sloane Coffin has said: If young people "grow up to despise what was given them in the house of God, either in words or in tunes, their respect for the Christian church is seriously enfeebled."

The tunes in this book have come from many traditions, countries, and cultures. Some appear for the first time in print. These were chosen by the Hymnal Committee from a large number of manuscripts sent in and considered anonymously, with no knowledge of the composer's name until the copy was made ready for the printer. Many tunes new to this book are centuries old and their inclusion reminds one of Riemann's definition that a classic is "a work of art against which the destroying hand of time has proved powerless." It has been

vii

our aim to make more of such music available in the present book. At the same time, due attention has also been given to the wisdom of C. S. Phillips' words: "A church, after all, is a place to help the wayfaring man or woman along the rough road of life, not an academy of the fine arts. We are right to say that we must only offer our best to God; but we have no reason for supposing that God's idea of 'the best' is purely or even primarily aesthetic." A constant search in the hymnals of our day has been made in order to know what the churches at large are singing and which tunes are in most general use. It has been our concern to include hymns for every type of congregation.

To encourage the singing of hymns in unison, tunes have been set in as low a key as is practicable, so as to bring the melody within the range of men's voices. When a tune appears more than once, two different keys have been given in most cases to increase the book's usefulness. In some instances more than one harmonization has been included for the sake of variety. Wherever possible the committee has used the "proper," or established, melody for a hymn where the words and the music are traditionally associated together. When a hymn has been set to several different tunes, the one having the widest usage generally has been chosen. Time signatures have been omitted in those hymns where the music does not follow a measured pattern throughout. Amens have been omitted in some instances where their use would seem inappropriate, as for example, after certain folk melodies, Negro spirituals, and carols; and in some of the psalm tunes the "gathering note" at the start of each phrase has been restored.

The service music provides a wide variety of hymns suitable for introits and responses for choir and congregation. A full quota of choir responses for the Communion service and more canticles and chants have been supplied in response to requests from organists and choirmasters. The descants which appear are relatively simple and should meet the needs of small choirs as well as large.

"A minister should study the contents of the hymnal as he does those of the Bible if he is to employ hymns as means of his people's fellowship with God." It has been a rare privilege to work with a committee whose members have done this with devotion, discernment, and skill. The music editors are deeply indebted to them for the warm, cordial, and sympathetic consideration given to a large body of musical material, and for the feeling of unity and accord that has been maintained consistently throughout the years of work that have gone into the preparation of this hymnbook. May those who use it find an equal degree of satisfaction and growth as they "sing to the Lord with cheerful voice."

Ethel Porter
Hugh Porter
Music Editors

Contents

THE HYMNS

WORSHIP

Adoration and Praise	1–31
Morning	32–43
Evening	44–59
Close of Worship	60–63

GOD THE FATHER

Works in Creation	64–75
Providence	76–97
Grace	98–102

OUR LORD JESUS CHRIST

Advent	103–115
Birth	116–146
Life and Ministry	147–153
Passion and Cross	154–179
Resurrection	180–194
Ascension and Reign	195–206
Presence and Guidance	207–220
Character and Glory	221–230

THE HOLY SPIRIT — 231–245

THE TRINITY — 246–251

THE BIBLE — 252–259

THE CHURCH OF CHRIST

Nature and Unity	260–270
Fellowship	271–276
Sacraments	
Baptism	277–279
Lord's Supper	280–292
Mission in the World	293–305
Communion of Saints	306–312

THE CHRISTIAN LIFE

Gospel Call and Response	313–331
Prayer	332–336
Hope, Joy, Peace	337–345
Faith and Aspiration	346–361
Pilgrimage and Conflict	362–389
Consecration	390–408

THE KINGDOM OF GOD ON EARTH

Brotherhood and Service	409–423
Justice	424–428
The Nation	429–443
World Peace	444–452

SEASONS

New Year	453–454
Changing Seasons	455–459
Harvest and Thanksgiving	460–464

SPECIAL SERVICES AND OCCASIONS

Marriage and the Family	465–466
Funerals	467–469
Ordinations	470–471
Church Dedications and Anniversaries	472–477

CHILDREN — 478–487

YOUTH — 488–495

THE NATIONAL ANTHEM — 496

CONTENTS

SERVICE MUSIC

Morning	497–506	Communion	544–556
Evening	507–510	Communion Hymns	557–558
Doxologies	511–515	Morning Canticles	559–569
Scripture	516–518	Evening Canticles	570–574
Prayer	519–530	Hymns	575–580
Versicles	531–534	Descants	581–584
Offertory	535–538	Amens	585–594
Close of Worship	539–543		

SERVICES, PRAYERS, READINGS

Orders for Worship	*Page* 491
Prayers and Other Worship Aids	503
Psalter Readings	515
Unison Readings	540

ACKNOWLEDGMENTS AND SOURCES

Hymns and Service Music	*Page* 550
Services, Prayers, Readings	556

INDEXES

Authors, Translators, and Sources	*Page* 559
Composers, Arrangers, and Sources	563
Metrical Index	567
Alphabetical Index of Tunes	571
Topical Index	575
Index of First Lines	584

PILGRIM HYMNAL

Serve the Lord with gladness!
Come into his presence with singing!

Psalm 100:2

Our God, Our Help in Ages Past

1

Based on Psalm 90
Isaac Watts, 1674-1748

ST. ANNE C.M.
Attr. to William Croft, 1678-1727

1 Our God, our help in a - ges past, Our hope for years to come,
2 Un - der the shad-ow of thy throne Thy saints have dwelt se - cure;
3 Be - fore the hills in or - der stood, Or earth re - ceived her frame,
4 A thou - sand a - ges in thy sight Are like an eve - ning gone,

Our shel - ter from the storm-y blast, And our e - ter - nal home,
Suf - fi - cient is thine arm a - lone, And our de - fense is sure.
From ev - er - last-ing thou art God, To end-less years the same.
Short as the watch that ends the night Be - fore the ris - ing sun. A - men.

5 Time, like an ever-rolling stream,
  Bears all its sons away;
  They fly, forgotten, as a dream
  Dies at the opening day.

6 Our God, our help in ages past,
  Our hope for years to come,
  Be thou our guard while troubles last,
  And our eternal home.

A descant may be found at No.583

ADORATION AND PRAISE

2 All Glory Be to God on High

Attr. to Nicolaus Decius, d.1541
Tr. Catherine Winkworth, 1827-1878, alt.

ALLEIN GOTT IN DER HÖH' 8.7.8.7.8.8.7.
"Geistliche Lieder," Leipzig, 1539

1 All glo-ry be to God on high, Who hath our race be-friend-ed!
2 We praise, we wor-ship thee, we trust And give thee thanks for-ev-er,
3 O Je-sus Christ, our God and Lord, Be-got-ten of the Fa-ther,
4 O Ho-ly Spir-it, pre-cious Gift, Thou Com-fort-er un-fail-ing,

To us no harm shall now come nigh, The strife at last is end-ed;
O Fa-ther, that thy rule is just And wise, and chang-es nev-er;
O thou who hast our peace re-stored, And the lost sheep dost gath-er,
Do thou our trou-bled souls up-lift, A-gainst the foe pre-vail-ing;

God show-eth his good-will to men, And peace shall reign on
Thy bound-less power o'er all things reigns, Thou dost what-e'er thy
Thou Lamb of God, en-throned on high, Be-hold our need and
A-vert our woes and calm our dread: For us the Sav-ior's

earth a-gain; O thank him for his good-ness!
will or-dains; 'Tis well thou art our rul-er!
hear our cry; Have mer-cy on us, Je-sus!
blood was shed; Do thou in faith sus-tain us! A-men.

ADORATION AND PRAISE

God Himself Is With Us

3

Gerhardt Tersteegen, 1697-1769
Tr. Frederick W. Foster, 1760-1835, and others

ARNSBERG 6.6.8.6.6.8.3.3.6.6.
Melody by Joachim Neander, 1650-1680

1 God him-self is with us: Let us now a - dore him, And with awe ap-
2 God him-self is with us: Hear the harps re - sound - ing! See the crowds the
3 O thou Fount of bless - ing, Pu - ri - fy my spir - it; Trust-ing on - ly

pear be - fore him. God is in his tem - ple, All with-in keep
throne sur-round - ing! "Ho - ly, ho - ly, ho - ly," Hear the hymn as -
in thy mer - it, Like the ho - ly an - gels Who be-hold thy

si - lence, Pros-trate lie with deep-est rev - erence. Him a - lone God we own,
cend - ing, An-gels, saints, their voices blend - ing! Bow thine ear To us here:
glo - ry, May I cease-less-ly a - dore thee, And in all, Great and small,

Him, our God and Sav - ior; Praise his name for - ev - er.
Hear, O Christ, the prais - es That thy Church now rais - es.
Seek to do most near - ly What thou lov - est dear - ly. A - men.

4 All People That on Earth Do Dwell

Based on Psalm 100
William Kethe, d. 1608?, alt.

OLD HUNDREDTH L.M. (*altered rhythm*)
Attr. to Louis Bourgeois, c.1510-c.1561
"Genevan Psalter," 1551

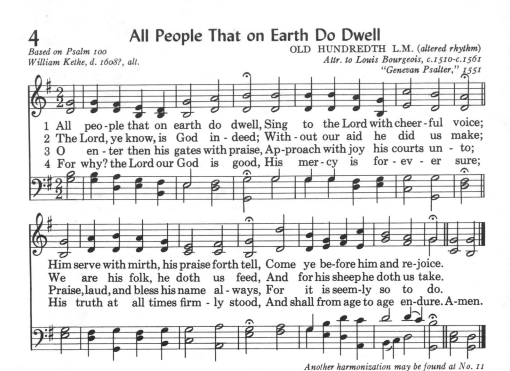

1 All peo-ple that on earth do dwell, Sing to the Lord with cheer-ful voice;
2 The Lord, ye know, is God in - deed; With - out our aid he did us make;
3 O en - ter then his gates with praise, Ap-proach with joy his courts un - to;
4 For why? the Lord our God is good, His mer - cy is for - ev - er sure;

Him serve with mirth, his praise forth tell, Come ye be-fore him and re-joice.
We are his folk, he doth us feed, And for his sheep he doth us take.
Praise, laud, and bless his name al - ways, For it is seem-ly so to do.
His truth at all times firm - ly stood, And shall from age to age en-dure. A-men.

Another harmonization may be found at No. 11

5 All People That on Earth Do Dwell

Melody in the Tenor

OLD HUNDREDTH L.M. (*altered rhythm*)
Arr. by John Dowland, 1562-1626

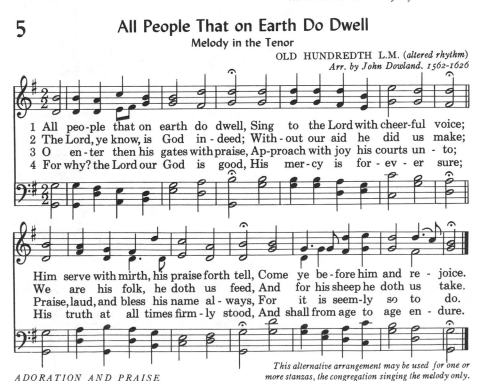

1 All peo-ple that on earth do dwell, Sing to the Lord with cheer-ful voice;
2 The Lord, ye know, is God in - deed; With - out our aid he did us make;
3 O en - ter then his gates with praise, Ap-proach with joy his courts un - to;
4 For why? the Lord our God is good, His mer - cy is for - ev - er sure;

Him serve with mirth, his praise forth tell, Come ye be-fore him and re - joice.
We are his folk, he doth us feed, And for his sheep he doth us take.
Praise, laud, and bless his name al - ways, For it is seem-ly so to do.
His truth at all times firm - ly stood, And shall from age to age en - dure.

ADORATION AND PRAISE

This alternative arrangement may be used for one or more stanzas, the congregation singing the melody only.

O Worship the King, All Glorious Above

6

Based on Psalm 104
Robert Grant, 1779-1838, alt.

LYONS 10.10.11.11.
Arr. from J. Michael Haydn ?, 1737-1806

1 O wor-ship the King, all glo-rious a-bove,
2 O tell of his might, O sing of his grace,
3 The earth with its store of won-ders un-told,
4 Thy boun-ti-ful care, what tongue can re-cite?
5 Frail chil-dren of dust, and fee-ble as frail,

O grate-ful-ly sing his power and his love;
Whose robe is the light, whose can-o-py space;
Al-might-y, thy power hath found-ed of old,
It breathes in the air, it shines in the light;
In thee do we trust, nor find thee to fail;

Our Shield and De-fend-er, the An-cient of Days,
His char-iots of wrath the deep thun-der-clouds form,
Hath stab-lished it fast by a change-less de-cree,
It streams from the hills, it de-scends to the plain,
Thy mer-cies how ten-der, how firm to the end,

Pa-vil-ioned in splen-dor, and gird-ed with praise.
And dark is his path on the wings of the storm.
And round it hath cast, like a man-tle, the sea.
And sweet-ly dis-tills in the dew and the rain.
Our Ma-ker, De-fend-er, Re-deem-er, and Friend! A-men.

Alternative tune, HANOVER, *No. 206*

ADORATION AND PRAISE

Immortal, Invisible, God Only Wise

Walter C. Smith, 1824-1908, alt.

ST. DENIO 11.11.11.11.
Welsh Hymn Melody

1 Im - mor - tal, in - vis - i - ble, God on - ly wise,
2 Un - rest - ing, un - hast - ing, and si - lent as light,
3 To all, life thou giv - est to both great and small;
4 Great Fa - ther of glo - ry, pure Fa - ther of light,

In light in - ac - ces - si - ble hid from our eyes,
Nor want - ing, nor wast - ing, thou rul - est in might;
In all life thou liv - est, the true life of all;
Thine an - gels a - dore thee, all veil - ing their sight;

Most bless - ed, most glo - rious, the An - cient of Days,
Thy jus - tice like moun - tains high soar - ing a - bove
We blos - som and flour - ish as leaves on the tree,
All praise we would ren - der; O help us to see

Al - might - y, vic - to - rious, thy great name we praise.
Thy clouds which are foun - tains of good - ness and love.
And with - er and per - ish, but naught chang - eth thee.
'Tis on - ly the splen - dor of light hid - eth thee. A - men.

ADORATION AND PRAISE

Joyful, Joyful, We Adore Thee

Henry van Dyke, 1852-1933

HYMN TO JOY 8.7.8.7.D.
Arr. from Ludwig van Beethoven, 1770-1827

1 Joy-ful, joy-ful, we a-dore thee, God of glo-ry, Lord of love;
2 All thy works with joy sur-round thee, Earth and heaven re-flect thy rays,
3 Thou art giv-ing and for-giv-ing, Ev-er bless-ing, ev-er blest,
4 Mor-tals, join the hap-py cho-rus Which the morn-ing stars be-gan;

Hearts un-fold like flowers be-fore thee, Open-ing to the sun a-bove.
Stars and an-gels sing a-round thee, Cen-ter of un-bro-ken praise.
Well-spring of the joy of liv-ing, O-cean depth of hap-py rest!
Fa-ther love is reign-ing o'er us, Broth-er love binds man to man.

Melt the clouds of sin and sad-ness, Drive the dark of doubt a-way;
Field and for-est, vale and moun-tain, Flow-ery mead-ow, flash-ing sea,
Thou our Fa-ther, Christ our Broth-er, All who live in love are thine;
Ev-er sing-ing, march we on-ward, Vic-tors in the midst of strife,

Giv-er of im-mor-tal glad-ness, Fill us with the light of day.
Chant-ing bird and flow-ing foun-tain, Call us to re-joice in thee.
Teach us how to love each oth-er, Lift us to the joy di-vine.
Joy-ful mu-sic leads us sun-ward In the tri-umph song of life. A-men.

ADORATION AND PRAISE

Before Jehovah's Aweful Throne
First Tune

Based on Psalm 100
Isaac Watts, 1674-1748
Alt. by John Wesley, 1703-1791

WINCHESTER NEW L.M.
Adapted from
"Musicalisches Handbuch," Hamburg, 1690

1 Be - fore Je - ho - vah's awe - ful throne, Ye
2 His sov - ereign power with - out our aid, Made
3 We are his peo - ple, we his care, Our
4 We'll crowd thy gates with thank - ful songs, High
5 Wide as the world is thy com - mand, Vast

na - tions bow with sa - cred joy; Know that the Lord is
us of clay, and formed us men; And when, like wan - dering
souls, and all our mor - tal frame; What last - ing hon - ors
as the heavens our voic - es raise; And earth, with her ten
as e - ter - ni - ty thy love; Firm as a rock thy

God a - lone, He can cre - ate, and he de - stroy.
sheep, we strayed, He brought us to his fold a - gain.
shall we rear, Al - might - y Mak - er, to thy name?
thou-sand tongues, Shall fill thy courts with sound-ing praise.
truth must stand, When roll - ing years shall cease to move. A - men.

Before Jehovah's Aweful Throne

Second Tune

Based on Psalm 100
Isaac Watts, 1674-1748
Alt. by John Wesley, 1703-1791

PARK STREET L.M.
Frederick M. A. Venua, 1788-1872

10

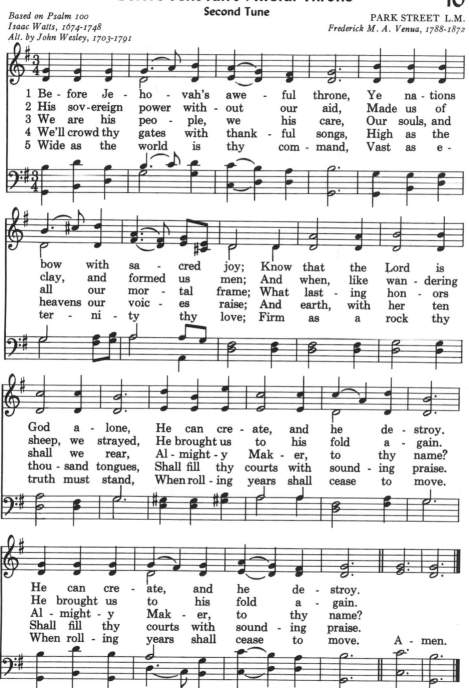

1 Be - fore Je - ho - vah's awe - ful throne, Ye na - tions
2 His sov-ereign power with - out our aid, Made us of
3 We are his peo - ple, we his care, Our souls, and
4 We'll crowd thy gates with thank - ful songs, High as the
5 Wide as the world is thy com - mand, Vast as e -

bow with sa - cred joy; Know that the Lord is
clay, and formed us men; And when, like wan - dering
all our mor - tal frame; What last - ing hon - ors
heavens our voic - es raise; And earth, with her ten
ter - ni - ty thy love; Firm as a rock thy

God a - lone, He can cre - ate, and he de - stroy.
sheep, we strayed, He brought us to his fold a - gain.
shall we rear, Al - might - y Mak - er, to thy name?
thou - sand tongues, Shall fill thy courts with sound - ing praise.
truth must stand, When roll - ing years shall cease to move.

He can cre - ate, and he de - stroy.
He brought us to his fold a - gain.
Al - might - y Mak - er, to thy name?
Shall fill thy courts with sound - ing praise.
When roll - ing years shall cease to move. A - men.

ADORATION AND PRAISE

From All That Dwell Below the Skies

First Tune

Based on Psalm 117
Isaac Watts, 1674-1748

OLD HUNDREDTH L.M.
Attr. to Louis Bourgeois, c.1510-c.1561
"Genevan Psalter," 1551

1 From all that dwell be - low the skies
2 E - ter - nal are thy mer - cies, Lord,

Let the Cre - a - tor's praise a - rise!
E - ter - nal truth at - tends thy word:

Let the Re - deem - er's name be sung
Thy praise shall sound from shore to shore

Through ev - ery land, by ev - ery tongue!
Till suns shall rise and set no more. A - men.

ADORATION AND PRAISE　　　　　　　*Another harmonization may be found at No. 4*

From All That Dwell Below the Skies

Second Tune

Based on Psalm 117
Isaac Watts, 1674-1748

LASST UNS ERFREUEN 8.8.4.4.8.8. *with Alleluias*
"Geistliche Kirchengesäng," Cologne, 1623

12

1 From all that dwell be-low the skies Let the Cre - a-tor's praise a-rise! Al-le-lu - ia! Al-le-lu - ia! Let the Re - deem-er's name be sung Through ev-ery land, by ev-ery tongue! Al-le-lu - ia! Al-le-lu - ia! Al-le-lu - ia! Al-le - lu - ia! Al-le-lu - ia!

2 E - ter-nal are thy mer-cies, Lord, E - ter-nal truth at-tends thy word! Al-le-lu - ia! Al-le-lu - ia! Thy praise shall sound from shore to shore Till suns shall rise and set no more! Al-le-lu - ia! Al-le-lu - ia! Al-le-lu - ia! Al-le - lu - ia! Al-le-lu - ia! A-men.

A lower setting may be found at No. 30

ADORATION AND PRAISE

Praise the Lord! Ye Heavens, Adore Him

Based on Psalm 148
"Foundling Hospital Collection," 1796

HYFRYDOL 8.7.8.7.D.
Melody by Rowland H. Prichard, 1811-1887

1 Praise the Lord! ye heavens, a - dore him; Praise him, an - gels, in the height;
2 Praise the Lord! for he is glo - rious; Nev - er shall his prom - ise fail;

Sun and moon, re-joice be - fore him; Praise him, all ye stars of light.
God hath made his saints vic-to - rious; Sin and death shall not pre-vail.

Praise the Lord! for he hath spo-ken; Worlds his might-y voice o - beyed;
Praise the God of our sal - va - tion! Hosts on high, his power pro-claim;

Laws which nev - er shall be bro-ken For their guid-ance he hath made.
Heaven, and earth, and all cre - a - tion, Laud and mag - ni - fy his name. A-men.

ADORATION AND PRAISE

Alternative tune, AUSTRIAN HYMN, *No. 267*

The God of Abraham Praise

14

Revised Version of the "Yigdal"
Daniel ben Judah, c.1400
Tr. Newton Mann, 1836-1926,
and Max Landsberg, 1845-1928

LEONI 6.6.8.4.D.
Traditional Hebrew Melody
Adapted by Meyer Lyon, 1751-1797

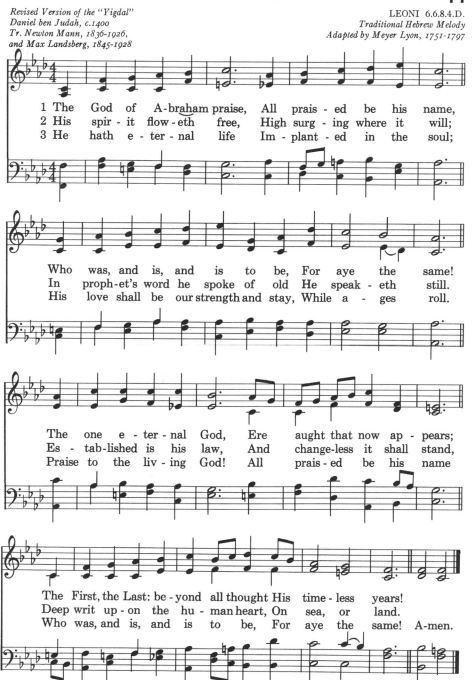

1 The God of A-braham praise, All prais-ed be his name,
2 His spir-it flow-eth free, High surg-ing where it will;
3 He hath e-ter-nal life Im-plant-ed in the soul;

Who was, and is, and is to be, For aye the same!
In proph-et's word he spoke of old He speak-eth still.
His love shall be our strength and stay, While a - ges roll.

The one e-ter-nal God, Ere aught that now ap-pears;
Es-tab-lished is his law, And change-less it shall stand,
Praise to the liv-ing God! All prais-ed be his name

The First, the Last: be-yond all thought His time-less years!
Deep writ up-on the hu-man heart, On sea, or land.
Who was, and is, and is to be, For aye the same! A-men.

15 Praise to the Lord, the Almighty

Joachim Neander, 1650-1680
Tr. Catherine Winkworth, 1827-1878, alt.

LOBE DEN HERREN 14.14.4.7.8.
"Stralsund Gesangbuch," 1665

1 Praise to the Lord, the Al-might-y, the King of cre-a-tion!
2 Praise to the Lord, who o'er all things so won-drous-ly reign-eth,
3 Praise to the Lord, who doth pros-per thy work and de-fend thee;
4 Praise to the Lord! O let all that is in me a-dore him!

O my soul, praise him, for he is thy health and sal-va-tion!
Shel-ters thee un-der his wings, yea, so gen-tly sus-tain-eth!
Sure-ly his good-ness and mer-cy here dai-ly at-tend thee.
All that hath life and breath, come now with prais-es be-fore him.

All ye who hear, Now to his tem-ple draw near;
Hast thou not seen How thy de-sires e'er have been
Pon-der a-new What the Al-might-y can do,
Let the A-men Sound from his peo-ple a-gain:

Join me in glad ad-o-ra-tion!
Grant-ed in what he or-dain-eth?
If with his love he be-friend thee.
Glad-ly for aye we a-dore him. A-men.

ADORATION AND PRAISE

Praise, My Soul, the King of Heaven

16

Based on Psalm 103
Henry F. Lyte, 1793-1847

PRAISE MY SOUL 8.7.8.7.8.7.
John Goss, 1800-1880

1 Praise, my soul, the King of heav - en, To his feet thy
2 Praise him for his grace and fa - vor To our fa - thers
3 Fa - ther-like, he tends and spares us; Well our fee - ble
4 An - gels, help us to a - dore him, Ye be - hold him

trib - ute bring; Ran - somed, healed, re - stored, for - giv - en,
in dis - tress; Praise him, still the same for - ev - er,
frame he knows; In his hands he gen - tly bears us,
face to face; Sun and moon, bow down be - fore him;

Who, like me, his praise should sing? Praise him! praise him!
Slow to chide, and swift to bless. Praise him! praise him!
Res - cues us from all our foes. Praise him! praise him!
Dwell - ers all in time and space, Praise him! praise him!

Praise him! praise him! Praise the ev - er - last - ing King!
Praise him! praise him! Glo - rious in his faith - ful - ness!
Praise him! praise him! Wide - ly as his mer - cy flows!
Praise him! praise him! Praise with us the God of grace! A - men.

Alternative tune, DULCE CARMEN, *No. 344*

ADORATION AND PRAISE

Praise Thou the Lord, O My Soul, Sing Praises

Based on Psalm 146
Johann D. Herrnschmidt, 1675-1723
Tr. Carl F. Pfatteicher, 1882-1957

LOBE DEN HERREN, O MEINE SEELE   10.8.10.8.8.8.4.4.
Freylinghausen's "Geistreiches Gesangbuch," 1704

1 Praise thou the Lord, O my soul, sing prais - es, Praise him from
2 Sing, all ye na - tions, ex - alt the glo - ry Of him whose

morn till fall of night. While o'er my life his strong
arm doth val - iant - ly! All that hath life and breath,

arm he rais - es, I shall sing thanks to God, my light.
tell the sto - ry In ac - cent strong, with voic - es free.

Who life and soul hath giv - en me, Be mag - ni - fied e -
Ye serv - ants of the Tri - une God, Fa - ther and Son and

ADORATION AND PRAISE

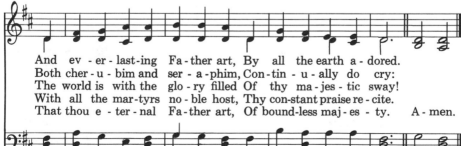

ter - nal - ly. Hal - le - lu - jah! Hal - le - lu - jah!
Spir - it laud! Hal - le - lu - jah! Hal - le - lu - jah! A - men.

O God, We Praise Thee, and Confess

18

Te Deum laudamus
"New Version, Supplement," 1703, alt.

TALLIS' ORDINAL C.M.
Thomas Tallis, d. 1585

1 O God, we praise thee, and con - fess That thou the on - ly Lord
2 To thee all an - gels cry a - loud; To thee the powers on high,
3 O ho - ly, ho - ly, ho - ly Lord, Whom heaven-ly hosts o - bey,
4 The a - pos - tles glo - rious com - pan - y, And proph-ets crowned with light,
5 The ho - ly Church through-out the world, O Lord, con - fess - es thee,

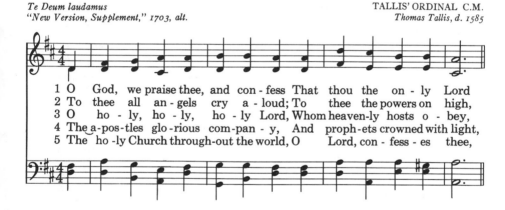

And ev - er - last-ing Fa - ther art, By all the earth a - dored.
Both cher - u - bim and ser - a - phim, Con - tin - u - ally do cry:
The world is with the glo - ry filled Of thy ma - jes - tic sway!
With all the mar-tyrs no - ble host, Thy con-stant praise re - cite.
That thou e - ter - nal Fa - ther art, Of bound-less maj - es - ty. A - men.

Praise the Lord, His Glories Show

Based on Psalm 150
Henry F. Lyte, 1793-1847

LLANFAIR 7.7.7.7. with Alleluias
Melody by Robert Williams, c.1781-1821

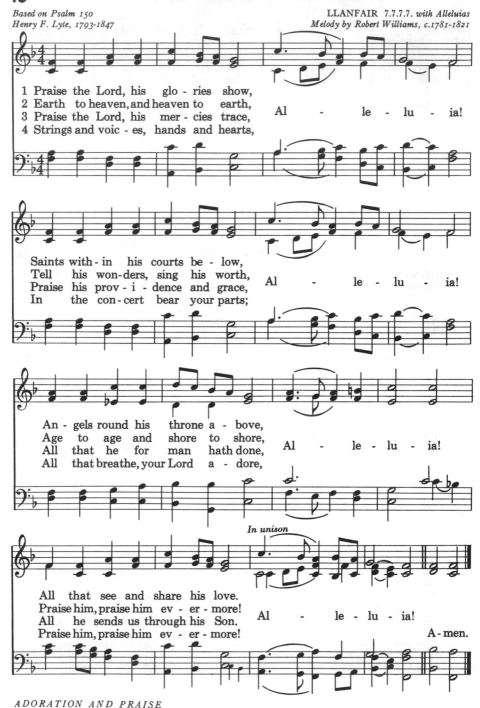

1 Praise the Lord, his glo-ries show,
2 Earth to heaven, and heaven to earth,
3 Praise the Lord, his mer-cies trace,
4 Strings and voic-es, hands and hearts,

Al - le - lu - ia!

Saints with-in his courts be-low,
Tell his won-ders, sing his worth,
Praise his prov-i-dence and grace,
In the con-cert bear your parts;

Al - le - lu - ia!

An-gels round his throne a-bove,
Age to age and shore to shore,
All that he for man hath done,
All that breathe, your Lord a-dore,

Al - le - lu - ia!

In unison

All that see and share his love.
Praise him, praise him ev-er-more!
All he sends us through his Son.
Praise him, praise him ev-er-more!

Al - le - lu - ia!

A - men.

ADORATION AND PRAISE

Sing Praise to God Who Reigns Above

20

Johann J Schütz, 1640-1690
Tr. Frances E. Cox, 1812-1897

MIT FREUDEN ZART 8.7.8.7.8.8.7.
Bohemian Brethren's "Kirchengesänge," 1566

1 Sing praise to God who reigns a-bove, The God of all cre - a - tion,
2 What God's al-might-y power hath made, His gra-cious mer - cy keep-eth;
3 Then all my glad-some way a - long, I sing a - loud thy prais-es,
4 O ye who name Christ's ho - ly name, Give God all praise and glo - ry;

The God of power, the God of love, The God of our sal - va - tion;
By morn-ing glow or eve-ning shade His watch-ful eye ne'er sleep-eth;
That men may hear the grate-ful song My voice un-wea - ried rais - es;
All ye who own his power, pro-claim A - loud the won - drous sto - ry!

With heal-ing balm my soul he fills, And ev - ery faith - less
With - in the king-dom of his might, Lo! all is just and
Be joy - ful in the Lord, my heart, Both soul and bod - y
Cast each false i - dol from his throne, The Lord is God, and

mur-mur stills: To God all praise and glo - ry.
all is right: To God all praise and glo - ry.
bear your part: To God all praise and glo - ry.
he a - lone: To God all praise and glo - ry. A - men.

ADORATION AND PRAISE

21 We Gather Together

KREMSER 12.11.12.11.

Netherlands Folk Song
Tr. Theodore Baker, 1851-1934

Netherlands Folk Song, 1626
Arr. by Edward Kremser, 1838-1914

1 We gath-er to-geth-er to ask the Lord's bless-ing, He chas-tens and
2 Be - side us to guide us, our God with us join - ing, Or - dain-ing, main-
3 We all do ex - tol thee, thou lead - er tri - um-phant, And pray that thou

has - tens his will to make known; The wick-ed op - press-ing now cease from dis-
tain - ing his king-dom di - vine, So from the be - gin-ning the fight we were
still our de - fend - er wilt be. Let thy con-gre - ga-tion es - cape trib-u-

tress-ing. Sing prais-es to his name; he for-gets not his own.
win-ning; Thou, Lord, wast at our side, all glo - ry be thine.
la - tion. Thy name be ev - er praised! O Lord, make us free! A - men.

22 We Praise Thee, O God

KREMSER 12.11.12.11.
Netherlands Folk Song, 1626
Arr. by Edward Kremser, 1838-1914

Julia C. Cory

1 We praise thee, O God, our Redeemer, Creator,
   In grateful devotion our tribute we bring.
We lay it before thee, we kneel and adore thee,
   We bless thy holy name, glad praises we sing.

2 We worship thee, God of our fathers, we bless thee;
   Through life's storm and tempest our guide hast thou been.
When perils o'ertake us, thou wilt not forsake us,
   And with thy help, O Lord, life's battles we win.

3 With voices united our praises we offer,
   And gladly our songs of true worship we raise.
Our sins now confessing, we pray for thy blessing;
   To thee, our great Redeemer, forever be praise. Amen.

ADORATION AND PRAISE

Ye Holy Angels Bright

23

Richard Baxter, 1615-1691, and others

DARWALL'S 148th 6.6.6.6.4.4.4.4.
John Darwall, 1731-1789

1 Ye ho - ly an - gels bright, Who wait at God's right hand,
2 Ye bless - ed souls at rest, Who ran this earth - ly race,
3 Ye saints who toil be - low, A - dore your heaven - ly King,
4 My soul, bear thou thy part, Tri - umph in God a - bove,

Or through the realms of light Fly at your Lord's com - mand,
And now, from sin re - leased, Be - hold the Sav - ior's face,
And on - ward as ye go Some joy - ful an - them sing;
And with a well-tuned heart Sing thou the songs of love.

As - sist our song, For else the theme Too
God's prais - es sound, As in his light With
Take what he gives And praise him still, Through
Let all thy days Till life shall end, What -

high doth seem For mor - tal tongue.
sweet de - light Ye do a - bound.
good and ill, Who ev - er lives.
e'er he send, Be filled with praise. A - men.

ADORATION AND PRAISE

24   # Now Let Every Tongue Adore Thee

Philipp Nicolai, 1556-1608
Tr. Paul English, d. 1932

WACHET AUF 8.9.8.8.9.8.6.6.4.8.8.
Melody by Philipp Nicolai, 1556-1608
Harm. by J. S. Bach, 1685-1750

Now let ev - ery tongue a - dore thee! Let men with an - gels

sing be - fore thee! Let harps and cym - bals now u - nite!

All thy gates with pearl are glo - rious, Where we par-take through

faith vic - to - rious, With an - gels round thy throne of light. No

ADORATION AND PRAISE

mor-tal eye hath seen, No mor-tal ear hath heard Such won-drous things; There-

fore with joy our song shall soar In praise to God for - ev-er-more. A-men.

Stand Up and Bless the Lord

25

James Montgomery, 1771-1854

CARLISLE S.M.
Charles Lockhart, 1745-1815

1 Stand up and bless the Lord, Ye peo - ple of his choice;
2 Though high a - bove all praise, A - bove all bless - ing high,
3 God is our strength and song, And his sal - va - tion ours;
4 Stand up and bless the Lord; The Lord your God a - dore;

Stand up and bless the Lord your God, With heart and soul and voice.
Who would not fear his ho - ly name, And laud and mag-ni - fy?
Then be his love in Christ pro-claimed With all our ran-somed powers.
Stand up and bless his glo-rious name, Hence-forth for ev - er - more. A-men.

O Be Joyful in the Lord!
First Tune

Based on Psalm 100
Curtis Beach, 1914-

ROCK OF AGES 7.7.7.7.5.7.6.7.
Traditional Hebrew Melody

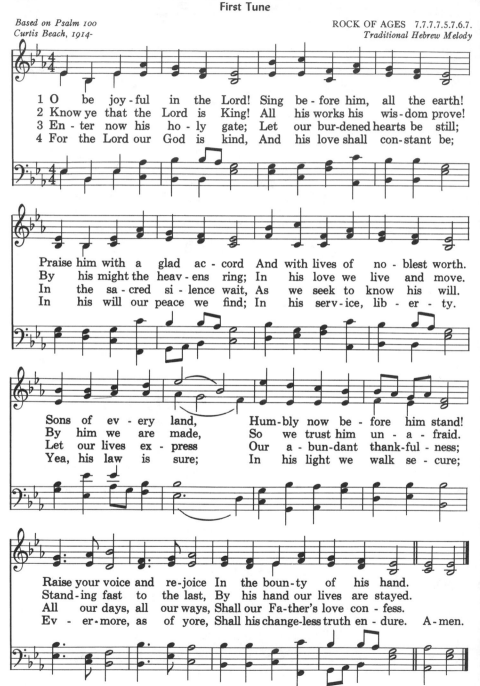

1 O be joy-ful in the Lord! Sing be-fore him, all the earth!
2 Know ye that the Lord is King! All his works his wis-dom prove!
3 En-ter now his ho-ly gate; Let our bur-dened hearts be still;
4 For the Lord our God is kind, And his love shall con-stant be;

Praise him with a glad ac-cord And with lives of no-blest worth.
By his might the heav-ens ring; In his love we live and move.
In the sa-cred si-lence wait, As we seek to know his will.
In his will our peace we find; In his serv-ice, lib-er-ty.

Sons of ev-ery land, Hum-bly now be-fore him stand!
By him we are made, So we trust him un-a-fraid.
Let our lives ex-press Our a-bun-dant thank-ful-ness;
Yea, his law is sure; In his light we walk se-cure;

Raise your voice and re-joice In the boun-ty of his hand.
Stand-ing fast to the last, By his hand our lives are stayed.
All our days, all our ways, Shall our Fa-ther's love con-fess.
Ev-er-more, as of yore, Shall his change-less truth en-dure. A-men.

ADORATION AND PRAISE

O Be Joyful in the Lord!

Second Tune

Based on Psalm 100
Curtis Beach, 1914-

FINLAY 7.7.7.7.5.7.6.7.
Harold W. Friedell, 1905-1958

27

In unison

1 O be joy-ful in the Lord! Sing be-fore him, all the earth!
2 Know ye that the Lord is King! All his works his wis-dom prove!
3 En-ter now his ho-ly gate; Let our bur-dened hearts be still;
4 For the Lord our God is kind, And his love shall con-stant be;

Praise him with a glad ac-cord And with lives of no-blest worth.
By his might the heav-ens ring; In his love we live and move.
In the sa-cred si-lence wait, As we seek to know his will.
In his will our peace we find; In his serv-ice, lib-er-ty.

Sons of ev-ery land, Hum-bly now be-fore him stand!
By him we are made, So we trust him un-a-fraid.
Let our lives ex-press Our a-bun-dant thank-ful-ness;
Yea, his law is sure; In his light we walk se-cure;

Raise your voice and re-joice In the boun-ty of his hand.
Stand-ing fast to the last, By his hand our lives are stayed.
All our days, all our ways, Shall our Fa-ther's love con-fess.
Ev-er-more, as of yore, Shall his change-less truth en-dure. A-men.

ADORATION AND PRAISE

28 We Worship Thee, Almighty Lord

Johann Olaf Wallin, 1779-1839
Tr. Charles Wharton Stork, 1881-

VI LOFVE DIG, O STORE GUD 8.8.10.10.
"Rostockerhandboken," 1529

In unison

1 We worship thee, almighty Lord,
2 Up-on a mountain build-ed high,
3 Through her shall ev-ery land pro-claim
4 All na-tions to thy throne shall throng

Our hearts re-vere thy gra-cious word When it goes forth from
Thy Church doth in thy strength re-ly, And stand-eth sure while
The sa-cred might of Je-sus' name, And all re-joice with
And raise on high the vic-tory song, While cher-u-bim re-

heaven o'er all the earth.
earth and time en-dure. Ho-ly, ho-ly,
Chris-tian heart and voice.
ply to ser-a-phim.

ho-ly art thou, O God! A-men.

ADORATION AND PRAISE

Now Thank We All Our God

29

Martin Rinckart, 1586-1649
Tr. Catherine Winkworth, 1827-1878

NUN DANKET 6.7.6.7.6.6.6.6.
Melody by Johann Crüger, 1598-1662

1 Now thank we all our God With heart and hands and voic - es,
2 O may this boun - teous God Through all our life be near us,
3 All praise and thanks to God The Fa - ther now be giv - en,

Who won-drous things hath done, In whom his world re - joic - es,
With ev - er joy - ful hearts And bless-ed peace to cheer us,
The Son, and him who reigns With them in high - est heav - en,

Who, from our moth-ers' arms, Hath blessed us on our way
And keep us in his grace, And guide us when per - plexed,
The one e - ter - nal God, Whom earth and heaven a - dore,

With count-less gifts of love, And still is ours to - day.
And free us from all ills In this world and the next.
For thus it was, is now, And shall be ev - er - more. A - men.

ADORATION AND PRAISE

Ye Watchers and Ye Holy Ones

Athelstan Riley, 1858-1945

LASST UNS ERFREUEN 8.8.4.4.8.8. *with Alleluias*
"Geistliche Kirchengesäng," Cologne, 1623

In unison

1 Ye watch-ers and ye ho-ly ones, Bright ser-aphs, cher-u-bim and
2 O high-er than the cher-u-bim, More glo-rious than the ser-a-
3 Re-spond, ye souls in end-less rest, Ye pa-tri-archs and proph-ets
4 O friends, in glad-ness let us sing, Su-per-nal an-thems ech-o-

thrones, Raise the glad strain, Al-le-lu-ia! Cry out, do-min-ions, prince-doms,
phim, Lead their prais-es, Al-le-lu-ia! Thou bear-er of the e-ter-nal
blest, Al-le-lu-ia, Al-le-lu-ia! Ye ho-ly twelve, ye mar-tyrs
ing, Al-le-lu-ia, Al-le-lu-ia! To God the Fa-ther, God the

powers, Vir-tues, arch-an-gels, an-gels' choirs,
Word, Most gra-cious, mag-ni-fy the Lord, Al-le-lu-ia,
strong, All saints tri-um-phant, raise the song,
Son, And God the Spir-it, Three in One,

Al-le-lu-ia, Al-le-lu-ia, Al-le-lu-ia, Al-le-lu-ia! A-men.

ADORATION AND PRAISE

A higher setting may be found at No. 12

Worship the Lord in the Beauty of Holiness

John S. B. Monsell, 1811-1875, alt.

MONSELL 12.10.12.10.
William F. Sherwin, 1826-1888

1 Wor - ship the Lord in the beau - ty of ho - li - ness,
2 Low at his feet lay thy bur - den of care - ful - ness,
3 Fear not to en - ter his courts in the slen - der - ness

Bow down be - fore him, his glo - ry pro - claim;
High on his heart he will bear it for thee;
Of the poor wealth thou wouldst reck - on as thine;

With gold of o - be - dience and in - cense of low - li - ness,
Com - fort thy sor - rows and an - swer thy prayer - ful - ness,
Truth in its beau - ty, and love in its ten - der - ness,

Kneel and a - dore him, the Lord is his name.
Guid - ing thy steps as may best for thee be.
These are the of - ferings to lay on his shrine. A - men.

ADORATION AND PRAISE

32   Awake, My Soul, and With the Sun

Thomas Ken, 1637-1711

MORNING HYMN L.M.
François H. Barthélémon, 1741-1808

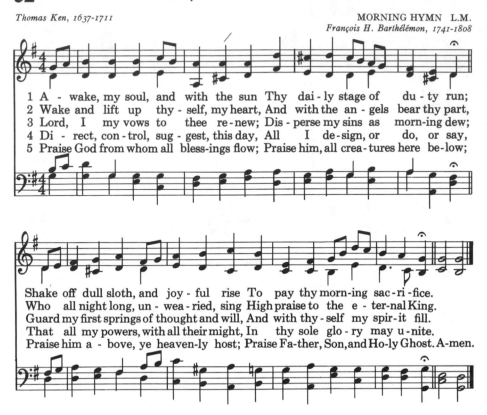

1 A - wake, my soul, and with the sun Thy dai - ly stage of du - ty run;
2 Wake and lift up thy - self, my heart, And with the an - gels bear thy part,
3 Lord, I my vows to thee re - new; Dis - perse my sins as morn-ing dew;
4 Di - rect, con - trol, sug - gest, this day, All I de - sign, or do, or say,
5 Praise God from whom all bless-ings flow; Praise him, all crea - tures here be - low;

Shake off dull sloth, and joy - ful rise To pay thy morn-ing sac - ri - fice.
Who all night long, un - wea - ried, sing High praise to the e - ter - nal King.
Guard my first springs of thought and will, And with thy - self my spir - it fill.
That all my powers, with all their might, In thy sole glo - ry may u - nite.
Praise him a - bove, ye heaven-ly host; Praise Fa - ther, Son, and Ho - ly Ghost. A-men.

33   As the Sun Doth Daily Rise

Latin: Matutinus altiora
Tr. O.B.C., alt.

INNOCENTS 7.7.7.7.
"The Parish Choir," 1850

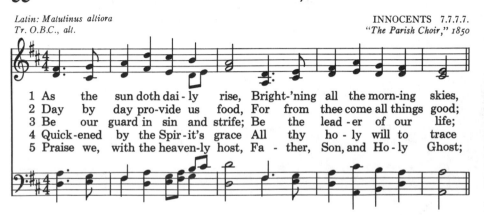

1 As the sun doth dai - ly rise, Bright-'ning all the morn-ing skies,
2 Day by day pro-vide us food, For from thee come all things good;
3 Be our guard in sin and strife; Be the lead - er of our life;
4 Quick-ened by the Spir-it's grace All thy ho - ly will to trace
5 Praise we, with the heaven-ly host, Fa - ther, Son, and Ho - ly Ghost;

MORNING

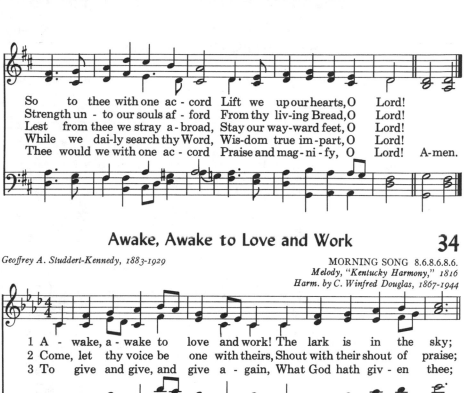

So to thee with one ac-cord Lift we up our hearts, O Lord!
Strength un-to our souls af-ford From thy liv-ing Bread, O Lord!
Lest from thee we stray a-broad, Stay our way-ward feet, O Lord!
While we dai-ly search thy Word, Wis-dom true im-part, O Lord!
Thee would we with one ac-cord Praise and mag-ni-fy, O Lord! A-men.

Awake, Awake to Love and Work 34

Geoffrey A. Studdert-Kennedy, 1883-1929

MORNING SONG 8.6.8.6.8.6.
Melody, "Kentucky Harmony," 1816
Harm. by C. Winfred Douglas, 1867-1944

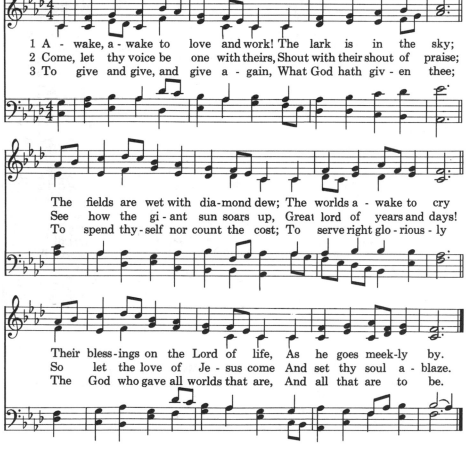

1 A-wake, a-wake to love and work! The lark is in the sky;
2 Come, let thy voice be one with theirs, Shout with their shout of praise;
3 To give and give, and give a-gain, What God hath giv-en thee;

The fields are wet with dia-mond dew; The worlds a-wake to cry
See how the gi-ant sun soars up, Great lord of years and days!
To spend thy-self nor count the cost; To serve right glo-rious-ly

Their bless-ings on the Lord of life, As he goes meek-ly by.
So let the love of Je-sus come And set thy soul a-blaze.
The God who gave all worlds that are, And all that are to be.

MORNING

When Morning Gilds the Skies

German: anon., 1828
Tr. Edward Caswall, 1814-1878, alt.

LAUDES DOMINI 6.6.6.6.6.6.
Joseph Barnby, 1838-1896

1 When morn-ing gilds the skies, My heart a-wak-ing cries,
2 The night be-comes as day, When from the heart we say,
3 Ye na-tions of man-kind, In this your con-cord find,
4 To God, the Word, on high, The hosts of an-gels cry,

May Je-sus Christ be praised! A-like at work and prayer,
May Je-sus Christ be praised! The powers of dark-ness fear,
May Je-sus Christ be praised! Let all the earth a-round
May Je-sus Christ be praised! Let mor-tals, too, up-raise

To Je-sus I re-pair; May Je-sus Christ be praised!
When this sweet chant they hear, May Je-sus Christ be praised!
Ring joy-ous with the sound, May Je-sus Christ be praised!
Their voice in hymns of praise, May Je-sus Christ be praised! A-men.

5 In heaven's eternal bliss
   The loveliest strain is this,
      May Jesus Christ be praised!
   Let air, and sea, and sky
   From depth to height reply
      May Jesus Christ be praised!

6 Be this, while life is mine,
   My canticle divine,
      May Jesus Christ be praised!
   Be this the eternal song
   Through all the ages long,
      May Jesus Christ be praised!

New Every Morning Is the Love

John Keble, 1792-1866, alt.

MELCOMBE L.M.
Samuel Webbe, 1740-1816

1 New ev - ery morn - ing is the love Our
2 New mer - cies, each re - turn - ing day, Hov -
3 If on our dai - ly course our mind Be
4 Old friends, old scenes, will love - lier be, As

wake - ning and up - ris - ing prove; Through sleep and dark - ness
er a - round us while we pray; New per - ils past, new
set to hal - low all we find, New treas - ures still, of
more of heaven in each we see; Some soft - 'ning gleam of

safe - ly brought, Re-stored to life and power and thought.
sins for-given, New thoughts of God, new hopes of heaven.
count - less price, God will pro - vide for sac - ri - fice.
love and prayer Shall dawn on ev - ery cross and care. A - men.

5 The trivial round, the common task,
Will furnish all we ought to ask;
Room to deny ourselves—a road
To bring us daily nearer God.

6 Only, O Lord, in thy dear love,
Fit us for perfect rest above;
And help us, this and every day,
To live more nearly as we pray.

MORNING

37

Still, Still With Thee

Harriet Beecher Stowe, 1812-1896

CONSOLATION 11.10.11.10.
Arr. from Felix Mendelssohn, 1809-1847

1 Still, still with thee, when pur - ple morn - ing break - eth,
2 A - lone with thee, a - mid the mys - tic shad - ows,
3 Still, still with thee! As to each new - born morn - ing
4 So shall it be at last, in that bright morn - ing,

When the bird wak - eth, and the shad - ows flee;
The sol - emn hush of na - ture new - ly born;
A fresh and sol - emn splen - dor still is given,
When the soul wak - eth and life's shad - ows flee;

Fair - er than morn - ing, love - li - er than day - light,
A - lone with thee in breath-less ad - o - ra - tion,
So does this bless - ed con - scious-ness, a - wak - ing,
O in that hour, fair - er than day - light dawn - ing,

Dawns the sweet con - scious-ness, I am with thee.
In the calm dew and fresh-ness of the morn.
Breathe each day near - ness un - to thee and heaven.
Shall rise the glo - rious thought, I am with thee. A - men.

MORNING

Morning Has Broken

Eleanor Farjeon, 1881-

BUNESSAN 5.5.5.4.D.
Gaelic Melody
Harm. by David Evans, 1874-1948

In unison

1 Morn-ing has bro - ken Like the first morn - ing, Black-bird has
2 Sweet the rain's new fall Sun - lit from heav - en, Like the first
3 Mine is the sun - light! Mine is the morn - ing Born of the

spo - ken Like the first bird. Praise for the sing - ing!
dew - fall On the first grass. Praise for the sweet - ness
one light E - den saw play! Praise with e - la - tion,

Praise for the morn - ing! Praise for them, spring - ing Fresh from the Word!
Of the wet gar - den, Sprung in com-plete - ness Where his feet pass.
Praise ev - ery morn - ing, God's re - cre - a - tion Of the new day!

MORNING

O Splendor of God's Glory Bright
First Tune

Latin: Splendor paternae gloriae
St. Ambrose, 340-397
Tr. Robert S. Bridges, 1844-1930

PUER NOBIS NASCITUR L.M.
Adapted by Michael Praetorius, 1571-1621

1 O Splen - dor of God's glo - ry bright, O thou that
2 O thou true Sun, on us thy glance Let fall in
3 The Fa - ther, too, our prayers im - plore, Fa - ther of
4 To guide what - e'er we no - bly do, With love all

bring - est light from light, O Light of light, light's liv - ing
roy - al ra - di - ance; The Spir - it's sanc - ti - fy - ing
glo - ry ev - er - more, The Fa - ther of all grace and
en - vy to sub - due; To make ill - for - tune turn to

spring, O Day, all days il - lu - min - ing,
beam Up - on our earth - ly sen - ses stream.
might, To ban - ish sin from our de - light:
fair, And give us grace our wrongs to bear. A - men.

MORNING

O Splendor of God's Glory Bright

Second Tune

Latin: *Splendor paternae gloriae*
St. Ambrose, 340-397
Tr. Robert S. Bridges, 1844-1930

SPLENDOR PATERNAE L.M.
Sarum Plainsong, Mode I

40

1 O Splen-dor of God's glo-ry bright, O thou that bring-est
2 O thou true Sun, on us thy glance Let fall in roy-al
3 The Fa-ther, too, our prayers im-plore, Fa-ther of glo-ry
4 To guide what-e'er we no-bly do, With love all en-vy

light from light, O Light of light, light's liv-ing spring,
ra-di-ance; The Spir-it's sanc-ti-fy-ing beam
ev-er-more, The Fa-ther of all grace and might,
to sub-due; To make ill-for-tune turn to fair,

O Day, all days il-lu-min-ing,
Up-on our earth-ly sen-ses stream.
To ban-ish sin from our de-light:
And give us grace our wrongs to bear. A-men.

41 Father, We Praise Thee, Now the Night Is Over

Latin: *Nocte surgentes*
Attr. to Gregory the Great, 540-604
Tr. Percy Dearmer, 1867-1936

CHRISTE SANCTORUM 11.11.11.5.
La Feillée's "Méthode du Plain-chant," 1782

In unison

1 Fa - ther, we praise thee, now the night is o - ver;
2 Mon - arch of all things, fit us for thy man - sions;
3 All - ho - ly Fa - ther, Son and e - qual Spir - it,

Ac - tive and watch - ful, stand we all be - fore thee;
Ban - ish our weak - ness, health and whole-ness send - ing;
Trin - i - ty bless - ed, send us thy sal - va - tion;

Sing - ing, we of - fer prayer and med - i - ta - tion:
Bring us to heav - en, where thy saints u - nit - ed
Thine is the glo - ry, gleam-ing and re - sound - ing

Thus we a - dore thee.
Joy with - out end - ing.
Through all cre - a - tion. A - men.

MORNING

High O'er the Lonely Hills

42

Jan Struther, 1901-1953

DAWN 6.4.6.4.6.6.6.4.
Thomas H. Ingham, 1878-1948

1 High o'er the lone - ly hills Black turns to gray,
2 So, o'er the hills of life, Storm - y, for - lorn,
3 Hear we no beat of drums, Fan - fare nor cry,
4 Bid then fare - well to sleep: Rise up and run!

Organ

Bird - song the val - ley fills, Mists fold a - way;
Out of the cloud and strife Sun - rise is born;
When Christ the her - ald comes Qui - et - ly nigh;
What though the hill be steep? Strength's in the sun.

Gray wakes to green a - gain; Beau - ty is seen a - gain,
Swift grows the light for us; End - ed is night for us;
Splen - dor he makes on earth; Col - or a - wakes on earth;
Now shall you find at last Night's left be - hind at last,

Gold and se - rene a - gain Dawn - eth the day.
Sound - less and bright for us Break - eth God's morn.
Sud - den - ly breaks on earth Light from the sky.
And for man - kind at last Day has be - gun!

MORNING

Christ, Whose Glory Fills the Skies

Charles Wesley, 1707-1788

RATISBON 7.7.7.7.7.7.
Johann Werner's "Choralbuch," 1815

1 Christ, whose glo - ry fills the skies, Christ, the true, the on - ly Light,
2 Dark and cheer-less is the morn Un - ac - com - pa - nied by thee;

Sun of right-eous-ness, a - rise, Tri-umph o'er the shades of night;
Joy - less is the day's re - turn, Till thy mer - cy's beams I see,

Day-spring from on high, be near; Day-star, in my heart ap-pear.
Till they in-ward light im - part, Glad my eyes, and warm my heart. A-men.

3 Visit, then, this soul of mine;
    Pierce the gloom of sin and grief;
Fill me, Radiancy divine,
    Scatter all my unbelief;
More and more thyself display,
    Shining to the perfect day.

Lord Jesus, in the Days of Old

44

James A. Noble, 1844-1896

VATER UNSER 8.8.8.8.8.8.
"Geistliche Lieder," Leipzig, 1539
Arr. from J.S. Bach, 1685-1750

1 Lord Je - sus, in the days of old Two walked with thee in
2 Did not their hearts with - in them burn? And though their Lord they

wan - ing light; And love's blind in - stinct made them bold To
failed to know, Did not their spir - its in - ly yearn? They

crave thy pres - ence through the night. As night de - scends, we
could not let the Stran - ger go. Much more must we who

too would pray, O leave us not at close of day.
know thee pray, O leave us not at close of day.

EVENING

45

Day Is Dying in the West

Mary A. Lathbury, 1841-1913

CHAUTAUQUA 7.7.7.7.4. *with Refrain*
William F. Sherwin, 1826-1888

1 Day is dy - ing in the west; Heaven is touch - ing
2 Lord of life, be - neath the dome Of the u - ni -
3 When for - ev - er from our sight Pass the stars, the

earth with rest; Wait and wor - ship while the night
verse, thy home, Gath - er us who seek thy face
day, the night, Lord of an - gels, on our eyes

Sets her eve - ning lamps a - light Through all the sky.
To the fold of thy em - brace, For thou art nigh.
Let e - ter - nal morn - ing rise, And shad - ows end.

REFRAIN

Ho - ly, ho - ly, ho - ly, Lord God of Hosts! Heaven and earth are full of thee!

EVENING

Heaven and earth are prais-ing thee, O Lord most high! A-men.

Again, as Evening's Shadow Falls

46

Samuel Longfellow, 1819-1892

CANONBURY L.M.
Arr. from Robert A. Schumann, 1810-1856

1 A - gain, as eve - ning's shad - ow falls, We gath - er
2 May strug - gling hearts that seek re - lease Here find the
3 O God, our Light, to thee we bow; With - in all
4 Life's tu - mult we must meet a - gain; We can - not

in these hal - lowed walls; And ves - per hymn and ves - per prayer
rest of God's own peace, And, strength-ened here by hymn and prayer,
shad - ows stand - est thou; Give deep - er calm than night can bring;
at the shrine re - main; But in the spir - it's se - cret cell

Rise min - gling on the ho - ly air.
Lay down the bur - den and the care.
Give sweet - er songs than lips can sing.
May hymn and prayer for ev - er dwell. A - men.

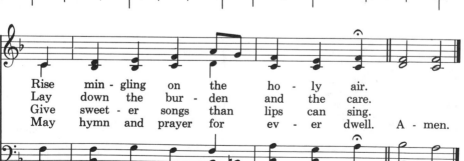

Another setting may be found at No.397
Alternative tune, SONG 5, No.509

EVENING

47 The Day Thou Gavest, Lord, Is Ended
First Tune

John Ellerton, 1826-1893, alt.

LES COMMANDEMENS DE DIEU 9.8.9.8.
Attr. to Louis Bourgeois, c.1510-c.1561
"Genevan Psalter," 1547

1 The day thou gav - est, Lord, is end - ed,
2 We thank thee that thy Church, un - sleep - ing
3 As o'er each con - ti - nent and is - land
4 The sun that bids us rest is wak - ing
5 So be it, Lord; thy throne shall nev - er,

The dark - ness falls at thy be - hest;
While earth rolls on - ward in - to light,
The dawn leads on an - oth - er day,
Our breth - ren 'neath the west - ern sky,
Like earth's proud em - pires, pass a - way;

To thee our morn - ing hymns as - cend - ed,
Through all the world her watch is keep - ing,
The voice of prayer is nev - er si - lent,
And hour by hour fresh lips are mak - ing
Thy king - dom stands, and grows for - ev - er,

Thy praise shall sanc - ti - fy our rest.
And rests not now by day or night.
Nor dies the strain of praise a - way.
Thy won-drous do - ings heard on high.
Till all thy crea - tures own thy sway. A - men.

The Day Thou Gavest, Lord, Is Ended
Second Tune

48

John Ellerton, 1826-1893, alt.

ST. CLEMENT 9.8.9.8.
Clement E. Scholefield, 1839-1904

1 The day thou gav - est, Lord, is end - ed,
2 We thank thee that thy Church, un - sleep - ing
3 As o'er each con - ti - nent and is - land
4 The sun that bids us rest is wak - ing
5 So be it, Lord; thy throne shall nev - er,

The dark - ness falls at thy be - hest;
While earth rolls on - ward in - to light,
The dawn leads on an - oth - er day,
Our breth - ren 'neath the west - ern sky,
Like earth's proud em - pires, pass a - way;

To thee our morn - ing hymns as - cend - ed,
Through all the world her watch is keep - ing,
The voice of prayer is nev - er si - lent,
And hour by hour fresh lips are mak - ing
Thy king - dom stands, and grows for - ev - er,

Thy praise shall sanc - ti - fy our rest.
And rests not now by day or night.
Nor dies the strain of praise a - way.
Thy won - drous do - ings heard on high.
Till all thy crea - tures own thy sway. A - men.

EVENING

49
O Gladsome Light

Greek: Phōs hilaron, 3rd century?
Tr. Robert S. Bridges, 1844-1930

NUNC DIMITTIS 6.6.7.6.6.7.
Attr. to Louis Bourgeois, c.1510-c.1561
Harm. adapted from Claude Goudimel, d.1572

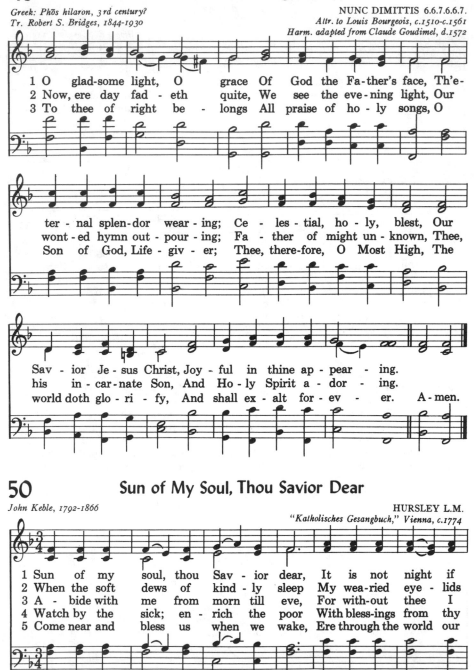

1 O glad-some light, O grace Of God the Fa-ther's face, Th'e-
2 Now, ere day fad - eth quite, We see the eve-ning light, Our
3 To thee of right be - longs All praise of ho - ly songs, O

ter - nal splen-dor wear - ing; Ce - les - tial, ho - ly, blest, Our
wont - ed hymn out - pour - ing; Fa - ther of might un - known, Thee,
Son of God, Life - giv - er; Thee, there-fore, O Most High, The

Sav - ior Je - sus Christ, Joy - ful in thine ap - pear - ing.
his in - car - nate Son, And Ho - ly Spirit a - dor - ing.
world doth glo - ri - fy, And shall ex - alt for - ev - er. A - men.

50
Sun of My Soul, Thou Savior Dear

John Keble, 1792-1866

HURSLEY L.M.
"Katholisches Gesangbuch," Vienna, c.1774

1 Sun of my soul, thou Sav - ior dear, It is not night if
2 When the soft dews of kind - ly sleep My wea-ried eye - lids
3 A - bide with me from morn till eve, For with-out thee I
4 Watch by the sick; en - rich the poor With bless-ings from thy
5 Come near and bless us when we wake, Ere through the world our

EVENING

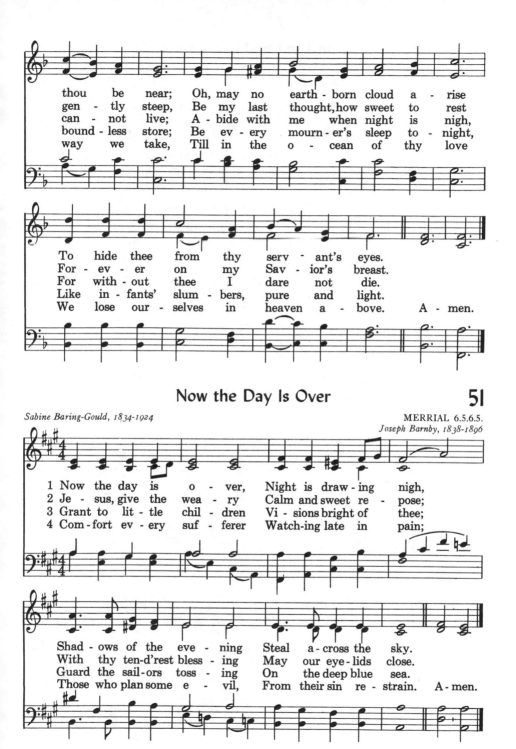

thou be near; Oh, may no earth-born cloud a - rise
gen - tly steep, Be my last thought, how sweet to rest
can - not live; A - bide with me when night is nigh,
bound - less store; Be ev - ery mourn - er's sleep to - night,
way we take, Till in the o - cean of thy love

To hide thee from thy serv - ant's eyes.
For - ev - er on my Sav - ior's breast.
For with - out thee I dare not die.
Like in - fants' slum - bers, pure and light.
We lose our - selves in heaven a - bove. A - men.

Now the Day Is Over

51

Sabine Baring-Gould, 1834-1924

MERRIAL 6.5.6.5.
Joseph Barnby, 1838-1896

1 Now the day is o - ver, Night is draw - ing nigh,
2 Je - sus, give the wea - ry Calm and sweet re - pose;
3 Grant to lit - tle chil - dren Vi - sions bright of thee;
4 Com - fort ev - ery suf - ferer Watch-ing late in pain;

Shad - ows of the eve - ning Steal a - cross the sky.
With thy ten-d'rest bless - ing May our eye - lids close.
Guard the sail-ors toss - ing On the deep blue sea.
Those who plan some e - vil, From their sin re - strain. A - men.

Alternative tune, EUDOXIA, *No. 510*

EVENING

52   Now, on Land and Sea Descending

Samuel Longfellow, 1819-1892, alt.

VESPER HYMN 8.7.8.7.8.6.8.7.
Attr. to Dmitri S. Bortniansky, 1751-1825
Arr. by John A. Stevenson, 1761-1833

1 Now, on land and sea de-scend-ing, Brings the night its peace pro-found;
2 Soon as dies the sun-set glo-ry, Stars of heaven shine out a-bove,
3 As the dark-ness deep-ens o'er us, Lo! e-ter-nal stars a-rise;

Let our ves-per hymn be blend-ing With the ho-ly calm a-round.
Tell-ing still the an-cient sto-ry, Their Cre-a-tor's change-less love.
Hope and faith and love rise glo-rious, Shin-ing in the spir-it's skies.

Ju - bi - la - te! Ju - bi - la - te! Ju - bi - la - te! A - men!

Let our ves-per hymn be blend-ing With the ho-ly calm a-round.
Tell-ing still the an-cient sto-ry Their Cre-a-tor's change-less love.
Hope and faith and love rise glo-rious, Shin-ing in the spir-it's skies. A-men.

EVENING

The Duteous Day Now Closeth 53

Paul Gerhardt, 1607-1676
Para. by Robert S. Bridges, 1844-1930

INNSBRUCK 7.7.6.7.7.8.
Attr. to Heinrich Isaak, c.1450-c.1527
Harm. by J.S. Bach, 1685-1750

1 The du-teous day now clos-eth, Each flower and tree re-
pos-eth, Shade creeps o'er wild and wood. Let
us, as night is fall-ing, On God, our Mak-er,
call-ing, Give thanks to him, the Giv-er good.

2 Now all the heaven-ly splen-dor Breaks forth in star-light
ten-der From myr-iad worlds un-known, And
man, the mar-vel see-ing, For-gets his self-ish
be-ing, For joy of beau-ty not his own.

3 A-while his mor-tal blind-ness May miss God's lov-ing-
kind-ness, And grope in faith-less strife, But
when life's day is o-ver Shall death's fair night dis-
cov-er The fields of ev-er-last-ing life. A-men.

EVENING

Now Cheer Our Hearts This Eventide

Nicolaus Selnecker, 1528-1592
Tr. from "Yattendon Hymnal," 1899

ACH BLEIB BEI UNS L.M.
"Geistliche Lieder," Leipzig, 1589
Harm. by J.S. Bach, 1685-1750

1 Now cheer our hearts this e - ven - tide, Lord Je - sus Christ, and with us bide; Thou that canst nev - er set in night, Our heaven - ly Sun, our glo - rious Light.

2 May we and all who bear thy name By gen - tle love thy cross pro - claim, Thy gift of peace on earth se - cure, And for thy truth the world en - dure. A - men.

EVENING

At Even, Ere the Sun Was Set

Henry Twells, 1823-1900

ANGELUS L.M.
Melody by Georg Joseph, c.1650
"Cantica Spiritualia," 1847

55

1 At e-ven, ere the sun was set, The sick, O
2 Once more 'tis e-ven-tide, and we, Op-pressed with
3 O Sav-ior Christ, our woes dis-pel, For some are
4 And none, O Lord, have per-fect rest, For none are

Lord, a-round thee lay; O in what di-vers pains they
va-rious ills, draw near; What if thy form we can-not
sick, and some are sad, And some have nev-er loved thee
whol-ly free from sin; And they who fain would serve thee

met! O with what joy they went a-way!
see? We know and feel that thou art here.
well, And some have lost the love they had;
best Are con-scious most of wrong with-in. A-men.

5 O Savior Christ, thou too art man;
   Thou hast been troubled, tempted, tried;
   Thy kind but searching glance can scan
   The very wounds that shame would hide.

6 Thy touch has still its ancient power;
   No word from thee can fruitless fall;
   Hear, in this solemn evening hour,
   And in thy mercy heal us all.

EVENING

56 All Praise to Thee, My God

Version when sung as a canon

Thomas Ken, 1637-1711, alt.

TALLIS' CANON L.M.
Thomas Tallis, d. 1585

1 All praise to thee, my God, this night, For all the bless-ings
2 For - give me, Lord, for thy dear Son, The ill that I this
3 O may my soul on thee re - pose, And with sweet sleep mine
4 Praise God, from whom all bless-ings flow; Praise him, all crea - tures

1 All praise to thee, my God, this night, For
2 For - give me, Lord, for thy dear Son, The
3 O may my soul on thee re - pose, And
4 Praise God, from whom all bless-ings flow; Praise

of the light! Keep me, O keep me, King of kings, Be -
day have done, That with the world, my - self, and thee, I,
eye - lids close, Sleep that may me more vig - orous make To
here be - low; Praise him a - bove, ye heaven - ly host; Praise

all the bless-ings of the light! Keep me, O keep me,
ill that I this day have done, That with the world, my -
with sweet sleep mine eye - lids close, Sleep that may me more
him, all crea - tures here be - low; Praise him a - bove, ye

EVENING

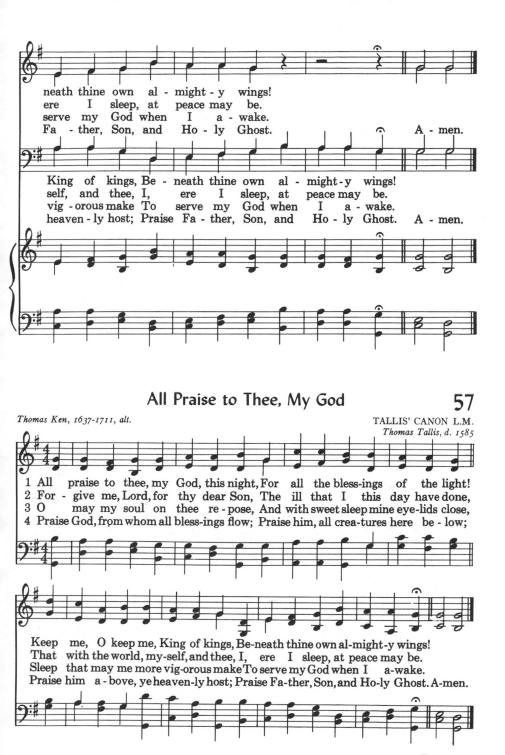

58 God That Madest Earth and Heaven

St. 1, *Reginald Heber, 1783-1826*

St. 2, *Frederick L. Hosmer, 1840-1929*

AR HYD Y NOS 8.4.8.4.8.8.8.4.

Traditional Welsh Melody

1 God, that mad-est earth and heav-en, Dark - ness and light,
2 When the con-stant sun re-turn-ing Un - seals our eyes,

Who the day for toil hast giv-en, For rest the night,
May we, born a - new like morn-ing, To la - bor rise;

May thine an - gel-guards de-fend us, Slum-ber sweet thy mer - cy send us;
Gird us for the task that calls us, Let not ease and self en-thrall us,

Ho - ly dreams and hopes at-tend us, This live - long night.
Strong through thee what-e'er be-fall us, O God most wise!

EVENING

Now God Be With Us

59

Petrus Herbert, d. *1571*
Tr. Catherine Winkworth, *1827-1878, alt.*

DIVA SERVATRIX 11.11.11.5.
"Bayeux Antiphoner," 1739

1 Now God be with us, for the night is clos - ing;
The light and dark - ness are of his dis - pos - ing,
And 'neath his shad - ow here to rest we yield us,
For he will shield us.

2 Let e - vil thoughts and spir - its flee be - fore us;
The morn - ing com - eth; watch, Pro-tec-tor, o'er us;
In soul and bod - y, thou from harm de-fend us;
Thine an - gels send us.

3 Let our last thoughts be thine when sleep o'er-takes us;
Our ear - liest thoughts be thine when morn-ing wakes us;
Let us serve thee, in all that we are do - ing
Thy praise pur - su - ing. A - men.

4 We have no refuge, none on earth to aid us,
  Save thee, O Father, who thine own hast made us;
  But thy dear presence will not leave them lonely
    Who seek thee only.

EVENING

60 Savior, Again to Thy Dear Name

John Ellerton, 1826-1893

ELLERS 10.10.10.10.
Edward J. Hopkins, 1818-1901

1 Sav - ior, a - gain to thy dear name we raise
2 Grant us thy peace up - on our home-ward way;
3 Grant us thy peace, Lord, through the com - ing night;
4 Grant us thy peace through - out our earth - ly life,

With one ac - cord our part - ing hymn of praise;
With thee be - gan, with thee shall end the day;
Turn thou for us its dark-ness in - to light;
Our balm in sor - row, and our stay in strife;

We stand to bless thee ere our wor - ship cease,
Guard thou the lips from sin, the hearts from shame,
From harm and dan - ger keep thy chil - dren free,
Then, when thy voice shall bid our con - flict cease,

Then, low - ly kneel - ing, wait thy word of peace.
That in this house have called up - on thy name.
For dark and light are both a - like to thee.
Call us, O Lord, to thine e - ter - nal peace. A - men.

CLOSE OF WORSHIP

God Be With You Till We Meet Again

First Tune

61

Jeremiah E. Rankin, 1828-1904, alt.

RANDOLPH 9.8.8.9.
R. Vaughan Williams, 1872-1958

In unison

1 God be with you till we meet a-gain; By his coun-sels guide, up-hold you,
2 God be with you till we meet a-gain; 'Neath his wings pro-tect-ing hide you,
3 God be with you till we meet a-gain; When life's per-ils thick con-found you,
4 God be with you till we meet a-gain; Keep love's ban-ner float-ing o'er you,

With his sheep se-cure-ly fold you: God be with you till we meet a-gain.
Dai - ly man-na still pro-vide you: God be with you till we meet a-gain.
Put his arms un-fail-ing round you: God be with you till we meet a-gain.
Smite death's threat-ening wave be-fore you: God be with you till we meet a-gain. A-men.

God Be With You Till We Meet Again

Second Tune

62

Jeremiah E. Rankin, 1828-1904, alt.

GOD BE WITH YOU 9.8.8.9.
William G. Tomer, 1832-1896

1 God be with you till we meet a - gain; By his coun-sels guide, up-hold you,
2 God be with you till we meet a - gain; 'Neath his wings pro-tect-ing hide you,
3 God be with you till we meet a - gain; When life's per-ils thick con-found you,
4 God be with you till we meet a - gain; Keep love's ban-ner float-ing o'er you,

With his sheep se-cure-ly fold you: God be with you till we meet a-gain.
Dai - ly man-na still pro-vide you: God be with you till we meet a-gain.
Put his arms un-fail-ing round you: God be with you till we meet a-gain.
Smite death's threat-ening wave be-fore you: God be with you till we meet a-gain. A-men.

CLOSE OF WORSHIP

63 Lord, Dismiss Us With Thy Blessing

Attr. to John Fawcett, 1739/40-1817, alt.

SICILIAN MARINERS 8.7.8.7.8.7.
Sicilian Melody

1 Lord, dis - miss us with thy bless - ing; Fill our hearts with
2 Thanks we give and ad - o - ra - tion For thy gos - pel's
3 So that when thy love shall call us, Sav - ior, from the

joy and peace; Let us each, thy love pos - sess - ing,
joy - ful sound; May the fruits of thy sal - va - tion
world a - way, Fear of death shall not ap - pall us,

Tri - umph in re - deem - ing grace: Oh, re - fresh us,
In our hearts and lives a - bound: Ev - er faith - ful,
Glad thy sum - mons to o - bey: May we ev - er,

oh, re - fresh us, Trav - eling through this wil - der - ness.
ev - er faith - ful To the truth may we be found.
may we ev - er Reign with thee in end - less day. A - men.

CLOSE OF WORSHIP

All Creatures of Our God and King

64

St. Francis of Assisi, 1182-1226
Tr. William H. Draper, 1855-1933

LASST UNS ERFREUEN 8.8.4.4.8.8. with Alleluias
Melody from "Geistliche Kirchengesäng," Cologne, 1623

In unison

1 All crea-tures of our God and King, Lift up your voice and with us sing
2 Thou rush-ing wind that art so strong, Ye clouds that sail in heaven a-long,
3 Thou flow-ing wa-ter, pure and clear, Make mu-sic for thy Lord to hear,
4 And all ye men of ten-der heart, For-giv-ing oth-ers, take your part,
5 Let all things their cre-a-tor bless, And wor-ship him in hum-ble-ness,

Al-le-lu-ia, Al-le-lu-ia! Thou burn-ing sun with gold-en
O praise him, Al-le-lu-ia! Thou ris-ing morn, in praise re-
Al-le-lu-ia, Al-le-lu-ia! Thou fire so mas-ter-ful and
O sing ye, Al-le-lu-ia! Ye who long pain and sor-row
O praise him, Al-le-lu-ia! Praise, praise the Fa-ther, praise the

beam, Thou sil-ver moon with soft-er gleam, O praise him, O
joice, Ye lights of eve-ning, find a voice, O praise him, O
bright, That giv-est man both warmth and light, O praise him, O
bear, Praise God and on him cast your care. O praise him, O
Son, And praise the Spir-it, three in One. O praise him, O

praise him, Al-le-lu-ia, Al-le-lu-ia, Al-le-lu-ia! A-men.

A lower setting may be found at No. 30

WORKS IN CREATION

65 Glory Be to God on High

Theodore C. Williams, 1855-1915

GWALCHMAI 7.7.7.7. *with Alleluias*
Joseph D. Jones, 1827-1870

1 Glo - ry be to God on high,
2 Crea - tures of the field and flood, Al - le - lu - ia!
3 Stars that have no voice to sing,

Let the whole cre - a - tion cry,
Earth and sea cry "God is good," Al - le - lu - ia!
Give their glo - ry to our King,

Peace and bless - ing he has given,
Toil - ing pil - grims raise the song, Al - le - lu - ia!
Si - lent powers and an - gels' song,

Earth re - peat the songs of heaven,
Saints in light the strain pro - long, Al - le - lu - ia!
All un - to our God be - long,
A - men.

WORKS IN CREATION

For the Beauty of the Earth

Folliott S. Pierpoint, 1835-1917, alt.

DIX 7.7.7.7.7.7.
Abridged from a chorale by
Conrad Kocher, 1786-1872

1 For the beau-ty of the earth, For the beau-ty of the skies,
2 For the beau-ty of each hour Of the day and of the night,
3 For the joy of ear and eye, For the heart and mind's de-light,
4 For the joy of hu-man love, Broth-er, sis-ter, par-ent, child,

For the love which from our birth O-ver and a-round us lies,
Hill and vale, and tree and flower, Sun and moon, and stars of light,
For the mys-tic har-mo-ny Link-ing sense to sound and sight,
Friends on earth, and friends a-bove, For all gen-tle thoughts and mild,

Lord of all, to thee we raise This our hymn of grate-ful praise. A-men.

5 For each perfect gift of thine
  Unto us so freely given,
  Graces, human and divine,
    Flowers of earth and buds of heaven,

6 For thy Church that evermore
  Lifteth holy hands above,
  Offering up on every shore
    Her pure sacrifice of love,

A higher setting may be found at No.119

WORKS IN CREATION

God of the Earth, the Sky, the Sea

Samuel Longfellow, 1819-1882

HERR JESU CHRIST, MEIN'S LEBENS LICHT L.M.
"As Hymnodus Sacer," Leipzig, 1625
Harm. by J. S. Bach, 1685-1750

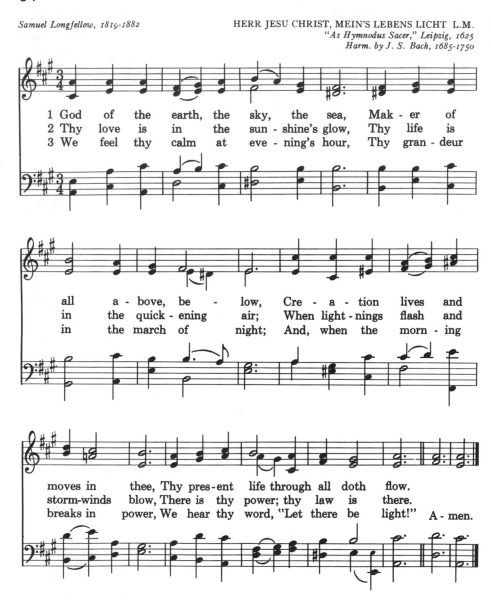

1 God of the earth, the sky, the sea, Mak-er of all a-bove, be-low, Cre-a-tion lives and moves in thee, Thy pres-ent life through all doth flow.

2 Thy love is in the sun-shine's glow, Thy life is in the quick-ening air; When light-nings flash and storm-winds blow, There is thy power; thy law is there.

3 We feel thy calm at eve-ning's hour, Thy gran-deur in the march of night; And, when the morn-ing breaks in power, We hear thy word, "Let there be light!" A-men.

4 But higher far, and far more clear,
Thee in man's spirit we behold;
Thine image and thyself are there,
The indwelling God, proclaimed of old.

WORKS IN CREATION

I Sing the Mighty Power of God

Isaac Watts, 1674-1748, alt.

ELLACOMBE C.M.D.
"Gesangbuch," Wirtemberg, 1784

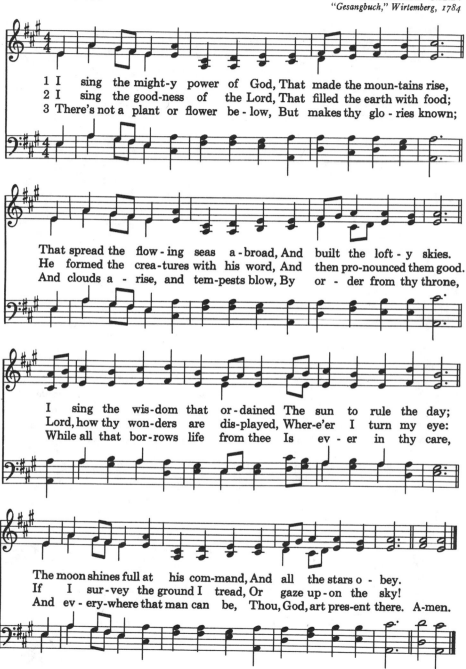

1 I sing the might-y power of God, That made the moun-tains rise,
2 I sing the good-ness of the Lord, That filled the earth with food;
3 There's not a plant or flower be-low, But makes thy glo-ries known;

That spread the flow-ing seas a-broad, And built the loft-y skies.
He formed the crea-tures with his word, And then pro-nounced them good.
And clouds a-rise, and tem-pests blow, By or-der from thy throne,

I sing the wis-dom that or-dained The sun to rule the day;
Lord, how thy won-ders are dis-played, Wher-e'er I turn my eye:
While all that bor-rows life from thee Is ev-er in thy care,

The moon shines full at his com-mand, And all the stars o-bey.
If I sur-vey the ground I tread, Or gaze up-on the sky!
And ev-ery-where that man can be, Thou, God, art pres-ent there. A-men.

A higher setting may be found at No. 459

WORKS IN CREATION

69 Let the Whole Creation Cry

Stopford A. Brooke, 1832-1916

SALZBURG 7.7.7.7.D.
Melody by Jacob Hintze, 1622-1702
Harm. by J. S. Bach, 1685-1750

1 Let the whole cre - a - tion cry, "Glo - ry to the Lord on high."
2 War-riors fight-ing for the Lord, Proph-ets burn-ing with his word,
3 Men and wom-en, young and old, Raise the an - them man - i - fold;

Heaven and earth, a - wake and sing, "God is good and there-fore King."
Those to whom the arts be - long, Add their voic - es to the song.
And let chil-dren's hap - py hearts In this wor-ship bear their parts;

Praise him, all ye hosts a - bove, Ev - er bright and fair in love;
Kings of knowl-edge and of law, To the glo - rious cir - cle draw;
From the north to south - ern pole Let the might - y cho - rus roll:

Sun and moon, up - lift your voice, Night and stars, in God re - joice!
All who work and all who wait, Sing, "The Lord is good and great!"
"Ho - ly, ho - ly, ho - ly One, Glo - ry be to God a - lone!" A - men.

WORKS IN CREATION

Let Us With a Gladsome Mind

First Tune

70

Based on Psalm 136
John Milton, 1608-1674, alt.

INNOCENTS 7.7.7.7.
"The Parish Choir," 1850

1 Let us with a glad-some mind Praise the Lord, for he is kind;
2 He, with all-com-mand-ing might, Filled the new-made world with light;
3 He the gold-en-tress-èd sun Caused all day his course to run;
4 The hornèd moon to shine by night, 'Mid her span-gled sis-ters bright;
5 All things liv-ing he doth feed; His full hand sup-plies their need;
6 Let us with a glad-some mind Praise the Lord, for he is kind;

For his mer-cies aye en-dure, Ev-er faith-ful, ev-er sure. A-men.

Alternative tune, MONKLAND, *No. 463*

Let Us With a Gladsome Mind

Second Tune

71

Based on Psalm 136
John Milton, 1608-1674, alt.

CHINESE MELODY 7.7.7.7.

1 Let us with a glad-some mind Praise the Lord, for he is kind;
2 He, with all-com-mand-ing might, Filled the new-made world with light;
3 He the gold-en-tress-èd sun Caused all day his course to run;
4 The hornèd moon to shine by night, 'Mid her span-gled sis-ters bright;
5 All things liv-ing he doth feed; His full hand sup-plies their need;
6 Let us with a glad-some mind Praise the Lord, for he is kind;

For his mer-cies aye en-dure, Ev-er faith-ful, ev-er sure.

WORKS IN CREATION

72
The Spacious Firmament on High

Based on Psalm 19
Joseph Addison, 1672-1719

CREATION L.M.D.
Franz J. Haydn, 1732-1809

1 The spa-cious fir-ma-ment on high, With all the
2 Soon as the eve-ning shades pre-vail, The moon takes
3 What though, in sol-emn si-lence, all Move round the

blue e-the-real sky, And span-gled heavens, a shin-ing frame,
up the won-drous tale; And night-ly, to the lis-tening earth,
dark ter-res-trial ball? What though no re-al voice nor sound

Their great O-rig-i-nal pro-claim. The un-wea-ried sun, from
Re-peats the sto-ry of her birth; Whilst all the stars that
A-midst their ra-diant orbs be found? In rea-son's ear they

day to day, Does his cre-a-tor's power dis-play, And pub-lish
round her burn, And all the plan-ets in their turn, Con-firm the
all re-joice, And ut-ter forth a glo-rious voice; For-ev-er

WORKS IN CREATION

es to ev - ery land The work of an al-might-y hand.
ti - dings as they roll, And spread the truth from pole to pole.
sing - ing, as they shine, "The hand that made us is di-vine." A-men.

Angels Holy, High and Lowly

73

Based on Benedicite
John S. Blackie, 1809-1895

LLANHERNE 8.7.8.8.7.
George T. Thalben-Ball, 1896-

1 An - gels ho - ly, high and low - ly, Sing the prais-es of the Lord!
2 Rock and high-land, wood and is - land, Crag where ea-gle's pride hath soared,
3 Roll-ing riv - er, praise him ev - er, From the moun-tain's deep vein poured;
4 Praise him ev - er, boun-teous giv-er! Praise him, Fa-ther, Friend, and Lord!

Earth and sky, all liv - ing na - ture, Man, the stamp of
Might - y moun-tains, pur - ple - breast-ed, Peaks cloud-cleav-ing,
Sil - ver foun - tain, clear - ly gush-ing, Trou - bled tor - rent,
Each glad soul its free course wing-ing, Each blithe voice its

thy Cre - a - tor, Praise ye, praise ye, God the Lord!
snow - y - crest - ed, Praise ye, praise ye, God the Lord!
mad - ly rush - ing, Praise ye, praise ye, God the Lord!
free song sing - ing, Praise the great and might - y Lord! A-men.

WORKS IN CREATION

O How Glorious, Full of Wonder

Based on Psalm 8
Curtis Beach, 1914-

IN BABILONE 8.7.8.7.D.
Traditional Dutch Melody

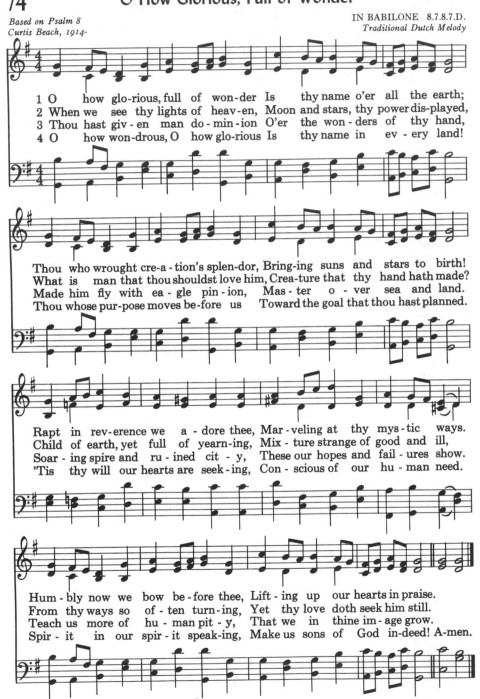

1 O how glo-rious, full of won-der Is thy name o'er all the earth;
2 When we see thy lights of heav-en, Moon and stars, thy power dis-played,
3 Thou hast giv-en man do-min-ion O'er the won-ders of thy hand,
4 O how won-drous, O how glo-rious Is thy name in ev-ery land!

Thou who wrought cre-a-tion's splen-dor, Bring-ing suns and stars to birth!
What is man that thou shouldst love him, Crea-ture that thy hand hath made?
Made him fly with ea-gle pin-ion, Mas-ter o-ver sea and land.
Thou whose pur-pose moves be-fore us Toward the goal that thou hast planned.

Rapt in rev-erence we a-dore thee, Mar-veling at thy mys-tic ways.
Child of earth, yet full of yearn-ing, Mix-ture strange of good and ill,
Soar-ing spire and ru-ined cit-y, These our hopes and fail-ures show.
'Tis thy will our hearts are seek-ing, Con-scious of our hu-man need.

Hum-bly now we bow be-fore thee, Lift-ing up our hearts in praise.
From thy ways so of-ten turn-ing, Yet thy love doth seek him still.
Teach us more of hu-man pit-y, That we in thine im-age grow.
Spir-it in our spir-it speak-ing, Make us sons of God in-deed! A-men.

WORKS IN CREATION

Heaven and Earth, and Sea and Air

75

Joachim Neander, 1650-1680
Tr. Catherine Winkworth, 1827-1878, alt.

GOTT SEI DANK 7.7.7.7.
Freylinghausen's "Gesangbuch," Halle, 1704

1 Heaven and earth, and sea and air, All their mak-er's praise de-clare;
2 See the glo-rious orb of day Break-ing through the clouds his way;
3 See how he hath ev-ery-where Made this earth so rich and fair;
4 Lord, great won-ders work-est thou! To thy sway all crea-tures bow;

Wake, my soul, a-wake and sing; Now thy grate-ful prais-es bring.
Moon and stars with sil-very light Praise him through the si-lent night.
Hill and vale and fruit-ful land, All things liv-ing, show his hand.
Write thou deep-ly in my heart What I am, and what thou art. A-men.

WORKS IN CREATION

How Gentle God's Commands

76

Philip Doddridge, 1702-1751, alt.

DENNIS S.M.
Melody by J. G. Nägeli, 1768?-1836
Arr. by Lowell Mason, 1792-1872

1 How gen-tle God's com-mands, How kind his pre-cepts are!
2 While prov-i-dence sup-ports, Let saints se-cure-ly dwell;
3 Why should this anx-ious load Press down your wea-ry mind?
4 His good-ness stands ap-proved, Down to the pres-ent day;

Come, cast your bur-dens on the Lord, And trust his con-stant care.
That hand which bears all na-ture up Shall guide his chil-dren well.
Haste to your heaven-ly Fa-ther's throne, And sweet re-fresh-ment find.
I'll drop my bur-den at his feet, And bear a song a-way. A-men.

PROVIDENCE

77

Be Still, My Soul

Katharina von Schlegel, 1697-?
Tr. Jane L. Borthwick, 1813-1897

FINLANDIA 10.10.10.10.10.10.
Jean Sibelius, 1865-1957

In unison

1 Be still, my soul: the Lord is on thy side; Bear pa-tient-ly the cross of grief or pain; Leave to thy God to or-der and pro-vide; In ev-ery change he faith-ful will re-main. Be still, my soul: thy best, thy heaven-ly

2 Be still, my soul: thy God doth un-der-take To guide the fu-ture as he has the past. Thy hope, thy con-fi-dence let noth-ing shake; All now mys-te-rious shall be bright at last. Be still, my soul: the waves and winds still

3 Be still, my soul: the hour is has-tening on When we shall be for-ev-er with the Lord, When dis-ap-point-ment, grief, and fear are gone, Sor-row for-got, love's pur-est joys re-stored. Be still, my soul: when change and tears are

PROVIDENCE

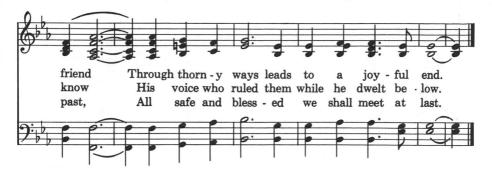

friend Through thorn-y ways leads to a joy-ful end.
know His voice who ruled them while he dwelt be·low.
past, All safe and bless-ed we shall meet at last.

Hast Thou Not Known

78

Based on Isaiah 40:28-31
Isaac Watts, 1674-1748
Alt. in "Scottish Paraphrases," 1781

ST. MAGNUS C.M.
Jeremiah Clark, c.1670-1707

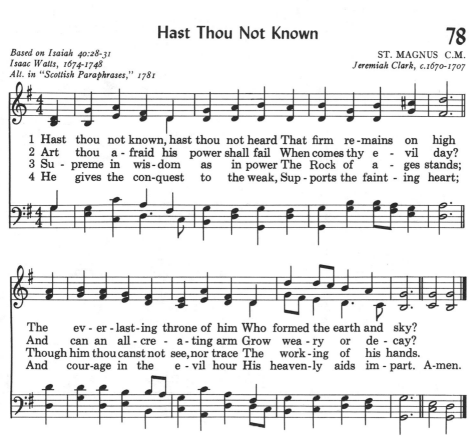

1 Hast thou not known, hast thou not heard That firm re-mains on high
2 Art thou a-fraid his power shall fail When comes thy e-vil day?
3 Su-preme in wis-dom as in power The Rock of a-ges stands;
4 He gives the con-quest to the weak, Sup-ports the faint-ing heart;

The ev-er-last-ing throne of him Who formed the earth and sky?
And can an all-cre-a-ting arm Grow wea-ry or de-cay?
Though him thou canst not see, nor trace The work-ing of his hands.
And cour-age in the e-vil hour His heaven-ly aids im-part. A-men.

5 Mere human power shall fast decay,
And youthful vigor cease;
But they who wait upon the Lord
In strength shall still increase.

6 They with unwearied feet shall tread
The path of life divine,
With growing ardor onward move,
With growing brightness shine.

PROVIDENCE

79

The King of Love My Shepherd Is
First Tune

Based on Psalm 23
Henry W. Baker, 1821-1877

DOMINUS REGIT ME 8.7.8.7.
John B. Dykes, 1823-1876

1 The King of love my shep - herd is, Whose
2 Where streams of liv - ing wa - ter flow, My
3 Per - verse and fool - ish oft I strayed, But
4 In death's dark vale I fear no ill, With

good - ness fail - eth nev - er; I noth - ing lack if
ran - somed soul he lead - eth, And where the ver - dant
yet in love he sought me, And on his shoul - der
thee, dear Lord, be - side me: Thy rod and staff my

I am his, And he is mine for - ev - er.
pas - tures grow, With food ce - les - tial feed - eth.
gen - tly laid, And home re - joic - ing brought me.
com - fort still, Thy cross be - fore to guide me. A - men.

5 Thou spread'st a table in my sight,
   Thy unction grace bestoweth,
   And O what transport of delight
   From thy pure chalice floweth!

6 And so through all the length of days
   Thy goodness faileth never;
   Good Shepherd, may I sing thy praise
   Within thy house forever.

PROVIDENCE

The King of Love My Shepherd Is

Second Tune

80

Based on Psalm 23
Henry W. Baker, 1821-1877

ST. COLUMBA 8.7.8.7
Ancient Irish Melody

1 The King of love my shep - herd is, Whose
2 Where streams of liv - ing wa - ter flow, My
3 Per - verse and fool - ish oft I strayed, But
4 In death's dark vale I fear no ill, With

good - ness fail - eth nev - er; I noth - ing lack if
ran - somed soul he lead - eth, And where the ver - dant
yet in love he sought me, And on his shoul - der
thee, dear Lord, be - side me: Thy rod and staff my

I am his, And he is mine for - ev - er.
pas - tures grow, With food ce - les - tial feed - eth.
gen - tly laid, And home re - joic - ing brought me.
com - fort still, Thy cross be - fore to guide me. A - men.

5 Thou spread'st a table in my sight,
Thy unction grace bestoweth,
And O what transport of delight
From thy pure chalice floweth!

6 And so through all the length of days
Thy goodness faileth never;
Good Shepherd, may I sing thy praise
Within thy house forever.

PROVIDENCE

81 Through All the Changing Scenes

Based on Psalm 34
"New Version," 1696

WILTSHIRE C.M.
George T. Smart, 1776-1867

1 Through all the chang-ing scenes of life, In
2 Oh mag-ni-fy the Lord with me, With
3 Oh make but tri-al of his love; Ex-
4 Fear him, ye saints, and you will then Have
5 To Fa-ther, Son, and Ho-ly Ghost, The

trou-ble and in joy, The prais-es of my
me ex-alt his name; When in dis-tress to
pe-rience will de-cide, How blest are they, and
noth-ing else to fear; Make you his serv-ice
God whom we a-dore, Be glo-ry, as it

God shall still My heart and tongue em-ploy.
him I called, He to my res-cue came.
on-ly they, Who in his truth con-fide.
your de-light, He'll make your wants his care.
was, is now, And shall be ev-er-more. A-men.

PROVIDENCE

High in the Heavens, Eternal God

82

Based on Psalm 36
Isaac Watts, 1674-1748, alt.

TRURO L.M.
Thomas Williams' "Psalmodia Evangelica," 1789

1 High in the heavens, e - ter - nal God, Thy good - ness
2 For - ev - er firm thy jus - tice stands, As moun - tains
3 My God, how ex - cel - lent thy grace, Whence all our
4 Life, like a foun - tain rich and free, Springs from the

in full glo - ry shines; Thy truth shall break through
their foun - da - tions keep; Wise are the won - ders
hope and com - fort spring! The sons of Ad - am
pres - ence of my Lord; And in thy light our

ev - ery cloud That veils and dark - ens thy de - signs.
of thy hands; Thy judg-ments are a might - y deep.
in dis - tress Fly to the shad - ow of thy wing.
souls shall see The glo - ries prom - ised in thy word. A-men.

A higher setting may be found at No. 114

PROVIDENCE

83 If Thou but Suffer God to Guide Thee

Georg Neumark, 1621-1681
Tr. Catherine Winkworth, 1827-1878

NEUMARK 9.8.9.8.8.8.
Melody by Georg Neumark, 1621-1681

1 If thou but suf - fer God to guide thee, And hope in
2 On - ly be still, and wait his lei - sure In cheer - ful
3 Sing, pray, and keep his ways un - swerv - ing; So do thine

him through all thy ways, He'll give thee strength, what-e'er be - tide thee,
hope, with heart con - tent To take what-e'er thy Fa - ther's pleas-ure
own part faith - ful - ly, And trust his word, though un - de - serv-ing;

And bear thee through the e - vil days; Who trusts in God's un-
And all - de - serv - ing love have sent; Nor doubt our in - most
Thou yet shalt find it true for thee; God nev - er yet for-

chang - ing love Builds on the rock that nought can move.
wants are known To him who chose us for his own.
sook at need The soul that trust - ed him in - deed. A-men.

PROVIDENCE

The Lord's My Shepherd

84

Based on Psalm 23
"Scottish Psalter," 1650, alt.

CRIMOND C.M.
Melody by Jessie S. Irvine, 1836-1887

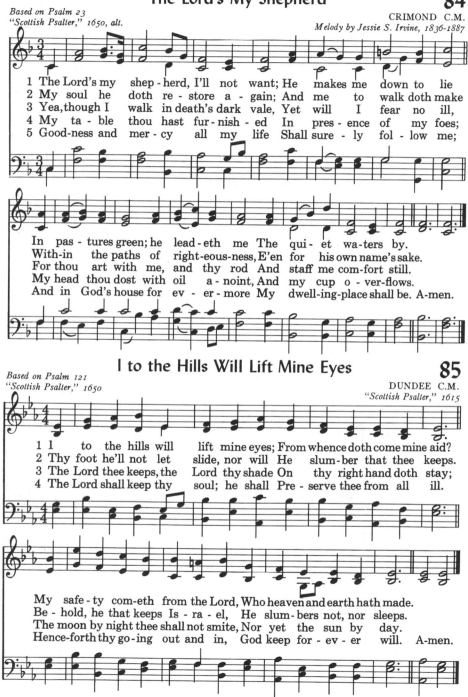

1 The Lord's my shep-herd, I'll not want; He makes me down to lie
2 My soul he doth re-store a-gain; And me to walk doth make
3 Yea, though I walk in death's dark vale, Yet will I fear no ill,
4 My ta-ble thou hast fur-nish-ed In pres-ence of my foes;
5 Good-ness and mer-cy all my life Shall sure-ly fol-low me;

In pas-tures green; he lead-eth me The qui-et wa-ters by.
With-in the paths of right-eous-ness, E'en for his own name's sake.
For thou art with me, and thy rod And staff me com-fort still.
My head thou dost with oil a-noint, And my cup o-ver-flows.
And in God's house for ev-er-more My dwell-ing-place shall be. A-men.

I to the Hills Will Lift Mine Eyes

85

Based on Psalm 121
"Scottish Psalter," 1650

DUNDEE C.M.
"Scottish Psalter," 1615

1 I to the hills will lift mine eyes; From whence doth come mine aid?
2 Thy foot he'll not let slide, nor will He slum-ber that thee keeps.
3 The Lord thee keeps, the Lord thy shade On thy right hand doth stay;
4 The Lord shall keep thy soul; he shall Pre-serve thee from all ill.

My safe-ty com-eth from the Lord, Who heaven and earth hath made.
Be-hold, he that keeps Is-ra-el, He slum-bers not, nor sleeps.
The moon by night thee shall not smite, Nor yet the sun by day.
Hence-forth thy go-ing out and in, God keep for-ev-er will. A-men.

Another arrangement may be found at No. 87

PROVIDENCE

86 Our God, to Whom We Turn

Edward Grubb, 1854-1939

STEADFAST 6.7.6.7.6.6.6.6.
"Neu Ordentlich Gesangbuch," 1646
Harm. from J. S. Bach, 1685-1750

1 Our God, to whom we turn When wea-ry with il - lu-sion,
2 Thou art thy-self the truth; Though we who fain would find thee,
3 All beau-ty speaks of thee: The moun-tains and the riv-ers,
4 Thou hid-den fount of love, Of peace, and truth, and beau-ty,

Whose stars se - rene-ly burn A - bove this earth's con - fu-sion,
Have tried, with thoughts un-couth, In fee - ble words to bind thee,
The line of lift-ed sea, Where spread-ing moon-light quiv-ers,
In - spire us from a - bove With joy and strength for du - ty.

Thine is the might - y plan, The stead-fast or - der sure
It is be - cause thou art We're driv-en to the quest;
The deep-toned or - gan blast That rolls through arch - es dim,
May thy fresh light a - rise With - in each cloud-ed heart,

In which the world be - gan, En - dures, and shall en - dure.
Till truth from false-hood part, Our souls can find no rest.
Hints of the mu-sic vast Of thine e - ter-nal hymn.
And give us o-pen eyes To see thee as thou art. A-men.

PROVIDENCE

God Moves in a Mysterious Way

William Cowper, 1731-1800

DUNDEE C.M.
"Scottish Psalter," 1615

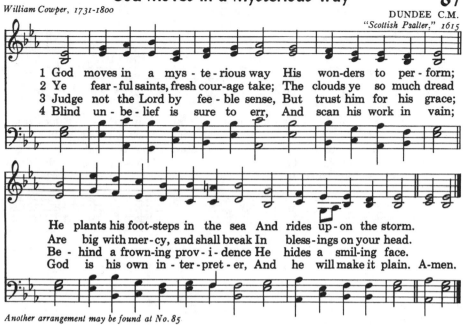

1 God moves in a mys - te - rious way His won-ders to per - form;
2 Ye fear - ful saints, fresh cour-age take; The clouds ye so much dread
3 Judge not the Lord by fee - ble sense, But trust him for his grace;
4 Blind un - be - lief is sure to err, And scan his work in vain;

He plants his foot-steps in the sea And rides up - on the storm.
Are big with mer - cy, and shall break In bless-ings on your head.
Be - hind a frown-ing prov - i - dence He hides a smil-ing face.
God is his own in - ter-pret - er, And he will make it plain. A-men.

Another arrangement may be found at No. 85

God Moves in a Mysterious Way

Melody in the Tenor

William Cowper, 1731-1800

DUNDEE C.M.
Arr. by Thomas Ravenscroft, c.1592-c.1635

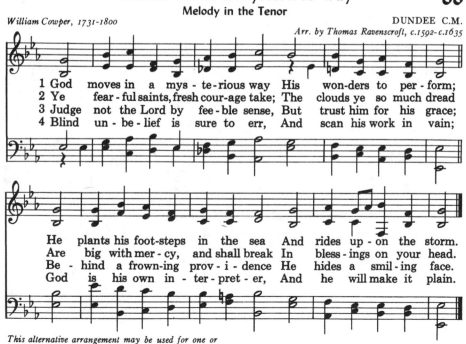

1 God moves in a mys - te - rious way His won-ders to per - form;
2 Ye fear - ful saints, fresh cour-age take; The clouds ye so much dread
3 Judge not the Lord by fee - ble sense, But trust him for his grace;
4 Blind un - be - lief is sure to err, And scan his work in vain;

He plants his foot-steps in the sea And rides up - on the storm.
Are big with mer - cy, and shall break In bless - ings on your head.
Be - hind a frown-ing prov - i - dence He hides a smil - ing face.
God is his own in - ter-pret - er, And he will make it plain.

*This alternative arrangement may be used for one or
more stanzas, the congregation singing the melody only.*

PROVIDENCE

Lord of All Being, Throned Afar
First Tune

Oliver Wendell Holmes, 1809-1894

UFFINGHAM L.M.
Jeremiah Clark, c.1670-1707

1 Lord of all be - ing, throned a - far, Thy glo - ry flames from
2 Sun of our life, thy quick - ening ray Sheds on our path the
3 Our mid-night is thy smile with - drawn; Our noon-tide is thy
4 Lord of all life, be - low, a - bove, Whose light is truth, whose
5 Grant us thy truth to make us free, And kin-dling hearts that

sun and star; Cen - ter and soul of ev - ery sphere,
glow of day; Star of our hope, thy soft - ened light
gra - cious dawn; Our rain - bow arch, thy mer - cy's sign;
warmth is love, Be - fore thy ev - er - blaz - ing throne
burn for thee, Till all thy liv - ing al - tars claim

Yet to each lov - ing heart how near!
Cheers the long watch - es of the night.
All, save the clouds of sin, are thine.
We ask no lus - ter of our own.
One ho - ly light, one heav - enly flame. A - men.

PROVIDENCE

Lord of All Being, Throned Afar

Second Tune

Oliver Wendell Holmes, 1809-1894

LOUVAN L.M.
Virgil C. Taylor, 1817-1891

1 Lord of all be-ing, throned a-far, Thy glo-ry flames from sun and star; Cen-ter and soul of ev-ery sphere, Yet to each lov-ing heart how near!

2 Sun of our life, thy quick-ening ray Sheds on our path the glow of day; Star of our hope, thy soft-ened light Cheers the long watch-es of the night.

3 Our mid-night is thy smile with-drawn; Our noon-tide is thy gra-cious dawn; Our rain-bow arch, thy mer-cy's sign; All, save the clouds of sin, are thine.

4 Lord of all life, be-low, a-bove, Whose light is truth, whose warmth is love, Be-fore thy ev-er-blaz-ing throne We ask no lus-ter of our own.

5 Grant us thy truth to make us free, And kin-dling hearts that burn for thee, Till all thy liv-ing al-tars claim One ho-ly light, one heav-en-ly flame. A-men.

PROVIDENCE

91 The Man Who Once Has Found Abode

Based on Psalm 91
Anonymous
"United Presbyterian Book of Psalms U.S.A.," 1871

TALLIS' CANON L.M.
Thomas Tallis, d.1585

1 The man who once has found abode
With in the se-cret place of God,
Shall with al-might-y God a-bide,
And in his shad-ow safe-ly hide.

2 I of the Lord my God will say, "He
is my ref-uge and my stay;
To him for safe-ty I will flee;
My God, in him my trust shall be."

3 He shall with all-pro-tect-ing care
Pre-serve thee from the fowl-er's snare;
When fear-ful plagues a-round pre-vail,
No fa-tal stroke shall thee as-sail.

4 His out-spread pin-ions shall thee hide;
Be-neath his wings shalt thou con-fide;
His faith-ful-ness shall ev-er be
A shield and buck-ler un-to thee. A-men.

5 No nightly terrors shall alarm,
   No deadly shaft by day shall harm,
   Nor pestilence that walks by night,
   Nor plagues that waste in noonday light.

6 Because thy trust is God alone,
   Thy dwelling-place the highest One,
   No evil shall upon thee come,
   Nor plague approach thy guarded home.

PROVIDENCE

I Look to Thee in Every Need

92

Samuel Longfellow, 1819-1892, alt.

O JESU 8.6.8.6.8.8.
Melody from "Hirschberg Gesangbuch," 1741

1 I look to thee in ev - ery need,
2 Dis - cour - aged in the work of life,
3 Thy calm - ness bends se - rene a - bove,
4 En - fold - ed deep in thy dear love,

And nev - er look in vain; I feel thy strong and ten - der love,
Dis - heart-ened by its load, Shamed by its fail - ures or its fears,
My rest - less-ness to still; A - round me flows thy quick - ening life,
Held in thy law, I stand; Thy hand in all things I be - hold,

And all is well a - gain: The thought of thee is might-ier far
I sink be - side the road; But let me on - ly think of thee
To nerve my fal-tering will: Thy pres - ence fills my sol - i - tude;
And all things in thy hand; Thou lead - est me by un-sought ways,

Than sin and pain and sor - row are.
And then new heart springs up in me.
Thy prov - i - dence turns all to good.
And turn'st my mourn - ing in - to praise. A - men.

PROVIDENCE

93 Guide Me, O Thou Great Jehovah

William Williams, 1717-1791
Tr. Peter Williams, 1727-1796, and others

CWM RHONDDA 8.7.8.7.8.7.7.
John Hughes, 1873-1932

1 Guide me, O thou great Je - ho - vah, Pil - grim through this
2 O - pen now the crys - tal foun - tain, Whence the heal - ing
3 When I tread the verge of Jor - dan, Bid my anx - ious

bar - ren land; I am weak, but thou art might-y; Hold me with thy
stream doth flow; Let the fire and cloud-y pil - lar Lead me all my
fears sub - side; Death of death, and hell's de-struc-tion, Land me safe on

power - ful hand; Bread of heav - en, bread of heav - en,
jour - ney through; Strong De - liv - erer, strong De - liv - erer,
Ca - naan's side; Songs of prais - es, songs of prais - es,

Feed me till I want no more, Feed me till I want no more.
Be thou still my strength and shield, Be thou still my strength and shield.
I will ev - er give to thee, I will ev - er give to thee. A-men.

PROVIDENCE

When All Thy Mercies, O My God

94

Joseph Addison, 1672-1719

TALLIS' ORDINAL C.M.
Thomas Tallis, d.1585

1 When all thy mer-cies, O my God, My ris-ing soul sur-veys, Trans-
2 Un-num-bered com-forts to my soul Thy ten-der care be-stowed, Be-
3 Ten thou-sand thou-sand pre-cious gifts My dai-ly thanks em-ploy; Nor
4 Through all e-ter-ni-ty to thee A joy-ful song I'll raise; For,

port-ed with the view, I'm lost In won-der, love, and praise.
fore my in-fant heart con-ceived From whom those com-forts flowed.
is the least a cheer-ful heart That tastes those gifts with joy.
oh, e-ter-ni-ty's too short To ut-ter all thy praise! A-men.

The Lord Will Come and Not Be Slow

95

YORK C.M.
"Scottish Psalter," 1615

Based on Psalms 82, 85, 86
John Milton, 1608-1674

Harm. by John Milton, Sr., c.1563-1647

1 The Lord will come and not be slow, His foot-steps can-not err;
2 Truth from the earth, like to a flower, Shall bud and blos-som then;
3 Rise, God, judge thou the earth in might, This wick-ed earth re-dress;
4 The na-tions all whom thou hast made Shall come, and all shall frame
5 For great thou art, and won-ders great By thy strong hand are done:

Be-fore him right-eous-ness shall go, His roy-al har-bin-ger.
And jus-tice, from her heaven-ly bower, Look down on mor-tal men.
For thou art he who shalt by right The na-tions all pos-sess.
To bow them low be-fore thee, Lord, And glo-ri-fy thy name.
Thou in thy ev-er-last-ing seat Re-main-est God a-lone. A-men.

A faux-bourdon may be found at No. 474

PROVIDENCE

96 Whate'er My God Ordains Is Right

Samuel Rodigast, 1649-1708
Tr. Catherine Winkworth, 1827-1878

WAS GOTT TUT 8.7.8.7.4.4.8.8.
Severus Gastorius, c.1675
"Weimar Gesangbuch," 1681

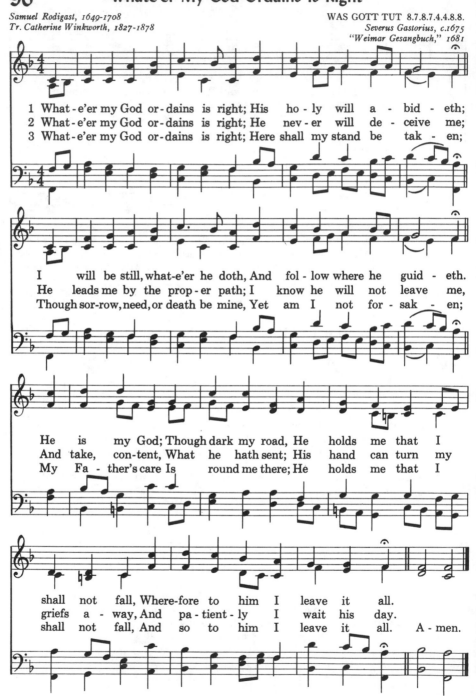

1 What-e'er my God or-dains is right; His ho-ly will a - bid - eth;
2 What-e'er my God or-dains is right; He nev-er will de - ceive me;
3 What-e'er my God or-dains is right; Here shall my stand be tak - en;

I will be still, what-e'er he doth, And fol - low where he guid - eth.
He leads me by the prop-er path; I know he will not leave me,
Though sor-row, need, or death be mine, Yet am I not for-sak - en;

He is my God; Though dark my road, He holds me that I
And take, con-tent, What he hath sent; His hand can turn my
My Fa - ther's care Is round me there; He holds me that I

shall not fall, Where-fore to him I leave it all.
griefs a - way, And pa - tient - ly I wait his day.
shall not fall, And so to him I leave it all. A - men.

PROVIDENCE

God of Our Life, Through All the Circling Years   97

Hugh T. Kerr, 1872-1950, alt.

SANDON 10.4.10.4.10.10.
Charles H. Purday, 1799-1885

1 God of our life, through all the cir-cling years, We trust in thee;
2 God of the past, our times are in thy hand; With us a-bide.
3 God of the com-ing years, through paths un-known We fol-low thee;

In all the past, through all our hopes and fears, Thy hand we see.
Lead us by faith to hope's true prom-ised land; Be thou our guide.
When we are strong, Lord, leave us not a-lone; Our ref-uge be.

With each new day, when morn-ing lifts the veil,
With thee to bless, the dark-ness shines as light,
Be thou for us in life our dai-ly bread,

We own thy mer-cies, Lord, which nev-er fail.
And faith's fair vi-sion chan-ges in-to sight.
Our heart's true home when all our years have sped. A-men.

PROVIDENCE

98 My God, I Thank Thee, Who Hast Made

Adelaide A. Procter, 1825-1864, alt.

WENTWORTH 8.4.8.4.8.4.
Frederick C. Maker, 1844-1927

1 My God, I thank thee, who hast made The earth so bright,
2 I thank thee, too, that thou hast made Joy to a - bound;
3 I thank thee more that all our joy Is touched with pain,
4 I thank thee, Lord, that thou hast kept The best in store;

So full of splen - dor and of joy, Beau - ty and light;
So man - y gen - tle thoughts and deeds Circ - ling us round,
That shad - ows fall on bright - est hours, That thorns re - main,
We have e - nough, yet not too much To long for more:

So man - y glo - rious things are here, No - ble and right.
That in the dark - est spot of earth Some love is found.
So that earth's bliss may be our guide, And not our chain.
A yearn - ing for a deep - er peace Not known be - fore. A-men.

99 O Love of God, How Strong and True

Horatius Bonar, 1808-1889

EISENACH L.M.
Melody by Johann H. Schein, 1586-1630

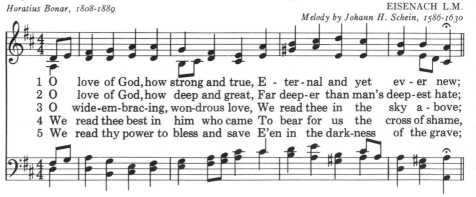

1 O love of God, how strong and true, E - ter - nal and yet ev - er new;
2 O love of God, how deep and great, Far deep - er than man's deep - est hate;
3 O wide-em-brac-ing, won-drous love, We read thee in the sky a - bove,
4 We read thee best in him who came To bear for us the cross of shame,
5 We read thy power to bless and save E'en in the dark-ness of the grave;

GRACE

Un - com-pre-hend-ed and un-bought, Be-yond all knowl-edge and all thought!
Self - fed, self-kin-dled like the light, Change-less, e-ter-nal, in - fi - nite!
We read thee in the earth be-low, In seas that swell and streams that flow.
Sent by the Fa-ther from on high, Our life to live, our death to die.
Still more in res - ur - rec-tion light We read the full-ness of thy might. A-men.

O My Soul, Bless God, the Father   100

Based on Psalm 103
Anonymous
"United Presbyterian Book of Psalms U.S.A.," 1871

STUTTGART 8.7.8.7.
Melody attr. to Christian F. Witt, 1660-1716
"Psalmodia Sacra," Gotha, 1715

1 O my soul, bless God, the Fa - ther; All with - in me bless his name;
2 Who for - giv - eth thy trans-gres-sions, Thy dis - ea - ses all who heals,
3 Far as east from west is dis - tant, He hath put a - way our sin;
4 As it was with - out be - gin-ning, So it lasts with - out an end;

Bless the Fa - ther, and for - get not All his mer - cies to pro-claim.
Who re-deems thee from de-struc-tion, Who with thee so kind-ly deals,
Like the pit - y of a fa - ther Hath the Lord's com-pas-sion been.
To their chil-dren's chil-dren ev - er Shall his right-eous-ness ex - tend: A-men.

5 Unto such as keep his covenant
   And are steadfast in his way,
Unto those who still remember
   His commandments and obey.

6 Bless the Father, all his creatures,
   Ever under his control;
All throughout his vast dominion
   Bless the Father, O my soul.

GRACE

101 There's a Wideness in God's Mercy

First Tune

Frederick W. Faber, 1814-1863

IN BABILONE 8.7.8.7.D.
Traditional Dutch Melody

1 There's a wide-ness in God's mer-cy, Like the wide-ness of the sea;
2 For the love of God is broad-er Than the meas-ure of man's mind;

There's a kind-ness in his jus-tice, Which is more than lib-er-ty.
And the heart of the E-ter-nal Is most won-der-ful-ly kind.

There is no place where earth's sor-rows Are more felt than up in heaven;
If our love were but more sim-ple, We should take him at his word;

There is no place where earth's fail-ings Have such kind-ly judg-ment given.
And our lives would be all sun-shine In the sweet-ness of our Lord. A-men.

GRACE

There's a Wideness in God's Mercy

Second Tune

102

Frederick W. Faber, 1814-1863

WELLESLEY 8.7.8.7.
Lizzie S. Tourjée, 1858-1913

1 There's a wide-ness in God's mer-cy, Like the wide-ness of the sea;
2 There is no place where earth's sor-rows Are more felt than up in heaven;
3 For the love of God is broad-er Than the meas-ure of man's mind;
4 If our love were but more sim-ple, We should take him at his word;

There's a kind-ness in his jus-tice, Which is more than lib-er-ty.
There is no place where earth's fail-ings Have such kind-ly judg-ment given.
And the heart of the E-ter-nal Is most won-der-ful-ly kind.
And our lives would be all sun-shine In the sweet-ness of our Lord. A-men.

Come, Thou Long-Expected Jesus

103

STUTTGART 8.7.8.7.

Charles Wesley, 1707-1788, alt.

Melody attr. to Christian F. Witt, 1660-1716
"Psalmodia Sacra," Gotha, 1715

1 Come, thou long-ex-pect-ed Je-sus, Born to set thy peo-ple free;
2 Is-rael's strength and con-so-la-tion, Hope of all the earth thou art;
3 Born thy peo-ple to de-liv-er, Born a child, and yet a king,
4 By thine own e-ter-nal Spir-it Rule in all our hearts a-lone;

From our fears and sins re-lease us; Let us find our rest in thee.
Dear de-sire of ev-ery na-tion, Joy of ev-ery long-ing heart.
Born to reign in us for-ev-er, Now thy gra-cious king-dom bring.
By thine all-suf-fi-cient mer-it Raise us to thy glo-rious throne. A-men.

ADVENT

104   Comfort, Comfort Ye My People

Based on Isaiah 40:1-8
Johann Olearius, 1611-1684
Tr. Catherine Winkworth, 1827-1878, alt.

PSALM 42 8.7.8.7.7.7.8.8.
"Genevan Psalter," 1551

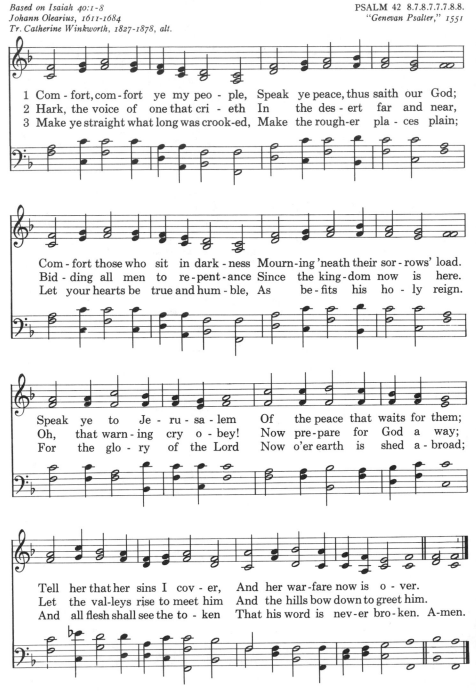

1 Com - fort, com - fort ye my peo - ple, Speak ye peace, thus saith our God;
2 Hark, the voice of one that cri - eth In the des - ert far and near,
3 Make ye straight what long was crook-ed, Make the rough-er pla - ces plain;

Com - fort those who sit in dark - ness Mourn-ing 'neath their sor - rows' load.
Bid - ding all men to re-pent-ance Since the king-dom now is here.
Let your hearts be true and hum - ble, As be - fits his ho - ly reign.

Speak ye to Je - ru - sa - lem Of the peace that waits for them;
Oh, that warn-ing cry o - bey! Now pre-pare for God a way;
For the glo - ry of the Lord Now o'er earth is shed a - broad;

Tell her that her sins I cov - er, And her war-fare now is o - ver.
Let the val-leys rise to meet him And the hills bow down to greet him.
And all flesh shall see the to - ken That his word is nev-er bro-ken. A-men.

ADVENT

Hail to the Lord's Anointed

105

Based on Psalm 72
James Montgomery, 1771-1854

ROCKPORT 7.6.7.6.D.
T. Tertius Noble, 1867-1953

1 Hail to the Lord's A - noint - ed, Great Da - vid's great-er Son!
2 He comes with suc - cor speed - y To those who suf - fer wrong;
3 He shall come down like show - ers Up - on the fruit - ful earth;
4 O'er ev - ery foe vic - to - rious, He on his throne shall rest,

Hail, in the time ap - point - ed, His reign on earth be - gun!
To help the poor and need - y, And bid the weak be strong;
And love, joy, hope, like flow - ers, Spring in his path to birth;
From age to age more glo - rious, All - bless - ing and all - blest;

He comes to break op - pres - sion, To set the cap - tive free,
To give them songs for sigh - ing, Their dark - ness turn to light,
Be - fore him on the moun - tains Shall peace, the her - ald, go;
The tide of time shall nev - er His cov - e - nant re - move;

To take a - way trans - gres - sion, And rule in eq - ui - ty.
Whose souls, con - demned and dy - ing, Were pre - cious in his sight.
And right - eous - ness, in foun - tains, From hill to val - ley flow.
His name shall stand for - ev - er: That name to us is Love. A-men.

ADVENT

106   Hills of the North, Rejoice

Charles E. Oakley, 1832-1865

LITTLE CORNARD 6.6.6.6.8.8.
Martin Shaw, 1875

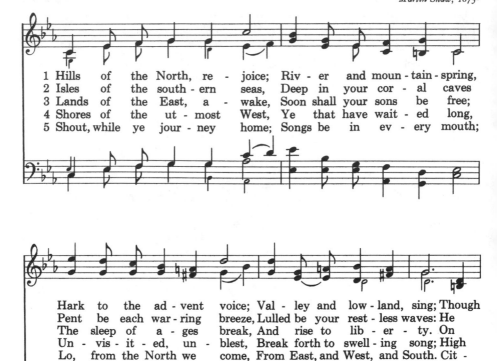

1 Hills of the North, re - joice; Riv - er and moun - tain-spring,
2 Isles of the south - ern seas, Deep in your cor - al caves
3 Lands of the East, a - wake, Soon shall your sons be free;
4 Shores of the ut - most West, Ye that have wait - ed long,
5 Shout, while ye jour - ney home; Songs be in ev - ery mouth;

Hark to the ad - vent voice; Val - ley and low - land, sing; Though
Pent be each war - ring breeze, Lulled be your rest - less waves: He
The sleep of a - ges break, And rise to lib - er - ty. On
Un - vis - it - ed, un - blest, Break forth to swell - ing song; High
Lo, from the North we come, From East, and West, and South. Cit -

ab - sent long, your Lord is nigh; He judg-ment brings and vic - to - ry.
comes to reign with bound-less sway, And makes your wastes his great high-way.
your far hills, long cold and gray, Has dawned the ev - er - last -ing day.
raise the note, that Je - sus died, Yet lives and reigns, the Cru - ci - fied.
y of God, the bond are free, We come to live and reign in thee! A-men.

ADVENT

Let All Mortal Flesh Keep Silence

Liturgy of St. James
Tr. Gerard Moultrie, 1829-1885

PICARDY 8.7.8.7.8.7.
Traditional French Carol

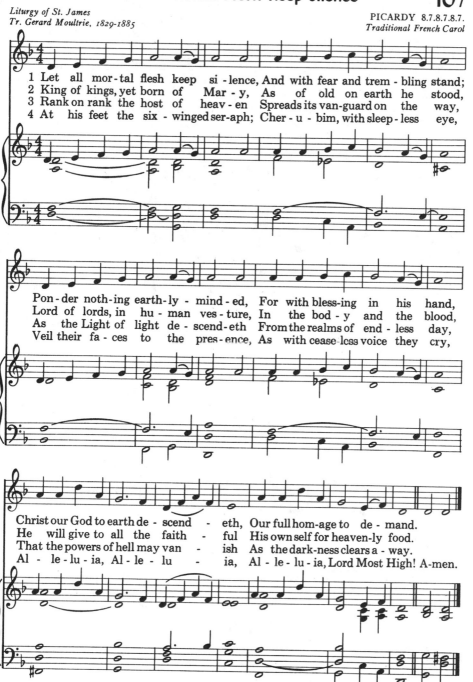

1 Let all mor-tal flesh keep si-lence, And with fear and trem-bling stand;
2 King of kings, yet born of Mar-y, As of old on earth he stood,
3 Rank on rank the host of heav-en Spreads its van-guard on the way,
4 At his feet the six-winged ser-aph; Cher-u-bim, with sleep-less eye,

Pon-der noth-ing earth-ly-mind-ed, For with bless-ing in his hand,
Lord of lords, in hu-man ves-ture, In the bod-y and the blood,
As the Light of light de-scend-eth From the realms of end-less day,
Veil their fa-ces to the pres-ence, As with cease-less voice they cry,

Christ our God to earth de-scend-eth, Our full hom-age to de-mand.
He will give to all the faith-ful His own self for heaven-ly food.
That the powers of hell may van-ish As the dark-ness clears a-way.
Al-le-lu-ia, Al-le-lu-ia, Al-le-lu-ia, Lord Most High! A-men.

ADVENT

108 Wake, Awake, for Night Is Flying

Philipp Nicolai, 1556-1608
Tr. Catherine Winkworth, 1827-1878, alt.

WACHET AUF 8.9.8.8.9.8.6.6.4.8.8.
Melody by Philipp Nicolai, 1556-1608
Harm. by J.S. Bach, 1685-1750

1 Wake, a-wake, for night is fly - ing; The watch-men on the
2 Zi - on hears the watch-men sing - ing; Her heart with deep de -

heights are cry - ing, A - wake, Je - ru - sa - lem, a - rise!
light is spring - ing, She wakes, she ris - es from her gloom,

Mid-night's sol - emn hour is toll - ing; His char-iot wheels are
For her Lord comes down all glo - rious, In grace ar - rayed, by

near - er roll - ing; He comes! O Church, lift up thine eyes!
truth vic - to - rious; Her star is risen, her light is come!

ADVENT

Rise up, with will-ing feet Go forth, the Bride-groom meet:
Ah, come thou bless-ed One, God's own be-lov - ed Son,

Hal - le - lu - jah! Lo, great and small, We an - swer all;
Hal - le - lu - jah! We haste a - long, An ea - ger throng,

We fol - low where thy voice shall call.
And glad - some join the ad - vent song. A - men.

3 Now let all the heavens adore thee,
   And men and angels sing before thee
      With harp and cymbal's clearest tone;
   Of one pearl each shining portal,
   Where we shall join the choirs immortal
      In praises round thy glorious throne;
   No vision ever brought,
   No ear hath ever caught
      Such great glory!
   Therefore will we, eternally,
   Sing hymns of joy and praise to thee.

109 Watchman, Tell Us of the Night

John Bowring, 1792-1872

ABERYSTWYTH 7.7.7.7.D.
Joseph Parry, 1841-1903

1 Watch-man, tell us of the night, What its signs of prom-ise are.
2 Watch-man, tell us of the night, High-er yet that star as-cends.
3 Watch-man, tell us of the night, For the morn-ing seems to dawn,

Trav-eler, o'er yon moun-tain's height, See that glo-ry-beam-ing star.
Trav-eler, bless-ed-ness and light, Peace and truth its course por-tends.
Trav-eler, dark-ness takes its flight, Doubt and ter-ror are with-drawn.

Watch-man, does its beau-teous ray Aught of joy or hope fore-tell?
Watch-man, will its beams a-lone Gild the spot that gave them birth?
Watch-man, let thy wan-derings cease; Hie thee to thy qui-et home.

Trav-eler, yes; it brings the day, Prom-ised day of Is-ra-el.
Trav-eler, a-ges are its own; See, it bursts o'er all the earth.
Trav-eler, lo, the Prince of peace, Lo, the Son of God is come. A-men.

ADVENT

Alternative tune, SALZBURG, No. 69

O Come, O Come, Emmanuel

Latin: c.9th century
Tr. John M. Neale, 1818-1866, Sts. 1,2, alt.
Tr. Henry S. Coffin, 1877-1954, Sts. 3,4

VENI EMMANUEL 8.8.8.8.8.8.
Adapted from Plainsong
Thomas Helmore, 1811-1890

110

1 O come, O come, Em-man-u-el, And ran-som cap-tive Is-ra-el, That mourns in lone-ly ex-ile here, Un-til the Son of God ap-pear.

2 O come, thou Day-spring, come and cheer Our spir-its by thine ad-vent here; Dis-perse the gloom-y clouds of night, And death's dark shad-ows put to flight.

3 O come, thou Wis-dom from on high, And or-der all things, far and nigh; To us the path of knowl-edge show, And cause us in her ways to go.

4 O come, De-sire of na-tions, bind All peo-ples in one heart and mind; Bid en-vy, strife and quar-rels cease; Fill the whole world with heav-en's peace.

REFRAIN

Re-joice! Re-joice! Em-man-u-el Shall come to thee, O Is-ra-el! A-men.

ADVENT

Of the Father's Love Begotten

Aurelius Clemens Prudentius, 348-c.410
Tr. John M. Neale, 1818-1866, St. 1, alt.
Tr. Henry W. Baker, 1821-1877, Sts. 2,3

DIVINUM MYSTERIUM 8.7.8.7.8.7.7.
13th century Plainsong, Mode V.

1 Of the Fa-ther's love be-got-ten, Ere the worlds be-gan to be,
2 O ye heights of heaven a-dore him; An-gel hosts, his prais-es sing;
3 Christ, to thee with God the Fa-ther, And, O Ho-ly Ghost, to thee,

He is Al-pha and O-me-ga, He the source, the end-ing he;
Powers, do-min-ions, bow be-fore him, And ex-tol our God and King;
Hymn and chant and high thanks-giv-ing, And un-wea-ried prais-es be:

Of the things that are, that have been, And that
Let no tongue on earth be si-lent, Ev-ery
Hon-or, glo-ry, and do-min-ion, And e-

fu - ture years shall see, Ev - er-more and ev - er - more!
voice in con - cert ring, Ev - er-more and ev - er - more!
ter - nal vic - to - ry, Ev - er-more and ev - er - more! A - men.

Ah! Think Not the Lord Delayeth

112

Percy Dearmer, 1867-1936

ALLES IST AN GOTTES SEGEN 8.8.7.D.
Attr. to J.B. König, 1691-1758
"Harmonischer Lieder-Schatz," 1738

1 Ah! think not the Lord de - lay - eth; "I am with you," still he say - eth,
2 For e'en now the reign of heav - en Spreads through-out the world like leav - en,
3 Not for us to find the rea - sons, Or to know the times and sea - sons,

"Do you yet not un - der-stand?" Look not back, the past re - gret-ting;
Un - ob-served, and ver - y near, Like the seed when no man know-eth,
Comes the Lord when strikes the hour; Ours to bear the faith - ful wit - ness

On the dawn your hearts be set-ting; Rise, and join the Lord's com-mand.
Like the shel-tering tree that grow-eth, Comes the life e - ter - nal here.
Which can shape the world to fit-ness, Thine, O God, to give the power. A-men.

113   Creator of the Stars of Night

Latin: anon. 9th century
Tr. John M. Neale, 1818-1866, alt.

CONDITOR ALME L.M.
Sarum Plainsong, Mode IV

1 Cre - a - tor of the stars of night, Thy peo-ple's ev - er - last-ing light,
2 To thee the trav - ail deep was known That made the whole cre - a - tion groan,
3 When the old world drew on toward night, Thou cam - est, not in splen-dor bright
4 At thy great name ex - alt - ed now All knees must bend, all hearts must bow;

O Christ, thou Sav-ior of us all, We pray thee, hear us when we call.
Till thou, Re-deem-er, should-est free Thine own in glo-rious lib - er - ty.
As mon-arch, but the hum-ble child Of Mar - y, blame-less moth-er mild.
And things ce - les-tial thee shall own, And things ter-res-trial, Lord a - lone. A - men.

114   Lift Up Your Heads, Ye Mighty Gates

Based on Psalm 24
Georg Weissel, 1590-1635
Tr. Catherine Winkworth, 1827-1878

TRURO L.M.
Thomas Williams', "Psalmodia Evangelica," 1789

1 Lift up your heads, ye might - y gates; Be - hold the
2 Fling wide the por - tals of your heart; Make it a
3 Re - deem - er, come! I o - pen wide My heart to
4 So come, my Sov - ereign; en - ter in! Let new and

ADVENT

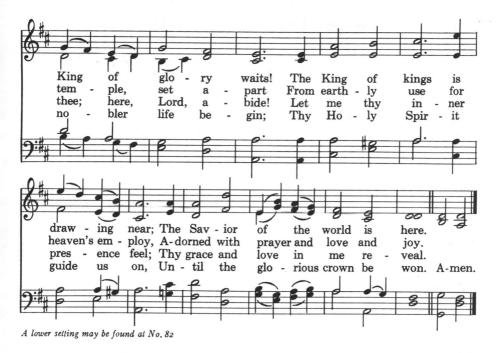

King of glo - ry waits! The King of kings is
tem - ple, set a - part From earth - ly use for
thee; here, Lord, a - bide! Let me thy in - ner
no - bler life be - gin; Thy Ho - ly Spir - it

draw - ing near; The Sav - ior of the world is here.
heaven's em - ploy, A-dorned with prayer and love and joy.
pres - ence feel; Thy grace and love in me re - veal.
guide us on, Un - til the glo - rious crown be won. A-men.

A lower setting may be found at No. 82

On Jordan's Bank the Baptist's Cry 115

Latin: Charles Coffin, 1676-1749
Tr. John Chandler, 1806-1876, alt.

WINCHESTER NEW L.M.
Adapted from "Musicalisches Handbuch," Hamburg, 1690

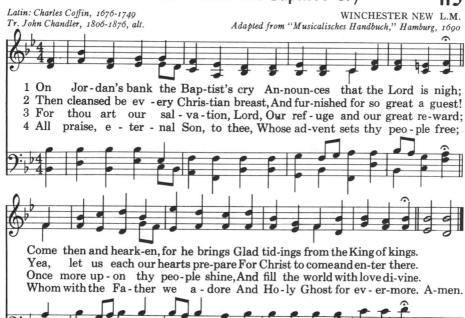

1 On Jor-dan's bank the Bap-tist's cry An-noun-ces that the Lord is nigh;
2 Then cleansed be ev - ery Chris-tian breast, And fur-nished for so great a guest!
3 For thou art our sal - va - tion, Lord, Our ref - uge and our great re-ward;
4 All praise, e - ter - nal Son, to thee, Whose ad-vent sets thy peo - ple free;

Come then and heark-en, for he brings Glad tid-ings from the King of kings.
Yea, let us each our hearts pre-pare For Christ to come and en-ter there.
Once more up - on thy peo-ple shine, And fill the world with love di-vine.
Whom with the Fa - ther we a - dore And Ho-ly Ghost for ev - er-more. A-men.

ADVENT

Angels We Have Heard on High

Traditional French Carol

GLORIA 7.7.7.7. *with Refrain*
French Carol Melody

1 An - gels we have heard on high Sweet - ly sing - ing o'er the plains,
2 Shep - herds, why this ju - bi - lee? Why your joy - ous strains pro - long?
3 Come to Beth - le - hem and see Him whose birth the an - gels sing;

And the moun - tains in re - ply Ech - o back their joy - ous strains.
Say what may the ti - dings be, Which in - spire your heaven - ly song.
Come a - dore on bend - ed knee, Christ, the Lord, the new - born King.

REFRAIN

Glo - - - - - - - - - - - ri - a

in ex - cel - sis De - o, Glo - - - - - - - - -

BIRTH

--- --- --- --- --- --- ri - a in ex - cel - sis De - o.

Angels, From the Realms of Glory

117

James Montgomery, 1771-1854

REGENT SQUARE 8.7.8.7.8.7.
Henry T. Smart, 1813-1879

1 An - gels, from the realms of glo - ry, Wing your flight o'er all the earth;
2 Shep-herds, in the fields a - bid-ing, Watch-ing o'er your flocks by night,
3 Sag - es, leave your con-tem-pla-tions, Bright-er vi - sions beam a - far;
4 Saints be - fore the al - tar bend-ing, Watch-ing long in hope and fear,

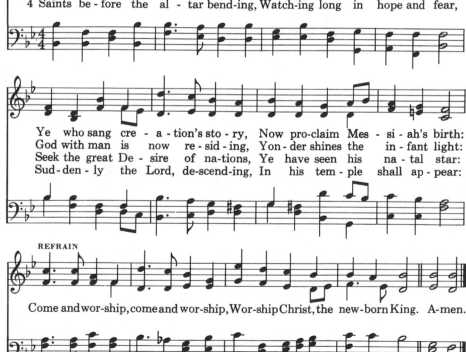

Ye who sang cre - a - tion's sto - ry, Now pro-claim Mes - si - ah's birth:
God with man is now re - sid - ing, Yon - der shines the in - fant light:
Seek the great De - sire of na-tions, Ye have seen his na - tal star:
Sud-den - ly the Lord, de-scend-ing, In his tem - ple shall ap - pear:

REFRAIN

Come and wor-ship, come and wor-ship, Wor-ship Christ, the new-born King. A-men.

BIRTH

118   # Break Forth, O Beauteous Heavenly Light

Johann Rist, 1607-1667
Tr. Attr. to John Troutbeck, 1832-1889

ERMUNTRE DICH 8.7.8.7.8.8.7.7.
Melody by Johann Schop, ?-c.1664
Harm. by J.S. Bach, 1685-1750

Break forth, O beau-teous heaven-ly light, And ush-er in the morn - ing; Ye shep-herds, shrink not with af-fright, But hear the an-gel's warn - ing. This child, now weak in in-fan-cy, Our con-fi-dence and joy shall be, The power of Sa-tan

BIRTH

break - ing, Our peace e - ter - nal mak - ing.

As With Gladness Men of Old 119

William C. Dix, 1837-1898, alt.

DIX 7.7.7.7.7.7.
Adapted from a chorale by Conrad Kocher, 1786-1872

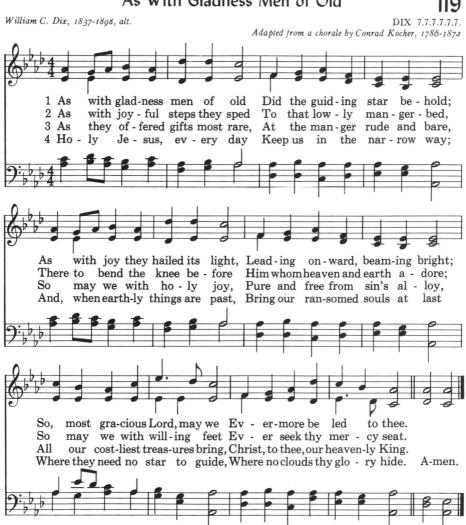

1 As with glad-ness men of old Did the guid-ing star be - hold;
2 As with joy - ful steps they sped To that low - ly man - ger - bed,
3 As they of - fered gifts most rare, At the man-ger rude and bare,
4 Ho - ly Je - sus, ev - ery day Keep us in the nar - row way;

As with joy they hailed its light, Lead-ing on-ward, beam-ing bright;
There to bend the knee be - fore Him whom heaven and earth a - dore;
So may we with ho - ly joy, Pure and free from sin's al - loy,
And, when earth-ly things are past, Bring our ran-somed souls at last

So, most gra-cious Lord, may we Ev - er-more be led to thee.
So may we with will-ing feet Ev - er seek thy mer - cy seat.
All our cost-liest treas-ures bring, Christ, to thee, our heaven-ly King.
Where they need no star to guide, Where no clouds thy glo - ry hide. A-men.

A lower setting may be found at No. 66

BIRTH

120   Hark! The Herald Angels Sing

Charles Wesley, 1707-1788, alt.

MENDELSSOHN 7.7.7.7.D. *with Refrain*
Felix Mendelssohn, 1809-1847
Arr. by William H. Cummings, 1831-1915

1 Hark! the her-ald an-gels sing, "Glo-ry to the new-born King;
2 Christ, by high-est heaven a-dored; Christ, the ev-er-last-ing Lord!
3 Hail the heaven-born Prince of peace! Hail the Sun of right-eous-ness!

Peace on earth, and mer-cy mild, God and sin-ners rec-on-ciled!"
Late in time be-hold him come, Off-spring of the Vir-gin's womb.
Light and life to all he brings, Risen with heal-ing in his wings,

Joy-ful, all ye na-tions, rise, Join the tri-umph of the skies;
Veiled in flesh the God-head see; Hail the in-car-nate De-i-ty,
Mild he lays his glo-ry by, Born that man no more may die,

With the an-gel-ic host pro-claim, "Christ is born in Beth-le-hem!"
Pleased as man with men to dwell, Je-sus, our Em-man-u-el.
Born to raise the sons of earth, Born to give them sec-ond birth.

BIRTH

REFRAIN

Hark! the her-ald an-gels sing, "Glo-ry to the new-born King!" A-men.

From Heaven Above to Earth I Come 121

Martin Luther, 1483-1546
Tr. Catherine Winkworth, 1827-1878

VOM HIMMEL HOCH L.M.
"Geistliche Lieder," Leipzig, 1539

1 From heaven a - bove to earth I come To bear good news to
2 To you, this night, is born a child Of Mar - y, chos - en
3 Ah, dear - est Je - sus, ho - ly child, Make thee a bed, soft,
4 Glo - ry to God in high - est heaven, Who un - to man his

ev - ery home; Glad tid - ings of great joy I bring,
moth - er mild; This lit - tle child, of low - ly birth,
un - de - filed With - in my heart, that it may be
son hath given, While an - gels sing with pi - ous mirth,

Where - of I now will say and sing.
Shall be the joy of all your earth.
A qui - et cham - ber kept for thee.
A glad new year to all the earth.

BIRTH

122 God Rest You Merry, Gentlemen

English Carol, 18th century

GOD REST YOU MERRY *Irregular with Refrain*
English Melody, 18th century

1 God rest you mer - ry, gen-tle-men, Let noth-ing you dis - may,
2 From God, our heaven-ly Fa - ther, A bless-ed an - gel came;
3 "Fear not, then," said the an - gel, "Let noth-ing you af - fright;
4 Now to the Lord sing prais - es, All you with - in this place,

Re - mem-ber Christ, our Sav - ior, Was born on Christ-mas Day,
And un - to cer - tain shep - herds Brought ti-dings of the same:
This day is born a Sav - ior, Of a pure vir - gin bright,
And with true love and broth-er-hood Each oth - er now em - brace;

To save us all from Sa-tan's power When we were gone a - stray.
How that in Beth - le - hem was born The Son of God by name.
To free all those who trust in him From Sa-tan's power and might."
This ho - ly tide of Christ - mas Doth bring re - deem-ing grace.

REFRAIN

O ti - dings of com - fort and joy, com-fort and joy;

BIRTH

O ti - dings of com - fort and joy!

All My Heart This Night Rejoices

123

Paul Gerhardt, 1607-1676
Tr. Catherine Winkworth, 1827-1878

WARUM SOLLT ICH 8.3.3.6.D.
Melody by Johann G. Ebeling, 1637-1676

1 All my heart this night re - joic - es As I hear, Far and near,
2 Hark! a voice from yon - der man - ger, Soft and sweet, Doth en - treat:
3 Come, then, let us has - ten yon - der! Here let all, Great and small,

Sweet-est an - gel voic - es. "Christ is born," their choirs are sing - ing,
"Flee from woe and dan - ger! Breth - ren, come! from all doth grieve you,
Kneel in awe and won - der! Love him who with love is yearn - ing!

Till the air Ev - ery-where Now with joy is ring - ing.
You are freed; All you need I will sure - ly give you."
Hail the star That from far Bright with hope is burn - ing! A-men.

BIRTH

Bring a Torch, Jeannette, Isabella

Traditional French Carol
Tr. E. Cuthbert Nunn, 1868-1914

BRING A TORCH *Irregular*
Harm. by E. Cuthbert Nunn, 1868-1914, alt.

In unison

1 Bring a torch, Jean-nette, Is-a-bel-la! Bring a torch, to the
2 It is wrong when the child is sleep-ing, It is wrong to
3 Soft-ly to the lit-tle sta-ble, Soft-ly for a

cra-dle run! It is Je-sus, good folk of the vil-lage;
talk so loud; Si-lence, all, as you gath-er a-round,
mo-ment come; Look and see how charm-ing is Je-sus,

Christ is born and Mar-y's call-ing. Ah! ah! beau-ti-ful
Lest your noise should wak-en Je-sus. Hush! hush! see how
How he is white, his cheeks are ros-y. Hush! hush! see how the

is the moth-er! Ah! ah! beau-ti-ful is her son!
fast he slum-bers; Hush! hush! see how fast he sleeps!
child is sleep-ing; Hush! hush! see how he smiles in dreams.

BIRTH

Good Christian Men, Rejoice

German-Latin Carol, 14th century
Para. by John M. Neale, 1818-1866

IN DULCI JUBILO *Irregular*
German Melody, 14th century

125

1 Good Chris-tian men, re - joice, With heart and soul and voice;
2 Good Chris-tian men, re - joice, With heart and soul and voice;
3 Good Chris-tian men, re - joice, With heart and soul and voice;

Give ye heed to what we say: Je - sus Christ is born to - day;
Now ye hear of end - less bliss; Je - sus Christ was born for this!
Now ye need not fear the grave; Je - sus Christ was born to save!

Ox and ass be - fore him bow, And he is in the man - ger now.
He hath oped the heaven-ly door, And man is bless - ed ev - er-more.
Calls you one and calls you all, To gain his ev - er-last - ing hall.

Christ is born to - day! Christ is born to - day!
Christ was born for this! Christ was born for this!
Christ was born to save! Christ was born to save!

BIRTH

126   Brightest and Best of the Sons of the Morning

Reginald Heber, 1783-1826, alt.

MORNING STAR 11.10.11.10.
James (John) P. Harding, ?-1911

1 Bright - est and best of the sons of the morn - ing,
2 Cold on his cra - dle the dew - drops are shin - ing,
3 Say, shall we yield him, in cost - ly de - vo - tion,
4 Vain - ly we of - fer each am - ple ob - la - tion;
5 Bright - est and best of the sons of the morn - ing,

Dawn on our dark - ness, and lend us thine aid;
Low lies his head with the beasts of the stall;
O - dors of E - dom and of - ferings di - vine,
Vain - ly with gifts would his fa - vor se - cure;
Dawn on our dark - ness, and lend us thine aid;

Star of the east, the ho - ri - zon a - dorn - ing,
An - gels a - dore him, in slum - ber re - clin - ing,
Gems of the moun - tain, and pearls of the o - cean,
Rich - er by far is the heart's ad - o - ra - tion,
Star of the east, the ho - ri - zon a - dorn - ing,

Guide where our in - fant Re - deem - er is laid!
Mak - er, and Mon - arch, and Sav - ior of all.
Myrrh from the for - est, or gold from the mine?
Dear - er to God are the prayers of the poor.
Guide where our in - fant Re - deem - er is laid! A - men.

BIRTH

Christians, Awake, Salute the Happy Morn

127

John Byrom, 1692-1763

YORKSHIRE 10.10.10.10.10.10.
John Wainwright, c.1723-1768

1 Chris-tians, a-wake, sa-lute the hap-py morn Where-on the
2 Then to the watch-ful shep-herds it was told, Who heard the an-
3 To Beth-lehem straight the en-lightened shep-herds ran, To see the
4 O may we keep and pon-der in our mind God's won-drous

Sav-ior of the world was born; Rise to a-dore the mys-ter-y of love,
gel-ic her-ald's voice:"Be-hold, I bring good ti-dings of a Sav-ior's birth
won-der God had wrought for man; And found, with Jo-seph and the bless-ed maid,
love in sav-ing lost man-kind: Trace we the babe, Who hath re-trieved our loss,

Which hosts of an-gels chant-ed from a-bove; With them the joy-ful
To you and all the na-tions up-on earth; This day hath God ful-
Her Son, the Sav-ior, in a man-ger laid; A-mazed, the won-drous
From his poor man-ger to his bit-ter cross; Tread-ing his steps, as-

ti-dings first be-gun Of God in-car-nate and the Vir-gin's Son.
filled his prom-ised word, This day is born a Sav-ior, Christ the Lord."
sto-ry they pro-claim, The first a-pos-tles of his in-fant fame.
sist-ed by his grace, Till man's first heaven-ly state a-gain takes place. A-men.

BIRTH

128   In the Bleak Midwinter

Christina G. Rossetti, 1830-1894, alt.

CRANHAM *Irregular*
Gustav T. Holst, 1874-1934

1 In the bleak mid - win - ter, Frost - y wind made moan,
2 Our God, heaven can - not hold him, Nor earth sus - tain;
3 An - gels and arch - an - gels May have gath - ered there,
4 What can I give him, Poor as I am?

Earth stood hard as i - ron, Wa - ter like a stone;
Heaven and earth shall flee a - way When he comes to reign;
Cher - u - bim and ser - a - phim Throng-ed the air;
If I were a shep - herd, I would bring a lamb;

Snow had fall - en, snow on snow, Snow on snow,
In the bleak mid - win - ter A sta - ble place suf - ficed The
But his moth - er on - ly, In her maid - en bliss,
If I were a wise man, I would do my part; Yet

In the bleak mid - win - ter, Long a - go.
Lord God al - might - y, Je - sus Christ.
Wor-shipped the be - lov - ed With a kiss.
what I can I give him— Give my heart.

BIRTH

It Came Upon the Midnight Clear

Edmund H. Sears, 1810-1876, alt.

CAROL C.M.D.
Richard S. Willis, 1819-1900

129

1 It came up-on the mid-night clear, That glo-rious song of old,
2 Still through the clo-ven skies they come, With peace-ful wings un-furled,
3 And ye, be-neath life's crush-ing load Whose forms are bend-ing low,
4 For lo, the days are hasten-ing on, By proph-et bards fore-told,

From an-gels bend-ing near the earth To touch their harps of gold;
And still their heaven-ly mu-sic floats O'er all the wea-ry world;
Who toil a-long the climb-ing way, With pain-ful steps and slow,
When with the ev-er-cir-cling years Comes round the age of gold;

"Peace on the earth, good will to men, From heaven's all gra-cious King."
A-bove its sad and low-ly plains They bend on hover-ing wing,
Look now, for glad and gold-en hours Come swift-ly on the wing;
When peace shall o-ver all the earth Its an-cient splen-dors fling,

The world in sol-emn still-ness lay To hear the an-gels sing.
And ev-er o'er its Ba-bel sounds The bless-ed an-gels sing.
O rest be-side the wea-ry road, And hear the an-gels sing!
And the whole world send back the song Which now the an-gels sing. A men.

BIRTH

130 Joy to the World! the Lord Is Come

Isaac Watts, 1674-1748

ANTIOCH C.M.
Attr. to Georg F. Handel, 1685-1759
Arr. by Lowell Mason, 1792-1872

1 Joy to the world! the Lord is come: Let earth re-
2 Joy to the earth! the Sav - ior reigns: Let men their
3 He rules the world with truth and grace, And makes the

ceive her King; Let ev - ery heart pre - pare him room,
songs em - ploy; While fields and floods, rocks, hills, and plains
na - tions prove The glo - ries of his right - eous - ness,

And heaven and na - ture sing, And heaven and na - ture
Re - peat the sound - ing joy, Re - peat the sound - ing
And won - ders of his love, And won - ders of his

And heaven and na - ture sing, And
Re - peat the sound-ing joy, Re -
And won - ders of his love, And

sing, And heaven, and heaven and na - ture sing.
joy, Re - peat, re - peat the sound - ing joy.
love, And won - ders, won - ders of his love. A - men.

heaven and na - ture sing.
peat the sound-ing joy,
won - ders of his love,

BIRTH

Lo, How a Rose E'er Blooming

German: anon., 15th century
Tr. Theodore Baker, 1851-1934

ES IST EIN' ROS' 7.6.7.6.6.7.6.
German: Melody, 16th century
Arr. by Michael Praetorius, 1571-1621

131

1 Lo, how a Rose e'er bloom-ing From ten-der stem hath sprung!
2 I - sa-iah 'twas fore-told it, The Rose I have in mind,

Of Jes-se's lin-eage com-ing As men of old have sung.
With Mar-y we be-hold it, The Vir-gin Moth - er kind.

It came, a flower-et bright, A - mid the cold of
To show God's love a - right, She bore to men a

win - ter, When half spent was the night.
Sav - ior, When half spent was the night.

BIRTH

O Come, All Ye Faithful

Latin: *John F. Wade, 1711-1786*
Tr. Frederick Oakeley, 1802-1880, and others

ADESTE FIDELES *Irregular*
John F. Wade's "Cantus Diversi," 1751

1 O come, all ye faith - ful, joy - ful and tri - um - phant, O
2 Sing, choirs of an - gels, sing in ex - ul - ta - tion,
3 Child, for us sin - ners poor and in the man - ger,
4 Yea, Lord, we greet thee, born this hap - py morn - ing,

come ye, O come ye to Beth - le - hem;
Sing, all ye cit - i - zens of heaven a - bove!
We would em - brace thee, with love and awe;
Je - sus, to thee be all glo - ry given;

Come and be - hold him, born the King of an - gels;
Glo - ry to God, all glo - ry in the high - est;
Who would not love thee, lov - ing us so dear - ly?
Word of the Fa - ther, now in flesh ap - pear - ing;

O come, let us a - dore him, O come, let us a - dore him,

BIRTH

O come, let us a - dore him, Christ, the Lord! A - men.

Adeste Fideles

Latin: John F. Wade, 1711-1786

ADESTE FIDELES *Irregular*
John F. Wade's "Cantus Diversi," 1751

133

1 Adeste fideles,
   Laeti triumphantes,
   Venite, venite in Bethlehem:
   Natum videte
   Regem angelorum:
   Venite, adoremus, venite, adoremus,
   Venite, adoremus Dominum.

2 Cantet nunc io
   Chorus angelorum,
   Cantet nunc aula caelestium:
   Gloria in
   Excelsis Deo:
   Venite, adoremus, venite, adoremus,
   Venite, adoremus Dominum.

3 Ergo qui natus
   Die hodierna,
   Jesu, tibi sit gloria:
   Patris aeterni
   Verbum caro factum:
   Venite, adoremus, venite, adoremus,
   Venite, adoremus Dominum.

134   O Little Town of Bethlehem

Phillips Brooks, 1835-1893

ST. LOUIS 8.6.8.6.7.6.8.6.
Lewis H. Redner, 1831-1908

1 O lit-tle town of Beth-le-hem, How still we see thee lie!
2 For Christ is born of Mar - y, And gath-ered all a-bove,
3 How si-lent-ly, how si-lent-ly, The won-drous gift is given!
4 O ho-ly Child of Beth-le-hem! De-scend to us, we pray;

A - bove thy deep and dream-less sleep The si-lent stars go by;
While mor-tals sleep, the an-gels keep Their watch of won-dering love.
So God im-parts to hu-man hearts The bless-ings of his heaven.
Cast out our sin and en-ter in; Be born in us to-day.

Yet in thy dark streets shin-eth The ev-er-last-ing Light;
O morn-ing stars, to-geth-er Pro-claim the ho-ly birth!
No ear may hear his com-ing, But in this world of sin,
We hear the Christ-mas an-gels The great glad ti-dings tell;

The hopes and fears of all the years Are met in thee to-night.
And prais-es sing to God the King, And peace to men on earth.
Where meek souls will re-ceive him, still The dear Christ en-ters in.
O come to us, a-bide with us, Our Lord Em-man-u-el! A-men.

O Jesu Sweet, O Jesu Mild

135

Valentin Thilo ?, 1607-1662
Tr. E. Harold Geer, 1886-1957

O JESULEIN SÜSS 8.8.8.8.8.8.
Melody, Cologne, 1623
Harm. by J. S. Bach, 1685-1750

1 O Je - su sweet, O Je - su mild, Thy
2 O Je - su sweet, O Je - su mild, Help

Fa - ther's will hast thou ful - filled. For thou hast
us to do as thou hast willed. What - e'er we

left thy heaven - ly throne Our low - ly state to
have be - longs to thee: O may we ev - er

make thine own, O Je - su sweet, O Je - su mild.
faith - ful be, O Je - su sweet, O Je - su mild.

BIRTH

136

On This Day Earth Shall Ring

"Piae Cantiones," 1582
Tr. Jane M. Joseph, c. 1894-1929

PERSONENT HODIE 6.6.6.6.6. *with Refrain*
"Piae Cantiones," 1582
Arr. by Gustav T. Holst, 1874-1934

1 On   this day   earth shall ring   With the song
2 His   the doom, ours the mirth;   When he came
3 God's bright star, o'er his head,   Wise men three
4 On   this day   an-gels sing;   With their song

chil-dren sing   To the Lord,   Christ our King,   Born on earth to
down to earth,   Beth-le-hem   saw his birth;   Ox and ass be-
to   him led,   Kneel-ing low   by his bed,   Lay their gifts be-
earth shall ring,   Prais-ing Christ,   heav-en's King,   Born on earth to

REFRAIN

save   us; Him the Fa-ther gave   us.
side   him From the cold would hide   him.   Id - e - o - o - o,
fore   him, Praise him and a-dore   him.
save   us. Peace and love he gave   us.

R.H.

R.H. L.H.

BIRTH

Id-e-o - o - o, Id-e-o glo-ri-a in ex-cel-sis De - o!

Away in a Manger

137

Anonymous

AWAY IN A MANGER 11.11.11.11.
Anonymous

1 A - way in a man - ger, no crib for his bed, The lit - tle Lord
2 The cat - tle are low - ing, the ba - by a - wakes, But lit - tle Lord

Je - sus laid down his sweet head. The stars in the sky looked
Je - sus, no cry - ing he makes. I love thee, Lord Je - sus, look

down where he lay, The lit - tle Lord Je - sus, a - sleep on the hay.
down from the sky, And stay by my cra - dle till morn - ing is nigh.

BIRTH

138

Silent Night, Holy Night

Joseph Mohr, 1792-1848
Tr. John F. Young, 1820-1885

STILLE NACHT *Irregular*
Franz Gruber, 1787-1863

1 Si - lent night, ho - ly night, All is calm, all is bright
2 Si - lent night, ho - ly night, Shep-herds quake at the sight,
3 Si - lent night, ho - ly night, Son of God, love's pure light

Round yon vir - gin moth-er and child. Ho - ly in-fant so ten-der and mild,
Glo - ries stream from heav-en a - far, Heaven-ly hosts sing al - le-lu - ia;
Ra - diant beams from thy ho-ly face, With the dawn of re - deem - ing grace,

Sleep in heav - en - ly peace, Sleep in heav - en - ly peace.
Christ, the Sav - ior, is born! Christ, the Sav - ior, is born!
Je - sus, Lord, at thy birth, Je - sus, Lord, at thy birth.

139

Stille Nacht, Heilige Nacht

Joseph Mohr, 1792-1848

STILLE NACHT *Irregular*
Franz Gruber, 1787-1863

1 Stille Nacht, heilige Nacht!
Alles schläft, einsam wacht
Nur das traute, hochheilige Paar
Holder Knabe im lockigen Haar,
Schlaf in himmlischer Ruh,
Schlaf in himmlischer Ruh!

2 Stille Nacht, heilige Nacht!
Hirten erst kundgemacht
Durch der Engel Halleluja,
Tönt es laut von fern und nah:
Christ der Retter ist da,
Christ der Retter ist da!

3 Stille Nacht, heilige Nacht!
Gottes Sohn, o wie lacht
Lieb' aus deinem göttlichen Mund,
Da uns schlägt die rettende Stund':
Christ, in deiner Geburt,
Christ, in deiner Geburt!

BIRTH

What Child Is This, Who, Laid to Rest

William C. Dix, 1837-1898

GREENSLEEVES 8.7.8.7. *with Refrain*
Traditional English Melody

140

In unison

1 What child is this, who, laid to rest, On Mar-y's lap is sleep-ing?
2 Why lies he in such mean es - tate Where ox and ass are feed-ing?
3 So bring him in-cense, gold, and myrrh, Come peas-ant, king, to own him;

Whom an - gels greet with an-thems sweet, While shep-herds watch are keep-ing?
Good Chris-tian, fear: for sin - ners here The si - lent Word is plead-ing.
The King of kings sal - va - tion brings, Let lov - ing hearts en-throne him.

REFRAIN

This, this is Christ the King, Whom shep-herds guard and an - gels sing:

Haste, haste to bring him laud, The babe, the son of Mar - y.

BIRTH

141 The First Nowell

Traditional English Carol

THE FIRST NOWELL *Irregular with Refrain*
Traditional English Melody

1 The first Now-ell, the an-gel did say, Was to
2 They look-ed up and saw a star Shin-ing
3 And by the light of that same star Three
4 This star drew nigh to the north-west, O'er
5 Then en-tered in those wise men three, Full

cer-tain poor shep-herds in fields as they lay; In fields where
in the east, be-yond them far, And to the
wise men came from coun-try far; To seek for a
Beth-le-hem it took its rest, And there it
rev-erent-ly up-on their knee, And of-fered

they lay keep-ing their sheep, On a cold win-ter's
earth it gave great light, And so it con-
king was their in-tent, And to fol-low the
did both stop and stay, Right o-ver the
there, in his pres-ence, Their gold and

REFRAIN

night that was so deep.
tin-ued both day and night.
star wher-ev-er it went. Now-ell, Now-ell, Now-
place where Je-sus lay.
myrrh and frank-in-cense.

BIRTH

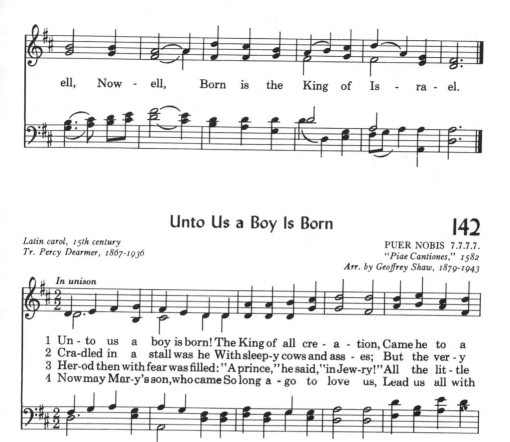

ell, Now - ell, Born is the King of Is - ra - el.

Unto Us a Boy Is Born

142

Latin carol, 15th century
Tr. Percy Dearmer, 1867-1936

PUER NOBIS 7.7.7.7.
"Piae Cantiones," 1582
Arr. by Geoffrey Shaw, 1879-1943

In unison

1 Un - to us a boy is born! The King of all cre - a - tion, Came he to a
2 Cra - dled in a stall was he With sleep-y cows and ass - es; But the ver - y
3 Her-od then with fear was filled: "A prince," he said, "in Jew-ry!" All the lit - tle
4 Now may Mar-y's son, who came So long a - go to love us, Lead us all with

world for-lorn, The Lord of ev - er - y na - - - - - - tion.
beasts could see That he all men sur - pass - - - - - - es.
boys he killed At Beth-lem in his fu - - - - - - ry.
hearts a-flame Un - to the joys a - bove - - - - - - us.

5   Alpha and Omega he!
    Let the organ thunder,
    While the choir with peals of glee
    Doth rend the air asunder.

143 We Three Kings of Orient Are

John H. Hopkins, Jr., 1820-1891, alt.

KINGS OF ORIENT 8.8.8.6. *with Refrain*
John H. Hopkins, Jr.; 1820-1891

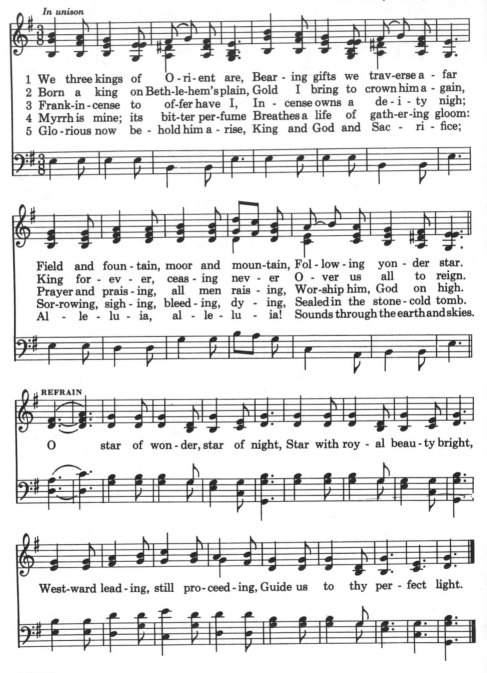

In unison

1 We three kings of O - ri - ent are, Bear - ing gifts we trav-erse a - far
2 Born a king on Beth-le-hem's plain, Gold I bring to crown him a - gain,
3 Frank-in-cense to of-fer have I, In - cense owns a de - i - ty nigh;
4 Myrrh is mine; its bit-ter per-fume Breathes a life of gath-er-ing gloom:
5 Glo-rious now be - hold him a - rise, King and God and Sac - ri - fice;

Field and foun - tain, moor and moun-tain, Fol - low - ing yon - der star.
King for - ev - er, ceas - ing nev - er O - ver us all to reign.
Prayer and prais - ing, all men rais - ing, Wor-ship him, God on high.
Sor-rowing, sigh - ing, bleed - ing, dy - ing, Sealed in the stone-cold tomb.
Al - le - lu - ia, al - le - lu - ia! Sounds through the earth and skies.

REFRAIN

O star of won - der, star of night, Star with roy - al beau - ty bright,

West-ward lead - ing, still pro-ceed-ing, Guide us to thy per - fect light.

BIRTH

What Star Is This, With Beams So Bright 144

Charles Coffin, 1676-1749
Tr. John Chandler, 1806-1876, alt.

PUER NOBIS NASCITUR L.M.
Adapted by Michael Praetorius, 1571-1621
Harm. by George R. Woodward, 1848-1934

1 What star is this, with beams so bright, More love - ly
2 'Tis now ful - filled what God de - creed, "From Ja - cob
3 O Je - sus, while the star of grace Im - pels us
4 To God the Fa - ther, heaven - ly Light, To Christ, re -

than the noon - day light? 'Tis sent to announce a new - born
shall a star pro - ceed"; And lo! the east - ern sa - ges
on to seek thy face, Let not our sloth - ful hearts re -
vealed in earth - ly night, To God the Ho - ly Ghost we

king, Glad ti - dings of our God to bring.
stand, To read in heaven the Lord's com - mand.
fuse The guid - ance of thy light to use.
raise An end - less song of thank - ful praise! A - men.

Another harmonization may be found at No. 39

BIRTH

145   O Morning Star, How Fair and Bright

Philipp Nicolai, 1556-1608
Tr. Catherine Winkworth, 1827-1878, alt.

WIE SCHÖN LEUCHTET   8.8.7.8.8.7.4.8.4.8.
Melody by Philipp Nicolai, 1556-1608
Harm. by J. S. Bach, 1685-1750

1 O Morn - ing Star, how fair and bright Thou beam - est forth in
2 Thou heaven-ly Bright - ness! Light di - vine! O deep with - in my

truth and light! O Sov-ereign meek and low - ly! Thou Root of Jes - se,
heart now shine, And make thee there an al - tar! Fill me with joy and

Da - vid's Son, My Lord and Mas - ter, thou hast won My heart to serve thee
strength to be Thy mem-ber, ev - er joined to thee In love that can-not

sole - ly! Thou art ho - ly, Fair and glo-rious, all - vic - to - rious,
fal - ter; Toward thee long - ing Doth pos - sess me; turn and bless me;

BIRTH

Rich in bless - ing, Rule and might o'er all pos - sess - ing.
Here in sad - ness Eye and heart long for thy glad - ness! A-men.

While Shepherds Watched Their Flocks 146

Nahum Tate, 1652-1715

WINCHESTER OLD C.M.
Thomas Este's "Whole Book of Psalms," 1592

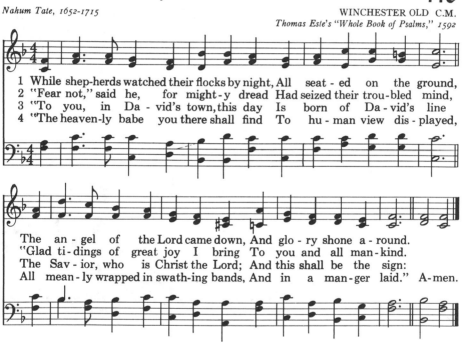

1 While shep-herds watched their flocks by night, All seat-ed on the ground,
2 "Fear not," said he, for might-y dread Had seized their trou-bled mind,
3 "To you, in Da-vid's town, this day Is born of Da-vid's line
4 "The heaven-ly babe you there shall find To hu-man view dis-played,

The an - gel of the Lord came down, And glo - ry shone a - round.
"Glad ti - dings of great joy I bring To you and all man - kind.
The Sav - ior, who is Christ the Lord; And this shall be the sign:
All mean - ly wrapped in swath-ing bands, And in a man - ger laid." A-men.

5 Thus spake the seraph; and forthwith
    Appeared a shining throng
  Of angels praising God, who thus
    Addressed their joyful song:

6 "All glory be to God on high,
    And to the earth be peace;
  Good will henceforth from heaven to men
    Begin and never cease."

Alternative tune, CHRISTMAS, *No. 362*

BIRTH

147　All Praise to Thee, for Thou, O King Divine

F. Bland Tucker, 1895-

ENGELBERG 10.10.10. *with Alleluia*
Charles V. Stanford, 1852-1924

1 All praise to thee, for thou, O King di - vine, Didst yield the
2 Thou cam'st to us in low - li - ness of thought; By thee the
3 Let this mind be in us which was in thee, Who wast a
4 Let ev - ery tongue con - fess with one ac - cord In heaven and

glo - ry that of right was thine, That in our dark-ened hearts thy
out - cast and the poor were sought, And by thy death was God's sal -
serv - ant that we might be free, Hum-bling thy - self to death on
earth that Je - sus Christ is Lord; And God the Fa-ther be by

grace might shine.
va - tion wrought. Al - le - lu - ia! Al - le - lu - ia!
Cal - va - ry.
all a - dored.

St. 1, 2, 3

St. 4

In harmony

A - men.

LIFE AND MINISTRY

Forty Days and Forty Nights

148

George H. Smyttan, 1822-1870
Alt. by Francis Pott, 1832-1909, and others

HEINLEIN 7.7.7.7.
Attr. to Martin Herbst, 1654-1681

1 For-ty days and for-ty nights Thou wast fast-ing in the wild;
2 Shall not we thy sor-row share, And from earth-ly joys ab-stain,
3 And if Sa-tan, vex-ing sore, Flesh or spir-it should as-sail,
4 Keep, O keep us, Sav-ior dear, Ev-er con-stant by thy side;

For-ty days and for-ty nights Temp-ted, and yet un-de-filed.
Fast-ing with un-ceas-ing prayer, Glad with thee to suf-fer pain?
Thou, his van-quish-er be-fore, Grant we may not faint nor fail.
That with thee we may ap-pear At the e-ter-nal East-er-tide. A-men.

I Know Not How That Bethlehem's Babe

149

Harry W. Farrington, 1879-1931

BANGOR C.M.
William Tans'ur, 1706?-1783

1 I know not how that Beth-lehem's babe Could in the God-head be;
2 I know not how that Cal-vary's cross A world from sin could free;
3 I know not how that Jos-eph's tomb Could solve death's mys-ter-y;

I on-ly know the man-ger child Has brought God's life to me.
I on-ly know its match-less love Has brought God's love to me.
I on-ly know a liv-ing Christ, Our im-mor-tal-i-ty. A-men.

LIFE AND MINISTRY

150 O Love, How Deep, How Broad, How High

First Tune

Latin: 15th century
Tr. Benjamin Webb, 1819-1885, alt.

DEUS TUORUM MILITUM L.M.
Grenoble Church Melody

1 O love, how deep, how broad, how high, How pass - ing
2 For us bap - tized, for us he bore His ho - ly
3 For us he prayed, for us he taught, For us his
4 For us to wick - ed men be - trayed, Scourged, mocked, in

thought and fan - ta - sy, That God, the Son of God, should
fast, and hun - gered sore; For us temp - ta - tions sharp he
dai - ly works he wrought, By words and signs and ac - tions,
pur - ple robe ar - rayed, He bore the shame - ful cross and

take Our mor - tal form for mor - tals' sake.
knew; For us the temp - ter o - ver - threw.
thus Still seek - ing not him - self, but us.
death; For us gave up his dy - ing breath. A - men.

5 For us he rose from death again,
  For us he went on high to reign;
  For us he sent his Spirit here
  To guide, to strengthen, and to cheer.

6 All glory to our Lord and God
  For love so deep, so high, so broad;
  The Trinity whom we adore
  For ever and for evermore.

LIFE AND MINISTRY

O Love, How Deep, How Broad, How High

Second Tune

151

Latin: 15th century
Tr. Benjamin Webb, 1819-1885, alt.

DEO GRACIAS L.M.
"The Agincourt Song," 15th century

In unison

1 O love, how deep, how broad, how high,
2 For us bap-tized, for us he bore
3 For us he prayed, for us he taught,
4 For us to wick-ed men be-trayed,

How pass-ing thought and fan-ta-sy,
His ho-ly fast, and hun-gered sore;
For us his dai-ly works he wrought,
Scourged, mocked, in pur-ple robe ar-rayed,

That God, the Son of God, should take
For us temp-ta-tions sharp he knew;
By words and signs and ac-tions, thus
He bore the shame-ful cross and death;

Our mor-tal form for mor-tals' sake.
For us the temp-ter o-ver-threw.
Still seek-ing not him-self, but us.
For us gave up his dy-ing breath. A-men.

Stanzas 5 and 6 on preceding page

LIFE AND MINISTRY

We Would See Jesus; Lo! His Star Is Shining

J. Edgar Park, 1879-1956

CUSHMAN 11.10.11.10.
Herbert B. Turner, 1852-1927

1 We would see Jesus; lo! his star is shining
2 We would see Jesus; Mar-y's son most ho-ly,
3 We would see Jesus; on the moun-tain teach-ing,
4 We would see Jesus; in his work of heal-ing,
5 We would see Jesus; in the ear-ly morn-ing

A-bove the sta-ble while the an-gels sing;
Light of the vil-lage life from day to day,
With all the lis-tening peo-ple gath-ered round;
At e-ven-tide be-fore the sun was set;
Still as of old he call-eth, "Fol-low me";

There in a man-ger on the hay re-clin-ing,
Shin-ing re-vealed through ev-ery task most low-ly,
While birds and flowers and sky a-bove are preach-ing
Di-vine and hu-man, in his deep re-veal-ing,
Let us a-rise, all mean-er serv-ice scorn-ing;

Haste, let us lay our gifts be-fore the King.
The Christ of God, the Life, the Truth, the Way.
The bless-ed-ness which sim-ple trust has found.
Of God and man in lov-ing serv-ice met.
Lord, we are thine, we give our-selves to thee! A-men.

LIFE AND MINISTRY

Lord, Who Throughout These Forty Days

153

Claudia F. Hernaman, 1838-1898

ST. FLAVIAN C.M.
"Day's Psalter," 1562

1 Lord, who through-out these for - ty days For us didst fast and pray,
2 As thou with Sa - tan didst con - tend, And didst the vic - tory win,
3 And through these days of pen - i - tence, And through thy pas - sion - tide,
4 A - bide with us, that so, this life Of suf-fering o - ver - past,

Teach us with thee to mourn our sins, And close by thee to stay.
O give us strength in thee to fight, In thee to con - quer sin.
Yea, ev - er - more, in life and death, Je - sus! with us a - bide.
An East-er of un - end - ing joy We may at - tain at last! A-men.

LIFE AND MINISTRY

O Thou Who Through This Holy Week

154

John M. Neale, 1818-1866

WALSALL C.M.
William Anchors' "Psalm Tunes," c.1721

1 O thou who through this ho - ly week Didst suf - fer for us all,
2 We can - not un - der - stand the woe Thy love was pleased to bear;
3 Thy feet the path of suf-fering trod; Thy hand the vic - tory won;

The sick to cure, the lost to seek, To raise up them that fall.
O Lamb of God, we on - ly know That all our hopes are there.
What shall we ren - der to our God For all that he hath done? A-men.

PASSION AND CROSS

155 All Glory, Laud, and Honor

Theodulph of Orleans, c.760-c.821
Tr. John M. Neale, 1818-1866, alt.

ST. THEODULPH 7.6.7.6.D.
Melody by Melchior Teschner, 1584-1635

1 All glo - ry, laud, and hon - or To thee, Re - deem - er, King,
2 Thou art the King of Is - rael, Thou Da - vid's roy - al son,
3 Thou didst ac - cept their prais - es; Ac - cept the prayers we bring,

To whom the lips of chil - dren Made sweet ho - san - nas ring!
Who in the Lord's name com - est, The King and bless - ed One;
Who in all good de - light - est, Thou good and gra - cious King.

The peo - ple of the He - brews With palms be - fore thee went;
To thee, be - fore thy pas - sion, They sang their hymns of praise;
All glo - ry, laud, and hon - or To thee, Re - deem - er, King,

Our praise and prayer and an - thems Be - fore thee we pre - sent.
To thee, now high ex - alt - ed, Our mel - o - dy we raise.
To whom the lips of chil - dren Made sweet ho - san - nas ring! A - men.

PASSION AND CROSS

Draw Nigh to Thy Jerusalem

156

Jeremy Taylor, 1613-1667, alt.

WOODLANDS 10.10.10.10.
Walter Greatorex, 1877-1949

1 Draw nigh to thy Je-ru-sa-lem, O Lord, Thy faith-ful peo-ple cry with one ac-cord; Ride on in tri-umph; Lord, be-hold we lay Our pas-sions, lusts, and proud wills in thy way!

2 Thy road is read-y; and thy paths made straight, With long-ing ex-pec-ta-tion seem to wait The con-se-cra-tion of thy beau-teous feet, And si-lent-ly thy prom-ised ad-vent greet!

3 Ho-san-na! wel-come to our hearts! for here Thou hast a tem-ple, too, as Zi-on dear; O en-ter in, dear Lord, un-bar the door; And in that tem-ple dwell for-ev-er-more. A men.

PASSION AND CROSS

157   In the Cross of Christ I Glory

John Bowring, 1792-1872

RATHBUN 8.7.8.7.
Ithamar Conkey, 1815-1867

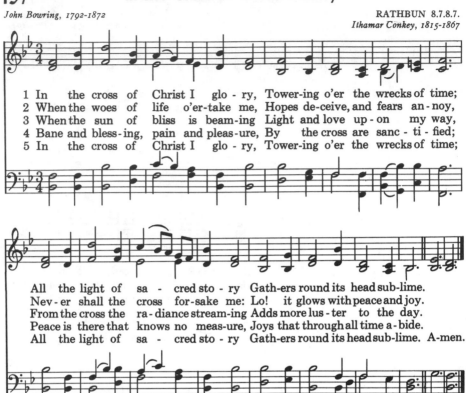

1 In the cross of Christ I glo - ry, Tower-ing o'er the wrecks of time;
2 When the woes of life o'er-take me, Hopes de-ceive, and fears an-noy,
3 When the sun of bliss is beam-ing Light and love up-on my way,
4 Bane and bless-ing, pain and pleas-ure, By the cross are sanc-ti-fied;
5 In the cross of Christ I glo - ry, Tower-ing o'er the wrecks of time;

All the light of sa - cred sto - ry Gath-ers round its head sub-lime.
Nev - er shall the cross for-sake me: Lo! it glows with peace and joy.
From the cross the ra - diance stream-ing Adds more lus - ter to the day.
Peace is there that knows no meas-ure, Joys that through all time a-bide.
All the light of sa - cred sto - ry Gath-ers round its head sub-lime. A-men.

158   Go to Dark Gethsemane

James Montgomery, 1771-1854, alt.

REDHEAD NO.76 7.7.7.7.7.7.
Richard Redhead, 1820-1901

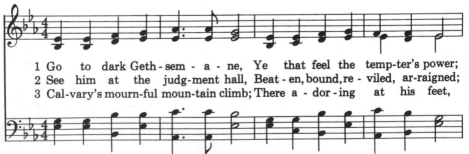

1 Go to dark Geth - sem - a - ne, Ye that feel the temp-ter's power;
2 See him at the judg-ment hall, Beat - en, bound, re - viled, ar-raigned;
3 Cal-vary's mourn-ful moun-tain climb; There a - dor-ing at his feet,

Your Re-deem-er's con-flict see; Watch with him one bit-ter hour;
See him meek-ly bear-ing all! Love to man his soul sus-tained.
Mark that mir-a-cle of time, God's own sac-ri-fice com-plete;

Turn not from his griefs a-way; Learn of Je-sus Christ to pray.
Shun not suf-fering, shame, or loss; Learn of Christ to bear the cross.
"It is fin-ished!" hear him cry; Learn of Je-sus Christ to die. A-men.

Alone Thou Goest Forth, O Lord 159

Peter Abelard, 1079-1142
Tr. F. Bland Tucker, 1895-

BANGOR C.M.
William Tans'ur, 1706?-1783

1 A-lone thou go-est forth, O Lord, In sac-ri-fice to die;
2 Our sins, not thine, thou bear-est, Lord, Make us thy sor-row feel,
3 This is earth's dark-est hour, but thou Dost light and life re-store;
4 Give us com-pas-sion for thee, Lord, That, as we share this hour,

Is this thy sor-row naught to us Who pass un-heed-ing by?
Till through our pit-y and our shame Love an-swers love's ap-peal.
Then let all praise be giv-en thee Who liv-est ev-er-more.
Thy cross may bring us to thy joy And res-ur-rec-tion power. A-men.

PASSION AND CROSS

Beneath the Cross of Jesus

Elizabeth C. Clephane, 1830-1869

ST. CHRISTOPHER 7.6.8.6.8.6.8.6.
Frederick C. Maker, 1844-1927

1 Be-neath the cross of Je - sus I fain would take my stand,
2 Up - on that cross of Je - sus Mine eye at times can see
3 I take, O cross, thy shad - ow For my a - bid - ing place;

The shad - ow of a might - y rock With - in a wea - ry land;
The ver - y dy - ing form of one Who suf - fered there for me;
I ask no oth - er sun - shine than The sun - shine of his face;

A home with - in the wild - er - ness, A rest up - on the way,
And from my smit - ten heart with tears Two won - ders I con - fess —
Con - tent to let the world go by, To know no gain nor loss,

From the burn-ing of the noon-tide heat, And the bur-den of the day.
The won-ders of his glo-rious love And my un-wor-thi-ness.
My sin - ful self my on - ly shame, My glo - ry all the cross. A-men.

PASSION AND CROSS

Before the Cross of Jesus

161

Ferdinand Q. Blanchard, 1876-

ST. CHRISTOPHER 7.6.8.6.8.6.8.6.
Frederick C. Maker, 1844-1927

1 Before the cross of Jesus
    Our lives are judged today;
The meaning of our eager strife
    Is tested by his Way.
Across our restless living
    The light streams from his cross,
And by its clear, revealing beams
    We measure gain and loss.

2 The hopes that lead us onward,
    The fears that hold us back,
Our will to dare great things for God,
    The courage that we lack,
The faith we keep in goodness,
    Our love, as low or pure,
On all, the judgment of the cross
    Falls steady, clear, and sure.

3 Yet humbly, in our striving,
    O God, we face its test.
We crave the power to do thy will
    With him who did it best.
On us let now the healing
    Of his great Spirit fall,
And make us brave and full of joy
    To answer to his call. Amen.

When My Love to God Grows Weak

162

John R. Wreford, 1800-1881, alt.

SONG 13 7.7.7.7.
Adapted from Orlando Gibbons, 1583-1625

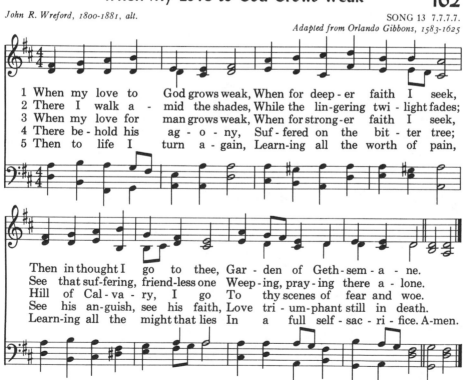

1 When my love to God grows weak, When for deep-er faith I seek,
2 There I walk a-mid the shades, While the lin-gering twi-light fades;
3 When my love for man grows weak, When for strong-er faith I seek,
4 There be-hold his ag-o-ny, Suf-fered on the bit-ter tree;
5 Then to life I turn a-gain, Learn-ing all the worth of pain,

Then in thought I go to thee, Gar-den of Geth-sem-a-ne.
See that suf-fering, friend-less one Weep-ing, pray-ing there a-lone.
Hill of Cal-va-ry, I go To thy scenes of fear and woe.
See his an-guish, see his faith, Love tri-um-phant still in death.
Learn-ing all the might that lies In a full self-sac-ri-fice. A-men.

PASSION AND CROSS

163 ## Ah, Holy Jesus, How Hast Thou Offended

Johann Heermann, 1585-1647
Tr. Robert S. Bridges, 1844-1930

HERZLIEBSTER JESU 11.11.11.5.
Johann Crüger, 1598-1662

1 Ah, ho - ly Je - sus, how hast thou of - fend - ed,
2 Who was the guilt - y? Who brought this up - on thee?
3 For me, kind Je - sus, was thy in - car - na - tion,
4 There - fore, kind Je - sus, since I can - not pay thee,

That man to judge thee hath in hate pre - tend - ed? By foes de-
A - las, my trea - son, Je - sus, hath un - done thee! 'Twas I, Lord
Thy mor - tal sor - row, and thy life's ob - la - tion; Thy death of
I do a - dore thee, and will ev - er pray thee, Think on thy

rid - ed, by thine own re - ject - ed, O most af - flict - ed!
Je - sus, I it was de - nied thee; I cru - ci - fied thee.
an - guish and thy bit - ter pas - sion, For my sal - va - tion.
pit - y and thy love un - swerv - ing, Not my de - serv - ing. A-men.

164 ## O Come and Mourn With Me Awhile

Frederick W. Faber, 1814-1863, alt.

ST. CROSS L.M.
John B. Dykes, 1823-1876

1 O come and mourn with me a - while! O come ye to the Sav - ior's side;
2 Have we no tears to shed for him, While sol - diers scoff and foes de - ride?
3 Seven times he spake, seven words of love, And all three hours his si - lence cried
4 O love of God! O sin of man! In this dread act your strength is tried,

PASSION AND CROSS

O come, to-geth-er let us mourn; Je-sus, our Lord, is cru-ci-fied.
Ah! look how pa-tient-ly he hangs; Je-sus, our Lord, is cru-ci-fied.
For mer-cy on the souls of men; Je-sus, our Lord, is cru-ci-fied.
And vic-to-ry re-mains with love, For he, our Lord, is cru-ci-fied.

Sunset to Sunrise Changes Now 165

Clement of Alexandria, c.170-220
Para. by Howard C. Robbins, 1876-1952

KEDRON L.M.
"Southern Harmony," 1835

In unison

1 Sun - set to sun - rise chang - es now, For
2 E'en though the sun with - holds its light, Lo!
3 Here in o'er - whelm - ing fi - nal strife The

God doth make his world a - new; On the Re - deem - er's
a more heaven - ly lamp shines here, And from the cross on
Lord of life hath vic - to - ry; And sin is slain, and

thorn-crowned brow The won - ders of that dawn we view.
Cal - vary's height Gleams of e - ter - ni - ty ap - pear.
death brings life, And sons of earth hold heaven in fee.

PASSION AND CROSS

166 Jesus, in Thy Dying Woes
First Tune

Words on the Cross
Thomas B. Pollock, 1836-1896, alt.

I

SWEDISH LITANY 7.7.7.6.
Swedish Melody, 1697

"Father, forgive them; for they know not what they do." *St. Luke 23:34*

1 Je - sus, in thy dy - ing woes, E - ven while thy life-blood flows,
2 Sav - ior, for our par - don sue, When our sins thy pangs re - new,
3 O may we, who mer - cy need, Be like thee in heart and deed,

Crav - ing par-don for thy foes: Hear us, ho - ly Je - sus.
For we know not what we do: Hear us, ho - ly Je - sus.
When with wrong our spir - its bleed: Hear us, ho - ly Je - sus. A - men.

167 Jesus, in Thy Dying Woes
Second Tune

Words on the Cross
Thomas B. Pollock, 1836-1896, alt.

TON-MÂN 7.7.7.6.
David Evans, 1874-1948

1 Je - sus, in thy dy - ing woes, E - ven while thy life-blood flows,
2 Sav - ior, for our par - don sue, When our sins thy pangs re - new,
3 O may we, who mer - cy need, Be like thee in heart and deed,

Crav - ing par - don for thy foes: Hear us, ho - ly Je - sus.
For we know not what we do: Hear us, ho - ly Je - sus.
When with wrong our spir - its bleed: Hear us, ho - ly Je - sus. A-men.

PASSION AND CROSS   *The tunes may be alternated if desired*

II

"To day shalt thou be with me in paradise."
St. Luke 23:43

1 Jesus, pitying the sighs
   Of the thief, who near thee dies,
   Promising him paradise:
      Hear us, holy Jesus.

2 May we, in our guilt and shame,
   Still thy love and mercy claim,
   Calling humbly on thy name:
      Hear us, holy Jesus.

3 O remember us who pine,
   Looking from our cross to thine;
   Cheer our souls with hope divine:
      Hear us, holy Jesus.

III

"Woman, behold thy son!" "Behold thy mother!"
St. John 19:26, 27

1 Jesus, loving to the end
   Her whose heart thy sorrows rend,
   And thy dearest human friend:
      Hear us, holy Jesus.

2 May we in thy sorrows share,
   And for thee all peril dare,
   And enjoy thy tender care:
      Hear us, holy Jesus.

3 May we all thy loved ones be,
   All one holy family,
   Loving for the love of thee.
      Hear us, holy Jesus.

IV

"My God, my God, why hast thou forsaken me?"
St. Matthew 27:46

1 Jesus, whelmed in fears unknown,
   With our evil left alone,
   While no light from heaven is shown:
      Hear us, holy Jesus.

2 When we vainly seem to pray,
   And our hope seems far away,
   In the darkness be our stay:
      Hear us, holy Jesus.

3 Though no Father seems to hear,
   Though no light our spirits cheer,
   Tell our faith that God is near:
      Hear us, holy Jesus.

V

"I thirst."
St. John 19:28

1 Jesus, in thy thirst and pain,
   While thy wounds thy life-blood drain,
   Thirsting more our love to gain:
      Hear us, holy Jesus.

2 Thirst for us in mercy still;
   All thy holy work fulfil;
   Satisfy thy loving will:
      Hear us, holy Jesus.

3 May we thirst thy love to know;
   Lead us in our sin and woe
   Where the healing waters flow:
      Hear us, holy Jesus.

VI

"It is finished."
St. John 19:30

1 Jesus, all our ransom paid,
   All thy Father's will obeyed,
   By thy sufferings perfect made:
      Hear us, holy Jesus.

2 Save us in our soul's distress,
   Be our help to cheer and bless,
   While we grow in holiness:
      Hear us, holy Jesus.

3 Brighten all our heavenward way
   With an ever holier ray,
   Till we pass to perfect day:
      Hear us, holy Jesus.

VII

"Father, into thy hands I commend my spirit."
St. Luke 23:46

1 Jesus, all thy labor vast,
   All thy woe and conflict past,
   Yielding up thy soul at last:
      Hear us, holy Jesus.

2 When the death shades round us lower,
   Guard us from the tempter's power,
   Keep us in that trial hour:
      Hear us, holy Jesus.

3 May thy life and death supply
   Grace to live and grace to die,
   Grace to reach the home on high:
      Hear us, holy Jesus.

168 Lord, Through This Holy Week

William H. Draper, 1855-1933

PSALM 80 11.10.11.10.
"Scottish Psalter," 1564
Adapted by James S. Anderson, 1853-1945

1 Lord, through this ho - ly week of our sal - va - tion
2 We would not leave thee, though our weak en - dur - ance
3 A - long that sa - cred way where thou art lead - ing,
4 Un - til thou see thy bit - ter tra - vail's end - ing,

Which thou hast won for us who went a - stray,
Make us un - wor - thy here to take our part;
Which thou didst take to save our souls from loss,
The world re - deemed, the will of God com - plete,

In all the con - flict of thy sore temp - ta - tion
Yet give us strength to trust the sweet as - sur - ance
Let us go al - so, till we see thee plead - ing
And, to thy Fa - ther's hands thy soul com - mend - ing,

We would con - tin - ue with thee day by day.
That thou, O Lord, art great - er than our heart.
In all - pre - vail - ing prayer up - on thy cross.
Thou lay the work he gave thee at his feet. A - men.

PASSION AND CROSS

My Song Is Love Unknown

Samuel Crossman, c.1624-1684

RHOSYMEDRE 6.6.6.6.4.4.4.4.
John D. Edwards, 1806-1885

1 My song is love un-known, My Sav-ior's love to me,
2 He came from his blest throne, Sal-va-tion to be-stow;
3 Some-times they strew his way, And his sweet prais-es sing;
4 Why, what hath my Lord done? What makes this rage and spite?
5 Here might I stay and sing, No sto-ry so di-vine;

Love to the love-less shown, That they might love-ly be.
But men made strange, and none The longed-for Christ would know.
Re-sound-ing all the day Ho-san-nas to their king.
He made the lame to run, He gave the blind their sight.
Nev-er was love, dear King, Nev-er was grief like thine.

O who am I, That for my sake My Lord should take Frail
But O, my friend, My friend in-deed, Who at my need His
Then "Cru-ci-fy!" Is all their breath, And for his death They
Sweet in-jur-ies! Yet they at these Them-selves dis-please, And
This is my friend, In whose sweet praise I all my days Could

flesh, and die? My Lord should take Frail flesh, and die?
life did spend! Who at my need His life did spend!
thirst and cry. And for his death They thirst and cry.
'gainst him rise. Them-selves dis-please, And 'gainst him rise.
gai-ly spend. I all my days Could gai-ly spend. A-men.

A lower setting may be found at No. 466

PASSION AND CROSS

170 O Sacred Head, Now Wounded

Latin: 12th century
German: Paul Gerhardt, 1607-1676
Tr. James W. Alexander, 1804-1859, alt.

PASSION CHORALE 7.6.7.6.D.
Melody by Hans Leo Hassler, 1564-1612
Harm. by J.S. Bach, 1685-1750

1 O sa-cred Head, now wound-ed, With grief and shame weighed down,
2 What thou, my Lord, hast suf-fered Was all for sin-ners' gain;
3 What lan-guage shall I bor-row To thank thee, dear-est friend;

Now scorn-ful-ly sur-round-ed With thorns, thy on-ly crown,
Mine, mine was the trans-gres-sion, But thine the dead-ly pain.
For this thy dy-ing sor-row, Thy pit-y with-out end?

How art thou pale with an-guish, With sore a-buse and scorn!
Lo, here I fall, my Sav-ior! 'Tis I de-serve thy place;
O make me thine for-ev-er; And, should I faint-ing be,

How does that vis-age lan-guish Which once was bright as morn!
Look on me with thy fa-vor, Vouch-safe to me thy grace.
Lord, let me nev-er, nev-er, Out-live my love to thee! A-men.

PASSION AND CROSS

There Is a Green Hill Far Away

171

First Tune

Cecil F. Alexander, 1818-1895

HORSLEY C.M.
William Horsley, 1774-1858

1 There is a green hill far a - way, With-out a cit - y wall,
2 We may not know, we can - not tell What pains he had to bear,
3 He died that we may be for - given, He died to make us good,
4 O dear - ly, dear - ly has he loved! And we must love him too,

Where the dear Lord was cru - ci - fied, Who died to save us all.
But we be - lieve it was for us He hung and suf - fered there.
That we might go at last to heaven, Saved by his pre-cious blood.
And trust in his re - deem-ing blood, And try his works to do. A-men.

There Is a Green Hill Far Away

172

Second Tune

Cecil F. Alexander, 1818-1895

MEDITATION C.M.
John H. Gower, 1855-1922

1 There is a green hill far a - way, With - out a cit - y wall,
2 We may not know, we can - not tell What pains he had to bear,
3 He died that we may be for-given, He died to make us good,
4 O dear - ly, dear - ly has he loved! And we must love him too,

Where the dear Lord was cru - ci - fied, Who died to save us all.
But we be - lieve it was for us He hung and suf-fered there.
That we might go at last to heaven, Saved by his pre-cious blood.
And trust in his re - deem-ing blood, And try his works to do. A-men.

PASSION AND CROSS

173 O Word of Pity, for Our Pardon Pleading

Ada R. Greenaway, *1861-1937*

ZU MEINEM HERRN 11.10.11.10.
Johann G. Schicht, 1753-1823
Harm. by David Evans, 1874-1948

1 O word of pit - y, for our par-don plead-ing, Breathed in the
hour of lone - li - ness and pain; O voice, which, through the a - ges in - ter-
ced - ing, Calls us to fel - low-ship with God a - gain;

2 O word of com - fort, through the si - lence steal-ing, As the dread
act of sac - ri - fice be - gan; O in - fi - nite com-pas-sion, still re-
veal - ing The in - fi - nite for-give-ness won for man;

3 O word of hope, to raise us near - er heav-en, When cour-age
fails us, and when faith is dim; The souls for whom Christ prays to Christ are
giv - en, To find their par-don and their joy in him. A-men.

4 O Intercessor, who art ever living
   To plead for dying souls that they may live,
   Teach us to know our sin which needs forgiving,
   Teach us to know the love which can forgive.

PASSION AND CROSS

Alternative tune, PSALM 80, *No. 168*

Throned Upon the Awful Tree

174

John Ellerton, 1826-1893, alt.

ARFON 7.7.7.7.7.7.
Welsh Hymn Melody

1 Throned up - on the aw - ful tree, King of grief, I watch with thee.
2 Si - lent through those three dread hours, Wres-tling with the e - vil powers,
3 Hark, that cry that peals a - loud Up-ward through the whelm-ing cloud!

Dark - ness veils thine an-guished face; None its lines of woe can trace;
Left a - lone with hu - man sin, Gloom a - round thee and with-in,
Thou, the Fa-ther's on - ly Son, Thou, his own a - noint-ed one,

None can tell what pangs un-known Hold thee si - lent and a - lone.
Till the ap-point-ed time is nigh, Till the Lamb of God may die.
Thou dost ask him—can it be? "Why hast thou for - sak - en me?" A-men.

4 Lord, should fear and anguish roll
   Darkly o'er my sinful soul,
Thou, who once wast thus bereft
   That thine own might ne'er be left,
Teach me by that bitter cry
   In the gloom to know thee nigh.

PASSION AND CROSS

175

Ride on, Ride on in Majesty!

First Tune

Henry H. Milman, 1791-1868, alt.

ST. DROSTANE L.M.
John Dykes, 1823-1876

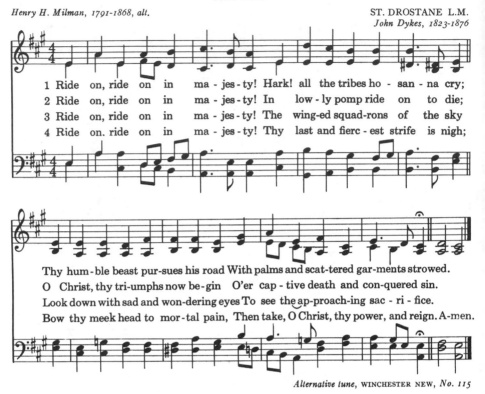

1 Ride on, ride on in ma - jes - ty! Hark! all the tribes ho - san - na cry;
2 Ride on, ride on in ma - jes - ty! In low - ly pomp ride on to die;
3 Ride on, ride on in ma - jes - ty! The wing-ed squad-rons of the sky
4 Ride on, ride on in ma - jes - ty! Thy last and fierc - est strife is nigh;

Thy hum - ble beast pur-sues his road With palms and scat-tered gar-ments strowed.
O Christ, thy tri-umphs now be-gin O'er cap - tive death and con-quered sin.
Look down with sad and won-dering eyes To see the ap-proach-ing sac - ri - fice.
Bow thy meek head to mor-tal pain, Then take, O Christ, thy power, and reign. A-men.

Alternative tune, WINCHESTER NEW, *No. 115*

176

Ride on, Ride on in Majesty!

Second Tune

Henry H. Milman, 1791-1868, alt.

THE KING'S MAJESTY L.M.
Graham George, 1912-

1 Ride on, ride on in ma - - jes - ty! Hark! all the
2 Ride on, ride on in ma - - jes - ty! In low - ly
3 Ride on, ride on in ma - - jes - ty! The wing - ed

PASSION AND CROSS

tribes ho - san - na cry; Thy hum - ble beast pur - sues his
pomp ride on to die; O Christ, thy tri - umphs now be -
squad - rons of the sky Look down with sad and won - dering

road With palms and scat - tered gar - ments strowed.
gin O'er cap - tive death and con - quered sin.
eyes To see the ap - proach-ing sac - ri - fice. A - men.

4 Ride on, ride on in majesty!
Thy last and fiercest strife is nigh;
Bow thy meek head to mortal pain,
Then take, O Christ, thy power, and reign.

177   When I Survey the Wondrous Cross

Isaac Watts, 1674-1748

HAMBURG L.M.
Arr. by Lowell Mason, 1792-1872

1 When I sur - vey the won - drous cross On which the Prince of glo - ry died, My rich - est gain I count but loss, And pour con - tempt on all my pride.

2 For - bid it, Lord, that I should boast, Save in the death of Christ, my God; All the vain things that charm me most I sac - ri - fice them to his blood.

3 See, from his head, his hands, his feet, Sor - row and love flow min - gled down! Did e'er such love and sor - row meet, Or thorns com - pose so rich a crown? A - men.

4 Were the whole realm of nature mine,
That were a present far too small;
Love so amazing, so divine,
Demands my soul, my life, my all.

PASSION AND CROSS

Alternative tune, ROCKINGHAM, *No. 357*

'Tis Midnight, and on Olive's Brow

William B. Tappan, 1794-1849, alt.

178

OLIVE'S BROW L.M.
William B. Bradbury, 1816-1868

1 'Tis mid-night, and on Ol-ive's brow The star is dimmed that late-ly shone; 'Tis mid-night, in the gar-den now The suf-fering Sav-ior prays a-lone.

2 'Tis mid-night, and, from all re-moved, The Sav-ior wres-tles lone with fears; E'en that dis-ci-ple whom he loved Heeds not his Mas-ter's grief and tears.

3 'Tis mid-night, and, for oth-ers' guilt, The Man of Sor-rows weeps in blood; Yet he that hath in an-guish knelt Is not for-sak-en by his God. A-men.

4 'Tis midnight, and from heavenly plains
Is borne the song that angels know;
Unheard by mortals are the strains
That sweetly soothe the Savior's woe.

PASSION AND CROSS

179 Were You There?

Negro Spiritual

WERE YOU THERE *Irregular*
Negro Melody

1 Were you there when they cru-ci-fied my Lord? Were you
2 Were you there when they nailed him to the tree? Were you
3 Were you there when they laid him in the tomb? Were you

there when they cru-ci-fied my Lord?
there when they nailed him to the tree? Oh! · · · ·
there when they laid him in the tomb?

Some-times it caus-es me to trem-ble, trem-ble, trem-ble.

Were you there when they cru-ci-fied my Lord?
Were you there when they nailed him to the tree?
Were you there when they laid him in the tomb?

PASSION AND CROSS

Alleluia! Alleluia! Hearts to Heaven

180

Christopher Wordsworth, 1807-1885, alt.

WEISSE FLAGGEN 8.7.8.7.D.
"Tochter Sion," Cologne, 1741

1 Al - le - lu - ia! Al - le - lu - ia! Hearts to heaven and voic - es raise;
2 Now the i - ron bars are bro - ken, Christ from death to life is born;
3 Al - le - lu - ia! Al - le - lu - ia! Glo - ry be to God on high;

Sing to God a hymn of glad-ness, Sing to God a hymn of praise.
Glo-rious life, and life im - mor-tal On this ho - ly East-er morn;
Al - le - lu - ia to the Sav - ior Who has won the vic - to - ry;

He who on the cross as Sav-ior For the world's sal - va - tion bled,
Christ has tri-umphed, and we con-quer By his might-y en - ter-prise,
Al - le - lu - ia to the Spir-it, Fount of love and sanc - ti - ty;

Je - sus Christ, the King of glo-ry, Now is ris - en from the dead.
We with him to life e - ter-nal By his res - ur - rec-tion rise.
Al - le - lu - ia! Al - le - lu - ia! To the Tri - une Ma - jes - ty. A - men.

A higher setting may be found at No. 413

RESURRECTION

Alleluia! The Strife Is O'er

Latin: 17th century
Tr. Francis Pott, 1832-1909

VICTORY 8.8.8. *with Alleluias*
Arr. from G. P. Sante da Palestrina, 1525-1594
William H. Monk, 1823-1889

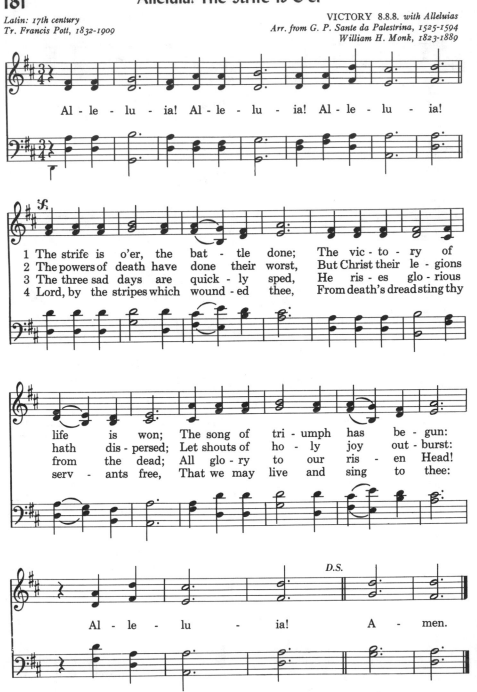

Al - le - lu - ia! Al - le - lu - ia! Al - le - lu - ia!

1 The strife is o'er, the bat - tle done; The vic - to - ry of
2 The powers of death have done their worst, But Christ their le - gions
3 The three sad days are quick - ly sped, He ris - es glo - rious
4 Lord, by the stripes which wound - ed thee, From death's dread sting thy

life is won; The song of tri - umph has be - gun:
hath dis - persed; Let shouts of ho - ly joy out - burst:
from the dead; All glo - ry to our ris - en Head!
serv - ants free, That we may live and sing to thee:

Al - le - lu - ia! A - men.

RESURRECTION

Christ the Lord Is Risen Today

182

Charles Wesley, 1707-1788 alt.

EASTER HYMN 7.7.7.7. *with Alleluias*
Arr. from "Lyra Davidica," 1708

1 Christ the Lord is risen to - day,
2 Lives a - gain our glo - rious King,
3 Love's re - deem-ing work is done, Al - - le - lu - ia!
4 Soar we now where Christ has led,
5 Hail the Lord of earth and heaven!

Sons of men and an - gels say:
Where, O death, is now thy sting?
Fought the fight, the bat - tle won, Al - - le - lu - ia!
Fol - lowing our ex - alt - ed Head,
Praise to thee by both be given,

Raise your joys and tri-umphs high,
Dy - ing once, he all doth save,
Death in vain for - bids him rise, Al - - le - lu - ia!
Made like him, like him we rise,
Thee we greet tri - um-phant now,

Sing, ye heavens, and earth re - ply:
Where thy vic - to - ry, O grave?
Christ has o - pened Par - a - dise, Al - - le - lu - ia!
Ours the cross, the grave, the skies,
Hail, the Res - ur - rec - tion thou!

A - men.

A descant may be found at No. 582
Alternative tune, LLANFAIR, *No. 187*

RESURRECTION

183 Christ the Lord Is Risen Again

Michael Weisse, c. 1488-1534
Tr. Catherine Winkworth, 1827-1878, alt.

CHRIST IST ERSTANDEN 7.7.7.7. *with Alleluias*
Traditional German Melody, c. 13th century

In unison

1 Christ the Lord is risen a - gain, Christ hath bro - ken ev - ery chain,
2 He who bore all pain and loss Com - fort - less up - on the cross,
3 He who slum-bered in the grave Is ex - alt - ed now to save;

Hark, the an - gels shout for joy, Sing - ing ev - er - more on high:
Lives in glo - ry now on high, Pleads for us and hears our cry: Al -
Now through Christ-en-dom it rings That the Lamb is King of kings:

REFRAIN

le - lu - ia! Al - le - lu - ia! Al - le -

lu - ia! Al - le - lu - ia! Hark, the an - gels shout for joy,
Lives in glo - ry now on high,
Now through Christ-en-dom it rings

RESURRECTION

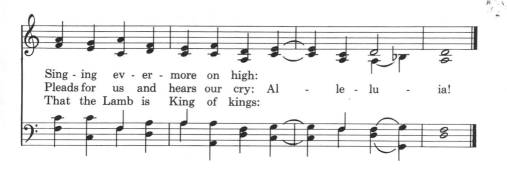

Singing evermore on high:
Pleads for us and hears our cry: Alleluia!
That the Lamb is King of kings:

Good Christian Men Rejoice and Sing! 184

Cyril A. Alington, 1872-1955

GELOBT SEI GOTT 8.8.8. *with Alleluias*
Melody by Melchior Vulpius, c.1560-1616

1 Good Christian men rejoice and sing! Now is the
2 The Lord of life is risen for aye; Bring flowers of
3 Praise we in songs of victory That love, that
4 Thy name we bless, O risen Lord, And sing to-

triumph of our King! To all the world glad
song to strew his way; Let all mankind re-
life which cannot die, And sing with hearts up-
day with one accord The life laid down, the

REFRAIN

news we bring:
joice and say: Alleluia! Alleluia! Alleluia!
lifted high:
life restored:

RESURRECTION

185 Come, Ye Faithful, Raise the Strain

First Tune

Attr. to John of Damascus, c.696-c.754
Tr. John M. Neale, 1818-1866

ST. KEVIN 7.6.7.6.D.
Arthur S. Sullivan, 1842-1900

1 Come, ye faith - ful, raise the strain Of tri - umph - ant glad - ness;
2 'Tis the spring of souls to - day; Christ hath burst his pris - on,
3 Now the queen of sea - sons, bright With the day of splen - dor,
4 Neith - er might the gates of death, Nor the tomb's dark por - tal,

God hath brought his Is - ra - el In - to joy from sad - ness;
And from three days' sleep in death As a sun hath ris - en;
With the roy - al feast of feasts, Comes its joy to ren - der;
Nor the watch - ers, nor the seal Hold thee as a mor - tal;

Loosed from Pha - raoh's bit - ter yoke Ja - cob's sons and daugh - ters;
All the win - ter of our sins, Long and dark, is fly - ing
Comes to glad Je - ru - sa - lem Who with true af - fec - tion
But to - day a - midst the twelve Thou didst stand, be - stow - ing

Led them with un-moist-ened foot Through the Red Sea wa - ters.
From his light, to whom we give Laud and praise un - dy - ing.
Wel-comes in un - wea-ried strains Je - sus' res - ur - rec - tion.
That thy peace which ev - er - more Pass - eth hu - man know - ing. A-men.

RESURRECTION

Come, Ye Faithful, Raise the Strain

186

Second Tune

Attr. to John of Damascus, c.696-c.754
Tr. John M. Neale, 1818-1866

AVE VIRGO VIRGINUM 7.6.7.6.D.
Leisentritt's "Gesangbuch," 1584

1 Come, ye faith-ful, raise the strain Of tri-umph-ant glad-ness;
2 'Tis the spring of souls to-day; Christ hath burst his pris-on,
3 Now the queen of sea-sons, bright With the day of splen-dor,
4 Neith-er might the gates of death, Nor the tomb's dark por-tal,

God hath brought his Is-ra-el In-to joy from sad-ness;
And from three days' sleep in death As a sun hath ris-en;
With the roy-al feast of feasts, Comes its joy to ren-der;
Nor the watch-ers, nor the seal Hold thee as a mor-tal;

Loosed from Pha-raoh's bit-ter yoke Ja-cob's sons and daugh-ters;
All the win-ter of our sins, Long and dark, is fly-ing
Comes to glad Je-ru-sa-lem Who with true af-fec-tion
But to-day a-midst the twelve Thou didst stand, be-stow-ing

Led them with un-moist-ened foot Through the Red Sea wa-ters.
From his light, to whom we give Laud and praise un-dy-ing.
Wel-comes in un-wea-ried strains Je-sus' res-ur-rec-tion.
That thy peace which ev-er-more Pass-eth hu-man know-ing. A-men.

RESURRECTION

187 Jesus Christ Is Risen Today

Latin: 14th century
English translation, "New Version," 1698
Charles Wesley, 1707-1788, St. 4

LLANFAIR 7.7.7.7. with Alleluias
Melody by Robert Williams, c.1781-1821
Harm. by John Roberts, 1822-1877

1 Je - sus Christ is risen to - day, Al - le - lu - ia!
2 Hymns of praise then let us sing:
3 But the pains which he en - dured,
4 Sing we to our God a - bove:

Our tri - umph-ant ho - ly day, Al - le - lu - ia!
Un - to Christ, our heaven-ly King,
Our sal - va - tion have pro - cured,
Praise e - ter - nal as his love,

Who did once up - on the cross, Al - le - lu - ia!
Who en - dured the cross and grave,
Now a - bove the sky he's King,
Praise him, all ye heaven - ly host,

In unison

Suf - fer to re - deem our loss.
Sin - ners to re - deem and save. Al - le - lu - ia!
Where the an - gels ev - er sing:
Fa - ther, Son, and Ho - ly Ghost.

A - men.

RESURRECTION

Alternative tune, EASTER HYMN, *No. 182*

Joy Dawned Again on Easter Day

188

Latin: 5th century?
Tr. John M. Neale, 1818-1866, alt.

PUER NOBIS NASCITUR L.M.
Adapted by Michael Praetorius, 1571-1621
Harm. by George R. Woodward, 1848-1934

1 Joy dawned a - gain on East - er Day, The sun shone
2 O Je - sus, King of gen - tle - ness, Do thou thy -
3 O Lord of all, with us a - bide In this our

out with fair ar - ray, When to their long - ing eyes re -
self our hearts pos - sess That we may give thee all our
joy - ful East - er - tide; From ev - ery wea - pon death can

stored, The A-pos - tles saw their ris - en Lord.
days The will - ing trib - ute of our praise.
wield Thine own re - deemed for ev - er shield. A - men.

RESURRECTION

189

Lift Up Your Hearts, Ye People
First Tune

Leonard A. Parr, 1880-

DU MEINE SEELE, SINGE 7.6.7.6.D.
Melody by Johann G. Ebeling, 1637-1676

1 Lift up your hearts, ye peo - ple, In songs of glad ac - cord,
2 Now let the earth be joy - ful In spring-time's bright ar - ray,

And in your ad - o - ra - tion Praise Christ, your ris - en Lord.
Let hearts down-cast and lone - ly Re - joice this East - er day;

For he hath won the vic - tory O'er sin and death's dark night,
The grave has lost its tri - umph, And death has lost its sting,

And filled the gloom and dark - ness With res - ur - rec - tion light.
O, sing in ex - ul - ta - tion To Christ, your ris - en King! A-men.

RESURRECTION

Lift Up Your Hearts, Ye People

Second Tune

190

Leonard A. Parr, 1880-

GREENLAND 7.6.7.6.D.
Attr. to J. Michael Haydn, 1737-1806

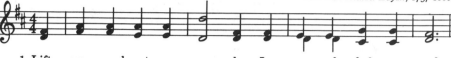

1 Lift up your hearts, ye peo - ple, In songs of glad ac - cord,
2 Now let the earth be joy - ful In spring-time's bright ar - ray,

And in your ad - o - ra - tion Praise Christ, your ris - en Lord.
Let hearts down-cast and lone - ly Re - joice this East - er day;

For he hath won the vic - tory O'er sin and death's dark night,
The grave has lost its tri - umph, And death has lost its sting,

And filled the gloom and dark-ness With res - ur - rec - tion light.
O, sing in ex - ul - ta - tion To Christ, your ris - en King! A-men.

RESURRECTION

191 O Sons and Daughters, Let Us Sing

Jean Tisserand, d.1494
Tr. John M. Neale, 1818-1866, alt.

O FILII ET FILIAE 8.8.8. *with Alleluias*
French: *15th century?*

Al - le - lu - ia! Al - le - lu - ia! Al - le - lu - ia!

1 O sons and daugh - ters, let us sing! The King of
2 That East - er morn at break of day, The faith - ful
3 An an - gel clad in white they see, Who sat and
4 How blest are they who have not seen, And yet whose
5 On this most ho - ly day of days, Our hearts and

heaven, the glo - rious King, O'er death to - day rose
wom - en went their way To seek the tomb where
spake un - to the three, "Your Lord doth go to
faith hath con - stant been; For they e - ter - nal
voic - es, Lord, we raise To thee, in ju - bi -

tri - umph - ing,
Je - sus lay,
Gal - i - lee," Al - le - lu - ia!
life shall win,
lee and praise,

RESURRECTION

The Day of Resurrection

192

John of Damascus, c.696-c.754
Tr. John M. Neale, 1818-1866, alt.

LANCASHIRE 7.6.7.6.D.
Henry T. Smart, 1813-1879

1 The day of res-ur-rec-tion! Earth, tell it out a-broad;
2 Our hearts be pure from e-vil, That we may see a-right
3 Now let the heavens be joy-ful, Let earth her song be-gin,

The Pass-o-ver of glad-ness, The Pass-o-ver of God.
The Lord in rays e-ter-nal Of res-ur-rec-tion light;
The round world keep high tri-umph, And all that is there-in;

From death to life e-ter-nal, From earth un-to the sky,
And, lis-tening to his ac-cents, May hear so calm and plain
Let all things seen and un-seen Their notes of glad-ness blend,

Our Christ hath brought us o-ver With hymns of vic-to-ry.
His own "All hail," and, hear-ing, May raise the vic-tor-strain.
For Christ the Lord is ris-en, Our joy that hath no end. A-men.

A lower setting may be found at No. 375
Alternative tune, GREENLAND, *No. 190*

RESURRECTION

193

Thine Is the Glory

Edmond L. Budry, 1854-1932
Tr. R. Birch Hoyle, 1875-1939

JUDAS MACCABEUS 5.5.6.5.6.5.6.5. *with Refrain*
Georg F. Handel, 1685-1759

1 Thine is the glo - ry, Ris - en, con-quering Son;
End - less is the

2 Lo! Je - sus meets thee, Ris - en from the tomb;
Lov - ing - ly he

3 No more we doubt thee, Glo - rious Prince of life!
Life is nought with-

vic - tory Thou o'er death hast won. An - gels in bright rai - ment
greets thee, Scat - ters fear and gloom; Let his church with glad - ness
out thee; Aid us in our strife; Make us more than con-querors,

Rolled the stone a way, Kept the fold - ed grave - clothes
Hymns of tri - umph sing, For her Lord now liv - eth;
Through thy death - less love; Bring us safe through Jor - dan

REFRAIN

Where thy bod - y lay.
Death hath lost its sting. Thine is the glo - ry, Ris - en, con-quering Son;
To thy home a - bove.

RESURRECTION

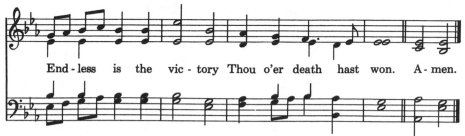

Endless is the victory Thou o'er death hast won. Amen.

The Whole Bright World Rejoices Now 194

Percy Dearmer, 1867-1936
"Oxford Book of Carols," 1928

HILARITER L.M.
Traditional German Melody
Martin Shaw, 1875-

1 The whole bright world rejoices now, Hilariter, Hilariter; The birds do sing on every bough, Alleluia, Alleluia!

2 Then shout beneath the racing skies, Hilariter, Hilariter; To him who rose that we might rise, Alleluia, Alleluia!

3 And all you living things make praise, Hilariter, Hilariter; He guideth you on all your ways, Alleluia, Alleluia!

4 He, Father, Son, and Holy Ghost, Hilariter, Hilariter; Our God most high, our joy and boast, Alleluia, Alleluia!

RESURRECTION

195 All Hail the Power of Jesus' Name
First Tune

Edward Perronet, 1726-1792
Alt. by John Rippon, 1751-1836

CORONATION C.M.
Oliver Holden, 1765-1844

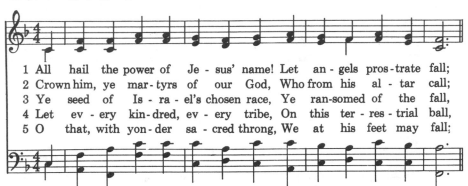

1 All hail the power of Je-sus' name! Let an-gels pros-trate fall;
2 Crown him, ye mar-tyrs of our God, Who from his al-tar call;
3 Ye seed of Is-ra-el's chosen race, Ye ran-somed of the fall,
4 Let ev-ery kin-dred, ev-ery tribe, On this ter-res-trial ball,
5 O that, with yon-der sa-cred throng, We at his feet may fall;

Bring forth the roy-al di-a-dem, And crown him Lord of all.
Ex-tol the stem of Jes-se's rod, And crown him Lord of all.
Hail him who saves you by his grace, And crown him Lord of all.
To him all maj-es-ty as-cribe, And crown him Lord of all.
We'll join the ev-er-last-ing song, And crown him Lord of all.

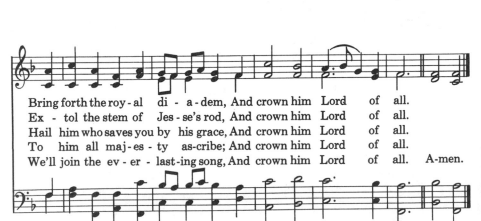

Bring forth the roy-al di-a-dem, And crown him Lord of all.
Ex-tol the stem of Jes-se's rod, And crown him Lord of all.
Hail him who saves you by his grace, And crown him Lord of all.
To him all maj-es-ty as-cribe; And crown him Lord of all.
We'll join the ev-er-last-ing song, And crown him Lord of all. A-men.

ASCENSION AND REIGN

A descant may be found at No. 581

All Hail the Power of Jesus' Name

Second Tune

196

Edward Perronet, 1726-1792
Alt. by John Rippon, 1751-1836

MILES LANE C.M.
William Shrubsole, 1760-1806

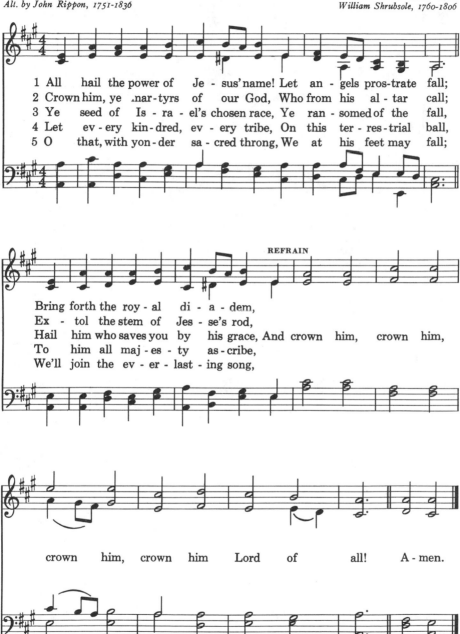

1 All hail the power of Jesus' name! Let angels prostrate fall;
2 Crown him, ye martyrs of our God, Who from his altar call;
3 Ye seed of Israel's chosen race, Ye ransomed of the fall,
4 Let every kindred, every tribe, On this terrestrial ball,
5 O that, with yonder sacred throng, We at his feet may fall;

REFRAIN

Bring forth the royal diadem,
Extol the stem of Jesse's rod,
Hail him who saves you by his grace, And crown him, crown him,
To him all majesty ascribe,
We'll join the everlasting song,

crown him, crown him Lord of all! A-men.

ASCENSION AND REIGN

197 At the Name of Jesus

Caroline M. Noel, 1817-1877

KING'S WESTON 6.5.6.5.D.
R. Vaughan Williams, 1872-1958

1 At the name of Je - sus Ev - ery knee shall bow,
2 At his voice cre - a - tion Sprang at once to sight
3 Hum-bled for a sea - son, To re - ceive a name
4 Bore it up tri - umph - ant, With its hu - man light,
5 In your hearts en - throne him; There let him sub - due

Ev - ery tongue con - fess him King of glo - ry now;
All the an - gel fa - ces, All the hosts of light,
From the lips of sin - ners, Un - to whom he came.
Through all ranks of crea - tures, To the cen - tral height,
All that is not ho - ly, All that is not true.

'Tis the Fa - ther's pleas - ure We should call him Lord,
Thrones and dom - i - na - tions, Stars up - on their way,
Faith - ful - ly he bore it, Spot - less to the last,
To the throne of God - head, To the Fa - ther's breast;
Crown him as your cap - tain In temp - ta - tion's hour;

Who from the be - gin - ning Was the might - y Word.
All the heaven-ly or - ders, In their great ar - ray.
Brought it back vic - to - rious, When from death he passed;
Filled it with the glo - ry Of that per - fect rest.
Let his will en - fold you In its light and power. A-men.

ASCENSION AND REIGN

Christ Is the World's True Light

198

George W. Briggs, 1875-1959

O GOTT, DU FROMMER GOTT 6.7.6.7.6.6.6.6.
Melody by Ahasuerus Fritsch, 1649-1701
Harm. by J.S. Bach, 1685-1750

1 Christ is the world's true light, Its cap-tain of sal-va-tion,
2 In Christ all ra-ces meet, Their an-cient feuds for-get-ting,
3 One Lord, in one great name U-nite us all who own thee;

The day-star clear and bright Of ev-ery man and na-tion;
The whole round world com-plete, From sun-rise to its set-ting;
Cast out our pride and shame That hin-der to en-throne thee;

New life, new hope a-wakes Wher-e'er men own his sway;
When Christ is throned as Lord, Men shall for-sake their fear
The world has wait-ed long, Has tra-vailed long in pain;

Free-dom her bond-age breaks, And night is turned to day.
To plough-share beat the sword, To prun-ing-hook the spear.
To heal its an-cient wrong, Come, Prince of peace, and reign. A-men.

ASCENSION AND REIGN

Crown Him With Many Crowns

Matthew Bridges, 1800-1894
Godfrey Thring, 1823-1903, St. 3

DIADEMATA S.M.D.
George J. Elvey, 1816-1893

1 Crown him with man-y crowns, The Lamb up-on his throne;
2 Crown him the Lord of love; Be-hold his hands and side,
3 Crown him the Lord of life, Who tri-umphed o'er the grave,
4 Crown him the Lord of years, The po-ten-tate of time,

Hark! how the heaven-ly an-them drowns All mu-sic but its own;
Rich wounds, yet vis-i-ble a-bove, In beau-ty glo-ri-fied;
And rose vic-to-rious in the strife For those he came to save;
Cre-a-tor of the roll-ing spheres, In-eff-a-bly sub-lime.

A-wake, my soul, and sing Of him who died for thee,
No an-gel in the sky Can ful-ly bear that sight,
His glo-ries now we sing Who died and rose on high,
All hail, Re-deem-er, hail! For thou hast died for me;

And hail him as thy match-less King Through all e-ter-ni-ty.
But down-ward bends his burn-ing eye At mys-ter-ies so bright.
Who died, e-ter-nal life to bring, And lives that death may die.
Thy praise shall nev-er, nev-er fail Through-out e-ter-ni-ty. A-men.

ASCENSION AND REIGN   *A higher setting may be found at No. 384*

The Head That Once Was Crowned With Thorns 200

Thomas Kelly, 1769-1855

ST. MAGNUS C.M.
Jeremiah Clark, c.1670-1707

1 The head that once was crowned with thorns Is crowned with glo - ry now;
2 The high - est place that heaven af - fords Is his, is his by right;
3 The joy of all who dwell a - bove, The joy of all be - low,
4 To them the cross, with all its shame, With all its grace, is given;

A roy - al di - a - dem a-dorns The might-y vic-tor's brow.
The King of kings, and Lord of lords, And heaven's e - ter - nal light.
To whom he man - i - fests his love, And grants his name to know.
Their name an ev - er - last-ing name, Their joy the joy of heaven. A-men.

The King Shall Come When Morning Dawns 201

Greek: anonymous
Tr. John Brownlie, 1857-1925

ST. STEPHEN C.M.
William Jones, 1726-1800

1 The King shall come when morn-ing dawns And light tri - um-phant breaks,
2 Not as of old a lit - tle child To bear, and fight, and die,
3 O bright-er than the ris - ing morn When he, vic - to - rious, rose,
4 O bright-er than that glo-rious morn Shall this fair morn-ing be,
5 The King shall come when morn-ing dawns, And light and beau-ty brings;

When beau - ty gilds the east - ern hills And life to joy a-wakes.
But crowned with glo - ry like the sun That lights the morn-ing sky.
And left the lone-some place of death, De - spite the rage of foes.
When Christ, our King, in beau - ty comes, And we his face shall see!
Hail, Christ the Lord! thy peo - ple pray, Come quick-ly, King of kings! A-men.

ASCENSION AND REIGN

202 Jesus Shall Reign Where'er the Sun

Isaac Watts, 1674-1748

DUKE STREET L.M.
John Hatton, d.1793

1 Je - sus shall reign wher - e'er the sun Doth his suc -
2 For him shall end - less prayer be made, And prais - es
3 Peo - ple and realms of ev - ery tongue Dwell on his

ces - sive jour - neys run; His king - dom stretch from
throng to crown his head; His name like sweet per -
love with sweet - est song, And in - fant voic - es

shore to shore Till moons shall wax and wane no more.
fume shall rise With ev - ery morn - ing sac - ri - fice.
shall pro - claim Their ear - ly bless - ings on his name. A-men.

4 Blessings abound where'er he reigns;
The prisoner leaps to lose his chains,
The weary find eternal rest,
And all the sons of want are blest.

5 Let every creature rise and bring
Peculiar honors to our King;
Angels descend with songs again,
And earth repeat the loud Amen.

ASCENSION AND REIGN

Look, Ye Saints, the Sight Is Glorious

203

Thomas Kelly, *1769-1855*

CORONAE 8.7.8.7.4.7.
William H. Monk, 1823-1889

1 Look, ye saints, the sight is glo-rious; See the Man of Sor-rows now;
2 Crown the Sav - ior, an - gels, crown him; Rich the tro-phies Je - sus brings;
3 Sin - ners in de - ri-sion crowned him, Mock-ing thus the Sav-ior's claim;

From the fight re-turned vic - to - rious, Ev - ery knee to him shall bow:
In the seat of power en-throne him, While the vault of heav - en rings:
Saints and an - gels throng a - round him, Own his ti - tle, praise his name:

Crown him! crown him! Crowns be-come the vic - tor's brow.
Crown him! crown him! Crown the Sav - ior King of kings.
Crown him! crown him! Spread a-broad the vic - tor's fame. A - men.

4 Hark! those bursts of acclamation!
  Hark! those loud triumphant chords!
Jesus takes the highest station;
  O what joy the sight affords!'
  Crown him! crown him
  King of kings, and Lord of lords.

ASCENSION AND REIGN

204 Rejoice, the Lord Is King

Charles Wesley, 1707-1788

DARWALL'S 148th 6.6.6.6.8.8.
John Darwall, 1731-1789

1 Re - joice, the Lord is King! Your Lord and King a - dore!
2 The Lord, our Sav - ior, reigns, The God of truth and love;
3 His king - dom can - not fail, He rules o'er earth and heaven;

Re - joice, give thanks, and sing, And tri - umph ev - er -
When he had purged our stains, He took his seat a -
The keys of death and hell Are to our Je - sus

more:
bove: Lift up your heart, lift up your voice! Re -
given:

joice, a - gain I say, re - joice! A - men.

ASCENSION AND REIGN

Hail the Day That Sees Him Rise

205

Charles Wesley, 1707-1788
Alt. by Thomas Cotterill, 1779-1823

GWALCHMAI 7.7.7.7. with Alleluias
Joseph D. Jones, 1827-1870

1 Hail the day that sees him rise,
2 There the glo - rious tri - umph waits, Al - le - lu - ia!
3 See, the heaven its Lord re - ceives,

Glo - rious to his na - tive skies,
Lift your heads, e - ter - nal gates, Al - le - lu - ia!
Yet he loves the earth he leaves,

Christ, a - while to mor - tals given,
Christ hath van - quished death and sin, Al - le - lu - ia!
Though re - turn - ing to his throne,

En - ters now the high - est heaven.
Take the King of glo - ry in. Al - le - lu - ia!
Still he calls man - kind his own.

A - men.

ASCENSION AND REIGN

206   Ye Servants of God, Your Master Proclaim

Charles Wesley, 1707-1788, alt.

HANOVER 10.10.11.11.
Attr. to William Croft, 1678-1727

1 Ye serv - ants of God, your Mas - ter pro - claim,
2 God rul - eth on high, al - might - y to save,
3 Sal - va - tion to God who sits on the throne!
4 Then let us a - dore and give him his right,

And pub - lish a - broad his won - der - ful name.
And still he is nigh, his pres - ence we have;
Let all cry a - loud and hon - or the Son;
All glo - ry and power, all wis - dom and might,

The name, all vic - to - rious, of Je - sus ex - tol;
The great con - gre - ga - tion his tri - umph shall sing,
The prais - es of Je - sus the an - gels pro - claim,
All hon - or and bless - ing with an - gels a - bove,

His king - dom is glo - rious, he rules o - ver all.
As - crib - ing sal - va - tion to Je - sus, our King.
Fall down on their fa - ces and wor - ship the Lamb.
And thanks nev - er ceas - ing and in - fi - nite love. A - men.

ASCENSION AND REIGN

A descant may be found at No. 584
Alternative tune, LYONS, No. 6

I Greet Thee, Who My Sure Redeemer Art   207

Attr. to John Calvin, 1509-1564
Tr. Elizabeth L. Smith, 1817-1898, alt.

SONG 24 10.10.10.10.
Orlando Gibbons, 1583-1625

1 I greet thee, who my sure Re - deem - er art,
2 Thou art the King of mer - cy and of grace,
3 Thou art the life, by which a - lone we live,
4 Thou hast the true and per - fect gen - tle - ness,
5 Our hope is in no oth - er save in thee;

My on - ly trust and sav - ior of my heart,
Reign - ing om - ni - po - tent in ev - ery place;
And all our sub - stance and our strength re - ceive;
No harsh - ness hast thou and no bit - ter - ness;
Our faith is built up - on thy prom - ise free;

Who pain didst un - der - go for my poor sake;
So come, O King, and our whole be - ing sway;
Sus - tain us by thy faith and by thy power,
O grant to us the grace we find in thee,
Lord, give us peace, and make us calm and sure,

I pray thee from our hearts all cares to take.
Shine on us with the light of thy pure day.
And give us strength in ev - ery try - ing hour.
That we may dwell in per - fect u - ni - ty.
That in thy strength we ev - er - more en - dure. A - men.

Alternative tune, TOULON, *No. 432*   *PRESENCE AND GUIDANCE*

208

Dear Master, in Whose Life I See

John Hunter, 1848-1917, alt.

O JESU CHRISTE, WAHRES LICHT L.M.
Melody, Nürnberg, 1676

1 Dear Mas - ter, in whose life I see
2 Though what I dream and what I do

All that I would, but fail, to be,
In all my days are of - ten two,

Let thy clear light for - ev - er shine,
Help me, op - pressed by things un - done,

To shame and guide this life of mine.
O thou whose deeds and dreams were one. A - men.

PRESENCE AND GUIDANCE　　　　　　　　　*Alternative tune,* HURSLEY, *No. 50*

Abide With Me

Henry F. Lyte, 1793-1847, alt.

EVENTIDE 10.10.10.10.
William H. Monk, 1823-1889

1 A - bide with me; fast falls the e - ven - tide; The dark-ness deep-ens,
2 Swift to its close ebbs out life's lit - tle day; Earth's joys grow dim, its
3 I need thy pres-ence ev - ery pass-ing hour; What but thy grace can
4 I fear no foe, with thee at hand to bless; Ills have no weight, and

Lord, with me a - bide; When oth - er help - ers fail, and com-forts flee,
glo - ries pass a - way; Change and de - cay in all a-round I see;
foil the temp-ter's power? Who like thy - self my guide and stay can be?
tears no bit - ter - ness; Where is death's sting? where, grave, thy vic-to - ry?

Help of the help - less, O a - bide with me.
O thou who chang-est not, a - bide with me.
Through cloud and sun - shine, O a - bide with me.
I tri - umph still if thou a - bide with me. A - men.

5 Hold thou thy cross before my closing eyes;
Shine through the gloom, and point me to the skies;
Heaven's morning breaks, and earth's vain shadows flee;
In life, in death, O Lord, abide with me.

PRESENCE AND GUIDANCE

210

Jesus, Lover of My Soul
First Tune

Charles Wesley, 1707-1788

MARTYN 7.7.7.7.D.
Simeon B. Marsh, 1798-1875

1 Je - sus, lov - er of my soul, Let me to thy bos - om fly,
2 Oth - er ref - uge have I none; Hangs my help-less soul on thee;
3 Plen-teous grace with thee is found, Grace to cov - er all my sin;

While the near - er wa - ters roll, While the tem-pest still is high;
Leave, ah! leave me not a - lone, Still sup-port and com - fort me.
Let the heal - ing streams a - bound, Make and keep me pure with - in.

Hide me, O my Sav - ior, hide, Till the storm of life is past;
All my trust on thee is stayed, All my help from thee I bring;
Thou of life the foun - tain art, Free - ly let me take of thee;

Safe in - to the ha - ven guide, O re - ceive my soul at last!
Cov - er my de - fense-less head With the shad - ow of thy wing.
Spring thou up with - in my heart, Rise to all e - ter - ni - ty. A - men.

PRESENCE AND GUIDANCE

Jesus, Lover of My Soul

Second Tune

Charles Wesley, 1707-1788

ABERYSTWYTH 7.7.7.7.D.
Joseph Parry, 1841-1903

1 Je - sus, lov - er of my soul, Let me to thy bos - om fly,
2 Oth - er ref - uge have I none; Hangs my help - less soul on thee;
3 Plen - teous grace with thee is found, Grace to cov - er all my sin;

While the near - er wa - ters roll, While the tem - pest still is high;
Leave, ah! leave me not a - lone, Still sup - port and com - fort me.
Let the heal - ing streams a - bound, Make and keep me pure with - in.

Hide me, O my Sav - ior, hide, Till the storm of life is past;
All my trust on thee is stayed, All my help from thee I bring;
Thou of life the foun - tain art, Free - ly let me take of thee;

Safe in - to the ha - ven guide, O re - ceive my soul at last!
Cov - er my de - fense - less head With the shad - ow of thy wing.
Spring thou up with - in my heart, Rise to all e - ter - ni - ty. A-men.

PRESENCE AND GUIDANCE

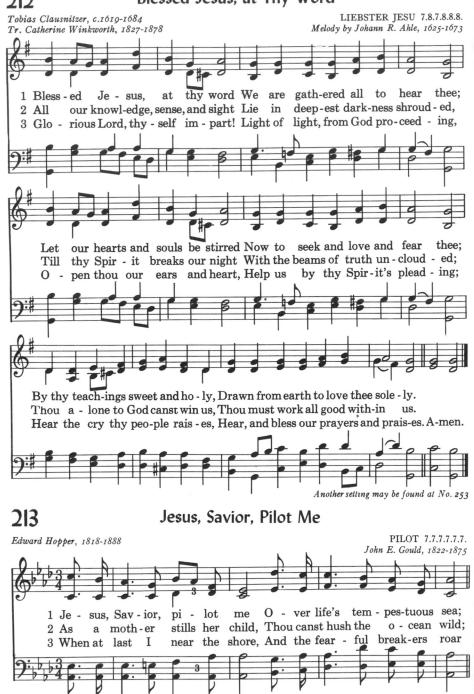

212 Blessed Jesus, at Thy Word

Tobias Clausnitzer, c.1619-1684
Tr. Catherine Winkworth, 1827-1878

LIEBSTER JESU 7.8.7.8.8.8.
Melody by Johann R. Ahle, 1625-1673

1 Bless-ed Je - sus, at thy word We are gath-ered all to hear thee;
2 All our knowl-edge, sense, and sight Lie in deep-est dark-ness shroud-ed,
3 Glo - rious Lord, thy - self im - part! Light of light, from God pro-ceed - ing,

Let our hearts and souls be stirred Now to seek and love and fear thee;
Till thy Spir - it breaks our night With the beams of truth un - cloud-ed;
O - pen thou our ears and heart, Help us by thy Spir-it's plead - ing;

By thy teach-ings sweet and ho - ly, Drawn from earth to love thee sole - ly.
Thou a - lone to God canst win us, Thou must work all good with-in us.
Hear the cry thy peo-ple rais - es, Hear, and bless our prayers and prais-es. A-men.

Another setting may be found at No. 253

213 Jesus, Savior, Pilot Me

Edward Hopper, 1818-1888

PILOT 7.7.7.7.7.7.
John E. Gould, 1822-1875

1 Je - sus, Sav - ior, pi - lot me O - ver life's tem - pes-tuous sea;
2 As a moth - er stills her child, Thou canst hush the o - cean wild;
3 When at last I near the shore, And the fear - ful break-ers roar

PRESENCE AND GUIDANCE

Un-known waves be-fore me roll, Hid-ing rock and treacherous shoal;
Bois-terous waves o-bey thy will When thou sayest to them, "Be still."
'Twixt me and the peace-ful rest, Then, while lean-ing on thy breast,

Chart and com-pass come from thee; Je-sus, Sav-ior, pi-lot me.
Won-drous Sov-ereign of the sea, Je-sus, Sav-ior, pi-lot me.
May I hear thee say to me, "Fear not, I will pi-lot thee." A-men.

Blest Are the Pure in Heart — 214

John Keble, 1792-1866, Sts. 1 and 3, alt.
William J. Hall, 1793-1861, Sts. 2 and 4

FRANCONIA S.M.
Melody by J. B. König, 1691-1758
Arr. by William H. Havergal, 1793-1870

1 Blest are the pure in heart, For they shall see our God;
2 The Lord, who left the heavens Our life and peace to bring,
3 Still to the low-ly soul He doth him-self im-part,
4 Lord, we thy pres-ence seek; May ours this bless-ing be:

The se-cret of the Lord is theirs, Their soul is Christ's a-bode.
To dwell in low-li-ness with men, Their pat-tern and their King,
And for his dwell-ing and his throne Choos-eth the pure in heart.
Give us a pure and low-ly heart, A tem-ple meet for thee. A-men.

PRESENCE AND GUIDANCE

Lead, Kindly Light
First Tune

John H. Newman, 1801-1890

LUX BENIGNA 10.4.10.4.10.10.
John B. Dykes, 1823-1876

1 Lead, kind-ly Light, a - mid the en-cir-cling gloom, Lead thou me on;
2 I was not ev - er thus, nor prayed that thou Shouldst lead me on;
3 So long thy power hath blest me, sure it still Will lead me on

The night is dark, and I am far from home; Lead thou me on!
I loved to choose and see my path, but now Lead thou me on.
O'er moor and fen, o'er crag and tor - rent, till The night is gone;

Keep thou my feet; I do not ask to see
I loved the gar - ish day, and, spite of fears,
And with the morn those an - gel fa - ces smile

The dis - tant scene: one step e - nough for me.
Pride ruled my will: re - mem - ber not past years.
Which I have loved long since, and lost a - while. A-men.

PRESENCE AND GUIDANCE

Lead, Kindly Light

Second Tune

John H. Newman, 1801-1890

SANDON 10.4.10.4.10.10.
Charles H. Purday, 1799-1885

1 Lead, kind-ly Light, a - mid the en-cir - cling gloom, Lead thou me on;
2 I was not ev - er thus, nor prayed that thou Shouldst lead me on;
3 So long thy power hath blest me, sure it still Will lead me on

The night is dark, and I am far from home; Lead thou me on!
I loved to choose and see my path, but now Lead thou me on.
O'er moor and fen, o'er crag and tor - rent, till The night is gone;

Keep thou my feet; I do not ask to see The
I loved the gar - ish day, and, spite of fears, Pride
And with the morn those an - gel fa - ces smile Which

dis - tant scene: one step e - nough for me.
ruled my will: re - mem - ber not past years.
I have loved long since, and lost a - while. A - men.

PRESENCE AND GUIDANCE

217 Lord of All Hopefulness

Jan Struther, 1901-1953

SLANE 10.11.11.12.
Traditional Irish Melody
Harm. by David Evans, 1874-1948

In unison

1 Lord of all hope-ful-ness, Lord of all joy,
2 Lord of all ea-ger-ness, Lord of all faith,
3 Lord of all kind-li-ness, Lord of all grace,
4 Lord of all gen-tle-ness, Lord of all calm,

Whose trust, ev-er child-like, no cares could de-stroy,
Whose strong hands were skilled at the plane and the lathe,
Your hands swift to wel-come, your arms to em-brace,
Whose voice is con-tent-ment, whose pres-ence is balm,

Be there at our wak-ing, and give us, we pray, Your
Be there at our la-bors, and give us, we pray, Your
Be there at our hom-ing, and give us, we pray, Your
Be there at our sleep-ing, and give us, we pray, Your

bliss in our hearts, Lord, at the break of the day.
strength in our hearts, Lord, at the noon of the day.
love in our hearts, Lord, at the eve of the day.
peace in our hearts, Lord, at the end of the day. A-men.

PRESENCE AND GUIDANCE

O Jesus, I Have Promised

218

John E. Bode, 1816-1874

ANGEL'S STORY 7.6.7.6.D.
Arthur H. Mann, 1850-1929

1 O Je - sus, I have prom - ised To serve thee to the end;
2 O let me hear thee speak - ing In ac - cents clear and still,
3 O Je - sus, thou hast prom - ised To all who fol - low thee

Be thou for - ev - er near me, My mas - ter and my friend;
A - bove the storms of pas - sion, The mur - murs of self - will;
That where thou art in glo - ry There shall thy serv ant be;

I shall not fear the bat - tle If thou art by my side,
O speak to re - as - sure me, To has - ten or con - trol;
And, Je - sus, I have prom - ised To serve thee to the end;

Nor wan - der from the path - way If thou wilt be my guide.
O speak, and make me lis - ten, Thou guard-ian of my soul.
O give me grace to fol - low, My mas - ter and my friend. A-men.

Alternative tune, LLANGLOFFAN, *No. 436*   *PRESENCE AND GUIDANCE*

O Thou Great Friend

Theodore Parker, *1810-1860*

FFIGYSBREN 10.10.10.10.
Welsh Hymn Melody

1 O thou great friend to all the sons of men,
2 Thee would I sing: thy truth is still the light
3 Yes, thou art still the Life; thou art the Way

Who once ap - peared in hum - blest guise be - low,
Which guides the na - tions grop - ing on their way,
The ho - liest know — Light, Life, and Way of heaven;

Sin to re - buke, to break the cap - tive's chain,
Stum - bling and fall - ing in dis - as - trous night,
And they who dear - est hope and deep - est pray

To call thy breth - ren forth from want and woe,
Yet hop - ing ev - er for the per - fect day.
Toil by the truth, life, way that thou hast given. A - men.

PRESENCE AND GUIDANCE

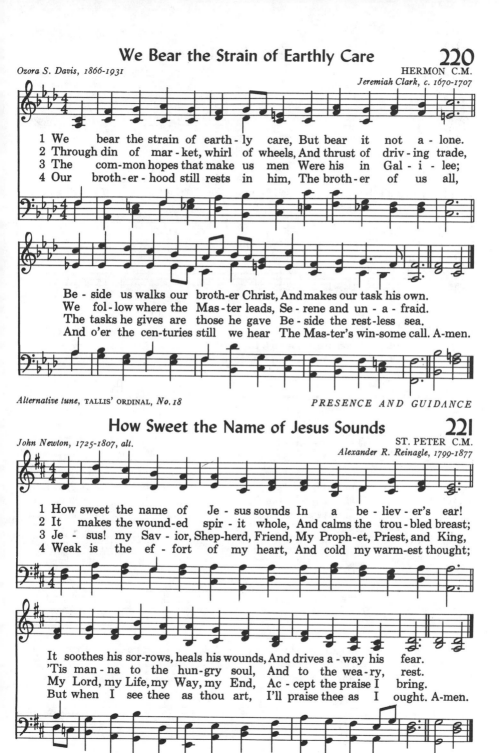

We Bear the Strain of Earthly Care

220 HERMON C.M.

Ozora S. Davis, 1866-1931

Jeremiah Clark, c. 1670-1707

1 We bear the strain of earth-ly care, But bear it not a-lone.
2 Through din of mar-ket, whirl of wheels, And thrust of driv-ing trade,
3 The com-mon hopes that make us men Were his in Gal-i-lee;
4 Our broth-er-hood still rests in him, The broth-er of us all,

Be-side us walks our broth-er Christ, And makes our task his own.
We fol-low where the Mas-ter leads, Se-rene and un-a-fraid.
The tasks he gives are those he gave Be-side the rest-less sea.
And o'er the cen-turies still we hear The Mas-ter's win-some call. A-men.

Alternative tune, TALLIS' ORDINAL, *No. 18*

PRESENCE AND GUIDANCE

How Sweet the Name of Jesus Sounds

221 ST. PETER C.M.

John Newton, 1725-1807, alt.

Alexander R. Reinagle, 1799-1877

1 How sweet the name of Je-sus sounds In a be-liev-er's ear!
2 It makes the wound-ed spir-it whole, And calms the trou-bled breast;
3 Je-sus! my Sav-ior, Shep-herd, Friend, My Proph-et, Priest, and King,
4 Weak is the ef-fort of my heart, And cold my warm-est thought;

It soothes his sor-rows, heals his wounds, And drives a-way his fear.
'Tis man-na to the hun-gry soul, And to the wea-ry, rest.
My Lord, my Life, my Way, my End, Ac-cept the praise I bring.
But when I see thee as thou art, I'll praise thee as I ought. A-men.

A higher setting may be found at No. 414

CHARACTER AND GLORY

222 Jesus, Priceless Treasure

Johann Franck, 1618-1677
Tr. Catherine Winkworth, 1827-1878

JESU, MEINE FREUDE 6.6.5.6.6.5.7.8.6.
Traditional German Melody
Adapted by Johann Crüger, 1598-1662

1 Je - sus, price - less treas - ure, Source of pur - est pleas-ure,
2 In thine arm I rest me; Foes who would mo - lest me
3 Hence, all thoughts of sad - ness! For the Lord of glad - ness,

Tru - est friend to me, Long my heart hath pant - ed, Till it well-nigh
Can - not reach me here. Though the earth be shak - ing, Ev - ery heart be
Je - sus, en - ters in; Those who love the Fa - ther, Though the storms may

faint - ed, Thirst-ing aft - er thee. Thine I am, O spot-less Lamb,
quak-ing, God dis-pels our fear; Sin and hell in con - flict fell
gath - er, Still have peace with - in; Yea, what-e'er we here must bear,

I will suf-fer nought to hide thee, Ask for nought be-side thee.
With their heav-iest storms as-sail us; Je - sus will not fail us.
Still in thee lies pur - est pleas - ure, Je - sus, price-less treas - ure! A-men.

CHARACTER AND GLORY

O for a Thousand Tongues to Sing

Charles Wesley, 1707-1788, alt.

AZMON C.M.
Carl G. Gläser, 1784-1829
Mason's "Modern Psalmody," 1839

1 O for a thou-sand tongues to sing My great Re-deem-er's praise,
2 My gra-cious Mas-ter and my God, As-sist me to pro-claim,
3 Glo-ry to God and praise and love Be ev-er, ev-er given

The glo-ries of my God and King, The tri-umphs of his grace!
To spread through all the earth a-broad The hon-ors of thy name.
By saints be-low and saints a-bove, The Church in earth and heaven. A-men.

A lower setting may be found at No. 346

O Lord and Master of Us All

John Greenleaf Whittier, 1807-1892

WALSALL C.M.
William Anchors' "Psalm Tunes," c. 1721

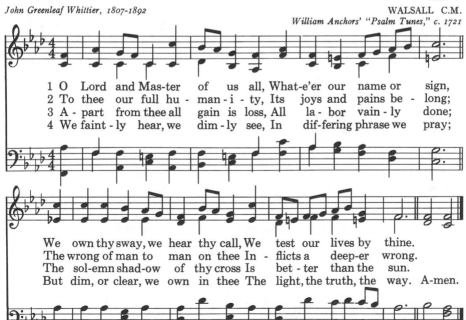

1 O Lord and Mas-ter of us all, What-e'er our name or sign,
2 To thee our full hu-man-i-ty, Its joys and pains be-long;
3 A-part from thee all gain is loss, All la-bor vain-ly done;
4 We faint-ly hear, we dim-ly see, In dif-fering phrase we pray;

We own thy sway, we hear thy call, We test our lives by thine.
The wrong of man to man on thee In-flicts a deep-er wrong.
The sol-emn shad-ow of thy cross Is bet-ter than the sun.
But dim, or clear, we own in thee The light, the truth, the way. A-men.

Alternative tune, st. agnes. No. 225

CHARACTER AND GLORY

Jesus, the Very Thought of Thee
First Tune

Latin: 12th century
Tr. Edward Caswall, 1814-1878, alt.

ST. AGNES C.M.
John B. Dykes, 1823-1876

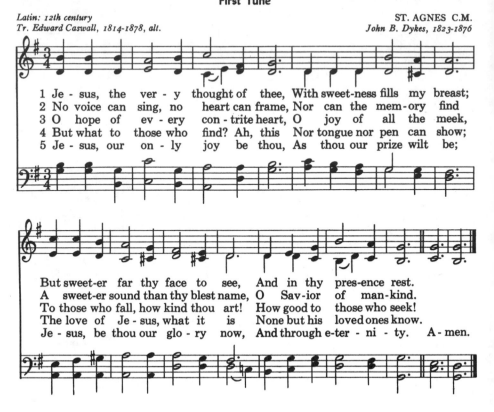

1 Je - sus, the ver - y thought of thee, With sweet-ness fills my breast;
2 No voice can sing, no heart can frame, Nor can the mem-ory find
3 O hope of ev - ery con - trite heart, O joy of all the meek,
4 But what to those who find? Ah, this Nor tongue nor pen can show;
5 Je - sus, our on - ly joy be thou, As thou our prize wilt be;

But sweet-er far thy face to see, And in thy pres-ence rest.
A sweet-er sound than thy blest name, O Sav-ior of man-kind.
To those who fall, how kind thou art! How good to those who seek!
The love of Je - sus, what it is None but his loved ones know.
Je - sus, be thou our glo - ry now, And through e-ter - ni - ty. A - men.

Jesus, the Very Thought of Thee
Second Tune

Latin: 12th century
Tr. Edward Caswall, 1814-1878, alt.

WINDSOR C.M.
Melody, Damon's "Psalmes," 1591

1 Je - sus, the ver - y thought of thee, With sweet-ness fills my breast;
2 No voice can sing, no heart can frame, Nor can the mem-ory find
3 O hope of ev - ery con - trite heart, O joy of all the meek,
4 But what to those who find? Ah, this Nor tongue nor pen can show;
5 Je sus, our on - ly joy be thou, As thou our prize wilt be;

CHARACTER AND GLORY

But sweet-er far thy face to see, And in thy pres-ence rest.
A sweet-er sound than thy blest name, O Sav-ior of man - kind.
To those who fall, how kind thou art! How good to those who seek!
The love of Je - sus, what it is None but his loved ones know.
Je - sus, be thou our glo - ry now, And through e-ter - ni - ty. A-men.

Fairest Lord Jesus 227

German: 17th century

SCHÖNSTER HERR JESU 5.6.8.5.5.8.
Silesian Melody

1 Fair - est Lord Je - sus, Rul - er of all na - ture,
2 Fair are the mead - ows, Fair - er still the wood - lands,
3 Fair is the sun - shine, Fair - er still the moon - light,

O thou of God and man the Son, Thee will I cher - ish,
Robed in the bloom - ing garb of spring: Je - sus is fair - er,
And all the twink - ling, star - ry host: Je - sus shines bright-er,

Thee will I hon - or, Thou, my soul's glo-ry, joy, and crown.
Je - sus is pur - er, Who makes the woe-ful heart to sing.
Je - sus shines pur - er, Than all the an-gels heaven can boast. A-men.

CHARACTER AND GLORY

228 Love Divine, All Loves Excelling

Charles Wesley, 1707-1788, alt.

BEECHER 8.7.8.7.D.
John Zundel, 1815-1882

1 Love di-vine, all loves ex-cel-ling, Joy of heaven, to earth come down,
2 Breathe, O breathe thy lov-ing Spir-it In-to ev-ery trou-bled breast;
3 Come, al-might-y to de-liv-er, Let us all thy life re-ceive;
4 Fin-ish, then, thy new cre-a-tion; Pure and spot-less let us be;

Fix in us thy hum-ble dwell-ing, All thy faith-ful mer-cies crown;
Let us all in thee in-her-it, Let us find thy prom-ised rest;
Sud-den-ly re-turn, and nev-er, Nev-er-more thy tem-ples leave.
Let us see thy great sal-va-tion Per-fect-ly re-stored in thee;

Je-sus, thou art all com-pas-sion, Pure, un-bound-ed love thou art;
Take a-way the love of sin-ning; Al-pha and O-me-ga be;
Thee we would be al-ways bless-ing, Serve thee as thy hosts a-bove,
Changed from glo-ry in-to glo-ry, Till in heaven we take our place,

Vis-it us with thy sal-va-tion, En-ter ev-ery trem-bling heart.
End of faith, as its be-gin-ning, Set our hearts at lib-er-ty.
Pray, and praise thee with-out ceas-ing, Glo-ry in thy per-fect love.
Till we cast our crowns be-fore thee, Lost in won-der, love, and praise. A-men.

CHARACTER AND GLORY

Alternative tune, HYFRYDOL, No. 13

Join All the Glorious Names

Isaac Watts, 1674-1748

CROFT'S 136th 6.6.6.6.8.8.
William Croft, 1678-1727

1 Join all the glo-rious names Of wis-dom, love, and power,
2 Great Proph-et of my God, My tongue would bless thy name;
3 Be thou my coun-sel-lor, My pat-tern and my guide;

That ev-er mor-tals knew, That an-gels ev-er bore;
By thee the joy-ful news Of our sal-va-tion came:
And through this des-ert land Still keep me near thy side;

All are too mean to speak his worth, Too mean to set my Sav-ior forth.
The joy-ful news of sins for-given, Of hell sub-dued and peace with heaven.
O let my feet ne'er run a-stray, Nor rove, nor seek the crook-ed way. A-men.

4 My dear almighty Lord,
My Conqueror and my King,
Thy scepter and thy sword,
Thy reigning grace I sing.
Thine is the power; behold I sit
In willing bonds before thy feet.

Alternative tune, DARWALL'S 148th, *No. 204*

CHARACTER AND GLORY

230 Immortal Love, Forever Full

John Greenleaf Whittier, 1807-1892

SERENITY C.M.
Arr. from William V. Wallace, 1814-1865

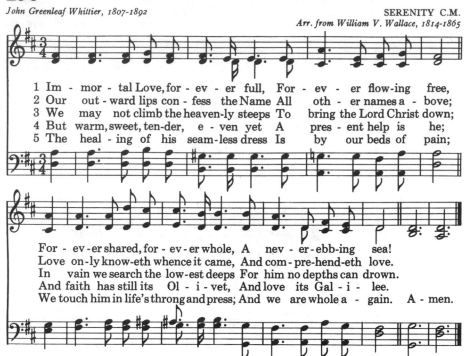

1 Im - mor - tal Love, for - ev - er full, For - ev - er flow-ing free,
2 Our out - ward lips con - fess the Name All oth - er names a - bove;
3 We may not climb the heaven-ly steeps To bring the Lord Christ down;
4 But warm, sweet, ten-der, e - ven yet A pres - ent help is he;
5 The heal - ing of his seam-less dress Is by our beds of pain;

For - ev-er shared, for - ev - er whole, A nev - er-ebb-ing sea!
Love on-ly know-eth whence it came, And com - pre-hend-eth love.
In vain we search the low-est deeps For him no depths can drown.
And faith has still its Ol - i - vet, And love its Gal - i - lee.
We touch him in life's throng and press; And we are whole a - gain. A - men.

6 Through him the first fond prayers are said
Our lips of childhood frame;
The last low whispers of our dead
Are burdened with his name.

CHARACTER AND GLORY

Alternative tune, BEATITUDO, *No. 350*

231 Come, Holy Ghost, Our Souls Inspire

Latin: 9th century
Tr. John Cosin, 1594-1672

DAS WALT' GOTT VATER L.M.
Melody by Daniel Vetter, ?-c.1730

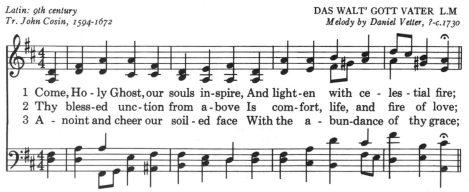

1 Come, Ho - ly Ghost, our souls in-spire, And light-en with ce - les - tial fire;
2 Thy bless-ed unc-tion from a-bove Is com-fort, life, and fire of love;
3 A - noint and cheer our soil - ed face With the a - bun-dance of thy grace;

THE HOLY SPIRIT

Thou the a-noint-ing Spir-it art, Who dost thy seven-fold gifts im-part.
En - a - ble with per-pet-ual light The dull-ness of our blind-ed sight.
Keep far our foes, give peace at home; Where thou art guide no ill can come. A-men.

Spirit of God, Descend Upon My Heart 232

Attr. to George Croly, 1780-1860

MORECAMBE 10.10.10.10.
Frederick C. Atkinson, 1841-1897

1 Spir - it of God, de-scend up - on my heart; Wean it from earth, through
2 I ask no dream, no proph-et ec - sta - sies, No sud-den rend - ing
3 Hast thou not bid us love thee, God and King? All, all thine own: soul,
4 Teach me to feel that thou art al - ways nigh; Teach me the strug - gles
5 Teach me to love thee as thine an - gels love, One ho - ly pas - sion

all its puls - es move; Stoop to my weak-ness, might-y as thou art,
of the veil of clay, No an - gel vis - it - ant, no o-pening skies,
heart, and strength, and mind; I see thy cross—there teach my heart to cling;
of the soul to bear: To check the ris - ing doubt, the reb - el sigh;
fill - ing all my frame; The bap-tism of the heaven-de-scend-ed Dove.

And make me love thee as I ought to love.
But take the dim - ness of my soul a - way.
O let me seek thee, and O let me find!
Teach me the pa - tience of un - an - swered prayer.
My heart an al - tar, and thy love the flame. A - men.

THE HOLY SPIRIT

233

Breathe on Me, Breath of God
First Tune

Edwin Hatch, 1835-1889, alt.

POTSDAM S.M.
"Church Psalter and Hymn Book," 1854

1 Breathe on me, Breath of God, Fill me with life a - new,
2 Breathe on me, Breath of God, Un - til my heart is pure,
3 Breathe on me, Breath of God, Till I am whol - ly thine,
4 Breathe on me, Breath of God, So shall I nev - er die,

That I may love what thou dost love, And do what thou wouldst do.
Un - til with thee I will one will To do and to en - dure.
Un - til this earth-ly part of me Glows with thy fire di - vine.
But live with thee the per-fect life Of thine e - ter - ni - ty. A-men.

234

Breathe on Me, Breath of God
Second Tune

Edwin Hatch, 1835-1889, alt.

TRENTHAM S.M.
Robert Jackson, 1840-1914

1 Breathe on me, Breath of God, Fill me with life a - new,
2 Breathe on me, Breath of God, Un - til my heart is pure,
3 Breathe on me, Breath of God, Till I am whol - ly thine,
4 Breathe on me, Breath of God, So shall I nev - er die,

That I may love what thou dost love, And do what thou wouldst do.
Un - til with thee I will one will To do and to en - dure.
Un - til this earth-ly part of me Glows with thy fire di - vine.
But live with thee the per-fect life Of thine e - ter - ni - ty. A-men.

THE HOLY SPIRIT

Come, Holy Spirit, God and Lord! 235

Martin Luther, 1483-1546
Tr. Catherine Winkworth, 1827-1878, alt.

DAS NEUGEBORNE KINDELEIN L.M.
Melody by Melchior Vulpius, c.1560-1616
Harm. by J. S. Bach, 1685-1750

1 Come, Ho - ly Spir - it, God and Lord!
2 Lord, by the bright - ness of thy light,
3 Thou strong De - fense, thou ho - ly Light,
4 That we may love not doc - trines strange,

Be all thy gra - ces now out - poured
Thou in the faith dost men u - nite
Teach us to know our God a - right,
Nor e'er to oth - er teach - ers range,

On the be - liev - er's mind and soul,
Of ev - ery land and ev - ery tongue;
And call him Fa - ther from the heart.
But Je - sus for our Mas - ter own,

To strength-en, save, and make us whole.
This to thy praise, O Lord, be sung.
The Word of life and truth im - part,
And put our trust in him a - lone. A - men.

Alternative tune, DAS WALT' GOTT VATER, *No. 231*

THE HOLY SPIRIT

236 Life of Ages, Richly Poured

Samuel Johnson, 1822-1882

BUCKLAND 7.7.7.7.
Leighton G. Hayne, 1836-1883

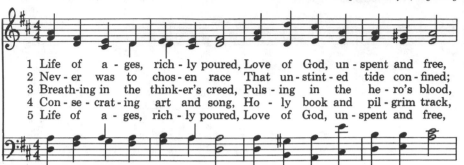

1 Life of a - ges, rich - ly poured, Love of God, un - spent and free,
2 Nev - er was to chos - en race That un - stint - ed tide con - fined;
3 Breath-ing in the think-er's creed, Puls - ing in the he - ro's blood,
4 Con - se - crat - ing art and song, Ho - ly book and pil - grim track,
5 Life of a - ges, rich - ly poured, Love of God, un - spent and free,

Flow-ing in the proph-et's word, And the peo-ple's lib - er - ty!
Thine is ev - ery time and place, Foun-tain sweet of heart and mind,
Nerv-ing sim-plest thought and deed, Freshen-ing time with truth and good,
Hurl-ing floods of ty-rant wrong From the sa - cred lim - its back.
Flow still in the proph-et's word, And the peo-ple's lib - er - ty! A - men.

Alternative tune, VIENNA, *No. 243*

237 Send Down Thy Truth, O God

Edward R. Sill, 1841-1887

ST. MICHAEL S.M.
Adapted from "Genevan Psalter," 1551

1 Send down thy truth, O God, Too long the shad - ows frown!
2 Send down thy Spir - it free Till wil - der - ness and town
3 Send down thy love, thy life, Our less - er lives to crown,
4 Send down thy peace, O Lord, Earth's bit - ter voic - es drown

THE HOLY SPIRIT

Too long the dark-ened way we've trod: Thy truth, O Lord, send down!
One tem-ple for thy wor-ship be: Thy Spir-it, O send down!
And cleanse them of their hate and strife: Thy liv-ing love send down!
In one deep o-cean of ac-cord: Thy peace, O God, send down! A-men.

Come, Gracious Spirit, Heavenly Dove 238

Simon Browne, 1680-1732, alt.

MENDON L.M.
German Melody
Arr. by Samuel Dyer, 1785-1835

1 Come, gra-cious Spir-it, heaven-ly Dove, With light and com-fort
2 The light of truth to us dis-play And make us know and
3 Lead us to Christ, the liv-ing Way, Nor let us from his
4 Lead us to heaven, that we may share Ful-ness of joy for

from a-bove; Be thou our guard-ian, thou our guide,
choose thy way; Plant ho-ly fear in ev-ery heart,
pre-cepts stray; Lead us to ho-li-ness, the road
ev-er there; Lead us to God, our fi-nal rest,

O'er ev-ery thought and step pre-side.
That we from thee may ne'er de-part.
That we must take to dwell with God.
To be with him for ev-er blest. A-men.

A higher setting may be found at No. 477

THE HOLY SPIRIT

239 Come Down, O Love Divine

Bianco da Siena, c. 1367
Tr. Richard F. Littledale, 1833-1890

DOWN AMPNEY 6.6.11.D.
R. Vaughan Williams, 1872-1958

1 Come down, O Love di - vine, Seek thou this soul of
2 O let it free - ly burn, Till earth - ly pas - sions
3 And so the yearn - ing strong With which the soul will

mine, And vis - it it with thine own ar - dor glow - ing;
turn To dust and ash - es in its heat con - sum - ing;
long, Shall far out - pass the power of hu - man tell - ing;

O Com - fort - er, draw near, With - in my heart ap - pear,
And let thy glo - rious light Shine ev - er on my sight,
For none can guess its grace, Till he be - come the place

And kin - dle it, thy ho - ly flame be - stow - ing.
And clothe me round, the while my path il - lum - ing.
Where - in the Ho - ly Spir - it makes his dwell - ing. A - men.

THE HOLY SPIRIT

Come, Holy Spirit, Heavenly Dove 240

Isaac Watts, 1674-1748

ST. AGNES C.M.
John B. Dykes, 1823-1876

1 Come, Ho-ly Spir-it, heaven-ly Dove, With all thy quick-ening powers;
2 In vain we tune our for-mal songs, In vain we strive to rise;
3 Come, Ho-ly Spir-it, heaven-ly Dove, With all thy quick-ening powers;

Kin-dle a flame of sa-cred love In these cold hearts of ours.
Ho-san-nas lan-guish on our tongues, And our de-vo-tion dies.
Come, shed a-broad a Sav-ior's love, And that shall kin-dle ours. A-men.

Spirit Divine, Attend Our Prayers 241

Andrew Reed, 1787-1862

NUN DANKET ALL' C.M.
Melody by Johann Crüger, 1598-1662

1 Spir-it di-vine, at-tend our prayers And make this house thy home;
2 Come as the fire, and purge our hearts Like sac-ri-fi-cial flame;
3 Come as the dove, and spread thy wings, The wings of peace-ful love,
4 Spir-it di-vine, at-tend our prayers And make this world thy home;

De-scend with all thy gra-cious powers, O come, great Spir-it, come!
Let our whole soul an offer-ing be To our Re-deem-er's name.
And let thy Church on earth be-come Blest as the Church a-bove.
De-scend with all thy gra-cious powers, O come, great Spir-it, come! A-men.

Another setting may be found at No. 256

THE HOLY SPIRIT

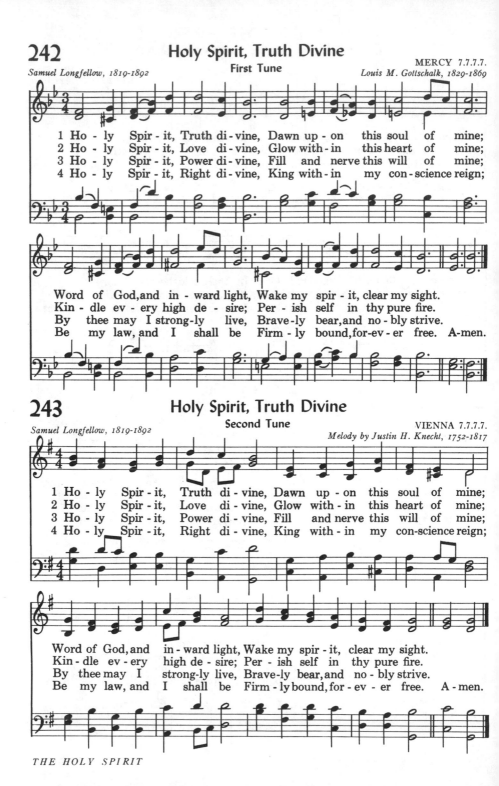

242

Holy Spirit, Truth Divine
First Tune

Samuel Longfellow, 1819-1892

MERCY 7.7.7.7.
Louis M. Gottschalk, 1829-1869

1 Ho-ly Spir-it, Truth di-vine, Dawn up-on this soul of mine;
2 Ho-ly Spir-it, Love di-vine, Glow with-in this heart of mine;
3 Ho-ly Spir-it, Power di-vine, Fill and nerve this will of mine;
4 Ho-ly Spir-it, Right di-vine, King with-in my con-science reign;

Word of God, and in-ward light, Wake my spir-it, clear my sight.
Kin-dle ev-ery high de-sire; Per-ish self in thy pure fire.
By thee may I strong-ly live, Brave-ly bear, and no-bly strive.
Be my law, and I shall be Firm-ly bound, for-ev-er free. A-men.

243

Holy Spirit, Truth Divine
Second Tune

Samuel Longfellow, 1819-1892

VIENNA 7.7.7.7.
Melody by Justin H. Knecht, 1752-1817

1 Ho-ly Spir-it, Truth di-vine, Dawn up-on this soul of mine;
2 Ho-ly Spir-it, Love di-vine, Glow with-in this heart of mine;
3 Ho-ly Spir-it, Power di-vine, Fill and nerve this will of mine;
4 Ho-ly Spir-it, Right di-vine, King with-in my con-science reign;

Word of God, and in-ward light, Wake my spir-it, clear my sight.
Kin-dle ev-ery high de-sire; Per-ish self in thy pure fire.
By thee may I strong-ly live, Brave-ly bear, and no-bly strive.
Be my law, and I shall be Firm-ly bound, for-ev-er free. A-men.

THE HOLY SPIRIT

O Holy Spirit, Enter In

244

Michael Schirmer, 1606-1673
Tr. Catherine Winkworth, 1827-1878

WIE SCHÖN LEUCHTET 8.8.7.8.8.7.8.4.4.8.
Melody by Philipp Nicolai, 1556-1608

1 O Ho - ly Spir-it, en - ter in, A-mong these hearts thy work be - gin,
2 O might-y Rock, O Source of life, Let thy dear word 'mid doubt and strife

Thy tem-ple deign to make us; Sun of the soul, thou Light di - vine
Be so with-in us burn-ing That we be faith-ful un - to death,

A - round and in us bright-ly shine, To strength and glad-ness wake us.
In thy pure love and ho - ly faith, From thee true wis-dom learn - ing!

Where thou shin - est life from heav - en There is giv - en;
Lord, thy gra - ces on us show - er; By thy pow - er

We be - fore thee For that pre-cious gift im - plore thee.
Christ con - fess - ing, Let us win his grace and bless - ing. A-men.

THE HOLY SPIRIT

Gracious Spirit, Dwell With Me

Thomas T. Lynch, 1818-1871

REDHEAD NO. 76 7.7.7.7.7.7.
Richard Redhead, 1820-1901

1 Gra - cious Spir - it, dwell with me, I my - self would
2 Truth - ful Spir - it, dwell with me, I my - self would
3 Might - y Spir - it, dwell with me, I my - self would
4 Ho - ly Spir - it, dwell with me, I my - self would

gra - cious be; And with words that help and heal
truth - ful be; And with wis - dom kind and clear
might - y be; Might - y so as to pre - vail
ho - ly be; Sep - a - rate from sin, I would

Would thy life in mine re - veal, And with ac - tions
Let thy life in mine ap - pear, And with ac - tions
Where un - aid - ed man must fail; Ev - er by a
Choose and cher - ish all things good, And what - ev - er

bold and meek Would for Christ my Sav - ior speak.
broth - er - ly Speak my Lord's sin - cer - i - ty.
might - y hope, Press - ing on and bear - ing up.
I can be Give to him who gave me thee! A - men.

THE HOLY SPIRIT

Alternative tune, RATISBON, *No. 43*

Come, Thou Almighty King

246

Anonymous, c. 1757

ITALIAN HYMN 6.6.4.6.6.6.4.
Felice de Giardini, 1716-1796

1 Come, thou al - might - y King, Help us thy
2 Come, thou in - car - nate Word, Gird on thy
3 Come, ho - ly Com - fort - er, Thy sa - cred
4 To the great One in Three E - ter - nal

name to sing; Help us to praise: Fa - ther, all
might - y sword; Our prayer at - tend: Come, and thy
wit - ness bear In this glad hour! Thou who al -
prais - es be Hence ev - er - more! His sov - ereign

glo - ri - ous, O'er all vic - to - ri - ous, Come, and reign
peo - ple bless, And give thy word suc - cess; Spir - it of
might - y art, Now rule in ev - ery heart, And ne'er from
maj - es - ty May we in glo - ry see, And to e -

o - ver us, An - cient of Days.
ho - li - ness, On us de - scend.
us de - part, Spir - it of power.
ter - ni - ty Love and a - dore. A - men.

Another setting may be found at No. 295

THE TRINITY

247 Holy God, We Praise Thy Name

Attr. to Ignaz Franz, 1719-1790
Tr. Clarence Walworth, 1820-1900, alt.

GROSSER GOTT, WIR LOBEN DICH 7.8.7.8.7.7.
"Katholisches Gesangbuch," Vienna, c. 1774

1 Ho - ly God, we praise thy name; Lord of all, we
2 Hark, the glad ce - les - tial hymn, An - gel choirs a -
3 Lo! the ap - os - tol - ic train Joins thy sa - cred
4 Ho - ly Fa - ther, ho - ly Son, Ho - ly Spir - it:

bow be - fore thee; All on earth thy scep - ter claim,
bove are rais - ing; Cher - u - bim and ser - a - phim,
name to hal - low; Proph-ets swell the glad re - frain,
Three we name thee, While in es - sence on - ly One;

All in heaven a - bove a - dore thee. In - fi - nite thy
In un - ceas - ing cho - rus prais-ing, Fill the heavens with
And the bless - ed mar - tyrs fol - low, And from morn to
Un - di - vid - ed God we claim thee, And a - dor - ing

vast do - main, Ev - er - last - ing is thy reign.
sweet ac - cord: Ho - ly, ho - ly, ho - ly Lord.
set of sun, Through the Church the song goes on.
bend the knee While we sing our praise to thee. A - men.

THE TRINITY

O God, Thou Art the Father

248

St. Columba, c. 521-597
Tr. Duncan Macgregor, 1854-1923

DURROW 7.6.7.6.D.
Traditional Irish Melody
Harm. by David Evans, 1874-1948

1 O God, thou art the Father Of all that have be-lieved,
2 High in the heaven-ly Zi - on Thou reign-est God a-dored,
3 Thou to the meek and low - ly Thy se-crets dost un - fold;

From whom all hosts of an - gels Have life and power re-ceived.
And in the com-ing glo - ry Thou shalt be Sov-ereign Lord.
O God, thou do-est all things, All things both new and old.

O God, thou art the Mak - er Of all cre - a - ted things,
Be-yond our ken thou shin - est, The ev - er-last-ing Light:
I walk se - cure and bless - ed In ev-ery clime or coast,

The right-eous Judge of jud - ges, The al-might-y King of kings.
In - ef - fa - ble in lov - ing, Un - think - a - ble in might.
In name of God the Fa - ther, And Son, and Ho - ly Ghost. A-men.

THE TRINITY

249 Ancient of Days, Who Sittest Throned in Glory

William C. Doane, 1832-1913

ANCIENT OF DAYS 11.10.11.10.
J. Albert Jeffery, 1855-1929

In unison

1 An - cient of Days, who sit - test throned in glo - ry,
2 O ho - ly Fa - ther, who hast led thy chil - dren
3 O ho - ly Je - sus, Prince of peace and Sav - ior,
4 O Ho - ly Ghost, the Lord and the Life - giv - er,
5 O Tri - une God, with heart and voice a - dor - ing

To thee all knees are bent, all voic - es pray;
In all the a - ges with the fire and cloud,
To thee we owe the peace that still pre - vails,
Thine is the quick - ening power that gives in - crease;
Praise we the good - ness that doth crown our days;

Thy love has blessed the wide world's won - drous sto - ry
Through seas dry - shod, through wea - ry wastes be - wil - dering;
Still - ing the rude wills of men's wild be - hav - ior,
From thee have flowed, as from a pleas - ant riv - er,
Pray we that thou wilt hear us, still im - plor - ing

THE TRINITY

With light and life since Eden's dawning day.
To thee in reverent love, our hearts are bowed.
And calming passion's fierce and stormy gales.
Our plenty, wealth, prosperity, and peace.
Thy love and favor, kept to us always. A-men.

We All Believe in One True God 250

Tobias Clausnitzer, c.1619-1684
Tr. Catherine Winkworth, 1827-1878, alt.

WIR GLAUBEN ALL' AN EINEN GOTT 8.7.7.7.7.7.
"Kirchengesangbuch," Darmstadt, 1699

1 We all believe in one true God, Father, Son, and Holy Ghost,
2 We all believe in Jesus Christ, Son of God and Mary's son,
3 We all confess the Holy Ghost, Who from both for-e'er pro-ceeds,

Ev-er-pres-ent help in need, Praised by all the heaven-ly host,
Who de-scend-ed from his throne And for us sal-va-tion won,
Who up-holds and com-forts us In all tri-als, fears, and needs.

By whose might-y power a-lone All is made and wrought and done.
By whose cross and death are we Res-cued from all mis-er-y.
Blest and Ho-ly Trin-i-ty, Praise for-ev-er be to thee! A-men.

THE TRINITY

251 Holy, Holy, Holy! Lord God Almighty

Reginald Heber, 1783-1826

NICAEA 11.12.12.10.
John B. Dykes, 1823-1876

1 Ho - ly, ho - ly, ho - ly! Lord God Al - might - y!
2 Ho - ly, ho - ly, ho - ly! all the saints a - dore thee,
3 Ho - ly, ho - ly, ho - ly! though the dark - ness hide thee,
4 Ho - ly, ho - ly, ho - ly! Lord God Al - might - y!

Ear - ly in the morn - ing our song shall rise to thee;
Cast - ing down their gold - en crowns a - round the glass - y sea;
Though the eye of sin - ful man thy glo - ry may not see;
All thy works shall praise thy name in earth and sky and sea;

Ho - ly, ho - ly, ho - ly! mer - ci - ful and might - y;
Cher - u - bim and ser - a - phim fall - ing down be - fore thee,
On - ly thou art ho - ly; there is none be - side thee,
Ho - ly, ho - ly, ho - ly! mer - ci - ful and might - y;

God in three per - sons, bless - ed Trin - i - ty!
Which wert, and art, and ev - er - more shalt be.
Per - fect in power, in love, and pur - i - ty.
God in three per - sons, bless - ed Trin - i - ty! A - men.

THE TRINITY

O Word of God Incarnate

252

William W. How, 1823-1897

MUNICH 7.6.7.6.D.
"Neu-vermehrtes Gesangbuch," Meiningen, 1693
Harm. by Felix Mendelssohn, 1809-1847

1. O Word of God in-car-nate, O Wis-dom from on high,
2. The Church from her dear Mas-ter Re-ceived the gift di-vine,
3. It float-eth like a ban-ner Be-fore God's host un-furled;
4. O make thy Church, dear Sav-ior, A lamp of bur-nished gold,

O Truth un-changed, un-chang-ing, O Light of our dark sky,
And still that light she lift-eth O'er all the earth to shine.
It shin-eth like a bea-con A-bove the dark-ling world;
To bear a-mong the na-tions Thy true light as of old!

We praise thee for the ra-diance That from the hal-lowed page,
It is the gold-en cas-ket Where gems of truth are stored;
It is the chart and com-pass That o'er life's surg-ing sea,
O teach thy wan-dering pil-grims By this their path to trace,

A lan-tern to our foot-steps, Shines on from age to age.
It is the heaven-drawn pic-ture Of Christ, the liv-ing Word.
'Mid mists, and rocks, and quick-sands Still guides, O Christ, to thee.
Till, clouds and dark-ness end-ed, They see thee face to face! A-men.

THE BIBLE

Book of Books, Our People's Strength

Percy Dearmer, 1867-1936

LIEBSTER JESU 7.8.7.8.8.8.
Melody by Johann R. Ahle, 1625-1673

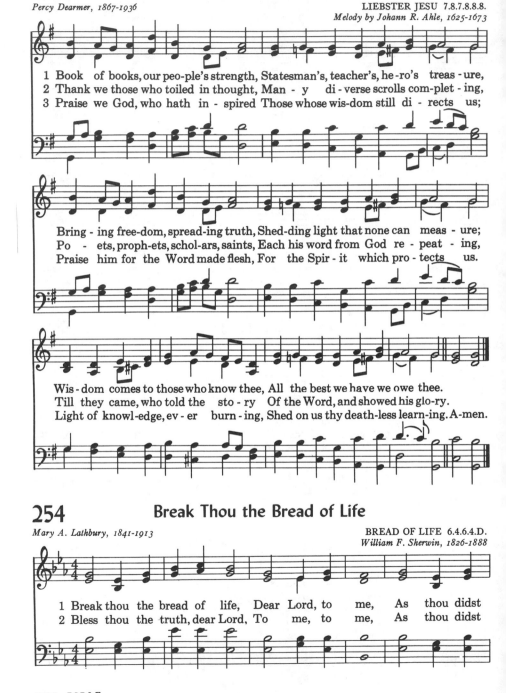

1 Book of books, our peo-ple's strength, Statesman's, teacher's, he-ro's treas-ure,
2 Thank we those who toiled in thought, Man - y di - verse scrolls com-plet - ing,
3 Praise we God, who hath in - spired Those whose wis-dom still di - rects us;

Bring - ing free-dom, spread-ing truth, Shed-ding light that none can meas - ure;
Po - ets, proph-ets, schol-ars, saints, Each his word from God re - peat - ing,
Praise him for the Word made flesh, For the Spir - it which pro - tects us.

Wis - dom comes to those who know thee, All the best we have we owe thee.
Till they came, who told the sto - ry Of the Word, and showed his glo-ry.
Light of knowl-edge, ev - er burn - ing, Shed on us thy death-less learn-ing. A-men.

254

Break Thou the Bread of Life

Mary A. Lathbury, 1841-1913

BREAD OF LIFE 6.4.6.4.D.
William F. Sherwin, 1826-1888

1 Break thou the bread of life, Dear Lord, to me, As thou didst
2 Bless thou the truth, dear Lord, To me, to me, As thou didst

THE BIBLE

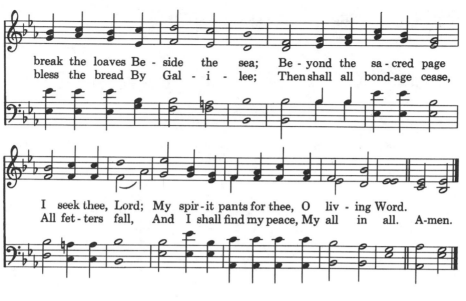

break the loaves Be - side the sea; Be - yond the sa - cred page
bless the bread By Gal - i - lee; Then shall all bond-age cease,

I seek thee, Lord; My spir-it pants for thee, O liv - ing Word.
All fet - ters fall, And I shall find my peace, My all in all. A-men.

Most Perfect Is the Law of God 255

Based on Psalm 19
"The Psalter," 1912

STRACATHRO C.M.
Melody by Charles Hutcheson, 1792-1860
Harm. by Geoffrey Shaw, 1879-1943

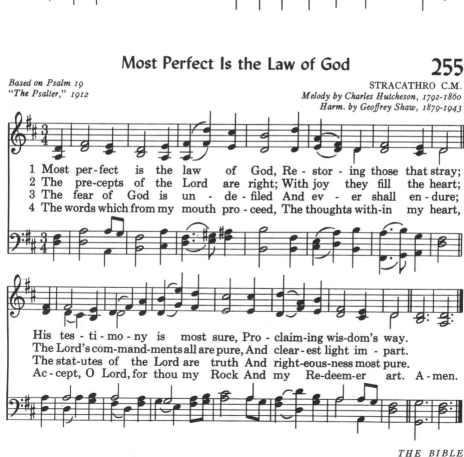

1 Most per-fect is the law of God, Re - stor-ing those that stray;
2 The pre-cepts of the Lord are right; With joy they fill the heart;
3 The fear of God is un - de-filed And ev - er shall en-dure;
4 The words which from my mouth pro - ceed, The thoughts with-in my heart,

His tes - ti - mo - ny is most sure, Pro - claim-ing wis-dom's way.
The Lord's com-mand-ments all are pure, And clear-est light im - part.
The stat-utes of the Lord are truth And right-eous-ness most pure.
Ac - cept, O Lord, for thou my Rock And my Re - deem-er art. A - men.

THE BIBLE

Lamp of Our Feet, Whereby We Trace

Bernard Barton, 1784-1849, alt.

NUN DANKET ALL' C.M.
Melody by Johann Crüger, 1598-1662

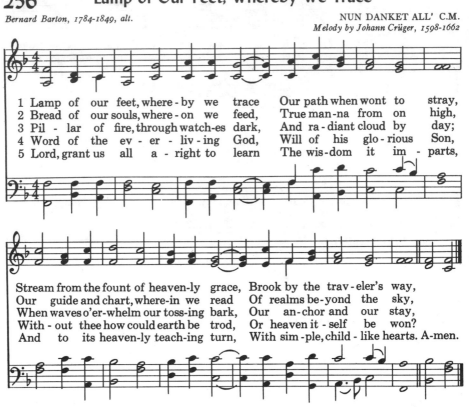

1 Lamp of our feet, where-by we trace Our path when wont to stray,
2 Bread of our souls, where-on we feed, True man-na from on high,
3 Pil - lar of fire, through watch-es dark, And ra-diant cloud by day;
4 Word of the ev - er - liv-ing God, Will of his glo-rious Son,
5 Lord, grant us all a - right to learn The wis-dom it im - parts,

Stream from the fount of heaven-ly grace, Brook by the trav-eler's way,
Our guide and chart, where-in we read Of realms be-yond the sky,
When waves o'er-whelm our toss-ing bark, Our an-chor and our stay,
With - out thee how could earth be trod, Or heaven it - self be won?
And to its heaven-ly teach-ing turn, With sim-ple, child - like hearts. A-men.

Another harmonization may be found at No. 241

The Heavens Declare Thy Glory, Lord

Based on Psalm 19
Isaac Watts, 1674-1748

UXBRIDGE L.M.
Lowell Mason, 1792-1872

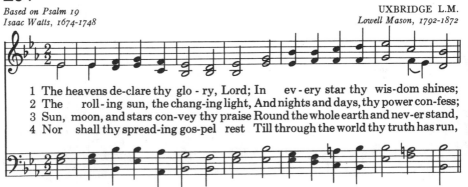

1 The heavens de-clare thy glo - ry, Lord; In ev - ery star thy wis-dom shines;
2 The roll-ing sun, the chang-ing light, And nights and days, thy power con-fess;
3 Sun, moon, and stars con-vey thy praise Round the whole earth and nev-er stand,
4 Nor shall thy spread-ing gos-pel rest Till through the world thy truth has run,

THE BIBLE

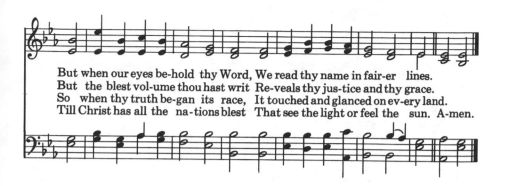

But when our eyes be-hold thy Word, We read thy name in fair-er lines.
But the blest vol-ume thou hast writ Re-veals thy jus-tice and thy grace.
So when thy truth be-gan its race, It touched and glanced on ev-ery land.
Till Christ has all the na-tions blest That see the light or feel the sun. A-men.

Lord, Thy Word Abideth 258

Henry W. Baker, 1821-1877

RAVENSHAW 6.6.6.6.
"Ave Hierarchia," 1531
Arr. by William H. Monk, 1823-1889

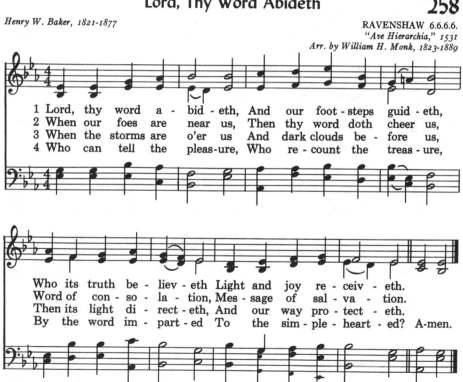

1 Lord, thy word a - bid - eth, And our foot-steps guid - eth,
2 When our foes are near us, Then thy word doth cheer us,
3 When the storms are o'er us And dark clouds be - fore us,
4 Who can tell the pleas-ure, Who re - count the treas - ure,

Who its truth be - liev - eth Light and joy re - ceiv - eth.
Word of con - so - la - tion, Mes - sage of sal - va - tion.
Then its light di - rect - eth, And our way pro - tect - eth.
By the word im - part - ed To the sim - ple - heart - ed? A-men.

5 Word of mercy, giving
Succor to the living;
Word of life, supplying
Comfort to the dying!

6 O, that we discerning
Its most holy learning,
Lord, may love and fear thee,
Evermore be near thee!

THE BIBLE

259   We Limit Not the Truth of God

George Rawson, 1807–1889

OLD 22nd C.M.D.
"Anglo-Genevan Psalter," 1556

1 We lim-it not the truth of God To our poor reach of mind,
2 Dark-ling our great fore-fa-thers went The first steps of the way;
3 The val-leys passed, as-cend-ing still, Our souls would high-er climb,
4 O Fa-ther, Son, and Spir-it, send Us in-crease from a-bove;

By no-tions of our day and sect, Crude, par-tial, and con-fined.
'Twas but the dawn-ing yet to grow In-to the per-fect day.
And look down from su-per-nal heights On all the by-gone time.
En-large, ex-pand all Chris-tian souls To com-pre-hend thy love,

No, let a new and bet-ter hope With-in our hearts be stirred:
And grow it shall, our glo-rious sun More fer-vid rays af-ford:
Up-ward we press, the air is clear, And the sphere-mu-sic heard:
And make us to go on, to know With no-bler powers con-ferred:

The Lord hath yet more light and truth To break forth from his Word. A-men.

Based on parting words of Pastor John Robinson to the Pilgrim Fathers, 1620.

THE BIBLE   *Alternative tune*, ELLACOMBE, *No. 459*

The Church's One Foundation

Samuel J. Stone, 1839-1900

AURELIA 7.6.7.6.D.
Samuel S. Wesley, 1810-1876

1 The Church's one foun-da-tion Is Je-sus Christ her Lord;
2 E-lect from ev-ery na-tion, Yet one o'er all the earth,
3 'Mid toil and trib-u-la-tion, And tu-mult of her war,
4 Yet she on earth hath un-ion With God, the Three in One,

She is his new cre-a-tion By wa-ter and the word;
Her char-ter of sal-va-tion, One Lord, one faith, one birth,
She waits the con-sum-ma-tion Of peace for ev-er-more;
And mys-tic sweet com-mun-ion With those whose rest is won.

From heaven he came and sought her To be his ho-ly bride;
One ho-ly name she bless-es, Par-takes one ho-ly food,
Till with the vi-sion glo-rious, Her long-ing eyes are blest,
O hap-py ones and ho-ly! Lord, give us grace that we

With his own blood he bought her, And for her life he died.
And to one hope she press-es, With ev-ery grace en-dued.
And the great Church vic-to-rious Shall be the Church at rest.
Like them, the meek and low-ly, On high may dwell with thee. A-men.

NATURE AND UNITY

261   City of God, How Broad and Far

Samuel Johnson, 1822-1882

RICHMOND C.M.
Thomas Haweis, 1734-1820

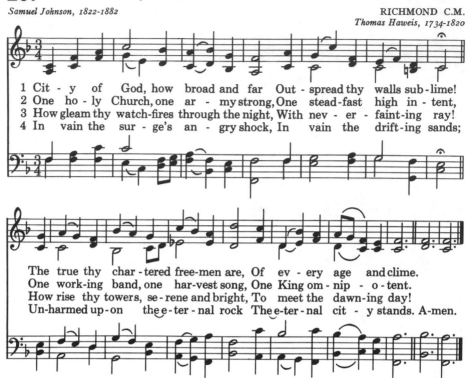

1 Cit-y of God, how broad and far Out-spread thy walls sub-lime!
2 One ho-ly Church, one ar-my strong, One stead-fast high in-tent,
3 How gleam thy watch-fires through the night, With nev-er-faint-ing ray!
4 In vain the sur-ge's an-gry shock, In vain the drift-ing sands;

The true thy char-tered free-men are, Of ev-ery age and clime.
One work-ing band, one har-vest song, One King om-nip-o-tent.
How rise thy towers, se-rene and bright, To meet the dawn-ing day!
Un-harmed up-on the e-ter-nal rock The e-ter-nal cit-y stands. A-men.

Alternative tune, NUN DANKET ALL', *No. 241*

262   Forgive, O Lord, Our Severing Ways

John Greenleaf Whittier, 1807-1892, and others

O MENSCH SIEH 8.8.8.
Bohemian Brethren's "Kirchengesänge," 1566

1 For-give, O Lord, our sev-ering ways, The ri-val
2 Thy grace im-part; in time to be Shall one great
3 A sweet-er song shall then be heard, Con-fess-ing,
4 That song shall swell from shore to shore, One hope, one

al - tars that we raise, The wran-gling tongues that mar thy praise.
tem - ple rise to thee—One Church for all hu-man-i - ty.
in a world's ac - cord, The in - ward Christ, the liv-ing Word.
faith, one love re - store The seam-less robe that Je - sus wore. A-men.

Christ Is Made the Sure Foundation 263

Latin: 7th century
Tr. John M. Neale, 1818-1866, alt.

REGENT SQUARE 8.7.8.7.8.7.
Henry T. Smart, 1813-1879

1 Christ is made the sure foun-da - tion, Christ the head and cor - ner stone,
2 To this tem - ple, where we call thee, Come, O Lord of hosts, to - day!
3 Here vouch-safe to all thy serv-ants What they ask of thee to gain:
4 Laud and hon - or to the Fa - ther, Laud and hon - or to the Son,

Chos - en of the Lord and prec-ious, Bind-ing all the Church in one;
With thy wont-ed lov - ing-kind-ness Hear thy peo - ple as they pray;
What they gain from thee for - ev - er With the bless - ed to re - tain,
Laud and hon - or to the Spir - it, Ev - er Three and ev - er One;

Ho - ly Zi - on's help for - ev - er, And her con - fi - dence a - lone.
And thy full-est ben - e - dic - tion Shed with-in its walls al - way.
And here-af - ter in thy glo - ry Ev - er-more with thee to reign.
One in might, and One in glo - ry, While un-end - ing a - ges run. A-men.

NATURE AND UNITY

264 O Where Are Kings and Empires Now

Arthur C. Coxe, 1818-1896, alt.

ST. ANNE C.M.
Attr. to William Croft, 1678-1727

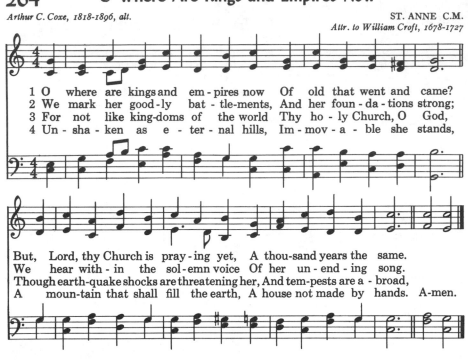

1 O where are kings and em-pires now Of old that went and came?
2 We mark her good-ly bat-tle-ments, And her foun-da-tions strong;
3 For not like king-doms of the world Thy ho-ly Church, O God,
4 Un-sha-ken as e-ter-nal hills, Im-mov-a-ble she stands,

But, Lord, thy Church is pray-ing yet, A thou-sand years the same.
We hear with-in the sol-emn voice Of her un-end-ing song.
Though earth-quake shocks are threatening her, And tem-pests are a-broad,
A moun-tain that shall fill the earth, A house not made by hands. A-men.

265 O God, Within Whose Sight

John Oxenham, 1852-1941

SERUG 6.6.4.6.6.6.4.
S. S. Wesley's "European Psalmist," 1872

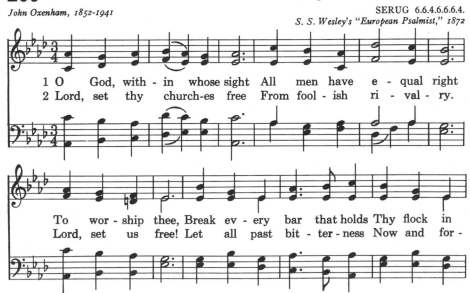

1 O God, with-in whose sight All men have e-qual right
2 Lord, set thy church-es free From fool-ish ri-val-ry.

To wor-ship thee, Break ev-ery bar that holds Thy flock in
Lord, set us free! Let all past bit-ter-ness Now and for-

NATURE AND UNITY

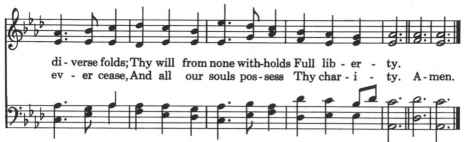

di - verse folds; Thy will from none with-holds Full lib - er - ty.
ev - er cease, And all our souls pos-sess Thy char - i - ty. A-men.

One Holy Church of God Appears 266

Samuel Longfellow, 1819-1892

ST. JAMES C.M.
Raphael Courteville, ?-c.1735

1 One ho - ly Church of God ap - pears Through
2 From old - est time, on far - thest shores, Be -
3 The truth is her pro - phet - ic gift, The
4 O liv - ing Church, thine er - rand speed, Ful -

ev - ery age and race, Un - wast - ed by the
neath the pine or palm, One un - seen Pres - ence
soul, her sa - cred page; And feet on mer - cy's
fill thy task sub - lime; With Bread of life earth's

lapse of years, Un - changed by chang - ing place.
she a - dores, With si - lence, or with psalm.
er - rands swift Do make her pil - grim - age.
hun - ger feed; Re - deem the e - vil time! A-men.

NATURE AND UNITY

267 Glorious Things of Thee Are Spoken

John Newton, 1725-1807

AUSTRIAN HYMN 8.7.8.7.D.
Franz J. Haydn, 1732-1809

1 Glo-rious things of thee are spo-ken, Zi - on, cit - y of our God;
2 See, the streams of liv-ing wa-ters, Springing from e - ter - nal love,
3 Round each hab-i-ta-tion hov-ering, See the cloud and fire ap-pear

He whose word can-not be bro-ken Formed thee for his own a - bode.
Well sup-ply thy sons and daughters, And all fear of want re - move.
For a glo-ry and a covering, Show - ing that the Lord is near!

On the Rock of A - ges founded, What can shake thy sure re-pose?
Who can faint, while such a riv - er Ev - er flows their thirst to as-suage?
Thus de - riv - ing from their ban-ner Light by night and shade by day,

With sal-va-tion's walls surrounded, Thou may'st smile at all thy foes.
Grace, which like the Lord, the Giver, Nev - er fails from age to age.
Safe they feed up - on the man-na Which he gives them when they pray. A-men.

NATURE AND UNITY

Lord, We Thank Thee for Our Brothers

268

Roger K. Powell, 1914-

AUSTRIAN HYMN 8.7.8.7.D.
Franz J. Haydn, 1732-1809

1 Lord, we thank thee for our brothers
  Keeping faith with us and thee,
Joining heart to heart with others,
  Making strong our company.
With the cross our only standard
  Let us sing with one great voice,
Glory, glory, thine the kingdom;
  Churches in thy Church rejoice.

2 God be praised for congregations
  Coming side by side to thee;
Many tongues of many nations
  Sing the greater unity.
Sweet the psalm and sweet the carol
  When our song is raised as one.
Glory, glory, thine the power,
  As in heaven thy will be done.

3 Hallowed be thy name forever!
  Heal our differences of old;
Bless thy Church's new endeavor;
  For thy kingdom make us bold.
One our Christ and one our gospel,
  Make us one we now implore.
Glory, glory, thine the glory
  Through the ages evermore.

I Love Thy Kingdom, Lord

269

Timothy Dwight, 1752-1817

ST. THOMAS S.M.
Williams' "New Universal Psalmodist," 1770

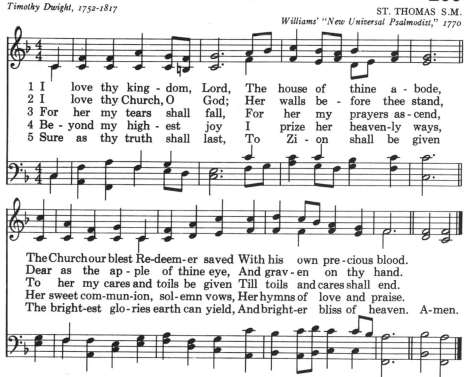

1 I love thy king-dom, Lord, The house of thine a-bode,
2 I love thy Church, O God; Her walls be-fore thee stand,
3 For her my tears shall fall, For her my prayers as-cend,
4 Be-yond my high-est joy I prize her heaven-ly ways,
5 Sure as thy truth shall last, To Zi-on shall be given

The Church our blest Re-deem-er saved With his own pre-cious blood.
Dear as the ap-ple of thine eye, And grav-en on thy hand.
To her my cares and toils be given Till toils and cares shall end.
Her sweet com-mun-ion, sol-emn vows, Her hymns of love and praise.
The bright-est glo-ries earth can yield, And bright-er bliss of heaven. A-men.

NATURE AND UNITY

270

Built on the Rock

Nicolai F. S. Grundtvig, 1783-1872
Tr. Carl Döving, 1867-1937, alt.

KIRKEN DEN ER ET 8.8.8.8.8.8.8.8.
Ludvig M. Lindeman, 1812-1887

1 Built on the Rock the Church doth stand, E - ven when stee-ples are
2 Sure - ly in tem - ples made with hands, God, the Most High, is not
3 Now we may gath - er with our King E'en in the low - li - est

fall - ing; Crum-bled have spires in ev - ery land, Bells still are
dwell - ing; High a - bove earth his tem - ple stands, All earth-ly
dwell - ing; Prais-es to him we there may bring, His won-drous

chim-ing and call - ing, Call-ing the young and old to rest, But a-bove
tem - ples ex - cell - ing. Yet he whom heavens can-not con-tain Chose to a-
mer - cy forth - tell - ing. Je - sus his grace to us ac-cords; Spir-it and

all the soul dis-tressed, Long-ing for rest ev - er - last - ing.
bide on earth with men, Built in our bod-ies his tem - ple.
life are all his words; His truth doth hal-low the tem - ple. A - men.

NATURE AND UNITY

We Come Unto Our Fathers' God

271

Thomas H. Gill, 1819-1906

NUN FREUT EUCH 8.7.8.7.8.8.7.
Klug's "Geistliche Lieder," Wittenberg, 1535

1 We come un-to our fa-thers' God; Their Rock is our sal-va-tion;
2 Their joy un-to their Lord we bring; Their song to us de-scend-eth;
3 Ye saints to come, take up the strain, The same sweet theme en-deav-or;

The e-ter-nal arms, their dear a-bode, We make our hab-i-ta-tion.
The Spir-it who in them did sing To us his mu-sic lend-eth:
Un-bro-ken be the gold-en chain! Keep on the song for-ev-er!

We bring thee, Lord, the praise they brought, We seek thee as thy
His song in them, in us, is one; We raise it high, we
Safe in the same dear dwell-ing place, Rich with the same e-

saints have sought In ev-ery gen-er-a-tion.
send it on, The song that nev-er end-eth.
ter-nal grace, Bless the same bound-less Giv-er. A-men.

FELLOWSHIP

Blest Be the Tie That Binds
First Tune

John Fawcett, 1739/40-1817

DENNIS S.M.
Melody by J. G. Nägeli, 1768?-1836
Adapted by Lowell Mason, 1792-1872

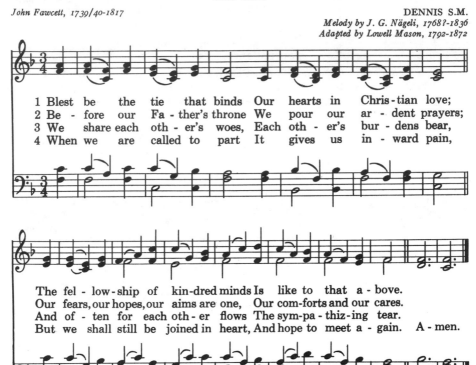

1 Blest be the tie that binds Our hearts in Chris-tian love;
2 Be - fore our Fa - ther's throne We pour our ar - dent prayers;
3 We share each oth - er's woes, Each oth - er's bur - dens bear,
4 When we are called to part It gives us in - ward pain,

The fel - low-ship of kin-dred minds Is like to that a - bove.
Our fears, our hopes, our aims are one, Our com-forts and our cares.
And of - ten for each oth - er flows The sym-pa - thiz-ing tear.
But we shall still be joined in heart, And hope to meet a - gain. A - men.

Blest Be the Tie That Binds
Second Tune

John Fawcett, 1739/40-1817

BOYLSTON S.M.
Lowell Mason, 1792-1872

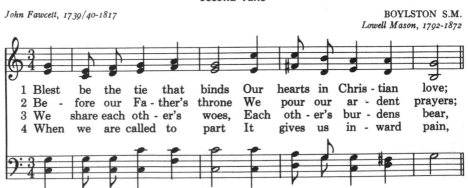

1 Blest be the tie that binds Our hearts in Chris - tian love;
2 Be - fore our Fa - ther's throne We pour our ar - dent prayers;
3 We share each oth - er's woes, Each oth - er's bur - dens bear,
4 When we are called to part It gives us in - ward pain,

FELLOWSHIP

The fel-low-ship of kin-dred minds Is like to that a - bove.
Our fears, our hopes, our aims are one, Our com-forts and our cares.
And of-ten for each oth-er flows The sym-pa-thiz-ing tear.
But we shall still be joined in heart, And hope to meet a - gain. A - men.

How Lovely Are Thy Dwellings Fair 274

Psalm 84
John Milton, 1608-1674

BISHOPTHORPE C.M.
Jeremiah Clark, c.1670-1707

1 How love - ly are thy dwell - ings fair, O
2 Hap - py, who in thy house re - side, Where
3 They jour - ney on from strength to strength With
4 Lord God of hosts that reign'st on high, That

Lord of hosts; how dear The pleas - ant tab - er -
thee they ev - er praise! Hap - py, whose strength in
joy and glad - some cheer, Till all be - fore our
man is tru - ly blest Who on - ly on thee

nac - les are Where thou dost dwell so near!
thee they doth bide, And in their hearts thy ways!
God at length In Zi - on do ap - pear.
doth re - ly, And in thee on - ly rest. A - men.

FELLOWSHIP

275 Eternal Ruler of the Ceaseless Round

John W. Chadwick, 1840-1904

SONG 1 10.10.10.10.10.10.
Orlando Gibbons, 1583-1625

1 E - ter - nal Rul - er of the cease - less round Of cir - cling
2 We are of thee, the chil - dren of thy love, The broth - ers
3 We would be one in ha - tred of all wrong, One in our

plan - ets sing - ing on their way, Guide of the na - tions
of thy well - be - lov - ed Son; De - scend, O Ho - ly
love of all things sweet and fair, One with the joy that

from the night pro - found In - to the glo - ry of the
Spir - it, like a dove In - to our hearts, that we may
break - eth in - to song, One with the grief that trem - bleth

per - fect day, Rule in our hearts, that we may ev - er
be as one: As one with thee, to whom we ev - er
in - to prayer, One in the power that makes the chil - dren

FELLOWSHIP

be Guid - ed and strength-ened and up - held by thee.
tend; As one with him, our broth-er and our friend.
free To fol - low truth, and thus to fol - low thee. A - men.

Unto Thy Temple, Lord, We Come 276

Robert Collyer, 1823-1912, alt.

EISENACH L.M.
Melody by Johann H. Schein, 1586-1630

1 Un - to thy tem - ple, Lord, we come With thank - ful hearts
2 The com - mon home of rich and poor, Of bond and free,
3 And dwell thou with us in this place, Thou and thy Christ,
4 May thy whole truth be spo - ken here; Thy gos - pel light

to wor - ship thee; And pray that this may be our home
and great and small, Large as thy love for - ev - er - more,
to guide and bless. Here make the well-springs of thy grace
for - ev - er shine; Thy per - fect love cast out all fear,

Un - til we touch e - ter - ni - ty:
And warm and bright and good to all.
Like foun - tains in the wil - der - ness.
And hu - man life be - come di - vine. A - men.

Alternative tune, MENDON, No. 238

FELLOWSHIP

277 Jesus, Friend, So Kind and Gentle

Philip E. Gregory, 1886-

SICILIAN MARINERS 8.7.8.7.8.7.
Sicilian Melody

1 Je - sus, Friend, so kind and gen - tle, Lit - tle ones we
bring to thee; Grant to them thy dear - est bless - ing,
Let thine arms a - round them be; Now en - fold them
in thy good - ness, From all dan - ger keep them free.

2 Thou who didst re - ceive the chil - dren To thy - self so
ten - der - ly, Give to all who teach and guide them,
Wis - dom and hu - mil - i - ty, Vi - sion true to
keep them no - ble, Love to serve them faith - ful - ly.

3 Grant to us a deep com - pas - sion For thy chil - dren
ev - ery - where. May we see our hu - man fam - ily
Free from sor - row and de - spair, And be - hold thy
king - dom glo - rious, In our world so bright and fair. A - men.

BAPTISM

Lord Jesus Christ, Our Lord Most Dear

Heinrich von Laufenburg, c.1400-c.1458
Tr. Catherine Winkworth, 1827-1878, alt.

VOM HIMMEL HOCH L.M.
"Geistliche Lieder," Leipzig, 1539

278

Lord Je - sus Christ, our Lord most dear,

As thou wast once an in - fant here,

So give this child of thine, we pray,

Thy grace and bless - ing day by day. A - men.

BAPTISM

279 Blessed Jesus, Here Are We

Benjamin Schmolck, 1672-1737
Tr. C. Winfred Douglas, 1867-1944

LIEBSTER JESU 7.8.7.8.8.8.
Melody by Johann R. Ahle, 1625-1673

In unison

Bless - ed Je - sus, here are we, Thy be - lov - ed word o - bey - ing.

Now these chil-dren come to thee As thou bid-dest in thy say - ing,
(this child doth)

"Let the lit - tle ones be giv - en Un - to me; of such is heav-en." A-men.

BAPTISM

280 Be Known to Us in Breaking Bread

James Montgomery, 1771-1854

ST. FLAVIAN C.M.
"Day's Psalter," 1562

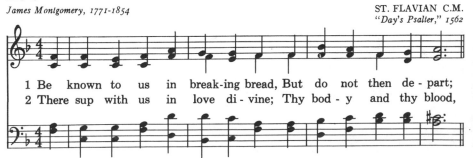

1 Be known to us in break-ing bread, But do not then de - part;
2 There sup with us in love di - vine; Thy bod - y and thy blood,

LORD'S SUPPER

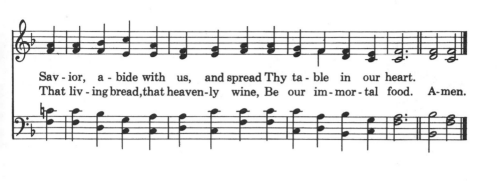

Sav - ior, a - bide with us, and spread Thy ta - ble in our heart.
That liv - ing bread, that heaven-ly wine, Be our im - mor - tal food. A-men.

Bread of Heaven, on Thee We Feed 281

Josiah Conder, 1789-1855, alt.

NICHT SO TRAURIG 7.7.7.7.7.7.
J. S. Bach, 1685-1750

1 Bread of heaven, on thee we feed, For thou art our food in - deed;
2 Vine of heaven, thy love sup - plies This blest cup of sac - ri - fice;

Ev - er may our souls be fed With this true and liv - ing bread,
'Tis thy wounds our heal - ing give; To thy cross we look and live;

Day by day with strength sup-plied Through the life of him who died.
Thou our life! O let us be Root-ed, graft-ed, built on thee. A-men.

LORD'S SUPPER

282 Bread of the World, in Mercy Broken

First Tune

Reginald Heber, *1783-1826*

RENDEZ À DIEU 9.8.9.8.D.
Attr. to Louis Bourgeois, c.1510-c.1561

Bread of the world, in mer - cy bro - ken, Wine of the

soul, in mer - cy shed, By whom the words of life were spo - ken,

And in whose death our sins are dead, Look on the heart by sor-row

bro - ken, Look on the tears by sin - ners shed, And be thy

LORD'S SUPPER

feast to us the to-ken That by thy grace our souls are fed. A-men.

Bread of the World, in Mercy Broken   283
Second Tune

Reginald Heber, 1783-1826

EUCHARISTIC HYMN 9.8.9.8.
J.S.B. Hodges, 1830-1915

1 Bread of the world, in mer - cy bro - ken, Wine of the
2 Look on the heart by sor - row bro - ken, Look on the

soul, in mer - cy shed, By whom the words of life were spo-ken,
tears by sin - ners shed, And be thy feast to us the to - ken

And in whose death our sins are dead,
That by thy grace our souls are fed. A - men.

284 According to Thy Gracious Word

First Tune

James Montgomery, 1771-1854

BANGOR C.M.
William Tans'ur, 1706?-1783

1 Ac - cord-ing to thy gra - cious word, In meek hu - mil - i - ty,
2 Thy bod - y, bro - ken for my sake, My bread from heaven shall be;
3 Re - mem-ber thee, and all thy pains, And all thy love to me;
4 And when these fail - ing lips grow dumb, And mind and mem - ory flee,

This will I do, my dy - ing Lord, I will re - mem - ber thee.
Thy tes - ta - men - tal cup I take, And thus re - mem - ber thee:
Yea, while a breath, a pulse re-mains, Will I re - mem - ber thee.
When thou shalt in thy king-dom come, Je - sus, re - mem - ber me. A-men.

285 According to Thy Gracious Word

Second Tune

James Montgomery, 1771-1854

MARTYRDOM C.M.
Hugh Wilson, 1764-1824

1 Ac - cord-ing to thy gra - cious word, In meek hu - mil - i - ty,
2 Thy bod - y, bro - ken for my sake, My bread from heaven shall be;
3 Re - mem-ber thee, and all thy pains, And all thy love to me;
4 And when these fail - ing lips grow dumb, And mind and mem - ory flee,

This will I do, my dy - ing Lord, I will re - mem - ber thee.
Thy tes - ta - men - tal cup I take, And thus re - mem - ber thee:
Yea, while a breath, a pulse re-mains, Will I re - mem - ber thee.
When thou shalt in thy king-dom come, Je - sus, re - mem - ber me. A-men.

LORD'S SUPPER

Come, Risen Lord

286

George W. Briggs, 1875-1959

SURSUM CORDA 10.10.10.10.
Alfred M. Smith, 1879-

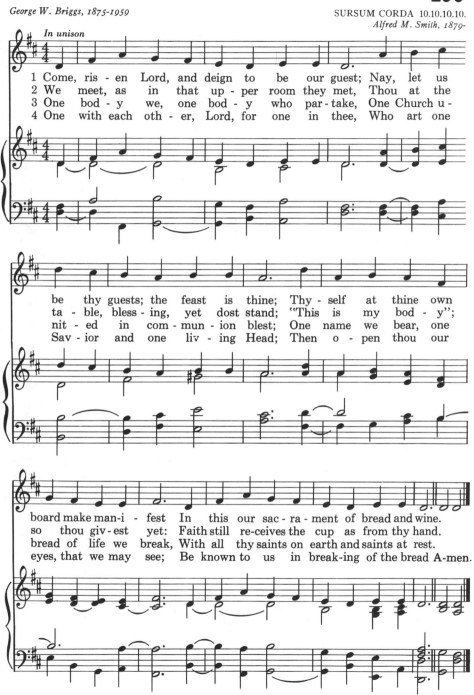

In unison

1 Come, ris-en Lord, and deign to be our guest; Nay, let us
2 We meet, as in that up-per room they met, Thou at the
3 One bod-y we, one bod-y who par-take, One Church u-
4 One with each oth-er, Lord, for one in thee, Who art one

be thy guests; the feast is thine; Thy-self at thine own
ta-ble, bless-ing, yet dost stand; "This is my bod-y";
nit-ed in com-mun-ion blest; One name we bear, one
Sav-ior and one liv-ing Head; Then o-pen thou our

board make man-i-fest In this our sac-ra-ment of bread and wine.
so thou giv-est yet: Faith still re-ceives the cup as from thy hand.
bread of life we break, With all thy saints on earth and saints at rest.
eyes, that we may see; Be known to us in break-ing of the bread A-men.

LORD'S SUPPER

287 Here, O My Lord, I See Thee Face to Face

Horatius Bonar, 1808-1889

LANGRAN 10.10.10.10.
James Langran, 1835-1909

1 Here, O my Lord, I see thee face to face;
2 Here would I feed up - on the bread of God,
3 This is the hour of ban - quet and of song;
4 Too soon we rise; the sym - bols dis - ap - pear;
5 I have no help but thine, nor do I need

Here would I touch and han - dle things un - seen;
Here drink with thee the roy - al wine of heaven;
This is the heaven - ly ta - ble spread for me;
The feast, though not the love is past and gone;
An - oth - er arm save thine to lean up - on.

Here grasp with firm - er hand the e - ter - nal grace,
Here would I lay a - side each earth - ly load,
Here let me feast, and, feast - ing, still pro - long
The bread and wine re - move, but thou art here,
It is e - nough, my Lord, e - nough in - deed;

And all my wea - ri - ness up - on thee lean.
Here taste a - fresh the calm of sin for - given.
The brief, bright hour of fel - low - ship with thee.
Near - er than ev - er, still my shield and sun.
My strength is in thy might, thy might a - lone. A - men.

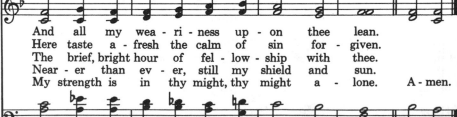

Alternative tune, MORECAMBE, *No. 232*
A plainsong setting may be found at No. 557

LORD'S SUPPER

Let Us Break Bread Together

Negro Spiritual

LET US BREAK BREAD 7.3.7.3. *with Refrain*
Negro Melody

In unison

1 Let us break bread to-geth-er on our knees;
2 Let us drink wine to-geth-er on our knees;
3 Let us praise God to-geth-er on our knees;

Let us break bread to-geth-er on our knees.
Let us drink wine to-geth-er on our knees.
Let us praise God to-geth-er on our knees.

REFRAIN

When I fall on my knees, with my face to the ris-ing sun,

O Lord, have mer-cy on me.

LORD'S SUPPER

289 Father, We Thank Thee Who Hast Planted

Greek: 2nd century
Tr. F. Bland Tucker, 1895-

RENDEZ À DIEU 9.8.9.8.D.
Attr. to Louis Bourgeois, c.1510-c.1561

1 Fa - ther, we thank thee who hast plant - ed Thy ho - ly
2 Watch o'er thy Church, O Lord, in mer - cy; Save it from

name with - in our hearts. Knowl-edge and faith and life im - mor - tal
e - vil, guard it still; Per - fect it in thy love, u - nite it,

Je - sus thy Son to us im - parts. Thou, Lord, didst make all for thy
Cleansed and con-formed un - to thy will. As grain, once scat - tered on the

pleas - ure, Didst give man food for all his days, Giv - ing in
hill - sides, Was in this bro - ken bread made one, So from all

LORD'S SUPPER

Christ the bread e-ter-nal; Thine is the power, be thine the praise.
lands thy Church be gath-ered In-to thy king-dom by thy Son. A-men.

Jesus, Thou Joy of Loving Hearts 290

Latin: 12th century
Tr. Ray Palmer, 1808-1887

FEDERAL STREET L.M.
Henry K. Oliver, 1800-1885

1 Je-sus, thou joy of lov-ing hearts, Thou 'fount of
2 Thy truth un-changed hath ev-er stood; Thou sav-est
3 Our rest-less spir-its yearn for thee, Wher-e'er our
4 O Je-sus, ev-er with us stay; Make all our

life, thou light of men, From the best bliss that
those that on thee call; To them that seek thee,
change-ful lot is cast: Glad when thy gra-cious
mo-ments calm and bright; Chase the dark night of

earth im-parts We turn un-filled to thee a-gain.
thou art good; To them that find thee, all in all.
smile we see; Blest when our faith can hold thee fast.
sin a-way; Shed o'er the world thy ho-ly light. A-men.

A lower setting may be found at No. 402
Alternative tune, HESPERUS, No. 447

LORD'S SUPPER

Lord, Enthroned in Heavenly Splendor

George H. Bourne, 1840-1925, Sts. 1 and 2
Percy Dearmer, 1867-1936, St. 3

BRYN CALFARIA 8.7.8.7.4.7.
Melody by William Owen, 1814-1893

1 Lord, en-throned in heaven-ly splen-dor, First-be-got-ten from the dead,
2 Here our hum-blest hom-age pay we; Here in lov-ing rev-erence bow;
3 Draw us in the Spir-it's teth-er For when hum-bly, in thy name,

Thou a-lone, our strong de-fend-er, Lift-est up thy peo-ple's head.
Here for faith's dis-cern-ment pray we Lest we fail to know thee now.
Two or three are met to-geth-er, Thou art in the midst of them.

Al-le-lu-ia! Al-le-lu-ia! Al-le-lu-ia!
Al-le-lu-ia! Al-le-lu-ia! Al-le-lu-ia!
Al-le-lu-ia! Al-le-lu-ia! Al-le-lu-ia!

Je-sus, true and liv-ing Bread. Je-sus, true and liv-ing Bread.
Thou art here, we ask not how. Thou art here, we ask not how.
Touch we now thy gar-ment's hem. Touch we now thy gar-ment's hem. A-men.

LORD'S SUPPER

And Now, O Father, Mindful of the Love

292

William Bright, 1824-1901, alt.

SONG 1 10.10.10.10.10.10.
Orlando Gibbons, 1583-1625

1 And now, O Fa-ther, mind-ful of the love That bought us, once for all, on
2 Look, Fa-ther, look on his a-noint-ed face, And on-ly look on us as
3 And so we come; O draw us to thy feet, Most pa-tient Sav-ior who canst

Cal-vary's tree, And hav-ing with us him that pleads a-bove,
found in him; Look not on our mis-us-ings of thy grace,
love us still! And by this food, so awe-ful and so sweet,

We here pre-sent, we here spread forth to thee, That on-ly of-fering
Our prayer so lan-guid, and our faith so dim; For lo! be-tween our
De-liv-er us from ev-ery touch of ill; In thine own serv-ice

per-fect in thine eyes, The one true, pure, im-mor-tal sac-ri-fice.
sins and their re-ward, We set the pas-sion of thy Son, our Lord.
make us glad and free, And grant us nev-er-more to part with thee. A-men.

LORD'S SUPPER

293 Come, Labor On

Jane L. Borthwick, 1813-1897, alt.

ORA LABORA 4.10.10.10.4.
T. Tertius Noble, 1867-1953

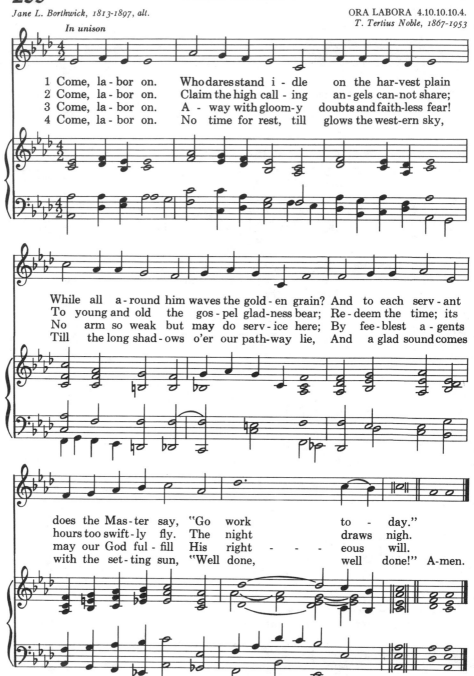

1 Come, la-bor on. Who dares stand i-dle on the har-vest plain
2 Come, la-bor on. Claim the high call-ing an-gels can-not share;
3 Come, la-bor on. A - way with gloom-y doubts and faith-less fear!
4 Come, la-bor on. No time for rest, till glows the west-ern sky,

While all a-round him waves the gold-en grain? And to each serv-ant
To young and old the gos-pel glad-ness bear; Re-deem the time; its
No arm so weak but may do serv-ice here; By fee-blest a-gents
Till the long shad-ows o'er our path-way lie, And a glad sound comes

does the Mas-ter say, "Go work to - day."
hours too swift-ly fly. The night draws nigh.
may our God ful-fill His right - - - eous will.
with the set-ting sun, "Well done, well done!" A-men.

MISSION IN THE WORLD

Eternal God, Whose Power Upholds

Henry H. Tweedy, 1868-1953

294

HALIFAX C.M.D.
Melody by Georg F. Handel, 1685-1759
Harm. by C. Winfred Douglas, 1867-1944

1 E - ter - nal God, whose power up-holds Both flower and flam - ing star,
2 O God of love, whose spir - it wakes In ev - ery hu - man breast,
3 O God of right-eous-ness and grace, Seen in the Christ, thy Son,

To whom there is no here nor there, No time, no near nor far,
Whom love, and love a - lone can know, In whom all hearts find rest,
Whose life and death re - veal thy face, By whom thy will was done,

No a - lien race, no for - eign shore, No child un-sought, un - known,
Help us to spread thy gra-cious reign Till greed and hate shall cease,
In - spire thy her - alds of good news To live thy life di - vine,

In unison

O send us forth, thy proph-ets true, To make all lands thine own!
And kind-ness dwell in hu-man hearts, And all the earth find peace!
Till Christ is formed in all man-kind And ev - ery land is thine! A - men.

MISSION IN THE WORLD

295   Christt for the World We Sing!

Samuel Wolcott, 1813-1886

ITALIAN HYMN 6.6.4.6.6.6.4.
Adapted from Felice de Giardini, 1716-1796

1 Christ for the world we sing! The world to Christ we bring
2 Christ for the world we sing! The world to Christ we bring
3 Christ for the world we sing! The world to Christ we bring
4 Christ for the world we sing! The world to Christ we bring

With lov-ing zeal: The poor, and them that mourn, The faint and
With fer-vent prayer: The way-ward and the lost, By rest-less
With one ac-cord: With us the work to share, With us re-
With joy-ful song: The new-born souls, whose days, Re-claimed from

o-ver-borne, Sin-sick and sor-row-worn, Whom Christ doth heal.
pas-sions tossed, Re-deemed at count-less cost From dark de-spair.
proach to dare, With us the cross to bear, For Christ our Lord.
er-ror's ways, In-spired with hope and praise, To Christ be-long. A-men.

Another setting may be found at No.246

296   Fling Out the Banner!

George W. Doane, 1799-1859, alt.

WALTHAM L.M.
John B. Calkin, 1827-1905

1 Fling out the ban-ner! let it float Sky-ward and sea-ward, high and wide:
2 Fling out the ban-ner! dis-tant lands Shall see from far the glo-rious sight,
3 Fling out the ban-ner! let it float Sky-ward and sea-ward, high and wide:
4 Fling out the ban-ner! wide and high, Sea-ward and sky-ward, let it shine.

MISSION IN THE WORLD

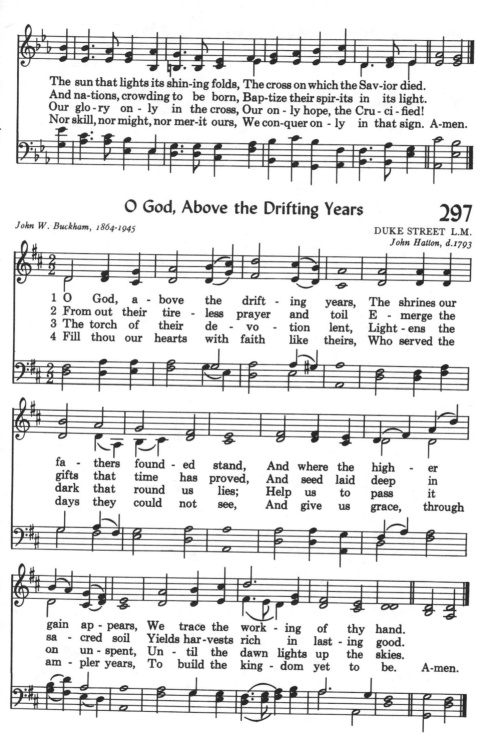

The sun that lights its shin-ing folds, The cross on which the Sav-ior died.
And na-tions, crowding to be born, Bap-tize their spir-its in its light.
Our glo-ry on-ly in the cross, Our on-ly hope, the Cru-ci-fied!
Nor skill, nor might, nor mer-it ours, We con-quer on-ly in that sign. A-men.

O God, Above the Drifting Years

297

John W. Buckham, 1864-1945

DUKE STREET L.M.
John Hatton, d.1793

1 O God, a-bove the drift-ing years, The shrines our
2 From out their tire-less prayer and toil E-merge the
3 The torch of their de-vo-tion lent, Light-ens the
4 Fill thou our hearts with faith like theirs, Who served the

fa-thers found-ed stand, And where the high-er
gifts that time has proved, And seed laid deep in
dark that round us lies; Help us to pass it
days they could not see, And give us grace, through

gain ap-pears, We trace the work-ing of thy hand.
sa-cred soil Yields har-vests rich in last-ing good.
on un-spent, Un-til the dawn lights up the skies.
am-pler years, To build the king-dom yet to be. A-men.

MISSION IN THE WORLD

298 God Is Working His Purpose Out

Arthur C. Ainger, 1841-1919

PURPOSE *Irregular*
Martin Shaw, 1875-

1 God is work-ing his pur-pose out As year suc-
2 From ut-most east to ut-most west, Wher-e'er man's
3 March we forth in the strength of God With the ban-ner of
4 All we can do is noth-ing worth Un-less God

Octaves to the end

ceeds to year; God is work-ing his
foot hath trod, By the mouth of man-y
Christ un-furled, That the light of the glo-rious
bless-es the deed; Vain-ly we hope for the

pur-pose out, And the time is draw-ing near; Near-er and
mes-sen-gers Goes forth the voice of God; Give ear to
gos-pel of truth May shine through-out the world; Fight we the
har-vest-tide Till God gives life to the seed; Yet near-er and

MISSION IN THE WORLD

near-er draws the time, The time that shall sure-ly be,
me, ye con-ti-nents, Ye isles, give ear to me,
fight with sorrow and sin To set their cap-tives free,
near-er draws the time, The time that shall sure-ly be,

When the earth shall be filled with the glo-ry of God
That the earth may be filled with the glo-ry of God
That the earth may be filled with the glo-ry of God
When the earth shall be filled with the glo-ry of God

St. 1, 2, 3 | St. 4

As the wa-ters cov-er the sea.
As the wa-ters cov-er the sea.
As the wa-ters cov-er the sea.
As the wa-ters cov-er the sea.

MISSION IN THE WORLD

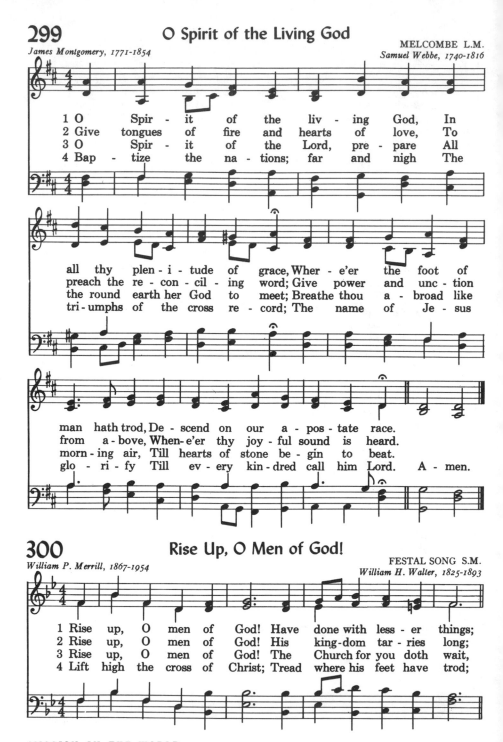

299 — O Spirit of the Living God

James Montgomery, 1771-1854

MELCOMBE L.M.
Samuel Webbe, 1740-1816

1 O Spir - it of the liv - ing God, In all thy plen - i - tude of grace, Wher - e'er the foot of man hath trod, De - scend on our a - pos - tate race.

2 Give tongues of fire and hearts of love, To preach the re - con - cil - ing word; Give power and unc - tion from a - bove, When-e'er thy joy - ful sound is heard.

3 O Spir - it of the Lord, pre - pare All the round earth her God to meet; Breathe thou a - broad like morn - ing air, Till hearts of stone be - gin to beat.

4 Bap - tize the na - tions; far and nigh The tri - umphs of the cross re - cord; The name of Je - sus glo - ri - fy Till ev - ery kin - dred call him Lord. A - men.

300 — Rise Up, O Men of God!

William P. Merrill, 1867-1954

FESTAL SONG S.M.
William H. Walter, 1825-1893

1 Rise up, O men of God! Have done with less - er things;

2 Rise up, O men of God! His king-dom tar - ries long;

3 Rise up, O men of God! The Church for you doth wait,

4 Lift high the cross of Christ; Tread where his feet have trod;

MISSION IN THE WORLD

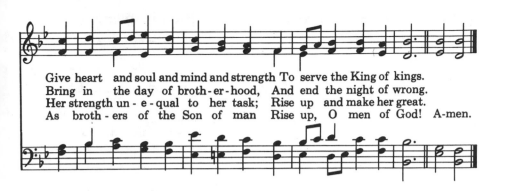

Give heart   and soul and mind and strength To serve the King of kings.
Bring in   the day of broth-er-hood, And end the night of wrong.
Her strength un - e-qual to her task; Rise up and make her great.
As broth-ers of the Son of man Rise up, O men of God! A-men.

Jesus, With Thy Church Abide

301

Thomas B. Pollock, 1836-1896

VIENNA 7.7.7.7.
Melody by Justin H. Knecht, 1752-1817

1 Je - sus, with thy   Church a - bide; Be   her sav - ior, lord, and guide,
2 May she guide the   poor and blind, Seek the lost un - til she find,
3 May her scat-tered chil - dren be From re-proach of e - vil free,
4 May she one in   doc - trine be, One in truth and char - i - ty,

While on earth her faith is   tried. We be-seech thee, hear us.
And the bro-ken - heart-ed bind. We be-seech thee, hear us.
Blame-less wit-ness-es for thee. We be-seech thee, hear us.
Win - ning all to faith in thee. We be-seech thee, hear us.   A - men.

5 May she holy triumphs win,
   Overthrow the hosts of sin,
   Gather all the nations in.
   We beseech thee, hear us.

MISSION IN THE WORLD

302   O Zion, Haste, Thy Mission High Fulfilling

Mary A. Thomson, 1834-1923

TIDINGS 11.10.11.10. *with Refrain*
James Walch, 1837-1901

1 O Zi - on, haste, thy mis - sion high ful - fill - ing,
2 Pro - claim to ev - ery peo - ple, tongue, and na - tion
3 Give of thy sons to bear the mes - sage glo - rious;

To tell to all the world that God is light, That he who
That God, in whom they live and move, is love, Tell how he
Give of thy wealth to speed them on their way; Pour out thy

made all na - tions is not will - ing One soul should per - ish,
stooped to save his lost cre - a - tion, And died on earth that
soul for them in prayer vic - to - rious, And all thou spend - est

REFRAIN

lost in shades of night.
man might live a - bove. Pub - lish glad ti - dings: Ti - dings of peace,
Je - sus will re - pay.

MISSION IN THE WORLD

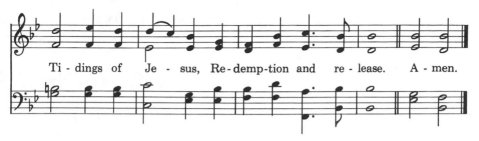

Ti - dings of Je - sus, Re - demp-tion and re - lease. A - men.

Creation's Lord, We Give Thee Thanks 303

William De Witt Hyde, 1858-1917, alt.

RAMWOLD L.M.
Richard Warner, 1908-

1 Cre - a-tion's Lord, we give thee thanks   That this thy world is
2 That thou hast not yet fin-ished man,   That we are in the
3 Be - yond the pres-ent sin and shame,   Wrong's bit-ter, cru - el,
4 What though the king-dom long de - lay,   And still with haugh-ty

in - com-plete,   That bat - tle   calls our mar-shaled ranks,
mak - ing still,   As friends who share the Mak-er's plan,
scorch-ing blight,   We see the beck-oning vi - sion flame,
foes must cope?   It gives us   that for which to pray,

In unison

That work a - waits our hands and feet,
As   sons who   know the Fa - ther's will.
The bless - ed   king - dom of the right.
A   field for   toil and faith and hope. A - men.

Alternative tune, ROCKINGHAM, *No. 357*

MISSION IN THE WORLD

304 Rejoice, O People, in the Mounting Years

Albert F. Bayly, 1901-

YORKSHIRE 10.10.10.10.10.10.
John Wainwright, c.1723-1768

1 Re - joice, O peo - ple, in the mount-ing years, Where - in God's
2 Re - joice, O peo - ple, in the years of old, When proph-ets'
3 Re - joice, O peo - ple, in this liv - ing hour; Low lies man's
4 Re - joice, O peo - ple, in the days to be, When o'er the

might-y pur-pos-es un - fold; From age to age his right-eous reign ap-pears,
glow-ing vi-sion lit the way, Till saint and mar - tyr sped the ven-ture bold,
pride and hu-man wis-dom dies; But on the cross God's love re-veals his power,
strife of na-tions sound-ing clear, Shall ring love's gra-cious song of vic - to - ry,

From land to land the love of Christ is told. Re-joice, O peo - ple,
And ea - ger hearts a-woke to greet the day. Re-joice in God's glad
And from his wait-ing Church new hopes a - rise. Re-joice that while the
To east and west his king-dom bring - ing near. Re-joice, re - joice, his

in your glo-rious Lord; Lift up your hearts in ju - bi - lant ac - cord.
mes - sen-gers of peace, Who bore the Sav-ior's gos-pel of re - lease.
sin of man di-vides, One Chris-tian fel-low-ship of love a - bides.
Church on earth is one, And binds the ran-somed na-tions 'neath the sun. A-men.

MISSION IN THE WORLD

The Morning Light Is Breaking

305

Samuel F. Smith, 1808-1895, alt.

WEBB 7.6.7.6.D.
George J. Webb, 1803-1887

1 The morn-ing light is break-ing, The dark-ness dis-ap-pears,
2 See all the na-tions bend-ing Be-fore the God we love,
3 Blest riv-er of sal-va-tion, Pur-sue thy on-ward way;

The sons of earth are wak-ing To pen-i-ten-tial tears;
And thou-sand hearts as-cend-ing In grat-i-tude a-bove,
Flow thou to ev-ery na-tion, Nor in thy rich-ness stay;

Each breeze that sweeps the o-cean Brings ti-dings from a-far
While sin-ners, now con-fess-ing, The gos-pel call o-bey,
Stay not till all the low-ly Tri-um-phant reach their home;

Of na-tions in com-mo-tion, Pre-pared for Zi-on's war.
And seek the Sav-ior's bless-ing, A na-tion in a day.
Stay not till all the ho-ly Pro-claim,"The Lord is come!" A-men.

A higher setting may be found at No. 385

MISSION IN THE WORLD

306

For All the Saints

First Tune

William W. How, 1823-1897, alt.

SINE NOMINE 10.10.10.4.
R. Vaughan Williams, 1872-1958

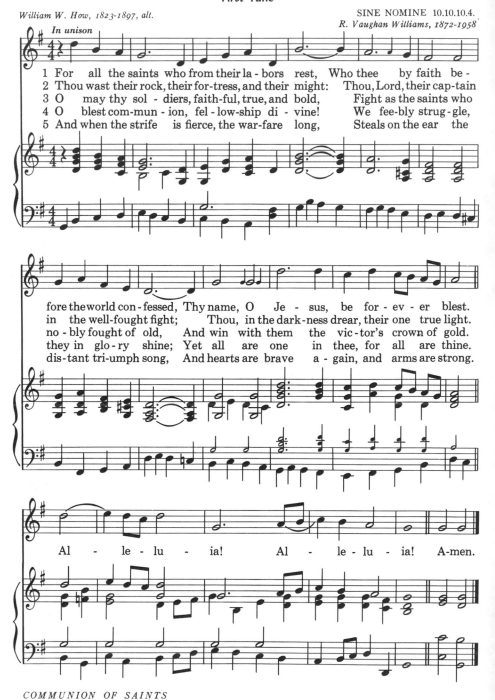

In unison

1 For all the saints who from their la - bors rest, Who thee by faith be -
2 Thou wast their rock, their for-tress, and their might: Thou, Lord, their cap-tain
3 O may thy sol - diers, faith-ful, true, and bold, Fight as the saints who
4 O blest com-mun - ion, fel - low-ship di - vine! We fee-bly strug-gle,
5 And when the strife is fierce, the war-fare long, Steals on the ear the

fore the world con - fessed, Thy name, O Je - sus, be for - ev - er blest.
in the well-fought fight; Thou, in the dark-ness drear, their one true light.
no - bly fought of old, And win with them the vic-tor's crown of gold.
they in glo - ry shine; Yet all are one in thee, for all are thine.
dis-tant tri-umph song, And hearts are brave a - gain, and arms are strong.

Al - le - lu - ia! Al - le - lu - ia! A - men.

COMMUNION OF SAINTS

For All the Saints

Second Tune

William W. How, 1823-1897, alt.

SARUM 10.10.10.4.
Joseph Barnby, 1838-1896

307

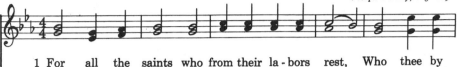

1 For all the saints who from their la-bors rest, Who thee by
2 Thou wast their rock, their for-tress, and their might: Thou, Lord, their
3 O may thy sol - diers, faith-ful, true, and bold, Fight as the
4 O blest com - mun - ion, fel - low-ship di - vine! We fee-bly
5 And when the strife is fierce, the war-fare long, Steals on the

faith be - fore the world con - fessed, Thy name, O Je - sus,
cap - tain in the well - fought fight; Thou, in the dark - ness
saints who no - bly fought of old, And win with them the
strug - gle, they in glo - ry shine; Yet all are one in
ear the dis - tant tri - umph song, And hearts are brave a -

be for - ev - er blest. Al - le - lu - ia! Al - le - lu - ia!
drear, their one true light. Al - le - lu - ia! Al - le - lu - ia!
vic - tor's crown of gold. Al - le - lu - ia! Al - le - lu - ia!
thee, for all are thine. Al - le - lu - ia! Al - le - lu - ia!
gain, and arms are strong. Al - le - lu - ia! Al - le - lu - ia! A-men.

COMMUNION OF SAINTS

308 For the Brave of Every Race

George W. Briggs, 1875-1959

SALZBURG 7.7.7.7.D.
Melody by Jacob Hintze, 1622-1702
Harm. by J. S. Bach, 1685-1750

1 For the brave of ev - ery race, All who served and fell on sleep,
2 Prince and peas-ant, bond and free, War - riors wield-ing free-dom's sword,
3 Val - iant - ly o'er sea and land Trod they the un - trod - den way,
4 Ev - er - more their life a - bides Who have lived to do thy will;

Whose for - got - ten rest - ing place Roll - ing years have bur -ied deep,
Bold ad - ven-turers on the sea, Faith - ful stew-ards of the word,
True and faith-ful to com-mand, Swift and fear - less to o - bey;
High a - bove the rest - less tides Stands their cit - y on the hill;

Broth - er - hood and sis - ter - hood Of earth's age-long chiv - al - ry,
Toil - ers in the mine and mill, Toil - ers at the fur - nace-blaze,
Strong in heart and hand and brain, Strong, yet bat-tling for the weak,
Lord and light of ev - ery age, By thy same sure coun - sel led,

Source and giv - er of all good, Lord, we praise, we wor-ship thee.
Long for - got - ten, liv - ing still, All thy serv-ants tell thy praise.
Recked they not of their own gain, Their own safe-ty scorned to seek.
Heirs of their great her - it - age, In their foot-steps will we tread. A-men.

COMMUNION OF SAINTS

Jerusalem the Golden

St. Bernard of Cluny, *12th century*
Tr. John M. Neale, 1818-1866, alt.

EWING 7.6.7.6.D.
Alexander Ewing, 1830-1895

309

1 Je - ru - sa - lem the gold - en, With milk and hon - ey blest,
2 They stand, those halls of Zi - on, All ju - bi - lant with song,
3 There is the throne of Da - vid, And there, from care re - leased,
4 O sweet and bless - ed coun - try, The home of God's e - lect!

Be - neath thy con - tem - pla - tion Sink heart and voice op - pressed.
And bright with man - y an an - gel, And all the mar - tyr throng.
The shout of them that tri - umph, The song of them that feast,
O sweet and bless - ed coun - try, That ea - ger hearts ex - pect!

I know not, O I know not, What joys a - wait us there,
The Prince is ev - er in them; The day - light is se - rene;
And they, who with their lead - er, Have con - quered in the fight,
Je - sus, in mer - cy bring us To that dear land of rest,

What ra - dian - cy of glo - ry, What bliss be - yond com - pare!
The pas - tures of the bless - ed Are decked in glo - rious sheen.
For - ev - er and for - ev - er Are clad in robes of white.
Who art, with God the Fa - ther And Spir - it, ev - er blest! A-men.

COMMUNION OF SAINTS

310 O What Their Joy and Their Glory Must Be

Peter Abelard, 1079-1142
Tr. John M. Neale, 1818-1866

O QUANTA QUALIA 10.10.10.10.
La Feillée's "Méthode du Plain-chant," 1808

1 O what their joy and their glo - ry must be,
2 Tru - ly Je - ru - sa - lem name we that shore,
3 We, where no trou - ble dis - trac - tion can bring,
4 Low be - fore him with our prais - es we fall,

Those end - less sab - baths the bless - ed ones see:
Vi - sion of peace, that brings joy ev - er - more;
Safe - ly the an - thems of Zi - on shall sing,
Of whom, and in whom, and through whom are all:

Crown for the val - iant, to wea - ry ones rest;
Wish and ful - fill - ment can sev - ered be ne'er,
While for thy grace, Lord, their voic - es of praise
Of whom, the Fa - ther; and in whom, the Son;

God shall be all, and in all ev - er blest.
Nor the thing prayed for come short of the prayer.
Thy bless - ed peo - ple shall ev - er - more raise.
Through whom, the Spir - it, with these ev - er One.   A-men.

COMMUNION OF SAINTS

Ten Thousand Times Ten Thousand

Henry Alford, 1810-1871

ALFORD 7.6.8.6.D.
John B. Dykes 1823-1876

311

1 Ten thou-sand times ten thou-sand, In spar-kling rai-ment bright,
2 What rush of al-le-lu-ias Fills all the earth and sky!
3 Bring near thy great sal-va-tion, Thou Lamb for sin-ners slain;

The ar-mies of the ran-somed saints Throng up the steeps of light;
What ring-ing of a thou-sand harps Be-speaks the tri-umph nigh!
Fill up the roll of thine e-lect, Then take thy power and reign;

'Tis fin-ished, all is fin-ished, Their fight with death and sin;
O day, for which cre-a-tion And all its tribes were made!
Ap-pear, De-sire of na-tions, Thine ex-iles long for home;

Fling o-pen wide the gold-en gates, And let the vic-tors in!
O joy, for all its for-mer woes, A thou-sand-fold re-paid!
Show in the heavens thy promised sign, Thou Prince and Savior, come! A-men.

COMMUNION OF SAINTS

312 Jerusalem, My Happy Home

F. B. P., c. 16th century, alt.

LAND OF REST C.M.
Traditional American Melody
Harm. by Annabel Morris Buchanan, 1888-

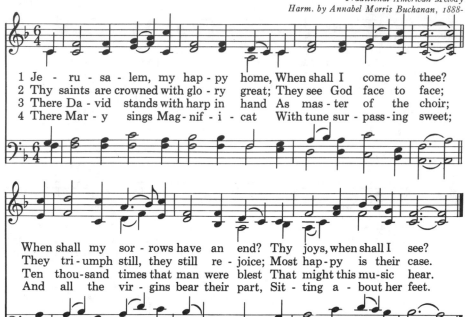

1 Je - ru - sa - lem, my hap - py home, When shall I come to thee?
2 Thy saints are crowned with glo - ry great; They see God face to face;
3 There Da - vid stands with harp in hand As mas - ter of the choir;
4 There Mar - y sings Mag - nif - i - cat With tune sur - pass - ing sweet;

When shall my sor - rows have an end? Thy joys, when shall I see?
They tri - umph still, they still re - joice; Most hap - py is their case.
Ten thou - sand times that man were blest That might this mu - sic hear.
And all the vir - gins bear their part, Sit - ting a - bout her feet.

5 There Magdalen hath left her moan,
   And cheerfully doth sing
With blessèd saints, whose harmony
   In every street doth ring.

6 Jerusalem, Jerusalem,
   God grant that I may see
Thine endless joy, and of the same
   Partaker ever be!

COMMUNION OF SAINTS

313 My God, I Love Thee

Attr. to Francis Xavier, 1506-1552
Tr. Edward Caswall, 1814-1878, alt.

ABBEY C.M.
"Scottish Psalter," 1615

1 My God, I love thee: not be - cause I hope for heaven there - by,
2 Not with the hope of gain - ing aught; Not seek - ing a re - ward;
3 E'en so I love thee, and will love, And in thy praise will sing,

GOSPEL CALL AND RESPONSE

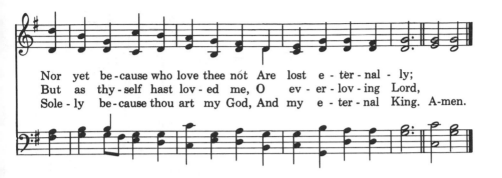

Nor yet be-cause who love thee nót Are lost e - tèr - nal - ly;
But as thy - self hast lov - ed me, O ev - er - lov - ing Lord,
Sole - ly be - cause thou art my God, And my e - ter - nal King. A-men.

Lord Jesus, Think on Me

314

Synesius of Cyrene, c.375-430
Tr. Allen W. Chatfield, 1808-1896, alt.

SOUTHWELL S.M.
Adapted from Damon's "Psalmes," 1579

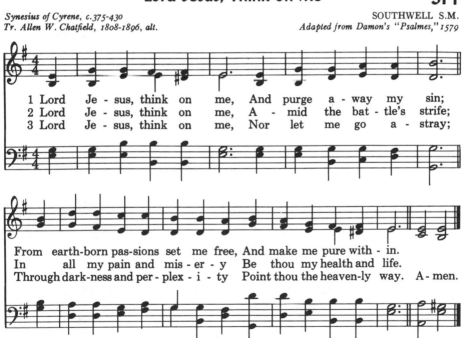

1 Lord Je - sus, think on me, And purge a - way my sin;
2 Lord Je - sus, think on me, A - mid the bat - tle's strife;
3 Lord Je - sus, think on me, Nor let me go a - stray;

From earth-born pas-sions set me free, And make me pure with - in.
In all my pain and mis - er - y Be thou my health and life.
Through dark-ness and per - plex - i - ty Point thou the heaven-ly way. A - men.

4 Lord Jesus, think on me,
   That, when this life is past,
I may the eternal brightness see,
   And share thy joy at last.

GOSPEL CALL AND RESPONSE

315 Come Unto Me, Ye Weary

William C. Dix, 1837-1898, alt.

WHITFORD 7.6.7.6.D.
John A. Lloyd, 1815-1874

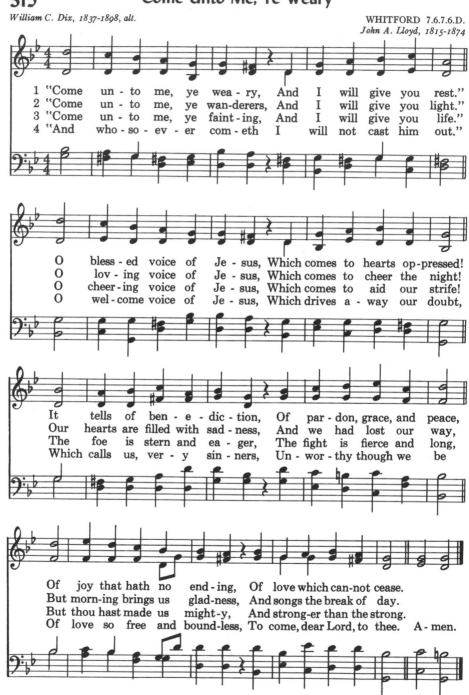

1 "Come un - to me, ye wea - ry, And I will give you rest."
2 "Come un - to me, ye wan-derers, And I will give you light."
3 "Come un - to me, ye faint-ing, And I will give you life."
4 "And who - so - ev - er com - eth I will not cast him out."

O bless - ed voice of Je - sus, Which comes to hearts op-pressed!
O lov - ing voice of Je - sus, Which comes to cheer the night!
O cheer-ing voice of Je - sus, Which comes to aid our strife!
O wel - come voice of Je - sus, Which drives a - way our doubt,

It tells of ben - e - dic - tion, Of par - don, grace, and peace,
Our hearts are filled with sad - ness, And we had lost our way,
The foe is stern and ea - ger, The fight is fierce and long,
Which calls us, ver - y sin - ners, Un - wor - thy though we be

Of joy that hath no end - ing, Of love which can-not cease.
But morn-ing brings us glad-ness, And songs the break of day.
But thou hast made us might-y, And strong-er than the strong.
Of love so free and bound-less, To come, dear Lord, to thee. A - men.

GOSPEL CALL AND RESPONSE

Alternative tune, LLANGLOFFAN, *No. 436*

God of Earth and Sea and Heaven

316

Frank Edwards, 1898-

LLANSANNAN 8.7.8.7.D.
Welsh Melody
Harm. by David Evans, 1874-1948

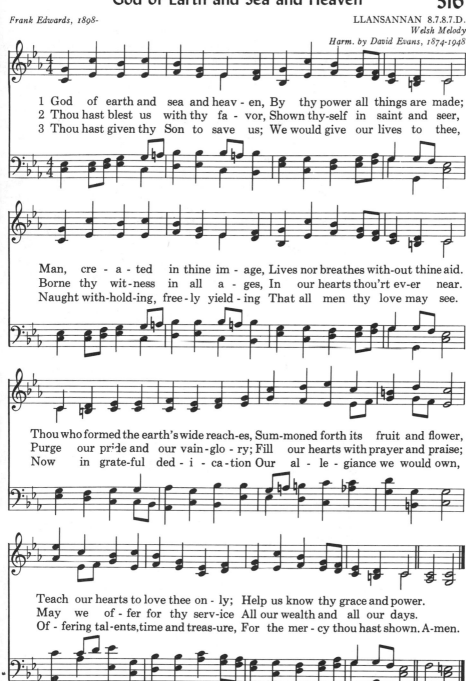

1 God of earth and sea and heav - en, By thy power all things are made;
2 Thou hast blest us with thy fa - vor, Shown thy-self in saint and seer,
3 Thou hast given thy Son to save us; We would give our lives to thee,

Man, cre - a - ted in thine im - age, Lives nor breathes with-out thine aid.
Borne thy wit-ness in all a - ges, In our hearts thou'rt ev - er near.
Naught with-hold-ing, free - ly yield - ing That all men thy love may see.

Thou who formed the earth's wide reach-es, Sum-moned forth its fruit and flower,
Purge our pride and our vain-glo - ry; Fill our hearts with prayer and praise;
Now in grate-ful ded - i - ca-tion Our al - le - giance we would own,

Teach our hearts to love thee on - ly; Help us know thy grace and power.
May we of - fer for thy serv-ice All our wealth and all our days.
Of - fering tal-ents, time and treas-ure, For the mer - cy thou hast shown. A-men.

Alternative tune, HYFRYDOL, *No. 13*

GOSPEL CALL AND RESPONSE

317 I Love to Tell the Story

Katherine Hankey, 1834-1911

HANKEY 7.6.7.6.D. *with Refrain*
William G. Fischer, 1835-1912

1 I love to tell the sto - ry Of un - seen things a - bove,
2 I love to tell the sto - ry, For those who know it best

Of Je - sus and his glo - ry, Of Je - sus and his love.
Seem hun - ger - ing and thirst - ing To hear it, like the rest.

I love to tell the sto - ry, Be - cause I know it's true;
And when, in scenes of glo - ry, I sing the new, new song,

It sat - is - fies my long - ings As noth - ing else would do.
'Twill be the old, old sto - ry That I have loved so long.

REFRAIN

I love to tell the sto - ry; 'Twill be my theme in glo - ry

GOSPEL CALL AND RESPONSE

To tell the old, old sto-ry Of Je-sus and his love. A-men.

Draw Thou My Soul, O Christ 318

Lucy Larcom, 1826-1893

ST. EDMUND 6.4.6.4.6.6.6.4.
Arthur S. Sullivan, 1842-1900

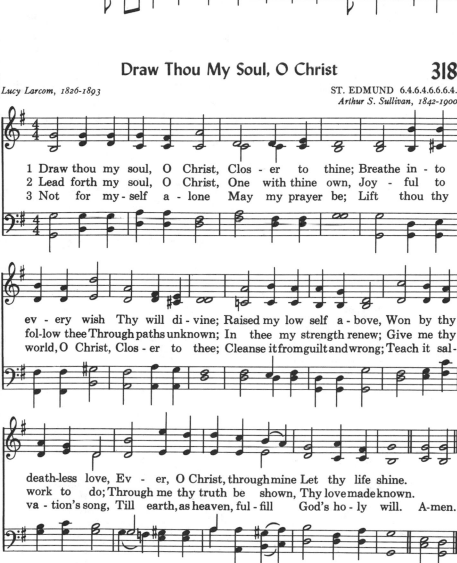

1 Draw thou my soul, O Christ, Clos-er to thine; Breathe in-to
2 Lead forth my soul, O Christ, One with thine own, Joy-ful to
3 Not for my-self a-lone May my prayer be; Lift thou thy

ev-ery wish Thy will di-vine; Raised my low self a-bove, Won by thy
fol-low thee Through paths unknown; In thee my strength renew; Give me thy
world, O Christ, Clos-er to thee; Cleanse it from guilt and wrong; Teach it sal-

death-less love, Ev-er, O Christ, through mine Let thy life shine.
work to do; Through me thy truth be shown, Thy love made known.
va-tion's song, Till earth, as heaven, ful-fill God's ho-ly will. A-men.

GOSPEL CALL AND RESPONSE

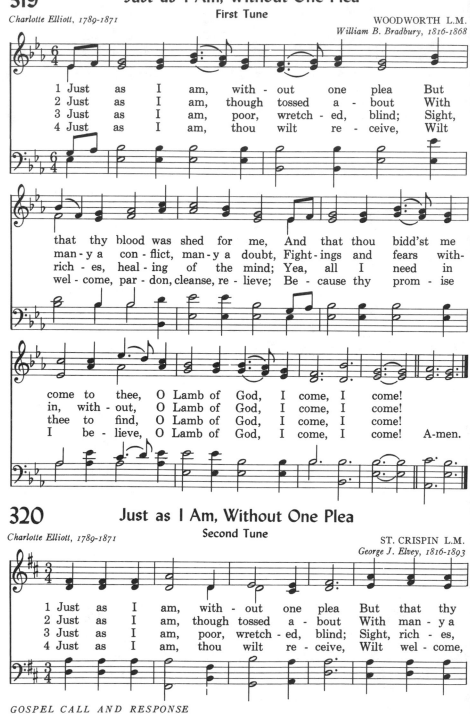

319
Just as I Am, Without One Plea
First Tune

Charlotte Elliott, 1789-1871

WOODWORTH L.M.
William B. Bradbury, 1816-1868

1 Just as I am, with-out one plea But
2 Just as I am, though tossed a-bout With
3 Just as I am, poor, wretch-ed, blind; Sight,
4 Just as I am, thou wilt re-ceive, Wilt

that thy blood was shed for me, And that thou bidd'st me
man-y a con-flict, man-y a doubt, Fight-ings and fears with-
rich-es, heal-ing of the mind; Yea, all I need in
wel-come, par-don, cleanse, re-lieve; Be-cause thy prom-ise

come to thee, O Lamb of God, I come, I come!
in, with-out, O Lamb of God, I come, I come!
thee to find, O Lamb of God, I come, I come!
I be-lieve, O Lamb of God, I come, I come! A-men.

320
Just as I Am, Without One Plea
Second Tune

Charlotte Elliott, 1789-1871

ST. CRISPIN L.M.
George J. Elvey, 1816-1893

1 Just as I am, with-out one plea But that thy
2 Just as I am, though tossed a-bout With man-y a
3 Just as I am, poor, wretch-ed, blind; Sight, rich-es,
4 Just as I am, thou wilt re-ceive, Wilt wel-come,

GOSPEL CALL AND RESPONSE

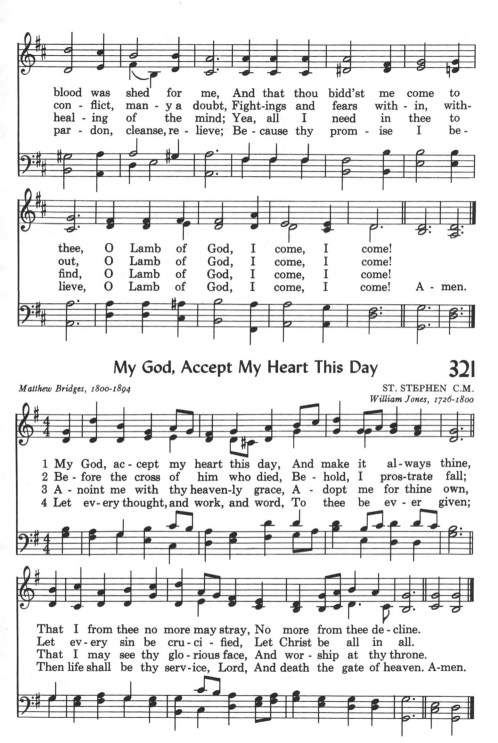

blood was shed for me, And that thou bidd'st me come to
con - flict, man - y a doubt, Fight-ings and fears with - in, with-
heal - ing of the mind; Yea, all I need in thee to
par - don, cleanse, re - lieve; Be - cause thy prom - ise I be -

thee, O Lamb of God, I come, I come!
out, O Lamb of God, I come, I come!
find, O Lamb of God, I come, I come!
lieve, O Lamb of God, I come, I come! A - men.

My God, Accept My Heart This Day 321

Matthew Bridges, 1800-1894

ST. STEPHEN C.M.
William Jones, 1726-1800

1 My God, ac - cept my heart this day, And make it al - ways thine,
2 Be - fore the cross of him who died, Be - hold, I pros-trate fall;
3 A - noint me with thy heaven-ly grace, A - dopt me for thine own,
4 Let ev - ery thought, and work, and word, To thee be ev - er given;

That I from thee no more may stray, No more from thee de - cline.
Let ev - ery sin be cru - ci - fied, Let Christ be all in all.
That I may see thy glo - rious face, And wor - ship at thy throne.
Then life shall be thy serv-ice, Lord, And death the gate of heaven. A-men.

GOSPEL CALL AND RESPONSE

322

Jesus Calls Us, O'er the Tumult
First Tune

Cecil F. Alexander 1818-1895

GALILEE 8.7.8.7.
William H. Jude, 1851-1922

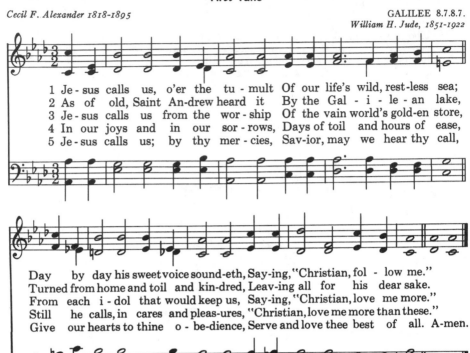

1 Je-sus calls us, o'er the tu-mult Of our life's wild, rest-less sea;
2 As of old, Saint An-drew heard it By the Gal-i-le-an lake,
3 Je-sus calls us from the wor-ship Of the vain world's gold-en store,
4 In our joys and in our sor-rows, Days of toil and hours of ease,
5 Je-sus calls us; by thy mer-cies, Sav-ior, may we hear thy call,

Day by day his sweet voice sound-eth, Say-ing, "Christian, fol-low me."
Turned from home and toil and kin-dred, Leav-ing all for his dear sake.
From each i-dol that would keep us, Say-ing, "Christian, love me more."
Still he calls, in cares and pleas-ures, "Christian, love me more than these."
Give our hearts to thine o-be-dience, Serve and love thee best of all. A-men.

323

Jesus Calls Us, O'er the Tumult
Second Tune

Cecil F. Alexander, 1818-1895

GOTT DES HIMMELS 8.7.8.7.
Adapted from Heinrich Albert, 1604-1651

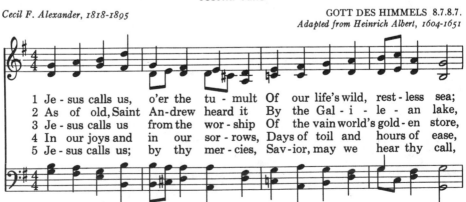

1 Je-sus calls us, o'er the tu-mult Of our life's wild, rest-less sea;
2 As of old, Saint An-drew heard it By the Gal-i-le-an lake,
3 Je-sus calls us from the wor-ship Of the vain world's gold-en store,
4 In our joys and in our sor-rows, Days of toil and hours of ease,
5 Je-sus calls us; by thy mer-cies, Sav-ior, may we hear thy call,

GOSPEL CALL AND RESPONSE

Day by day his sweet voice sound-eth, Say-ing, "Christian, fol - low me."
Turned from home and toil and kin-dred, Leav-ing all for his dear sake.
From each i - dol that would keep us, Say-ing, "Christian, love me more."
Still he calls, in cares and pleas-ures, "Christian, love me more than these."
Give our hearts to thine o - be-dience, Serve and love thee best of all. A-men.

O Thou to Whose All-Searching Sight   324

Nicolaus L. von Zinzendorf, 1700-1760
Tr. John Wesley, 1703-1791, alt.

GRACE CHURCH L.M.
Attr. to Ignaz J. Pleyel, 1757-1831

1 O thou to whose all - search - ing sight The dark - ness
2 Wash out its stains, re - fine its dross, Nail my af -
3 If in this dark - some wild I stray, Be thou my
4 Sav - ior, wher - e'er thy steps I see, Daunt-less, un -

shin - eth as the light, Search, prove my heart; it longs for
fec - tions to the cross; Hal - low each thought; let all with -
light, be thou my way; No foes, no e - vils need I
tired, I fol - low thee. O let thy hand sup - port me

thee; O burst these bonds, and set it free!
in Be clean, as thou, my Lord, art clean.
fear, No harm, while thou, my God, art near.
still, And lead me to thy ho - ly hill! A - men.

GOSPEL CALL AND RESPONSE

325 Lord Christ, When First Thou Cam'st

W. Russell Bowie, 1882-

MIT FREUDEN ZART 8.7.8.7.8.8.7.
Bohemian Brethren's "Kirchengesänge," 1566

1 Lord Christ, when first thou cam'st to men, Up - on a cross they bound thee,
2 O awe - ful love, which found no room In life where sin de - nied thee,
3 New ad - vent of the love of Christ, Shall we a - gain re - fuse thee,
4 O wound - ed hands of Je - sus, build In us thy new cre - a - tion;

And mocked thy sav - ing king-ship then By thorns with which they crowned thee;
And, doomed to death, must bring to doom The power which cru - ci - fied thee,
Till in the night of hate and war We per - ish as we lose thee?
Our pride is dust; our vaunt is stilled; We wait thy rev - e - la - tion.

And still our wrongs may weave thee now New thorns to pierce that
Till not a stone was left on stone, And all a na - tion's
From old un - faith our souls re - lease To seek the king - dom
O love that tri - umphs o - ver loss, We bring our hearts be -

stead - y brow, And robe of sor - row round thee.
pride o'erthrown, Went down to dust be - side thee!
of thy peace, By which a - lone we choose thee.
fore thy cross, To fin - ish thy sal - va - tion. A - men.

GOSPEL CALL AND RESPONSE

Thou Didst Leave Thy Throne

326

Emily E. S. Elliott, 1836-1897, alt.

MARGARET *Irregular*
Timothy R. Matthews, 1826-1910

1 Thou didst leave thy throne and thy king - ly crown When thou cam - est to earth for me, But in Beth - le-hem's home there was found no room For thy ho - ly na - tiv - i - ty. O come to my heart, Lord Je - sus; There is room in my heart for thee!

2 Heav-en's arch - es rang when the an - gels sang, Pro - claim-ing thy roy - al de - gree, But in low - ly birth didst thou come to earth, And in great hu - mil - i - ty. O come to my heart, Lord Je - sus; There is room in my heart for thee!

3 The fox - es found rest, and the birds their nest In the shade of the for - est tree, But thy couch was the sod, O thou Son of God, In the des - erts of Gal - i - lee. O come to my heart, Lord Je - sus; There is room in my heart for thee!

4 Thou cam - est, O Lord, with the liv - ing word That should set thy peo - ple free, But with mock - ing scorn and with crown of thorn They bore thee to Cal - va - ry. O come to my heart, Lord Je - sus; There is room in my heart for thee!

5 When the heavens shall ring and the an - gels sing At thy com - ing to vic - to - ry, Let thy voice call me home, say - ing, "Yet there is room, There is room at my side for thee." And my heart shall re-joice, Lord Je - sus; When thou com-est and call-est me. A-men.

GOSPEL CALL AND RESPONSE

327   Savior, Like a Shepherd Lead Us

Attr. to Dorothy A. Thrupp, 1779-1847

BRADBURY 8.7.8.7.D.
William B. Bradbury, 1816-1868

1 Sav-ior, like a shep-herd lead us, Much we need thy ten-der care;
2 We are thine; do thou be-friend us; Be the guard-ian of our way;
3 Ear-ly let us seek thy fa - vor; Ear-ly let us do thy will;

In thy pleas-ant pas-tures feed us, For our use thy folds pre-pare.
Keep thy flock; from sin de - fend us; Seek us when we go a - stray.
Bless-ed Lord and on - ly Sav - ior, With thy love our bos-oms fill.

Bless-ed Je - sus, Bless-ed Je - sus, Thou hast bought us, thine we are;
Bless-ed Je - sus, Bless-ed Je - sus, Hear thy chil-dren when they pray;
Bless-ed Je - sus, Bless-ed Je - sus, Thou hast loved us, love us still;

Bless-ed Je - sus, Bless-ed Je - sus, Thou hast bought us, thine we are.
Bless-ed Je - sus, Bless-ed Je - sus, Hear thy chil-dren when they pray.
Bless-ed Je - sus, Bless-ed Je - sus, Thou hast loved us, love us still. A-men.

GOSPEL CALL AND RESPONSE

The Lord Is Rich and Merciful

328

Thomas T. Lynch, 1818-1871

SHEPHERDS' PIPES C.M.D.
Annabeth McClelland Gay, 1925-

1 The Lord is rich and mer-ci-ful; The Lord is ver-y kind;
2 The Lord is glo-ri-ous and strong; Our God is ver-y high;
3 The Lord is won-der-ful and wise, As all the a-ges tell;

O come to him, come now to him With a be-liev-ing mind.
O trust in him, trust now in him, And have se-cu-ri-ty.
O learn of him, learn now of him, Then with thee it is well,

His com-forts, they shall strengthen thee, Like flow-ing wa-ters cool,
He shall be to thee like the sea, And thou shalt sure-ly feel
And with his light thou shalt be blest, There-in to work and live,

And he shall for thy spir-it be A foun-tain ev-er full.
His wind, that blow-eth health-i-ly, Thy sick-ness-es to heal.
And he shall be to thee a rest When eve-ning hours ar-rive.

GOSPEL CALL AND RESPONSE

329
O Jesus, Thou Art Standing

William W. How, 1823-1897

ST. HILDA 7.6.7.6.D.
Justin H. Knecht, 1752-1817, and
Edward Husband, 1843-1908

1 O Je - sus, thou art stand - ing Out - side the fast-closed door,
2 O Je - sus, thou art knock - ing, And lo! that hand is scarred,
3 O Je - sus, thou art plead - ing In ac - cents meek and low,

In low - ly pa - tience wait - ing To pass the thresh - old o'er.
And thorns thy brow en - cir - cle, And tears thy face have marred.
"I died for you, my chil - dren, And will ye treat me so?"

Shame on us, Chris - tian broth - ers, His name and sign who bear;
O love that pass - eth knowl - edge, So pa - tient - ly to wait!
O Lord, with shame and sor - row We o - pen now the door;

O shame, thrice shame up - on us, To keep him stand - ing there!
O sin that hath no e - qual, So fast to bar the gate!
Dear Sav - ior, en - ter, en - ter, And leave us nev - er - more! A-men.

GOSPEL CALL AND RESPONSE

One Who Is All Unfit to Count

330

Narayan V. Tilak, 1862-1919
Tr. Nicol Macnicol, 1870-1952

WIGTOWN C.M.
"Scottish Psalter," 1635

1 One who is all un-fit to count
2 Thou dwell-est in un-shad-owed light,
3 Ah, did not he the heaven-ly throne

As schol-ar in thy school, Thou of thy
All sin and shame a-bove. That thou shouldst
A lit-tle thing es-teem, And not un-

love hast named a friend, O kind-ness won-der-ful!
bear our sin and shame, How can I tell such love?
wor-thy for my sake A mor-tal bod-y deem? A-men.

4 So, Love itself in human form,
   For love of me he came;
   I cannot look upon his face
   For shame, for bitter shame.

5 If there is aught of worth in me,
   It comes from thee alone;
   Then keep me safe, for so, O Lord,
   Thou keepest but thine own.

GOSPEL CALL AND RESPONSE

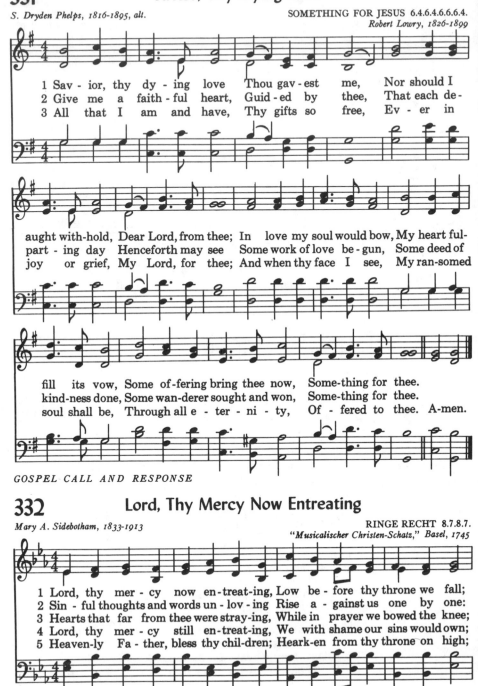

331 Savior, Thy Dying Love

S. Dryden Phelps, 1816-1895, alt.

SOMETHING FOR JESUS 6.4.6.4.6.6.6.4.
Robert Lowry, 1826-1899

1 Sav-ior, thy dy-ing love Thou gav-est me, Nor should I
2 Give me a faith-ful heart, Guid-ed by thee, That each de-
3 All that I am and have, Thy gifts so free, Ev-er in

aught with-hold, Dear Lord, from thee; In love my soul would bow, My heart ful-
part-ing day Henceforth may see Some work of love be-gun, Some deed of
joy or grief, My Lord, for thee; And when thy face I see, My ran-somed

fill its vow, Some of-fering bring thee now, Some-thing for thee.
kind-ness done, Some wan-derer sought and won, Some-thing for thee.
soul shall be, Through all e-ter-ni-ty, Of-fered to thee. A-men.

GOSPEL CALL AND RESPONSE

332 Lord, Thy Mercy Now Entreating

Mary A. Sidebotham, 1833-1913

RINGE RECHT 8.7.8.7.
"Musicalischer Christen-Schatz," Basel, 1745

1 Lord, thy mer-cy now en-treat-ing, Low be-fore thy throne we fall;
2 Sin-ful thoughts and words un-lov-ing Rise a-gainst us one by one;
3 Hearts that far from thee were stray-ing, While in prayer we bowed the knee;
4 Lord, thy mer-cy still en-treat-ing, We with shame our sins would own;
5 Heaven-ly Fa-ther, bless thy chil-dren; Heark-en from thy throne on high;

PRAYER

Our mis-deeds to thee con-fess-ing, On thy name we hum-bly call.
Acts un-wor-thy, deeds un-think-ing, Good that we have left un-done.
Lips that, while thy prais-es sound-ing, Lift-ed not the soul to thee.
From hence-forth, the time re-deem-ing, May we live to thee a-lone.
Lov-ing Sav-ior, Ho-ly Spir-it, Hear and heed our hum-ble cry. A-men.

Father Almighty, Bless Us With Thy Blessing 333

Anonymous
"Berwick Hymnal," 1886

INTEGER VITAE 11.11.11.5.
Friedrich F. Flemming, 1778-1813

1 Fa-ther al-might-y, bless us with thy bless-ing; An-swer in
2 Shep-herd of souls, who bring-est all who seek thee To pas-tures
3 Fa-ther of mer-cy, from thy watch and keep-ing No place can

love thy chil-dren's sup-pli-ca-tion; Hear thou our prayer, the
green be-side the peace-ful wa-ters, Ten-der-est guide, in
part, nor hour of time re-move us; Give us thy good, and

spo-ken and un-spo-ken; Hear us, our Fa-ther.
ways of cheer-ful du-ty Lead us, good Shep-herd.
save us from our e-vil, In-fi-nite Spir-it. A-men.

PRAYER

334 Father, in Thy Mysterious Presence

Samuel Johnson, 1822-1882

DONNE SECOURS 11.10.11.10.
"Genevan Psalter," 1551

In unison

1 Fa - ther, in thy mys - te - rious pres - ence kneel - ing,
2 Lord, we have wan - dered forth through doubt and sor - row,
3 Now, Fa - ther, now, in thy dear pres - ence kneel - ing,

Fain would our souls feel all thy kin - dling love,
And thou hast made each step an on - ward one,
Our spir - its yearn to feel thy kin - dling love;

For we are weak, and need some deep re - veal - ing
And we will ev - er trust each un - known mor - row;
Now make us strong, we need thy deep re - veal - ing

Of trust and strength and calm - ness from a - bove.
Thou wilt sus - tain us till its work is done.
Of trust and strength and calm - ness from a - bove. A-men.

PRAYER

What a Friend We Have in Jesus

335

Joseph Scriven, 1819-1886

ERIE 8.7.8.7.D.
Charles C. Converse, 1832-1918

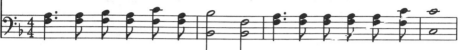

1 What a friend we have in Je - sus, All our sins and griefs to bear!
2 Have we tri - als and temp - ta - tions? Is there trou-ble an - y - where?
3 Are we weak and heav - y lad - en, Cum-bered with a load of care?

What a priv - i - lege to car - ry Ev - ery-thing to God in prayer!
We should nev - er be dis - cour - aged; Take it to the Lord in prayer!
Pre - cious Sav - ior, still our ref - uge, Take it to the Lord in prayer!

Oh, what peace we of - ten for - feit, Oh, what need-less pain we bear,
Can we find a friend so faith - ful, Who will all our sor - rows share?
Do thy friends de-spise, for - sake thee? Take it to the Lord in prayer!

All be-cause we do not car - ry Ev - ery-thing to God in prayer.
Je - sus knows our ev - ery weak-ness; Take it to the Lord in prayer!
In his arms he'll take and shield thee, Thou wilt find a sol - ace there. A-men.

PRAYER

336   O Thou by Whom We Come to God

James Montgomery, 1771-1854, alt.

SONG 67 C.M.
Orlando Gibbons, 1583-1625

1 O thou by whom we come to God, The Life, the Truth, the Way,
2 We per-ish if we cease from prayer; O grant us power to pray;
3 God of all grace, we come to thee With bro-ken, con-trite hearts;
4 Give deep hu-mil-i-ty; the sense Of god-ly sor-row give;
5 Give these, and then thy will be done; Thus strength-ened with all might,

The path of prayer thy-self hast trod, Lord, teach us how to pray.
And, when to meet thee we pre-pare, Lord, meet us by the way.
Give, what thine eye de-lights to see, Truth in the in-ward parts.
A strong, de-sir-ing con-fi-dence To hear thy voice and live.
We by thy Spir-it, and thy Son, Shall pray, and pray a-right. A-men.

PRAYER   *A higher setting may be found at No. 360*

337   Give to the Winds Thy Fears
First Tune

Paul Gerhardt, 1607-1676
Tr. John Wesley, 1703-1791, alt.

ICH HALTE TREULICH STILL S.M.D.
Johann S. Bach, 1685-1750

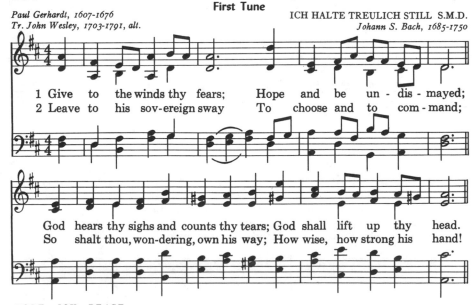

1 Give to the winds thy fears; Hope and be un-dis-mayed;
2 Leave to his sov-ereign sway To choose and to com-mand;

God hears thy sighs and counts thy tears; God shall lift up thy head.
So shalt thou, won-dering, own his way; How wise, how strong his hand!

HOPE, JOY, PEACE

Through waves, and clouds, and storms, He gen-tly clears thy way;
Far, far a-bove thy thought His coun-sel shall ap-pear,

Wait thou his time; so shall this night Soon end in joy-ous day.
When ful-ly he the work hath wrought That caused thy need-less fear. A-men.

Alternative tune, DIADEMATA, *No. 199*

Give to the Winds Thy Fears   338
Second Tune

Paul Gerhardt, 1607-1676
Tr. John Wesley, 1703-1791, alt.

ST. BRIDE S.M.
Samuel Howard, 1710-1782

1 Give to the winds thy fears; Hope and be un-dis-mayed;
2 Through waves, and clouds, and storms, He gen-tly clears thy way;
3 Leave to his sov-ereign sway To choose and to com-mand;
4 Far, far a-bove thy thought His coun-sel shall ap-pear,

God hears thy sighs and counts thy tears; God shall lift up thy head.
Wait thou his time; so shall this night Soon end in joy-ous day.
So shalt thou, won-dering, own his way How wise, how strong his hand!
When ful-ly he the work hath wrought That caused thy need-less fear. A-men.

HOPE, JOY, PEACE

339 All My Hope on God Is Founded

Joachim Neander, 1650-1680
Para. by Robert S. Bridges, 1844-1930

MEINE HOFFNUNG 8.7.8.7.3.3.7.
Melody by Joachim Neander, 1650-1680

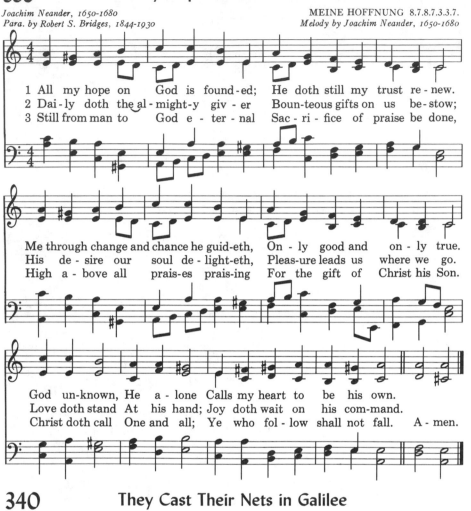

1 All my hope on God is found-ed; He doth still my trust re-new.
2 Dai-ly doth the al-might-y giv-er Boun-teous gifts on us be-stow;
3 Still from man to God e-ter-nal Sac-ri-fice of praise be done,

Me through change and chance he guid-eth, On-ly good and on-ly true.
His de-sire our soul de-light-eth, Pleas-ure leads us where we go.
High a-bove all prais-es prais-ing For the gift of Christ his Son.

God un-known, He a-lone Calls my heart to be his own.
Love doth stand At his hand; Joy doth wait on his com-mand.
Christ doth call One and all; Ye who fol-low shall not fall. A-men.

340 They Cast Their Nets in Galilee

William A. Percy, 1885-1942, alt.

GEORGETOWN C.M.
David McK. Williams, 1887-

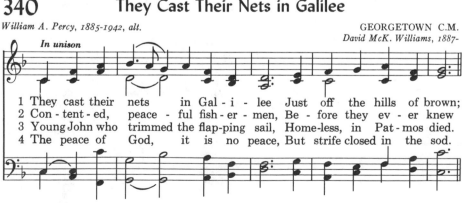

In unison

1 They cast their nets in Gal-i-lee Just off the hills of brown;
2 Con-tent-ed, peace-ful fish-er-men, Be-fore they ev-er knew
3 Young John who trimmed the flap-ping sail, Home-less, in Pat-mos died.
4 The peace of God, it is no peace, But strife closed in the sod.

HOPE, JOY, PEACE

Such hap-py, sim-ple fish-er-folk, Be-fore the Lord came down.
The peace of God that filled their hearts Brim-ful, and broke them too.
Pe-ter, who hauled the teem-ing net, Head down was cru-ci-fied.
Yet, broth-ers, pray for but one thing: The mar-velous peace of God. A-men.

Dear Lord and Father of Mankind 341

John Greenleaf Whittier, 1807-1892

REST 8.6.8.8.6.
Frederick C. Maker, 1844-1927

1 Dear Lord and Fa-ther of man-kind, For-give our fool-ish ways.
2 In sim-ple trust like theirs who heard, Be-side the Syr-ian sea,
3 O sab-bath rest by Gal-i-lee! O calm of hills a-bove!
4 Drop thy still dews of qui-et-ness, Till all our striv-ings cease;
5 Breathe through the puls-es of de-sire Thy cool-ness and thy balm;

Re-clothe us in our right-ful mind; In pur-er lives thy
The gra-cious call-ing of the Lord, Let us, like them, with-
Where Je-sus knelt to share with thee The si-lence of e-
Take from our souls the strain and stress, And let our or-dered
Let sense be dumb, let flesh re-tire: Speak through the earth-quake,

serv-ice find, In deep-er rev-erence, praise.
out a word, Rise up and fol-low thee.
ter-ni-ty, In-ter-pret-ed by love.
lives con-fess The beau-ty of thy peace.
wind, and fire, O still, small voice of calm. A-men.

HOPE, JOY, PEACE

342

I Need Thee Every Hour

Annie S. Hawks, 1835-1918
Robert Lowry, 1826-1899, Refrain

NEED 6.4.6.4. *with Refrain*
Robert Lowry, 1826-1899

1 I need thee ev - ery hour, Most gra - cious Lord;
2 I need thee ev - ery hour; Stay thou near by;
3 I need thee ev - ery hour In joy or pain;
4 I need thee ev - ery hour; Teach me thy will,

No ten - der voice like thine Can peace af - ford.
Temp - ta - tions lose their power When thou art nigh.
Come quick - ly, and a - bide Or life is vain.
And thy rich prom - is - es In me ful - fill.

REFRAIN

I need thee, oh, I need thee; Ev - ery hour I need thee;

O bless me now, my Sav - ior, I come to thee. A - men.

HOPE, JOY, PEACE

In Heavenly Love Abiding

343

Anna L. Waring 1823-1910

NYLAND 7.6.7.6.D.
Traditional Finnish Melody
Harm. by David Evans, 1874-1948

1 In heaven-ly love a-bid-ing, No change my heart shall fear,
2 Wher-ev-er he may guide me, No want shall turn me back;
3 Green pas-tures are be-fore me, Which yet I have not seen;

And safe is such con-fid-ing, For noth-ing chang-es here.
My shep-herd is be-side me, And noth-ing can I lack.
Bright skies will soon be o'er me, Where the dark clouds have been.

The storm may roar with-out me, My heart may low be laid,
His wis-dom ev-er wak-eth; His sight is nev-er dim;
My hope I can-not meas-ure; The path to life is free;

But God is round a-bout me, And can I be dis-mayed?
He knows the way he tak-eth, And I will walk with him.
My Sav-ior has my treas-ure, And he will walk with me. A-men.

Alternative tune, EWING, *No. 309*

HOPE, JOY, PEACE

344 Lead Us, Heavenly Father, Lead Us

James Edmeston, 1791-1867

DULCE CARMEN 8.7.8.7.8.7.
"An Essay on the Church Plain Chant," 1782

1 Lead us, heaven-ly Fa-ther, lead us O'er the world's tem-
2 Sav-ior, breathe for-give-ness o'er us; All our weak-ness
3 Spir-it of our God, de-scend-ing, Fill our hearts with

pes-tuous sea; Guard us, guide us, keep us, feed us,
thou dost know; Thou didst tread this earth be-fore us;
heaven-ly joy; Love with ev-ery pas-sion blend-ing,

For we have no help but thee, Yet pos-sess-ing
Thou didst feel its keen-est woe; Lone and drear-y,
Pleas-ure that can nev-er cloy; Thus pro-vid-ed,

ev-ery bless-ing, If our God our Fa-ther be.
faint and wea-ry, Through the des-ert thou didst go.
par-doned, guid-ed, Noth-ing can our peace de-stroy. A-men.

HOPE, JOY, PEACE

Rejoice, Ye Pure in Heart

345

Edward H. Plumptre, 1821-1891

MARION S.M. *with Refrain*
Arthur H. Messiter, 1834-1916

1 Re - joice, ye pure in heart; Re - joice, give thanks and sing;
2 Bright youth and snow-crowned age, Strong men and maid - ens meek,
3 With voice as full and strong As o - cean's surg - ing praise,
4 Yes, on through life's long path, Still chant - ing as ye go,

Your fes - tal ban - ner wave on high, The cross of Christ your King!
Raise high your free, ex - ult - ing song, God's won-drous prais-es speak.
Send forth the hymns our fa - thers loved, The psalms of an - cient days.
From youth to age, by night and day, In glad-ness and in woe.

REFRAIN

Re - joice, re - joice, Re - joice, give thanks and sing. A-men.

Re - joice, re - joice,

5 Still lift your standard high,
Still march in firm array,
As warriors through the darkness toil
Till dawns the golden day!

6 Praise him who reigns on high,
The Lord whom we adore,
The Father, Son, and Holy Ghost,
One God for evermore!

HOPE, JOY, PEACE

346   Come, Let Us Join With Faithful Souls

William G. Tarrant, 1853-1928

AZMON C.M.
Carl G. Gläser, 1784-1829
Mason's "Modern Psalmody," 1839

1 Come, let us join with faith-ful souls Our song of faith to sing;
2 Faith-ful are all who love the truth And dare the truth to tell,
3 And faith-ful are the gen-tle hearts To whom the power is given
4 O Lord of hosts, our faith re - new, And grant us, in thy love,

One brother-hood in heart are we, And one our Lord and King.
Who steadfast stand at God's right hand And strive to serve him well.
Of ev-ery hearth to make a home, Of ev-ery home a heaven.
To sing the songs of vic - to - ry With faith-ful souls a - bove. A-men.

A higher setting may be found at No. 223

347   Lord, As to Thy Dear Cross

John H. Gurney, 1802-1862

ST. BERNARD C.M.
"Tochter Sion," Cologne, 1741

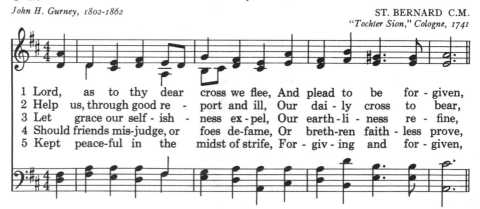

1 Lord, as to thy dear cross we flee, And plead to be for - given,
2 Help us, through good re - port and ill, Our dai - ly cross to bear,
3 Let grace our self - ish - ness ex - pel, Our earth - li - ness re - fine,
4 Should friends mis-judge, or foes de-fame, Or breth-ren faith - less prove,
5 Kept peace-ful in the midst of strife, For - giv - ing and for - given,

FAITH AND ASPIRATION

So let thy life our pat-tern be, And form our souls for heaven.
Like thee, to do our Fa-ther's will, Our brethren's grief to share.
And kind-ness in our bos-oms dwell As free and true as thine.
Then, like thine own, be all our aim To con-quer them by love.
O may we lead the pil-grim's life, And fol-low thee to heaven. A-men.

My Faith Looks Up to Thee 348

Ray Palmer, 1808-1887, alt.

OLIVET 6.6.4.6.6.6.4.
Lowell Mason, 1792-1872

1 My faith looks up to thee, Thou Lamb of Cal - va - ry,
2 May thy rich grace im - part Strength to my faint - ing heart,
3 While life's dark maze I tread, And griefs a - round me spread,
4 When ends life's tran - sient dream, When death's cold; sul - len stream

Sav - ior di - vine! Now hear me while I pray; Take all my
My zeal in - spire; As thou hast died for me, Oh, may my
Be thou my guide; Bid dark-ness turn to day; Wipe sor-row's
Shall o'er me roll, Blest Sav - ior, then, in love, Fear and dis -

guilt a - way; Oh, let me from this day Be whol - ly thine.
love to thee Pure, warm, and changeless be, A liv - ing fire.
tears a - way; Nor let me ev - er stray From thee a - side.
trust re-move; Oh, bear me safe a - bove, A ran - somed soul. A-men.

FAITH AND ASPIRATION

349

O for a Closer Walk With God
First Tune

William Cowper, 1731-1800

CAITHNESS C.M.
"Scottish Psalter," 1635

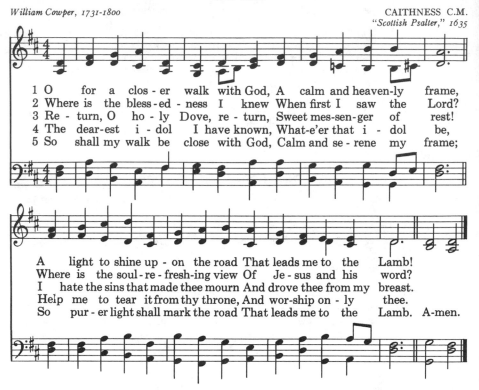

1 O for a clos-er walk with God, A calm and heaven-ly frame,
2 Where is the bless-ed-ness I knew When first I saw the Lord?
3 Re-turn, O ho-ly Dove, re-turn, Sweet mes-sen-ger of rest!
4 The dear-est i-dol I have known, What-e'er that i-dol be,
5 So shall my walk be close with God, Calm and se-rene my frame;

A light to shine up-on the road That leads me to the Lamb!
Where is the soul-re-fresh-ing view Of Je-sus and his word?
I hate the sins that made thee mourn And drove thee from my breast.
Help me to tear it from thy throne, And wor-ship on-ly thee.
So pur-er light shall mark the road That leads me to the Lamb. A-men.

350

O for a Closer Walk With God
Second Tune

William Cowper, 1731-1800

BEATITUDO C.M.
John B. Dykes, 1823-1876

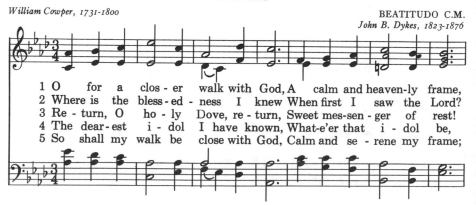

1 O for a clos-er walk with God, A calm and heaven-ly frame,
2 Where is the bless-ed-ness I knew When first I saw the Lord?
3 Re-turn, O ho-ly Dove, re-turn, Sweet mes-sen-ger of rest!
4 The dear-est i-dol I have known, What-e'er that i-dol be,
5 So shall my walk be close with God, Calm and se-rene my frame;

FAITH AND ASPIRATION

A light to shine up-on the road That leads me to the Lamb!
Where is the soul-re-fresh-ing view Of Je-sus and his word?
I hate the sins that made thee mourn And drove thee from my breast.
Help me to tear it from thy throne, And wor-ship on-ly thee.
So pur-er light shall mark the road That leads me to the Lamb. A-men.

Nearer, My God, to Thee 351

Sarah F. Adams, 1805-1848

BETHANY 6.4.6.4.6.6.6.4.
Lowell Mason, 1792-1872

1 Near-er, my God, to thee, Near-er to thee, E'en though it be a cross
2 Though like the wan-der-er, The sun gone down, Dark-ness be o-ver me,
3 There let the way ap-pear Steps un-to heaven; All that thou send-est me
4 Then, with my wak-ing thoughts Bright with thy praise, Out of my ston-y griefs
5 Or if on joy-ful wing Cleav-ing the sky, Sun, moon, and stars for-got,

That rais-eth me; Still all my song would be, Near-er, my God, to thee,
My rest a stone, Yet in my dreams I'd be, Near-er, my God, to thee,
In mer-cy given; An-gels to beck-on me Near-er, my God, to thee,
Beth-el I'll raise; So by my woes to be Near-er, my God, to thee,
Up-ward I fly, Still all my song shall be, Near-er, my God, to thee,

Near-er, my God, to thee, Near-er to thee. A-men.

FAITH AND ASPIRATION

352

Lift Up Your Hearts!

Henry M. Butler, 1833-1918, alt.

WOODLANDS 10.10.10.10.
Walter Greatorex, 1877-1949

In unison

1 "Lift up your hearts!" We lift them, Lord, to thee;
2 A - bove the lev - el of the for - mer years,
3 Lift ev - ery gift that thou thy - self hast given;
4 Then, as the trum - pet call, in aft - er years,

Here at thy feet none oth - er may we see.
The mire of sin, the weight of guilt - y fears,
Low lies the best till lift - ed up to heaven;
"Lift up your hearts!" rings peal - ing in our ears,

"Lift up your hearts!" E'en so, with one ac - cord,
The mist of doubt, the blight of love's de - cay,
Low lie the bound - ing heart, the teem - ing brain,
Still shall those hearts re - spond, with full ac - cord,

We lift them up, we lift them to the Lord.
O Lord of light, lift all our hearts to - day!
Till, sent from God, they mount to God a - gain.
"We lift them up, we lift them to the Lord!" A-men.

FAITH AND ASPIRATION

Alternative tune, SURSUM CORDA, *No. 286*

Lord, I Want to Be a Christian

353

Negro Spiritual

I WANT TO BE A CHRISTIAN *Irregular*
Negro Melody

1 Lord, I want to be a Chris-tian In my heart, in my heart;
2 Lord, I want to be more lov-ing In my heart, in my heart;
3 Lord, I want to be more ho-ly In my heart, in my heart;
4 Lord, I want to be like Je-sus In my heart, in my heart;

Lord, I want to be a Chris-tian In my heart.
Lord, I want to be more lov-ing In my heart.
Lord, I want to be more ho-ly In my heart.
Lord, I want to be like Je-sus In my heart.

In my heart,   In my heart,
In my heart,   In my heart,

Lord, I want to be a Chris-tian In my heart.
Lord, I want to be more lov-ing In my heart.
Lord, I want to be more ho-ly In my heart.
Lord, I want to be like Je-sus In my heart.

FAITH AND ASPIRATION

354
Who Trusts in God, a Strong Abode
First Tune

Joachim Magdeburg, c.1525-?
Tr. B. H. Kennedy, 1804-1889
Alt. by William W. How, 1823-1897

WAS MEIN GOTT WILL 8.7.8.7.D.
Melody by Claude de Sermisy, c.1490-1562
Harm. from J. S. Bach, 1685-1750

1 Who trusts in God, a strong a-bode In heaven and earth pos-sess-es;
2 Though Sa-tan's wrath be-set our path And world-ly scorn as-sail us,
3 In all the strife of mor-tal life Our feet shall stand se-cure-ly;

Who looks in love to Christ a-bove, No fear his heart op-press-es.
While thou art near we will not fear, Thy strength shall nev-er fail us.
Temp-ta-tion's hour shall lose its power, For thou shalt guard us sure-ly.

In thee a-lone, dear Lord, we own Sweet hope and con-so-la-tion:
Thy rod and staff shall keep us safe, And guide our steps for-ev-er,
O God, re-new with heaven-ly dew Our bod-y, soul, and spir-it

Our shield from foes, our balm for woes, Our great and sure sal-va-tion.
Nor shades of death, nor hell be-neath, Our souls from thee shall sev-er.
Un-til we stand at thy right hand, Through Je-sus' sav-ing mer-it. A-men.

FAITH AND ASPIRATION

Who Trusts in God, a Strong Abode
Second Tune

Joachim Magdeburg, c.1525-?
Tr. B. H. Kennedy, 1804-1889
Alt. by William W. How, 1823-1897

BISHOPGARTH 8.7.8.7.D.
Arthur S. Sullivan, 1842-1900

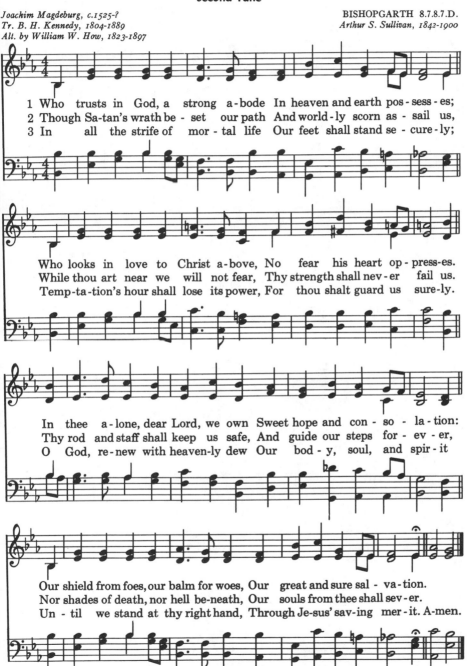

1 Who trusts in God, a strong a-bode In heaven and earth pos-sess-es;
2 Though Sa-tan's wrath be-set our path And world-ly scorn as-sail us,
3 In all the strife of mor-tal life Our feet shall stand se-cure-ly;

Who looks in love to Christ a-bove, No fear his heart op-press-es.
While thou art near we will not fear, Thy strength shall nev-er fail us.
Temp-ta-tion's hour shall lose its power, For thou shalt guard us sure-ly.

In thee a-lone, dear Lord, we own Sweet hope and con-so-la-tion:
Thy rod and staff shall keep us safe, And guide our steps for-ev-er,
O God, re-new with heaven-ly dew Our bod-y, soul, and spir-it

Our shield from foes, our balm for woes, Our great and sure sal-va-tion.
Nor shades of death, nor hell be-neath, Our souls from thee shall sev-er.
Un-til we stand at thy right hand, Through Je-sus' sav-ing mer-it. A-men.

FAITH AND ASPIRATION

356 Make Me a Captive, Lord

George Matheson, 1842-1906

LLANLLYFNI S.M.D.
John Jones, 1797-1857
Adapted by David Jenkins, 1849-1915

1 Make me a cap-tive, Lord, And then I shall be free;
2 My heart is weak and poor Un-til it mas-ter find;
3 My will is not my own Till thou hast made it thine;

Force me to ren-der up my sword, And I shall con-queror be.
It has no spring of ac-tion sure, It va-ries with the wind.
If it would reach a mon-arch's throne It must its crown re - sign;

I sink in life's a - larms When by my-self I stand;
It can-not free-ly move Till thou hast wrought its chain;
It on - ly stands un-bent A - mid the clash-ing strife,

Im - pris-on me with-in thine arms, And strong shall be my hand.
En - slave it with thy match-less love, And death-less it shall reign.
When on thy bos-om it has leant And found in thee its life. A - men.

FAITH AND ASPIRATION

Strong Son of God, Immortal Love

357

Alfred Tennyson, 1809-189?

ROCKINGHAM L.M.
Adapted by Edward Miller, 1731-1807

1 Strong Son of God, im - mor - tal Love, Whom we, that have not seen thy face, By faith, and faith a - lone, em - brace, Be - liev - ing where we can - not prove,

2 Thou wilt not leave us in the dust; Thou mad - est man, he knows not why. He thinks he was not made to die; And thou hast made him, thou art just.

3 Thou seem - est hu - man and di - vine, The high - est, ho - liest man - hood, thou. Our wills are ours, we know not how; Our wills are ours to make them thine.

4 Our lit - tle sys - tems have their day; They have their day and cease to be; They are but bro - ken lights of thee, And thou, O Lord, art more than they. A - men.

5 We have but faith; we cannot know,
For knowledge is of things we see;
And yet we trust it comes from thee,
A beam in darkness; let it grow.

6 Let knowledge grow from more to more,
But more of reverence in us dwell;
That mind and soul, according well,
May make one music as before.

Alternative tune, ST. CRISPIN, *No. 320*

FAITH AND ASPIRATION

358

Rock of Ages
First Tune

Augustus M. Toplady, 1740-1778, alt.

TOPLADY 7.7.7.7.7.7.
Thomas Hastings, 1784-1872

1 Rock of a - ges, cleft for me, Let me hide my-self in thee;
2 Not the la - bors of my hands Can ful - fill thy law's de-mands;
3 Noth-ing in my hand I bring, Sim-ply to thy cross I cling;

Let the wa - ter and the blood, From thy riv - en side which flowed,
Could my zeal no res - pite know, Could my tears for - ev - er flow,
Na - ked, come to thee for dress; Help-less, look to thee for grace;

Be of sin the dou - ble cure, Cleanse me from its guilt and power.
All for sin could not a - tone; Thou must save, and thou a - lone.
Foul, I to the foun-tain fly; Wash me, Sav-ior, or I die! A-men.

4 While I draw this fleeting breath,
    When mine eyes shall close in death,
When I soar to worlds unknown,
    See thee on thy judgment throne,
Rock of ages, cleft for me,
    Let me hide myself in thee!

FAITH AND ASPIRATION

Rock of Ages

Second Tune

Augustus M. Toplady, 1740-1778, alt.

REDHEAD NO. 76 7.7.7.7.7.7.
Richard Redhead, 1820-1901

359

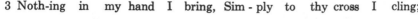

1 Rock of a - ges, cleft for me, Let me hide my - self in thee;
2 Not the la - bors of my hands Can ful - fill thy law's de-mands;
3 Noth-ing in my hand I bring, Sim - ply to thy cross I cling;

Let the wa - ter and the blood, From thy riv - en side which flowed,
Could my zeal no res - pite know, Could my tears for - ev - er flow,
Na - ked, come to thee for dress; Help-less, look to thee for grace;

Be of sin the dou - ble cure, Cleanse me from its guilt and power.
All for sin could not a - tone; Thou must save, and thou a - lone.
Foul, I to the foun-tain fly; Wash me, Sav-ior, or I die! A - men.

4 While I draw this fleeting breath,
   When mine eyes shall close in death,
When I soar to worlds unknown,
   See thee on thy judgment throne,
Rock of ages, cleft for me,
   Let me hide myself in thee!

FAITH AND ASPIRATION

360 Within the Maddening Maze of Things

John Greenleaf Whittier, 1807-1892

SONG 67 C.M.
Orlando Gibbons, 1583-1625

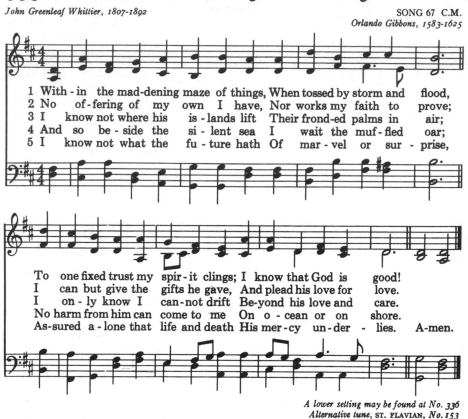

1 With-in the mad-dening maze of things, When tossed by storm and flood,
2 No of-fering of my own I have, Nor works my faith to prove;
3 I know not where his is-lands lift Their frond-ed palms in air;
4 And so be-side the si-lent sea I wait the muf-fled oar;
5 I know not what the fu-ture hath Of mar-vel or sur-prise,

To one fixed trust my spir-it clings; I know that God is good!
I can but give the gifts he gave, And plead his love for love.
I on-ly know I can-not drift Be-yond his love and care.
No harm from him can come to me On o-cean or on shore.
As-sured a-lone that life and death His mer-cy un-der-lies. A-men.

A lower setting may be found at No. 336
Alternative tune, ST. FLAVIAN, No. 153

361 Have Faith in God

Bryn A. Rees, 1911-

SOUTHWELL S.M.
Adapted from Damon's "Psalmes," 1579

1 Have faith in God, my heart; Trust and be un-a-fraid;
2 Have faith in God, my mind, Though oft thy light burns low;
3 Have faith in God, my soul; His cross for-ev-er stands;
4 Lord Je-sus, make me whole; Grant me no rest-ing place,

FAITH AND ASPIRATION

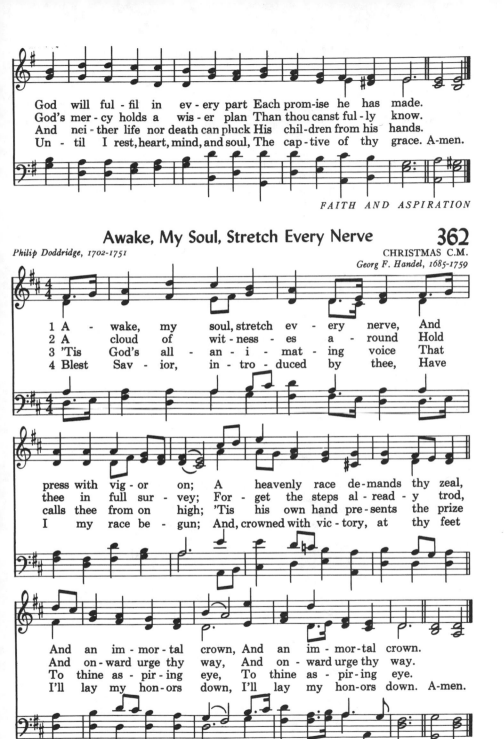

God will ful - fil in ev - ery part Each prom - ise he has made.
God's mer - cy holds a wis - er plan Than thou canst ful - ly know.
And nei - ther life nor death can pluck His chil - dren from his hands.
Un - til I rest, heart, mind, and soul, The cap - tive of thy grace. A - men.

FAITH AND ASPIRATION

Awake, My Soul, Stretch Every Nerve 362

Philip Doddridge, 1702-1751

CHRISTMAS C.M.
Georg F. Handel, 1685-1759

1 A - wake, my soul, stretch ev - ery nerve, And
2 A cloud of wit - ness - es a - round Hold
3 'Tis God's all - an - i - mat - ing voice That
4 Blest Sav - ior, in - tro - duced by thee, Have

press with vig - or on; A heavenly race de - mands thy zeal,
thee in full sur - vey; For - get the steps al - read - y trod,
calls thee from on high; 'Tis his own hand pre - sents the prize
I my race be - gun; And, crowned with vic - tory, at thy feet

And an im - mor - tal crown, And an im - mor - tal crown.
And on - ward urge thy way, And on - ward urge thy way.
To thine as - pir - ing eye, To thine as - pir - ing eye.
I'll lay my hon - ors down, I'll lay my hon - ors down. A - men.

PILGRIMAGE AND CONFLICT

363

A Mighty Fortress Is Our God

Based on Psalm 46
Martin Luther, 1483-1546
Tr. Frederick H. Hedge, 1805-1890

EIN' FESTE BURG 8.7.8.7.6.6.6.6.7.
Melody by Martin Luther, 1483-1546

1 A might-y for-tress is our God, A bul-wark nev-er fail-ing;
2 Did we in our own strength con-fide, Our striv-ing would be los-ing,
3 And though this world, with dev-ils filled, Should threat-en to un-do us,
4 That word a-bove all earth-ly powers, No thanks to them, a-bid-eth;

Our help-er he a-mid the flood Of mor-tal ills pre-vail-ing.
Were not the right man on our side, The man of God's own choos-ing.
We will not fear, for God hath willed His truth to tri-umph through us.
The Spir-it and the gifts are ours Through him who with us sid-eth.

For still our an-cient foe Doth seek to work us woe; His craft and power are
Dost ask who that may be? Christ Je-sus, it is he; Lord Sab-a-oth his
The prince of dark-ness grim, We trem-ble not for him; His rage we can en-
Let goods and kin-dred go, This mor-tal life al-so; The bod-y they may

great, And armed with cru-el hate, On earth is not his e-qual.
name. From age to age the same, And he must win the bat-tle.
dure, For lo, his doom is sure: One lit-tle word shall fell him.
kill; God's truth a-bid-eth still, His king-dom is for-ev-er. A-men.

PILGRIMAGE AND CONFLICT

Christian, Dost Thou See Them

364

Attr. to St. Andrew of Crete, c.660-c.732
Tr. John M. Neale, 1818-1866, alt.

ST. ANDREW OF CRETE 6.5.6.5.D.
John B. Dykes, 1823-1876

1 Chris-tian, dost thou see them On the ho-ly ground,
2 Chris-tian, dost thou feel them, How they work with-in,
3 Chris-tian, dost thou hear them, How they speak thee fair,
4 "Well I know thy trou-ble, O my serv-ant true;

How the powers of dark-ness Com-pass thee a-round?
Striv-ing, tempt-ing, lur-ing, Goad-ing in-to sin?
"Al-ways fast and vig-il, Al-ways watch and prayer?"
Thou art ver-y wea-ry; I was wea-ry, too.

Chris-tian, up and smite them, Count-ing gain but loss,
Chris-tian, nev-er trem-ble, Nev-er be down-cast;
Chris-tian, an-swer bold-ly, "While I breathe I pray!"
But that toil shall make thee Some day all mine own,

In the strength that com-eth By the ho-ly cross.
Gird thee for the bat-tle; Watch and pray and fast.
Peace shall fol-low bat-tle; Night shall end in day.
And the end of sor-row Shall be near my throne." A-men.

PILGRIMAGE AND CONFLICT

365

Faith of Our Fathers

Frederick W. Faber, 1814-1863, alt.

ST. CATHERINE 8.8.8.8.8.8.
Henri F. Hemy, 1818-1888
Adapted by James G. Walton, 1821-1905

1 Faith of our fa - thers, liv - ing still In spite of dun - geon,
2 Our fa - thers, chained in pris - ons dark, Were still in heart and
3 Faith of our fa - thers, God's great power Shall win all na - tions
4 Faith of our fa - thers, we will love Both friend and foe in

fire, and sword. O how our hearts beat high with joy
con-science free, And blest would be their chil - dren's fate,
un - to thee, And through the truth that comes from God,
all our strife, And preach thee, too, as love knows how,

When-e'er we hear that glo - rious word! Faith of our fa - thers,
If they, like them, should die for thee. Faith of our fa - thers,
Man - kind shall then in - deed be free. Faith of our fa - thers,
By kind - ly words and vir - tuous life. Faith of our fa - thers,

ho - ly faith, We will be true to thee till death. A - men.

PILGRIMAGE AND CONFLICT

God of Grace and God of Glory

Harry Emerson Fosdick, 1878-

CWM RHONDDA 8.7.8.7.8.7.7.
John Hughes, 1873-1932

1 God of grace and God of glo - ry, On thy peo - ple
2 Lo! the hosts of e - vil round us Scorn thy Christ, as -
3 Cure thy chil - dren's war - ring mad - ness; Bend our pride to
4 Set our feet on loft - y pla - ces; Gird our lives that
5 Save us from weak res - ig - na - tion To the e - vils

pour thy power; Crown thine an - cient church's sto - ry; Bring her bud to
sail his ways! From the fears that long have bound us, Free our hearts to
thy con - trol; Shame our wan - ton, self - ish glad - ness, Rich in things and
they may be Arm-ored with all Christ-like gra - ces In the fight to
we de - plore; Let the search for thy sal - va - tion Be our glo - ry

glo - rious flower. Grant us wis - dom, Grant us cour - age,
faith and praise. Grant us wis - dom, Grant us cour - age,
poor in soul. Grant us wis - dom, Grant us cour - age,
set men free. Grant us wis - dom, Grant us cour - age,
ev - er - more. Grant us wis - dom, Grant us cour - age,

For the fac - ing of this hour, For the fac - ing of this hour.
For the liv - ing of these days, For the liv - ing of these days.
Lest we miss thy king-dom's goal, Lest we miss thy king-dom's goal.
That we fail not man nor thee, That we fail not man nor thee.
Serv-ing thee whom we a - dore, Serv-ing thee whom we a - dore. A-men.

Alternative tune, REGENT SQUARE, *No. 263*

PILGRIMAGE AND CONFLICT

367

Fight the Good Fight

John S. B. Monsell, 1811-1875, alt.

PENTECOST L.M.
William Boyd, 1847-1928

1 Fight the good fight with all thy might! Christ is thy strength, and Christ thy right. Lay hold on life, and it shall be Thy joy and crown e-ter-nal-ly.

2 Run the straight race through God's good grace; Lift up thine eyes, and seek his face. Life with its way be-fore us lies; Christ is the path, and Christ the prize.

3 Cast care a-side, lean on thy guide; His bound-less mer-cy will pro-vide. Trust, and thy trust-ing soul shall prove Christ is its life, and Christ its love.

4 Faint not nor fear, his arms are near; He chang-eth not, and thou art dear. On-ly be-lieve, and thou shalt see That Christ is all in all to thee. A-men.

368

Father, Hear the Prayer We Offer

Love M. Willis, 1824-1908, and others

REGENSBURG 8.7.8.7.
Melody by Johann Crüger, 1598-1662

1 Fa-ther, hear the prayer we of-fer: Not for ease that prayer shall be,

2 Not for-ev-er in green pas-tures Do we ask our way to be,

3 Not for-ev-er by still wa-ters Would we i-dly rest and stay,

4 Be our strength in hours of weak-ness, In our wan-derings be our guide;

PILGRIMAGE AND CONFLICT

But for strength that we may ev - er Live our lives cou - ra - geous - ly.
But the steep and rug-ged path-way May we tread re - joic - ing - ly.
But would smite the liv-ing foun-tains From the rocks a - long our way.
Through en-deav - or, fail-ure, dan-ger, Fa - ther, be thou at our side. A - men.

God's Glory Is a Wondrous Thing 369

Frederick W. Faber, 1814-1863

HUMMEL C.M.
Heinrich C. Zeuner, 1795-1875

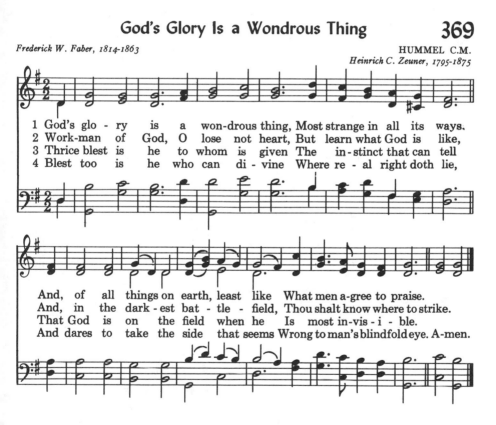

1 God's glo - ry is a won-drous thing, Most strange in all its ways.
2 Work-man of God, O lose not heart, But learn what God is like,
3 Thrice blest is he to whom is given The in-stinct that can tell
4 Blest too is he who can di - vine Where re - al right doth lie,

And, of all things on earth, least like What men a-gree to praise.
And, in the dark - est bat - tle - field, Thou shalt know where to strike.
That God is on the field when he Is most in-vis - i - ble.
And dares to take the side that seems Wrong to man's blindfold eye. A - men.

5 For right is right, since God is God,
   And right the day must win;
   To doubt would be disloyalty,
   To falter would be sin.

370 He Leadeth Me, O Blessed Thought

Joseph H. Gilmore, 1834-1918

HE LEADETH ME L.M. *with Refrain*
William B. Bradbury, 1816-1868

1 He lead-eth me, O bless-ed thought! O words with heaven-ly com-fort fraught!
2 Lord, I would clasp thy hand in mine, Nor ev - er mur - mur nor re-pine;
3 And when my task on earth is done, When, by thy grace, the vic-tory's won,

What-e'er I do, wher-e'er I be, Still 'tis God's hand that lead-eth me.
Con-tent, what-ev - er lot I see, Since 'tis my God that lead-eth me.
E'en death's cold wave I will not flee, Since God through Jor-dan lead-eth me.

REFRAIN

He lead-eth me, he lead-eth me, By his own hand he lead-eth me;

His faith-ful fol-lower I would be, For by his hand he lead-eth me. A-men.

PILGRIMAGE AND CONFLICT

He Who Would Valiant Be

371

John Bunyan, 1628-1688, alt.

ST. DUNSTAN'S 6.5.6.5.6.6.6.5.
C. Winfred Douglas, 1867-1944

1 He who would val - iant be 'Gainst all dis - as - ter,
2 Who so be - set him round With dis - mal sto - ries,
3 Since, Lord, thou dost de - fend Us with thy Spir - it,

Let him in con - stan - cy Fol - low the Mas - ter.
Do but them - selves con - found; His strength the more is.
We know we at the end Shall life in - her - it.

There's no dis - cour - age - ment Shall make him once re - lent
No foes shall stay his might, Though he with gi - ants fight;
Then fan - cies, flee a - way! I'll fear not what men say;

His first a - vowed in - tent To be a pil - grim.
He will make good his right To be a pil - grim.
I'll la - bor night and day To be a pil - grim. A-men.

PILGRIMAGE AND CONFLICT

How Firm a Foundation

K.
Rippon's "A Selection of Hymns," 1787, alt.

ADESTE FIDELES 11.11.11.11.
John F. Wade's "Cantus Diversi," 1751

1 How firm a foun - da - tion, ye saints of the Lord,
2 "Fear not, I am with thee, oh, be not dis - mayed,
3 "When through the deep wa - ters I call thee to go,
4 "When through fi - ery tri - als thy path - way shall lie,

Is laid for your faith in his ex - cel - lent word!
For I am thy God, and will still give thee aid.
The riv - ers of woe shall not thee o - ver - flow;
My grace, all - suf - fi - cient, shall be thy sup - ply.

What more can he say than to you he hath said,
I'll strength - en thee, help thee, and cause thee to stand,
For I will be near thee, thy trou - bles to bless,
The flame shall not hurt thee; I on - ly de - sign

To you who for ref - uge to Je - sus have fled?
Up - held by my right - eous, om - nip - o - tent hand,
And sanc - ti - fy to thee thy deep - est dis - tress,
Thy dross to con - sume, and thy gold to re - fine,

PILGRIMAGE AND CONFLICT

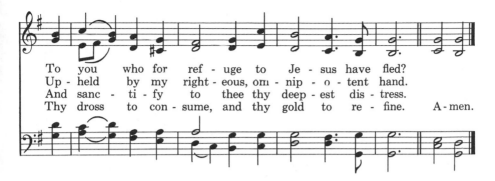

To you who for ref - uge to Je - sus have fled?
Up - held by my right - eous, om - nip - o - tent hand.
And sanc - ti - fy to thee thy deep - est dis - tress.
Thy dross to con - sume, and thy gold to re - fine. A - men.

5 "The soul that on Jesus hath leaned for repose,
   I will not, I will not desert to his foes;
   That soul, though all hell should endeavor to shake,
   I'll never, no, never, no, never forsake.
   I'll never, no, never, no, never forsake!"

God Is My Strong Salvation 373

Based on Psalm 27
James Montgomery, 1771-1854
MEIN LEBEN 7.6.7.6.
Melody by Melchior Vulpius, c.1560-1616

1 God is my strong sal - va - tion; What foe have I to fear?
2 Though hosts en - camp a - round me, Firm in the fight I stand;
3 Place on the Lord re - li - ance, My soul, with cour - age wait;
4 His might thy heart shall strength-en, His love thy joy in - crease;

In dark-ness and temp-ta - tion My light, my help is near.
What ter-ror can con - found me, With God at my right hand?
His truth be thine af - fi - ance, When faint and des - o - late.
Mer-cy thy days shall length-en; The Lord will give thee peace. A-men.

PILGRIMAGE AND CONFLICT

374 In the Hour of Trial

James Montgomery, 1771-1854, alt.

PENITENCE 6.5.6.5.D.
Spencer Lane, 1843-1903

1 In the hour of tri - al, Je - sus, plead for me,
2 With for - bid - den pleas - ures Would this vain world charm,
3 Should thy mer - cy send me Sor - row, toil, or woe,

Lest by base de - ni - al I de - part from thee;
Or its sor - did treas - ures Spread to work me harm;
Or should pain at - tend me On my path be - low,

When thou seest me wa - ver, With a look re - call,
Bring to my re - mem - brance Sad Geth - sem - a - ne,
Grant that I may nev - er Fail thy hand to see;

Nor for fear or fa - vor Suf - fer me to fall.
Or, in dark - er sem - blance, Cross-crowned Cal - va - ry.
Grant that I may ev - er Cast my care on thee. A-men.

PILGRIMAGE AND CONFLICT

Lead On, O King Eternal

Ernest W. Shurtleff, 1862-1917

LANCASHIRE 7.6.7.6.D.
Henry T. Smart, 1813-1879

375

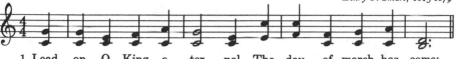

1 Lead on, O King e - ter - nal, The day of march has come;
2 Lead on, O King e - ter - nal, Till sin's fierce war shall cease,
3 Lead on, O King e - ter - nal, We fol - low, not with fears,

Hence-forth in fields of con - quest Thy tents shall be our home.
And ho - li - ness shall whis - per The sweet a - men of peace.
For glad - ness breaks like morn - ing Wher-e'er thy face ap - pears.

Through days of prep - a - ra - tion Thy grace has made us strong,
For not with swords' loud clash - ing, Nor roll of stir - ring drums,
Thy cross is lift - ed o'er us; We jour - ney in its light;

And now, O King e - ter - nal, We lift our bat - tle song.
But deeds of love and mer - cy, The heavenly king-dom comes.
The crown a - waits the con - quest; Lead on, O God of might. A-men.

A higher setting may be found at No. 192
Alternative tune, LLANGLOFFAN, *No. 436*

PILGRIMAGE AND CONFLICT

376

Lead Us, O Father

William H. Burleigh, 1812-1871

LANGRAN 10.10.10.10.
James Langran, 1835-1909

1 Lead us, O Fa - ther, in the paths of peace;
2 Lead us, O Fa - ther, in the paths of truth;
3 Lead us, O Fa - ther, in the paths of right;
4 Lead us, O Fa - ther, to thy heaven - ly rest,

With - out thy guid - ing hand we go a - stray,
Un - helped by thee, in er - ror's maze we grope,
Blind - ly we stum - ble when we walk a - lone,
How - ev - er rough and steep the path may be,

And doubts ap - pall, and sor - rows still in - crease;
While pas - sion stains and fol - ly dims our youth,
In - volved in shad - ows of a mor - tal night;
Through joy or sor - row, as thou deem - est best,

Lead us through Christ, the true and liv - ing Way.
And age comes on un-cheered by faith and hope.
On - ly with thee we jour - ney safe - ly on.
Un - til our lives are per - fect - ed in thee. A - men.

PILGRIMAGE AND CONFLICT

Lift Thy Head, O Zion, Weeping

377

Karoly Jeszensky, c.1674
Tr. William Toth, 1905-

MAGYAR 8.7.8.7.7.7.8.8.
Hymn of the Hungarian Galley Slaves, 1674

1 Lift thy head, O Zi-on, weep-ing, Still the Lord thy Fa-ther is;
2 Though the sea his waves as-sem-ble And in fu-ry fall on thee,
3 Though the hills and vales be riv-en God cre-a-ted with his hand,
4 Though in chains thou now art griev-ing, Though a tor-tured slave thou die,

Thou art dai-ly in his keep-ing, And thine ev-ery care is his.
Though thou cry, with heart a-trem-ble, "O my Sav-ior, suc-cor me!"
Though the mov-ing signs of heav-en Wars pre-sage in ev-ery land,
Zi-on, if thou die be-liev-ing, Heav-en's path shall o-pen lie.

Rise and be of glad-some heart, And with cour-age play thy part;
Though un-trou-bled still he sleep Who thy hope is on the deep,
Yet, O Zi-on, have no fear: Ev-er is thy help-er near;
Up-ward gaze and hap-py be, God hath not for-sak-en thee;

Soon a-gain his arms will fold thee To his lov-ing heart and hold thee.
Zi-on, calm the breast that quaketh; Nev-er God his own for-sak-eth.
He hath sought thee, he hath found thee; Lo! his wings are walls a-round thee.
Thou his peo-ple art, and sure-ly He will fold his own se-cure-ly. A-men.

PILGRIMAGE AND CONFLICT

378 Lord of Our Life, and God of Our Salvation
First Tune

Matthäus von Löwenstern, 1594-1648
Tr. Philip Pusey, 1799-1855

ISTE CONFESSOR (ROUEN) 11.11.11.5.
Poitiers Antiphoner, 1746

1 Lord of our life, and God of our sal - va - tion, Star of our
night, and hope of ev - ery na - tion, Hear and re - ceive thy
Church's sup - pli - ca - tion, Lord God al - might - y.

2 Lord, thou canst help when earth-ly ar - mor fail - eth; Lord, thou canst
save when sin it - self as - sail - eth; Lord, o'er thy rock nor
death nor hell pre - vail - eth; Grant us thy peace, Lord:

3 Peace, in our hearts, our e - vil thoughts as - suag - ing; Peace, in thy
Church, where broth-ers are en - gag - ing; Peace, when the world its
bus - y war is wag - ing; Calm thy foes' rag - ing! A-men.

4 Grant us thy help till backward they are driven;
Grant them thy truth, that they may be forgiven;
Grant peace on earth, or after we have striven,
Peace in thy heaven.

PILGRIMAGE AND CONFLICT

Lord of Our Life, and God of Our Salvation

Second Tune

379

Matthäus von Löwenstern, *1594-1648*
Tr. Philip Pusey, *1799-1855*

CLOISTERS 11.11.11.5.
Joseph Barnby, *1838-1896*

1 Lord of our life, and God of our sal-va-tion, Star of our
2 Lord, thou canst help when earth-ly ar-mor fail-eth; Lord, thou canst
3 Peace, in our hearts, our e-vil thoughts as-suag-ing; Peace, in thy

night, and hope of ev-ery na-tion, Hear and re-ceive thy
save when sin it-self as-sail-eth; Lord, o'er thy rock nor
Church, where broth-ers are en-gag-ing; Peace, when the world its

Church's sup-pli-ca-tion, Lord God al-might-y.
death nor hell pre-vail-eth; Grant us thy peace, Lord:
bus-y war is wag-ing; Calm thy foes' rag-ing! A-men.

4 Grant us thy help till backward they are driven;
   Grant them thy truth, that they may be forgiven;
   Grant peace on earth, or after we have striven,
       Peace in thy heaven.

PILGRIMAGE AND CONFLICT

March on, O Soul, With Strength

George T. Coster, 1835-1912, alt.

ARTHUR'S SEAT 6.6.6.6.8.8.
Arr. from John Goss, 1800-1880

1 March on, O soul, with strength, Like those strong men of old
2 The sons of fa - thers we By whom our faith is taught
3 March on, O soul, with strength, As strong the bat - tle rolls;
4 Not long the con - flict; soon The ho - ly war shall cease;

Who 'gainst en - thron - ed wrong Stood con - fi - dent and bold,
To fear no ill, to fight The ho - ly fight they fought;
'Gainst lies and lusts and wrongs, Let cour - age rule our souls;
Faith's war - fare end - ed: won The home of end - less peace.

Who, thrust in prison or cast to flame,
He - ro - ic war - riors, ne'er from Christ
In keen - est strife, Lord, may we stand,
Look up, the vic - tor's crown at length;

Still made their glo - ry in thy name.
By an - y lure or guile en - ticed.
Up - held and strength - ened by thy hand.
March on, O soul, march on with strength. A-men.

PILGRIMAGE AND CONFLICT

My Faith, It Is an Oaken Staff

Thomas T. Lynch, 1818-1871

THE STAFF OF FAITH 8.6.8.6.8.8.8.6.
Traditional Swiss Melody

1 My faith, it is an oak-en staff, The trav-eler's well-loved aid;
2 I have a guide, and in his steps When trav-el-ers have trod,
3 My faith, it is an oak-en staff, O let me on it lean!

My faith, it is a weap-on stout, The sol-dier's trust-y blade.
Wheth-er be-neath was flint-y rock Or yield-ing grass-y sod,
My faith, it is a trust-y sword, May false-hood find it keen!

I'll trav-el on, and still be sti..red By si-lent thought or so-cial word;
They cared not, but with force un-spent, Un-moved by pain, they on-ward went,
Thy spir-it, Lord, to me im-part, O make me what thou ev-er art,

By all my per-ils un-de-terred, A sol-dier-pil-grim staid.
Un-stayed by pleas-ures, still they bent Their zeal-ous course to God.
Of pa-tient and cou-ra-geous heart, As all true saints have been.

PILGRIMAGE AND CONFLICT

382 Onward, Christian Soldiers

Sabine Baring-Gould, 1834-1924

ST. GERTRUDE 6.5.6.5.D. *with Refrain*
Arthur S. Sullivan, 1842-1900

1 On-ward, Chris-tian sol - diers, March-ing as to war, With the cross of
2 Like a might-y ar - my Moves the Church of God; Broth-ers, we are
3 Crowns and thrones may per-ish, King-doms rise and wane, But the Church of
4 On-ward, then, ye peo - ple, Join our hap-py throng, Blend with ours your

Je - sus Go - ing on be - fore; Christ the roy - al Mas - ter Leads a-
tread - ing Where the saints have trod; We are not di - vid - ed, All one
Je - sus Con-stant will re - main; Gates of hell can nev - er 'Gainst that
voic - es In the tri-umph song; Glo - ry, laud, and hon - or Un - to

gainst the foe; For - ward in - to bat - tle, See his ban-ners go.
bod - y we, One in hope and doc - trine, One in char - i - ty.
Church pre - vail; We have Christ's own prom-ise, And that can - not fail.
Christ the King; This through count-less a - ges Men and an - gels sing.

REFRAIN

On - ward, Chris - tian sol - diers, March-ing as to war,

PILGRIMAGE AND CONFLICT

With the cross of Je-sus Go-ing on be-fore. A-men.

Forward Through the Ages 383

Frederick L. Hosmer, 1840-1929

ST. GERTRUDE 6.5.6.5.D. *with Refrain*
Arthur S. Sullivan, 1842-1900

1 Forward through the ages,
   In unbroken line,
Move the faithful spirits
   At the call divine.
Gifts in differing measure,
   Hearts of one accord,
Manifold the service,
   One the sure reward;
Forward through the ages,
   In unbroken line,
Move the faithful spirits
   At the call divine.

2 Wider grows the kingdom,
   Reign of love and light;
For it we must labor,
   Till our faith is sight.
Prophets have proclaimed it,
   Martyrs testified,
Poets sung its glory,
   Heroes for it died.
Forward through the ages,
   In unbroken line,
Move the faithful spirits
   At the call divine.

3 Not alone we conquer,
   Not alone we fall;
In each loss or triumph
   Lose or triumph all.
Bound by God's far purpose
   In one living whole,
Move we on together
   To the shining goal!
Forward through the ages,
   In unbroken line,
Move the faithful spirits
   At the call divine.

PILGRIMAGE AND CONFLICT

Soldiers of Christ, Arise

Charles Wesley, 1707-1788, alt.

DIADEMATA S.M.D.
George J. Elvey, 1816-1893

1 Sol - diers of Christ, a - rise, And put your ar - mor on;
2 Stand, then, in his great might, With all his strength en - dued,
3 Leave no un - guard - ed place, No weak - ness of the soul,

Strong in the strength which God sup - plies Through his e - ter - nal Son,
And take, to arm you for the fight, The pan - o - ply of God,
Take ev - ery vir - tue, ev - ery grace, And for - ti - fy the whole.

Strong in the Lord of hosts, And in his might - y power,
That, hav - ing all things done, And all your con - flicts past,
From strength to strength go on; Wres - tle and fight and pray;

Who in the strength of Je - sus trusts Is more than con-quer - or.
Ye may o'er-come through Christ a-lone And stand en-tire at last.
Tread all the powers of dark-ness down And win the well-fought day. A-men.

PILGRIMAGE AND CONFLICT

A lower setting may be found at No. 199

Stand up, Stand up for Jesus

George Duffield, 1818-1888

WEBB 7.6.7.6.D.
George J. Webb, 1803-1887

385

1 Stand up, stand up for Je - sus, Ye sol - diers of the cross;
2 Stand up, stand up for Je - sus, The trum - pet call o - bey,
3 Stand up, stand up for Je - sus, Stand in his strength a - lone,
4 Stand up, stand up for Je - sus, The strife will not be long;

Lift high his roy - al ban - ner, It must not suf - fer loss.
Forth to the might - y con - flict, In this his glo - rious day.
The arm of flesh will fail you, Ye dare not trust your own.
This day the noise of bat - tle, The next the vic - tor's song.

From vic - tory un - to vic - tory His ar - my shall he lead,
Ye that are men now serve him A - gainst un - num-bered foes;
Put on the gos - pel ar - mor, Each piece put on with prayer;
To him that o - ver - com - eth A crown of life shall be;

Till ev - ery foe is van-quished, And Christ is Lord in - deed.
Let cour - age rise with dan - ger, And strength to strength op-pose.
Where du - ty calls, or dan - ger, Be nev - er want-ing there.
He with the King of glo - ry Shall reign e - ter - nal - ly. A-men.

A lower setting may be found at No. 305

PILGRIMAGE AND CONFLICT

386

Lighten the Darkness

Frances M. Owen, 1842-1883

SONG 24 10.10.10.10.
Orlando Gibbons, 1583-1625

1 Light-en the dark-ness of our life's long night, Through which we
2 Light-en the dark-ness of our self-con-ceit, The sub-tle
3 Light-en our dark-ness when we bow the knee To all the

blind-ly stum-ble to the day. Shad-ows mis-lead us; Fa-ther,
dark-ness that we love so well, Which shrouds the path of wis-dom
gods we ig-no-rant-ly make And wor-ship, dream-ing that we

send thy light To set our foot-steps in the home-ward way.
from our feet, And lulls our spir-its with its bane-ful spell.
wor-ship thee, Till clear-er light our slum-bering souls a-wake. A-men.

4 Lighten our darkness when we fail at last,
And in the midnight lay us down to die;
We trust to find thee when the night is past,
And daylight breaks across the morning sky.

PILGRIMAGE AND CONFLICT

Through the Night of Doubt and Sorrow

387

Bernard S. Ingemann, 1789-1862
Tr. Sabine Baring-Gould, 1834-1924

ST. ASAPH 8.7.8.7.D.
William S. Bambridge, 1842-1923

1 Through the night of doubt and sor - row On-ward goes the pil-grim band,
2 One the light of God's own pres-ence, O'er his ran-somed peo - ple shed,
3 One the strain that lips of thou-sands Lift as from the heart of one,

Sing-ing songs of ex - pec - ta - tion, March-ing to the prom-ised land.
Chas-ing far the gloom and ter - ror, Bright-ening all the path we tread;
One the con - flict, one the per - il, One the march in God be - gun;

Clear be - fore us through the dark-ness Gleams and burns the guid-ing light;
One the ob - ject of our jour-ney, One the faith which nev - er tires,
One the glad-ness of re-joic-ing On the far e - ter - nal shore,

Broth-er clasps the hand of broth-er, Step-ping fear-less through the night.
One the ear - nest look-ing for-ward, One the hope our God in-spires.
Where the one al-might-y Fa - ther Reigns in love for - ev - er-more. A men.

PILGRIMAGE AND CONFLICT

388 The Son of God Goes Forth to War

Reginald Heber, 1783-1826

ALL SAINTS NEW C.M.D.
Henry S. Cutler, 1824-1902

1 The Son of God goes forth to war, A king-ly crown to gain;
2 The mar-tyr first, whose ea-gle eye Could pierce be-yond the grave,
3 A glo-rious band, the cho-sen few On whom the Spir-it came,
4 A no-ble ar-my, men and boys, The ma-tron and the maid,

His blood-red ban-ner streams a-far; Who fol-lows in his train?
Who saw his Mas-ter in the sky, And called on him to save,
Twelve val-iant saints, their hope they knew, And mocked the cross and flame;
A-round the Sav-ior's throne re-joice, In robes of light ar-rayed;

Who best can drink his cup of woe, Tri-um-phant o-ver pain,
Like him, with par-don on his tongue, In midst of mor-tal pain,
They met the ty-rant's brandished steel, The li-on's gor-y mane;
They climbed the steep as-cent of heaven Through per-il, toil, and pain:

Who pa-tient bears his cross be-low, He fol-lows in his train.
He prayed for them that did the wrong: Who fol-lows in his train?
They bowed their necks the death to feel: Who fol-lows in their train?
O God, to us may grace be given To fol-low in their train. A-men.

PILGRIMAGE AND CONFLICT

O God of Bethel, by Whose Hand 389

Philip Doddridge, 1702-1751
Alt. by John Logan, 1748-1788, and others

DUNDEE C.M.
"Scottish Psalter," 1615

1 O God of Beth-el, by whose hand Thy peo-ple still are fed,
2 Our vows, our prayers, we now pre-sent Be-fore thy throne of grace;
3 Through each per-plex-ing path of life Our wan-dering foot-steps guide;
4 Oh, spread thy cov-ering wings a-round Till all our wan-derings cease,

Who through this earth-ly pil-grim-age Hast all our fa-thers led,
God of our fa-thers, be the God Of their suc-ceed-ing race.
Give us each day our dai-ly bread, And rai-ment fit pro-vide.
And at our Fa-ther's loved a-bode Our souls ar-rive in peace. A-men.

PILGRIMAGE AND CONFLICT

As Pants the Hart 390

Based on Psalm 42
"New Version," 1696, alt.

MARTYRDOM C.M.
Hugh Wilson, 1764-1824

1 As pants the hart for cool-ing streams When heat-ed in the chase,
2 For thee, my God, the liv-ing God, My thirst-y soul doth pine.
3 Why rest-less, why cast down, my soul? Hope still, and thou shalt sing

So longs my soul, O God, for thee, And thy re-fresh-ing grace.
O when shall I be-hold thy face, Thou maj-es-ty di-vine?
The praise of him who is thy God, Thy health's e-ter-nal spring. A-men.

Another harmonization may be found at No. 285
Alternative tune, ST. BERNARD, No. 347

CONSECRATION

391

Be Thou My Vision

Ancient Irish
Tr. by Mary E. Byrne, 1880-1931
Versified by Eleanor H. Hull, 1860-1935

SLANE 10.10.9.10.
Traditional Irish Melody
Harm. by David Evans, 1874-1948

In unison

1 Be thou my vi-sion, O Lord of my heart;
2 Be thou my wis-dom, and thou my true word;
3 Rich-es I heed not, nor man's emp-ty praise,
4 High King of heav-en, my vic-to-ry won,

Nought be all else to me save that thou art.
I ev-er with thee and thou with me, Lord;
Thou mine in-her-it-ance, now and al-ways;
May I reach heaven's joys, O bright heav-en's Sun!

Thou my best thought, by day or by night,
Thou my great Fa-ther, I thy true son;
Thou and thou on-ly, first in my heart,
Heart of my own heart, what-ev-er be-fall,

Wak-ing or sleep-ing, thy pres-ence my light.
Thou in me dwell-ing, and I with thee one.
High King of heav-en, my treas-ure thou art.
Still be my vi-sion, O Rul-er of all. A-men.

CONSECRATION

Father in Heaven, Who Lovest All

392

Rudyard Kipling, 1865-1936

SAXBY L.M.
Timothy R. Matthews, 1826-1910

1 Fa - ther in heaven, who lov - est all, O help thy
2 Teach us to bear the yoke in youth, With stead - fast -
3 Teach us to rule our - selves al - way, Con - trolled and
4 Teach us to look in all our ends On thee for
5 Teach us the strength that can - not seek, By deed or
6 Teach us de - light in sim - ple things, And mirth that

chil - dren when they call, That they may build from age to
ness and care - ful truth, That, in our time, thy grace may
clean - ly night and day, That we may bring, if need a -
judge and not our friends, That we, with thee, may walk un -
thought, to hurt the weak, That, un - der thee, we may pos -
has no bit - ter springs, For - give - ness free of e - vil

age An un - de - fil - ed her - it - age.
give The truth where - by the na - tions live.
rise, No maimed or worth - less sac - ri - fice.
cowed By fear or fa - vor of the crowd.
sess Man's strength to com - fort man's dis - tress.
done, And love to all men 'neath the sun. A - men.

This may be sung as a young people's patriotic hymn by using the following as the first and last stanzas:

Land of our birth, we pledge to thee
  Our love and toil in the years to be
When we are grown and take our place,
  As men and women with our race.

Land of our birth, our faith, our pride,
  For whose dear sake our fathers died;
O Motherland, we pledge to thee
  Head, heart, and hand through the years to be.

Alternative tune, HESPERUS, *No. 447*

CONSECRATION

393 God Be in My Head

"Sarum Primer," 1558

LYTLINGTON *Irregular*
Sydney H. Nicholson, 1875-1947

God be in my head, And in my un-der-stand-ing;

God be in mine eyes, And in my look-ing;

God be in my mouth, And in my speak-ing;

God be in my heart, And in my think-ing;

God be at mine end, And at my de-part-ing.

CONSECRATION

Another setting may be found at No. 543

Heart and Mind, Possessions, Lord

394

Krishnarao Rathnaji Sangle, 1834-1908
Tr. Alden H. Clark, 1878-, and others

TANA MANA DHANA (Marathi) Irregular
Ancient Indian Melody
Adapted by Marion Jean Chute, 1901-

1 Heart and mind, pos - ses - sions, Lord, I of - fer un - to thee;
2 Heart and mind, pos - ses - sions, Lord, I of - fer un - to thee;

All these were thine, Lord; thou didst give them all to me.
Thou art the Way, the Truth; thou art the Life.

Won-drous are thy do - ings un - to me. Plans and my thoughts and
Sin - ful, I com - mit my - self to thee. Je - sus Christ is fill - ing

ev - ery - thing I ev - er do are de - pend - ent on thy
all the heart of me. He can give me vic - tory o'er

will and love a - lone. I com - mit my spir - it un - to thee.
all that threat-ens me. Je - sus Christ is fill - ing all my heart.

CONSECRATION

395 Behold Us, Lord, a Little Space

John Ellerton, 1826-1893

DUNFERMLINE C.M.
"Scottish Psalter," 1615

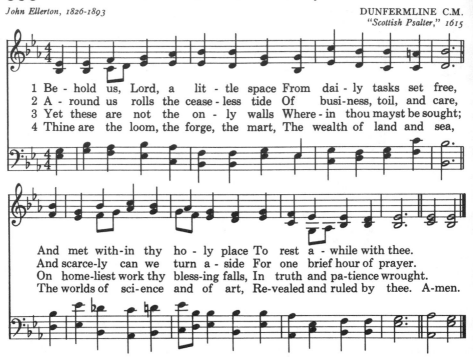

1 Be - hold us, Lord, a lit - tle space From dai - ly tasks set free,
2 A - round us rolls the cease - less tide Of busi - ness, toil, and care,
3 Yet these are not the on - ly walls Where - in thou mayst be sought;
4 Thine are the loom, the forge, the mart, The wealth of land and sea,

And met with - in thy ho - ly place To rest a - while with thee.
And scarce - ly can we turn a - side For one brief hour of prayer.
On home - liest work thy bless - ing falls, In truth and pa - tience wrought.
The worlds of sci - ence and of art, Re - vealed and ruled by thee. A - men.

5 Then let us prove our heavenly birth,
    In all we do and know;
  And claim the kingdom of the earth
    For thee and not thy foe.

6 Work shall be prayer, if all be wrought
    As thou wouldst have it done;
  And prayer, by thee inspired and taught,
    Itself with work be one.

Alternative tune, WINCHESTER OLD, *No. 146*

396 Fill Thou My Life, O Lord

Horatius Bonar, 1808-1889

WIGTOWN C.M.
"Scottish Psalter," 1635

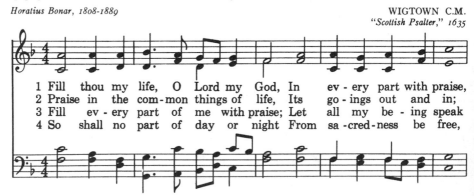

1 Fill thou my life, O Lord my God, In ev - ery part with praise,
2 Praise in the com - mon things of life, Its go - ings out and in;
3 Fill ev - ery part of me with praise; Let all my be - ing speak
4 So shall no part of day or night From sa - cred - ness be free,

CONSECRATION

That my whole be-ing may pro-claim Thy be-ing and thy ways:
Praise in each du-ty and each deed, How-ev-er small and mean.
Of thee and of thy love, O Lord, Poor though I be and weak.
But all my life, in ev-ery step, Be fel-low-ship with thee. A-men.

Lord, Speak to Me, That I May Speak 397

Frances R. Havergal, 1836-1879

CANONBURY L.M.
Arr. from Robert A. Schumann, 1810-1856

1 Lord, speak to me, that I may speak In
2 O strength-en me, that while I stand Firm
3 O teach me, Lord, that I may teach The
4 O fill me with thy full-ness, Lord, Un-

liv-ing ech-oes of thy tone; As thou hast sought, so
on the rock, and strong in thee, I may stretch out a
pre-cious things thou dost im-part; And wing my words, that
til my ver-y heart o'er-flow In kin-dling thought and

let me seek Thy err-ing chil-dren lost and lone.
lov-ing hand To wres-tlers with the trou-bled sea!
they may reach The hid-den depths of man-y a heart!
glow-ing word, Thy love to tell, thy praise to show! A-men.

A lower setting may be found at No. 46

CONSECRATION

398

Hope of the World

Georgia Harkness, 1891-

DONNE SECOURS 11.10.11.10.
"Genevan Psalter," 1551

1 Hope of the world, thou Christ of great com - pas - sion,
2 Hope of the world, God's gift from high - est heav - en,
3 Hope of the world, a - foot on dust - y high - ways,
4 Hope of the world, who by thy cross didst save us
5 Hope of the world, O Christ, o'er death vic - to - rious,

Speak to our fear - ful hearts by con - flict rent.
Bring - ing to hun - gry souls the bread of life,
Show - ing to wan - dering souls the path of light,
From death and dark de - spair, from sin and guilt,
Who by this sign didst con - quer grief and pain,

Save us, thy peo - ple, from con - sum - ing pas - sion,
Still let thy Spir - it un - to us be giv - en
Walk thou be - side us lest the tempt - ing by - ways
We ren - der back the love thy mer - cy gave us;
We would be faith - ful to thy gos - pel glo - rious;

Who by our own false hopes and aims are spent.
To heal earth's wounds and end her bit - ter strife.
Lure us a - way from thee to end - less night.
Take thou our lives and use them as thou wilt.
Thou art our Lord! Thou dost for - ev - er reign! A-men.

CONSECRATION

Alternative tune, ANCIENT OF DAYS, *No. 249*

O Love That Wilt Not Let Me Go

399

George Matheson, 1842-1906

ST. MARGARET 8.8.8.8.6.
Albert L. Peace, 1844-1912

1 O Love that wilt not let me go,
2 O Light that fol-lowest all my way,
3 O Joy that seek-est me through pain,
4 O Cross that lift-est up my head,

I rest my wea-ry soul in thee;
I yield my flick-ering torch to thee;
I can-not close my heart to thee;
I dare not ask to fly from thee;

I give thee back the life I owe,
My heart re-stores its bor-rowed ray,
I trace the rain-bow through the rain,
I lay in dust life's glo-ry dead,

That in thine o-cean depths its flow May rich-er, full-er be.
That in thy sun-shine's blaze its day May bright-er, fair-er be.
And feel the prom-ise is not vain That morn shall tear-less be.
And from the ground there blos-soms red Life that shall end-less be. A-men.

CONSECRATION

400   More Love to Thee, O Christ

Elizabeth P. Prentiss, 1818-1878

MORE LOVE TO THEE 6.4.6.4.6.6.4.
William H. Doane, 1832-1915

1 More love to thee, O Christ, More love to thee! Hear thou the
2 Once earth-ly joy I craved, Sought peace and rest; Now thee a-
3 Then shall my lat - est breath Whis - per thy praise; This be the

prayer I make On bend - ed knee; This is my ear - nest plea,
lone I seek, Give what is best; This all my prayer shall be,
part - ing cry My heart shall raise; This still its prayer shall be,

More love, O Christ, to thee, More love to thee, More love to thee! A-men

401   Teach Me, My God and King

George Herbert, 1593-1633

MORNINGTON S.M.
Garret Wellesley, 1735-1781

1 Teach me, my God and King, In all things thee to see, And what I
2 A man that looks on glass On it may stay his eye; Or if he
3 All may of thee par - take: Noth-ing can be so mean, Which with this
4 A serv-ant with this clause Makes drudg-er - y di-vine: Who sweeps a
5 This is the fam-ous stone That turn - eth all to gold: For that which

CONSECRATION

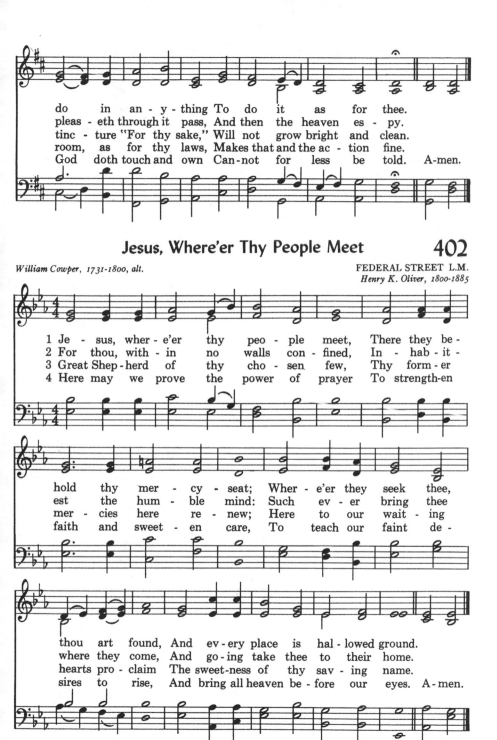

do   in an - y - thing To do   it   as   for   thee.
pleas - eth through it pass, And then the heaven es -   py.
tinc - ture "For thy sake," Will not grow bright and clean.
room,   as   for thy laws, Makes that and the ac - tion fine.
God   doth touch and own Can-not for   less   be   told. A-men.

Jesus, Where'er Thy People Meet   402

William Cowper, 1731-1800, alt.

FEDERAL STREET L.M.
Henry K. Oliver, 1800-1885

1 Je - sus, wher - e'er   thy   peo - ple   meet, There they be -
2 For thou, with - in   no   walls con - fined, In - hab - it -
3 Great Shep - herd of   thy cho - sen few,   Thy form - er
4 Here may we prove the power of prayer To strength-en

hold thy   mer - cy - seat; Wher - e'er they seek thee,
est   the   hum - ble mind: Such ev - er bring thee
mer - cies here   re - new; Here   to our   wait - ing
faith and   sweet - en care, To   teach our faint de -

thou art found, And ev - ery place is hal - lowed ground.
where they come, And go - ing take thee to their home.
hearts pro - claim The sweet-ness of thy sav - ing name.
sires to rise, And bring all heaven be - fore our eyes. A - men.

A higher setting may be found at No. 290

CONSECRATION

Those Who Love and Those Who Labor

Geoffrey Dearmer, 1893-

ALTA TRINITA BEATA 8.7.8.7.D.
Adapted from a melody in
"Laudi Spirituali," Florence, 14th century

In unison

1 Those who love and those who la-bor fol - low
2 Where the man - y work to - geth - er, they with

in the way of Christ: Thus the first dis -
God him - self a - bide, But the lone - ly

ci - ples found him, thus the gift of love suf - ficed.
work - er al - so finds him ev - er at his side.

Je - sus says to those who seek him, I will
Lo, the Prince of com - mon wel - fare dwells with -

CONSECRATION

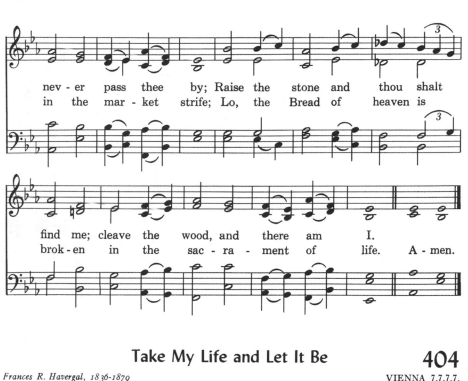

nev-er pass thee by; Raise the stone and thou shalt
in the mar-ket strife; Lo, the Bread of heaven is

find me; cleave the wood, and there am I.
brok-en in the sac-ra-ment of life. A-men.

Take My Life and Let It Be

404

Frances R. Havergal, 1836-1879

VIENNA 7.7.7.7.
Melody by Justin H. Knecht, 1752-1817

1 Take my life, and let it be Con-se-crat-ed, Lord, to thee;
2 Take my hands, and let them move At the im-pulse of thy love;
3 Take my will, and make it thine; It shall be no long-er mine;
4 Take my love: my Lord I pour At thy feet its treas-ure store;

Take my mo-ments and my days, Let them flow in cease-less praise.
Take my feet, and let them be Swift and beau-ti-ful for thee.
Take my heart, it is thine own; It shall be thy roy-al throne.
Take my-self, and I will be Ev-er, on-ly, all for thee. A-men.

CONSECRATION

405 Master, No Offering Costly and Sweet

Edwin P. Parker, 1836-1925

LOVE'S OFFERING 6.4.6.4.6.6.4.4.
Edwin P. Parker, 1836-1925

1 Mas - ter, no of - fer - ing Cost - ly and sweet May we, like
2 Dai - ly our lives would show Weak-ness made strong, Toil - some and
3 Some word of hope for hearts Bur - dened with fears, Some balm of
4 Thus, in thy serv - ice, Lord, Till e - ven - tide Clos - es the

Mag - da-lene, Lay at thy feet, Yet may love's in-cense rise, Sweet-er than
gloom - y ways Brightened with song, Some deeds of kindness done, Some souls by
peace for eyes Blind - ed with tears, Some dews of mer-cy shed, Some wayward
day of life, May we a - bide; And when earth's labors cease, Bid us de-

sac - ri - fice, Dear Lord, to thee, Dear Lord, to thee.
pa - tience won, Dear Lord, to thee, Dear Lord, to thee.
foot-steps led, Dear Lord, to thee, Dear Lord, to thee.
part in peace, Dear Lord, to thee, Dear Lord, to thee. A-men.

406 Forth in Thy Name, O Lord, I Go

Charles Wesley, 1707-1788, alt.

MORNING HYMN L.M.
François H. Barthélémon, 1741-1808

1 Forth in thy name, O Lord, I go, My dai - ly la - bor to pur - sue,
2 The task thy wis - dom hath assigned, O let me cheer-ful - ly ful - fill,
3 Thee may I set at my right hand, Whose eyes my in - most substance see,
4 Give me to bear thy eas - y yoke, And ev - ery mo-ment watch and pray,

CONSECRATION

Thee, on-ly thee, re-solved to know In all I think or speak or do.
In all my works thy presence find, And prove thy good and perfect will.
And la-bor on at thy command, And of-fer all my works to thee.
And still to things e - ter-nal look, And has-ten to thy glo-rious day. A-men.

Alternative tune, CANONBURY, *No. 397*

O Light That Knew No Dawn 407

Gregory Nazianzen, c.329-389
Tr. John Brownlie, 1857-1925

HAREWOOD 6.6.6.6.8.8.
Samuel S. Wesley, 1810-1876

1 O Light that knew no dawn, That shines to end - less day,
2 Thy grace, O Fa - ther, give, That I may serve with fear;
3 That, cleansed from stain of sin, I may meet hom - age give,
4 Thy grace, O Fa - ther, give, I hum - bly thee im - plore,

All things in earth and heaven Are lus-tered by thy ray; No eye can to thy
A - bove all boons, I pray, Grant me thy voice to hear. From sin thy child in
And, pure in heart, be - hold Thy beau-ty while I live, Clean hands in ho - ly
And let thy mer - cy bless Thy serv-ant more and more. All grace and glo - ry

throne as - cend, Nor mind thy bright-ness com - pre - hend.
mer - cy free, And let me dwell in light with thee,
wor - ship raise, And thee, O Christ, my Sav - ior, praise.
be to thee From age to age e - ter - nal - ly. A - men.

CONSECRATION

408 I Sought the Lord and Afterward I Knew

Unknown
"The Pilgrim Hymnal," 1904

GENEVAN PSALM 22 10.10.10.6.
Abridged from "Genevan Psalter," 1549

1 I sought the Lord, and aft - er - ward I knew
2 Thou didst reach forth thy hand and mine en - fold;
3 I find, I walk, I love, but oh, the whole

He moved my soul to seek him, seek - ing me;
I walked and sank not on the storm - vexed sea;
Of love is but my an - swer, Lord, to thee!

It was not I that found, O Sav - ior true;
'Twas not so much that I on thee took hold
For thou wert long be - fore - hand with my soul;

No, I was found of thee.
As thou, dear Lord, on me.
Al - ways thou lov - edst me. A - men.

CONSECRATION

Jesus, Thou Divine Companion

409

Henry van Dyke, 1852-1933

PLEADING SAVIOR 8.7.8.7.D.
Melody, "The Christian Lyre," 1831

1 Je - sus, thou di - vine com - pan - ion, By thy low - ly hu - man birth
2 They who tread the path of la - bor Fol - low where thy feet have trod;
3 Ev - ery task, how - ev - er sim - ple, Sets the soul that does it free;

Thou hast come to join the work - ers, Bur - den - bear - ers of the earth.
They who work with - out com - plain - ing Do the ho - ly will of God.
Ev - ery deed of love and kind - ness Done to man is done to thee.

Thou, the car - pen - ter of Naz - areth, Toil - ing for thy dai - ly food,
Thou, the peace that pass - eth knowledge, Dwell - est in the dai - ly strife;
Je - sus, thou di - vine com - pan - ion, Help us all to work our best;

By thy pa - tience and thy cour - age, Thou hast taught us toil is good.
Thou, the Bread of heaven, art bro - ken In the sac - ra - ment of life.
Bless us in our dai - ly la - bor, Lead us to our sab - bath rest. A - men.

BROTHERHOOD AND SERVICE

410 · O Brother Man, Fold to Thy Heart

John Greenleaf Whittier, 1807-1892

INTERCESSOR 11.10.11.10.
C. Hubert H. Parry, 1848-1918

1 O broth - er man, fold to thy heart thy broth - er:
2 Fol - low with rev - erent steps the great ex - am - ple
3 Then shall all shack - les fall: the storm - y clang - or

Where pit - y dwells, the peace of God is there;
Of him whose ho - ly work was do - ing good:
Of wild war mu - sic o'er the earth shall cease;

To wor - ship right - ly is to love each oth - er,
So shall the wide earth seem our Fa - ther's tem - ple,
Love shall tread out the bale - ful fire of an - ger,

Each smile a hymn, each kind - ly deed a prayer.
Each lov - ing life a psalm of grat - i - tude.
And in its ash - es plant the tree of peace. A - men.

BROTHERHOOD AND SERVICE

Alternative tune, WELWYN, *No. 411*

Lord God of Hosts, Whose Purpose

411

Shepherd Knapp, 1873-1946

WELWYN 11.10.11.10.
Alfred Scott-Gatty, 1847-1918

1 Lord God of hosts, whose pur-pose, nev-er swerv-ing,
2 Strong Son of God, whose work was his that sent thee,
3 O Prince of peace, thou bring-er of good ti-dings,
4 Lord God, whose grace has called us to thy serv-ice,

Leads toward the day of Je-sus Christ thy Son,
One with the Fa-ther, thought and deed and word,
Teach us to speak thy word of hope and cheer:
How good thy thoughts toward us, how great their sum!

Grant us to march a-mong thy faith-ful le-gions,
One make us all, true com-rades in thy serv-ice,
Rest for the soul, and strength for all man's striv-ing,
We work with thee, we go where thou wilt lead us,

Armed with thy cour-age, till the world is won.
And make us one in thee with God the Lord.
Light for the path of life, and God brought near.
Un-til in all the earth thy king-dom come. A-men.

Alternative tune, DONNE SECOURS, *No. 398*

BROTHERHOOD AND SERVICE

412 O Master Workman of the Race

Jay T. Stocking, 1870-1936

KINGSFOLD C.M.D.
Traditional English Melody
Arr. by R. Vaughan Williams, 1872-1958

1 O Mas-ter Work-man of the race, Thou Man of Gal - i - lee,
2 O Car-pen-ter of Naz - a - reth, Build-er of life di - vine,
3 O thou who didst the vi - sion send And gives to each his task,

Who with the eyes of ear - ly youth E - ter - nal things did see,
Who shap-est man to God's own law, Thy - self the fair de - sign,
And with the task suf - fi-cient strength, Show us thy will, we ask.

We thank thee for thy boy - hood faith That shone thy whole life through;
Build us a tower of Christ-like height, That we the land may view,
Give us a con-science bold and good, Give us a pur - pose true,

"Did ye not know it is my work My Fa-ther's work to do?"
And see like thee our no - blest work Our Fa-ther's work to do.
That it may be our high - est joy Our Fa-ther's work to do. A-men.

BROTHERHOOD AND SERVICE

Son of God, Eternal Savior

413

Somerset C. Lowry, 1855-1932, alt.

WEISSE FLAGGEN 8.7.8.7.D.
"Tochter Sion," Cologne, 1741.

1 Son of God, e - ter - nal Sav - ior, Source of life and truth and grace,
2 Lord, as thou hast lived for oth - ers, So may we for oth - ers live;
3 Come, O Christ, and reign a - bove us, King of love, and Prince of peace;
4 See the Christ-like host ad - vanc - ing, High and low - ly, great and small,

Son of man, whose birth in - car - nate Hal - lows all our hu - man race,
Free - ly have thy gifts been grant - ed, Free - ly may thy serv-ants give.
Hush the storm of strife and pas - sion, Bid its cru - el dis-cords cease;
Linked in bonds of com-mon serv - ice For the com - mon Lord of all.

Thou, our head, who, throned in glo - ry, For thine own dost ev - er plead,
Thine the gold and thine the sil - ver, Thine the wealth of land and sea,
By thy pa - tient years of toil - ing, By thy si - lent hours of pain,
Thou who pray - edst, thou who will - est That thy peo - ple should be one,

Fill us with thy love and pit - y, Heal our wrongs, and help our need.
We but stew-ards of thy boun - ty, Held in sol - emn trust for thee.
Quench our fe-vered thirst of pleas-ure, Shame our sel - fish greed of gain.
Grant, O grant our hope's fru-i-tion: Here on earth thy will be done. A - men.

A lower setting may be found at No. 180
Alternative tune, IN BABILONE, *No. 74*

BROTHERHOOD AND SERVICE

414
In Christ There Is No East or West
First Tune

John Oxenham, *1852-1941*

ST. PETER C.M.
Alexander R. Reinagle, *1799-1877*

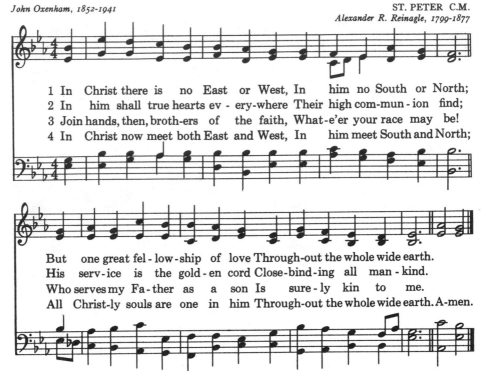

1 In   Christ there is   no East or West, In   him no South or North;
2 In   him shall true hearts ev - ery-where Their high com-mun - ion find;
3 Join hands, then, broth-ers of   the faith, What-e'er your race may be!
4 In   Christ now meet both East and West, In   him meet South and North;

But   one great fel - low-ship of love Through-out the whole wide earth.
His   serv-ice is the gold - en cord Close-bind-ing all man - kind.
Who serves my Fa-ther as   a   son Is   sure-ly kin   to   me.
All   Christ-ly souls are one in him Through-out the whole wide earth. A-men.

A lower setting may be found at No. 221

415
In Christ There Is No East or West
Second Tune

John Oxenham, *1852-1941*

McKEE C.M.
Negro Melody
Adapted by Harry T. Burleigh, *1866-1949*

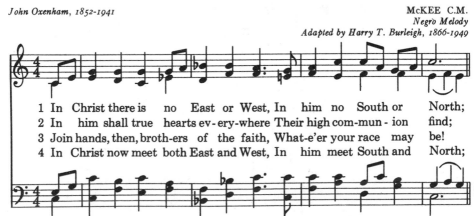

1 In   Christ there is   no   East or West, In   him no   South or   North;
2 In   him shall true   hearts ev-ery-where Their high com-mun - ion   find;
3 Join hands, then, broth-ers of   the faith, What-e'er your race may   be!
4 In   Christ now meet both East and West, In   him meet South and   North;

BROTHERHOOD AND SERVICE

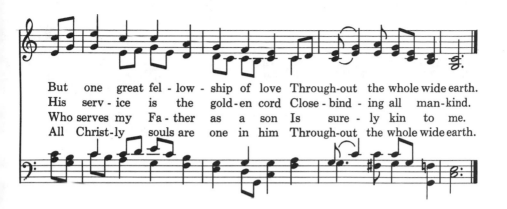

But one great fel - low - ship of love Through-out the whole wide earth.
His serv - ice is the gold-en cord Close - bind - ing all man-kind.
Who serves my Fa - ther as a son Is sure - ly kin to me.
All Christ-ly souls are one in him Through-out the whole wide earth.

Christian, Rise and Act Thy Creed 416

F. A. Rollo Russell, 1849-1914

INNOCENTS 7.7.7.7.
"The Parish Choir," 1850

1 Chris-tian, rise and act thy creed; Let thy prayer be in thy deed;
2 Hearts a-round thee sink with care; Thou canst help their load to bear;
3 Let thine alms be hope and joy, And thy wor-ship God's em-ploy;

Seek the right, per-form the true, Raise thy work and life a - new.
Thou canst bring in-spir-ing light, Arm their fal-tering wills to fight.
Give him thanks in hum-ble zeal, Learn-ing all his will to feel. A-men.

4 Come then, law divine, and reign;
Freest faith assailed in vain,
Perfect love bereft of fear,
Born in heaven and radiant here.

417
The Day of the Lord Is at Hand

Charles Kingsley, 1819-1875

REMEMBER THE POOR *Irregular*
Traditional Irish Melody

1 The day of the Lord is at hand, at hand; Its storms roll up the
2 Who would sit down and sigh for a lost age of gold, While the Lord of all a - ges is

sky; The na - tions sleep starv - ing on heaps of gold; All
here? True hearts will leap at the trum - pet of God, And

dream - ers toss and sigh; The night is dark - est be -
those who can suf - fer can dare. Each old age of gold was an

fore the morn; When the pain is sor - est the child is born, And the
i - ron age too, And the meek - est of saints may find stern work to do In the

BROTHERHOOD AND SERVICE

day of the Lord at hand, at hand, The day of the Lord at hand.
day of the Lord at hand, at hand, In the day of the Lord at hand.

O Master, Let Me Walk With Thee 418

Washington Gladden, 1836-1918

MARYTON L.M.
H. Percy Smith, 1825-1898

1 O Mas - ter, let me walk with thee In low - ly
2 Help me the slow of heart to move By some clear,
3 Teach me thy pa - tience; still with thee In clos - er,
4 In hope that sends a shin - ing ray Far down the

paths of serv - ice free; Tell me thy se - cret, help me
win - ning word of love; Teach me the way - ward feet to
dear - er com - pa - ny, In work that keeps faith sweet and
fu - ture's broad-ening way, In peace that on - ly thou canst

bear The strain of toil, the fret of care.
stay, And guide them in the home - ward way.
strong, In trust that tri - umphs o - ver wrong.
give, With thee, O Mas - ter, let me live. A - men.

BROTHERHOOD AND SERVICE

419   Thou God of All, Whose Spirit Moves

John Haynes Holmes, 1879-1964

OLD 22nd C.M.D.
"Anglo-Genevan Psalter," 1556

1 Thou God of all, whose spir - it moves From pole to si - lent pole,
2 One in the pa - tient com - pa - ny Of those who heed thy will,
3 One in the truth that makes men free, The faith that makes men brave;

Whose pur-pose binds the star-ry spheres In one stu - pen - dous whole,
And stead-fast - ly pur - sue the way Of thy com-mand-ments still;
One in the love that suf-fers long To seek, and serve, and save;

Whose life, like light, is free - ly poured On all be-neath the sun,
One in the ho - ly fel - low - ship Of those who chal-lenge wrong,
One in the vi - sion of thy peace, The king-dom yet to be,

To thee we lift our hearts, and pray That thou wilt make us one:
And lift the spir-it's sword to shield The weak a - gainst the strong;
When thou shalt be the God of all, And all be one in thee. A-men.

BROTHERHOOD AND SERVICE

O Holy City, Seen of John

W. Russell Bowie, 1882-

MORNING SONG 8.6.8.6.8.6.
Melody, "Kentucky Harmony," 1816
Harm. by C. Winfred Douglas, 1867-1944

420

1 O ho-ly cit-y, seen of John, Where Christ, the Lamb, doth reign,
2 O shame to us who rest con-tent While lust and greed for gain
3 Give us, O God, the strength to build The cit-y that hath stood

With-in whose four-square walls shall come No night, nor need, nor pain,
In street and shop and ten-e-ment Wring gold from hu-man pain,
Too long a dream, whose laws are love, Whose ways are broth-er-hood,

And where the tears are wiped from eyes That shall not weep a-gain,
And bit-ter lips in blind de-spair Cry, "Christ hath died in vain!"
And where the sun that shin-eth is God's grace for hu-man good.

4 Already in the mind of God
   That city riseth fair:
Lo, how its splendor challenges
   The souls that greatly dare,
Yea, bids us seize the whole of life
   And build its glory there.

BROTHERHOOD AND SERVICE

421 We Thank Thee, Lord, Thy Paths of Service

Calvin W. Laufer, 1874-1938

FIELD 10.10.10.10.
Calvin W. Laufer, 1874-1938

1 We thank thee, Lord, thy paths of serv-ice lead
2 We've sought and found thee in the se-cret place
3 We've felt thy touch in sor-row's dark-ened way
4 We've seen thy glo-ry like a man-tle spread

To bla-zoned heights and down the slopes of need;
And mar-veled at the ra-diance of thy face;
A-bound with love and sol-ace for the day;
O'er hill and dale in saf-fron flame and red;

They reach thy throne, en-com-pass land and sea,
But of-ten in some far off Gal-i-lee
And, 'neath the bur-dens there, thy sov-ereign-ty
But in the eyes of men, re-deemed and free,

And he who jour-neys in them walks with thee.
Be-held thee fair-er yet while serv-ing thee.
Has held our hearts enthralled while serv-ing thee.
A splen-dor great-er yet while serv-ing thee. A-men.

BROTHERHOOD AND SERVICE

When Through the Whirl of Wheels 422

Geoffrey A. Studdert-Kennedy, 1883-1929

LOMBARD STREET 11.10.11.10.
Frederick G. Russell, 1867-1929

In unison

1 When through the whirl of wheels, and en-gines hum - ming,
2 When through the night the furn-ace fires a - flar - ing,
3 When in the depths the pa-tient min-er striv - ing
4 When on the sweat of la-bor and its sor - row,
5 Then will he come with meek-ness for his glo - ry,

Pa - tient-ly power - ful for the sons of men,
Shoot - ing out tongues of flame like leap - ing blood,
Feels in his arms the vig - or of the Lord,
Toil - ing in twi - light flick - er - ing and dim,
God in a work - man's jack - et as be - fore,

Peals like a trum - pet prom - ise of his com - ing
Speak to the heart of love, a - live and dar - ing,
Strikes for a king - dom and his King's ar - riv - ing,
Flames out the sun - shine of the great to - mor - row,
Liv - ing a - gain the e - ter - nal gos - pel sto - ry,

Who in the clouds is pledged to come a - gain,
Sing of the bound - less en - er - gy of God,
Hold - ing his pick more splen - did than the sword,
When all the world looks up be-cause of him,
Sweep-ing the shav - ings from his work - shop floor. A - men.

BROTHERHOOD AND SERVICE

423 Where Cross the Crowded Ways of Life

Frank Mason North, 1850-1935

GERMANY L.M.
Gardiner's "Sacred Melodies," 1815

1 Where cross the crowd-ed ways of life, Where sound the
2 In haunts of wretch-ed - ness and need, On shad-owed
3 From ten-der child-hood's help-less - ness, From wom-an's
4 The cup of wa-ter given for thee Still holds the

cries of race and clan, A-bove the noise of self-ish
thresh-olds dark with fears, From paths where hide the lures of
grief, man's bur - dened toil, From fam-ished souls, from sor-rows'
fresh-ness of thy grace; Yet long these mul - ti-tudes to

strife, We hear thy voice, O Son of man.
greed, We catch the vi - sion of thy tears.
stress, Thy heart has nev - er known re - coil.
see The sweet com - pas - sion of thy face. A - men.

5 O Master, from the mountain side,
   Make haste to heal these hearts of pain;
   Among these restless throngs abide,
   O tread the city's streets again,

6 Till sons of men shall learn thy love,
   And follow where thy feet have trod,
   Till glorious from thy heaven above,
   Shall come the city of our God.

BROTHERHOOD AND SERVICE

Hail the Glorious Golden City

Felix Adler, 1851-1933, alt.

LLANSANNAN 8.7.8.7.D.
Welsh Melody
Harm. by David Evans, 1874-1948

424

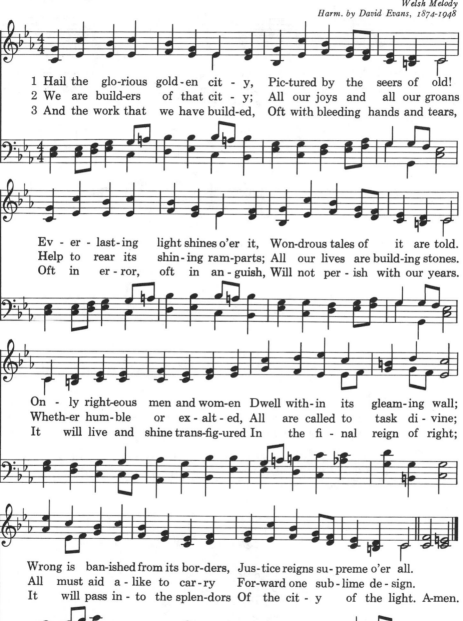

1 Hail the glo-rious gold-en cit - y, Pic-tured by the seers of old!
2 We are build-ers of that cit - y; All our joys and all our groans
3 And the work that we have build-ed, Oft with bleeding hands and tears,

Ev - er - last-ing light shines o'er it, Won-drous tales of it are told.
Help to rear its shin-ing ram-parts; All our lives are build-ing stones.
Oft in er - ror, oft in an - guish, Will not per - ish with our years.

On - ly right-eous men and wom-en Dwell with-in its gleam-ing wall;
Wheth-er hum-ble or ex - alt - ed, All are called to task di - vine;
It will live and shine trans-fig-ured In the fi - nal reign of right;

Wrong is ban-ished from its bor-ders, Jus-tice reigns su-preme o'er all.
All must aid a - like to car-ry For-ward one sub - lime de - sign.
It will pass in - to the splen-dors Of the cit - y of the light. A-men.

Alternative tune, AUSTRIAN HYMN, No. 267

JUSTICE

425

Men, Whose Boast It Is

James Russell Lowell, 1819-1891

IVES 7.7.7.7.D.
"Plymouth Collection," 1855

1 Men, whose boast it is that ye Come of fa - thers brave and free,
2 Is true free-dom but to break Fet - ters for our own dear sake,
3 They are slaves who fear to speak For the fall - en and the weak;

If there breathe on earth a slave, Are ye tru - ly free and brave?
And, with leath-ern hearts, for - get That we owe man - kind a debt?
They are slaves who will not choose Ha - tred, scoff - ing, and a - buse,

If ye do not feel the chain When it works a broth-er's pain,
No! true free-dom is to share All the chains our broth-ers wear,
Ra - ther than in si - lence shrink From the truth they needs must think;

Are ye not base slaves in - deed, Slaves un - wor - thy to be freed?
And, with heart and hand, to be Ear - nest to make oth - ers free.
They are slaves who dare not be In the right with two or three.

JUSTICE

427 We Are Living, We Are Dwelling

Arthur C. Coxe, 1818-1896, alt.

BLAENHAFREN 8.7.8.7.D.
Traditional Welsh Melody

1 We are liv-ing, we are dwell-ing In a grand and aw-ful time,
2 Will ye play then? will ye dal-ly Far be-hind the bat-tle line?
3 Sworn to yield, to wa-ver, nev-er, Con-se-crat-ed, born a-gain,

In an age on a-ges tell-ing; To be liv-ing is sub-lime.
Up! it is Je-ho-vah's ral-ly; God's own arm hath need of thine.
Sworn to be Christ's sol-diers ev-er, O for Christ at least be men!

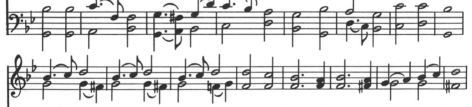

Hark! the wak-ing up of na-tions, Hosts ad-vanc-ing to the fray;
Worlds are charg-ing, heaven be-hold-ing; Thou hast but an hour to fight;
O let all the soul with-in you For the truth's sake go a-broad!

Hark! what sound-eth is cre-a-tion's Groan-ing for the lat-ter day.
Now, the bla-zoned cross un-fold-ing, On, right on-ward for the right!
Strike! let ev-ery nerve and sin-ew Tell on a-ges, tell for God. A-men.

JUSTICE

The Voice of God Is Calling

John Haynes Holmes, 1879-1964

MEIRIONYDD 7.6.7.6.D.
Welsh Hymn Melody
Attr. to William Lloyd, 1786-1852

426

1 The voice of God is call-ing Its sum-mons un-to men;
2 I hear my peo-ple cry-ing In cot and mine and slum;
3 We heed, O Lord, thy sum-mons, And an-swer: Here are we!
4 From ease and plen-ty save us; From pride of place ab-solve;

As once he spake in Zi-on, So now he speaks a-gain:
No field or mart is si-lent, No cit-y street is dumb.
Send us up-on thine er-rand; Let us thy serv-ants be.
Purge us of low de-sire; Lift us to high re-solve;

Whom shall I send to suc-cor My peo-ple in their need?
I see my peo-ple fall-ing In dark-ness and de-spair.
Our strength is dust and ash-es, Our years a pass-ing hour,
Take us, and make us ho-ly; Teach us thy will and way.

Whom shall I send to loos-en The bonds of shame and greed?
Whom shall I send to shat-ter The fet-ters which they bear?
But thou canst use our weak-ness To mag-ni-fy thy power.
Speak, and, be-hold! we an-swer; Command, and we o-bey! A-men.

Alternative tune, WEBB, *No. 305*

JUSTICE

When Israel Was in Egypt's Land

428

Negro Spiritual

GO DOWN MOSES *Irregular*
Negro Melody

1 When Is-rael was in E-gypt's land,
2 Thus saith the Lord, bold Mo-ses said, Let my peo-ple go,
3 No more in bond-age shall they toil,

Op-pressed so hard they could not stand,
If not I'll smite your first-born dead, Let my peo-ple go.
Let them come out with E-gypt's spoil,

REFRAIN

Go down, Mo-ses, 'Way down in E-gypt's land,

Tell old Phar-aoh, To let my peo-ple go.

JUSTICE

429 Eternal Father, Strong to Save

William Whiting, 1825-1878, alt.

MELITA 8.8.8.8.8.8.
John B. Dykes, 1823-1876

1 E - ter - nal Fa - ther, strong to save, Whose arm doth bind the
2 O Sav - ior, whose al - might - y word, The winds and waves sub -
3 O Ho - ly Spir - it, who didst brood Up - on the cha - os
4 O Trin - i - ty of love and power! Our breth - ren shield in

rest - less wave, Who bidd'st the might - y o - cean deep Its
mis - sive heard, Who walk - edst on the foam - ing deep, And
dark and rude, Who bad'st its an - gry tu - mult cease, And
dan - ger's hour; From rock and tem - pest, fire and foe, Pro -

own ap - point - ed lim - its keep, O hear us when we
calm a - mid its rage didst sleep, O hear us when we
gav - est light, and life, and peace, O hear us when we
tect them where - so - e'er they go; Thus ev - er - more shall

cry to thee, For those in per - il on the sea.
cry to thee, For those in per - il on the sea.
cry to thee, For those in per - il on the sea.
rise to thee Glad hymns of praise from land and sea. A - men.

THE NATION

Rejoice, O Land, in God Thy Might

430

Robert S. Bridges, 1844-1930

WAREHAM L.M.
William Knapp, 1698?-1768

1 Re - joice, O land, in God thy might;
2 Glad shalt thou be, with bless - ing crowned;
3 He shall for - give thy sins un - told;

His will o - bey, him serve a - right;
With joy and peace thou shalt a - bound;
Re - mem - ber thou his love of old;

For thee the saints up - lift their voice:
Yea, love with thee shall make his home
Walk in his way, his word a - dore,

Fear not, O land: in God re - joice.
Un - til thou see God's king - dom come.
And keep his truth for ev - er - more. A - men.

THE NATION

431 God of Our Fathers, Known of Old

Rudyard Kipling, 1865-1936

FOLKINGHAM 8.8.8.8.8.8.
"Supplement to the New Version," 1708

1 God of our fa - thers, known of old, Lord of our
2 The tu - mult and the shout-ing dies; The cap - tains
3 Far - called, our na - vies melt a - way; On dune and
4 If drunk with sight of power, we loose Wild tongues that
5 For hea - then heart that puts her trust In reek - ing

far - flung bat - tle line, Be - neath whose aw - ful
and the kings de - part; Still stands thine an - cient
head - land sinks the fire; Lo, all our pomp of
have not thee in awe, Such boast - ings as the
tube and i - ron shard, All val - iant dust that

hand we hold Do - min - ion o - ver palm and pine,
sac - ri - fice, An hum - ble and a con - trite heart.
yes - ter - day Is one with Nin - e - veh and Tyre!
Gen - tiles use, Or less - er breeds with-out the law,
builds on dust, And guard-ing, calls not thee to guard,

Lord God of hosts, be with us yet, Lest we for-get, lest we for-get!
Lord God of hosts, be with us yet, Lest we for-get, lest we for-get!
Judge of the na-tions, spare us yet, Lest we for-get, lest we for-get!
Lord God of hosts, be with us yet, Lest we for-get, lest we for-get!
For fran-tic boast and fool-ish word, Thy mer-cy on thy peo-ple, Lord! A-men.

THE NATION

God of the Nations, Who From Dawn of Days 432

W. Russell Bowie, 1882-

TOULON 10.10.10.10.
Abridged from "Genevan Psalter," 1551

1 God of the nations, who from dawn of days
2 Thine an-cient might de-stroyed the Phar-aoh's boast;
3 Thy hand has led a-cross the hun-gry sea
4 Then, for thy grace to grow in broth-er-hood,

Hast led thy peo-ple in their wid-ening ways,
Thou wast the shield for Is-rael's march-ing host,
The ea-ger peo-ples flock-ing to be free,
For hearts a-flame to serve thy des-tined good,

Through whose deep pur-pose stran-ger thou-sands stand
And, all the a-ges through, past crum-bling throne
And from the breeds of earth, thy si-lent sway
For faith, and will to win what faith shall see,

Here in the bor-ders of our prom-ised land,
And bro-ken fet-ter, thou hast brought thine own.
Fash-ions the na-tion of the broad-ening day.
God of thy peo-ple, hear us cry to thee! A-men.

THE NATION

433 **God of Our Fathers, Whose Almighty Hand**

Daniel C. Roberts, 1841-1907

NATIONAL HYMN 10.10.10.10.
George W. Warren, 1828-1902

Trumpets, before each stanza
(optional)

1 God of our fa-thers, whose al-might-y hand
2 Thy love di-vine hath led us in the past;
3 From war's a-larms, from dead-ly pes-ti-lence,
4 Re-fresh thy peo-ple on their toil-some way;

Leads forth in beau-ty all the star-ry band
In this free land by thee our lot is cast;
Be thy strong arm our ev-er sure de-fense;
Lead us from night to nev-er-end-ing day;

Of shin-ing worlds in splen-dor through the skies,
Be thou our rul-er, guard-ian, guide, and stay,
Thy true re-li-gion in our hearts in-crease;
Fill all our lives with love and grace di-vine,

Our grate-ful songs be-fore thy throne a-rise.
Thy word our law, thy paths our cho-sen way.
Thy boun-teous good-ness nour-ish us in peace.
And glo-ry, laud, and praise be ev-er thine. A-men.

THE NATION

God Send Us Men Whose Aim 'Twill Be 434

Frederick J. Gillman, 1866-1949, alt.

MELROSE L.M.
Frederick C. Maker, 1844-1927

1 God send us men whose aim 'twill be,
2 God send us men a - lert and quick
3 God send us men of stead - fast will,
4 God send us men with hearts a - blaze,

Not to de - fend some an - cient creed,
His loft - y pre - cepts to trans - late,
Pa - tient, cou - ra - geous, strong and true,
All truth to love, all wrong to hate;

But to live out the laws of Christ
Un - til the laws of Christ be - come
With vi - sion clear and mind e - quipped
These are the pa - triots na - tions need;

In ev - ery thought and word and deed.
The laws and hab - its of the state.
His will to learn, his work to do.
These are the bul - warks of the state. A - men.

Alternative tune, DAS WALT' GOTT VATER, No. 231

THE NATION

435   Judge Eternal, Throned in Splendor

Henry S. Holland, 1847-1918, alt.

RHUDDLAN 8.7.8.7.8.7.
Traditional Welsh Melody

1 Judge e - ter - nal, throned in splen - dor, Lord of lords and
2 Still the wea - ry folk are pin - ing For the hour that
3 Crown, O God, thine own en - deav - or; Cleave our dark - ness

King of kings, With thy liv - ing fire of judg - ment
brings re - lease; And the cit - y's crowd - ed clan - gor
with thy sword; Feed the faint and hun - gry peo - ples

Purge this land of bit - ter things; Sol - ace all its
Cries a - loud for sin to cease; And the home-steads
With the rich - ness of thy Word; Cleanse the bod - y

wide do - min - ion With the heal - ing of thy wings.
and the wood-lands Plead in si - lence for their peace.
of this na - tion Through the glo - ry of the Lord. A - men.

THE NATION

O God of Earth and Altar

Gilbert K. Chesterton, 1874-1936

436

LLANGLOFFAN 7.6.7.6.D.
Traditional Welsh Melody

1 O God of earth and al - tar, Bow down and hear our cry;
2 From all that ter - ror teach - es, From lies of tongue and pen,
3 Tie in a liv - ing teth - er The prince and priest and thrall;

Our earth - ly rul - ers fal - ter, Our peo - ple drift and die;
From all the eas - y speech - es That com - fort cru - el men,
Bind all our lives to - geth - er, Smite us and save us all;

The walls of gold en - tomb us, The swords of scorn di - vide;
From sale and prof - a - na - tion Of hon - or and the sword,
In ire and ex - ul - ta - tion A - flame with faith, and free,

Take not thy thun - der from us, But take a - way our pride.
From sleep and from dam - na - tion, De - liv - er us, good Lord!
Lift up a liv - ing na - tion, A sin - gle sword to thee. A - men.

THE NATION

437 My Country, 'Tis of Thee

Samuel F. Smith, 1808-1895

AMERICA 6.6.4.6.6.6.4.
Source Unknown

1 My coun-try, 'tis of thee, Sweet land of lib-er-ty,
2 My na-tive coun-try, thee, Land of the no-ble free,
3 Let mu-sic swell the breeze, And ring from all the trees

Of thee I sing; Land where my fa-thers died, Land of the
Thy name I love; I love thy rocks and rills, Thy woods and
Sweet free-dom's song; Let mor-tal tongues a-wake; Let all that

pil-grims' pride, From ev-ery moun-tain side Let free-dom ring.
tem-pled hills; My heart with rap-ture thrills Like that a-bove.
breathe par-take; Let rocks their si-lence break; The sound pro-long. A-men.

4 Our father's God, to thee,
Author of liberty,
To thee we sing;
Long may our land be bright
With freedom's holy light;
Protect us by thy might,
Great God, our King.

THE NATION

O God, Beneath Thy Guiding Hand

438

Leonard Bacon, 1802-1881

DUKE STREET L.M.
John Hatton, d.1793

1 O God, be-neath thy guid-ing hand Our ex-iled
2 Thou heard'st, well-pleased, the song, the prayer; Thy bless-ing
3 Laws, free-dom, truth, and faith in God Came with those

fa-thers crossed the sea, And when they trod the
came, and still its power Shall on-ward through all
ex-iles o'er the waves, And where their pil-grim

win-try strand, With prayer and psalm they wor-shiped thee.
a-ges bear The mem-ory of that ho-ly hour.
feet have trod, The God they trust-ed guards their graves. A-men.

4 And here thy name, O God of love,
   Their children's children shall adore,
   Till these eternal hills remove,
      And spring adorns the earth no more.

THE NATION

439   # Not Alone for Mighty Empire

William P. Merrill, 1867-1954

AUSTRIAN HYMN 8.7.8.7.D.
Franz J. Haydn, 1732-1809

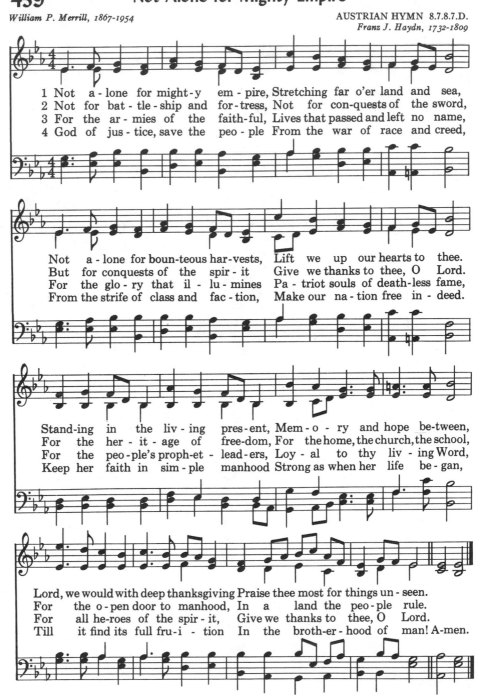

1 Not a-lone for might-y em-pire, Stretching far o'er land and sea,
2 Not for bat-tle-ship and for-tress, Not for con-quests of the sword,
3 For the ar-mies of the faith-ful, Lives that passed and left no name,
4 God of jus-tice, save the peo-ple From the war of race and creed,

Not a-lone for boun-teous har-vests, Lift we up our hearts to thee.
But for conquests of the spir-it Give we thanks to thee, O Lord.
For the glo-ry that il-lu-mines Pa-triot souls of death-less fame,
From the strife of class and fac-tion, Make our na-tion free in-deed.

Stand-ing in the liv-ing pres-ent, Mem-o-ry and hope be-tween,
For the her-it-age of free-dom, For the home, the church, the school,
For the peo-ple's proph-et-lead-ers, Loy-al to thy liv-ing Word,
Keep her faith in sim-ple manhood Strong as when her life be-gan,

Lord, we would with deep thanksgiving Praise thee most for things un-seen.
For the o-pen door to manhood, In a land the peo-ple rule.
For all he-roes of the spir-it, Give we thanks to thee, O Lord.
Till it find its full fru-i-tion In the broth-er-hood of man! A-men.

THE NATION   *Alternative tune,* HYFRYDOL, *No. 13*

O Beautiful for Spacious Skies

Katharine Lee Bates, 1859-1929

MATERNA C.M.D.
Samuel A. Ward, 1848-1903

440

1 O beau-ti-ful for spa-cious skies, For am-ber waves of grain,
2 O beau-ti-ful for pil-grim feet, Whose stern, im-pas-sioned stress
3 O beau-ti-ful for he-roes proved In lib-er-at-ing strife,
4 O beau-ti-ful for pa-triot dream That sees be-yond the years

For pur-ple moun-tain maj-es-ties A-bove the fruit-ed plain!
A thor-ough-fare for free-dom beat A-cross the wil-der-ness!
Who more than self their coun-try loved, And mer-cy more than life!
Thine al-a-bas-ter cit-ies gleam, Un-dimmed by hu-man tears!

A-mer-i-ca! A-mer-i-ca! God shed his grace on thee,
A-mer-i-ca! A-mer-i-ca! God mend thine ev-ery flaw,
A-mer-i-ca! A-mer-i-ca! May God thy gold re-fine,
A-mer-i-ca! A-mer-i-ca! God shed his grace on thee,

And crown thy good with broth-er-hood From sea to shin-ing sea.
Con-firm thy soul in self-con-trol, Thy lib-er-ty in law.
Till all suc-cess be no-ble-ness, And ev-ery gain di-vine.
And crown thy good with broth-er-hood From sea to shin-ing sea. A-men.

THE NATION

441 Once to Every Man and Nation

James Russell Lowell, 1819-1891, alt.

EBENEZER (TON-Y-BOTEL) 8.7.8.7.D.
Thomas J. Williams, 1869-1944

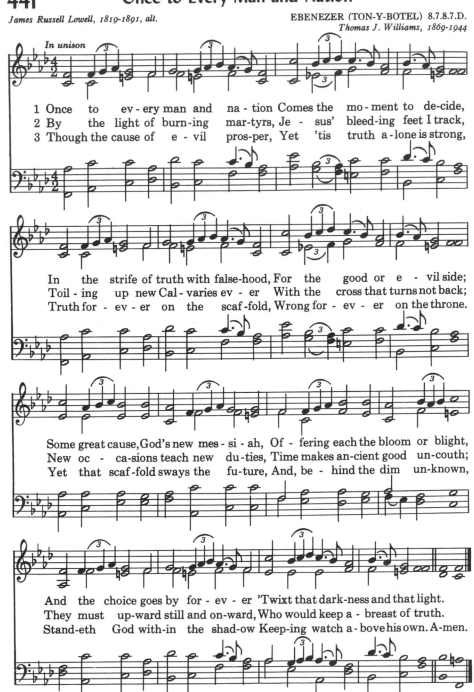

1 Once to ev-ery man and na-tion Comes the mo-ment to de-cide,
2 By the light of burn-ing mar-tyrs, Je-sus' bleed-ing feet I track,
3 Though the cause of e-vil pros-per, Yet 'tis truth a-lone is strong,

In the strife of truth with false-hood, For the good or e-vil side;
Toil-ing up new Cal-varies ev-er With the cross that turns not back;
Truth for-ev-er on the scaf-fold, Wrong for-ev-er on the throne.

Some great cause, God's new mes-si-ah, Of-fering each the bloom or blight,
New oc-ca-sions teach new du-ties, Time makes an-cient good un-couth;
Yet that scaf-fold sways the fu-ture, And, be-hind the dim un-known,

And the choice goes by for-ev-er 'Twixt that dark-ness and that light.
They must up-ward still and on-ward, Who would keep a-breast of truth.
Stand-eth God with-in the shad-ow Keep-ing watch a-bove his own. A-men.

THE NATION

Thou Judge by Whom Each Empire Fell

442

Percy Dearmer, 1867-1936

NUN FREUT EUCH 8.7.8.7.8.8.7.
Klug's "Geistliche Lieder," Wittenberg, 1535

1 Thou Judge by whom each em-pire fell, When pride of power o'er-came it,
2 Search, Lord, our spir-its in thy sight, In best and worst re-veal us;
3 Lo, fear-ing nought we come to thee, Though by our fault con-found-ed;

Con-vict us now, if we re-bel, Our na-tion judge, and shame it.
Shed on our souls a blaze of light, And judge, that thou may'st heal us.
Though self-ish, mean, and base we be, Thy jus-tice is un-bound-ed:

In each sharp cri-sis, Lord, ap-pear, For-give, and show our
The pres-ent be our judg-ment day, When all our lack thou
So large, it nought but love re-quires, And, judg-ing, pard-ons,

du-ty clear: To serve thee by re-pent-ance.
dost sur-vey: Show us our-selves and save us.
frees, in-spires. De-liv-er us from e-vil! A-men.

THE NATION

Mine Eyes Have Seen the Glory

Julia Ward Howe, 1819-1910

BATTLE HYMN OF THE REPUBLIC *Irregular*
William Steffe?, c.1852

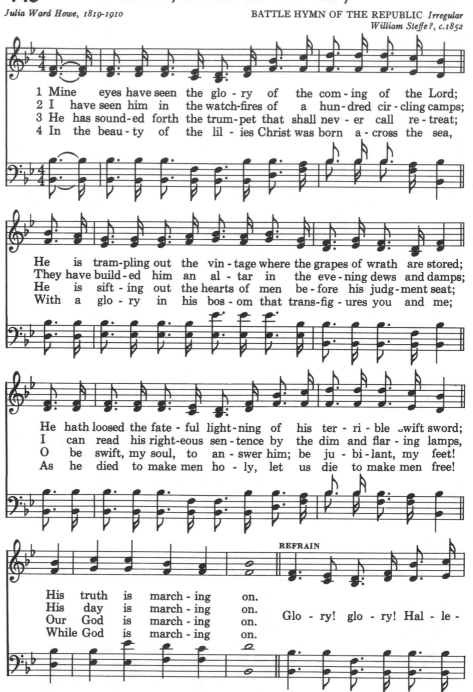

1 Mine eyes have seen the glo-ry of the com-ing of the Lord;
2 I have seen him in the watch-fires of a hun-dred cir-cling camps;
3 He has sound-ed forth the trum-pet that shall nev-er call re-treat;
4 In the beau-ty of the lil-ies Christ was born a-cross the sea,

He is tram-pling out the vin-tage where the grapes of wrath are stored;
They have build-ed him an al-tar in the eve-ning dews and damps;
He is sift-ing out the hearts of men be-fore his judg-ment seat;
With a glo-ry in his bos-om that trans-fig-ures you and me;

He hath loosed the fate-ful light-ning of his ter-ri-ble swift sword;
I can read his right-eous sen-tence by the dim and flar-ing lamps,
O be swift, my soul, to an-swer him; be ju-bi-lant, my feet!
As he died to make men ho-ly, let us die to make men free!

REFRAIN

His truth is march-ing on.
His day is march-ing on.
Our God is march-ing on.
While God is march-ing on.

Glo-ry! glo-ry! Hal-le-

THE NATION

lu - jah! Glo - ry! glo - ry! Hal - le - lu - jah!

Glo - ry! glo - ry! Hal - le - lu - jah! His truth is march - ing on.

THE NATION

O Day of God, Draw Nigh 444

R. B. Y. Scott, 1899- ,alt.

ST. MICHAEL S.M.
Adapted from "Genevan Psalter," 1551

1 O Day of God, draw nigh In beau - ty and in power,
2 Bring to our trou - bled minds, Un - cer - tain and a - fraid,
3 Bring jus - tice to our land, That all may dwell se - cure,
4 Bring to our world of strife Thy sov-ereign word of peace,
5 O Day of God, draw nigh As at cre - a - tion's birth;

Come with thy time-less judg-ment now To match our pres-ent hour.
The qui - et of a stead-fast faith, Calm of a call o - beyed.
And fine - ly build for days to come Foun-da-tions that en - dure.
That war may haunt the earth no more And des - o - la - tion cease.
Let there be light a - gain, and set Thy judg-ments in the earth. A - men.

WORLD PEACE

445 Father Eternal, Ruler of Creation

Laurence Housman, 1865-1959

LANGHAM 11.10.11.10.10.
Geoffrey Shaw, 1879-1943

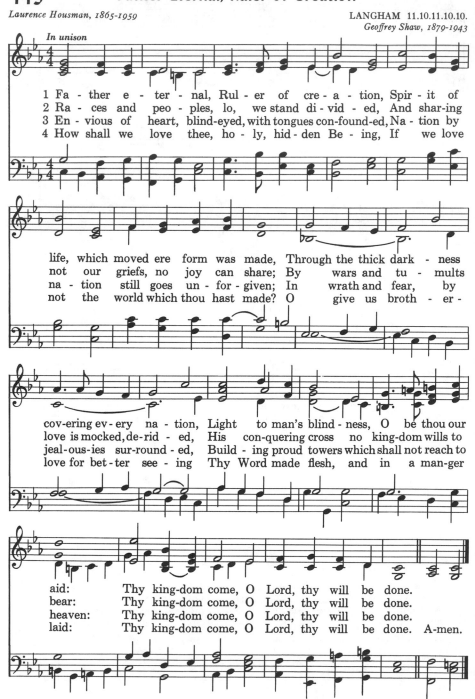

In unison

1 Fa - ther e - ter - nal, Rul - er of cre - a - tion, Spir - it of
2 Ra - ces and peo - ples, lo, we stand di - vid - ed, And shar - ing
3 En - vious of heart, blind-eyed, with tongues con-found-ed, Na - tion by
4 How shall we love thee, ho - ly, hid - den Be - ing, If we love

life, which moved ere form was made, Through the thick dark - ness
not our griefs, no joy can share; By wars and tu - mults
na - tion still goes un - for - given; In wrath and fear, by
not the world which thou hast made? O give us broth - er -

cov-ering ev - ery na - tion, Light to man's blind - ness, O be thou our
love is mocked, de-rid - ed, His con-quering cross no king-dom wills to
jeal-ous-ies sur-round - ed, Build - ing proud towers which shall not reach to
love for bet - ter see - ing Thy Word made flesh, and in a man-ger

aid: Thy king-dom come, O Lord, thy will be done.
bear: Thy king-dom come, O Lord, thy will be done.
heaven: Thy king-dom come, O Lord, thy will be done.
laid: Thy king-dom come, O Lord, thy will be done. A-men.

WORLD PEACE

God the Omnipotent

446

Henry F. Chorley, *1808-1872*, Sts. *1,2, alt.*
John Ellerton, *1826-1893*, Sts. *3,4, alt.*

RUSSIAN HYMN 11.10.11.9.
Alexis F. Lvov, 1799-1870

1 God the Om - nip - o - tent! King, who or - dain - est
2 God the All - mer - ci - ful! earth hath for - sak - en
3 God the all - right - eous One! man hath de - fied thee;
4 God the All - prov - i - dent! earth by thy chas - tening

Thun - der thy clar - ion, the light - ning thy sword,
Thy ways all ho - ly, and slight - ed thy word;
Yet to e - ter - ni - ty stand - eth thy word;
Yet shall to free - dom and truth be re - stored;

Show forth thy pit - y on high where thou reign - est:
Bid not thy wrath in its ter - rors a - wak - en:
False - hood and wrong shall not tar - ry be - side thee:
Through the thick dark - ness thy king - dom is has - tening:

Give to us peace in our time, O Lord.
Give to us peace in our time, O Lord.
Give to us peace in our time, O Lord.
Thou wilt give peace in thy time, O Lord. A - men.

WORLD PEACE

447   O God of Love, O King of Peace

Henry W. Baker, 1821-1877

HESPERUS L.M.
Henry Baker, 1835-1910

1 O God of love, O King of peace, Make wars through-out the
2 Re-mem-ber, Lord, thy works of old, The won-ders that our
3 Whom shall we trust but thee, O Lord? Where rest but on thy

world to cease; The wrath of sin - ful man re - strain:
fa - thers told; Re - mem - ber not our sin's dark stain:
faith - ful word? None ev - er called on thee in vain:

Give peace, O God, give peace a - gain!
Give peace, O God, give peace a - gain!
Give peace, O God, give peace a - gain! A - men.

448   Thy Kingdom Come, O Lord

Frederick L Hosmer, 1840-1929

ST. CECILIA 6.6.6.6.
Leighton G. Hayne, 1836-1883

1 Thy king-dom come, O Lord, Wide-cir-cling as the sun;
2 One in the bond of peace, The serv-ice glad and free
3 Speed, speed the longed-for time Fore-told by rap-tured seers,
4 Till rise in or-dered plan On firm foun-da-tions broad,

WORLD PEACE

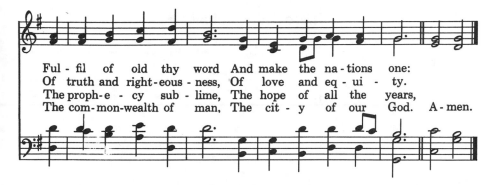

Ful - fil of old thy word And make the na - tions one:
Of truth and right-eous - ness, Of love and eq - ui - ty.
The proph-e - cy sub - lime, The hope of all the years,
The com-mon-wealth of man, The cit - y of our God. A - men.

Let There Be Light, Lord God of Hosts 449

William M. Vories, 1880- , alt.

ELTON L.M.
Lowell Mason, 1792-1872

1 Let there be light, Lord God of hosts! Let there be
2 With - in our pas - sioned hearts in - still The calm that
3 Give us the peace of vi - sion clear To see our
4 Let woe and waste of war - fare cease, That use - ful

wis - dom on the earth! Let broad hu - man - i - ty have birth!
end - eth strain and strife; Make us thy min - is - ters of life;
broth-ers' good our own, To joy and suf - fer not a - lone:
la - bor yet may build Its homes with love and laugh-ter filled!

Let there be deeds, in - stead of boasts!
Purge us from lusts that curse and kill!
The love that cast - eth out all fear!
God, give thy way - ward chil - dren peace! A - men.

Alternative tune, PENTECOST, *No. 367*

WORLD PEACE

450 These Things Shall Be

John A. Symonds, 1840-1893, alt.

TRURO L.M.
Thomas Williams' "Psalmodia Evangelica," 1789

1 These things shall be: a loft-ier race Than e'er the
2 They shall be gen-tle, brave, and strong To spill no
3 Na-tion with na-tion, land with land, In-armed shall

world hath known shall rise With flame of free-dom
drop of blood, but dare All that may plant man's
live as com-rades free; In ev-ery heart and

in their souls, And light of knowl-edge in their eyes;
lord-ship firm On earth and fire and sea and air;
brain shall throb The pulse of one fra-ter-ni-ty; A-men.

4 There shall be no more sin, nor shame,
    Though pain and passion may not die,
For man shall be at one with God
    In bonds of firm necessity.

WORLD PEACE   *A higher setting may be found at No. 454*

Turn Back, O Man, Forswear Thy Foolish Ways 451

Clifford Bax, 1886-1962

OLD 124th 10.10.10.10.10.
"Genevan Psalter," 1551

1 Turn back, O man, for-swear thy fool-ish ways. Old now is
2 Earth might be fair and all men glad and wise. Age aft-er
3 Earth shall be fair, and all her peo-ple one; Nor till that

earth, and none may count her days; Yet thou, her child, whose
age their trag-ic em-pires rise, Built while they dream, and
hour shall God's whole will be done. Now, e-ven now, once

head is crowned with flame, Still wilt not hear thine in-ner God pro-
in that dream-ing weep; Would man but wake from out his haunt-ed
more from earth to sky, Peals forth in joy man's old un-daunt-ed

claim: "Turn back, O man, for-swear thy fool-ish ways!"
sleep, Earth might be fair and all men glad and wise.
cry: "Earth shall be fair, and all her folk be one!" A-men.

WORLD PEACE

Lord, Save Thy World

Albert F. Bayly, 1901-

UFFINGHAM L.M.
Jeremiah Clark, c.1670-1707

1 Lord, save thy world: in bit-ter need Thy chil-dren lift their cry to thee; We wait thy lib-er-at-ing deed To sig-nal hope and set us free.

2 Lord, save thy world: our souls are bound In i-ron chains of fear and pride; High walls of ig-nor-ance a-round Our fa-ces from each oth-er hide.

3 Lord, save thy world: we strive in vain To save our-selves with-out thine aid; What skill and sci-ence slow-ly gain, Is soon to e-vil ends be-trayed. A-men.

4 Lord, save thy world: but thou hast sent
The Savior whom we sorely need;
For us his tears and blood were spent,
That from our bonds we might be freed.

5 Then save us now, by Jesus' power,
And use the lives thy love sets free
To bring at last the glorious hour
When all men find thy liberty.

WORLD PEACE

Ring Out, Wild Bells

Alfred Tennyson, 1809-1892

DEUS TUORUM MILITUM L.M.
Grenoble Church Melody

In unison

1 Ring out, wild bells, to the wild sky, The fly - ing
2 Ring out the old, ring in the new, Ring, hap - py
3 Ring out the grief that saps the mind, For those that

cloud, the frost - y light: The year is dy - ing in the
bells, a - cross the snow! The year is go - ing, let him
here we see no more; Ring out the feud of rich and

night; Ring out, wild bells, and let him die.
go; Ring out the false, ring in the true.
poor; Ring in re - dress to all man - kind. A - men.

4 Ring out false pride in place and blood,
The civic slander and the spite;
Ring in the love of truth and right;
Ring in the common love of good.

5 Ring in the valiant man and free,
The larger heart, the kindlier hand;
Ring out the darkness of the land;
Ring in the Christ that is to be.

Alternative tune, MENDON, *No. 477*

NEW YEAR

454 Great God, We Sing That Mighty Hand

Philip Doddridge, 1702-1751

TRURO L.M.
Thomas Williams' "Psalmodia Evangelica," 1789

1 Great God, we sing that might-y hand By which sup-
2 By day, by night, at home, a - broad, Still are we
3 With grate-ful hearts the past we own; The fu - ture,

port - ed still we stand; The open - ing year thy
guard - ed by our God: By his in - ces - sant
all to us un - known, We to thy guard - ian

mer - cy shows; That mer - cy crowns it till it close.
boun - ty fed, By his un - err - ing coun - sel led.
care com - mit, And, peace-ful, leave be - fore thy feet. A-men.

4 In scenes exalted or depressed,
Thou art our joy, and thou our rest;
Thy goodness all our hopes shall raise,
Adored through all our changing days.

NEW YEAR

A lower setting may be found at No. 450

'Tis Winter Now; the Fallen Snow

Samuel Longfellow, 1819-1892

DANBY L.M.
Traditional English Melody
Arr. by R. Vaughan Williams, 1872-1958

In unison

1 'Tis win-ter now; the fal-len snow Has left the
2 And yet God's love is not with-drawn; His life with-
3 And though a-broad the sharp winds blow, And skies are

heavens all cold-ly clear; Through leaf-less boughs the sharp winds
in the keen air breathes; His beau-ty paints the crim-son
chill, and frosts are keen, Home clos-er draws her cir-cle

blow, And all the earth lies dead and drear.
dawn, And clothes the boughs with glit-tering wreaths.
now, And warm-er glows her light with-in. A-men.

4 O God! who givest the winter's cold,
As well as summer's joyous rays,
Us warmly in thy love enfold,
And keep us through life's wintry days.

Alternative tune, PUER NOBIS NASCITUR, *No. 188*

CHANGING SEASONS

456 All Beautiful the March of Days

Frances W. Wile, 1878-1939

FOREST GREEN C.M.D.
Traditional English Melody
Arr. by R. Vaughan Williams, 1872-1958

1 All beau - ti - ful the march of days, As sea - sons come and go;
2 O'er white ex - pan - ses spark-ling pure The ra - diant morns un - fold;
3 O thou from whose un - fath - omed law The year in beau-ty flows,

The hand that shaped the rose hath wrought The crys - tal of the snow,
The sol - emn splen - dors of the night Burn bright-er through the cold.
Thy-self the vi - sion pass-ing by In crys - tal and in rose,

Hath sent the hoar - y frost of heaven, The flow - ing wa - ters sealed,
Life mounts in ev - ery throbbing vein, Love deep-ens round the hearth,
Day un - to day doth ut - ter speech, And night to night pro - claim,

And laid a si - lent love-li - ness On hill and wood and field.
And clear-er sounds the an - gel hymn, "Good will to men on earth."
In ev - er-chang-ing words of light, The won - der of thy name. A-men.

CHANGING SEASONS

The Summer Days Are Come Again 457

Samuel Longfellow, 1819-1892, alt.

FOREST GREEN C.M.D.
Traditional English Melody
Arr. by R. Vaughan Williams, 1872-1958

1 The summer days are come again;
   Once more the glad earth yields
Her golden wealth of ripening grain,
   And breath of clover fields,
And deepening shade of summer woods,
   And glow of summer air,
And winging thoughts, and happy moods
   Of love and joy and prayer.

2 The summer days are come again;
   The birds are on the wing;
God's praises, in their loving strain,
   Unconsciously they sing.
We know who giveth all the good
   That doth our cup o'erbrim;
For summer joy in field and wood
   We lift our song to him.   Amen.

Praise to God, Your Praises Bring 458

William C. Gannett, 1840-1923, alt.

SAVANNAH 7.7.7.7.
"The Foundery Collection," 1742

1 Praise to God, your prais-es bring; Hearts, bow down and voic-es, sing
2 Praise him for his budding green, A - pril's res-ur - rec-tion-scene;
3 Praise him for his sum-mer rain, Feed - ing, day and night, the grain;
4 Praise him for his gar - den root, Mead - ow grass and or - chard fruit:

Prais-es to the glo-rious One, All his year of won-der done.
Praise him for his shin-ing hours, Star-ring all the land with flowers.
Praise him for his ti - ny seed, Hold-ing all his world shall need.
Praise for hills and val-leys broad, Each the ta - ble of our God. A-men.

5 Praise him for the winter's rest,
   Snow that falls on nature's breast;
Praise for happy dreams of birth,
   Brooding in the quiet earth.

6 For his year of wonder done,
   Praise to the all-glorious One!
Hearts, bow down and voices, sing
Praise and love to nature's King!

Alternative tune, MONKLAND, *No. 463*

CHANGING SEASONS

459 With Songs and Honors Sounding Loud

Isaac Watts, 1674-1748, alt.

ELLACOMBE C.M.D.
"Gesangbuch," Wirtemberg, 1784

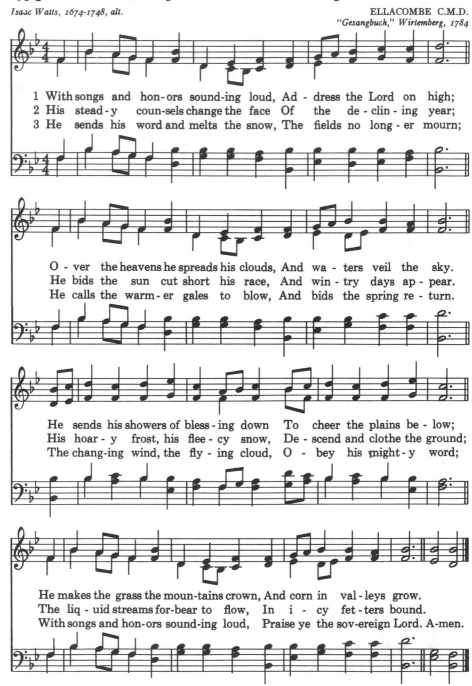

1 With songs and hon-ors sound-ing loud, Ad - dress the Lord on high;
2 His stead - y coun-sels change the face Of the de - clin - ing year;
3 He sends his word and melts the snow, The fields no long - er mourn;

O - ver the heavens he spreads his clouds, And wa - ters veil the sky.
He bids the sun cut short his race, And win - try days ap - pear.
He calls the warm - er gales to blow, And bids the spring re - turn.

He sends his showers of bless - ing down To cheer the plains be - low;
His hoar - y frost, his flee - cy snow, De - scend and clothe the ground;
The chang-ing wind, the fly - ing cloud, O - bey his might - y word;

He makes the grass the moun-tains crown, And corn in val - leys grow.
The liq - uid streams for-bear to flow, In i - cy fet - ters bound.
With songs and hon-ors sound-ing loud, Praise ye the sov-ereign Lord. A-men.

CHANGING SEASONS   *A lower setting may be found at No. 68*

We Plow the Fields and Scatter

460

Matthias Claudias, 1740-1815
Tr. Jane M. Campbell, 1817-1878, alt.

WIR PFLÜGEN 7.6.7.6.D. *with Refrain*
Johann A. P. Schulz, 1747-1800

1 We plow the fields and scat-ter The good seed on the land, But it is
2 He on-ly is the mak-er Of all things near and far; He paints the
3 We thank thee, then, O Fa-ther, For all things bright and good: The seed-time

fed and wa-tered By God's al-might-y hand. He sends the snow in
way-side flow-er, He lights the eve-ning star. The winds and waves o-
and the har-vest, Our life, our health, our food. Ac-cept the gifts we

win-ter, The warmth to swell the grain, The breez-es and the sun-shine, And
bey him, By him the birds are fed; Much more, to us his chil-dren, He
of-fer, For all thy love im-parts, And, what thou most de-sir-est, Our

REFRAIN

soft, re-fresh-ing rain.
gives our dai-ly bread. All good gifts a-round us Are sent from heaven a-
hum-ble, thank-ful hearts.

bove; Then thank the Lord, O thank the Lord For all his love. A-men.

HARVEST AND THANKSGIVING

461 Come, Ye Thankful People, Come

Henry Alford, 1810-1871

ST. GEORGE'S WINDSOR 7.7.7.7.D.
George J. Elvey, 1816-1893

1 Come, ye thank-ful peo-ple, come, Raise the song of har-vest home;
2 All the world is God's own field, Fruit un-to his praise to yield;
3 For the Lord our God shall come, And shall take his har-vest home;
4 E-ven so, Lord, quick-ly come To thy fi-nal har-vest home;

All is safe-ly gath-ered in, Ere the win-ter storms be-gin;
Wheat and tares to-geth-er sown, Un-to joy or sor-row grown;
From his field shall in that day All of-fens-es purge a-way,
Gath-er thou thy peo-ple in, Free from sor-row, free from sin;

God, our Mak-er, doth pro-vide For our wants to be sup-plied;
First the blade, and then the ear, Then the full corn shall ap-pear;
Give his an-gels charge at last In the fire the tares to cast,
There for-ev-er pu-ri-fied, In thy pres-ence to a-bide;

Come to God's own tem-ple, come, Raise the song of har-vest home.
Lord of har-vest, grant that we Whole-some grain and pure may be.
But the fruit-ful ears to store In his gar-ner ev-er-more.
Come, with all thine an-gels, come, Raise the glo-rious har-vest home. A-men.

HARVEST AND THANKSGIVING

Come, Ye Thankful People, Come

462

Henry Alford, 1810-1871
Anna L. Barbauld, 1743-1825, and others

ST. GEORGE'S WINDSOR 7.7.7.7.D.
George J. Elvey, 1816-1893

1 Come, ye thankful people, come,
 Raise the song of harvest home;
All is safely gathered in
 Ere the winter storms begin;
God, our Maker, doth provide
 For our wants to be supplied;
Come to God's own temple, come,
 Raise the song of harvest home.

2 All the blessings of the field,
 All the stores the gardens yield,
All the fruits in full supply,
 Ripened 'neath the summer sky,
All that spring with bounteous hand
 Scatters o'er the smiling land,
All that liberal autumn pours
 From her rich o'er-flowing stores,

3 These to thee, our God, we owe,
 Source whence all our blessings flow;
And for these our souls shall raise
 Grateful vows and solemn praise.
Come, then, thankful people, come,
 Raise the song of harvest home;
Come to God's own temple, come,
 Raise the song of harvest home. Amen.

Praise, O Praise Our God and King

463

Henry W. Baker, 1821-1877

MONKLAND 7.7.7.7.
"Hymn Tunes of the United Brethren," 1824
Arr. by John B. Wilkes, 1785-1869

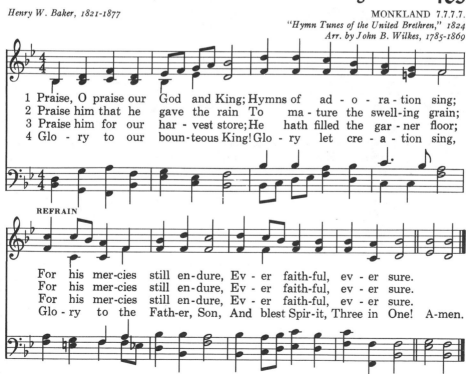

1 Praise, O praise our God and King; Hymns of ad-o-ra-tion sing;
2 Praise him that he gave the rain To ma-ture the swell-ing grain;
3 Praise him for our har-vest store; He hath filled the gar-ner floor;
4 Glo-ry to our boun-teous King! Glo-ry let cre-a-tion sing,

REFRAIN

For his mer-cies still en-dure, Ev-er faith-ful, ev-er sure.
For his mer-cies still en-dure, Ev-er faith-ful, ev-er sure.
For his mer-cies still en-dure, Ev-er faith-ful, ev-er sure.
Glo-ry to the Fath-er, Son, And blest Spir-it, Three in One! A-men.

HARVEST AND THANKSGIVING

464 Praise to God, Immortal Praise

Anna L. Barbauld, 1743-1825, alt.

DIX 7.7.7.7.7.7.
Adapted from a chorale by
Conrad Kocher, 1743-1872

1 Praise to God, im-mor-tal praise, For the love that crowns our days!
2 For the bless-ings of the field, For the stores the gar-dens yield,

Boun-teous source of ev-ery joy, Let thy praise our tongues em-ploy:
Flocks that whit-en all the plain, Yel-low sheaves of rip-ened grain,

Sing-ing thus through all our days, Praise to God, im-mor-tal praise.
Lord, for these, our souls shall raise, Grate-ful vows and sol-emn praise. A-men.

3 All that spring with bounteous hand
   Scatters o'er the smiling land,
All that liberal autumn pours
   From her rich o'erflowing stores,
All to thee, our God, we owe,
   Source whence all our blessings flow.

HARVEST AND THANKSGIVING

O Perfect Love

465

Dorothy F. Gurney, 1858-1932

O PERFECT LOVE 11.10.11.10.
Joseph Barnby, 1838-1896

1 O per - fect Love, all hu - man thought tran - scend - ing,
2 O per - fect Life, be thou their full as - sur - ance
3 Grant them the joy which bright - ens earth - ly sor - row;

Low - ly we kneel in prayer be - fore thy throne,
Of ten - der char - i - ty and stead - fast faith,
Grant them the peace which calms all earth - ly strife,

That theirs may be the love which knows no end - ing,
Of pa - tient hope, and qui - et, brave en - dur - ance,
And to life's day the glo - rious un - known mor - row

Whom thou for - ev - er - more dost join in one.
With child - like trust that fears nor pain nor death.
That dawns up - on e - ter - nal love and life. A-men.

MARRIAGE AND THE FAMILY

466 Our Father, by Whose Name

F. Bland Tucker, 1895-

RHOSYMEDRE 6.6.6.6.8.8.8.
John D. Edwards, 1806-1885

1 Our Fa - ther, by whose name All fa - ther - hood is known,
2 O Christ, thy - self a child With - in an earth - ly home,
3 O Spir - it, who dost bind Our hearts in u - ni - ty,

Who dost in love pro - claim Each fam - i - ly thine own,
With heart still un - de - filed, Thou didst to man - hood come;
Who teach - est us to find The love from self set free,

Bless thou all par - ents, guard - ing well, With con - stant love as
Our chil - dren bless, in ev - ery place, That they may all be -
In all our hearts such love in - crease, That ev - ery home, by

sen - ti - nel, The homes in which thy peo - ple dwell.
hold thy face, And know - ing thee may grow in grace.
this re - lease, May be the dwell - ing place of peace. A - men.

MARRIAGE AND THE FAMILY   *A higher setting may be found at No. 169*

Father, to Thee We Look in All Our Sorrow 467

Frederick L. Hosmer, 1840-1929

L'OMNIPOTENT 11.10.11.10.
"Genevan Psalter," 1551

1 Fa - ther, to thee we look in all our sor - row;
2 When fond hopes fail and skies are dark be - fore us,
3 Nought shall af - fright us, on thy good - ness lean - ing;
4 Pa - tient, O heart, though heav - y be thy sor - rows,

Thou art the foun - tain whence our heal - ing flows;
When the vain cares that vex our life in - crease,
Low in the heart faith sing - eth still her song;
Be not cast down, dis - qui - et - ed in vain;

Dark though the night, joy com - eth with the mor - row;
Comes with its calm the thought that thou art o'er us,
Chast - ened by pain we learn life's deep - er mean - ing,
Yet shall thou praise him, when these dark - ened fur - rows,

Safe - ly they rest who on thy love re - pose.
And we grow qui - et, fold - ed in thy peace.
And in our weak - ness thou dost make us strong.
Where now he plow - eth, wave with gold - en grain. A - men.

FUNERALS

468   God of the Living, in Whose Eyes

John Ellerton, 1826-1893, alt.

GOTTLOB, ES GEHT 8.8.8.8.8.8.
German Chorale
Harm. by J. S. Bach, 1685-1750

In unison

1 God of the liv - ing, in whose eyes Un - veiled thy
2 Re - leased from earth - ly toil and strife, With thee is
3 Not spilt like wa - ter on the ground, Not wrapped in
4 Thy word is true, thy will is just; To thee we

whole cre - a - tion lies, All souls are thine; we must not say
hid - den still their life; Thine are their thoughts, their works, their powers,
dream - less sleep pro-found, Not wan-dering in un - known de - spair
leave them, Lord, in trust, And bless thee for the love which gave

That those are dead who pass a - way; From this our
All thine, and yet most tru - ly ours, For well we
Be - yond thy voice, thine arm, thy care, Not left to
Thy Son to fill a hu - man grave, That none might

world of flesh set free, We know them liv-ing un - to thee.
know, wher-e'er they be, Our dead are liv-ing un - to thee.
lie like fall - en tree, Not dead, but liv-ing un - to thee.
fear that world to see, Where all are liv-ing un - to thee. A-men.

FUNERALS

O Lord of Life, Where'er They Be

469

Frederick L. Hosmer, 1840-1929

GELOBT SEI GOTT 8.8.8. *with Alleluias*
Melody by Melchior Vulpius, c.1560-1616
Harm. by Henry G. Ley, 1887-

1 O Lord of life, wher-e'er they be, Safe in thine own e-ter-ni-ty, Our dead are liv-ing un-to thee:

2 All souls are thine, and here or there They rest with-in thy shel-ter-ing care; One prov-i-dence a-like they share:

3 Thy word is true, thy ways are just; A-bove the re-quiem, "Dust to dust," Shall rise our psalm of grate-ful trust:

REFRAIN

Al-le-lu-ia! Al-le-lu-ia! Al-le-lu-ia! A-men.

4 O happy they in God who rest,
No more by fear and doubt oppressed,
Living or dying, they are blest:
Alleluia! Alleluia! Alleluia!

FUNERALS

470 God of the Prophets

Denis Wortman, 1835-1922

TOULON 10.10.10.10.
Abridged from "Genevan Psalter," 1551

1 God of the proph - ets, bless the proph - ets' sons:
2 A - noint them proph - ets! Make their ears at - tent
3 A - noint them priests! Strong in - ter - ces - sors they
4 A - noint them kings! Aye, king - ly kings, O Lord!
5 Make them a - pos - tles! Her - alds of thy cross,

E - li - jah's man - tle o'er E - li - sha cast.
To thy di - vin - est speech; their hearts a - wake
For par - don, and for char - i - ty and peace!
A - noint them with the Spir - it of thy Son:
Forth may they go to tell all realms thy grace;

Each age its sol - emn task may claim but once:
To hu - man need; their lips make el - o - quent
Ah, if with them the world might pass a - stray,
Theirs not a jew - eled crown, a blood-stained sword;
In - spired of thee, may they count all but loss,

Make each one no - bler, strong - er than the last!
To as - sure the right, and ev - ery e - vil break.
In - to the dear Christ's life of sac - ri - fice.
Theirs, by sweet love, for Christ a king - dom won.
And stand at last with joy be - fore thy face. A - men.

ORDINATIONS

Henry R. Moxley, 1881-

WELWYN 11.10.11.10.
Alfred Scott-Gatty, 1847-1918

1 Lord of true light, we grate-ful-ly a-dore thee
2 We praise thee, Lord, that now the light is fall-ing
3 Be in his mind, the truth of all his teach-ing;
4 Be in his heart, the fount of all his lov-ing;
5 Be in his will, his strength for self-de-ni-al;

For all thy gifts be-stowed up-on our race,
Here on thy serv-ant in this sol-emn hour;
Give him the faith that wel-comes all the light,
Make him a shep-herd, kind to young and old,
Fit him to fol-low thee through pain and loss,

For saints of old, who made their vows be-fore thee,
Con-firm in him his high and ho-ly call-ing,
Till, from the shad-ows to thy pres-ence reach-ing,
Pa-tient and watch-ful when thy sheep are rov-ing,
Serv-ing the world, un-til through ev-ery tri-al

And told the world the won-ders of thy grace.
En-due him with thy wis-dom, love, and power.
He sees the glo-ry that shall end our night.
Tend-ing with care the lambs with-in the fold.
He learns at length the tri-umph of the cross. A-men.

Alternative tune, L'OMNIPOTENT, *No. 467*

ORDINATIONS

472   Lord, Thou Hast Known Our Joy

Charles S. Mills, 1861-1942

ITALIAN HYMN 6.6.4.6.6.6.6.4.
Felice de Giardini, 1716-1796

1 Lord, thou hast known our joy, Build-ing for
2 Now as we give it thee Thine ev - er -
3 May this new tem - ple prove True wit - ness
4 O Christ, the Church - 's head, Who for us
5 Lord, though these hours of praise, And all our

thine em - ploy This house of prayer; As we thy
more to be, Who giv - est all, Come, thou, O
of thy love, To all men free; May all who
all hast bled That we might live, Thy cross we
earth - ly days Will soon be o'er, Still may these

help have sought, With la - bor long have wrought, Our will - ing
Lord di - vine, Make this thy ho - ly shrine Where thy pure
seek this door, And sav - ing grace im - plore, Love one an -
lift on high This house to glo - ri - fy; On thee our
courts pro - claim The glo - ry of thy name, O thou, who

of - ferings brought This work to share.
light may shine; O hear our call!
oth - er more As they seek thee.
hearts re - ly Thy power to give.
art the same For - ev - er - more! A - men.

CHURCH DEDICATIONS AND ANNIVERSARIES   *A lower setting may be found at No. 246*

O Lord, Almighty God, Thy Works 473

"The Whole Booke of Psalmes," 1647
(The Bay Psalm Book)

YORK C.M.
"Scottish Psalter," 1615
Harm. by John Milton, Sr., c.1563-1647

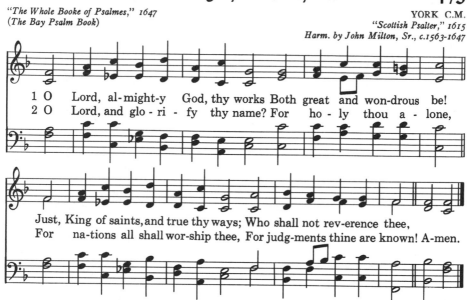

1 O Lord, al-might-y God, thy works Both great and won-drous be!
2 O Lord, and glo-ri-fy thy name? For ho-ly thou a-lone,

Just, King of saints, and true thy ways; Who shall not rev-erence thee,
For na-tions all shall wor-ship thee, For judg-ments thine are known! A-men.

This hymn, called "The Song of Moses and the Lamb," was sung at the close of the meeting of the Cambridge Synod in 1648, the first great council of the Congregational churches in New England.

O Lord, Almighty God, Thy Works 474
Melody in the Tenor

"The Whole Booke of Psalmes," 1647
(The Bay Psalm Book)

YORK C.M.
Arr. by Simon Stubbs, c. 16th century
"Ravenscroft's Psalter," 1621

1 O Lord, al-might-y God, thy works Both great and won-drous be!
2 O Lord, and glo-ri-fy thy name? For ho-ly thou a-lone,

Just, King of saints, and true thy ways; Who shall not rev-erence thee,
For na-tions all shall wor-ship thee, For judg-ments thine are known!

This alternative arrangement may be used for one or both stanzas, the congregation singing the melody only

CHURCH DEDICATIONS AND ANNIVERSARIES

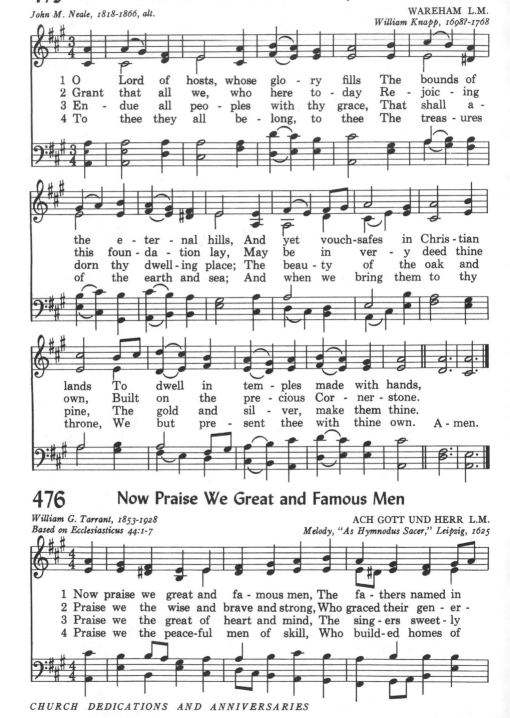

475 O Lord of Hosts, Whose Glory Fills

John M. Neale, 1818-1866, alt.

WAREHAM L.M.
William Knapp, 1698?-1768

1 O Lord of hosts, whose glo-ry fills The bounds of
2 Grant that all we, who here to-day Re-joic-ing
3 En-due all peo-ples with thy grace, That shall a-
4 To thee they all be-long, to thee The treas-ures

the e-ter-nal hills, And yet vouch-safes in Chris-tian
this foun-da-tion lay, May be in ver-y deed thine
dorn thy dwell-ing place; The beau-ty of the oak and
of the earth and sea; And when we bring them to thy

lands To dwell in tem-ples made with hands,
own, Built on the pre-cious Cor-ner-stone.
pine, The gold and sil-ver, make them thine.
throne, We but pre-sent thee with thine own. A-men.

476 Now Praise We Great and Famous Men

William G. Tarrant, 1853-1928
Based on Ecclesiasticus 44:1-7

ACH GOTT UND HERR L.M.
Melody, "As Hymnodus Sacer," Leipzig, 1625

1 Now praise we great and fa-mous men, The fa-thers named in
2 Praise we the wise and brave and strong, Who graced their gen-er-
3 Praise we the great of heart and mind, The sing-ers sweet-ly
4 Praise we the peace-ful men of skill, Who build-ed homes of

CHURCH DEDICATIONS AND ANNIVERSARIES

sto - ry; And praise the Lord, who now as then Re -
a - tion, Who helped the right, and fought the wrong, And
gift - ed, Whose mu - sic like a might - y wind The
beau - ty, And, rich in art, made rich - er still The

veals in man his glo - ry.
made our folk a na - tion.
souls of men up - lift - ed.
broth - er - hood of du - ty. A - men.

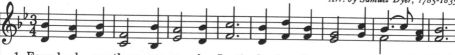

Founded on Thee, Our Only Lord   477

Samuel F. Smith, 1808-1895

MENDON L.M.
German Melody
Arr. by Samuel Dyer, 1785-1835

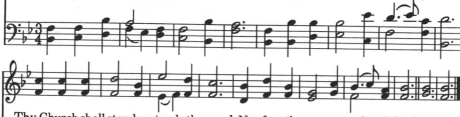

1 Found-ed on thee, our on - ly Lord, On thee, the ev - er - last - ing Rock,
2 For thee our wait - ing spir - its yearn, For thee this house of praise we rear;
3 Come, with thy Spir - it and thy power, The Con-queror, once the Cru - ci - fied;
4 Ac - cept the work our hands have wrought; Ac-cept, O God, this earth-ly shrine;

Thy Church shall stand as stands thy word, Nor fear the storm, nor dread the shock.
To thee with long-ing hearts we turn; Come, fix thy glo-rious pres-ence here.
Our God, our Strength, our King, our Tower, Here plant thy throne, and here a-bide.
Be thou our rock, our life, our thought, And we, as liv - ing tem-ples, thine. A-men.

A lower setting may be found at No. 238   CHURCH DEDICATIONS AND ANNIVERSARIES

478 All Things Bright and Beautiful

Cecil F. Alexander, 1818-1895

ROYAL OAK 7.6.7.6. with Refrain
Traditional English Melody
Adapted by Martin Shaw, 1875-

In unison

REFRAIN

All things bright and beau-ti-ful, All crea-tures great and small,

All things wise and won-der-ful, The Lord God made them all.

Fine

1 Each lit-tle flower that o-pens, Each lit-tle bird that sings,
2 The pur-ple-head-ed moun-tain, The riv-er run-ning by,
3 The cold wind in the win-ter, The pleas-ant sum-mer sun,

He made their glow-ing col-ors, He made their ti-ny wings.
The sun-set, and the morn-ing That bright-ens up the sky,
The ripe fruits in the gar-den, He made them ev-er-y one.

Repeat Refrain

CHILDREN

Father, We Thank Thee for the Night

479

Attr. to Rebecca J. Weston, dates unknown

ONSLOW L.M.
Melody, Daniel Batchellor, dates unknown
"Manual for Teachers," 1885

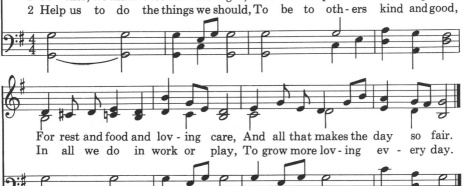

1 Fa - ther, we thank thee for the night, And for the pleas-ant morn-ing light,
2 Help us to do the things we should, To be to oth - ers kind and good,

For rest and food and lov - ing care, And all that makes the day so fair.
In all we do in work or play, To grow more lov - ing ev - ery day.

I Love to Think That Jesus Saw

480

Ada Skemp, 1857-1927

CHILDHOOD 8.8.8.6.
"A Students' Hymnal," University of Wales, 1923
H. Walford Davies, 1869-1941

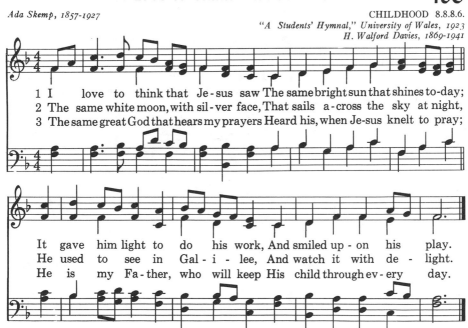

1 I love to think that Je - sus saw The same bright sun that shines to-day;
2 The same white moon, with sil - ver face, That sails a-cross the sky at night,
3 The same great God that hears my prayers Heard his, when Je-sus knelt to pray;

It gave him light to do his work, And smiled up - on his play.
He used to see in Gal - i - lee, And watch it with de - light.
He is my Fa - ther, who will keep His child through ev - ery day.

CHILDREN

481   I Sing a Song of the Saints of God

Lesbia Scott, 1898- , alt.

GRAND ISLE *Irregular*
John H. Hopkins, 1861-1945

In unison

1 I sing a song of the saints of God Pa-tient and brave and true,
2 They loved their Lord so dear, so dear, And his love made them strong;
3 They lived not on - ly in a - ges past, There are hun-dreds of thou-sands still;

Who toiled and fought and lived and died For the Lord they loved and
And they fol-lowed the right, for Je - sus' sake, The whole of their good lives
The world is bright with the joy-ous saints Who love to do Je - sus'

knew. And one was a doc - tor, and one was a queen, And
long. And one was a sol - dier, and one was a priest, And
will. You can meet them in school, or in lanes, or at sea, In

one was a shep-herd-ess on the green: They were all of them
one was slain by a fierce wild beast: And there's not an - y
church, or in trains, or in shops, or at tea; For the saints of

CHILDREN

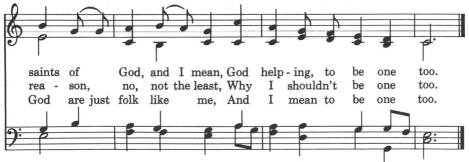

saints of God, and I mean, God help-ing, to be one too.
rea - son, no, not the least, Why I shouldn't be one too.
God are just folk like me, And I mean to be one too.

Little Jesus, Sweetly Sleep

482

Czech Carol
Tr. Percy Dearmer, 1867-1936

ROCKING 10.7.8.8.7.7.
Czech Melody
Arr. by Martin Shaw, 1875-

1 Lit - tle Je - sus, sweet - ly sleep, do not stir; We will lend a
2 Mar-y's lit - tle ba - by, sleep, sweet - ly sleep; Sleep in com - fort,

coat of fur; We will rock you, rock you, rock you, We will rock you, rock you,
slum - ber deep; We will rock you, rock you, rock you, We will rock you, rock you,

rock you: See the fur to keep you warm, Snug-ly round your ti - ny form.
rock you: We will serve you all we can, Dar-ling, dar - ling lit - tle man.

CHILDREN

483   I Think When I Read That Sweet Story

Jemima Luke, 1813-1906, alt.

SWEET STORY *Irregular*
Greek Melody
Arr. by William B. Bradbury, 1816-1868

In unison

1 I think when I read that sweet sto-ry of old,
2 I wish that his hands had been placed on my head,

When Je-sus was here a-mong men,
That his arm had been thrown a-round me,

How he called lit-tle chil-dren as lambs to his fold,
And that I might have seen his kind look when he said,

I should like to have been with him then.
"Let the lit-tle ones come un-to me."

CHILDREN

Remember All the People

484

Percy Dearmer, 1867-1936

FAR-OFF LANDS 7.6.7.6.D.
Melody of the Bohemian Brethren
Arr. by C. Winfred Douglas, 1867-1944

1 Re - mem - ber all the peo - ple Who live in far - off lands,
2 Some work in sul - try for - ests Where apes swing to and fro;
3 God bless the men and wom - en Who serve him o - ver - sea;

In strange and love - ly cit - ies, Or roam the des - ert sands,
Some fish in might - y riv - ers, Some hunt a - cross the snow.
God raise up more to help them To set the na - tions free,

Or farm the moun - tain pas - tures, Or till the end - less plains
Re - mem - ber all God's chil - dren Who yet have nev - er heard
Till all the dis - tant peo - ple In ev - ery for - eign place

Where chil - dren wade through rice fields And watch the cam - el trains.
The truth that comes from Je - sus, The glo - ry of his Word.
Shall un - der - stand his king - dom And come in - to his grace.

CHILDREN

485 This Is My Father's World

Maltbie D. Babcock, 1858-1901, alt.

TERRA BEATA S.M.D.
Traditional English Melody
Adapted by Franklin L. Sheppard, 1852-1930

In unison

1 This is my Fa-ther's world; And to my lis-tening ears, All
2 This is my Fa-ther's world; The birds their car-ols raise, The
3 This is my Fa-ther's world; Oh, let me ne'er for-get That

na - ture sings, and round me rings The mu - sic of the spheres.
morn - ing light, the lil - y white, De - clare their Mak-er's praise.
though the wrong seems oft so strong, God is the rul - er yet.

This is my Fa-ther's world; I rest me in the thought Of
This is my Fa-ther's world; He shines in all that's fair; In the
This is my Fa-ther's world; Why should my heart be sad? The

rocks and trees, of skies and seas, His hand the won-ders wrought.
rus - tling grass I hear him pass; He speaks to me ev-ery-where.
Lord is king; let the heav-ens ring. God reigns; let the earth be glad.

CHILDREN

Golden Breaks the Dawn

486

T. C. Chao, 1888-
Tr. Frank W. Price, 1895-

LE P'ING 5.5.5.5.D.
Chinese Folk Melody
Adapted by Hu Te-ngai, dates unknown

1 Gold - en breaks the dawn, Comes the east - ern sun
2 Give me dai - ly bread While I do my part;

Like a man of brawn Set his course to run.
Bright skies o - ver - head, Glad - ness in my heart.

Birds a - bove me fly, Flow - ers bloom be - low;
Sim - ple wants pro - vide, E - vil let me shun,

Through the earth and sky God's great mer - cies flow.
Je - sus at my side Till the day is done.

Praise Our God Above

487

T. C. Chao, 1888-
Tr. Frank W. Price, 1895-

HSUAN P'ING 5.5.5.5.D.
Confucian Temple Chant

1 Praise our God a - bove For his bound - less love,
2 God's care like a cloak Wraps us coun - try folk;

Spring wind, sum - mer rain, Then the har - vest grain,
He makes green things grow, Rip - ens what we sow.

Pearl - y rice and corn, Fra - grant au - tumn morn.
Through him we are strong, Sing our har - vest song;

Though our work is hard, God gives us re - ward.
Praise him, field and flower, Praise his might - y power.

CHILDREN

Go, Tell It on the Mountain

Negro Spiritual

GO TELL IT ON THE MOUNTAIN *Irregular*
Negro Melody

REFRAIN

Go, tell it on the moun-tain, O-ver the hills and ev-ery-where;

Go, tell it on the moun-tain That Je-sus Christ is born! *Fine*

1 While shep-herds kept their watch-ing O'er si-lent flocks by night, Be-
2 The shep-herds feared and trem-bled When lo! a-bove the earth Rang
3 Down in a low-ly man-ger The hum-ble Christ was born, And

hold through-out the heav-ens There shone a ho-ly light. *D.C.*
out the an-gel cho-rus That hailed our Sav-ior's birth.
God sent us sal-va-tion That bless-ed Christ-mas morn.

I Would Be True

Howard A. Walter, 1883-1918

PEEK 11.10.11.10.10.
Joseph Y. Peek, 1843-1911

489

1 I would be true, for there are those who trust me;
2 I would be friend of all, the foe, the friend-less;

I would be pure, for there are those who care;
I would be giv-ing, and for-get the gift;

I would be strong, for there is much to suf-fer;
I would be hum-ble, for I know my weak-ness;

I would be brave, for there is much to dare,
I would look up, and laugh, and love, and lift,

I would be brave, for there is much to dare.
I would look up, and laugh, and love, and lift. A-men.

YOUTH

490 Now in the Days of Youth

Walter J. Mathams, 1853-1932

DIADEMATA S.M.D.
George J. Elvey, 1816-1893

1 Now in the days of youth, When life flows fresh and free,
2 Teach us wher-e'er we live, To act as in thy sight,
3 Teach us to love the true, The beau - ti - ful and pure,
4 Spir - it of Christ, do thou Our first bright days in - spire,

Thou Lord of all our hearts and lives We give our-selves to thee;
And do what thou wouldst have us do With ra - di - ant de - light,
And let us not for one short hour An e - vil thought en - dure;
That we may live the life of love And loft - i - est de - sire;

Our fer - vent gift re - ceive, And fit us to ful - fill,
Not choos - ing what is great, Nor spurn - ing what is small,
But give us grace to stand De - cid - ed, brave, and strong,
And be by thee pre - pared For larg - er years to come,

Through all our days, in all our ways, Our heavenly Fa-ther's will.
But take as from thy hands our tasks And glo - ri - fy them all.
The lov - ers of all ho - ly things, The foes of all things wrong.
And for the life in - ef - fa - ble With-in the Fa-ther's home. A-men.

YOUTH

A lower setting may be found at No. 199

O God of Youth, Whose Spirit

491

Bates G. Burt, 1878-1948

LYNNE 13.10.11.10.
Bates G. Burt, 1878-1948

In unison

1 O God of youth, whose Spir-it in our hearts is stir - ring
2 Fill thou our hearts with zeal in ev-ery brave en-deav - or
3 Teach us to know the way of Je-sus Christ, our Mas - ter;
4 May we be true to him, our Cap-tain of sal-va - tion,

Hope and de - sire for no - ble lives and true,
To right the wrongs that shame this mor - tal life;
Give us his clear - eyed faith, his fear - less heart,
Bear - ing his cross in serv - ice glad and free,

Keep us, we pray thee, stead-fast and un - err - ing;
Give us the val - iant spir - it that shall nev - er
And through life's dark - ness, dan - ger, and dis - as - ter,
Win - ning the world to that last con - sum - ma - tion

With light and love di - vine our souls en - due.
Fal - ter or fail how - ev - er long the strife.
Oh, may we nev - er from his side de - part.
When all its king-doms shall his king - dom be. A - men.

YOUTH

492   O Gracious God, Whose Constant Care

Harry T. Stock, 1891-1958, alt.

LOBT GOTT IHR CHRISTEN 8.6.8.8.6.
Melody by Nicolaus Hermann, c.1485-1561

1 O gra-cious God, whose con - stant care Sup -
2 We thank thee, Fa - ther, for each word, Each
3 Com - pan - ion of this sa - cred hour, Re -

plies our gold - en days, Whose joy - ous fel - low -
thought-re - veal - ing truth, For proph - et voic - es
new in us each day Our loft - y pur - pose;

ship we share At work, at rest, in
glad - ly heard, For dar - ing dreams, for
grant us power That wor - thy thoughts in

play and prayer, Ac - cept our heart - felt praise.
friends who stirred The frag - ile wills of youth.
deeds may flower, In Christ - like lives, we pray. A - men.

YOUTH

When Stephen, Full of Power and Grace 493

Jan Struther, 1901-1953

WELLINGTON SQUARE C.M.D.
Guy Warrack, 1900-

In unison

1 When Ste-phen, full of power and grace, Went forth through-out the land,
2 When Ste-phen preached a-gainst the laws And by those laws was tried,
3 When Ste-phen, young and doomed to die, Fell crushed be-neath the stones,
4 Let me, O Lord, thy cause de-fend, A knight with-out a sword;

He bore no shield be-fore his face, No wea-pon in his hand;
He had no friend to plead his cause, No spokes-man at his side;
He had no curse nor venge-ful cry For those who broke his bones;
No shield I ask, no faith-ful friend, No ven-geance, no re-ward;

But on-ly in his heart a flame And on his lips a sword
But on-ly in his heart a flame And in his eyes a light
But on-ly in his heart a flame And on his lips a prayer
But on-ly in my heart a flame And in my soul a dream,

Where-with he smote and o-ver-came The foe-men of the Lord.
Where-with God's day-break to pro-claim And rend the veils of night.
That God, in sweet for-give-ness' name, Should un-der-stand and spare.
So that the stones of earth-ly shame A jew-elled crown may seem. A-men.

YOUTH

494   We Would Be Building

Purd E. Deitz, 1897-

FINLANDIA 10.10.10.10.10.10.
Jean Sibelius, 1865-1957

1 We would be build-ing; tem-ples still un-done O'er crum-bling
2 Teach us to build; up-on the sol-id rock We set the
3 O keep us build-ing, Mas-ter; may our hands Ne'er fal-ter

walls their cross-es scarce-ly lift, Wait-ing till love can
dream that hard-ens in-to deed, Ribbed with the steel that
when the dream is in our hearts, When to our ears there

raise the bro-ken stone, And hearts cre-a-tive bridge the hu-man rift.
time and change doth mock, The un-fail-ing pur-pose of our no-blest creed.
come di-vine com-mands And all the pride of sin-ful will de-parts.

We would be build-ing; Mas-ter, let thy plan
Teach us to build; O Mas-ter, lend us sight
We build with thee, O grant en-dur-ing worth

YOUTH

Re - veal the life that God would give to man.
To see the tow - ers gleam - ing in the light.
Un - til the heaven - ly king - dom comes on earth. A-men.

A lower setting may be found at No. 77

We Are Climbing Jacob's Ladder 495

Negro Spiritual

JACOB'S LADDER 8.8.8.5.
Negro Melody

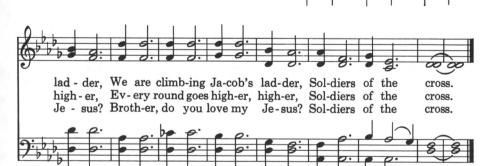

1 We are climb-ing Ja-cob's lad - der, We are climb-ing Ja-cob's
2 Ev - ery round goes high-er, high-er, Ev - ery round goes high-er,
3 Broth-er, do you love my Je - sus? Broth-er, do you love my

lad - der, We are climb-ing Ja-cob's lad-der, Sol-diers of the cross.
high - er, Ev-ery round goes high-er, high-er, Sol-diers of the cross.
Je - sus? Broth-er, do you love my Je - sus? Sol-diers of the cross.

4 If you love him, why not serve him?
  If you love him, why not serve him?
  If you love him, why not serve him?
  Soldiers of the cross.

YOUTH

496   The National Anthem

Francis Scott Key, 1779-1843

STAR-SPANGLED BANNER *Irregular*
Unknown

1 O say can you see by the dawn's ear - ly light,
2 O thus be it ev - er when free men shall stand

What so proud - ly we hailed at the twi - light's last gleam - ing,
Be - tween their loved homes and the war's des - o - la - tion!

Whose broad stripes and bright stars through the per - il - ous fight,
Blest with vic - tory and peace, may the heaven - res - cued land

O'er the ram - parts we watched were so gal - lant - ly stream - ing?
Praise the power that hath made and pre - served us a na - tion.

And the rock - ets' red glare, the bombs burst - ing in air,
Then con - quer we must, when our cause it is just,

Gave proof through the night that our flag was still there.
And this be our mot - to, "In God is our trust."

O say does that star - span - gled ban - ner yet wave
And the star - span - gled ban - ner in tri - umph shall wave

O'er the land of the free and the home of the brave?
O'er the land of the free and the home of the brave!

SERVICE MUSIC

497 ## Praise to the Holiest in the Height

John H. Newman, 1801-1890

ST. MARY C.M.
Melody, "Prys' Psalter," 1621

Praise to the Ho-liest in the height And in the depth be praise; In all his words most won-der-ful, Most sure in all his ways.

498 ## Each Morning Brings

Johannes Zwick, 1496-1542
Tr. Margaret Barclay, 1951

ALL MORGEN IST L.M.
Melody, Wittenberg, 1537

1 Each morn-ing brings us fresh out-poured, The lov-ing-kind-ness of the Lord.
2 O God, thou star of dawn-ing day Give us that light for which we pray;

It ends not as the day goes past, But gives us strength while life shall last.
Make thou thy flame in us to glow, That we no lack of grace may know.

MORNING

Lo, God Is Here!

499

Gerhard Tersteegen, 1697-1769
Tr. John Wesley, 1703-1791, alt.

AUS GNADEN SOLL ICH 8.8.8.8.8.8.
Justin H. Knecht, 1752-1817

1 Lo, God is here! Let us a - dore And own how sol - emn is this place! Let all with - in us feel his power, And si - lent bow be - fore his face; Who know his power, his grace who prove, Serve him with awe, with rev - erence, love.

2 Lo, God is here! Him day and night The u - nit - ed choirs of an - gels sing; To him, en-throned a - bove all height, Heaven's hosts their no - blest prais - es bring; To him may all our thoughts a - rise, In nev - er - ceas - ing sac - ri - fice.

MORNING

500   Lord God of Morning and of Night

Francis T. Palgrave, 1824-1897, alt.

MACH'S MIT MIR, GOTT L.M.
Melody by Johann H. Schein, 1586-1630

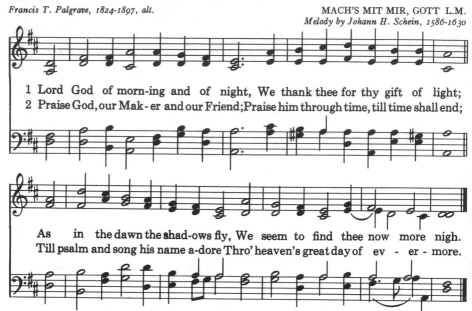

1 Lord God of morn-ing and of night, We thank thee for thy gift of light;
2 Praise God, our Mak-er and our Friend; Praise him through time, till time shall end;

As in the dawn the shad-ows fly, We seem to find thee now more nigh.
Till psalm and song his name a-dore Thro' heaven's great day of ev - er - more.

501   Lord, for the Mercies of the Night

John Mason, c.1645-1694

FARRANT C.M.
Attr. to Richard Farrant, c.1530-1580

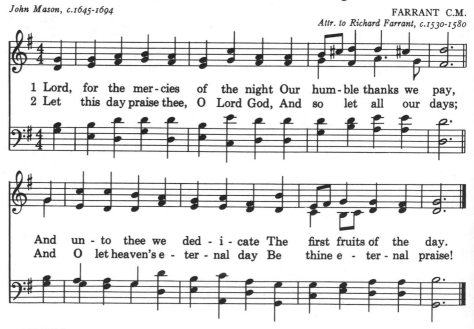

1 Lord, for the mer-cies of the night Our hum-ble thanks we pay,
2 Let this day praise thee, O Lord God, And so let all our days;

And un-to thee we ded-i-cate The first fruits of the day.
And O let heaven's e-ter-nal day Be thine e-ter-nal praise!

We Praise Thee, Lord

502

Johann Franck, 1618-1677
Tr. Catherine Winkworth, 1827-1878, alt.

AINSWORTH 97 10.10.10.10.
Melody, "Genevan Psalter," 1562
Harm. from Claude Le Jeune, c.1523-c.1600

1 We praise thee, Lord, with ear - liest morn - ing ray;
2 Thy peo - ple, Lord, are sing - ing night and day:

We praise thee with the glow - ing light of day.
"All hail to him, the might - y God, for aye,

All things that live and move, by sea and land,
By whom, through whom, in whom all be - ings are!"

For - ev - er read - y at thy serv - ice stand.
O may we ech - o on the song a - far.

MORNING

503 Open Now Thy Gates of Beauty

Benjamin Schmolak, 1672-1737
Tr. Catherine Winkworth, 1827-1878

UNSER HERRSCHER 8.7.8.7.7.7.
Melody by Joachim Neander, 1650-1680

1 O - pen now thy gates of beau - ty, Zi - on, let me en - ter there,
2 Gra-cious God, I come be - fore thee, Come thou al - so un - to me;

Where my soul in joy - ful du - ty, Waits for him who an-swers prayer.
Where we find thee and a - dore thee, There a heaven on earth must be.

O how bless - ed is this place, Filled with sol - ace, light, and grace!
To my heart O en - ter thou, Let it be thy tem - ple now.

504 This Is the Day the Lord Hath Made

Isaac Watts, 1674-1748

NUN DANKET ALL' C.M.
Melody by Johann Crüger, 1598-1662

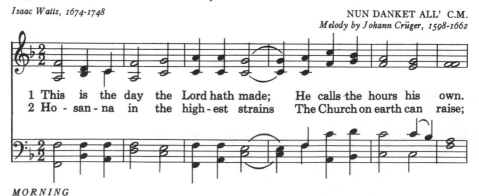

1 This is the day the Lord hath made; He calls the hours his own.
2 Ho - san - na in the high - est strains The Church on earth can raise;

MORNING

Let heaven re-joice, let earth be glad, And praise sur-round the throne.
The high-est heavens, in which he reigns, Shall give him no-bler praise.

You That Have Spent the Silent Night 505

Based on George Gascoigne, c.1525-1577, alt.
"The Oxford Hymn Book," 1925

OLD 22nd C.M.D.
"Anglo-Genevan Psalter," 1556

You that have spent the si-lent night In sleep and qui-et rest,

And joy to see the cheer-ful light That ris-eth in the east;

Now lift your hearts, your voic-es raise, Your morn-ing trib-ute bring,

And pay a grate-ful song of praise To heaven's al-might-y King.

MORNING

506 Come, My Soul, Thou Must Be Waking

Friedrich R. L. von Canitz, 1654-1699
Tr. Henry J. Buckoll, 1803-1871, alt.

VENI, ANIMA MEA 8.4.7.D.
Mark Dickey, 1885-1961

1 Come, my soul, thou must be wak-ing, Now is break-ing O'er the
2 Glad-ly hail the sun re-turn-ing, Read-y burn-ing Be the

earth an-oth-er day; Come to him who made this splen-dor,
in-cense of thy powers; For the night is safe-ly end-ed,

See thou ren-der All thy fee-ble strength can pay.
God hath tend-ed With his care thy help-less hours.

MORNING

507 To Thee Before the Close of Day

Latin: c.7th century
Tr. John David Chambers, 1805-1893

JAM LUCIS L.M.
Plainsong, Mode VI

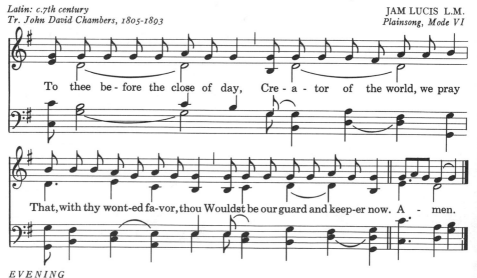

To thee be-fore the close of day, Cre-a-tor of the world, we pray

That, with thy wont-ed fa-vor, thou Wouldst be our guard and keep-er now. A - men.

EVENING

Before the Day Draws Near Its Ending **508**

John Ellerton, 1826-1893

RENDEZ À DIEU 9.8.9.8.D.
Attr. to Louis Bourgeois, c.1510-c.1561

1 Be - fore the day draws near its end - ing, And eve-ning steals o'er earth and sky;
2 O Light all clear, O Truth most ho - ly, O bound-less Mer-cy par-doning all,

Once more to thee our hymns as-cend - ing Shall speak thy prais-es, Lord most high.
Be - fore thy feet, a-bashed and low - ly, With one last prayer thy chil-dren fall.

Thy name is blessed by count-less num - bers, In vast-er worlds un-seen, un-known,
And through the swell of chant-ing voic - es, The blend-ed notes of age and youth,

Whose du-teous serv-ice nev-er slum - bers, In per-fect love and fault-less tone.
Thine ear dis-cerns, thy love re - joic - es, When hearts rise up to thee in truth.

EVENING

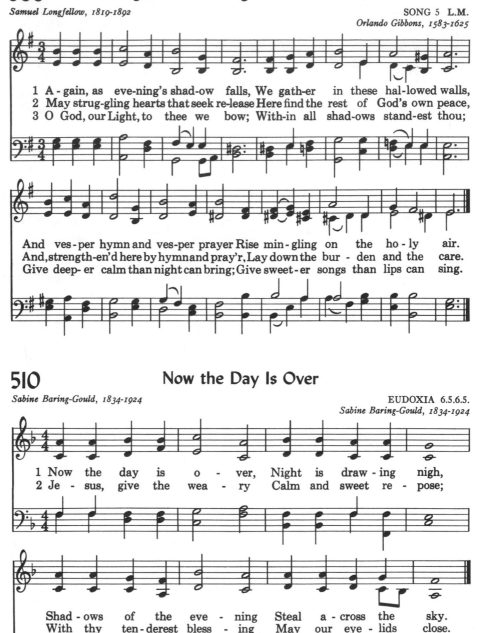

509 Again, as Evening's Shadow Falls

Samuel Longfellow, 1819-1892

SONG 5 L.M.
Orlando Gibbons, 1583-1625

1 A-gain, as eve-ning's shad-ow falls, We gath-er in these hal-lowed walls,
2 May strug-gling hearts that seek re-lease Here find the rest of God's own peace,
3 O God, our Light, to thee we bow; With-in all shad-ows stand-est thou;

And ves-per hymn and ves-per prayer Rise min-gling on the ho-ly air.
And, strength-en'd here by hymn and pray'r, Lay down the bur-den and the care.
Give deep-er calm than night can bring; Give sweet-er songs than lips can sing.

510 Now the Day Is Over

Sabine Baring-Gould, 1834-1924

EUDOXIA 6.5.6.5.
Sabine Baring-Gould, 1834-1924

1 Now the day is o-ver, Night is draw-ing nigh,
2 Je-sus, give the wea-ry Calm and sweet re-pose;

Shad-ows of the eve-ning Steal a-cross the sky.
With thy ten-derest bless-ing May our eye-lids close.

EVENING

Gloria Patri

Old Scottish Chant

Gloria Patri

512

"Pilgrim Hymnal," 1931

Gloria Patri

513

Henry W. Greatorex, 1813-1858

DOXOLOGIES

514   Praise God From Whom All Blessings Flow

Thomas Ken, *1637-1711*

OLD HUNDREDTH L.M. *(original rhythm)*
Attr. to Louis Bourgeois, c.1510-c.1561
"Genevan Psalter," 1551

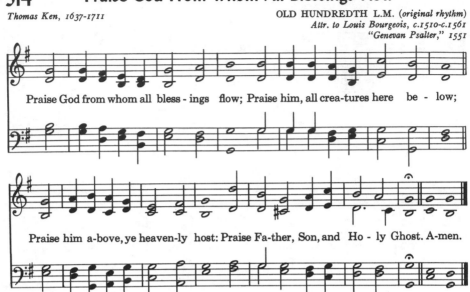

Praise God from whom all bless - ings flow; Praise him, all crea-tures here be - low;

Praise him a-bove, ye heaven-ly host: Praise Fa-ther, Son, and Ho - ly Ghost. A-men.

Another harmonization may be found at No. 11

515   Praise God From Whom All Blessings Flow

Thomas Ken, *1637-1711*

OLD HUNDREDTH L.M. *(altered rhythm)*
Attr. to Louis Bourgeois, c.1510-c.1561
"Genevan Psalter," 1551

Praise God from whom all bless-ings flow; Praise him, all crea-tures here be - low;

Praise him a-bove, ye heaven-ly host: Praise Fa-ther, Son, and Ho - ly Ghost. A-men.

DOXOLOGIES

Thy Word Is a Lamp Unto My Feet 516

Psalm 119:105

Hugh Porter, 1897-1960

Thy word is a lamp un-to my feet And a light un-to my path.

Teach Me, O Lord, the Way of Thy Statutes 517

Psalm 119:33

Arr. from Thomas Attwood, 1765-1838

Teach me, O Lord, the way of thy stat - utes, And

I shall keep it un - to the end.

Let Thy Word Abide in Us, O Lord 518

D. Tait Patterson, 1877-1956

George Dyson, 1883-1964

Let thy word a - bide in us, O Lord.

SCRIPTURE

519

To My Humble Supplication

Joseph Bryan, *17th century*

MON DIEU, PRÊTE-MOI L'OREILLE 8.8.7.7.
"Genevan Psalter," 1543

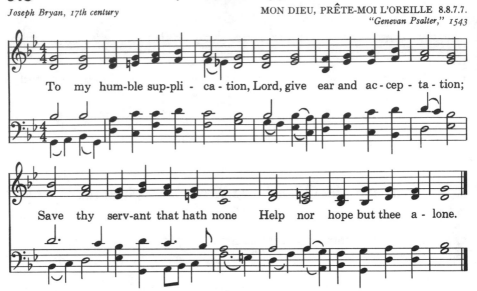

To my hum-ble sup-pli - ca - tion, Lord, give ear and ac-cep - ta - tion;

Save thy serv-ant that hath none Help nor hope but thee a - lone.

520

Almighty Father, Hear Our Prayer

Arr. from Felix Mendelssohn, *1809-1847*

Al-might-y Fa-ther, hear our prayer, and bless all souls that wait be - fore thee. A-men.

521

Lord Jesus Christ, Be Present Now

J. Niedling's *"Lutherisch Handbüchlein,"* 1638
Tr. Catherine Winkworth, *1827-1878, alt.*

HERR JESU CHRIST L.M.
"Pensum Sacrum," 1648
Harm. from *"Cantionale Sacrum,"* 1651

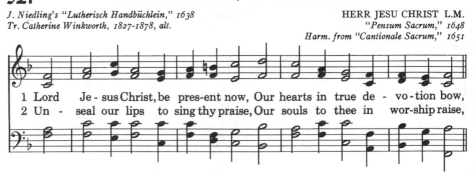

1 Lord Je - sus Christ, be pres-ent now, Our hearts in true de - vo-tion bow,
2 Un - seal our lips to sing thy praise, Our souls to thee in wor-ship raise,

PRAYER

Thy Spir-it send with grace di-vine, And let thy truth with-in us shine.
Make strong our faith, in-crease our light That we may know thy name a-right.

Another form of this tune may be found at No. 537

Let the Words of My Mouth 522

Psalm 19:14

Richard Langdon, c.1729-1803

Let the words of my mouth, and the medi-ta-tion of my heart,

Be acceptable in thy sight, { O Lord, my } my re-deem-er. A-men.
{ strength, and }

May the Words of Our Mouths 523

Psalm 19:14, alt.

Alan Walker, 1927-

In unison

May the words of our mouths, And the med-i-ta-tion of our hearts

Be ac-cept-a-ble in thy sight, O Lord, our strength, and our re-deem-er. A-men.

PRAYER

524

Lead Me, Lord

Based on Psalms 5:8 and 4:8

Samuel S. Wesley, 1810-1876

Lead me, Lord, lead me in thy right-eous-ness, make thy way plain be-fore my face. For it is thou, Lord, thou, Lord, on - ly, that mak - est me dwell in safe - ty.

525

Come, and Let Us Sweetly Join

Charles Wesley, 1707-1788

SAVANNAH 7.7.7.7.
"The Foundery Collection," 1742

Come, and let us sweet-ly join Christ to praise, in hymns di-vine.

Give we all, with one ac - cord, Glo - ry to our com-mon Lord. A-men.

PRAYER

O Thou Who Hearest Prayer

Unknown

6.6.6.6.8.8.
Welsh Melody

O thou who hear-est prayer, Give ear un-to our cry;

O let thy chil-dren share thy bless-ing from on high.

We plead the prom-ise of thy word, O grant us peace, al - might-y Lord!

Enrich, Lord, Heart, Mouth, Hands in Me

George Herbert, 1593-1633, alt.

WULFRUN 8.8.8.
George W. Briggs, 1875-1959

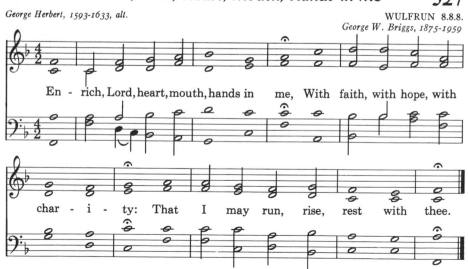

En - rich, Lord, heart, mouth, hands in me, With faith, with hope, with char - i - ty: That I may run, rise, rest with thee.

PRAYER

Create in Me a Clean Heart, O God

Psalm 51:10-12

Tonus Regius

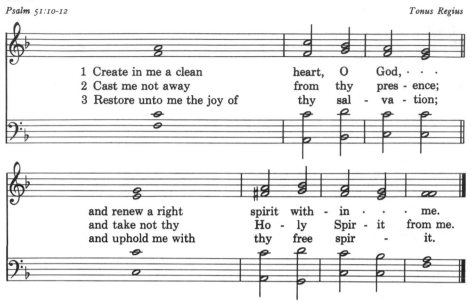

1 Create in me a clean heart, O God, . . .
2 Cast me not away from thy pres - ence;
3 Restore unto me the joy of thy sal - va - tion;

and renew a right spirit with - in . . . me.
and take not thy Ho - ly Spir - it from me.
and uphold me with thy free spir - it.

The Sacrifices of God

Psalm 51:17

Tonus Regius

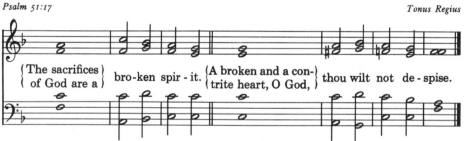

{The sacrifices / of God are a} bro-ken spir - it. {A broken and a con- / trite heart, O God,} thou wilt not de - spise.

O Thou by Whom We Come to God

James Montgomery, 1771-1854

WIGTOWN C.M.
"Scottish Psalter," 1635

O thou by whom we come to God, The Life, the Truth, the Way;

PRAYER

The path of prayer thy-self hast trod, Lord: teach us how to pray.

The Lord Be With You 531

To be said or sung: *Choir and Congregation:*

The {Lord be / with you,} And with thy spir - it. Let us pray.

(O Lord, show / thy mercy up-) on us, And grant us thy sal - va - tion.

(O God, make clean / our hearts with-) in us. And take not thy Ho - ly Spir-it from us.

Have Mercy Upon Us 532
For use with a litany

Have mercy up-	on	· · · ·	us.
Good Lord, de-	liv -	er	us.
Spare	us,	good	Lord.
Son of God, we beseech thee to	hear	· · · ·	us.
We beseech thee to hear	us,	O	Lord.
Grant	us	thy	peace.

533

The Lord Be With You

Thomas Tallis, d. 1585

534

O Lord, Open Thou Our Lips

VERSICLES

We Give Thee But Thine Own 535

William W. How, 1823-1897

YATTENDON 46 S.M.
Harry E. Wooldridge, 1845-1917

We give thee but thine own, What-e'er the gift may be; All that we
have is thine a - lone, A trust, O Lord, from thee. A - men.

Alternative tune, ST. MICHAEL, *No. 237*

All Things Come of Thee, O Lord 536

From 1 Chronicles 29:14

Ascribed to Ludwig van Beethoven, 1770-1827

All things come of thee, O Lord, and of thine own have we giv-en thee. A-men.

All Things Are Thine 537

John Greenleaf Whittier, 1807-1892

HERR JESU CHRIST L.M.
"Pensum Sacrum," 1648

All things are thine; no gift have we, Lord of all gifts, to of - fer thee;

And hence with grate-ful hearts to-day Thine own be-fore thy feet we lay. A-men.

OFFERTORY

538

Bless Thou the Gifts

Samuel Longfellow, 1819-1892, alt.

BRESLAU L.M.
Melody, Leipzig, 1625

Bless thou the gifts our hands have brought, Bless thou the work our hearts have planned;

Ours is the faith, the will, the thought, The rest, O God, is in thy hand. A-men.

OFFERTORY

539

May the Grace of Christ Our Savior

John Newton, 1725-1807

OMNI DIE 8.7.8.7.
Corner's "Gesangbuch," 1631
Harm. by Hubert Lamb, 1909-

1 May the grace of Christ our Sav - ior And the Fa-ther's bound-less love,
2 Thus may we a - bide in un - ion With each oth - er and the Lord,

With the Ho - ly Spir-it's fav - or, Rest up - on us from a - bove.
And pos - sess in sweet com-mun-ion Joys which earth can-not af - ford. A - men.

CLOSE OF WORSHIP

Father, Give Thy Benediction

540

Samuel Longfellow, 1819-1892

ALTA TRINITA BEATA 8.7.8.7.
"Laudi Spirituali," 14th century

Fa - ther, give thy ben - e - dic - tion, Give thy peace be - fore we part;

Still our minds with truth's con-vic-tion, Calm with trust each anx-ious heart. A-men.

Thou Wilt Keep Him in Perfect Peace

541

Isaiah 26:3

DUKE'S TUNE 8.6.
"Scottish Psalter," 1615, abridged

Thou wilt keep him in per-fect peace Whose mind is stayed on thee. A - men.

CLOSE OF WORSHIP

542

Sweet Savior, Bless Us Ere We Go

Frederick W. Faber, 1814-1863

GOTTLOB, ES GEHT 8.8.8.8.8.8.
German Chorale
Harm. by J. S. Bach, 1685-1750

Sweet Sav-ior, bless us ere we go, Thy word in - to our

minds in - stil, And make our luke-warm hearts to glow With low-ly

love and fer - vent will. Through life's long day and death's dark night,

O gen - tle Je - sus, be our light. A - men.

God Be in My Head

543

"Sarum Primer," 1558

GOD BE IN MY HEAD Irregular
H. Walford Davies, 1869-1941

God be in my head, and in my un-der-stand-ing;

God be in mine eyes and in my look-ing; God be in my mouth, and in my

speak - ing; God be in my heart, and in my think - ing;

God be at mine end, and at my de-part - ing.

CLOSE OF WORSHIP

544   Responses After the Commandments

After each Commandment except the tenth   *Thomas Tallis, d. 1585*

Lord, have mercy up - on · · · us, and in-cline our hearts to keep this law.

After the tenth Commandment

{Lord, have } on · · · us, {and write all these thy } hearts, we be - seech thee.
{ mercy up- }   { laws in our }

545   Lord, Have Mercy Upon Us

John Merbecke, c.1510-c.1585

Lord, have mer-cy up-on us; Christ, have mer-cy up-on us; Lord, have mer-cy up-on us.

546   Glory Be to Thee

Thomas Tallis, d. 1585

Glo - ry be to thee, O Lord.

547   Glory Be to Thee

Thomas Tallis, d. 1585

Glo - ry be to thee, O Lord.

548   Thanks Be to Thee

Thomas Tallis, d. 1585

{Thanks be to thee, O } ho - ly gos - pel.
{Christ, for this thy }

549   Praise Be to Thee

John Playford, 1674-1730

Praise be to thee, O Christ.

COMMUNION

Samuel Wesley, 1766-1837

Ho - ly, ho - ly, ho - ly, Lord God of hosts, Heaven and earth are full of thy

glo - ry: Glo - ry be to thee, O Lord most high. A - men.

Holy, Holy, Holy
Sanctus
551

Peter C. Lutkin, 1858-1931

In unison

Ho - ly, ho - ly, ho - ly, Lord

God of hosts, Heaven and earth are full of thy

glo - ry: Glo - ry be to thee, O Lord most high. A - men.

552

Lift Up Your Hearts
Sursum Corda

John Merbecke, c.1510-c.1585

Lift up your hearts. We lift them up un-to the Lord.

{Let us give / thanks unto the} Lord our God. It is meet and right so to do.

553

Holy, Holy, Holy
Sanctus

John Merbecke, c.1510-c.1585

Ho-ly, ho-ly, ho-ly, Lord God of hosts, Heaven and earth are full of thy glo-ry: Glo-ry be to thee, O Lord most high. A-men.

Glory Be to God on High

Gloria in Excelsis

554

Old Scottish Chant

1 Glory be to God on high, and on earth peace, good
2 {We praise thee, we / bless thee, we} wor-ship thee, {we glorify thee, we / give thanks to thee for} thy . . .

will towards men. 3 O Lord God, heaven-ly King,
great . . . . glory, 4 {O Lord, the only / begotten Son,} Je - sus Christ;

God the Fa-ther al - mighty. 5 That takest away the
{O Lord God, Lamb / of God,} Son . . . of the Father, 6 Thou that takest away the
7 {Thou that sittest at the / right hand of}

sins of the world, have mercy up - on . . . us. 8 For thou
sins of the world, re - ceive our prayer. 9 {Thou only, O / Christ, with the}
God the Father, have mercy up - on . . . us.

only art holy, thou on - ly art the Lord;
Ho - ly Ghost, {art most high / in the glory of} God the Fa - ther. A-men.

COMMUNION

555 O Lamb of God

Agnus Dei

John Merbecke, c.1510-c.1585

In unison

O Lamb of God, that tak-est a-way the sins of the world,

have mer-cy up-on us. O Lamb of God, that tak-est a-way the

sins of the world, have mer-cy up-on us. O Lamb of God,

that tak-est a-way the sins of the world, grant us thy peace.

COMMUNION

O Christ, Thou Lamb of God

Braunschweig, 1528
Arr. by Healey Willan, 1880-

556

In unison

O Christ, thou Lamb of God, that tak-est a-way the sins of the world,
have mer-cy up-on us. O Christ, thou Lamb of God, that
tak-est a-way the sins of the world, grant us thy
peace. A - - - - - men.

COMMUNION

557 Here, O My Lord, I See Thee

Horatius Bonar, 1808-1889

ADORO TE 10.10.10.10.
Benedictine Plainsong, Mode V, 13th century

In unison

1 Here, O my Lord, I see thee face to face;
2 Here would I feed up-on the bread of God,
3 I have no help but thine, nor do I need

Here would I touch and han-dle things un-seen;
Here drink with thee the roy-al wine of heaven;
An-oth-er arm save thine to lean up-on.

Here grasp with firm-er hand e-ter-nal grace,
Here would I lay a-side each earth-ly load,
It is e-nough, my Lord, e-nough in-deed;

And all my wea-ri-ness up-on thee lean.
Here taste a-fresh the calm of sin for-given.
My strength is in thy might, thy might a-lone. A-men.

COMMUNION HYMNS

'Twas on That Dark and Doleful Night

558

Isaac Watts, 1674-1748

BOURBON L.M.
Melody, "Hesperian Harp," 1848
Harm. by Louise McAllister, 1913-1960

1 'Twas on that dark and dole-ful night, When powers of earth and
2 Be - fore the mourn-ful scene be - gan, He took the bread and
3 "This is my bod - y, broke for sin, Re - ceive and eat the
4 "Do this," he cried, "till time shall end, In mem-ory of your
5 Je - sus, thy feast we cel - e - brate; We show thy death, we

hell a - rose A - gainst the Son of
blest and brake; What love through all his
liv - ing food"; Then took the cup and
dy - ing friend: Meet at my ta - ble
sing thy name, Till thou re - turn, and

God's de - light, And friends be-trayed him to his foes.
ac - tions ran, What won-drous words of love he spake!
blessed the wine, "'Tis the new cove - nant in my blood."
and re - cord The love of your de - part - ed Lord."
we shall eat The mar-riage sup - per of the Lamb. A - men.

COMMUNION HYMNS

559 We Praise Thee, O God
Te Deum Laudamus

Edwin G. Monk, 1819-1900

1. {We praise thee, O God; we acknowl-edge thee to} be the Lord. {All the earth doth worship thee: the Fa-ther} ev-er-last - ing.

2. {To thee all angels cry aloud; the heav-ens and all the} powers there-in. {To thee cher-ubim and sera-phim con-} tin-ual-ly do cry,

3. {Holy, holy, holy, Lord God of} Sab - a - oth; {heaven and earth are full of the majesty} of thy glo - - ry.

4. {The glorious com-pany of the apostles} praise · thee; {the goodly fel-lowship of the} proph-ets praise · · thee;

5. {The noble army of martyrs} praise · thee; {the holy Church throughout all the world} doth ac - knowl-edge thee;

6. {The Father, of an infinite majesty; thine adorable, true and} on - ly Son; also the Holy Ghost, the Com - fort - er.

William Croft, 1678-1727

7. {Thou art the King of} glory, O Christ, {Thou art the ev-erlasting} Son of the Fa - ther.

8. {When thou took-est upon thee to de-} liv - er man, {Thou didst hum-ble thyself to be} born of a vir - gin.

9. {When thou hadst overcome the} sharpness of death, {Thou didst open the kingdom of heaven to} all be - liev - ers.

MORNING CANTICLES

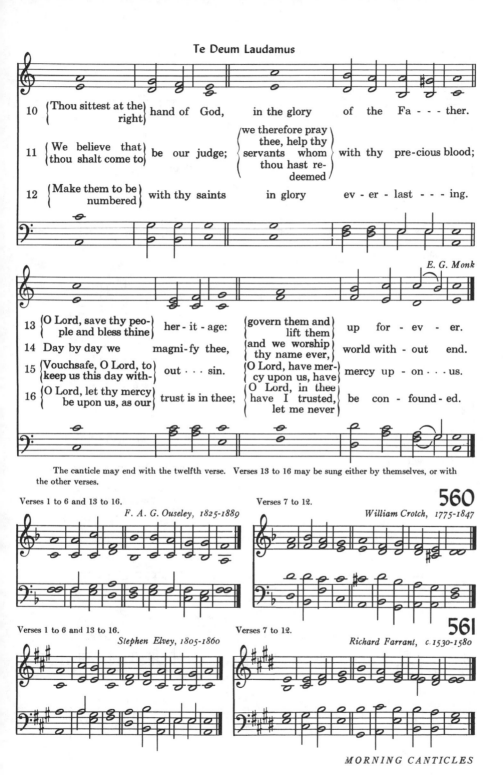

Te Deum Laudamus

10 {Thou sittest at the / right} hand of God, in the glory of the Fa - - - ther.

11 {We believe that / thou shalt come to} be our judge; {we therefore pray thee, help thy servants whom thou hast re-deemed} with thy pre-cious blood;

12 {Make them to be / numbered} with thy saints in glory ev - er - last - - - ing.

E. G. Monk

13 {O Lord, save thy peo-ple and bless thine} her - it - age: {govern them and lift them} up for - ev - er.

14 Day by day we magni-fy thee, {and we worship thy name ever,} world with - out end.

15 {Vouchsafe, O Lord, to keep us this day with-} out . . . sin. {O Lord, have mer-cy upon us, have} mercy up - on . . . us.

16 {O Lord, let thy mercy be upon us, as our} trust is in thee; {O Lord, in thee have I trusted, let me never} be con - found - ed.

The canticle may end with the twelfth verse. Verses 13 to 16 may be sung either by themselves, or with the other verses.

Verses 1 to 6 and 13 to 16.   *F. A. G. Ouseley, 1825-1889*   Verses 7 to 12.   *William Crotch, 1775-1847*   **560**

Verses 1 to 6 and 13 to 16.   *Stephen Elvey, 1805-1860*   Verses 7 to 12.   *Richard Farrant, c.1530-1580*   **561**

MORNING CANTICLES

562

O Come, Let Us Sing
Venite

William Boyce, 1710-1779

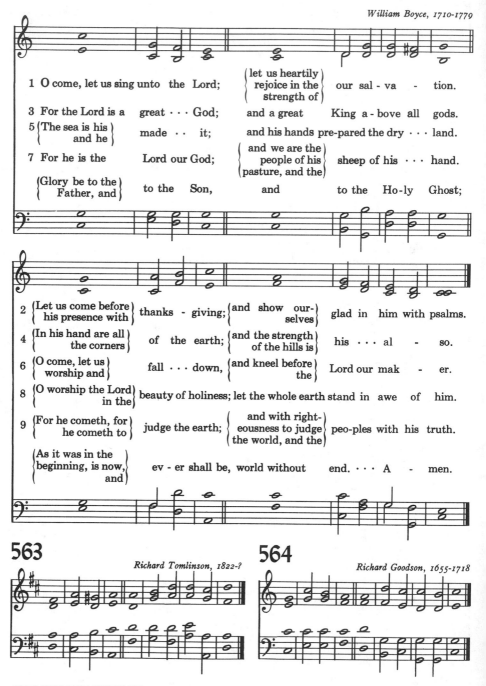

1 O come, let us sing unto the Lord; {let us heartily rejoice in the strength of} our sal-va-tion.

3 For the Lord is a great · · · God; and a great King a-bove all gods.

5 {The sea is his and he} made · · it; and his hands pre-pared the dry · · · land.

7 For he is the Lord our God; {and we are the people of his pasture, and the} sheep of his · · · hand.

{Glory be to the Father, and} to the Son, and to the Ho-ly Ghost;

2 {Let us come before his presence with} thanks-giving; {and show our-selves} glad in him with psalms.

4 {In his hand are all the corners} of the earth; {and the strength of the hills is} his · · · al - so.

6 {O come, let us worship and} fall · · · down, {and kneel before the} Lord our mak - er.

8 {O worship the Lord in the} beauty of holiness; let the whole earth stand in awe of him.

9 {For he cometh, for he cometh to} judge the earth; {and with right-eousness to judge the world, and the} peo-ples with his truth.

{As it was in the beginning, is now, and} ev - er shall be, world without end. · · · A - men.

563

Richard Tomlinson, 1822-?

564

Richard Goodson, 1655-1718

MORNING CANTICLES

O Be Joyful in the Lord
Jubilate Deo

565

Henry Aldrich, 1647-1710

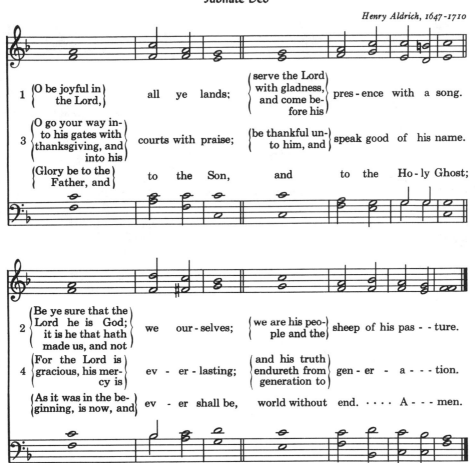

1 {O be joyful in the Lord,} all ye lands; {serve the Lord with gladness, and come before his} pres-ence with a song.

3 {O go your way in-to his gates with thanksgiving, and into his} courts with praise; {be thankful un-to him, and} speak good of his name.

{Glory be to the Father, and} to the Son, and to the Ho-ly Ghost;

2 {Be ye sure that the Lord he is God; it is he that hath made us, and not} we our-selves; {we are his peo-ple and the} sheep of his pas - -ture.

4 {For the Lord is gracious, his mer-cy is} ev - er-lasting; {and his truth endureth from generation to} gen - er - a - - -tion.

{As it was in the be-ginning, is now, and} ev - er shall be, world without end. . . . . A - - -men.

566

Oxford Chant

567

George J. Elvey, 1816-1893

MORNING CANTICLES

568

Blessed Be the Lord God
Benedictus

Joseph Barnby, 1838-1896

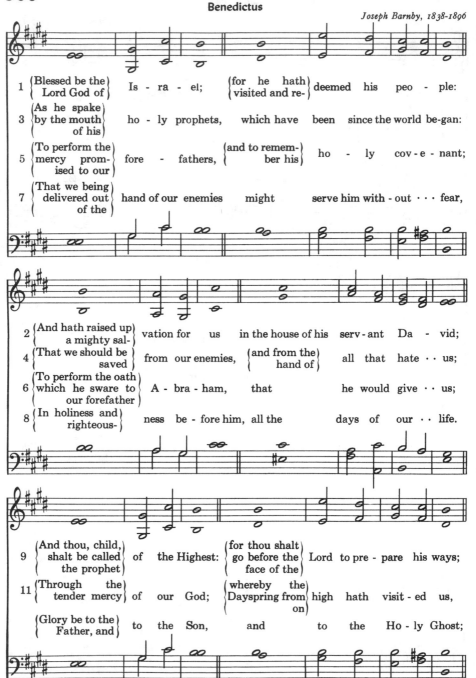

1 {Blessed be the / Lord God of} Is - ra - el; {for he hath / visited and re-} deemed his peo - ple:

3 {As he spake / by the mouth / of his} ho - ly prophets, which have been since the world be-gan:

5 {To perform the / mercy prom- / ised to our} fore - fathers, {and to remem- / ber his} ho - ly cov - e - nant;

7 {That we being / delivered out / of the} hand of our enemies might serve him with - out · · · fear,

2 {And hath raised up / a mighty sal-} vation for us in the house of his serv - ant Da - vid;

4 {That we should be / saved} from our enemies, {and from the / hand of} all that hate · · us;

6 {To perform the oath / which he sware to / our forefather} A - bra - ham, that he would give · · us;

8 {In holiness and / righteous-} ness be - fore him, all the days of our · · life.

9 {And thou, child, / shalt be called / the prophet} of the Highest: {for thou shalt / go before the / face of the} Lord to pre - pare his ways;

11 {Through the / tender mercy} of our God; {whereby the / Dayspring from / on} high hath visit - ed us,

{Glory be to the / Father, and} to the Son, and to the Ho - ly Ghost;

MORNING CANTICLES

10 { To give knowledge / of salvation } unto his people by the re - mis-sion of their sins,

12 { To give light to them / that sit in darkness / and in the } shadow of death, { and to guide / our feet } into the way of peace.

{ As it was in the be- / ginning, is now, and } ev - er shall be, world without end. · · · A - - men.

Blessed Art Thou, O Lord 569
Benedictus es, Domine
John Randall, 1715-1799

1 { Blessed art / thou, O Lord } God of our fathers: { Praised and / exalted above } all for ev - - - er.

3 { Blessed art / thou in the / temple } of thy holiness: { Praised and / exalted above } all for ev - - - er.

5 { Blessed art / thou on the / glorious } throne of thy kingdom: { Praised and / exalted above } all for ev - - - er.

{ Glory be to / the Father, and } to the Son, and to the Ho - ly Ghost;

2 { Blessed art / thou for the } name of thy majesty; { Praised and / exalted above } all for ev - - - er.

4 { Blessed art thou / that beholdest / the depths, and / dwellest be- } tween the cherubim: { Praised and / exalted above } all for ev - - - er.

6 { Blessed art thou / in the firma- } ment of heaven: { Praised and / exalted above } all for ev - - - er.

{ As it was in / the beginning, / is now, and } ev - er shall be, world without end. · · A - - - men.

MORNING CANTICLES

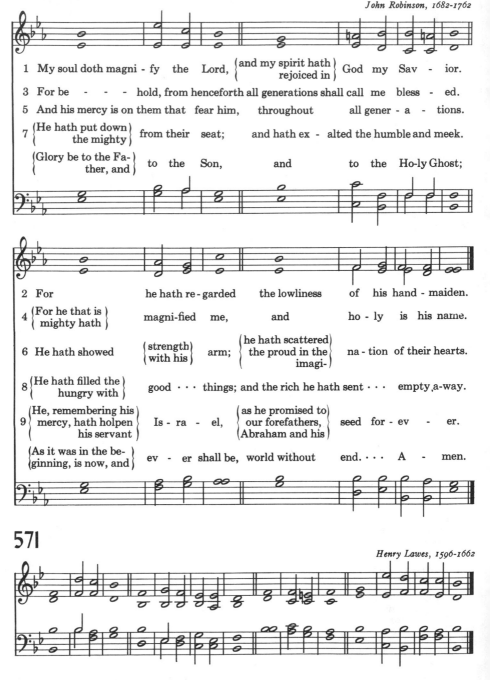

570 My Soul Doth Magnify the Lord
Magnificat

John Robinson, 1682-1762

1 My soul doth magni - fy the Lord, {and my spirit hath / rejoiced in} God my Sav - ior.

3 For be - - - hold, from henceforth all generations shall call me bless - ed.

5 And his mercy is on them that fear him, throughout all gener - a - tions.

7 {He hath put down / the mighty} from their seat; and hath ex - alted the humble and meek.

{Glory be to the Fa- / ther, and} to the Son, and to the Ho-ly Ghost;

2 For he hath re - garded the lowliness of his hand - maiden.

4 {For he that is / mighty hath} magni-fied me, and ho - ly is his name.

6 He hath showed {strength / with his} arm; {he hath scattered / the proud in the / imagi-} na - tion of their hearts.

8 {He hath filled the / hungry with} good · · · things; and the rich he hath sent · · · empty a-way.

9 {He, remembering his / mercy, hath holpen / his servant} Is - ra - el, {as he promised to / our forefathers, / Abraham and his} seed for - ev - er.

{As it was in the be- / ginning, is now, and} ev - er shall be, world without end. · · · A - men.

571

Henry Lawes, 1596-1662

EVENING CANTICLES

Lord, Now Lettest Thou Thy Servant Depart

572

Nunc dimittis

Joseph Barnby, 1838-1896

1 Lord, now lettest thou thy servant de - - part in peace
2 For mine eyes have seen
3 Which thou hast pre - pared
4 To be a light to lighten the Gentiles
  Glory be to the Father, and to the Son,
  As it was in the beginning, is now, and ev - er shall be,

ac - - - - cord - ing to thy word.
thy sal - - va - - tion,
before the face of all · · · peo - ple;
and to be the glory of thy peo - ple Is - ra - el.
and to the Ho - ly Ghost;
world without end. · · · A - men.

573

Richard Farrant, c.1530-1580

574

Tonus Regius

EVENING CANTICLES

575   Come, Holy Ghost, Our Souls Inspire

Latin: 9th century
Tr. John Cosin, 1594-1672

VENI CREATOR L.M.
Plainsong
"Vesperale Romanum" (Mechlin)

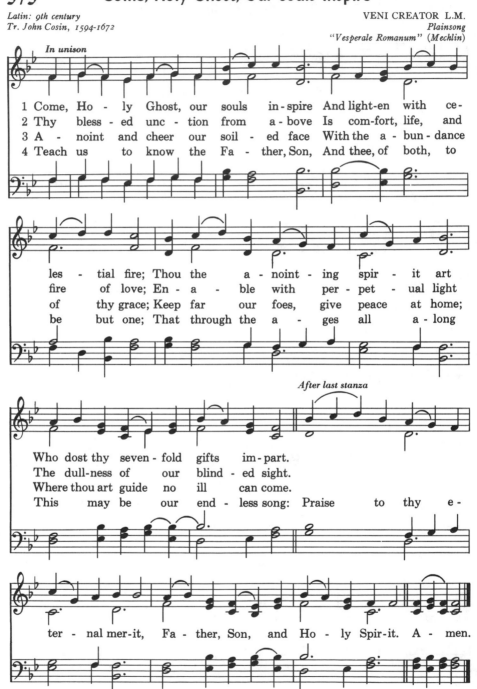

In unison

1 Come, Ho - ly Ghost, our souls in-spire And light-en with ce -
2 Thy bless - ed unc - tion from a - bove Is com-fort, life, and
3 A - noint and cheer our soil - ed face With the a - bun - dance
4 Teach us to know the Fa - ther, Son, And thee, of both, to

les - tial fire; Thou the a - noint - ing spir - it art
fire of love; En - a - ble with per - pet - ual light
of thy grace; Keep far our foes, give peace at home;
be but one; That through the a - ges all a - long

After last stanza

Who dost thy seven - fold gifts im - part.
The dull-ness of our blind - ed sight.
Where thou art guide no ill can come.
This may be our end - less song: Praise to thy e -

ter - nal mer-it, Fa - ther, Son, and Ho - ly Spir-it. A - men.

HYMNS

Lord, Thou Hast Searched Me

576

Based on Psalm 139
"The Psalter Hymnal," 1927

TENDER THOUGHT L.M.
"Kentucky Harmony," 1816

1 Lord, thou hast searched me and dost know
2 My words from thee I can - not hide;
3 Where can I go a - part from thee,
4 If I the wings of morn - ing take,
5 If deep - est dark - ness cov - er me,

Wher - e'er I rest, wher - e'er I go;
I feel thy power on ev - ery side;
Or whith - er from thy pres - ence flee?
And far a - way my dwell - ing make,
The dark - ness hid - eth not from thee;

Thou know - est all that I have planned,
O won - drous knowl - edge, aw - ful might,
In heaven? It is thy dwell - ing fair;
The hand that lead - eth me is thine,
To thee both night and day are bright,

And all my ways are in thy hand.
Un - fath - omed depth, un - meas - ured height!
In death's a - bode? Lo, thou art there.
And my sup - port thy power di - vine.
The dark - ness shin - eth as the light.

HYMNS

577

Great God Who Hast Delivered Us

Unknown

PSALM 36 (68) 8.8.7.8.8.7.D.
Melody attr. to M. Greiter, c.1500-1552

Great God who hast de - liv-ered us   By   thy great love and might-y power
Make man - i - fest in this dread time   Thy power su-preme, thy love sub-lime,

In many an e - vil hour,   Then   to thy name be glo - ry given,
That love that nev - er fail - eth.

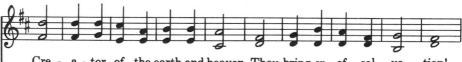

Cre - a - tor of the earth and heaven, Thou bring-er of sal - va - tion!

To thee, the source of all our joy,   To   thee we sing, O Lord most high,

HYMNS

Glad praise and ad - o - ra - tion.

This tune when set to Psalm 68 by Théodore Béza (1519-1605), became known as the "Battle Song of the Huguenots."

I Sought the Lord, and Afterward I Knew 578

Unknown
"The Pilgrim Hymnal," 1904

PEACE 10.10.10.6.
"The Revivalist," 1869
Adapted by George Brandon, 1924-

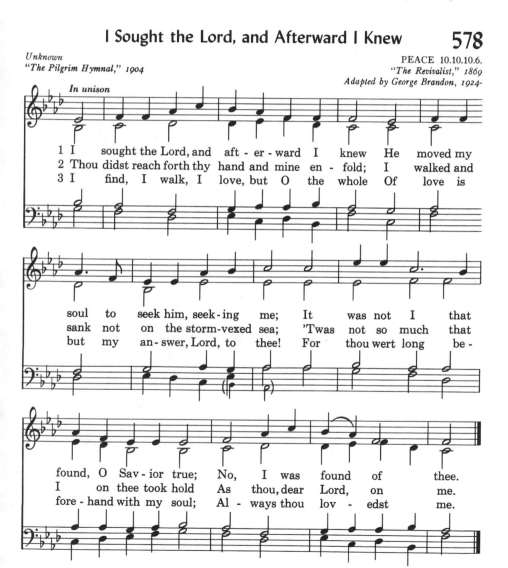

1 I sought the Lord, and aft - er - ward I knew He moved my
2 Thou didst reach forth thy hand and mine en - fold; I walked and
3 I find, I walk, I love, but O the whole Of love is

soul to seek him, seek - ing me; It was not I that
sank not on the storm-vexed sea; 'Twas not so much that
but my an - swer, Lord, to thee! For thou wert long be -

found, O Sav - ior true; No, I was found of thee.
I on thee took hold As thou, dear Lord, on me.
fore - hand with my soul; Al - ways thou lov - edst me.

HYMNS

579

Summer Ended, Harvest O'er

Greville Phillimore, 1821-1884

FREUEN WIR UNS ALL IN EIN 7.7.7.7.
Bohemian Melody, 1457
Harm. by George R. Woodward, 1848-1934

1 Sum - mer end - ed, har - vest o'er, Lord, to thee our song we pour,
2 For the prom - ise ev - er sure That, while heav'n and earth en - dure,

For the val - ley's gold - en yield, For the fruits of tree and field;
Seed - time, har - vest, cold, and heat Shall their year - ly round com - plete. A - men.

580

O Lord, Turn Not Thy Face From Them

John Marckant, 16th century, alt.

CONTRITION C.M.
Vincent Persichetti, 1915-

1 O Lord, turn not thy face from them, Who lie in woe - ful state,
2 A gate which o - pens wide to those That do la - ment their sin;
3 Have mer - cy, now, up - on my soul, Hear this my hum - ble prayer;

La - ment - ing all their sin - ful lives, Be - fore thy mer - cy gate.
Shut not that gate a - gainst me, Lord, But let me en - ter in.
For mer - cy, Lord, is all my suit, O let thy mer - cy spare. A - men.

All Hail the Power of Jesus' Name

581

Edward Perronet, 1726-1792
Alt. by John Rippon, 1751-1836

CORONATION C.M.
Oliver Holden, 1765-1844
Descant: David McK. Williams, 1887-

1 All hail the power of Je-sus' name! Let an-gels pros-trate fall;
2 Crown him, ye mar-tyrs of our God, Who from his al-tar call;
3 Let ev-ery kin-dred, ev-ery tribe, On this ter-res-trial ball,
4 O that, with yon-der sa-cred throng, We at his feet may fall;

the roy-al di-a-dem, And crown him Lord of all.
the stem of Jes-se's rod, And crown him Lord of all.
all maj-es-ty as-cribe, And crown him Lord of all.
the ev-er-last-ing song, And crown him Lord of all.

Bring forth
Ex-tol
To him
We'll join

DESCANTS

582 Christ the Lord Is Risen Today

Charles Wesley, 1707-1788

EASTER HYMN 7.7.7.7. *with Alleluias*
Arr. from "Lyra Davidica," 1708
Descant: Ethel and Hugh Porter

Al - - le - lu - - ia!

1 Christ the Lord is risen to - day, Al - - le - lu - ia!
2 Lives a - gain our glo-rious King, Al - - le - lu - ia!
3 Love's re-deem-ing work is done, Al - - le - lu - ia!
4 Soar we now, where Christ has led, Al - - le - lu - ia!
5 Hail the Lord of earth and heaven! Al - - le - lu - ia!

Al - - le - lu - - ia!

Sons of men and an-gels say: Al - - le - lu - ia!
Where, O death, is now thy sting? Al - - le - lu - ia!
Fought the fight, the bat - tle won, Al - - le - lu - ia!
Fol-low-ing our ex - alt - ed Head, Al - - le - lu - ia!
Praise to thee by both be given, Al - - le - lu - ia!

Raise your joys and tri-umphs high, Al - - le - lu - ia!
Dy - ing once, he all doth save, Al - - le - lu - ia!
Death in vain for - bids him rise, Al - - le - lu - ia!
Made like him, like him we rise, Al - - le - lu - ia!
Thee we greet tri - um-phant now, Al - - le - lu - ia!

Raise your joys and tri-umphs high, Al - - le - lu - ia!
Dy - ing once, he all doth save, Al - - le - lu - ia!
Death in vain for - bids him rise, Al - - le - lu - ia!
Made like him, like him we rise, Al - - le - lu - ia!
Thee we greet tri - um-phant now, Al - - le - lu - ia!

DESCANTS

Ah - - - - - Al - le - lu - ia! A-men.

Sing, ye heavens, and earth re - ply: Al - - - le - lu - ia!
Where thy vic - to - ry, O grave? Al - - - le - lu - ia!
Christ has o-pened Par - a - dise, Al - - - le - lu - ia!
Ours the cross, the grave, the skies, Al - - - le - lu - ia!
Hail, the Res - ur - rec - tion thou! Al - - - le lu - ia! A-men.

Harmonization for this tune, No. 182

Our God, Our Help in Ages Past 583

Isaac Watts, 1674-1748

ST. ANNE C.M.
Attr. to William Croft, 1678-1727
Descant: Donald D. Kettring, 1907-

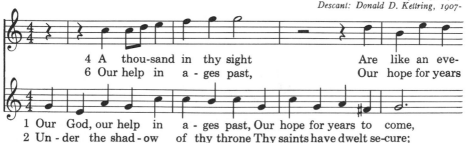

4 A thou-sand in thy sight Are like an eve-
6 Our help in a - ges past, Our hope for years

1 Our God, our help in a - ges past, Our hope for years to come,
2 Un - der the shad - ow of thy throne Thy saints have dwelt se-cure;
3 Be - fore the hills in or - der stood, Or earth re-ceived her frame,
4 A thou-sand a - ges in thy sight Are like an eve-ning gone,
5 Time, like an ev - er - roll-ing stream, Bears all its sons a - way;
6 Our God, our help in a - ges past, Our hope for years to come,

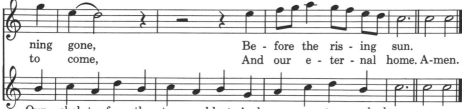

ning gone, Be - fore the ris - ing sun.
to come, And our e - ter - nal home. A-men.

Our shel-ter from the storm-y blast, And our e - ter - nal home.
Suf - fi - cient is thine arm a - lone, And our de-fense is sure.
From ev - er - last-ing thou art God, To end - less years the same.
Short as the watch that ends the night Be - fore the ris - ing sun.
They fly, for-got-ten, as a dream Dies at the o - pening day.
Be thou our guard while trou-bles last, And our e - ter - nal home. A-men.

Harmonization for this tune, No. 1

DESCANTS

584 Ye Servants of God, Your Master Proclaim

Charles Wesley, 1707-1788

HANOVER 10.10.11.11.
William Croft, 1678-1727
Descant: Donald D. Kettring, 1907-

Ah .... Ah ....

1 Ye serv-ants of God, your Mas-ter pro-claim, And pub-lish a-
2 God rul-eth on high, al-might-y to save, And still he is
3 Then let us a-dore and give him his right, All glo-ry and

Ah .... Ah ·

broad his won-der-ful name; The name, all-vic-to-rious, of
nigh, his pres-ence we have; The great con-gre-ga-tion his
power, all wis-dom and might, All hon-or and bless-ing with

.... Ah .... Ah .... A - men.

Je-sus ex-tol; His king-dom is glo-rious, he rules o-ver all.
tri-umph shall sing, As-crib-ing sal-va-tion to Je-sus, our King.
an-gels a-bove, And thanks nev-er ceas-ing and in-fi-nite love. A-men.

DESCANTS

592   Twofold Amen

593   Threefold Amen

594   Sevenfold Amen

AMENS

SERVICES

PRAYERS

READINGS

for

Congregational

Worship

Table of Selections

Orders for Worship

An Order for Worship   491

A Second Order for Worship   492

An Order for Worship with Communion   494

An Order for the Reception of Members into the Church   497

An Order for the Sacrament of Baptism for Infants or Children   498

An Order for Confirmation   501

Prayers and Other Worship Aids

Opening Sentences	503	Offertory Sentences	511
Prayers of Preparation	503	Offertory Prayers	511
Prayers for Illumination	504	Affirmations of Faith	511
Prayers of Adoration	504	Salem Church Covenant, 1629	512
Prayers of Confession	505	The Ten Commandments	513
Prayers for Pardon	505	The Great Commandment	513
Prayers for the Church	506	The Lord's Prayer	513
Prayers for Peace	507	Benedictions	513
General Prayers	508	Litany for the Church	514
Collects and Short Prayers	510		

Psalter Readings

515–539

Unison Readings

540–549

ORDERS FOR WORSHIP

I An Order for Worship

PRELUDE
CALL TO WORSHIP*
INVOCATION
LORD'S PRAYER
HYMN
RESPONSIVE READING
GLORIA PATRI
SCRIPTURE LESSON
ANTHEM
PASTORAL PRAYER
OFFERING AND DEDICATION*
HYMN
SERMON
PRAYER
HYMN
BENEDICTION
POSTLUDE

* The Doxology may be sung in place of the Call to Worship or at the Offering.

2 A Second Order for Worship*

This service begins with a Call to Worship, the minister saying:

Our help is in the name of the Lord, who made heaven and earth.
Let us worship God.

HYMN *If this is not a processional hymn, it should be sung following the scriptural sentences.*

All standing, he reads one or more sentences of Holy Scripture:

O give thanks unto the Lord, for he is good: for his mercy endureth forever. Be thankful unto him and bless his name. For the Lord is good; his mercy is everlasting, and his truth endureth to all generations. Praise ye the Lord.

Give unto the Lord, O ye kindreds of the people, give unto the Lord glory and strength. Give unto the Lord the glory due unto his name: bring an offering and come into his courts.

The hour cometh, and now is, when the true worshipers shall worship the Father in spirit and in truth, for the Father seeketh such to worship him. God is a Spirit, and they that worship him must worship him in spirit and in truth.

PRAYER OF ADORATION AND CONFESSION
Minister and people

Almighty God, whose glory the heavens are telling, the earth thy power, and the sea thy might, and whose greatness all feeling and thinking creatures everywhere proclaim; to thee belongeth glory, honor, power, and love, now and forever, and unto ages of ages, through Jesus Christ our Lord. Amen.[1]

O God, whose goodness is great, and the multitude of thy mercies innumerable, we have sinned against thee, and done evil in thy sight; yet because thou art the God of mercy and the Fountain of eternal purity we present unto thee the sacrifice of a troubled spirit, beseeching thee to let the fire of thy love cleanse our sins and purify our souls. Make us clean hearts, O God; though our sins be as scarlet, yet make them like wool; though they be as purple, yet make them white as snow. Restore the voice of joy and gladness to us; give us the comforts of thy help again, and let thy free spirit establish us in the liberty of the sons of God; so shall we sing of thy righteousness, and our lips shall give thee praise in the congregation of thy redeemed, now, henceforth, and forever. Amen.[2]

AN ASSURANCE OF PARDON *Read by the minister*

The Lord is merciful and gracious, slow to anger and plenteous in mercy. If we confess our sins, he is faithful and just to forgive us our sins and to cleanse us from all unrighteousness. Amen.

* See p. 556 for all acknowledgments and sources.

ANTHEM

PRAYER FOR ILLUMINATION

Almighty God, by whose grace we hear the word of thy kingdom, and who hast taught us that they that hear the Word of God and keep it are blessed; grant us so to hear it and to understand it that it may be the rule of our faith and lives, and that we may love it and meditate in it day and night: through Jesus Christ our Lord. Amen.[3]

READING FROM THE PSALTER

GLORIA PATRI

OLD TESTAMENT LESSON

NEW TESTAMENT LESSON *This lesson may consist of two passages of scriptures, the first taken from the Epistles, the Acts or Apocalypse, and the second from one of the Gospels. Here, if desired, a children's address may be given.*

HYMN *Children may leave during the singing of this hymn.*

PRAYER OF INTERCESSION

CALL TO PRAYER
SILENT PRAYER
PRAYER

Almighty and everliving God, which by thy holy apostle hast taught us to make prayers and supplications, and to give thanks for all men; we humbly beseech thee most mercifully to receive these our prayers, which we offer unto thy divine Majesty; beseeching thee to inspire continually the universal Church with the spirit of truth, unity, and concord: and grant that all they that do confess thy holy name may agree in the truth of thy holy Word, and live in unity and godly love. We beseech thee also to save and defend thy servant, the President of the United States, that under him we may be godly and quietly governed: and grant unto all in authority that they may truly and indifferently minister justice, to the suppression of wickedness and vice, and to the maintenance of thy true religion and virtue. Give grace (O heavenly Father) to all ministers, that they may both by their life and doctrine set forth thy true and lively word, and rightly and duly administer thy holy sacraments; and to all thy people give thy heavenly grace; and especially to this congregation here present, that with meek heart and due reverence, they may hear and receive thy holy Word, truly serving thee in holiness and righteousness all the days of their life. And we most humbly beseech thee of thy goodness (O Lord) to comfort and succor all them which in this life be in trouble, sorrow, need, sickness, or any other adversity. Grant this, O Father, for Jesus Christ's sake, our only mediator and advocate. Amen.[4]

493

SERMON

AN AFFIRMATION OF FAITH *Here one of the affirmations to be found in "Prayers and Other Worship Aids," Numbers 51–53, may be used by the minister and people.*

OFFERING

SENTENCES

COLLECTION OF GIFTS AND ANTHEM

PRESENTATION *Some congregations may wish to make the presentation with the Doxology.*

When the foregoing ministry of the Word is followed by Holy Communion, the service then proceeds according to the order normally used by the church for the administration of the sacrament of the Lord's Supper. If desired, it may follow with the section of "An Order for Worship with Communion," beginning with "The Invitation."

PRAYERS OF THANKSGIVING, SUPPLICATION, DEDICATION, AND THE LORD'S PRAYER

HYMN

BENEDICTION

3 An Order for Worship with Communion

ORGAN PRELUDE

HYMN OR PROCESSIONAL

PROCLAMATION OF GOD'S LOVE IN CHRIST

For God so loved the world, that he gave his only begotten Son, that whosoever believeth in him should not perish, but have everlasting life.

INVITATION OF CHRIST

Come unto me, all ye that labor and are heavy laden, and I will give you rest. Ask, and it shall be given you; seek and ye shall find; knock, and it shall be opened unto you. For everyone that asketh, receiveth; and he that seeketh, findeth; and to him that knocketh, it shall be opened. Thou shalt love the Lord thy God with all thy heart, and with all thy soul, and with all thy mind, and with all thy strength; and thy neighbor as thyself.

COMMUNION COLLECT

Almighty God, unto whom all hearts are open, all desires known, and from whom no secrets are hid; cleanse the thoughts of our hearts by the inspiration of thy Holy Spirit, that we may perfectly love thee, and worthily magnify thy holy name; through Christ our Lord. Amen.[1]

GENERAL CONFESSION *Minister and congregation*

Almighty and most merciful Father, we have erred and strayed from thy ways like lost sheep. We have followed too much the devices and desires of our own hearts. We have offended against thy holy laws. We have left undone those things which we ought to have done; and we have done those things which we ought not to have done. But thou, O Lord, have mercy upon us. Spare thou those, O God, who confess their faults. Restore thou those who are penitent; according to thy promises declared unto mankind in Christ Jesus our Lord. And grant, O most merciful Father, for his sake, that we may hereafter live a godly, righteous, and sober life, to the glory of thy holy name. Amen.[2]

ASSURANCE OF GOD'S FORGIVENESS

THE LORD'S PRAYER *Minister and congregation*

CALL TO PRAISE

MINISTER: O Lord, open thou our lips.
PEOPLE: *And our mouth shall show forth thy praise.*
MINISTER: Praise ye the Lord.
PEOPLE: *The Lord's name be praised.*

GLORIA PATRI

SCRIPTURE LESSON*

ANTHEM OR HYMN

CALL TO PRAYER

PRAYERS**

OFFERING

SENTENCES
COLLECTION OF GIFTS
DOXOLOGY

SERMON

THE INVITATION

* Suggested readings will be found in "The Lectionary" in *A Book of Worship for Free Churches*, Oxford University Press, New York, N.Y., 1948, pp. 403–408.
** *A Book of Worship for Free Churches*, op. cit., pp. 105–106; or the minister's own may be used.

495

SURSUM CORDA AND SANCTUS

MINISTER: Lift up your hearts.
PEOPLE: *We lift them up unto the Lord.*
MINISTER: Let us give thanks unto our Lord God.
PEOPLE: *It is meet and right so to do.*

It is very meet, right, and our bounden duty, that we should at all times, and in all places give thanks unto thee, O Lord, holy Father, almighty, everlasting God.* Therefore with angels and archangels, and with all the company of heaven, we laud and magnify thy glorious name; evermore praising thee, and saying:

Holy, holy, holy, Lord God of hosts,
Heaven and earth are full of thy glory:
Glory be to thee, O Lord most high. Amen.

PRAYER OF CONSECRATION OR EUCHARISTIC PRAYER

THE WORDS OF INSTITUTION

Giving of the Bread

The Lord Jesus the same night in which he was betrayed took bread: And when he had given thanks, he brake it, and said, Take, eat: this is my body, which is broken for you: this do in remembrance of me.

Ministering to you in his name, I give you this bread.

Giving of the Cup

After the same manner also he took the cup, when he had supped, saying, This cup is the new testament in my blood: this do ye, as oft as ye drink it in remembrance of me. For as often as ye eat this bread, and drink this cup, ye do show the Lord's death till he come.

Ministering to you in his name, I give you this cup.

PRAYER OF THANKSGIVING *Unison*

We give thanks to thee, almighty God, that thou hast refreshed us with this memorial of thy love, and hast granted to us the presence of thy Son, even Jesus Christ our Lord; and we beseech thee to strengthen our faith in thee and to increase our love toward one another; through him who is our redeemer. Amen.

* After the words "Father, almighty, everlasting God," the minister may, if he so desires, read the proper preface for the season of the Christian year. The Sanctus may be sung by the choir or the entire congregation.

HYMN

If a second offering is desired, it should be taken during the singing of this hymn.

PRAYER OF DEDICATION

BENEDICTION

ORGAN POSTLUDE

4 An Order for the Reception of Members into the Church

This order may be used at any worship service, but it is recommended that it be used in connection with the celebration of Holy Communion.

THE ROLL CALL OF CANDIDATES *Each rises as his name is called. When the roll call is finished, all shall present themselves before the minister.*

THE CONFESSION OF FAITH

MINISTER: Dearly beloved, do you confess your faith in Jesus Christ as your personal Lord and Savior, and make him your example, and take for your rule of life his words: Thou shalt love the Lord thy God with all thy heart, and with all thy soul, and with all thy mind. And . . . thy neighbor as thyself?

RESPONSE: *I do.*

THE COVENANT OF WORSHIP AND SERVICE
Or the church's own covenant may be used.

MINISTER: In the presence of God and these witnesses, do you give yourself unreservedly to his service, and take this to be your church? Ever mindful of the welfare of your fellow members, do you promise to walk with them in faithfulness and Christian love? And do you promise that, so far as able, you will attend the services of this church, observe its sacraments, share in its work, support, and benevolences, and endeavor to make it a fruitful body of Christians?

RESPONSE: *I do.*

WELCOME TO THE CHURCH *The congregation will stand.* The members will say with the minister:*

We then as members of this church, gladly welcome you to a part with us in the hopes, the labors, and the joys of the Church of Christ. We promise to walk with you in Christian love and sympathy, and to promote, as far as in us lies, your growth in the Christian life.

* Some churches may prefer to have only the members stand for the welcome to the local church and to have members of other churches stand when the welcome to the Church Universal is extended.

Members of other churches will join, as all say:

We as members of the Church Universal bid you welcome and renew our covenant with Christ and his Church. May God keep us true to him, and bring us at length into the Church Triumphant.

> *Here, if desired, may be used the Apostles' Creed, the Nicene Creed, the Kansas City Statement of Faith or the church's own statement of faith. See "Prayers and Other Worship Aids," Numbers 51–53.*

THE RIGHT HAND OF FELLOWSHIP *To be extended by the minister*

DECLARATION TO THE MEMBERS

So then you are no longer strangers and sojourners, but you are fellow citizens with the saints and members of the household of God, built upon the foundation of the apostles and prophets, Christ Jesus himself being the chief cornerstone, in whom the whole structure is joined together and grows into a holy temple in the Lord. (Ephesians 2: 19–21)

> *The new members resume their seats.*

5 An Order for the Sacrament of Baptism for Infants or Children

> *Baptism should ordinarily be administered during the service of the church and may follow the New Testament lesson. After the singing of a baptismal hymn, the minister says:*

Our help is in the name of the Lord, who made heaven and earth.

The mercy of the Lord is from everlasting to everlasting upon them that fear him, and his righteousness unto children's children.

He shall feed his flock like a shepherd; he shall gather the lambs with his arm.

And Jesus called a little child unto him, and set him in the midst of them. Jesus said, Suffer little children to come unto me, and forbid them not: for of such is the kingdom of God.

Address

Dearly beloved, you have brought your child here desiring for him Christian baptism. This is a service of thanksgiving as we offer to God the gratitude of our hearts for the hope and happiness which come into our lives by the presence of a child. It is a recognition of God as the giver of life and a testimony that children belong, with us who believe, to the church; and that Christ claims them as his own, calling them to himself. Also, this service is one of dedication and consecration: the dedication of your child to God; and your own consecration to new and holier fidelity. From the days of our fathers the church has taught that the sacrament of baptism is a sign and seal of the covenant of grace, of union with Christ in his body, of cleansing of heart and soul, of resurrection unto eternal life, of our calling and engagement to be his forever, and of our welcome in the household of faith.

You do now engage upon your part to perform those things needful that the good will and love of the heavenly Father be not hidden from him, but rather that they may be made evident; that he may grow into the love and nurture and admonition of the Lord.

Do you thus engage?

RESPONSE: *I do.*

MINISTER: Do you promise to instruct this child in the Word of God, and by precept and example to bring him up in the nurture and admonition of the Lord, to teach him the principles of our Christian religion, to pray with him and for him and to rear him up in the fellowship of the church?

RESPONSE: *I do.*

MINISTER: *To be used when sponsors participate in the service* You, who stand sponsors, solemnly engage to strive diligently to hold up the hands of these parents in the fulfillment of their covenant that this child be instructed in the Word of God, brought up in the nurture and admonition of the Lord, kept in communion with the church, and strengthened to live in godly manner all the days of his life. Do you thus engage?

RESPONSE: *We do.*

MINISTER: Do you, the members of this church as of the whole Church of Christ, receive this child into your love and care, and do you promise that so far as in you lies you will uphold and encourage the parents in the fulfillment of their covenant?

RESPONSE: *We do.*

MINISTER: Grant, O Lord, unto these thy servants, the grace to perform that which they have promised before thee. And sanctify with thy spirit this child now to be baptized and committed in Christian faith to thee. Amen.

The Baptism

By what name shall this child be called?

N———, I baptize thee in the name of the Father, and of the Son, and of the Holy Spirit. Amen.

This child is now received into the love and care of the church in the good hope that hereafter he may never be ashamed to confess the faith of Christ crucified but may be kept steadfast in his love and service.

Let us pray:

Almighty and everlasting God, who of thine infinite mercy and goodness dost give little ones unto us to increase our joy, and hast promised that thou wilt be not only our God, but also the God and Father of our children; keep, guard, and bless this child evermore. As he has been baptized by our ministry into the Christian church, so may he, by thy guidance, become one with Christ. Breathe upon him now and always thy Holy Spirit. Grant that he may be a blessing to the home and the world into which he has been born.

O God our Father, give unto thy servants to whom thou hast committed this blessed trust a wise, loving, devout, and faithful spirit. Guide them with thy counsel as they teach and train their child; and help them to lead their household into an ever-increasing knowledge of Christ, and a more steadfast obedience to thy will. Grant that they may serve thy Church with renewed devotion and steadfast loyalty.

We commend to thy fatherly care the children and families of this congregation. Help us in our homes to honor thee, and by love to serve one another. And to thy name be all blessing and glory; through Jesus Christ our Lord. Amen.

> *This Order may be concluded with the Lord's Prayer or a benediction by the minister.*

6 An Order for Confirmation

This service presupposes baptism and, also, careful and complete instruction of the candidates in a confirmation or church membership class. In the case of adults who have been baptized previously, but have not been received into the full communion of the church, this order may be used for their profession of faith and reception as members.

At the appointed time in a general service of the church, preferably in connection with the celebration of the Holy Communion, the minister shall read the names of those to be confirmed, requesting them to stand with him before the congregation.

MINISTER: What shall I render unto the Lord for all his benefits toward me? I will take the cup of salvation and call upon the name of the Lord. I will pay my vows unto the Lord now in the presence of all his people.

Our Lord Jesus Christ said, If any man will come after me, let him deny himself, and take up his cross and follow me.

Dearly beloved, following the example of the apostles of our Lord, the church bestows upon those who have been baptized, and have been properly instructed, the blessing of confirmation by prayer and the laying on of hands.

In this sacred ordinance you, on your part, renew and ratify the promise and vow made in your baptism; while the church, in God's stead, claims you publicly for his service, blesses you in his name, confirms you in his covenant, and invokes upon you in larger measure the Holy Spirit, by whose help alone you are able to fulfill your vows by leading holy and obedient lives.

Do you believe in God as your heavenly Father?
RESPONSE: *I do.*
MINISTER: Do you accept Jesus as your Savior and Master?
RESPONSE: *I do.*
MINISTER: Do you believe in the Holy Spirit as your Comforter and Guide?
RESPONSE: *I do.*
MINISTER: Will you continue striving to know and to do the will of God as taught in the Holy Scriptures?
RESPONSE: *I will.*
MINISTER: Will you be loyal to the Church of Christ, wherever you are, and uphold it by your prayers, your presence, your gifts, and your service?
RESPONSE: *I will.*

Reading and Owning of the Covenant

Then shall the minister read the covenant of the local church.

MINISTER: Do you accept and own with us this the covenant of our church?
RESPONSE: *I do.*

*Then shall the minister ask the confirmands to kneel or bow, and
laying his hands upon the head of each one, shall say:*

Confirm, O Lord, this thy child with thy heavenly grace; that he may continue
thine forever; and daily increase in thy Holy Spirit more and more, until he
comes unto thy everlasting kingdom. Amen.

or

Almighty and eternal God, strengthen this thy servant, we beseech thee, with
the Holy Spirit the Comforter, and daily increase in him thy manifold gifts of
grace: the spirit of wisdom and understanding, the spirit of counsel and might,
the spirit of knowledge and of the fear of the Lord; and keep him in thy mercy
unto life eternal; through Jesus Christ our Lord. Amen.[1]

CHORAL RESPONSE

The Lord bless you and keep you; the Lord make his face to shine upon you,
and be gracious unto you; the Lord lift up his countenance upon you, and give
you peace.

The Right Hand of Fellowship

Then shall the minister extend the right hand of fellowship and say:

I now receive and welcome you into membership in this congregation and into
the fellowship of the Church Universal. I invite you to partake of the Holy
Communion, and to participate in all the privileges and obligations of the Church
of Christ.

PRAYERS AND OTHER WORSHIP AIDS

Opening Sentences

7 Serve the LORD with gladness: come before his presence with singing. Enter into his gates with thanksgiving, and into his courts with praise: be thankful unto him, and bless his name. For the LORD is good; his mercy is everlasting; and his truth endureth to all generations.

8 Seek ye the LORD while he may be found, call ye upon him while he is near: let the wicked forsake his way, and the unrighteous man his thoughts: and let him return unto the LORD, and he will have mercy upon him; and to our God, for he will abundantly pardon.

9 The hour cometh, and now is, when the true worshipers shall worship the Father in spirit and in truth: for the Father seeketh such to worship him. God is a Spirit: and they that worship him must worship him in spirit and truth.

Prayers of Preparation

10 O almighty God, from whom every good prayer cometh, and who pourest out on all who desire it the spirit of grace and supplication; deliver us, when we draw nigh to thee, from coldness of heart and wanderings of mind, that with steadfast thoughts and kindled affections we may worship thee in spirit and in truth, through Jesus Christ our Lord. Amen.

11 O God, thou source of all pure desires and holy affections, give me now a quiet mind and a reverent and devout heart, that I may worthily worship thee at this time. Amen.

12 Almighty, ever gracious Father, forasmuch as all our salvation depends upon our having truly understood thy holy Word: therefore grant us that our hearts be set free from worldly things, so that we may with all diligence and faith hear and apprehend thy holy Word, that thereby we may rightly understand thy gracious will, and in all sincerity live according to the same, to thy praise and glory, through our Lord Jesus Christ. Amen.

503

13 O Lord our God, great, eternal, wonderful in glory, who keepest covenant and promise for those that love thee with their whole heart, who art the life of all, the help of those that flee to thee, the hope of those that cry unto thee, cleanse us from our sins, and from every thought displeasing to thy goodness. Cleanse our souls and bodies, our hearts and consciences, that with pure heart and a clear mind, with perfect love and calm hope we may confidently and fearlessly pray to thee, through Jesus Christ our Lord. Amen.

Prayers for Illumination

14 O Lord God, who hast left unto us thy holy Word to be a lamp unto our feet and a light unto our path, give unto us all thy holy spirit, we humbly pray thee, that out of the same Word we may learn what is thy blessed will, and frame our lives in all holy obedience to the same, to thine honor and glory and the increase of our faith, through Jesus Christ our Lord. Amen.

15 O God, whose word is quick and powerful, and sharper than any two-edged sword, grant us grace to receive thy truth in faith and love, that by it we may be taught and guided, upheld and comforted, and prepared unto every good word and work, to the glory of thy name, through Jesus Christ our Lord. Amen.

Prayers of Adoration

16 Almighty God, whose glory the heavens are telling, the earth thy power, and the sea thy might, and whose greatness all feeling and thinking creatures everywhere proclaim, to thee belongeth glory, honor, power, and love, now and for ever, and unto ages of ages, through Jesus Christ our Lord. Amen.

17 Eternal God, most blessed and most holy, we worship and adore thee. We acknowledge thine infinite glory; we celebrate thy divine majesty; we praise thee for the wonder of thy love in Jesus Christ our Lord. Accept, we beseech thee, the adoration of our hearts; and by thy holy spirit enable us to worship thee in the beauty of holiness; for to thee, Father, Son, and Holy Ghost, we ascribe all honor and glory, now and for ever. Amen.

Prayers of Confession

18 Almighty and most merciful Father, we have erred and strayed from thy ways like lost sheep. We have followed too much the devices and desires of our own hearts. We have offended against thy holy laws. We have left undone those things which we ought to have done, and we have done those things which we ought not to have done. But thou, O Lord, have mercy upon us. Spare thou those, O God, who confess their faults. Restore thou those who are penitent, according to thy promises declared unto mankind in Christ Jesus our Lord. And grant, O most merciful Father, for his sake, that we may hereafter live a godly, righteous, and sober life, to the glory of thy holy name. Amen.

19 Almighty and most merciful God, we acknowledge and confess that we have sinned against thee in thought and word and deed, that we have not loved thee with all our heart and soul, with all our mind and strength, and that we have not loved our neighbor as ourselves. We beseech thee, O God, to be forgiving to what we have been, to help us to amend what we are, and of thy mercy to direct what we shall be, so that the love of goodness may ever be first in our hearts, that we may always walk in thy commandments and ordinances blameless, and follow unto our life's end in the steps of Jesus Christ our Lord. Amen.

20 We confess to thee, almighty God, Father, Son, and Holy Spirit, that we have grievously sinned in thought, word, and deed. Make us truly contrite. Fill us with holy fear, and give us grace to amend our lives according to thy Word, for the glory of thy holy name, through Jesus Christ our Lord. Amen.

Prayers for Pardon

21 Almighty and everlasting God, who art always more ready to hear than we to pray, and art wont to give more than either we desire or deserve, pour down upon us the abundance of thy mercy, forgiving us those things whereof our conscience is afraid, and giving us those good things which we are not worthy to ask, but through the merits and mediation of Jesus Christ, thy Son, our Lord. Amen.

22 Almighty God, our heavenly Father, who of his great mercy hath promised forgiveness of sins to all them, who with hearty repentance and true faith, turn unto him, have mercy upon you; pardon and deliver you from all your sins; confirm and strengthen you in all goodness; and bring you to everlasting life, through Jesus Christ our Lord. Amen.

Prayers for the Church

23 Endue thy Church, O God, with the spirit of wisdom and power in Christ, that where others question, thy Church may affirm, where others flee, thy Church may advance, and where others fall, thy Church may stand, through the same Jesus Christ our Lord. Amen.

24 Thou Father of our Lord Jesus Christ, who is head of the Church, give us grace to lay to heart the great dangers we are in by our unhappy divisions. Take away all hatred and prejudice, and whatsoever else may hinder us from godly union and concord, that, as there is but one body, and one spirit, and one hope of our calling, one Lord, one faith, one baptism, one God and Father of us all, so we may henceforth be all of one heart, and of one soul, united in one holy bond of truth and peace, of faith and charity, and may with one mind and one mouth glorify thee, through Jesus Christ our Lord. Amen.

25 Gracious Father, we humbly beseech thee for thy universal Church. Fill it with all truth, in all truth with all peace. Where it is corrupt, purge it, and where it is in error, direct it; where it is superstitious, rectify it; where anything is amiss, reform it; where it is right, strengthen and confirm it; where it is in want, furnish it; where it is divided and rent asunder, make up the breaches thereof, O thou holy One of Israel, for the sake of Jesus Christ our Lord and Savior. Amen.

26 O God, who didst send thy word to speak in the prophets and live in thy Son, and appoint thy Church to be witness of divine things in all the world; revive the purity and deepen the power of its testimony; and through the din of earthly interests and the storm of human passions, let it make the still small voice of thy spirit inly felt. Nearer and nearer may thy kingdom come from age to age, meeting the face of the young as a rising dawn, and brightening the song of the old, "Lord, now lettest thou thy servant depart in peace." Already let its light abash our guilty negligence, and touch with hope each secret sorrow of the earth. By the cleansing spirit of thy Son, make this world a fitting forecourt to that sanctuary not made with hands, where our life is hid with Christ in God. Amen.

27 O almighty God, whose dearly beloved Son after his resurrection sent his apostles into all the world, and on the day of Pentecost endued them with special gifts of the Holy Spirit, that they might gather in the spiritual harvest, we beseech thee to look down from heaven upon the fields now white unto the harvest, and to send forth more laborers to gather fruit unto eternal life. And grant us grace so to help them with our prayers and offerings that, when the harvest of the earth is ripe and the time for reaping is come, we, together with them, may rejoice before thee according to the joy in harvest, through Jesus Christ our Lord. Amen.

28 Almighty and everliving God, who by thy holy apostle hast taught us to make prayers and supplications, and to give thanks for all men; we humbly beseech thee most mercifully to receive these our prayers, which we offer unto thy divine Majesty, beseeching thee to inspire continually the universal Church with the spirit of truth, unity, and concord; and grant that all they that do confess thy holy name may agree in the truth of thy holy Word, and live in unity and godly love. We beseech thee also to save and defend thy servant the President of the United States of America, that under him we may be godly and quietly governed; and grant unto all in authority, that they may truly and indifferently minister justice, to the suppression of wickedness and vice, and to the maintenance of thy true religion and virtues. Give grace, O heavenly Father, to all ministers, that they may both by their life and doctrine set forth thy true and lively word, and rightly and duly administer thy holy sacraments; and to all thy people give thy heavenly grace; and especially to this congregation here present, that with meek heart and due reverence, they may hear and receive thy holy Word, truly serving thee in holiness and righteousness all the days of their life. And we most humbly beseech thee of thy goodness, O Lord, to comfort and succor all them who in this life be in trouble, sorrow, need, sickness, or any other adversity. Grant this, O Father, for Jesus Christ's sake, our only mediator and advocate. Amen.

29 We beseech thee, O Lord, for thy church through the world. May it grow in the faith of the cross and the power of the resurrection. May thy spirit minister to it continually the redemption and reconciliation of all things. Keep it in thy eternal unity, in great humility, in godly fear, and in thine own pure and peaceable wisdom so easy to be entreated. Make it swift and mighty in the cause of the kingdom of heaven. Cover, establish, and enlighten it, that it may see through all that darkens the time, and move in the shadow of thy wing, with faith, obedience, sacrifice, and godly power, through Christ our Lord. Amen.

Prayers for Peace

30 O God, from whom all holy desires, all good counsels, and all just works do proceed, give unto thy servants that peace which the world cannot give, that our hearts may be set to obey thy commandments, and also that by thee, we, being defended from the fear of our enemies, may pass our time in rest and quietness, through the merits of Jesus Christ our Savior. Amen.

31 O God, who callest the peacemakers thy children, we beseech thee that as thou didst send thy Son with the heavenly voice of peace on earth to be the Prince of peace to man, so thou wilt keep our hearts and minds in his peace, and make us both to love and defend the same. Guide the counsels of the President and of all leaders and governors in equity and steadfastness to establish unity and concord among the nations, that all mankind may render thee the fruits of peace and righteousness, through Jesus Christ our Lord. Amen.

General Prayers

32 Eternal God, who hast neither dawn nor evening, yet sendest us the alternate mercies of the darkness and the day, there is no light but thine without, within. As thou liftest the curtain of night from our abodes, take also the veil from all our hearts. Rise with thy morning upon our souls; quicken all our labor and our prayer, and though all else declines, let the noontide of thy grace and peace remain. May we walk while it is yet day in the steps of him who, with fewest hours, finished thy divinest work. Amen.

33 O God, who hast drawn over weary day the restful veil of night, wrap our consciences in heavenly peace. Lift from our hands our tasks, and all through the night bear in thy bosom the full weight of our burdens and sorrows, that in untroubled slumber we may press our weakness close to thy strength, and win new power for the morrow's duty from thee who givest thy beloved sleep. Amen.

34 Almighty God, Father of all mercies, we, thine unworthy servants, do give thee most humble and hearty thanks for all thy goodness and loving-kindness to us, and to all men. We bless thee for our creation, preservation, and all the blessings of this life, but above all for thine inestimable love in the redemption of the world by our Lord Jesus Christ, for the means of grace, and for the hope of glory. And, we beseech thee, give us that due sense of all thy mercies, that our hearts may be unfeignedly thankful, and that we show forth thy praise, not only with our lips, but in our lives, by giving up ourselves to thy service, and by walking before thee in holiness and righteousness all our days, through Jesus Christ our Lord, to whom, with thee and the Holy Ghost, be all honor and glory, world without end. Amen.

35 O God, the Creator and Preserver of all mankind, we humbly beseech thee for all sorts and conditions of men, that thou wouldest be pleased to make thy ways known unto them, thy saving health unto all nations. More especially we pray for thy holy Church Universal; that it may be so guided and governed by thy good Spirit, that all who profess and call themselves Christians may be led into the way of truth, and hold the faith in unity of spirit, in the bond of peace, and in righteousness of life. Finally we commend to thy fatherly goodness all those who are any ways afflicted, or distressed, in mind, body, or estate, that it may please thee to comfort and relieve them, according to their several necessities, giving them patience under their sufferings, and a happy issue out of all their afflictions. And this we beg for Jesus Christ's sake. Amen.

36 O thou who art the light of the minds that know thee, the life of the souls that love thee, and the strength of the wills that serve thee, help us so to know thee that we may truly love thee, so to love thee that we may fully serve thee, whom to serve is perfect freedom, through Jesus Christ our Lord. Amen.

37 Almighty Father, enter thou our hearts and so fill us with thy love that, forsaking all evil desires, we may embrace thee, our only good. Show unto us for thy mercies' sake, O Lord our God, what thou art unto us. Say unto our souls: I am thy salvation. So speak that we may hear. Our hearts are before thee; open thou our ears; let us hasten after thy voice, and take hold on thee. Hide not thy face from us, we beseech thee, O Lord. Enlarge thou the narrowness of our souls, that thou mayest enter in. Repair the ruinous mansions, that thou mayest dwell there. Hear us, O heavenly Father, for the sake of thine only Son, Jesus Christ, our Lord, who liveth and reigneth with thee and the Holy Ghost, now and for ever. Amen.

38 Almighty and everlasting God, we be taught by thy holy Word that the hearts of rulers are in thy rule and governance and that thou dost dispose, and turn them as it seemeth best to thy godly wisdom; we humbly beseech thee, so to dispose and govern the heart of the President of the United States, thy servant, our chosen leader, that in all his thoughts, words, and works, he may ever seek thy honor and glory, and study to preserve thy people committed to his charge, in wealth, peace, and godliness. Grant this, O merciful Father, for thy dear Son's sake, Jesus Christ our Lord. Amen.

39 O God, the Father of us all, who has taught us to bear one another's burdens and so to fulfill the law of Christ, grant that, in humility of mind and purity of heart, we may always follow the example of our Savior Christ, who went about among men doing good. Give us grace to deny ourselves, to be helpers one of another, and to be forgiving to those who have done us wrong. Enable us to put away all bitterness, and wrath, and anger, and evil speaking, with all malice; and grant that, in honor preferring one another, we may walk in love, even as Christ loved us and gave himself for us, to whom with thee, O Father, and the Holy Ghost, be all honor and glory, world without end. Amen.

Collects and Short Prayers

40 Almighty God, unto whom all hearts are open, all desires known, and from whom no secrets are hid, cleanse the thoughts of our hearts by the inspiration of thy holy spirit, that we may perfectly love thee, and worthily magnify thy holy name, through Christ our Lord. Amen.

41 O Lord, our heavenly Father, almighty and everlasting God, who hast safely brought us to the beginning of this day, defend us in the same with thy mighty power and grant that this day we fall into no sin, neither run into any kind of danger, but that all our doings, being ordered by thy governance, may be righteous in thy sight, through Jesus Christ our Lord. Amen.

42 Direct us, O Lord, in all our doings, with thy most gracious favor, and further us with thy continual help, that in all our works begun, continued, and ended in thee, we may glorify thy holy name, and finally, by thy mercy, obtain everlasting life, through Jesus Christ our Lord. Amen.

43 Grant, we beseech thee, almighty God, that the words which we have heard this day with our outward ears, may, through thy grace, be so grafted inwardly in our hearts, that they may bring forth in us the fruit of good living, to the honor and praise of thy name, through Jesus Christ our Lord. Amen.

44 Almighty God, who hast given us grace at this time with one accord to make our common supplications unto thee, and dost promise that when two or three are gathered together in thy name thou wilt grant their requests, fulfil now, O Lord, the desires and petitions of thy servants, as may be most expedient for them, granting us in this world knowledge of thy truth, and in the world to come life everlasting. Amen.

45 O Lord, support us all the day long of this troublous life, until the shadows lengthen and the evening comes, and the busy world is hushed, and the fever of life is over, and our work is done. Then in thy mercy grant us a safe lodging and a holy rest, and peace at the last, through Jesus Christ our Lord. Amen.

Offertory Sentences

46 Remember the words of the Lord Jesus, how he said, It is more blessed to give than to receive.

47 Freely ye have received, freely give. Let your light so shine before men that they may see your good works, and glorify your Father which is in heaven.

48 Every man according as he purposeth in his heart, so let him give; not grudgingly, or of necessity: for God loveth a cheerful giver.

Offertory Prayers

49 Accept, O Lord, these offerings which thy people make unto thee; and grant that the cause to which they are devoted may prosper under thy guidance, to the glory of thy name, through Jesus Christ our Lord. Amen.

50 O God, most merciful and gracious, of whose bounty we have all received, accept, we beseech thee, this offering of thy people. Remember in thy love those who have brought it and those for whom it is given, and so follow it with thy blessing that it may promote peace and goodwill among men, and advance the kingdom of our Lord and Savior, Jesus Christ. Amen.

Affirmations of Faith

51 I believe in God the Father Almighty, maker of heaven and earth, and in Jesus Christ his only Son our Lord, who was conceived by the Holy Ghost, born of the Virgin Mary, suffered under Pontius Pilate, was crucified, dead, and buried. He descended into hell; the third day he rose again from the dead; he ascended into heaven, and sitteth on the right hand of God the Father Almighty. From thence he shall come to judge the quick and the dead.

I believe in the Holy Ghost, the holy Catholic Church, the communion of saints, the forgiveness of sins, the resurrection of the body, and the life everlasting. Amen. *The Apostles' Creed*

511

52 I believe in one God the Father Almighty, maker of heaven and earth, and of all things visible and invisible:

And in one Lord Jesus Christ, the only-begotten Son of God, begotten of his Father before all worlds, God of God, Light of Light, very God of very God; begotten, not made, being of one substance with the Father by whom all things were made, who for us men and for our salvation came down from heaven, and was incarnate by the Holy Ghost of the Virgin Mary, and was made man, and was crucified also for us under Pontius Pilate. He suffered and was buried, and the third day he rose again according to the Scriptures and ascended into heaven, and sitteth on the right hand of the Father; and he shall come again, with glory, to judge both the quick and the dead, whose kingdom shall have no end.

And I believe in the Holy Ghost, the Lord, and Giver of life, who proceedeth from the Father and the Son, who with the Father and Son together is worshiped and glorified, who spake by the prophets. And I believe one holy Catholic and Apostolic Church; I acknowledge one baptism for the remission of sins, and I look for the resurrection of the dead, and the life of the world to come. Amen.   *The Nicene Creed*

53 We believe in God the Father, infinite in wisdom, goodness and love, and in Jesus Christ, his Son, our Lord and Savior, who for us and our salvation lived and died and rose again and liveth evermore, and in the Holy Spirit, who taketh of the things of Christ and revealeth them to us, renewing, comforting, and inspiring the souls of men.

We are united in striving to know the will of God as taught in the holy Scriptures, and in our purpose to walk in the ways of the Lord, made known or to be made known to us.

We hold it to be the mission of the Church of Christ to proclaim the gospel to all mankind, exalting the worship of the one true God, and laboring for the progress of knowledge, the promotion of justice, the reign of peace, and the realization of human brotherhood.

Depending, as did our fathers, upon the continued guidance of the Holy Spirit to lead us into all truth, we work and pray for the transformation of the world into the kingdom of God, and we look with faith for the triumph of righteousness, and the life everlasting.

The Kansas City Statement of Faith, 1913

54   Salem Church Covenant, 1629

We covenant with the Lord and one with an other and doe bynd our selves in the presence of God, to walke together in all his waies, according as he is pleased to reveale himself unto us in his blessed word of truth.

55   The Ten Commandments

God spake all these words, saying, I am the LORD thy God, who brought thee out of the land of Egypt, out of the house of bondage.

Thou shalt have no other gods before me.
Thou shalt not make unto thee any graven image.
Thou shalt not take the name of the LORD thy God in vain.
Remember the sabbath day, to keep it holy.
Honor thy father and thy mother.
Thou shalt not kill.
Thou shalt not commit adultery.
Thou shalt not steal.
Thou shalt not bear false witness against thy neighbor.
Thou shalt not covet thy neighbor's house, thou shalt not covet thy neighbor's wife, nor his manservant, nor his maidservant, nor his ox, nor his ass, nor anything that is thy neighbor's.

56   The Great Commandment

Thou shalt love the Lord thy God with all thy heart, and with all thy soul, and with all thy mind. This is the first and great commandment. And the second is like unto it, Thou shalt love thy neighbor as thyself. On these two commandments hang all the law and the prophets.

57   The Lord's Prayer

Our Father, which art in heaven, Hallowed be thy name. Thy kingdom come. Thy will be done in earth, as it is in heaven. Give us this day our daily bread. And forgive us our debts, as we forgive our debtors. And lead us not into temptation, but deliver us from evil: For thine is the kingdom, and the power, and the glory, for ever. Amen.

Benedictions

58   The LORD bless you and keep you: The LORD make his face to shine upon you, and be gracious unto you: The LORD lift up his countenance upon you, and give you peace. Amen.

59   The grace of the Lord Jesus Christ and the love of God and the fellowship of the Holy Spirit be with you all. Amen.

60   The peace of God, which passeth all understanding, keep your hearts and minds in the knowledge and love of God, and of his son Jesus Christ our Lord; and the blessing of God Almighty, the Father, the Son, and the Holy Spirit, be upon you, and remain with you always. Amen.

61   Litany for the Church

We, thy humble servants, do beseech thee, O Lord, that it may please thee to receive our supplications for thy Church, that it may be truly one, holy, and catholic;

We beseech thee to hear us, good Lord.

That it may please thee to purge the Church from all error, unbelief and want of faith; that it may be the pillar and ground of the truth;

We beseech thee to hear us, good Lord.

That thy Church may be delivered from all scandal, sin, and shame; from complicity with wrong and compromise with evil; from inconsistency, wavering, and fear; that it may shine as a light in the world, and be as a city set on a hill;

We beseech thee to hear us, good Lord.

That thy Church may preach the Gospel to every creature, set forth the truth that makes men free, and so lift up the cross of Christ that all mankind may be drawn together unto him;

We beseech thee to hear us, good Lord.

That thy Church may remember the sheep that are not of the fold, seek out the wandering and the lost, proclaim the forgiveness of sins to the penitent, keep a heart of compassion for all mankind, and defend the cause of the poor and the oppressed;

We beseech thee to hear us, good Lord.

That thy Church may remember to hear what the Spirit saith, so that it may teach only as it learns; to follow Christ, as it would lead mankind; to be itself the example of what it would commend to all societies and states of men;

We beseech thee to hear us, good Lord.

That it may be granted to thy Church to unite the nations of the world in one family, to bring deliverance to the peoples, and to gather all thy sheep together, so that there may be one flock and one Shepherd;

We beseech thee to hear us, good Lord.

O Eternal God, the Father of spirits and the Lover of souls, who didst send thy Holy Spirit upon thy Church on the day of Pentecost, and hast promised that he shall abide with it for ever; let that same Spirit lead us into all truth, defend us from all sin, enrich us with his gifts, refresh us with his comfort, rule our hearts in all things and lead us in the way everlasting; through Jesus Christ our Lord, who with thee and the same Spirit, liveth and reigneth one God, world without end. Amen.

PSALTER READINGS

62   *Psalm 1*

Blessed is the man who walks not in the counsel of the wicked, nor stands in the way of sinners, nor sits in the seat of scoffers;

But his delight is in the law of the Lord, and on his law he meditates day and night.

He is like a tree planted by streams of water, that yields its fruit in its season,

And its leaf does not wither.
In all that he does, he prospers.

The wicked are not so, but are like chaff which the wind drives away.

Therefore the wicked will not stand in the judgment, nor sinners in the congregation of the righteous;

For the LORD knows the way of the righteous,

But the way of the wicked will perish.

63   *Psalms 3, 4*

O LORD, how many are my foes!

Many are rising against me; many are saying of me, there is no help for him in God.

But thou, O LORD, art a shield about me, my glory, and the lifter of my head.

I cry aloud to the Lord, and he answers me from his holy hill.

I lie down and sleep; I wake again, for the LORD sustains me.

I am not afraid of ten thousands of people who have set themselves against me round about.

Answer me when I call, O God of my right!

Thou hast given me room when I was in distress.

Be gracious unto me, and hear my prayer.

O men, how long shall my honor suffer shame?

How long will you love vain words, and seek after lies?

But know that the Lord has set apart the godly for himself;

The LORD hears when I call to him.

There are many who say, " O that we might see some good!

Lift up the light of thy countenance upon us, O LORD! "

Thou hast put more joy in my heart than they have when their grain and wine abound.

In peace I will both lie down and sleep;

For thou alone, O Lord, makest me dwell in safety.

64   *Psalm 8*

O LORD, our Lord, how majestic is thy name in all the earth!

Thou whose glory above the heavens is chanted by the mouths of babes and infants,

Thou hast founded a bulwark because of thy foes,

To still the enemy and the avenger.

When I look at thy heavens, the work of thy fingers, the moon and the stars which thou hast established;

What is man that thou art mindful of him, and the son of man that thou dost care for him?

Yet thou hast made him little less than God, and dost crown him with glory and honor.

Thou hast given him dominion over the works of thy hands;

Thou hast put all things under his feet,

All sheep and oxen, and also the beasts of the field,

The birds of the air, and the fish of the sea, whatever passes along the paths of the sea.

O Lord, our Lord, how majestic is thy name in all the earth!

65   Psalm 10

Why dost thou stand afar off, O LORD? Why dost thou hide thyself in times of trouble?

For the wicked boasts of the desires of his heart, and the man greedy for gain curses and renounces the Lord.

In the pride of his countenance the wicked does not seek him;

All his thoughts are, " There is no God."

His ways prosper at all times; thy judgments are on high, out of his sight; as for all his foes, he puffs at them.

He thinks in his heart, " I shall not be moved; throughout all generations I shall not meet adversity."

The hapless is crushed, sinks down, and falls by his might.

He thinks in his heart, " God has forgotten, he has hidden his face, he will never see it."

Arise, O LORD, lift up thy hand; forget not the afflicted.

Thou dost see; yea, thou dost note trouble and vexation, and thou mayst take it into thy hands;

The hapless commits himself to thee; thou hast been the helper of the fatherless.

The Lord is king for ever and ever;

O LORD, thou wilt hear the desire of the meek; thou wilt strengthen their heart, thou wilt incline thine ear

To do justice to the fatherless and the oppressed, so that man who is of the earth may strike terror no more.

66   Psalms 13, 15

How long, O LORD? Wilt thou forget me for ever?

How long wilt thou hide thy face from me?

How long must I bear pain in my soul, and have sorrow in my heart all the day?

How long shall my enemy be exalted over me?

Consider and answer me, O LORD my God;

Lighten my eyes, lest I sleep the sleep of death;

Lest my enemy say, "I have prevailed over him."

Lest my foes rejoice because I am shaken.

But I have trusted in thy steadfast love; my heart shall rejoice in thy salvation.

I will sing to the Lord, because he has dealt bountifully with me.

O LORD, who shall sojourn in thy tent? Who shall dwell on thy holy hill?

He who walks blamelessly, and does what is right, and speaks truth from his heart;

Who does not slander with his tongue, and does no evil to his friend, nor takes up a reproach against his neighbor;

In whose eyes a reprobate is despised, but who honors those who fear the Lord;

Who swears to his own hurt and does not change, and who does not take a bribe against the innocent.

He who does these things shall never be moved.

67   *Psalm 16*

Preserve me, O God, for in thee I take refuge.

I say to the Lord, " Thou art my Lord; I have no good apart from thee."

The LORD is my chosen portion and my cup; thou holdest my lot.

The lines have fallen for me in pleasant places; yea, I have a goodly heritage.

I bless the LORD who gives me counsel; in the night also my heart instructs me.

I keep the Lord always before me; because he is at my right hand, I shall not be moved.

Therefore my heart is glad, and my soul rejoices; my body also dwells secure.

Thou dost show me the path of life;

In thy presence there is fulness of joy,

In thy right hand are pleasures for evermore.

68   *Psalm 19*

The heavens are telling the glory of God; and the firmament proclaims his handiwork.

Day to day pours forth speech, and night to night declares knowledge.

There is no speech, nor are there words; their voice is not heard;

Yet their voice goes out through all the earth, and their words to the end of the world.

In them he has set a tent for the sun, which comes forth like a bridegroom leaving his chamber,

And like a strong man runs its course with joy.

Its rising is from the end of the heavens, and its circuit to the end of them;

And there is nothing hid from its heat.

The law of the LORD is perfect, reviving the soul;

The testimony of the Lord is sure, making wise the simple;

The precepts of the LORD are right, rejoicing the heart;

The commandment of the Lord is pure, enlightening the eyes;

The fear of the LORD is clean, enduring for ever;

The ordinances of the Lord are true, and righteous altogether.

More to be desired are they than gold, even much fine gold;

Sweeter also than honey and drippings of the honeycomb.

Moreover by them is thy servant warned; in keeping them there is great reward.

But who can discern his errors? Clear thou me from hidden faults.

Keep back thy servant also from presumptuous sins; let them not have dominion over me!

Then I shall be blameless, and innocent of great transgression.

Unison Let the words of my mouth and the meditation of my heart be acceptable in thy sight, O LORD, my rock and my redeemer.

69 *In unison*   *Psalm 23*

The LORD is my shepherd,
I shall not want;
He makes me lie down in green pastures;
He leads me beside still waters.
He restores my soul;
He leads me in the paths of righteousness for his name's sake.
Even though I walk through the valley of the shadow of death, I fear no evil;
For thou art with me; thy rod and thy staff, they comfort me.
Thou preparest a table before me in the presence of my enemies;
Thou anointest my head with oil, my cup overflows.
Surely goodness and mercy shall follow me all the days of my life;
And I shall dwell in the house of the LORD for ever.

70   *Psalm 24*

The earth is the LORD's and the fulness thereof, the world and those who dwell therein;

For he has founded it upon the seas, and established it upon the rivers.

Who shall ascend the hill of the LORD? And who shall stand in his holy place?

He who has clean hands and a pure heart, who does not lift up his soul to what is false, and does not swear deceitfully.

He will receive blessing from the LORD, and vindication from the God of his salvation.

Such is the generation of those who seek him, who seek the face of the God of Jacob.

Lift up your heads, O gates! and be lifted up, O ancient doors! that the King of glory may come in.

Who is the King of glory? The Lord, strong and mighty, the Lord, mighty in battle!

Lift up your heads, O gates! and be lifted up, O ancient doors! that the King of glory may come in!

Who is this King of glory? The Lord of hosts, he is the King of glory!

71   *Psalm 25*

To thee, O LORD, I lift up my soul. O my God, in thee I trust.

Make me to know thy ways, O Lord; teach me thy paths.

Lead me in thy truth, and teach me, for thou art the God of my salvation; for thee I wait all the day long.

Be mindful of thy mercy, O Lord, and of thy steadfast love, for they have been from of old.

Remember not the sins of my youth, or my transgressions; according to thy steadfast love remember me, for thy goodness' sake, O LORD!

Good and upright is the Lord; therefore he instructs sinners in the way.

He leads the humble in what is right, and teaches the humble in his way.

All the paths of the Lord are steadfast love and faithfulness, for those who keep his covenant and his testimonies.

For thy name's sake, O LORD, pardon my guilt, for it is great.

Who is the man that fears the Lord? Him will he instruct in the way that he should choose.

He himself shall abide in prosperity, and his children shall possess the land.

The friendship of the Lord is for those who fear him, and he makes known to them his covenant.

My eyes are ever toward the LORD, for he will pluck my feet out of the net.

Turn thou to me, and be gracious to me; for I am lonely and afflicted.

Relieve the troubles of my heart, and bring me out of my distresses.

Consider my affliction and my trouble, and forgive all my sins.

Consider how many are my foes, and with what violent hatred they hate me.

Oh guard my life, and deliver me; let me not be put to shame, for I take refuge in thee.

May integrity and uprightness preserve me,

For I wait for thee.

72 *Psalm 32*

Blessed is he whose transgression is forgiven, whose sin is covered.

Blessed is the man to whom the Lord imputes no iniquity, and in whose spirit there is no deceit.

I acknowledged my sin to thee, and I did not hide my iniquity;

I said, " I will confess my transgressions to the Lord "; then thou didst forgive the guilt of my sin.

Therefore let every one who is godly offer prayer to thee;

At a time of distress, in the rush of great waters, they shall not reach him.

Thou art a hiding place for me, thou preservest me from trouble;

Thou dost encompass me with deliverance.

I will instruct you and teach you the way you should go;

I will counsel you with my eye upon you.

Many are the pangs of the wicked; but mercy surrounds him who trusts in the LORD.

Be glad in the Lord, and rejoice, O righteous, and shout for joy, all you upright in heart!

73 *Psalm 33*

Rejoice in the LORD, O you righteous! Praise befits the upright.

Praise the Lord with the lyre, make melody to him with the harp of ten strings!

Sing to him a new song, play skilfully on the strings, with loud shouts.

For the word of the Lord is upright; and all his work is done in faithfulness.

He loves righteousness and justice; the earth is full of the steadfast love of the LORD.

By the word of the Lord the heavens were made, and all their host by the breath of his mouth.

He gathered the waters of the sea as in a bottle; he put the deeps in storehouses.

Let all the earth fear the Lord, let all the inhabitants of the world stand in awe of him!

For he spoke, and it came to be; he commanded, and it stood forth.

The Lord *brings the counsel of the nations to nought; he frustrates the plans of the peoples.*

The counsel of the LORD stands for ever, the thoughts of his heart to all generations.

Blessed is the nation whose God is the Lord, *the people whom he has chosen as his heritage!*

The LORD looks down from heaven, he sees all the sons of men;

From where he sits enthroned he looks forth on all the inhabitants of the earth,

He who fashions the hearts of them all, and observes all their deeds.

A king is not saved by his great army; a warrior is not delivered by his great strength.

The war horse is a vain hope for victory, and by its great might it cannot save.

Behold, the eye of the Lord *is on those who fear him, on those who hope in his steadfast love.*

That he may deliver their soul from death, and keep them alive in famine.

Our soul waits for the Lord; *he is our help and shield.*

Yea, our heart is glad in him, because we trust in his holy name.

Let thy steadfast love, O Lord, *be upon us, even as we hope in thee.*

74 *Psalm 34*

I will bless the LORD at all times; his praise shall continually be in my mouth.

My soul makes its boast in the Lord; *let the afflicted hear and be glad.*

O magnify the LORD with me, and let us exalt his name together!

I sought the Lord, *and he answered me, and delivered me from all my fears.*

Look to him, and be radiant; so your faces shall never be ashamed.

This poor man cried, and the Lord *heard him, and saved him out of all his troubles.*

The angel of the LORD encamps around those who fear him, and delivers them.

O taste and see that the Lord *is good! Happy is the man who takes refuge in him!*

O fear the LORD, you his saints, for those who fear him have no want.

Come, O sons, listen to me, I will teach you the fear of the Lord.

Keep your tongue from evil, and your lips from speaking deceit.

Depart from evil, and do good; seek peace, and pursue it.

The eyes of the LORD are toward the righteous, and his ears toward their cry.

The face of the Lord *is against evildoers, to cut off the remembrance of them from the earth.*

When the righteous cry for help, the LORD hears, and delivers them out of all their troubles.

The Lord *is near to the brokenhearted, and saves the crushed in spirit.*

75 *Psalm 36*

Thy steadfast love, O LORD, extends to the heavens, thy faithfulness to the clouds.

Thy righteousness is like the mountains of God, thy judgments are like the great deep; man and beast thou savest, O Lord.

How precious is thy steadfast love, O God!

The children of men take refuge in the shadow of thy wings.

They feast on the abundance of thy house;

And thou givest them drink from the river of thy delights.

For with thee is the fountain of life; in thy light do we see light.

O continue thy steadfast love to those who know thee, and thy salvation to the upright of heart!

76 *Psalm 37*

Fret not yourself because of the wicked, be not envious of wrongdoers!

For they will soon fade like the grass, and wither like the green herb.

Trust in the LORD, and do good; so you will dwell in the land, and enjoy security.

Take delight in the Lord, and he will give you the desires of your heart.

Commit your way to the LORD; trust in him, and he will act.

He will bring forth your vindication as the light, and your right as the noonday.

Be still before the LORD, and wait patiently for him;

Fret not yourself over him who prospers in his way, over the man who carries out evil devices!

Refrain from anger, and forsake wrath! Fret not yourself; it tends only to evil.

The steps of a man are from the Lord, and he establishes him in whose way he delights.

Though he fall, he shall not be cast headlong, for the LORD is the stay of his hand.

Depart from evil, and do good, so shall you abide for ever.

For the LORD loves justice; he will not forsake his saints.

The righteous shall be preserved for ever, but the children of the wicked shall be cut off.

The righteous shall possess the land, and dwell upon it for ever.

The mouth of the righteous utters wisdom, and his tongue speaks justice.

The law of his God is in his heart; his steps do not slip.

Mark the blameless man, and behold the upright, for there is posterity for the man of peace.

But transgressors shall be altogether destroyed;

The posterity of the wicked shall be cut off.

The salvation of the righteous is from the LORD;

He is their refuge in the time of trouble.

The LORD helps them and delivers them;

He delivers them from the wicked, and saves them, because they take refuge in him.

77 *Psalm 40*

I waited patiently for the LORD; he inclined to me and heard my cry.

He drew me from the desolate pit, out of the miry bog, and set my feet upon a rock, making my steps secure.

He put a new song in my mouth, a song of praise to our God.

Many will see and fear, and put their trust in the Lord.

Blessed is the man who makes the LORD his trust, who does not turn to the proud, to those who go astray after false gods!

Thou hast multiplied, O Lord my God, thy wondrous deeds and thy thoughts toward us; none can compare with thee!

Were I to proclaim and tell of them, they would be more than can be numbered.

Sacrifice and offering thou dost not desire; but thou hast given me an open ear. Burnt offering and sin offering thou hast not required.

Then I said, "Lo, I come; in the roll of the book it is written of me;

I delight to do thy will, O my God; thy law is within my heart."

I have told the glad news of deliverance in the great congregation;

Lo, I have not restrained my lips, as thou knowest, O Lord.

I have not hid thy saving help within my heart, I have spoken of thy faithfulness and thy salvation;

I have not concealed thy steadfast love and thy faithfulness from the great congregation.

Do not thou, O LORD, withhold thy mercy from me, let thy steadfast love and thy faithfulness ever preserve me!

For evils have encompassed me without number; my iniquities have overtaken me, till I cannot see;

They are more than the hairs of my head; my heart fails me.

Be pleased, O Lord, to deliver me! O Lord, make haste to help me!

May all who seek thee rejoice and be glad in thee;

May those who love thy salvation say continually, "Great is the Lord!"

As for me, I am poor and needy; but the Lord takes thought for me.

Thou art my help and my deliverer; do not tarry, O my God!

78 *Psalms 42, 43*

As a hart longs for flowing streams, so longs my soul for thee, O God.

My soul thirsts for God, for the living God.

When shall I come and behold the face of God?

My tears have been my food day and night, while men say to me continually, "Where is your God?"

These things I remember, as I pour out my soul:

How I went with the throng, and led them in procession to the house of God, with glad shouts and songs of thanksgiving, a multitude keeping festival.

Why are you cast down, O my soul, and why are you disquieted within me?

Hope in God, for I shall again praise him, my help and my God.

Deep calls to deep at the thunder of thy cataracts;

All thy waves and thy billows have gone over me.

By day the LORD commands his stead-fast love;

And at night his song is with me, a prayer to the God of my life.

I say to God, my rock, "Why hast thou forgotten me? Why go I mourning because of the oppression of the enemy?"

As with a deadly wound in my body, my adversaries taunt me, while they say to me continually, "Where is your God?"

Why are you cast down, O my soul, and why are you disquieted within me?

Hope in God, for I shall again praise him, my help and my God.

Oh send out thy light and thy truth, let them lead me, let them bring me to thy holy hill and to thy dwelling!

Then will I go to the altar of God, to God my exceeding joy, and I will praise thee with the lyre, O God, my God.

Why are you cast down, O my soul, and why are you disquieted within me?

Hope in God, for I shall again praise him, my help and my God.

79   *Psalm 46*

God is our refuge and strength, a very present help in trouble. Therefore we will not fear though the earth should change, though the mountains shake in the heart of the sea; though its waters roar and foam, though the mountains tremble with its tumult.

The Lord of hosts is with us; the God of Jacob is our refuge.

There is a river whose streams make glad the city of God, the holy habitation of the Most High. God is in the midst of her, she shall not be moved; God will help her right early. The

nations rage, the kingdoms totter; he utters his voice, the earth melts.

The Lord of hosts is with us; the God of Jacob is our refuge.

Come, behold the works of the LORD, how he has wrought desolation in the earth. He makes wars cease to the end of the earth; he breaks the bow, and shatters the spear, he burns the chariots with fire! "Be still, and know that I am God; I am exalted among the nations, I am exalted in the earth!"

The Lord of hosts is with us; the God of Jacob is our refuge.

80   *Psalm 51*

Have mercy on me, O God, according to thy steadfast love; according to thy abundant mercy blot out my transgressions.

Wash me thoroughly from my iniquity, and cleanse me from my sin!

For I know my transgressions, and my sin is ever before me.

Against thee, thee only, have I sinned, and done that which is evil in thy sight,

So that thou art justified in thy sentence and blameless in thy judgment.

Behold, thou desirest truth in the inward being; therefore teach me wisdom in my secret heart.

Purge me with hyssop, and I shall be clean; wash me, and I shall be whiter than snow.

Fill me with joy and gladness; let the bones which thou hast broken rejoice.

Hide thy face from my sins, and blot out all my iniquities.

Create in me a clean heart, O God, and put a new and right spirit within me.

Cast me not away from thy presence, and take not thy holy Spirit from me.

Restore to me the joy of thy salvation, and uphold me with a willing spirit.

Then will I teach transgressors thy ways, and sinners will return to thee.

Deliver me from bloodguiltiness, O God, thou God of my salvation, and my tongue will sing aloud of thy deliverance.

O LORD, open thou my lips, and my mouth shall show forth thy praise.

For thou hast no delight in sacrifice; were I to give a burnt offering, thou wouldst not be pleased.

The sacrifice acceptable to God is a broken spirit;

A broken and contrite heart, O God, thou wilt not despise.

81 *Psalm 57*

Be merciful to me, O God, be merciful to me, for in thee my soul takes refuge;

In the shadow of thy wings I will take refuge, till the storms of destruction pass by.

I cry to God Most High, to God who fulfils his purpose for me.

He will send from heaven and save me. God will send forth his steadfast love and his faithfulness!

Be exalted, O God, above the heavens! Let thy glory be over all the earth!

My heart is steadfast, O God, my heart is steadfast! I will sing and make melody!

Awake, my soul! Awake, O harp and lyre! I will awake the dawn!

I will give thanks to thee, O Lord, among the peoples; I will sing praises to thee among the nations.

For thy steadfast love is great to the heavens, thy faithfulness to the clouds.

Be exalted, O God, above the heavens! Let thy glory be over all the earth!

82 *Psalms 61, 62*

Hear my cry, O God, listen to my prayer;

From the end of the earth I call to thee, when my heart is faint.

Lead thou me to the rock that is higher than I;

For thou art my refuge, a strong tower against the enemy.

Let me dwell in thy tent for ever! Oh to be safe under the shelter of thy wings!

For thou, O God, hast heard my vows, thou hast given me the heritage of those who fear thy name.

For God alone my soul waits in silence, for my hope is from him.

He only is my rock and my salvation, my fortress; I shall not be shaken.

On God rests my deliverance and my honor; my mighty rock, my refuge is God.

Trust in him at all times, O people; pour out your heart before him; God is a refuge for us.

Men of low estate are but a breath, men of high estate are a delusion;

In the balances they go up; they are together lighter than a breath.

Put no confidence in extortion, set no vain hopes on robbery;

If riches increase, set not your heart on them.

Once God has spoken; twice have I heard this: that power belongs to God.

And that to thee, O Lord, belongs steadfast love. For thou dost requite a man according to his work.

83 *Psalm 65*

Praise is due to thee, O God, in Zion; and to thee shall vows be performed.

O thou who hearest prayer! To thee shall all flesh come on account of sins.

When our transgressions prevail over us, thou dost forgive them.

Blessed is he whom thou dost choose and bring near, to dwell in thy courts!

We shall be satisfied with the goodness of thy house, thy holy temple!

By dread deeds thou dost answer us with deliverance, O God of our salvation,

Who art the hope of all the ends of the earth, and of the farthest seas;

Who by thy strength hast established the mountains, being girded with might;

Who dost still the roaring of the seas, the roaring of their waves, the tumult of the peoples;

So that those who dwell at earth's farthest bounds are afraid at thy signs;

Thou makest the outgoings of the morning and the evening to shout for joy.

Thou visitest the earth and waterest it, thou greatly enrichest it;

The river of God is full of water; thou providest their grain, for so thou hast prepared it.

Thou waterest its furrows abundantly, settling its ridges, softening it with showers, and blessing its growth.

Thou crownest the year with thy bounty; the tracks of thy chariot drip with fatness.

The pastures of the wilderness drip, the hills gird themselves with joy,

The meadows clothe themselves with flocks, the valleys deck themselves with grain,

They shout and sing together for joy.

84 *Psalms 66, 67*

Make a joyful noise to God, all the earth;

Sing the glory of his name; give to him glorious praise!

Say to God, "How terrible are thy deeds!

So great is thy power that thy enemies cringe before thee.

All the earth worships thee; they sing praises to thee, sing praises to thy name."

Come and see what God has done; he is terrible in his deeds among men.

He turned the sea into dry land; men passed through the river on foot; There did we rejoice in him.

Bless our God, O peoples, let the sound of his praise be heard, who has kept us among the living, and has not let our feet slip.

Come and hear, all you who fear God,

And I will tell you what he has done for me.

I cried aloud to him, and he was extolled with my tongue.

If I had cherished iniquity in my heart, the Lord would not have listened.

But truly God has listened; he has given heed to the voice of my prayer.

Blessed be God, because he has not rejected my prayer or removed his steadfast love from me.

May God be gracious to us and bless us and make his face to shine upon us,

That thy way may be known upon earth, thy saving power among all nations.

Let the peoples praise thee, O God; let all the peoples praise thee!

Let the nations be glad and sing for joy,

For thou dost judge the peoples with equity, and guide the nations upon earth.

Let the peoples praise thee, O God; let all the peoples praise thee!

The earth has yielded its increase; God, our God, has blessed us.

God has blessed us; let all the ends of the earth fear him!

85 *Psalm 72*

Give the king thy justice, O God, and thy righteousness to the royal son!

May he judge thy people with righteousness, and thy poor with justice!

Let the mountains bear prosperity for the people, and the hills, in righteousness!

May he defend the cause of the poor of the people, give deliverance to the needy, and crush the oppressor!

May he live while the sun endures, and as long as the moon, throughout all generations!

May he be like rain that falls on the mown grass, like showers that water the earth!

In his days may righteousness flourish, and peace abound, till the moon be no more!

May he have dominion from sea to sea, and from the River to the ends of the earth!

May all kings fall down before him, all nations serve him!

For he delivers the needy when he calls, the poor and him who has no helper.

He has pity on the weak and the needy, and saves the lives of the needy.

From oppression and violence he redeems their life; and precious is their blood in his sight.

May his name endure for ever, his fame continue as long as the sun!

May men bless themselves by him, all nations call him blessed!

Blessed be the LORD, the God of Israel, who alone does wondrous things.

Blessed be his glorious name for ever; may his glory fill the whole earth! Amen and Amen!

86 *Psalm 73*

Truly God is good to the upright, to those who are pure in heart.

But as for me, my feet had almost stumbled, my steps had well nigh slipped.

For I was envious of the arrogant, when I saw the prosperity of the wicked.

For they have no pangs; their bodies are sound and sleek.

They are not in trouble as other men are; they are not stricken like other men.

Therefore pride is their necklace; violence covers them as a garment.

Their eyes swell out with fatness, their hearts overflow with follies.

They scoff and speak with malice; loftily they threaten oppression.

They set their mouths against the heavens, and their tongue struts through the earth.

Therefore the people turn and praise them; they find no fault in them.

And they say, "How can God know? Is there knowledge in the Most High?"

Behold, these are the wicked; always at ease, they increase in riches.

All in vain have I kept my heart clean and washed my hands in innocence.

For all the day long I have been stricken, and chastened every morning.

If I had said, "I will speak thus," I would have been untrue to the generation of thy children.

But when I thought how to understand this, it seemed to me a wearisome task,

Until I went into the sanctuary of God; then I perceived their end.

Truly thou dost set them in slippery places; thou dost make them fall to ruin.

How they are destroyed in a moment, swept away utterly by terrors!

They are like a dream when one awakes, on awaking you despise their phantoms.

When my soul was embittered, when I was pricked in heart,

I was stupid and ignorant, I was like a beast toward thee.

Nevertheless I am continually with thee; thou dost hold my right hand.

Thou dost guide me with thy counsel, and afterward thou wilt receive me to glory.

Whom have I in heaven but thee? And there is nothing upon earth that I desire besides thee.

My flesh and my heart may fail, but God is the strength of my heart and my portion for ever.

87   *Psalm 84*

How lovely is thy dwelling place, O LORD of hosts!

My soul longs, yea, faints for the courts of the Lord; my heart and flesh sing for joy to the living God.

Even the sparrow finds a home, and the swallow a nest for herself, where she may lay her young, at thy altars, O LORD of hosts, my king and my God.

Blessed are those who dwell in thy house, ever singing thy praise!

Blessed are the men whose strength is in thee, in whose heart are the highways to Zion.

As they go through the valley of Baca they make it a place of springs; the early rain also covers it with pools.

They go from strength to strength; the God of gods will be seen in Zion.

O Lord God of hosts, hear my prayer; give ear, O God of Jacob!

Behold our shield, O God; look upon the face of thine anointed!

For a day in thy courts is better than a thousand elsewhere. I would rather be a doorkeeper in the house of my God than dwell in the tents of wickedness.

For the LORD God is a sun and a shield; he bestows favor and honor. No good thing does the LORD withhold from those who walk uprightly.

O Lord of hosts, blessed is the man who trusts in thee!

88 *Psalm 86*

Incline thy ear, O LORD, and answer me, for I am poor and needy.

Preserve my life, for I am godly; save thy servant who trusts in thee.

Thou art my God; be gracious to me, O Lord, for to thee do I cry all the day.

Gladden the soul of thy servant, for to thee, O Lord, do I lift up my soul.

For thou, O LORD, art good and forgiving,

Abounding in steadfast love to all who call on thee.

Give ear, O LORD, to my prayer; hearken to my cry of supplication.

In the day of my trouble I call on thee, for thou dost answer me.

There is none like thee among the gods, O Lord,

Nor are there any works like thine.

All the nations thou hast made shall come and bow down before thee, O Lord, and shall glorify thy name.

For thou art great and doest wondrous things, thou alone art God.

Teach me thy way, O LORD, that I may walk in thy truth;

Unite my heart to fear thy name.

I give thanks to thee, O Lord my God, with my whole heart,

And I will glorify thy name for ever.

Thou, O Lord, art a God merciful and gracious,

Slow to anger and abounding in steadfast love and faithfulness.

Turn to me and take pity on me;

Give thy strength to thy servant, and save the son of thy handmaid.

Show me a sign of thy favor, that those who hate me may see and be put to shame

Because thou, Lord, hast helped me and comforted me.

89 *Psalm 89*

I will sing of thy steadfast love, O LORD, for ever; with my mouth I will proclaim thy faithfulness to all generations.

For thy steadfast love was established for ever, thy faithfulness is firm as the heavens.

Thou hast said, "I have made a covenant with my chosen one, I have sworn to David my servant: 'I will establish your descendants for ever, and build your throne for all generations.'"

Let the heavens praise thy wonders, O Lord, thy faithfulness in the assembly of the holy ones!

For who in the skies can be compared to the LORD? Who among the heavenly beings is like the LORD, a God feared in the council of the holy ones, great and terrible above all that are round about him?

O Lord God of hosts, who is mighty as thou art, O Lord, with thy faithfulness round about thee?

Thou dost rule the raging of the sea; when its waves rise, thou stillest them.

The heavens are thine, the earth also is thine;

The world and all that is in it, thou hast founded them.

The north and the south, thou hast created them; Tabor and Hermon joyously praise thy name.

Thou hast a mighty arm; strong is thy hand, high thy right hand.

Righteousness and justice are the foundation of thy throne; steadfast love and faithfulness go before thee.

Blessed are the people who know the festal shout, who walk, O LORD, in the light of thy countenance,

Who exult in thy name all the day, and extol thy righteousness.

For thou art the glory of their strength; by thy favor our horn is exalted.

For our shield belongs to the Lord, our king to the Holy One of Israel.

90   *Psalm 90*

LORD, thou hast been our dwelling place in all generations.

Before the mountains were brought forth, or ever thou hadst formed the earth and the world, from everlasting to everlasting thou art God.

Thou turnest man back to the dust, and sayest, "Turn back, O children of men!"

For a thousand years in thy sight are but as yesterday when it is past, or as a watch in the night.

Thou dost sweep men away; they are like a dream, like grass which is renewed in the morning.

In the morning it flourishes and is renewed; in the evening it fades and withers.

For we are consumed by thy anger; by thy wrath we are overwhelmed.

Thou hast set our iniquities before thee, our secret sins in the light of thy countenance.

For all our days pass away under thy wrath, our years come to an end like a sigh.

The years of our life are three-score and ten, or even by reason of strength fourscore; yet their span is but toil and trouble; they are soon gone, and we fly away.

Who considers the power of thy anger, and thy wrath according to the fear of thee?

So teach us to number our days that we may get a heart of wisdom.

Return, O LORD! How long? Have pity on thy servants!

Satisfy us in the morning with thy steadfast love, that we may rejoice and be glad all our days.

Make us glad as many days as thou hast afflicted us, and as many years as we have seen evil.

Let thy work be manifest to thy servants, and thy glorious power to their children.

Let the favor of the Lord our God be upon us, and establish thou the work of our hands upon us,

Yea, the work of our hands establish thou it.

91   *Psalm 91*

He who dwells in the shelter of the Most High, who abides in the shadow of the Almighty, will say to the LORD,

" My refuge, and my fortress; my God, in whom I trust."

For he will deliver you from the snare of the fowler and from the deadly pestilence;

He will cover you with his pinions, and under his wings you will find refuge; his faithfulness is a shield and buckler.

You will not fear the terror of the night, nor the arrow that flies by day,

Nor the pestilence that stalks in darkness, nor the destruction that wastes at noonday.

A thousand may fall at your side, ten thousand at your right hand; but it will not come near you.

You will only look with your eyes and see the recompense of the wicked.

Because you have made the LORD your refuge, the Most High your habitation,

No evil shall befall you, no scourge come near your tent.

For he will give his angels charge of you to guard you in all your ways.

On their hands they will bear you up, lest you dash your foot against a stone.

You will tread on the lion and the adder, the young lion and the serpent you will trample under foot.

Because he cleaves to me in love, I will deliver him; I will protect him, because he knows my name.

When he calls to me, I will answer him; I will be with him in trouble, I will rescue him and honor him.

With long life I will satisfy him, and show him my salvation.

92 *In unison* Psalm 95

O come, let us sing to the LORD; let us make a joyful noise to the rock of our salvation!

Let us come into his presence with thanksgiving; let us make a joyful noise to him with songs of praise!

For the LORD is a great God, and a great King above all gods.

In his hand are the depths of the earth; the heights of the mountains are his also.

The sea is his, for he made it; for his hands formed the dry land.

O come, let us worship and bow down, let us kneel before the LORD, our Maker!

For he is our God, and we are the people of his pasture, and the sheep of his hand.

93 Psalm 96

O sing to the LORD a new song;

Sing to the Lord, all the earth!

Sing to the LORD, bless his name; tell of his salvation from day to day.

Declare his glory among the nations, his marvelous works among all the peoples!

For great is the LORD, and greatly to be praised; he is to be feared above all gods.

For all the gods of the people are idols; but the Lord made the heavens.

Honor and majesty are before him; strength and beauty are in his sanctuary.

Ascribe to the Lord, O families of the peoples, ascribe to the Lord glory and strength!

Ascribe to the LORD the glory due his name; bring an offering, and come into his courts!

Worship the Lord in holy array; tremble before him, all the earth!

Say among the nations, "The LORD reigns!

Yea, the world is established, it shall never be moved; he will judge the peoples with equity."

Let the heavens be glad, and let the earth rejoice;

Let the sea roar, and all that fills it;

Let the field exult, and everything in it!

Then shall all the trees of the wood sing for joy before the Lord,

For he comes, for he comes to judge the earth.

He will judge the world with righteousness, and the peoples with his truth.

94   Psalm 98

O sing to the LORD a new song, for he has done marvelous things!

His right hand and his holy arm have gotten him victory.

The LORD has made known his victory,

He has revealed his vindication in the sight of the nations.

He has remembered his steadfast love and faithfulness to the house of Israel.

All the ends of the earth have seen the victory of our God.

Make a joyful noise to the LORD, all the earth;

Break forth into joyous song and sing praises!

Sing praises to the LORD with the lyre, with the lyre and the sound of melody!

With trumpets and the sound of the horn make a joyful noise before the King, the Lord!

Let the sea roar, and all that fills it;

The world and those who dwell in it!

Let the floods clap their hands;

Let the hills sing for joy together before the Lord,

For he comes to rule the earth.

He will judge the world with righteousness, and the peoples with equity.

95 *In unison*   Psalm 100

Make a joyful noise to the LORD, all the lands!
Serve the LORD with gladness! Come into his presence with singing!
Know that the LORD is God! It is he that made us, and we are his;
We are his people, and the sheep of his pasture.
Enter his gates with thanksgiving, and his courts with praise!
Give thanks to him, bless his name!
For the LORD is good; his steadfast love endures for ever, and his faithfulness to all generations.

96   Psalm 103

Bless the LORD, O my soul; and all that is within me, bless his holy name!

Bless the Lord, O my soul, and forget not all his benefits,

Who forgives all your iniquity, who heals all your diseases,

Who redeems your life from the Pit, who crowns you with steadfast love and mercy,

Who satisfies you with good as long as you live so that your youth is renewed like the eagle's.

The Lord works vindication and justice for all who are oppressed.

He made known his ways to Moses, his acts to the people of Israel.

The Lord is merciful and gracious, slow to anger, and abounding in steadfast love.

He will not always chide, nor will he keep his anger for ever.

He does not deal with us according to our sins, nor requite us according to our iniquities.

For as the heavens are high above the earth, so great is his steadfast love toward those who fear him.

As far as the east is from the west, so far does he remove our transgressions from us.

As a father pities his children, so the LORD pities those who fear him.

For he knows our frame; he remembers that we are dust.

As for man, his days are like grass; he flourishes like a flower of the field.

For the wind passes over it, and it is gone, and its place knows it no more.

But the steadfast love of the LORD is from everlasting to everlasting upon those who fear him,

And his righteousness to children's children, to those who keep his covenant and remember to do his commandments.

The LORD has established his throne in the heavens, and his kingdom rules over all.

Bless the Lord, *O you his angels, you mighty ones who do his word, hearkening to the voice of his word!*

Bless the LORD, all his hosts, his ministers that do his will!

Bless the Lord, *all his works, in all places of his dominion. Bless the* Lord, *O my soul.*

97 Psalm 104

Bless the LORD, O my soul!

O Lord *my God, thou art very great!*

Thou art clothed with honor and majesty, who coverest thyself with light as with a garment,

Who hast stretched out the heavens like a tent, who hast laid the beams of thy chambers on the waters,

Who makest the clouds thy chariot, who ridest on the wings of the wind,

Who makest the winds thy messengers, fire and flame thy ministers.

Thou didst set the earth on its foundations, so that it should never be shaken.

Thou didst cover it with the deep as with a garment; the waters stood above the mountains.

At thy rebuke they fled; at the sound of thy thunder they took to flight.

The mountains rose, the valleys sank down to the place which thou didst appoint for them.

Thou didst set a bound which they should not pass, so that they might not again cover the earth.

Thou makest springs gush forth in the valleys; they flow between the hills,

They give drink to every beast of the field; the wild asses quench their thirst.

By them the birds of the air have their habitation; they sing among the branches.

From thy lofty abode thou waterest the mountains; the earth is satisfied with the fruit of thy work.

Thou dost cause the grass to grow for the cattle, and plants for man to cultivate,

That he may bring forth food from the earth, and wine to gladden the heart of man,

Oil to make his face shine, and bread to strengthen man's heart.

The trees of the LORD are watered abundantly, the cedars of Lebanon which he planted.

In them the birds build their nests, the stork has her home in the fir trees.

The high mountains are for the wild goats; the rocks are a refuge for the badgers.

Thou hast made the moon to mark the seasons; the sun knows its time for setting.

Thou makest darkness, and it is night, when all the beasts of the forest creep forth.

The young lions roar for their prey, seeking their food from God.

When the sun rises, they get them away and lie down in their dens.

Man goes forth to his work and to his labor until the evening.

98   *Psalm 104*

O LORD, how manifold are thy works!

In wisdom hast thou made them all; the earth is full of thy creatures.

Yonder is the sea, great and wide, which teems with things innumerable,

Living things both small and great.

There go the ships, and Leviathan which thou didst form to sport in it.

These all look to thee, to give them their food in due season.

When thou givest to them, they gather it up;

When thou openest thy hand, they are filled with good things.

When thou hidest thy face, they are dismayed;

When thou takest away their breath, they die and return to their dust.

When thou sendest forth thy Spirit, they are created;

And thou renewest the face of the ground.

May the glory of the LORD endure for ever, may the LORD rejoice in his works,

Who looks on the earth and it trembles, who touches the mountains and they smoke!

I will sing to the LORD as long as I live; I will sing praise to my God while I have being.

May my meditation be pleasing to him, for I rejoice in the Lord.

Let sinners be consumed from the earth, and let the wicked be no more!

Bless the Lord, O my soul! Praise the Lord!

99   *Psalm 107*

O give thanks to the LORD, for he is good;

For his steadfast love endures for ever!

Let the redeemed of the LORD say so, whom he has redeemed from trouble,

And gathered in from the lands, from the east and from the west, from the north and from the south.

Some wandered in desert wastes, finding no way to a city to dwell in;

Hungry and thirsty, their soul fainted within them.

Then they cried to the LORD in their trouble, and he delivered them from their distress;

He led them by a straight way, till they reached a city to dwell in.

Let them thank the LORD for his steadfast love, for his wonderful works to the sons of men!

For he satisfies him who is thirsty, and the hungry he fills with good things.

Some sat in darkness and in gloom, prisoners in affliction and in irons,

For they had rebelled against the words of God, and spurned the counsel of the Most High.

Their hearts were bowed down with hard labor, they fell down, with none to help.

Then they cried to the Lord *in their trouble, and he delivered them from their distress.*

He brought them out of darkness and gloom, and broke their bonds asunder.

Let them thank the Lord *for his steadfast love, for his wonderful works to the sons of men!*

Some were sick through their sinful ways, and because of their iniquities suffered affliction;

They loathed any kind of food, and they drew near to the gates of death.

Then they cried to the LORD in their trouble, and he delivered them from their distress;

He sent forth his word, and healed them, and delivered them from destruction.

Let them thank the LORD for his steadfast love, for his wonderful works to the sons of men!

And let them offer sacrifices of thanksgiving, and tell of his deeds in songs of joy!

Whoever is wise, let him give heed to these things,

Let men consider the steadfast love of the Lord.

100 *Psalm 116*

I love the LORD, because he has heard my voice and my supplications.

Because he inclined his ear to me, therefore I will call on him as long as I live.

The snares of death encompassed me; the pangs of Sheol laid hold on me; I suffered distress and anguish.

Then I called on the name of the Lord: *" O* Lord, *I beseech thee, save my life! "*

Gracious is the LORD, and righteous; our God is merciful.

The Lord *preserves the simple; when I was brought low, he saved me.*

Return, O my soul, to your rest; for the LORD has dealt bountifully with you.

For thou hast delivered my soul from death, my eyes from tears, my feet from stumbling.

I walk before the LORD in the land of the living.

I kept my faith, even when I said, " I am greatly afflicted."

I said in my consternation, "Men are all a vain hope."

What shall I render to the Lord *for all his bounty to me?*

I will lift up the cup of salvation and call on the name of the LORD,

I will pay my vows to the Lord *in the presence of all his people.*

Precious in the sight of the LORD is the death of his saints.

O Lord, *I am thy servant, the son of thy handmaid. Thou hast loosed my bonds.*

I will offer to thee the sacrifice of thanksgiving and call on the name of the LORD.

I will pay my vows to the Lord *in the presence of all his people,*

In the courts of the house of the LORD, in your midst, O Jerusalem.

Praise the Lord!

101 — Psalm 118

O give thanks to the LORD, for he is good; his steadfast love endures for ever!

Let Israel say, " His steadfast love endures for ever."

Let the house of Aaron say, "His steadfast love endures for ever."

Let those who fear the Lord *say, " His steadfast love endures for ever."*

Out of my distress I called on the LORD; the LORD answered and set me free.

With the Lord *on my side I do not fear. What can man do to me?*

The LORD is on my side to help me; I shall look in triumph on those who hate me.

It is better to take refuge in the Lord *than to put confidence in man.*

It is better to take refuge in the LORD than to put confidence in princes.

The Lord is my strength and my song; he has become my salvation.

Hark, glad songs of victory in the tents of the righteous:

" The right hand of the Lord *does valiantly, the right hand of the* Lord *is exalted, the right hand of the* Lord *does valiantly! "*

I shall not die, but I shall live, and recount the deeds of the LORD.

The Lord *has chastened me sorely, but he has not given me over to death.*

Open to me the gates of righteousness, that I may enter through them and give thanks to the LORD.

This is the gate of the Lord; *the righteous shall enter through it.*

The stone which the builders rejected has become the chief cornerstone.

This is the Lord's *doing; it is marvelous in our eyes.*

This is the day which the LORD has made;

Let us rejoice and be glad in it.

Thou art my God, and I will give thanks to thee;

Thou art my God, I will extol thee.

O give thanks to the LORD, for he is good;

For his steadfast love endures for ever!

102 — Psalm 119

Great peace have those who love thy law; nothing can make them stumble.

I hope for thy salvation, O Lord, *and I do thy commandments.*

My soul keeps thy testimonies; I love them exceedingly.

I keep thy precepts and testimonies, for all my ways are before thee.

Let my cry come before thee, O LORD; give me understanding according to thy word!

Let my supplication come before thee; deliver me according to thy word.

My lips will pour forth praise that thou dost teach me thy statutes.

My tongue will sing of thy word, for all thy commandments are right.

Let thy hand be ready to help me, for I have chosen thy precepts.

I long for thy salvation, O Lord, and thy law is my delight.

Let me live, that I may praise thee, and let thy ordinances help me.

I have gone astray like a lost sheep; seek thy servant, for I do not forget thy commandments.

103   *Psalms 121, 122*

I lift up my eyes to the hills. From whence does my help come?

My help comes from the Lord, who made heaven and earth.

He will not let your foot be moved, he who keeps you will not slumber.

Behold, he who keeps Israel will neither slumber nor sleep.

The LORD is your keeper; the LORD is your shade on your right hand.

The sun shall not smite you by day, nor the moon by night.

The LORD will keep you from all evil; he will keep your life.

The Lord will keep your going out and your coming in from this time forth and for evermore.

I was glad when they said to me, "Let us go to the house of the LORD!"

Our feet have been standing within your gates, O Jerusalem!

Jerusalem, built as a city which is bound firmly together,

To which the tribes go up, the tribes of the Lord,

As was decreed for Israel, to give thanks to the name of the LORD.

There thrones for judgment were set, the thrones of the house of David.

Pray for the peace of Jerusalem! "May they prosper who love you!"

Peace be within your walls, and security within your towers!"

For my brethren and companions' sake I will say, "Peace be within you!"

For the sake of the house of the Lord our God, I will seek your good.

104 *In unison*   *Psalm 130*

Out of the depths I cry to thee, O LORD!
LORD, hear my voice!
Let thy ears be attentive to the voice of my supplications!
If thou, O LORD, shouldst mark iniquities, Lord, who could stand?
But there is forgiveness with thee, that thou mayest be feared.
I wait for the LORD, my soul waits, and in his word I hope;
My soul waits for the LORD more than watchmen for the morning, more than watchmen for the morning.
O Israel, hope in the LORD!
For with the LORD there is steadfast love, and with him is plenteous redemption.
And he will redeem Israel from all his iniquities.

105   *Psalm 136*

O give thanks to the LORD, for he is good. O give thanks to the God of gods, O give thanks to the LORD of lords,

For his steadfast love endures for ever.

To him who alone does great wonders, to him who by understanding made the heavens; to him who spread out the earth upon the waters,

For his steadfast love endures for ever.

To him who made the great lights, the sun to rule over the day, the moon and stars to rule over the night,

For his steadfast love endures for ever.

To him who smote the first-born of Egypt, and brought Israel out from among them, with a strong hand and an outstretched arm,

For his steadfast love endures for ever.

To him who led his people through the wilderness, to him who smote great kings, and gave their land as a heritage to Israel his servant,

For his steadfast love endures for ever.

It is he who remembered us in our low estate, and rescued us from our foes; he who gives food to all flesh.

O give thanks to the God of heaven, for his steadfast love endures for ever.

106 *Psalm 139*

O LORD, thou hast searched me and known me!

Thou knowest when I sit down and when I rise up; thou discernest my thoughts from afar.

Thou searchest out my path and my lying down, and art acquainted with all my ways.

Even before a word is on my tongue, lo, O Lord, thou knowest it altogether.

Thou dost beset me behind and before, and layest thine hand upon me.

Such knowledge is too wonderful for me; it is high, I cannot attain it.

Whither shall I go from thy Spirit? Or whither shall I flee from thy presence?

If I ascend to heaven, thou art there! If I make my bed in Sheol, thou art there!

If I take the wings of the morning and dwell in the uttermost parts of the sea,

Even there thy hand shall lead me, and thy right hand shall hold me.

If I say, "Let only darkness cover me, and the light about me be night,"

Even the darkness is not dark to thee, the night is bright as the day, for darkness is as light with thee.

How precious to me are thy thoughts, O God! How vast is the sum of them!

If I would count them, they are more than the sand. When I awake, I am still with thee.

Search me, O God, and know my heart! Try me and know my thoughts!

And see if there be any wicked way in me, and lead me in the way everlasting!

107 *Psalm 145*

I will extol thee, my God and King, and bless thy name for ever and ever.

Every day I will bless thee, and praise thy name for ever and ever.

Great is the LORD, and greatly to be praised, and his greatness is unsearchable.

One generation shall laud thy works to another, and shall declare thy mighty acts.

Of the glorious splendor of thy majesty, and of thy wondrous works, I will meditate.

Men shall proclaim the might of thy terrible acts, and I will declare thy greatness.

They shall pour forth the fame of thy abundant goodness, and shall sing aloud of thy righteousness.

The Lord *is gracious and merciful, slow to anger and abounding in steadfast love.*

The LORD is good to all, and his compassion is over all that he has made.

All thy works shall give thanks to thee, O Lord, and all thy saints shall bless thee!

They shall speak of the glory of thy kingdom, and tell of thy power,

To make known to the sons of men thy mighty deeds, and the glorious splendor of thy kingdom.

Thy kingdom is an everlasting kingdom, and thy dominion endures throughout all generations.

The Lord *is faithful in all his words, and gracious in all his deeds.*

The LORD upholds all who are falling, and raises up all who are bowed down.

The eyes of all look to thee, and thou givest them their food in due season.

Thou openest thy hand, thou satisfiest the desire of every living thing.

The Lord *is just in all his ways, and kind in all his doings.*

The LORD is near to all who call upon him, to all who call upon him in truth.

He fulfils the desire of all who fear him, he also hears their cry, and saves them.

The LORD preserves all who love him; but all the wicked he will destroy.

My mouth will speak the praise of the Lord, *and let all flesh bless his holy name for ever and ever.*

108 Psalm 148

Praise the LORD! Praise the LORD from the heavens, praise him in the heights!

Praise him, all his angels, praise him, all his host!

Praise him, sun and moon, praise him, all you shining stars!

Praise him, you highest heavens, and you waters above the heavens!

Let them praise the name of the LORD! For he commanded and they were created;

And he established them for ever and ever; he fixed their bounds which cannot be passed.

Praise the LORD from the earth, you sea monsters and all deeps,

Fire and hail, snow and frost, stormy wind fulfilling his command!

Mountains and all hills, fruit trees and all cedars!

Beasts and all cattle, creeping things and flying birds!

Kings of the earth and all peoples, princes and all rulers of the earth!

Young men and maidens together, old men and children!

Let them praise the name of the LORD, for his name alone is exalted; his glory is above earth and heaven.

He has raised up a horn for his people, praise for all his saints, for the people of Israel who are near to him. Praise the Lord!

109 *In unison*   *Psalm 150*

Praise the LORD!
Praise God in his sanctuary; praise him in his mighty firmament!
Praise him for his mighty deeds; praise him according to his exceeding greatness!
Praise him with trumpet sound; praise him with lute and harp!
Praise him with timbrel and dance; praise him with strings and pipe!
Praise him with sounding cymbals, praise him with loud clashing cymbals!
Let everything that breathes praise the LORD!
Praise the LORD!

UNISON READINGS

110

Psalm 23
(King James Version)

The LORD is my shepherd; I shall not want.

He maketh me to lie down in green pastures: he leadeth me beside the still waters.

He restoreth my soul: he leadeth me in the paths of righteousness for his name's sake.

Yea, though I walk through the valley of the shadow of death, I will fear no evil: for thou art with me; thy rod and thy staff they comfort me.

Thou preparest a table before me in the presence of mine enemies: thou anointest my head with oil; my cup runneth over.

Surely goodness and mercy shall follow me all the days of my life: and I will dwell in the house of the LORD for ever.

111

Deuteronomy 32:1–3, 7, 9–12; 33:26–27a

Give ear, O heavens, and I will speak; and let the earth hear the words of my mouth. May my teaching drop as the rain, my speech distil as the dew, as the gentle rain upon the tender grass, and as the showers upon the herb.

For I will proclaim the name of the LORD. Ascribe greatness to our God!

Remember the days of old, consider the years of many generations; ask your father, and he will show you; your elders, and they will tell you.

For the LORD's portion is his people, Jacob his allotted heritage. He found him in a desert land, and in the howling waste of the wilderness; he encircled him, he cared for him, he kept him as the apple of his eye.

Like an eagle that stirs up its nest, that flutters over its young, spreading out its wings, catching them, bearing them on its pinions, the LORD alone did lead him, and there was no foreign god with him.

There is none like God, who rides through the heavens to your help, and in his majesty through the skies. The eternal God is your dwelling place, and underneath are the everlasting arms.

112

1 Chronicles 29:10b–13

Blessed art thou, O LORD, the God of Israel our father, for ever and ever.

Thine, O LORD, is the greatness, and the power, and the glory, and the victory, and the majesty;

For all that is in the heavens and in the earth is thine;

Thine is the kingdom, O LORD, and thou art exalted as head above all.

Both riches and honor come from thee, and thou rulest over all.

In thy hand are power and might; and in thy hand it is to make great and to give strength to all.

And now we thank thee, our God, and praise thy glorious name.

113

Proverbs 3:13–26

Happy is the man who finds wisdom, and the man who gets understanding, for the gain from it is better than gain from silver and its profit better than gold.

She is more precious than jewels, and nothing you desire can compare with her.

Long life is in her right hand; in her left hand are riches and honor.

Her ways are ways of pleasantness, and all her paths are peace.

She is a tree of life to those who lay hold of her; those who hold her fast are called happy.

The LORD by wisdom founded the earth; by understanding he established the heavens;

By his knowledge the deeps broke forth, and the clouds drop down the dew.

My son, keep sound wisdom and discretion; let them not escape from your sight, and they will be life for your soul and adornment for your neck.

Then you will walk on your way securely and your foot will not stumble.

If you sit down, you will not be afraid:

When you lie down, your sleep will be sweet.

Do not be afraid of sudden panic, or of the ruin of the wicked, when it comes;

For the LORD will be your confidence and will keep your foot from being caught.

114 *Isaiah 9:2, 6–7*

The people who walked in darkness have seen a great light.

Those who dwelt in a land of deep darkness, on them has light shined.

For to us a child is born, to us a son is given; and the government will be upon his shoulder, and his name will be called "Wonderful Counselor, Mighty God, Everlasting Father, Prince of Peace."

Of the increase of his government and of peace there will be no end, upon the throne of David, and over his kingdom, to establish it, and to uphold it with justice and with righteousness from this time forth and for evermore.

The zeal of the LORD of hosts will do this.

115 *Isaiah 11:1–9*

There shall come forth a shoot from the stump of Jesse, and a branch shall grow out of his roots.

And the Spirit of the LORD shall rest upon him, the spirit of wisdom and understanding, the spirit of counsel and might, the spirit of knowledge and the fear of the LORD.

And his delight shall be in the fear of the LORD.

He shall not judge by what his eyes see, or decide by what his ears hear;

But with righteousness he shall judge the poor, and decide with equity for the meek of the earth;

And he shall smite the earth with the rod of his mouth, and with the breath of his lips he shall slay the wicked.

Righteousness shall be the girdle of his waist, and faithfulness the girdle of his loins.

The wolf shall dwell with the lamb, and the leopard shall lie down with the kid, and the calf and the lion and the fatling together, and a little child shall lead them.

The cow and the bear shall feed; their young shall lie down together; and the lion shall eat straw like the ox.

The sucking child shall play over the hole of the asp, and the weaned child shall put his hand on the adder's den.

They shall not hurt or destroy in all my holy mountain; for the earth shall be full of the knowledge of the LORD as the waters cover the sea.

116 *Isaiah 25:1, 4, 8–9; 26:3–4*

O LORD, thou art my God; I will exalt thee, I will praise thy name; for thou hast done wonderful things, plans formed of old, faithful and sure.

For thou hast been a stronghold to the poor, a stronghold to the needy in his distress, a shelter from the storm and a shade from the heat.

He will swallow up death for ever, and the Lord GOD will wipe away tears from all faces, and the reproach of his people he will take away from all the earth; for the LORD has spoken.

It will be said on that day, "Lo, this is our God; we have waited for him, that he might save us.

This is the LORD; we have waited for him; let us be glad and rejoice in his salvation."

Thou dost keep him in perfect peace, whose mind is stayed on thee, because he trusts in thee.

Trust in the LORD for ever, for the LORD GOD is an everlasting rock.

117
Isaiah 40:1–5, 9–11

Comfort, comfort my people, says your God.

Speak tenderly to Jerusalem, and cry to her that her warfare is ended, that her iniquity is pardoned, that she has received from the LORD's hand double for all her sins.

A voice cries: "In the wilderness prepare the way of the LORD, make straight in the desert a highway for our God.

Every valley shall be lifted up, and every mountain and hill be made low; the uneven ground shall become level, and the rough places a plain.

And the glory of the LORD shall be revealed, and all flesh shall see it together, for the mouth of the LORD has spoken."

Get you up to a high mountain, O Zion, herald of good tidings;

Lift up your voice with strength, O Jerusalem, herald of good tidings, lift it up, fear not;

Say to the cities of Judah, "Behold your God!"

Behold, the Lord GOD comes with might, and his arm rules for him; behold, his reward is with him, and his recompense before him.

He will feed his flock like a shepherd, he will gather the lambs in his arms, he will carry them in his bosom, and gently lead those that are with young.

118
Isaiah 40:28–31

Have you not known? Have you not heard?

The LORD is the everlasting God, the Creator of the ends of the earth.

He does not faint or grow weary, his understanding is unsearchable.

He gives power to the faint, and to him who has no might he increases strength.

Even youths shall faint and be weary, and young men shall fall exhausted;

But they who wait for the LORD shall renew their strength, they shall mount up with wings like eagles, they shall run and not be weary, they shall walk and not faint.

119
Isaiah 53:1–6

Who has believed what we have heard? And to whom has the arm of the LORD been revealed?

For he grew up before him like a young plant, and like a root out of dry ground;

He had no form or comeliness that we should look at him, and no beauty that we should desire him.

He was despised and rejected by men; a man of sorrows, and acquainted with grief;

And as one from whom men hide their faces he was despised, and we esteemed him not.

Surely he has borne our griefs and carried our sorrows; yet we esteemed him stricken, smitten by God, and afflicted.

But he was wounded for our transgressions, he was bruised for our iniquities; upon him was the chastisement that made us whole, and with his stripes we are healed.

All we like sheep have gone astray; we have turned every one to his own way;

And the LORD has laid on him the iniquity of us all.

120 *Isaiah 55:6–13*

Seek the LORD while he may be found, call upon him while he is near;

Let the wicked forsake his way, and the unrighteous man his thoughts; let him return to the LORD, that he may have mercy on him, and to our God, for he will abundantly pardon.

For my thoughts are not your thoughts, neither are your ways my ways, says the LORD.

For as the heavens are higher than the earth, so are my ways higher than your ways and my thoughts than your thoughts.

For as the rain and the snow come down from heaven, and return not thither but water the earth, making it bring forth and sprout, giving seed to the sower and bread to the eater, so shall my word be that goes forth from my mouth;

It shall not return to me empty, but it shall accomplish that which I purpose, and prosper in the thing for which I sent it.

For you shall go out in joy, and be led forth in peace;

The mountains and the hills before you shall break forth into singing, and all the trees of the field shall clap their hands.

Instead of the thorn shall come up the cypress; instead of the brier shall come up the myrtle;

And it shall be to the LORD for a memorial, for an everlasting sign which shall not be cut off.

121 *Isaiah 61:1–4*

The Spirit of the Lord GOD is upon me, because the LORD has anointed me to bring good tidings to the afflicted;

He has sent me to bind up the brokenhearted, to proclaim liberty to the captives, and the opening of the prison to those who are bound;

To proclaim the year of the LORD's favor, and the day of vengeance of our God;

To comfort all who mourn; to grant to those who mourn in Zion — to give them a garland instead of ashes, the oil of gladness instead of mourning, the mantle of praise instead of a faint spirit;

That they may be called oaks of righteousness, the planting of the LORD, that he may be glorified.

They shall build up the ancient ruins, they shall raise up the former devastations; they shall repair the ruined cities, the devastations of many generations.

122 *Jeremiah 31:31, 32a, 33, 34*

Behold, the days are coming, says the LORD, when I will make a new covenant with the house of Israel and the house of Judah,

Not like the covenant which I made with their fathers when I took them by the hand to bring them out of the land of Egypt, my covenant which they broke.

But this is the covenant which I will make with the house of Israel after those days, says the LORD:

I will put my law within them, and I will write it upon their hearts;

And I will be their God, and they shall be my people.

And no longer shall each man teach his neighbor and each his brother, saying, "Know the LORD," for they

shall all know me, from the least of
them to the greatest, says the LORD;
For I will forgive their iniquity, and I
will remember their sin no more.

123   *Wisdom of Solomon 3:1–9*

The souls of the righteous are in the
hand of God, and no torment will
ever touch them.
In the eyes of the foolish they seemed
to have died, and their departure
was thought to be an affliction, and
their going from us to be their destruction; but they are at peace.
For though in the sight of men they
were punished, their hope was full
of immortality.
Having been disciplined a little, they
will receive great good, because God
tested them and found them worthy
of himself;
Like gold in the furnace he tried them,
and like a sacrificial burnt offering
he accepted them.
In the time of their visitation they will
shine forth, and will run like sparks
through the stubble.
They will govern nations and rule over
peoples, and the LORD will reign over
them for ever.
Those who trust in him will understand
truth, and the faithful will abide
with him in love, because grace and
mercy are upon his elect, and he
watches over his holy ones.

124   *Ecclesiasticus 44:1–15*

Let us now praise famous men, and
our fathers in their generations.
The LORD apportioned to them great
glory, his majesty from the beginning.
There were those who ruled in their
kingdoms, and were men renowned
for their power, giving counsel by
their understanding, and proclaim-
ing prophecies;

Leaders of the people in their delibera-
tions and in understanding of learn-
ing for the people, wise in their
words of instruction;
Those who composed musical tunes,
and set forth verses in writing;
Rich men furnished with resources,
living peaceably in their habita-
tions —
All these were honored in their generations, and were the glory of their
times.
There are some of them who have left
a name, so that men declare their
praise.
And there are some who have no memorial, who have perished as though
they had not lived; they have become as though they had not been
born, and so have their children
after them.
But these were men of mercy, whose
righteous deeds have not been forgotten; their prosperity will remain
with their descendants, and their
inheritance to their children's children.
Their descendants stand by the cove-
nants; their children also, for their
sake.
Their posterity will continue for ever,
and their glory will not be blotted out.
Their bodies were buried in peace, and
their name lives to all generations.
Peoples will declare their wisdom, and
the congregation proclaims their
praise.

125   *Matthew 5:3–16 The Beatitudes*

Blessed are the poor in spirit, for theirs
is the kingdom of heaven.
Blessed are those who mourn, for they
shall be comforted.
Blessed are the meek, for they shall in-
herit the earth.
Blessed are those who hunger and
thirst for righteousness, for they
shall be satisfied.

Blessed are the merciful, for they shall obtain mercy.

Blessed are the pure in heart, for they shall see God.

Blessed are the peacemakers, for they shall be called sons of God.

Blessed are those who are persecuted for righteousness' sake, for theirs is the kingdom of heaven.

Blessed are you when men revile you and persecute you and utter all kinds of evil against you falsely on my account. Rejoice and be glad, for your reward is great in heaven, for so men persecuted the prophets who were before you.

You are the salt of the earth; but if salt has lost its taste, how shall its saltness be restored? It is no longer good for anything except to be thrown out and trodden under foot by men.

You are the light of the world. A city set on a hill cannot be hid. Nor do men light a lamp and put it under a bushel, but on a stand, and it gives light to all in the house.

Let your light so shine before men, that they may see your good works and give glory to your Father who is in heaven.

126
Luke 1:46–55
The Magnificat

My soul magnifies the Lord, and my spirit rejoices in God my Savior, for he has regarded the low estate of his handmaiden.

For behold, henceforth all generations will call me blessed; for he who is mighty has done great things for me, and holy is his name.

And his mercy is on those who fear him from generation to generation.

He has shown strength with his arm, he has scattered the proud in the imagination of their hearts, he has put down the mighty from their thrones, and exalted those of low degree; he has filled the hungry with good things, and the rich he has sent empty away.

He has helped his servant Israel, in remembrance of his mercy, as he spoke to our fathers, to Abraham and to his posterity for ever.

127
Luke 1:68–79
The Benedictus

Blessed be the Lord God of Israel, for he has visited and redeemed his people, and has raised up a horn of salvation for us in the house of his servant David, as he spoke by the mouth of his holy prophets from of old, that we should be saved from our enemies, and from the hand of all who hate us; to perform the mercy promised to our fathers, and to remember his holy covenant, the oath which he swore to our father Abraham, to grant us that we, being delivered from the hand of our enemies, might serve him without fear, in holiness and righteousness before him all the days of our life.

And you, child, will be called the prophet of the Most High;

For you will go before the Lord to prepare his ways, to give knowledge of salvation to his people in the forgiveness of their sins,

Through the tender mercy of our God, when the day shall dawn upon us from on high to give light to those who sit in darkness and in the shadow of death, to guide our feet into the way of peace.

128
Luke 2:25–33
The Nunc Dimittis

Now there was a man in Jerusalem, whose name was Simeon, and this man was righteous and devout, looking for the consolation of Israel, and the Holy Spirit was upon him.

And it had been revealed to him by the Holy Spirit that he should not see death before he had seen the Lord's Christ.

And inspired by the Spirit he came into the temple; and when the parents brought in the child Jesus, to do for him according to the custom of the law, he took him up in his arms and blessed God and said;

" Lord, now lettest thou thy servant depart in peace, according to thy word;

For mine eyes have seen thy salvation which thou hast prepared in the presence of all peoples,

A light for revelation to the Gentiles,
And for glory to thy people Israel."

129 *John 1:1–14*

In the beginning was the Word, and the Word was with God, and the Word was God.

He was in the beginning with God; all things were made through him, and without him was not anything made that was made.

In him was life, and the life was the light of men.

The light shines in the darkness, and the darkness has not overcome it.

There was a man sent from God, whose name was John.

He came for testimony, to bear witness to the light, that all might believe through him.

He was not the light, but came to bear witness to the light.

The true light that enlightens every man was coming into the world.

He was in the world, and the world was made through him, yet the world knew him not.

He came to his own home, and his own people received him not.

But to all who received him, who believed in his name, he gave power to become children of God; who were born, not of blood nor of the will of the flesh nor of the will of man, but of God.

And the Word became flesh and dwelt among us, full of grace and truth; we have beheld his glory, glory as of the only Son from the Father.

130 *Romans 8:31b–32, 35, 37–39*

If God is for us, who is against us?

He who did not spare his own Son but gave him up for us all, will he not also give us all things with him?

Who shall separate us from the love of Christ?

Shall tribulation, or distress, or persecution, or famine, or nakedness, or peril, or sword?

No, in all these things we are more than conquerors through him who loved us.

For I am sure that neither death, nor life, nor angels, nor principalities, nor things present, nor things to come, nor powers, nor height, nor depth, nor anything else in all creation, will be able to separate us from the love of God in Christ Jesus our Lord.

131 *Romans 12:1–2, 9–21*

I appeal to you therefore, brethren, by the mercies of God, to present your bodies as a living sacrifice, holy and acceptable to God, which is your spiritual worship.

Do not be conformed to this world but be transformed by the renewal of your mind, that you may prove what is the will of God, what is good and acceptable and perfect.

Let love be genuine; hate what is evil, hold fast to what is good; love one another with brotherly affection; outdo one another in showing honor.

Never flag in zeal, be aglow with the Spirit, serve the Lord.

Rejoice in your hope, be patient in tribulation, be constant in prayer.

Contribute to the needs of the saints, practice hospitality.

Bless those who persecute you; bless and do not curse them.

Rejoice with those who rejoice, weep with those who weep.

Live in harmony with one another; do not be haughty, but associate with the lowly; never be conceited.

Repay no one evil for evil, but take thought for what is noble in the sight of all.

If possible, so far as it depends upon you, live peaceably with all.

Beloved, never avenge yourselves, but leave it to the wrath of God; for it is written, "Vengeance is mine, I will repay, says the Lord."

No, "if your enemy is hungry, feed him; if he is thirsty, give him drink; for by so doing you will heap burning coals upon his head."

Do not be overcome by evil, but overcome evil with good.

132   *1 Corinthians 13*

If I speak in the tongues of men and of angels, but have not love, I am a noisy gong or a clanging cymbal.

And if I have prophetic powers, and understand all mysteries and all knowledge, and if I have all faith, so as to remove mountains, but have not love, I am nothing.

If I give away all I have, and if I deliver my body to be burned, but have not love, I gain nothing.

Love is patient and kind; love is not jealous or boastful; it is not arrogant or rude.

Love does not insist on its own way; it is not irritable or resentful; it does not rejoice at wrong, but rejoices in the right.

Love bears all things, believes all things, hopes all things, endures all things.

Love never ends;

As for prophecy, it will pass away; as for tongues, they will cease; as for knowledge, it will pass away.

For our knowledge is imperfect and our prophecy is imperfect; but when the perfect comes, the imperfect will pass away.

When I was a child, I spoke like a child, I thought like a child, I reasoned like a child; when I became a man, I gave up childish ways.

For now we see in a mirror dimly, but then face to face.

Now I know in part; then I shall understand fully, even as I have been fully understood.

So faith, hope, love abide, these three; but the greatest of these is love.

133   *1 Corinthians 15: 20–22, 51, 53–57*

Christ has been raised from the dead, the first fruits of those who have fallen asleep.

For as by a man came death, by a man has come also the resurrection of the dead.

For as in Adam all die, so also in Christ shall all be made alive.

Lo! I tell you a mystery.

We shall not all sleep, but we shall all be changed.

For this perishable nature must put on the imperishable, and this mortal nature must put on immortality.

When the perishable puts on the imperishable, and the mortal puts on immortality, then shall come to pass the saying that is written:

"Death is swallowed up in victory.

O death, where is thy victory?

O death, where is thy sting?"

The sting of death is sin, and the power of sin is the law.

But thanks be to God, who gives us the victory through our Lord Jesus Christ.

134
Ephesians 4:1–7, 11–13

I therefore, a prisoner for the Lord, beg you to lead a life worthy of the calling to which you have been called, with all lowliness and meekness, with patience, forbearing one another in love, eager to maintain the unity of the Spirit in the bond of peace.

There is one body and one Spirit, just as you were called to the one hope that belongs to your call, one Lord, one faith, one baptism, one God and Father of us all, who is above all and through all and in all.

But grace was given to each of us according to the measure of Christ's gift.

And his gifts were that some should be apostles, some prophets, some evangelists, some pastors and teachers,

For the equipment of the saints, for the work of ministry, for building up the body of Christ,

Until we all attain to the unity of the faith and of the knowledge of the Son of God, to mature manhood, to the measure of the stature of the fullness of Christ.

135
Philippians 2:5–11

Have this mind among yourselves, which you have in Christ Jesus, who, though he was in the form of God, did not count equality with God a thing to be grasped, but emptied himself, taking the form of a servant, being born in the likeness of men.

And being found in human form he humbled himself and became obedient unto death, even death on a cross.

Therefore God has highly exalted him and bestowed on him the name which is above every name, that at the name of Jesus every knee should bow, in heaven and on earth and under the earth, and every tongue confess that Jesus Christ is Lord, to the glory of God the Father.

136
Revelation 21:1–7; 22:1, 5

I saw a new heaven and a new earth; for the first heaven and the first earth had passed away, and the sea was no more.

And I saw the holy city, new Jerusalem, coming down out of heaven from God, prepared as a bride adorned for her husband;

And I heard a great voice from the throne saying, "Behold, the dwelling of God is with men.

He will dwell with them, and they shall be his people, and God himself will be with them;

He will wipe away every tear from their eyes, and death shall be no more, neither shall there be mourning nor crying nor pain any more, for the former things have passed away."

And he who sat upon the throne said, "Behold, I make all things new. . .

I am the Alpha and the Omega, the beginning and the end.

To the thirsty I will give water without price from the fountain of the water of life.

He who conquers shall have this heritage, and I will be his God and he shall be my son."

Then he showed me the river of the water of life, bright as crystal, flowing from the throne of God and of the Lamb.

And night shall be no more; they need no light of lamp or sun, for the Lord God will be their light, and they shall reign for ever and ever.

137   Te Deum Laudamus*

An Early Christian Hymn

We praise thee, O God: we acknowledge thee to be the Lord.
All the earth doth worship thee, the Father everlasting.

> To thee all angels cry aloud, the heavens and all the powers therein;
> To thee cherubim and seraphim continually do cry.

Holy, holy, holy, Lord God of Sabaoth;
Heaven and earth are full of the majesty of thy glory.

> The glorious company of the apostles praise thee.
> The goodly fellowship of the prophets praise thee.
> The noble army of martyrs praise thee.

The holy Church throughout all the world doth acknowledge thee;
The Father of an infinite majesty; thine adorable true and only Son;
Also the Holy Ghost the Comforter.

> Thou art the King of glory, O Christ.
> Thou art the everlasting Son of the Father.

When thou tookest upon thee to deliver man,
Thou didst humble thyself to be born of a virgin.

> When thou hadst overcome the sharpness of death,
> Thou didst open the kingdom of heaven to all believers.

Thou sittest at the right hand of God, in the glory of the Father.

> We believe that thou shalt come to be our judge.

We therefore pray thee, help thy servants, whom thou hast redeemed with thy
precious blood.

> Make them to be numbered with thy saints, in glory everlasting.

O Lord, save thy people, and bless thine heritage.
Govern them and lift them up for ever.

> Day by day we magnify thee;
> And we worship thy name ever, world without end.

Vouchsafe, O Lord, to keep us this day without sin.
O Lord, have mercy upon us, have mercy upon us

> O Lord, let thy mercy be upon us, as our trust is in thee.
> O Lord, in thee have I trusted: let me never be confounded.

* This may be read responsively or in unison.

Acknowledgments and Sources

The publishers wish to express sincere gratitude and appreciation to those individuals and publishers who kindly granted permission for use of their copyrighted materials. Every effort has been made to trace the ownership of all copyrighted material, although in some instances exact ownership is obscure. If for this reason any omissions have been made, it is hoped that these will be brought to our attention so that proper acknowledgment may be made in future editions of the book.

The scripture quotations are from the *Revised Standard Version of the Bible*, copyrighted 1946 and 1952 by the Division of Christian Education, National Council of Churches, and used by permission.

Hymns and Service Music

8 Words reprinted from *The Poems of Henry van Dyke* (copyright, 1911, by Charles Scribner's Sons; 1939, by Tertius van Dyke) by permission of the publisher.

12 Music copyright. Reprinted from *The English Hymnal* by permission of the Oxford University Press, London.

15 Words from *Hymns of Western Europe*. Used by permission of the Oxford University Press, London.

17 Words and music from *The Oxford American Hymnal*. Used by permission of the Oxford University Press, Inc., New York.

21 Words used by permission of G. Schirmer, Inc., copyright owner.

22 Words used by permission of the author.

24 Words from *At Worship*. Used by permission of Harper & Brothers, New York.

28 Words used by permission of the translator. Translation made at the request of Archbishop Nathan Söderblom for a world convention at Stockholm.

30 Words and music copyright. Reprinted from *The English Hymnal* by permission of the Oxford University Press, London.

34 Words from *The Unutterable Beauty* by G. A. Studdert-Kennedy. Used by permission of Hodder & Stoughton Ltd., London. Music used by permission of The Church Pension Fund.

38 Words used by permission of the author. Harmony copyright. Reprinted from *The Church Hymnary*, Revised Edition, by permission of the Oxford University Press, London.

39 Words copyright. Reprinted from *The Yattendon Hymnal* by permission of The Clarendon Press, Oxford, England. Harmony copyright. Reprinted from *Songs of Praise*, Enlarged Edition, by permission of the Oxford University Press, London.

40 Words and music copyright. Reprinted from *The Yattendon Hymnal* by permission of The Clarendon Press, Oxford, England.

41 Words copyright. Reprinted from *The English Hymnal* by permission of the Oxford University Press, London. Harmony copyright. Reprinted from *The Church Hymnary*, Revised Edition, by permission of the Oxford University Press, London.

42 Words and music copyright. Reprinted from *Songs of Praise*, Enlarged Edition (where the tune is called "Watchman"), by permission of the Oxford University Press, London.

45 Words and music used by permission of the Chautauqua Institution.

49 Words copyright. Reprinted from *The Yattendon Hymnal* by permission of The Clarendon Press, Oxford, England.

51 Words used by permission of J. Curwen & Sons Ltd.

53 Words copyright. Reprinted from *The Yattendon Hymnal* by permission of The Clarendon Press, Oxford, England.

54 Words copyright. Reprinted from *The Yattendon Hymnal* by permission of The Clarendon Press, Oxford, England.

58 Words from the *Hymn and Tune Book*, The Beacon Press, Boston, 1914. Used by permission.

550

168 Words used by permission of the Proprietors of *Hymns Ancient and Modern.* Music copyright. Reprinted from *The Church Hymnary*, Revised Edition, by permission of the Oxford University Press, London.

173 Words used by permission of the Proprietors of *Hymns Ancient and Modern.* Harmony copyright. Reprinted from *The Church Hymnary*, Revised Edition, by permission of the Oxford University Press, London.

176 Music copyright, 1941, by The H. W. Gray Company, Inc. Used by permission.

184 Words used by permission of the Hon. Mrs. H. Alington.

188 Words used by permission of The Church Pension Fund. Music used by permission of A. R. Mowbray & Co., Ltd.

189 Music used by permission of the Verein zur Herausgabe des Gesangbuches der evangelisch-reformierten Kirchen der deutschsprachigen Schweiz.

193 Words from *Cantate Domino.* Used by permission of the World's Student Christian Federation.

194 Words and music copyright. Reprinted from *Songs of Praise*, Enlarged Edition, by permission of the Oxford University Press, London.

197 Music copyright. Reprinted from *Songs of Praise*, Enlarged Edition, by permission of the Oxford University Press, London.

198 Words copyright. Reprinted from *Songs of Praise*, Enlarged Edition, by permission of the Oxford University Press, London.

201 Words copyright. Reprinted from *Hymns of the Russian Church* by permission of the Oxford University Press, London.

208 Words used by permission of the Rt. Rev. L. S. Hunter. Music used by permission of the Verein zur Herausgabe des Gesangbuches der evangelisch-reformierten Kirchen der deutschsprachigen Schweiz.

217 Words copyright. Reprinted from *Songs of Praise*, Enlarged Edition, by permission of the Oxford University Press, London. Melody by P. W. Joyce. Used by permission of the publishers: The Educational Company of Ireland Ltd. Harmony copyright. Reprinted from *The Church Hymnary*, Revised Edition, by permission of the Oxford University Press, London.

218 Music used by permission of E. R. Goodliffe.

220 Words used by permission of Mrs. Elizabeth Davis Burford.

234 Music used by permission of Mrs. Ethel Taylor.

235 Words used by permission of the United Lutheran Church in America.

238 Words used by permission of The Church Pension Fund.

239 Music copyright. Reprinted from *Songs of Praise*, Enlarged Edition, by permission of the Oxford University Press, London.

248 Melody by P. W. Joyce. Used by permission of the publishers: The Educational Company of Ireland Ltd. Harmony copyright. Reprinted from *The Church Hymnary*, Revised Edition, by permission of the Oxford University Press, London.

250 Words and music from *The Lutheran Hymnal.* Used by permission of the Concordia Publishing House.

253 Words copyright. Reprinted from *Songs of Praise*, Enlarged Edition, by permission of the Oxford University Press, London.

254 Words and music used by permission of the Chautauqua Institution.

255 Arrangement copyright. Reprinted from *Songs of Praise*, Enlarged Edition, by permission of the Oxford University Press, London.

265 Words used by permission of Miss Erica Oxenham.

268 Words used by permission of the author.

270 Words from the *Lutheran Hymnary*, copyright by the Augsburg Publishing House. Used by permission.

277 Words used by permission of the author.

279 Words used by permission of The Church Pension Fund.

286 Words copyright. Reprinted from *Songs of Praise*, Enlarged Edition, by permission of the Oxford University Press, London. Music used by permission of the composer.

287 Music used by permission of Novello & Co., Ltd.

289 Words used by permission of The Church Pension Fund.

291 Words used by permission of Allan Bourne Webb, copyright owner.

293 Music copyright assigned, 1946, to The H. W. Gray Company, Inc. Used by permission.

294 Words used by permission of The Hymn Society of America. Music used by permission of The Church Pension Fund.

297 Words by permission of author's heirs.

298 Words copyright by the author's heirs. Music copyright. Reprinted from *Songs of Praise*, Enlarged Edition, by permission of the Oxford University Press, London.

300 Words used by permission of *The Presbyterian Outlook*.

303 Words used by permission of Mrs. George P. Hyde.

304 Words used by permission of the author, copyright owner.

306 Music copyright. Reprinted from *The Church Hymnary*, Revised Edition, by permission of the Oxford University Press, London.

308 Words used by permission of Loughborough Training College.

312 Music by permission of J. Fischer & Bro.

316 Harmony copyright. Reprinted from *The Church Hymnary*, Revised Edition, by permission of the Oxford University Press, London.

317 Words used by permission of Sybil Tremillen.

322 Music copyright. Used by permission of Ascherberg, Hopwood & Crew Limited, 16 Mortimer Street, London W.1.

325 Words from *Lift Up Your Hearts*, Enlarged Edition, by Walter Russell Bowie. Used by permission of Abingdon Press.

326 Music used by permission of Novello & Co., Ltd.

330 Words used by permission of Miss Helen Macnicol.

339 Words copyright. Reprinted from *The Yattendon Hymnal* by permission of The Clarendon Press, Oxford, England.

340 Words by permission of Leroy P. Percy. Music used by permission of The Church Pension Fund.

341 Music copyright. Used by permission of The Psalms and Hymns Trust.

343 Words copyright by the author's heirs. Harmony copyright. Reprinted from *The Church Hymnary*, Revised Edition, by permission of the Oxford University Press, London.

346 Words used by permission of Miss Dorothy Tarrant.

352 Words used by permission of the executors of the estate of E. M. Butler. Music copyright. Reprinted from *Songs of Praise*, Enlarged Edition, by permission of the Oxford University Press, London.

354 Music used by permission of the Yale University Press.

356 Music copyright. Reprinted from *Songs of Praise*, Enlarged Edition, by permission of the Oxford University Press, London.

361 Words copyright by the author. Used by permission.

366 Words used by permission of the author. Music used by permission of Mrs. John Hughes.

367 Music used by permission of Novello & Co., Ltd.

368 Music: extrait du Recueil *Louange et Prière* (Psaumes, chorals, cantiques, répons liturgiques), 4e édition, 1957, paru aux Editions Delachaux & Niestlé, Neuchâtel et Paris. Used by permission.

371 Words copyright. Reprinted from *The English Hymnal* by permission of the Oxford University Press, London. Music used by permission of The Church Pension Fund.

376 Music used by permission of Novello & Co., Ltd.

377 Words and music used by permission of the Eden Publishing House.

380 Words copyright by the author's heirs.

382 Words used by permission of J. Curwen & Sons Ltd.

383 Words from the *Hymn and Tune Book*, The Beacon Press, Boston, 1914. Used by permission.

387 Words used by permission of J. Curwen & Sons Ltd. Music used by permission of Marlborough College.

391 Words used by permission of Chatto & Windus Ltd. Melody by P. W. Joyce. Used by permission of the publishers: The Educational Company of Ireland Ltd. Harmony copyright. Reprinted from *The Church Hymnary*, Revised Edition, by permission of the Oxford University Press, London.

392 Words "The Children's Song" from *Puck of Pook's Hill* by Rudyard Kipling. Copyright, 1906, by Rudyard Kipling. Reprinted by permission of Mrs. George Bambridge, Doubleday and Company, Inc., Methuen & Co., Ltd., and the Macmillan Company of Canada Ltd. Music used by permission of Novello & Co., Ltd.

393 Music copyright by The Royal School of Church Music, Addington Palace, Croydon, England. Used by permission.

398 Words from "Eleven Ecumenical Hymns." Copyright, 1954, by The Hymn Society of America. Used by permission.

399 Music used by permission of Novello & Co., Ltd.

403 Words copyright. Reprinted from *Songs of Praise*, Enlarged Edition, by permission of the Oxford University Press, London.

407 Words copyright by Marshall, Morgan & Scott Ltd., London, England. Used by permission.

408 Music used by permission of the Yale University Press.

409 Words from *The Toiling of Felix* by Henry van Dyke. Used by permission of Charles Scribner's Sons.

410 Music used by permission of the Proprietors of *Hymns Ancient and Modern*.

411 Words used by permission of Mrs. Wilson M. Powell.
Music used by permission of the Rt. Rev. the Abbot of Downside.

412 Music copyright. Reprinted from *The Church Hymnary*, Revised Edition, by permission of the Oxford University Press, London.

413 Words copyright. Reprinted from *The BBC Hymn Book* by permission of the Oxford University Press, London.

414 Words used by permission of Miss Erica Oxenham.

415 Words used by permission of Miss Erica Oxenham.
Music used by permission of the Executor of the Estate of H. T. Burleigh.

417 Music used by permission of the Association for Promoting Christian Knowledge.

419 Words used by permission of the author.

420 Words from *Hymns of the Kingdom of God*, Coffin and Vernon. Used by permission of Harper & Brothers, New York.
Music used by permission of The Church Pension Fund.

422 Words used by permission of the Industrial Christian Fellowship.
Music copyright by the composer's heirs.

424 Words used by permission of Felix Adler's literary estate.
Harmony copyright. Reprinted from *The Church Hymnary*, Revised Edition, by permission of the Oxford University Press, London.

426 Words used by permission of the author.

428 Music from the book *American Negro Songs* by J. W. Work, copyrighted by J. W. Work, 1940, assigned Theodore Presser Company, 1948. Used by permission.

430 Words copyright. Reprinted from *The Yattendon Hymnal* by permission of The Clarendon Press, Oxford, England.

431 Words "Recessional" from *The Five Nations* by Rudyard Kipling. Copyright, 1903, by Rudyard Kipling. Reprinted by permission of Mrs. George Bambridge, Doubleday and Company, Inc., Methuen & Co., Ltd., and the Macmillan Company of Canada Ltd.

432 Words used by permission of the author.

434 Words and music used by permission of the Trustees of *The Fellowship Hymn Book*.

435 Words copyright. Reprinted from *Songs of Praise*, Enlarged Edition, by permission of the Oxford University Press, London.

436 Words copyright. Reprinted from *The English Hymnal* by permission of the Oxford University Press, London.

439 Words used by permission of the estate of William P. Merrill.

441 Music used by permission of Gwenlyn Evans Ltd.

442 Words copyright. Reprinted from *Songs of Praise*, Enlarged Edition, by permission of the Oxford University Press, London.

444 Words used by permission of the author.

445 Words copyright. Reprinted from *Songs of Praise*, Enlarged Edition, by permission of the Oxford University Press, London.
Music used by permission of the League of Nations Union.

448 Words used by permission of The Beacon Press, Boston.

449 Words used by permission of the American Peace Society.
Music used by permission of the Yale University Press.

451 Words used by permission of A. D. Peters.

452 Words used by permission of the author, copyright owner.

455 Music copyright. Reprinted from *Songs of Praise*, Enlarged Edition, by permission of the Oxford University Press, London.

456 Words used by permission of Mrs. Dorothy M. W. Bean.
Music copyright. Reprinted from *The English Hymnal* by permission of the Oxford University Press, London.

465 Words copyright. Reprinted by permission of the Oxford University Press, London.

466 Words used by permission of The Church Pension Fund.

467 Words used by permission of The Beacon Press, Boston.

468 Music from the *Harvard University Hymn Book* edited by E. C. Moore and A. T. Davison. Copyright, 1926, 1954, by the Harvard University Press. Reprinted by permission.

ACKNOWLEDGMENTS AND SOURCES

469 Words used by permission of The Beacon Press, Boston.

471 Words copyright by the Congregational Union of England and Wales. Used by permission of the Independent Press Ltd. Music used by permission of the Rt. Rev. the Abbot of Downside.

472 Words used by permission of Mrs. Charles M. Mills.

476 Words used by permission of Miss Dorothy Tarrant.

478 Music used by permission of J. Curwen & Sons Ltd.

480 Words reprinted by permission of the National Sunday School Union. Music copyright. Reprinted from *A Students Hymnal* by permission of the Oxford University Press, London.

481 Words used by permission of Morehouse-Gorham Company. Music used by permission of The Church Pension Fund.

482 Words and music copyright. Reprinted from *The Oxford Book of Carols* by permission of the Oxford University Press, London.

484 Words copyright. Reprinted from *Songs of Praise*, Enlarged Edition, by permission of the Oxford University Press, London. Music used by permission of The Church Pension Fund.

485 Words from *Thoughts for Everyday Living* by Maltbie D. Babcock. Used by permission of Charles Scribner's Sons.

486 Words and music copyright by Frank W. Price. Used by permission.

487 Words and music copyright by Frank W. Price. Used by permission.

488 Words and music from the book *American Negro Songs* by J. W. Work, copyrighted by J. W. Work, 1940, assigned Theodore Presser Company, 1948. Used by permission.

491 Words and music used by permission of John H. Burt.

492 Words used by permission of the author. Music used by permission of the Yale University Press.

493 Words and music copyright. Reprinted from *Songs of Praise*, Enlarged Edition, by permission of the Oxford University Press, London.

494 Words copyright, 1936, by Purd E. Deitz. Used by permission. Arrangement from *The Hymnal*. Copyright, 1933, by The Presbyterian Board of Christian Education. Used by permission.

498 Words and music from *Cantate Domino*. Used by permission of the World's Student Christian Federation.

499 Music from *The Oxford American Hymnal*. Used by permission of the Oxford University Press, Inc., New York.

500 Words and music used by permission of the Yale University Press.

502 Music used by permission of the Yale University Press.

505 Words from the *Oxford Hymn Book*. Used by permission of The Clarendon Press, Oxford, England.

507 Words and music used by permission of The Church Pension Fund.

510 Words and music used by permission of J. Curwen & Sons Ltd.

517 Words and music copyright, 1925, 1952, by E. C. Schirmer Music Company, Boston. Used by permission.

518 Words and music from *The Call to Worship*. Used by permission of Dr. J. W. T. Patterson and the Carey Kingsgate Press Ltd.

521 Words used by permission of the Yale University Press.

524 Words and music copyright, 1925, 1952, by E. C. Schirmer Music Company, Boston. Used by permission.

527 Music copyright. Reprinted from *Songs of Praise*, Enlarged Edition, by permission of the Oxford University Press, London.

535 Music copyright. Reprinted from *The Yattendon Hymnal* by permission of The Clarendon Press, Oxford, England.

538 Words from *Christian Hymns*. Used by permission of the Christian Foundation.

539 Music used by permission of Middlesex School and Milton Academy.

542 Words and music from the *Harvard University Hymn Book*, edited by E. C. Moore and A. T. Davison, copyright, 1926, 1954, by the Harvard University Press. Reprinted by permission.

543 Music used by permission of the Trustees of the late Sir H. Walford Davies.

551 Music used by permission of The Parish Press of the Fond du Lac Cathedral.

553 Harmonization used by permission of The Church Pension Fund.

555 Harmonization used by permission of The Church Pension Fund.

556 Arrangement reprinted from *We Praise Thee* by Healey Willan by permission of the Concordia Publishing House.

557 Music used by permission of the Yale University Press.

558 Harmony copyright by Miss Louise McAllister. Used by permission.

576 Words and music used by permission of the Yale University Press.

577 **Words and music: Extrait du Recueil** *Louange et Prière* (Psaumes, chorals, cantiques, répons liturgiques), 4e édition, 1957, paru aux Editions Delachaux & Niestlé, Neuchâtel et Paris. Used by permission.

579 Words and music from *Songs of Syon*. Used by permission of Schott & Co., Ltd., London.

580 Permission for reprint granted by Elkan-Vogel Co., Inc., Philadelphia 3, Pa. Reprinted from *Hymns and Responses for the Church Year* by Vincent Persichetti, published by Elkan-Vogel Co., Inc., Philadelphia 3, Pa.

581 Descant copyright by the Fleming H. Revell Company. Used by permission.

583 Descant from *Familiar Hymns with Descants*. Copyright, 1956, by W. L. Jenkins, The Westminster Press. Used by permission.

584 Descant from *Familiar Hymns with Descants*. Copyright, 1956, by W. L. Jenkins, The Westminster Press. Used by permission.

592 Permission for reprint granted by Elkan-Vogel Co., Inc., Philadelphia 3, Pa. Reprinted from *Hymns and Responses for the Church Year* by Vincent Persichetti, published by Elkan-Vogel Co., Inc., Philadelphia 3, Pa.

593 Permission for reprint granted by Elkan-Vogel Co., Inc., Philadelphia 3, Pa. Reprinted from *Hymns and Responses for the Church Year* by Vincent Persichetti, published by Elkan-Vogel Co., Inc., Philadelphia 3, Pa.

The following material is covered by the publisher's copyright:
Words: Nos. 26, 27, 74, 189, 190, 316
Music: Nos. 27, 303, 328, 506, 516, 523, 578 (harmonization), 582 (descant), 591

Services, Prayers, Readings

2 This order of worship is based upon "Third Order of Service" in *A Book of Public Worship*, compiled by John Huxtable, John Marsh, Remilly Micklem, and James Todd, Oxford University Press, London, 1949. It is altered and used by kind permission of the compilers and the Oxford University Press. The service also draws upon the early Reformed structure of worship adopted by our Congregational forefathers, and reflects the insights of William D. Maxwell in his book, *Concerning Worship*, Oxford University Press, London, 1948.

  [1] From *A Book of Public Worship*, p. 82. Used by permission of the compilers and the Oxford University Press, London.
  [2] From *A Book of Public Worship*, p. 93. Used by permission of the compilers and the Oxford University Press, London.
  [3] From *A Book of Public Worship*, p. 141. Used by permission of the compilers and the Oxford University Press, London.
  [4] Adapted from *The First and Second Prayer Books of Edward VI*, Everyman's Library, No. 448, E. P. Dutton & Co., Inc., New York, pp. 221–222. Used by permission.

3 This order of worship is taken from "An Order of Morning Worship with Communion" in *A Book of Worship for Free Churches*, Oxford University Press, New York, 1948, pp. 103–110. Used by permission of The Board of Home Missions of the Congregational and Christian Churches, New York.

  [1] Adapted from *The First and Second Prayer Books of Edward VI*, Everyman's Library, No. 448, E. P. Dutton & Co., Inc., New York, p. 212. Used by permission.
  [2] From *The Book of Common Prayer*, The Church Pension Fund, Protestant Episcopal Church, New York, 1945, p. 6. Altered.

5 This order of baptism is based on "The Sacrament of Baptism for Infants and Children" in *A Book of Worship for Free Churches*, pp. 117–120. Used by permission of The Board of Home Missions of the Congregational and Christian Churches, New York. An order for the baptism of adults may be found on page 124 in the above book.

6 [1] From *The Book of Common Order of the Church of Scotland*, Oxford University Press, London, 1940, p. 102. Used by permission of the Church of Scotland Committee on Public Worship and Aids to Devotion.

ACKNOWLEDGMENTS AND SOURCES

7 Psalm 100:2, 4–5. (K.J.V.)

8 Isaiah 55:6–7. (K.J.V.)

9 John 4:23–24. (K.J.V.)

10 From *A Book of Public Worship*, p. 87. Used by permission of the compilers and the Oxford University Press, London.

11 From the *Pilgrim Hymnal*, The Pilgrim Press, Boston, 1935, no. 553, a collect. Used by permission.

12 From *An Outline of Christian Worship*, William D. Maxwell, Oxford University Press, London, 1936, p. 104. Used by permission.

13 From *A Book of Public Worship*, p. 86. Used by permission of the compilers and the Oxford University Press, London.

14 From *A Book of Public Worship*, Oxford University Press, London, p. 142. Used by permission of the Presbyterian Church of England.

15 From *A Book of Public Worship*, p. 21. Used by permission of the compilers and the Oxford University Press, London.

16 From *A Book of Public Worship*, p. 82. Used by permission of the compilers and the Oxford University Press, London.

17 From *A Book of Public Worship*, p. 83. Used by permission of the compilers and the Oxford University Press, London.

18 From *The Book of Common Prayer*, op. cit., p. 6. Altered.

19 From *Devotional Services for Public Worship*, compiled by John Hunter, E. P. Dutton & Co., Inc., New York, p. 48. Used by permission.

20 From *The Book of Common Worship*, The Board of Christian Education of the Presbyterian Church in the U.S.A., Philadelphia, 1946, p. 118.

21 From *The Book of Common Prayer*, op. cit., p. 206.

22 Adapted from *The First and Second Prayer Books of Edward VI*, Everyman's Library, No. 448, E. P. Dutton & Co., Inc., New York, pp. 224–225. Used by permission.

23 From *Prayers of the Christian Life*, John Underwood Stephens, copyright, 1952, by the Oxford University Press, Inc., New York, p. 74. Reprinted by permission.

24 From the *Book of Worship*, approved by the General Synod of the Evangelical and Reformed Church, Eden Publishing House, St. Louis, 1947, p. 363. Used by permission.

25 From *A Chain of Prayer Across the Ages*, compiled by Selina F. Fox, E. P. Dutton & Co., Inc., New York, 1913, p. 10. Used by permission.

26 From *Prayers for Services*, compiled and edited by Morgan Phelps Noyes, Charles Scribner's Sons, New York, 1934, pp. 137–138.

27 From *The Book of Common Prayer* of the Anglican Church of Canada. Used by permission.

28 Adapted from *The First and Second Prayer Books of Edward VI*, Everyman's Library, No. 448, E. P. Dutton & Co., Inc., New York, pp. 221–222. Used by permission.

29 From *Intercessory Services for Aid in Public Worship*, P. T. Forsyth, John Heywood, Ltd., Manchester, England, 1896, p. 8. Used by permission of Mrs. J. Forsyth Andrews.

30 From *The Book of Common Prayer*, op. cit., p. 31.

31 Adapted from *A Chain of Prayer Across the Ages*, compiled by Selina F. Fox, E. P. Dutton & Co., Inc., New York, 1913, p. 200. Used by permission.

32 From *Prayers for Services*, op. cit., p. 37.

33 From *With God in Prayer*, Charles H. Brent, George W. Jacobs & Co., Philadelphia, 1907.

34 From *The Book of Common Prayer*, op. cit., p. 19.

35 From *The Book of Common Prayer*, op. cit., pp. 18–19.

36 From *The Book of Common Order of the Church of Scotland*, p. 271. Used by permission of the Church of Scotland Committee on Public Worship and Aids to Devotion.

37 From *The Communion of Prayer*, edited by William Boyd Carpenter, George W. Jacobs & Co., Philadelphia, p. 184.

38 Adapted from *The First and Second Prayer Books of Edward VI*, Everyman's Library, No. 448, E. P. Dutton & Co., Inc., New York, pp. 213–214. Used by permission.

39 From *A Book of Public Worship*, p. 104. Used by permission of the compilers and the Oxford University Press, London.

40 Adapted from *The First and Second Prayer Books of Edward VI*, Everyman's Library, No. 448, E. P. Dutton & Co., Inc., New York, p. 212. Used by permission.

41 From *The Book of Common Prayer*, op. cit., p. 17.

42 Ibid., p. 49.

43 Ibid.

44 Ibid., p. 34.

45 From *Prayers for Services*, op. cit., pp. 224–225. Altered.

46 Acts 20:35. (K.J.V.)

47 Matthew 10:8; 5:16. (K.J.V.)

48 2 Corinthians 9:7. (K.J.V.)

49 From *A Book of Public Worship*, p. 144. Used by permission of the compilers and the Oxford University Press, London.

50 From the *Service Book and Ordinal of the Presbyterian Church of South Africa*, Jackson Son & Co., Ltd. Used by permission.

51 From *The Book of Common Prayer*, op. cit., p. 15.

52 Ibid., pp. 15–16.

53 From the *Pilgrim Hymnal*, op. cit., no. 554, second affirmation of faith.

54 From *A History of the Congregational Churches in the United States*, Williston Walker, The Christian Literature Company, New York, 1894, p. 104.

55 Exodus 20:1–17. Arranged. (K.J.V.)

56 Matthew 22:37–40. (K.J.V.)

57 Matthew 6:9–13. (K.J.V.)

58 Numbers 6:24–26.

59 2 Corinthians 13:14.

60 From *The Book of Common Order of the Church of Scotland*, p. 311. Used by permission of the Church of Scotland Committee on Public Worship and Aids to Devotion.

61 From *The Order of Divine Service for Public Worship*, William E. Orchard, Oxford University Press, London, 1919, pp. 106–107. Used by permission.

Index of Authors, Translators, and Sources

Abelard, Peter (1079–1142), 159, 310
Adams, Sarah F. (1805–1848), 351
Addison, Joseph (1672–1719), 72, 94
Adler, Felix (1851–1933), 424
Ainger, Arthur C. (1841–1919), 298
Alexander, Cecil F. (1818–1895), 171, 172, 322, 323, 478
Alexander, James W. (1804–1859), 170
Alford, Henry (1810–1871), 311, 461, 462
Alington, Cyril A. (1872–1955), 184
Anonymous, 91, 100, 246, 333, 408, 473, 474, 526, 577, 578
  American, 137
  Czech, 482
  English, 122, 141
  French, 116, 124
  German, 35, 131, 227
  Greek, 49, 201, 289
  Irish, 391
  Latin, 33, 110, 113, 125, 142, 150, 151, 170, 181, 187, 188, 225, 226, 231, 263, 290, 507, 575

Babcock, Maltbie D. (1858–1901), 485
Bacon, Leonard (1802–1881), 438
Baker, Henry W. (1821–1877), 79, 80, 111, 258, 447, 463
Baker, Theodore (1851–1934), 21, 131
Barbauld, Anna L. (1743–1825), 462, 464
Barclay, Margaret (unknown), 498
Baring-Gould, Sabine (1834–1924), 51, 382, 387, 510
Barton, Bernard (1784–1849), 256
Bates, Katharine Lee (1859–1929), 440
Bax, Clifford (1886–1962), 451
Baxter, Richard (1615–1691), 23
Bayly, Albert F. (1901–   ), 304, 452
Beach, Curtis (1914–   ), 26, 27, 74
Berwick Hymnal (1886), 333
Bianco da Siena (c.1367), 239
Blackie, John S. (1809–1895), 73
Blanchard, Ferdinand Q. (1876–   ), 161
Bode, John E. (1816–1874), 218
Bonar, Horatius (1808–1889), 99, 287, 396, 557
Borthwick, Jane L. (1813–1897), 77, 293
Bourne, George H. (1840–1925), 291
Bowie, W. Russell (1882–   ), 325, 420, 432

Bowring, John (1792–1872), 109, 157
Bridges, Matthew (1800–1894), 199, 321
Bridges, Robert S. (1844–1930), 39, 40, 49, 53, 163, 339, 430
Briggs, George W. (1875–1959), 198, 286, 308
Bright, William (1824–1901), 292
Brooke, Stopford A. (1832–1916), 69
Brooks, Phillips (1835–1893), 134
Browne, Simon (1680–1732), 238
Brownlie, John (1857–1925), 201, 407
Bryan, Joseph (17th century), 519
Buckham, John W. (1864–1945), 297
Buckoll, Henry J. (1803–1871), 506
Budry, Edmond L. (1854–1932), 193
Bunyan, John (1628–1688), 371
Burleigh, William H. (1812–1871), 376
Burt, Bates G. (1878–1948), 491
Butler, Henry M. (1833–1918), 352
Byrne, Mary E. (1880–1931), 391
Byrom, John (1692–1763), 127

Calvin, John (1509–1564), 207
Campbell, Jane M. (1817–1878), 460
Canitz, Friedrich, R. L. von (1654–1699), 506
Caswall, Edward (1814–1878), 35, 225, 226, 313
Chadwick, John W. (1840–1904), 275
Chambers, John David (1805–1893), 507
Chandler, John (1806–1876), 115, 144
Chao, T. C. (1888–   ), 486, 487
Chatfield, Allen W. (1808–1896), 314
Chesterton, Gilbert K. (1874–1936), 436
Chorley, Henry F. (1808–1872), 446
Clark, Alden H. (1878–   ), 394
Claudius, Matthias (1740–1815), 460
Clausnitzer, Tobias (c.1619–1684), 212, 250
Clement of Alexandria (c.170–220), 165
Clephane, Elizabeth C. (1830–1869), 160
Coffin, Charles (1676–1749), 115, 144
Coffin, Henry S. (1877–1954), 110
Collyer, Robert (1823–1912), 276
Conder, Josiah (1789–1855), 281
Cory, Julia C. (unknown), 22
Cosin, John (1594–1672), 231, 575
Coster, George T. (1835–1912), 380

Cotterill, Thomas (1779–1823), 205
Cowper, William (1731–1800), 87, 88, 349, 350, 402
Cox, Frances E. (1812–1897), 20
Coxe, Arthur C. (1818–1896), 264, 427
Croly, George (1780–1860), 232
Crossman, Samuel (c.1624–1684), 169

Davis, Ozora S. (1866–1931), 220
Dearmer, Geoffrey (1893–   ), 403
Dearmer, Percy (1867–1936), 41, 112, 142, 194, 253, 442, 482, 484
Decius, Nicolaus (d.1541), 2
Deitz, Purd E. (1897–   ), 494
Dix, William C. (1837–1898), 119, 140, 315
Doane, George W. (1799–1859), 296
Doane, William C. (1832–1913), 249
Doddridge, Philip (1702–1751), 76, 362, 389, 454
Douglas, C. Winfred (1867–1944), 279
Döving, Carl (1867–1937), 270
Draper, William H. (1855–1933), 64, 168
Duffield, George (1818–1888), 385
Dwight, Timothy (1752–1817), 269

Edmeston, James (1791–1867), 344
Edwards, Frank (1898–   ), 316
Ellerton, John (1826–1893), 47, 48, 60, 174, 395, 446, 468, 508
Elliott, Charlotte (1789–1871), 319, 320
Elliott, Emily E. S. (1836–1897), 326
English, Paul (d.1932), 24

F. B. P. (c. 16th century), 312
Faber, Frederick W. (1814–1863), 101, 102, 164, 365, 369, 542
Farjeon, Eleanor (1881–   ), 38
Farrington, Harry W. (1879–1931), 149
Fawcett, John (1739/40–1817), 63, 272, 273
Fosdick, Harry Emerson (1878–   ), 366
Foster, Frederick W. (1760–1835), 3
Foundling Hospital Collection (1796), 13
Franck, Johann (1618–1677), 222, 502
Franz, Ignaz (1719–1790), 247

Gannett, William C. (1840–1923), 458
Gascoigne, George (c.1525–1577), 505
Geer, E. Harold (1886–1957), 135
Gerhardt, Paul (1607–1676), 53, 123, 170, 337, 338
Gill, Thomas H. (1819–1906), 271
Gillman, Frederick J. (1866–1949), 434
Gilmore, Joseph H. (1834–1918), 370
Gladden, Washington (1836–1918), 418
Grant, Robert (1779–1838), 6

Greenway, Ada R. (1861–1937), 173
Gregory, Philip E. (1886–   ), 277
Gregory the Great (540–604), 41
Grubb, Edward (1854–1939), 86
Grundtvig, Nicolai F. S. (1783–1872), 270
Gurney, Dorothy F. (1858–1932), 465
Gurney, John H. (1802–1862), 347

Hall, William J. (1793–1861), 214
Hankey, Katherine (1834–1911), 317
Harkness, Georgia (1891–   ), 398
Hatch, Edwin (1835–1889), 233, 234
Havergal, Frances R. (1836–1879), 397, 404
Hawks, Annie S. (1835–1918), 342
Heber, Reginald (1783–1826), 58, 126, 251, 282, 283, 388
Hedge, Frederick H. (1805–1890), 363
Heermann, Johann (1585–1647), 163
Herbert, George (1593–1633), 401, 527
Herbert, Petrus (d.1571), 59
Hernaman, Claudia F. (1838–1898), 153
Herrnschmidt, Johann D. (1675–1723), 17
Holland, Henry S. (1847–1918), 435
Holmes, John Haynes (1879–1964), 419, 426
Holmes, Oliver Wendell (1809–1894), 89, 90
Hopkins, John H., Jr. (1820–1891), 143
Hopper, Edward (1818–1888), 213
Hosmer, Frederick L. (1840–1929), 58, 383, 448, 467, 469
Housman, Laurence (1865–1959), 445
How, William W. (1823–1897), 252, 306, 307, 329, 354, 355, 535
Howe, Julia Ward (1819–1910), 443
Hoyle, R. Birch (1875–1939), 193
Hull, Eleanor H. (1860–1935), 391
Hunter, John (1848–1917), 208
Hyde, William DeWitt (1858–1917), 303

Ingemann, Bernard S. (1789–1862), 387

Jeszensky, Karoly (c.1674), 377
John of Damascus (c.696–c.754), 185, 186, 192
Johnson, Samuel (1822–1882), 236, 261, 334
Joseph, Jane M. (c.1894–1929), 136
Judah, Daniel ben (c. 1400), 14

K., 372
Keble, John (1792–1866), 36, 50, 214
Kelly, Thomas (1769–1855), 200, 203
Ken, Thomas (1637–1711), 32, 56, 57, 514, 515
Kennedy, B. H. (1804–1889), 354, 355
Kerr, Hugh T. (1872–1950), 97
Kethe, William (d.1608?), 4, 5
Key, Francis Scott (1779–1843), 496

Kingsley, Charles (1819–1875), 417
Kipling, Rudyard (1865–1936), 392, 431
Knapp, Shepherd (1873–1946), 411

Landsberg, Max (1845–1928), 14
Larcom, Lucy (1826–1893), 318
Lathbury, Mary A. (1841–1913), 45, 254
Laufenberg, Heinrich von (c.1400–c.1458), 278
Laufer, Calvin W. (1874–1938), 421
Littledale, Richard F. (1833–1890), 239
Liturgy of St. James, 107
Logan, John (1748–1788), 389
Longfellow, Samuel (1819–1892), 46, 52, 67, 92, 242, 243, 266, 455, 457, 509, 538, 540
Lowell, James Russell (1819–1891), 425, 441
Löwenstern, Matthäus von (1594–1648), 378, 379
Lowry, Robert (1826–1899), 342
Lowry, Somerset C. (1855–1932), 413
Luke, Jemima (1813–1906), 483
Luther, Martin (1483–1546), 121, 235, 363
Lynch, Thomas T. (1818–1871), 245, 328, 381
Lyte, Henry F. (1793–1847), 16, 19, 209

Macgregor, Duncan (1854–1923), 248
Macnicol, Nicol (1870–1952), 330
Magdeburg, Joachim (c.1525–?), 354, 355
Mann, Newton (1836–1926), 14
Marckant, John (16th century), 580
Mason, John (c.1645–1694), 501
Mathams, Walter J. (1853–1932), 490
Matheson, George (1842–1906), 356, 399
Merrill, William P. (1867–1954), 300, 439
Mills, Charles S. (1861–1942), 472
Milman, Henry H. (1791–1868), 175, 176
Milton, John (1608–1674), 70, 71, 95, 274
Mohr, Joseph (1792–1848), 138, 139
Monsell, John S. B. (1811–1875), 31, 367
Montgomery, James (1771–1854), 25, 105, 117, 158, 280, 284, 285, 299, 336, 373, 374, 530
Moultrie, Gerard (1829–1885), 107
Moxley, Henry R. (1881–   ), 471

Nazianzen, Gregory (c.329–389), 407
Neale, John M. (1818–1866), 110, 111, 113, 125, 154, 155, 185, 186, 188, 191, 192, 263, 309, 310, 364, 475
Neander, Joachim (1650–1680), 15, 75, 339
Negro Spirituals, 179, 288, 353, 428, 488, 495
Netherlands Folk Song, 21
Neumark, Georg (1621–1681), 83
New Version (*See* Tate and Brady *New Version*)

Newman, John H. (1801–1890), 215, 216, 497
Newton, John (1725–1807), 221, 267, 539
Nicolai, Philipp (1556–1608), 24, 108, 145
Niedling's, J., *Lutherisch Handbüchlein* (1638), 521
Noble, James A. (1844–1896), 44
Noel, Caroline M. (1817–1877), 197
North, Frank Mason (1850–1935), 423
Nunn, E. Cuthbert (1868–1914), 124

O. B. C., 33
Oakeley, Frederick (1802–1880), 132
Oakley, Charles E. (1832–1865), 106
Olearius, Johann (1611–1684), 104
Owen, Frances M. (1842–1883), 386
Oxenham, John (1852–1941), 265, 414, 415, 510
Oxford Book of Carols, 194
Oxford Hymn Book, The (1925), 505

Palgrave, Francis T., (1824–1897), 500
Palmer, Ray (1808–1887), 290, 348
Park, J. Edgar (1879–1956), 152
Parker, Edwin P. (1836–1925), 405
Parker, Theodore (1810–1860), 219
Parr, Leonard A. (1880–   ), 189, 190
Patterson, D. Tait (1877–1956), 518
Percy, William A. (1885–1942), 340
Perronet, Edward (1726–1792), 195, 196, 581
Pfatteicher, Carl F. (1882–1957), 17
Phelps, S. Dryden (1816–1895), 331
Phillimore, Greville (1821–1884), 579
Piae Cantiones (1582), 136
Pierpoint, Folliott S. (1835–1917), 66
Pilgrim Hymnal, The (1904), 408, 578
Plumptre, Edward H. (1821–1891), 345
Pollock, Thomas B. (1836–1896), 166, 167, 301
Pott, Francis (1832–1909), 148, 181
Powell, Roger K. (1914–   ), 268
Prentiss, Elizabeth P. (1818–1878), 400
Price, Frank W. (1895–   ), 486, 487
Procter, Adelaide A. (1825–1864), 98
Prudentius, Aurelius Clemens (348–c.410), 111
Psalms

5:8 and 4:8	524
8	74
19	72, 255, 257
19:14	522, 523
23	79, 80, 84
24	114
27	373
34	81
36	82

Psalms (*Cont.*)

42	390
46	363
51:10–12	528
51:17	529
72	105
82, 85, 86	95
84	274
90	1
91	91
100	4, 9, 10, 26
103	16, 100
104	6
117	11, 12
119:33	517
119:105	516
121	85
136	70, 71
139	576
146	17
148	13
150	19

Psalter, The (1912), 255
Psalter Hymnal, The (1927), 576
Pusey, Philip (1799–1855), 376, 379

Rankin, Jeremiah E. (1828–1904), 61, 62
Rawson, George (1807–1889), 259
Reed, Andrew (1787–1862), 241
Rees, Bryn A. (1911–   ), 361
Riley, Athelstan (1858–1945), 30
Rinckart, Martin (1586–1649), 29
Rippon, John (1751–1836), 195, 196, 581
Rippon's *A Selection of Hymns* (1787), 372
Rist, Johann (1607–1667), 118
Robbins, Howard C. (1876–1952), 165
Roberts, Daniel C. (1841–1907), 433
Rodigast, Samuel (1649–1708), 96
Rossetti, Christina G. (1830–1894), 128
Russell, F. A. Rollo (1849–1914), 416

St. Ambrose (340–397), 39, 40
St. Andrew of Crete (c.660–c.732), 364
St. Bernard of Cluny (12th century), 309
St. Columba (c.521–597), 248
St. Francis of Assisi (1182–1226), 64
Sangle, Krishnarao Rathnaji (1834–1908), 394
Sarum Primer (1558), 393, 543
Schirmer, Michael (1606–1673), 244
Schlegel, Katharina von (1697–?), 77
Schmolck, Benjamin (1672–1737), 279, 503
Schütz, Johann J. (1640–1690), 20
Scott, Lesbia (1898–   ), 481
Scott, R. B. Y. (1899–   ), 444
Scottish Paraphrases (1781), 78

Scottish Psalter (1650), 84, 85
Scriven, Joseph (1819–1886), 335
Sears, Edmund H. (1810–1876), 129
Selnecker, Nicolaus (1528–1592), 54
Shurtleff, Ernest W. (1862–1917), 375
Sidebotham, Mary A. (1833–1913), 332
Sill, Edward R. (1841–1887), 237
Skemp, Ada (1857–1927), 480
Smith, Elizabeth L. (1817–1898), 207
Smith, Samuel F. (1808–1895), 305, 437, 477
Smith, Walter C. (1824–1908), 7
Smyttan, George H. (1822–1870), 148
Stock, Harry T. (1891–1958), 492
Stocking, Jay T. (1870–1936), 412
Stone, Samuel J. (1839–1900), 260
Stork, Charles Wharton (1881–   ), 28
Stowe, Harriet Beecher (1812–1896), 37
Struther, Jan (1901–1953), 42, 217, 493
Studdert-Kennedy, Geoffrey A. (1883–1929), 34, 422
Symonds, John A. (1840–1893), 450
Synesius of Cyrene (c.375–430), 314

Tappan, William B. (1794–1849), 178
Tarrant, William G. (1853–1928), 346, 476
Tate and Brady *New Version*
   1696: 81, 390
   1698: 187
   Supplement (1703): 18
Tate, Nahum (1652–1715), 146
Taylor, Jeremy (1613–1667), 156
Tennyson, Alfred (1809–1892), 357, 453
Tersteegen, Gerhardt (1697–1769), 3, 499
Theodulph of Orleans (c.760–c.821), 155
Thilo, Valentin (1607–1662), 135
Thomson, Mary A. (1834–1923), 302
Thring, Godfrey (1823–1903), 199
Thrupp, Dorothy A. (1779–1847), 327
Tilak, Narayan V. (1862–1919), 330
Tisserand, Jean (d.1494), 191
Toplady, Augustus M. (1740–1778), 358, 359
Toth, William (1905–   ), 377
Troutbeck, John (1832–1889), 118
Tucker, F. Bland (1895–   ), 147, 159, 289, 466
Tweedy, Henry H. (1868–1953), 294
Twells, Henry (1823–1900), 55

United Presbyterian Book of Psalms U. S. A. (1871), 91, 100

van Dyke, Henry (1852–1933), 8, 409
Vories, William M. (1880–   ), 449

Wade, John F. (1711–1786), 132, 133
Wallin, Johann Olaf (1779–1839), 28
Walter, Howard A. (1883–1918), 489

Walworth, Clarence (1820–1900), 247

Waring, Anna L. (1823–1910), 343

Watts, Isaac (1674–1748), 1, 9, 10, 11, 12, 68, 78, 82, 130, 177, 202, 229, 240, 257, 459, 504, 558, 583

Webb, Benjamin (1819–1885), 150, 151

Weisse, Michael (c.1488–1534), 183

Weissel, Georg (1590–1635), 114

Wesley, Charles (1707–1788), 43, 103, 120, 182, 187, 204, 205, 206, 210, 211, 223, 228, 384, 406, 525, 582, 584

Wesley, John (1703–1791), 9, 10, 324, 337, 338, 499

Weston, Rebecca J. (dates unknown), 479

Whiting, William (1825–1878), 429

Whittier, John Greenleaf (1807–1892), 224, 230, 262, 341, 360, 410, 537

Whole Booke of Psalmes, The (1647) (*The Bay Psalm Book*), 473, 474

Wile, Frances W. (1878–1939), 456

Williams, Peter (1727–1796), 93

Williams, Theodore C. (1855–1915), 65

Williams, William (1717–1791), 93

Willis, Love M. (1824–1908), 368

Winkworth, Catherine (1827–1878), 2, 15, 29, 59, 75, 83, 96, 104, 108, 114, 121, 123, 145, 183, 212, 222, 235, 244, 250, 278, 502, 503, 521

Wolcott, Samuel (1813–1886), 295

Wordsworth, Christopher (1807–1885), 180

Wortman, Denis (1835–1922), 470

Wreford, John R. (1800–1881), 162

Xavier, Francis (1506–1552), 313

Yattendon Hymnal (1899), 54

Yigdal, The, 14

Young, John F. (1820–1885), 138

Zinzendorf, Nicolaus L. von (1700–1760), 324

Zwick, Johannes (1496–1542), 498

Index of Composers, Arrangers, and Sources

"Agincourt Song, The" (15th century), 151

Ahle, Johann R. (1625–1673), 212, 253, 279

Albert, Heinrich (1604–1651), 323

Aldrich, Henry (1647–1710), 565

American Melody, 312

Anchors', William, *Psalm Tunes*, (c.1721), 154, 224

Anderson, James S. (1853–1945), 168

Anglo-Genevan Psalter (1556), 259, 419, 505

Anonymous, 137, 437, 496, 528, 529

As Hymnodus Sacer, Leipzig (1625), 67, 476

Atkinson, Frederick C. (1841–1897), 232

Attwood, Thomas (1765–1838), 517

Ave Hierarchia (1531), 258

Bach, J. S. (1685–1750), 24, 44, 53, 54, 67, 69, 86, 108, 118, 135, 145, 170, 198, 235, 281, 308, 337, 354, 468, 542

Baker, Henry (1835–1910), 447

Bambridge, William S. (1842–1923), 387

Baring-Gould, Sabine (1834–1924), 510

Barnby, Joseph (1838–1896), 35, 51, 307, 379, 465, 568, 572

Barrow, Robert G. (1911–   ), 591

Barthélémon, François H. (1741–1808), 32, 406

Batchellor, Daniel (unknown), 479

Bayeux Antiphoner (1739), 59

Beethoven, Ludwig van (1770–1827), 8, 536

Bohemian Brethren's *Kirchengesänge* (1566), 20, 262, 325

Bohemian Melodies 484, 579

Bortniansky, Dmitri S. (1751–1825), 52

Bourgeois, Louis (c.1510–c.1561), 4, 11, 47, 49, 282, 289, 508, 514, 515

Boyce, William (1710–1779), 562

Boyd, William (1847–1928), 367

Bradbury, William B. (1816–1868), 178, 319, 327, 370, 483

Brandon, George (1924–   ), 578

Braunschweig Melody (1528), 556

Briggs, George W. (1875–1959), 527

Buchanan, Annabel Morris (1888–   ), 312

Burleigh, Harry T. (1866–1949), 415

Burt, Bates G. (1878–1948), 491

Calkin, John B. (1827–1905), 296

Cantica Spiritualia (1847), 55

Cantionale Sacrum (1651), 521

Chinese Melodies, 71, 486, 487

Christian Lyre, The (1831), 409

Church Psalter and Hymn Book (1854), 233

Chute, Marion Jean (1901–   ), 394

Clark, Jeremiah (c.1670–1707), 78, 89, 200, 220, 274, 452

Cologne Melody (1623), 135

Confucian Temple Chant, 487
Conkey, Ithamar (1815–1867), 157
Converse, Charles C. (1832–1918), 335
Corner's *Gesangbuch* (1631), 539
Courteville, Raphael (?–c.1735), 266
Croft, William (1678–1727), 1, 206, 229, 264, 559, 583, 584
Crotch, William (1775–1847), 560
Crüger, Johann (1598–1662), 29, 163, 222, 241, 256, 368, 504
Cummings, William H. (1831–1915), 120
Cutler, Henry S. (1824–1902), 388
Czech Melody, 482

Damon's *Psalmes*,
  1579: 314, 361
  1591: 226
Darwall, John (1731–1789), 23, 204
Davies, H. Walford (1869–1941), 480, 543
Day's Psalter (1562), 153, 280
Dickey, Mark (1885–1961), 506
Doane, William H. (1832–1915), 400
Douglas, C. Winfred (1867–1944), 34, 294, 371, 420, 484
Dowland, John (1562–1626), 5
Dutch Melody, 74, 101
Dyer, Samuel (1785–1835), 238, 477
Dykes, John B. (1823–1876), 79, 164, 175, 215, 225, 240, 251, 311, 350, 364, 429
Dyson, George (1883–1964), 518

Ebeling, Johann G. (1637–1676), 123, 189
Edwards, John D. (1806–1885), 169, 466
Elvey, George J. (1816–1893), 199, 320, 384, 461, 462, 490, 567
Elvey, Stephen (1805–1860), 561
English Melodies, 122, 140, 141, 151, 412, 455, 456, 457, 478, 485
Essay on the Church Plain Chant, An (1782), 344
Este's, Thomas, *Whole Book of Psalms* (1592), 146
Evans, David (1874–1948), 38, 167, 173, 217, 248, 316, 343, 391, 424
Ewing, Alexander (1830–1895), 309

Farrant, Richard (c.1530–1580), 501, 561, 573
Finnish Melody, 343
Fischer, William G. (1835–1912), 317
Flemming, Friedrich F. (1778–1813), 333
Foundery Collection, The (1742), 458, 525
French Melodies, 107, 116, 191
Freylinghausen's *Geistreiches Gesangbuch* (1704), 17, 75
Friedell, Harold W. (1905–1958), 27
Fritsch, Ahasuerus (1649–1701), 198

Gaelic Melody, 38
Gardiner's *Sacred Melodies* (1815), 423
Gastorius, Severus (c.1675), 96
Gay, Annabeth McClelland (1925–   ), 328
Geistliche Kirchengesäng, Cologne (1623), 12, 30, 64
Geistliche Lieder, Leipzig,
  1539: 2, 44, 121, 278
  1589: 54
Genevan Psalter,
  1543: 519
  1547: 47
  1551: 4, 11, 104, 237, 334, 398, 432, 444, 451, 467, 470, 514, 515
  1562: 502
George, Graham (1912–   ), 176
German Melodies, 125, 131, 183, 222, 238, 468, 477, 542
Gesangbuch, Wirtemberg (1784), 68, 459
Giardini, Felice de (1716–1796), 246, 295, 472
Gibbons, Orlando (1583–1625), 162, 207, 275, 292, 336, 360, 386, 509
Gläser, Carl G. (1784–1829), 223, 346
Goodson, Richard (1655–1718), 564
Goss, John (1800–1880), 16, 380
Gottschalk, Louis M. (1829–1869), 242
Goudimel, Claude (d.1572), 49
Gould, John E. (1822–1875), 213
Gower, John H. (1855–1922), 172
Greatorex, Henry W. (1813–1858), 513
Greatorex, Walter (1877–1949), 156, 352
Greek Melody, 483
Greiter, Mattaeus (c.1500–1552), 577
Grenoble Church Melody, 150, 453
Gruber, Franz (1787–1863), 138, 139

Handel, Georg F. (1685–1759), 130, 193, 294, 362
Harding, James (John) P. (?–1911), 126
Harmonischer Lieder-Schatz (1738), 112
Hassler, Hans Leo (1564–1612), 170
Hastings, Thomas (1784–1872), 358
Hatton, John (d. 1793), 202, 297, 438
Havergal, William H. (1793–1870), 214
Haweis, Thomas (1734–1820), 261
Haydn, Franz J. (1732–1809), 72, 267, 268, 439
Haydn, J. Michael (1737–1806), 6, 190
Hayne, Leighton G. (1836–1883), 236, 448
Hebrew Melodies, 14, 26
Helmore, Thomas (1811–1890), 110
Hemy, Henri F. (1818–1888), 365
Herbst, Martin (1654–1681), 148
Hermann, Nicholaus (c.1485–1561), 492

Hesperian Harp (1848), 558
Hintze, Jacob (1622–1702), 69, 308
Hirschberg *Gesangbuch* (1741), 92
Hodges, J. S. B. (1830–1915), 283
Holden, Oliver (1765–1844), 195, 581
Holst, Gustav T. (1874–1934), 128, 136
Hopkins, Edward J. (1818–1901), 60
Hopkins, John H. (1861–1945), 481
Hopkins, John H., Jr. (1820–1891), 143
Horsley, William (1774–1858), 171
Howard, Samuel (1710–1782), 338
Hu Te-ngai (unknown), 486
Hughes, John (1873–1932), 93, 366
Hungarian Melody, 377
Husband, Edward (1843–1908), 329
Hutcheson, Charles (1792–1860), 255
Hymn Tunes of the United Brethren (1824),
    463

Indian Melody, 394
Ingham, Thomas H. (1878–1948), 42
Irish Melodies, 8C, 217, 248, 391, 417
Irvine, Jessie S. (1836–1887), 84
Isaak, Heinrich (c.1450–c.1527), 53

Jackson, Robert (1840–1914), 234
Jeffery, J. Albert (1855–1929), 249
Jenkins, David (1849–1915), 356
Jones, John (1797–1857), 356
Jones, Joseph D. (1827–1870), 65, 205
Jones, William (1726–1800), 201, 321
Joseph, Georg (c.1650), 55
Jude, William H. (1851–1922), 322

Katholisches Gesangbuch, Vienna (c.1774),
    50, 247
Kentucky Harmony (1816), 34, 420, 576
Kettring, Donald D. (1907–   ), 583, 584
Kirchengesangbuch, Darmstadt (1699), 250
Klug's *Geistliche Lieder*, Wittenberg (1535)
    271, 442
Knapp, William (1698?–1768), 430, 475
Knecht, Justin H. (1752–1817), 243, 301,
    329, 404, 499
Kocher, Conrad (1786–1872), 66, 119, 464
König, J. B. (1691–1758), 112, 214
Kremser, Edward (1838–1914), 21, 22

La Feillée's *Méthode du Plain-chant*,
    1782: 41
    1808: 310
Lamb, Hubert (1909–   ), 539
Lane, Spencer (1843–1903), 374
Langdon, Richard (c.1729–1803), 522
Langran, James (1835–1909), 287, 376
Laudi Spirituali, Florence (14th century),
    403, 540

Laufer, Calvin W. (1874–1938), 421
Lawes, Henry (1596–1662), 571
Leipzig Melody (1625), 538
Leisentritt's *Gesangbuch* (1584), 186
LeJeune, Claude (c.1523–c.1600), 502
Ley, Henry G. (1887–   ), 469
Lindeman, Ludvig M. (1812–1887), 270
Lloyd, John A. (1815–1874), 315
Lloyd, William (1786–1852), 426
Lockhart, Charles (1745–1815), 25
Lowry, Robert (1826–1899), 331, 342
Luther, Martin (1483–1546), 363
Lutkin, Peter C. (1858–1931), 551
Lvov, Alexis F. (1799–1870), 446
Lyon, Meyer (1751–1797), 14
Lyra Davidica (1708), 182, 582

Maker, Frederick C. (1844–1927), 98, 160,
    161, 341, 434
Mann, Arthur H. (1850–1929), 218
Manual for Teachers (1885), 479
Marsh, Simeon B. (1798–1875), 210
Mason, Lowell (1792–1872), 76, 130, 177,
    257, 272, 273, 348, 351, 449
Mason's *Modern Psalmody* (1839), 223, 346
Matthews, Timothy R. (1826–1910), 326,
    392
McAllister, Louise (1913–1960), 558
Mendelssohn, Felix (1809–1847), 37, 120,
    252, 520
Merbecke, John (c.1510–c.1585), 545, 552,
    553, 555
Messiter, Arthur H. (1834–1916), 345
Miller, Edward (1731–1807), 357
Milton, John, Sr. (c.1563–1647), 95, 473
Monk, Edwin G. (1819–1900), 559
Monk, William H. (1823–1889), 181, 203,
    209, 258
Musicalischer Christen-Schatz, Basel (1745),
    332
Musicalisches Handbuch, Hamburg (1690),
    9, 115

Nägeli, J. G. (1768?–1836), 76, 272
Neander, Joachim (1650–1680), 3, 339, 503
Negro Melodies, 179, 288, 353, 415, 428,
    488, 495
Netherlands Melody (1626), 21, 22
Neu Ordentlich Gesangbuch (1646), 86
Neu-vermehrtes Gesangbuch, Meiningen
    (1693), 252
Neumark, Georg (1621–1681), 83
Nicholson, Sydney H. (1875–1947), 393
Nicolai, Philipp (1556–1608), 24, 108, 145,
    244
Noble, T. Tertius (1867–1953), 105, 293

Nunn, E. Cuthbert (1868–1914), 124
Nürnberg Melody (1676), 208

Oliver, Henry K. (1800–1885), 290, 402
Ouseley, F. A. G. (1825–1889), 560
Owen, William (1814–1893), 291
Oxford Chant, 566

Palestrina, G. P. Sante da (1525–1594), 181
Parish Choir, The (1850), 33, 70, 416
Parker, Edwin P. (1836–1925), 405
Parry, C. Hubert H. (1848–1918), 410
Parry, Joseph (1841–1903), 109, 211
Peace, Albert L. (1844–1912), 399
Peek, Joseph Y. (1843–1911), 489
Pensum Sacrum (1648), 521, 537
Persichetti, Vincent (1915–   ), 580, 592, 593
Piae Cantiones (1582), 136, 142
Pilgrim Hymnal (1931), 512
Plainsong, 40, 110, 111, 113, 507, 557, 575
Playford, John (1674–1730), 549
Pleyel, Ignaz J. (1757–1831), 324
Plymouth Collection (1855), 425
Poitiers Antiphoner (1746), 378
Porter, Ethel (1901–   ), 582
Porter, Hugh (1897–1960), 516, 582
Praetorius, Michael (1571–1621), 39, 131, 144, 188
Prichard, Rowland H. (1811–1887), 13
Prys' Psalter (1621), 497
Psalmodia Sacra, Gotha (1715), 100, 103
Purday, Charles H. (1799–1885), 97, 216

Ramsey, Robert (1600–1650), 586
Randall, John (1715–1799), 569
Ravenscroft, Thomas (c.1592–c.1635), 88
Ravenscroft's Psalter (1621), 474
Redhead, Richard (1820–1901), 158, 245, 359
Redner, Lewis H. (1831–1908), 134
Reinagle, Alexander R. (1799–1877), 221, 414
Revivalist, The (1869), 578
Roberts, John (1822–1877), 187
Robinson, John (1682–1762), 570
Rostockerhandboken (1529), 28
Russell, Frederick G. (1867–1929), 422

Schein, Johann H. (1586–1630), 99, 276, 500
Schicht, Johann G. (1753–1823), 173
Scholefield, Clement E. (1839–1904), 48
Schop, Johann (?–c.1644), 118
Schulz, Johann A. P. (1747–1800), 460

Schumann, Robert A. (1810–1856), 46, 397
Scott-Gatty, Alfred (1847–1918), 411, 471
Scottish Melodies, 511, 554
Scottish Psalter,
  1564: 168
  1615: 85, 87, 95, 313, 389,- 395, 473, 541
  1635: 330, 349, 396, 530
Sermisy, Claude de (c.1490–1562), 354
Shaw, Geoffrey (1879–1943), 142, 255, 445
Shaw, Martin (1875–1958), 106, 194, 298, 478, 482
Sheppard, Franklin L. (1852–1930), 485
Sherwin, William F. (1826–1888), 31, 45, 254
Shrubsole, William (1760–1806), 196
Sibelius, Jean (1865–1957), 77, 494
Sicilian Melody, 63, 277
Silesian Melody, 227
Smart, George T. (1776–1867), 81
Smart, Henry T. (1813–1879), 117, 192, 263, 375
Smith, Alfred M. (1879–   ), 286
Smith, H. Percy (1825–1898), 418
Southern Harmony (1835), 165
Stainer, John (1840–1901), 594
Stanford, Charles V. (1852–1924), 147
Steffe, William ? (c.1852), 443
Stevenson, John A. (1761–1833), 52
Stralsund Gesangbuch (1665), 15
Stubbs, Simon (c.16th century), 474
Students' Hymnal, A, University of Wales (1923), 480
Sullivan, Arthur S. (1842–1900), 185, 318, 355, 382, 383
Swedish Melody, 166
Swiss Melody, 381

Tallis, Thomas (d.1585), 18, 56, 57, 91, 94, 533, 544, 546, 547, 548
Tans'ur, William (1706?–1783), 149, 159, 284
Tate and Brady New Version, Supplement (1708), 431
Taylor, Virgil C. (1817–1891), 90
Teschner, Melchior (1584–1635), 155
Thalben-Ball, George T. (1896–   ), 73
Tochter Sion, Cologne (1741), 180, 347, 413
Tomer, William G. (1832–1896), 62
Tomlinson, Richard (1822–?), 563
Tourjée, Lizzie S. (1858–1913), 102
Traditional Carols, 116, 122, 124, 125, 137, 141, 194
Turner, Herbert B. (1852–1927), 152

Vaughan Williams, R. (1872–1958), 61, 197, 239, 306, 412, 455, 456, 457

Venua, Frederick M. A. (1788–1872), 10
Vesperale Romanum (Mechlin), 575
Vetter, Daniel (?–c.1730), 231
Vulpius, Melchior (c.1560–1616), 184, 235, 373, 469

Wade's, John F., *Cantus Diversi* (1751), 132, 133, 372
Wainwright, John (c.1723–1768), 127, 304
Walch, James (1837–1901), 302
Walker, Alan (1927–   ), 523
Wallace, William V. (1814–1865), 230
Walter, William H. (1825–1893), 300
Walton, James G. (1821–1905), 365
Ward, Samuel A. (1848–1903), 440
Warner, Richard (1908–   ), 303
Warrack, Guy (1900–   ), 493
Warren, George W. (1828–1902), 433
Webb, George J. (1803–1887), 305, 385
Webbe, Samuel (1740–1816), 36, 299
Weimar Gesangbuch (1681), 96
Wellesley, Garret (1735–1781), 401
Welsh Melodies, 7, 58, 174, 219, 316, 424, 426, 427, 435, 436, 526
Werner's, Johann, *Choralbuch* (1815), 43

Wesley, Samuel (1766–1837), 550
Wesley, Samuel S. (1810–1876), 260, 407, 524
Wesley's, S. S., *European Psalmist* (1872), 265
Wilkes, John B. (1785–1869), 463
Willan, Healey (1880–   ), 556
Williams, David McK. (1887–   ), 340, 581
Williams' *New Universal Psalmodist* (1770), 269
Williams, Robert (c.1781–1821), 19, 187
Williams', Thomas, *Psalmodia Evangelica* (1789), 82, 114, 450, 454
Williams, Thomas J. (1869–1944), 441
Willis, Richard S. (1819–1900), 129
Wilson, Hugh (1764–1824), 285, 390
Witt, Christian F. (1660–1716), 100, 103
Wittenberg Melody (1537), 498
Woodward, George R. (1848–1934), 144, 188, 579
Wooldridge, Harry E. (1845–1917), 535

Zeuner, Heinrich C. (1795–1875), 369
Zundel, John (1815–1882), 228

Metrical Index

SHORT METER
S.M. 6.6.8.6.
Boylston 273
Carlisle 25
Dennis 76, 272
Festal Song 300
Franconia 214
Mornington 401
Potsdam 233
St. Bride 338
St. Michael 237, 444
St. Thomas (Williams) 269
Southwell 314, 361
Trentham 234
Yattendon 46 535

SHORT METER
with Refrain
Marion 345

SHORT METER DOUBLE
S.M.D. 6.6.8.6.D.
Diademata 199, 384, 490
Ich halte treulich still 337

Llanllyfni 356
Terra beata 485

COMMON METER
C.M. 8.6.8.6.
Abbey 313
Antioch 130
Azmon 223, 346
Bangor 149, 159, 284
Beatitudo 350
Bishopthorpe 274
Caithness 349
Christmas 362
Contrition 580
Coronation 195, 581
Crimond 84
Dundee 85, 87, 88, 389
Dunfermline 395
Farrant 501
Georgetown 340
Hermon 220
Horsley 171
Hummel 369
Land of Rest 312
Martyrdom 285, 390

Meditation 172
Miles Lane 196
McKee 415
Nun danket all' 241, 256, 504
Richmond 261
St. Agnes 225, 240
St. Anne 1, 264, 583
St. Bernard 347
St. Flavian 153, 280
St. James 266
St. Magnus 78, 200
St. Mary 497
St. Peter 221, 414
St. Stephen 201, 321
Serenity 230
Song 67 336, 360
Stracathro 255
Tallis' Ordinal 18, 94
Walsall 154, 224
Wigtown 330, 396, 530
Wiltshire 81
Winchester Old 146
Windsor 226
York 95, 473, 474

COMMON METER DOUBLE
C.M.D. 8.6.8.6.D.

All Saints New 388
Carol 129
Ellacombe 68, 459
Forest Green 456, 457
Halifax 294
Kingsfold 412
Materna 440
Old 22nd 259, 419, 505
Shepherds' Pipes 328
Wellington Square 493

LONG METER
L.M. 8.8.8.8.

Ach bleib bei uns 54
Ach Gott und Herr 476
All morgen ist 498
Angelus 55
Bourbon 558
Breslau 538
Canonbury 46, 397
Conditor alme 113
Danby 455
Das neugeborne Kindelein 235
Das walt' Gott vater 231
Deo Gracias 151
Deus tuorum militum 150, 453
Duke Street 202, 297, 438
Eisenach 99, 276
Elton 449
Federal Street 290, 402
Germany 423
Grace Church 324
Hamburg 177
He leadeth me 370
Herr Jesu Christ 521, 537
Herr Jesu Christ, mein's Lebens Licht 67
Hesperus 447
Hilariter 194
Hursley 50
Jam lucis 507
Kedron 165
Louvan 90
Mach's mit mir, Gott 500
Maryton 418
Melcombe 36, 299
Melrose 434
Mendon 238, 477
Morning Hymn 32, 406
O Jesu Christe, wahres Licht 208
Old Hundredth 4, 5, 11, 514, 515
Olive's Brow 178
Onslow 479
Park Street 10
Pentecost 367
Puer nobis nascitur 39, 144, 188

Ramwold 303
Rockingham 357
St. Crispin 320
St. Cross 164
St. Drostane 175
Saxby 392
Song 5 509
Splendor Paternae 40
Tallis' Canon 56, 57, 91
Tender Thought 576
The King's Majesty 176
Truro 82, 114, 450, 454
Uffingham 89, 452
Uxbridge 257
Veni Creator 575
Vom Himmel hoch 121, 278
Waltham 296
Wareham 430, 475
Winchester New 9, 115
Woodworth 319

LONG METER DOUBLE
L.M.D. 8.8.8.8.D.

Creation 72

4.10.10.10.4.

Ora labora 293

5.5.5.4.D.

Bunessan 38

5.5.5.5.D.

Hsuan p'ing 487
Le p'ing 486

5.5.6.5.6.5.6.5. with Refrain

Judas Maccabeus 193

5.6.8.5.5.8.

Schönster Herr Jesu 227

6.4.6.4. with Refrain

Need 342

6.4.6.4.D.

Bread of Life 254

6.4.6.4.6.6.4.

More love to thee 400

6.4.6.4.6.6.4.4.

Love's Offering 405

6.4.6.4.6.6.6.4.

Bethany 351
Dawn 42
St. Edmund 318
Something for Jesus 331

6.5.6.5.

Eudoxia 510
Merrial 51

6.5.6.5.D.

King's Weston 197
Penitence 374
St. Andrew of Crete 364

6.5.6.5.D. with Refrain

St. Gertrude 382, 383

6.5.6.5.6.6.6.5.

St. Dunstan's 371

6.6.4.6.6.6.4.

America 437
Italian Hymn 246, 295, 472
Olivet 348
Serug 265

6.6.5.6.6.6.5.7.8.6.

Jesu, meine Freude 222

6.6.6.6.

Ravenshaw 258
St. Cecilia 448

6.6.6.6.4.4.4.4.

Darwall's 148th 23
Rhosymedre 169

6.6.6.6.6. with Refrain

Personent hodie 136

6.6.6.6.6.6.

Laudes Domini 35

6.6.6.6.8.8.

Arthur's Seat 380
Croft's 136th 229
Darwall's 148th 204
Harewood 407
Little Cornard 106
Welsh Melody 526

6.6.6.6.8.8.8.

Rhosymedre 466

6.6.7.6.6.7.

Nunc dimittis 49

6.6.8.4.D.

Leoni 14

6.6.8.6.6.8.3.3.6.6.

Arnsberg 3

6.6.11.D.

Down Ampney 239

6.7.6.7.6.6.6.6.

Nun danket 29
O Gott, du frommer Gott 198
Steadfast 86

7.3.7.3. with Refrain
Let us break bread   288

7.6.7.6.
Mein Leben   373

7.6.7.6. with Refrain
Royal Oak   478

7.6.7.6.D.
Angel's Story   218
Aurelia   260
Ave virgo virginum   186
Du meine Seele, singe   189
Durrow   248
Ewing   309
Far-Off Lands   484
Greenland   190
Lancashire   192, 375
Llangloffan   436
Meirionydd   426
Munich   252
Nyland   343
Passion Chorale   170
Rockport   105
St. Hilda   329
St. Kevin   185
St. Theodulph   155
Webb   305, 385
Whitford   315

7.6.7.6.D. with Refrain
Hankey   317
Wir pflügen   460

7.6.7.6.6.7.6.
Es ist ein' Ros'   131

7.6.8.6.D.
Alford   311

7.6.8.6.8.6.8.6.
St. Christopher   160, 161

7.7.6.7.7.8.
Innsbruck   53

7.7.7.6.
Swedish Litany   166
Ton-mân   167

7.7.7.7.
Buckland   236
Chinese Melody   71
Freuen wir uns all in ein   579
Gott sei Dank   75
Heinlein   148
Innocents   33, 70, 416
Mercy   242
Monkland   463

Puer nobis   142
Savannah   458, 525
Song 13   162
Vienna   243, 301, 404

7.7.7.7. with Alleluias
Christ ist erstanden   183
Easter Hymn   182, 582
Gwalchmai   65, 205
Llanfair   19, 187

7.7.7.7. with Refrain
Gloria   116

7.7.7.7.4. with Refrain
Chautauqua   45

7.7.7.7.5.7.6.7.
Finlay   27
Rock of Ages   26

7.7.7.7.7.7.
Arfon   174
Dix   66, 119, 464
Nicht so traurig   281
Pilot   213
Ratisbon   43
Redhead No. 76   158, 245, 359
Toplady   358

7.7.7.7.D.
Aberystwyth   109, 211
Ives   425
Martyn   210
St. George's Windsor   461, 462
Salzburg   69, 308

7.7.7.7.D. with Refrain
Mendelssohn   120

7.8.7.8.7.7.
Grosser Gott, wir loben dich   247

7.8.7.8.8.8.
Liebster Jesu   212, 253, 279

8.3.3.6.D.
Warum sollt ich   123

8.4.7.D.
Veni, anima mea   506

8.4.8.4.8.4.
Wentworth   98

8.4.8.4.8.8.8.4.
Ar hyd y nos   58

8.6.
Duke's Tune   541

8.6.8.6.7.6.8.6.
St. Louis   134

8.6.8.6.8.6.
Morning Song   34, 420

8.6.8.6.8.8.
O Jesu   92

8.6.8.6.8.8.8.6.
The Staff of Faith   381

8.6.8.8.6.
Lobt Gott ihr Christen   492
Rest   341

8.7.7.7.7.7.
Wir glauben all' an einen Gott   250

8.7.8.7.
Alta Trinita beata   540
Dominus regit me   79
Galilee   322
Gott des Himmels   323
Omni Die   539
Rathbun   157
Regensburg   368
Ringe recht   332
St. Columba   80
Stuttgart   100, 103
Wellesley   102

8.7.8.7. with Refrain
Greensleeves   140

8.7.8.7.3.3.7.
Meine Hoffnung   339

8.7.8.7.4.4.8.8.
Was Gott tut   96

8.7.8.7.4.7.
Bryn Calfaria   291
Coronae   203

8.7.8.7.6.6.6.6.7.
Ein' feste Burg   363

8.7.8.7.7.7.
Unser Herrscher   503

8.7.8.7.8.6.8.7.
Vesper Hymn   52

8.7.8.7.7.7.8.8.
Magyar   377
Psalm 42   104

8.7.8.7.8.7.
Dulce carmen 344
Picardy 107
Praise my soul 16
Regent Square 117, 263
Rhuddlan 435
Sicilian Mariners 63, 277

8.7.8.7.8.7.7.
Cwm Rhondda 93, 366
Divinum mysterium 111

8.7.8.7.D.
Alta Trinita beata 403
Austrian Hymn 267, 268, 439
Beecher 228
Bishopgarth 355
Blaenhafren 427
Bradbury 327
Ebenezer 441
Erie 335
Hyfrydol 13
Hymn to Joy 8
In Babilone 74, 101
Llansannan 316, 424
Pleading Savior 409
St. Asaph 387
Was mein Gott will 354
Weisse Flaggen 180, 413

8.7.8.7.8.8.7.
Allein Gott in der Höh' 2
Mit Freuden zart 20, 325
Nun freut euch 271, 442

8.7.8.7.8.8.7.7.
Ermuntre dich 118

8.7.8.8.7.
Llanherne 73

8.8.4.4.8.8. with Alleluias
Lasst uns erfreuen 12, 30, 64

8.8.7.7.
Mon Dieu, prête-moi l'oreille 519

8.8.7.D.
Alles ist an Gottes Segen 112

8.8.7.8.8.7.D.
Psalm 36 577

8.8.7.8.8.7.4.8.4.8.
Wie schön leuchtet 145

8.8.7.8.8.7.8.4.4.8.
Wie schön leuchtet 244

8.8.8.
O mensch sieh 262
Wulfrun 527

8.8.8. with Alleluias
Gelobt sei Gott 184, 469
O filii et filiae 191
Victory 181

8.8.8.5.
Jacob's Ladder 495

8.8.8.6.
Childhood 480

8.8.8.6. with Refrain
Kings of Orient 143

8.8.8.8.6.
St. Margaret 399

8.8.8.8.
O Jesulein süss 135

8.8.8.8.8.8.
Aus Gnaden soll ich 499
Folkingham 431
Gottlob, es geht 468, 542
Melita 429
St. Catherine 365
Vater unser 44
Veni Emmanuel 110

8.8.8.8.8.8.8.
Kirken den er et 270

8.8.10.10.
Vi lofve dig, o store Gud 28

8.9.8.8.9.8.6.6.4.8.8.
Wachet auf 24, 108

9.8.8.9.
God be with you 62
Randolph 61

9.8.9.8.
Eucharistic Hymn 283
Les Commandemens de Dieu 47
St. Clement 48

9.8.9.8.8.8.
Neumark 83

9.8.9.8.D.
Rendez à Dieu 282, 289, 508

10.4.10.4.10.10.
Lux benigna 215
Sandon 97, 216

10.7.8.8.7.7.
Rocking 482

10.8.10.8.8.8.4.4.
Lobe den Herren, O meine Seele 17

10.10.9.10.
Slane 391

10.10.10. with Alleluia
Engelberg 147

10.10.10.4.
Sarum 307
Sine nomine 306

10.10.10.6.
Genevan Psalm 22 408
Peace 578

10.10.10.10.
Adoro te 557
Ainsworth 97 502
Ellers 60
Eventide 209
Field 421
Ffigysbren 219
Langran 287, 376
Morecambe 232
National Hymn 433
O quanta qualia 310
Song 24 207, 386
Sursum corda 286
Toulon 432, 470
Woodlands 156, 352

10.10.10.10.10.
Old 124th 451

10.10.10.10.10.10.
Finlandia 77, 494
Song 1 275, 292
Yorkshire 127, 304

10.10.11.11.
Hanover 206, 584
Lyons 6

10.11.11.12.
Slane 217

11.10.11.9.
Russian Hymn 446

11.10.11.10.

Ancient of Days 249
Consolation 37
Cushman 152
Donne secours 334, 398
Intercessor 410
Lombard Street 422
L'Omnipotent 467
Morning Star 126
O Perfect Love 465
Psalm 80 168
Welwyn 411, 471
Zu meinem Herrn 173

11.10.11.10. with Refrain

Tidings 302

11.10.11.10.10.

Langham 445
Peek 489

11.11.11.5.

Christe sanctorum 41
Cloisters 379

Diva servatrix 59
Herzliebster Jesu 163
Integer vitae 333
Iste Confessor 378

11.11.11.11.

Adeste fideles 372
Away in a manger 137
St. Denio 7

11.12.12.10.

Nicaea 251

12.10.12.10.

Monsell 31

12.11.12.11.

Kremser 21, 22

13.10.11.10.

Lynne 491

14.14.4.7.8.

Lobe den Herren 15

IRREGULAR

Adeste fideles 132
Battle Hymn of the Republic 443
Bring a torch 124
Cranham 128
Go down Moses 428
Go tell it on the mountain 488
God be in my head 543
Grand Isle 481
I want to be a Christian 353
In dulci jubilo 125
Lytlington 393
Margaret 326
Purpose 298
Remember the Poor 417
Star-Spangled Banner 496
Stille Nacht 138
Sweet Story 483
Tana mana dhana 394
Were you there 179

IRREGULAR WITH REFRAIN

God rest you merry 122
The First Nowell 141

Alphabetical Index of Tunes

Abbey 313
Aberystwyth 109, 211
Ach bleib bei uns 54
Ach Gott und Herr 476
Adeste fideles (Portuguese Hymn) 132, 133, 372
Adoro te 557
Ainsworth 97 502
Albany (*See* Ancient of Days)
Alford 311
All morgen ist 498
All Saints New 388
Allein Gott in der Höh' 2
Alles ist an Gottes Segen 112
Alta Trinita beata 403, 540
America 437
Ancient of Days (Albany) 249
Angelic Songs (*See* Tidings)
Angel's Story 218
Angelus 55
Antioch 130
Ar hyd y nos 58
Arfon 174
Arnsberg (Gröningen, Wunderbarer König) 3
Arthur's Seat 380

Aurelia 260
Aus der Tiefe (*See* Heinlein)
Aus Gnaden soll ich 499
Austrian Hymn 267, 268, 439
Ave virgo virginum (Gaudeamus pariter) 186
Away in a manger 137
Azmon 223, 346

Bangor 149, 159, 284
Battle Hymn of the Republic 443
Batty (*See* Ringe recht)
Beatitudo 350
Beecher 228
Benedic anima mea (*See* Praise my soul)
Bethany 351
Bishopgarth 355
Bishopthorpe 274
Blaenhafren 427
Bohemian Brethren (*See* Mit Freuden zart)
Bonn (*See* Warum sollt ich)
Bourbon 558
Boylston 273
Bradbury 327

Bread of Life 254
Breslau 538
Bring a torch 124
Bryn Calfaria 291
Buckland 236
Bunessan 38

Caithness 349
Canonbury 46, 397
Canterbury (*See* Song 13)
Carlisle 25
Carol 129
Chautauqua 45
Childhood 480
Chinese Melody 71
Christ ist erstanden 183
Christe sanctorum 41
Christmas 362
Cloisters 379
Conditor alme 113
Consolation 37
Contrition 580
Corde natus (*See* Divinum mysterium)
Corinth (*See* Dulce carmen)
Coronae 203
Coronation 195, 581
Cranham 128

Crasselius (*See* Winchester New)
Creation 72
Crimond 84
Croft's 136th 229
Crusader's Hymn (*See* Schönster Herr Jesu)
Cushman 152
Cwm Rhondda 93, 366

Danby 455
Darwall's 148th 23, 204
Das neugeborne Kindelein (Jena) 235
Das walt' Gott vater 231
Dawn 42
Dennis 76, 272
Deo Gracias (The Agincourt Song) 151
Deus tuorum militum 150, 453
Diademata 199, 384, 490
Diva servatrix 59
Divinum mysterium (Corde natus) 111
Dix 66, 119, 464
Dominus regit me 79
Donne secours 334, 398
Down Ampney 239
Dresden (*See* Wir pflügen)
Du meine Seele, singe 189
Duke Street 202, 297, 438
Duke's Tune 541
Dulce carmen (Corinth, Tantum ergo) 344
Dundee (French) 85, 87, 88, 389
Dunfermline 395
Durrow 248

Easter Hymn (Worgan) 182, 582
Ebeling (*See* Warum sollt ich)
Ebenezer (Ton-y-botel) 441
Ecumenical (*See* Sursum corda)
Ein' feste Burg 363
Eisenach 99, 276
Ellacombe 68, 459
Ellers 60
Elton 449
Engelberg 147
Erfurt (*See* Vom Himmel hoch)
Erie (What a Friend) 335
Ermuntre dich (Schop) 118
Es ist ein' Ros' 131
Es ist gewisslich (*See* Nun freut euch)
Eucharistic Hymn 283
Eudoxia 510
Eventide 209
Ewing 309

Far-Off Lands 484
Farrant 501
Federal Street 290, 402
Festal Song 300
Festgesang (*See* Mendelssohn)
Ffigysbren 219
Field 421
Finlandia 77, 494
Finlay 27
Folkingham 431
Forest Green 456, 457
Franconia 214
Frankfort (*See* Wie schön leuchtet)
French (*See* Dundee)
Freu dich sehr (*See* Psalm 42)
Freuen wir uns all in ein 579

Galilee 322
Gardiner (*See* Germany)
Gaudeamus pariter (*See* Ave virgo virginum)
Gelobt sei Gott 184, 469
Genevan Psalm 22 408
Georgetown 340
Germany (Gardiner, Walton) 423
Gethsemane (*See* Redhead No. 76)
Gloria (Iris) 116
Go down Moses 428
Go tell it on the mountain 488
God be in my head 543
God be with you 62
God rest you merry 122
Gott des Himmels 323
Gott sei Dank 75
Gottlob, es geht 468, 542
Gottschalk (*See* Mercy)
Grace Church 324
Graefenberg (*See* Nun danket all')
Grand Isle 481
Greenland 190
Greensleeves 140
Gröningen (*See* Arnsberg)
Grosser Gott, wir loben dich 247
Gwalchmai 65, 205

Halifax 294
Hamburg 177
Hankey (I love to tell the story) 317
Hanover 206, 584
Harewood 407
He leadeth me 370
Heinlein (Aus der Tiefe) 148
Hermann (*See* Lobt Gott ihr Christen)
Hermon 220

Herr Jesu Christ 521, 537
Herr Jesu Christ, mein's Lebens Licht 67
Herzlich tut mich verlangen (*See* Passion Chorale)
Herzliebster Jesu 163
Hesperus (Quebec) 447
Hilariter 194
Holy Night (*See* Stille Nacht)
Horsley 171
Hsuan p'ing 487
Hummel 369
Hursley 50
Hyfrydol 13
Hymn to Joy 8

I love to tell the story (*See* Hankey)
I want to be a Christian 353
Ich halte treulich still 337
In Babilone 74, 101
In dulci jubilo 125
Innocents 33, 70, 416
Innsbruck (Nun ruhen alle Wälder) 53
Integer vitae 333
Intercessor 410
Iris (*See* Gloria)
Iste Confessor (Rouen) 378
Italian Hymn (Moscow, Trinity) 246, 295, 472
Ives 425

Jacob's Ladder 495
Jam lucis 507
Jena (*See* Das neugeborne Kindelein)
Jesu, meine Freude 222
Joanna (*See* St. Denio)
Judas Maccabeus 193

Kedron 165
Kings of Orient 143
King's Weston 197
Kingsfold 412
Kirken den er et 270
Kremser 21, 22

Lancashire 192, 375
Land of Rest 312
Langham 445
Langran 287, 376
Lasst uns erfreuen (Vigiles et sancti) 12, 30, 64
Laudes Domini 35
Leoni (Yigdal) 14
Le p'ing 486
Les Commandemens de Dieu 47
Let us break bread 288
Liebster Jesu 212, 253, 279
Little Cornard 106
Llanfair 19, 187

Llangloffan 436
Llanherne 73
Llanllyfni 356
Llansannan 316, 424
Lobe den Herren 15
Lobe den Herren, O meine Seele 17
Lobt Gott ihr Christen (Hermann) 492
Lombard Street 422
L'Omnipotent 467
Louvan 90
Lovely (*See* Rhosymedre)
Love's Offering 405
Luther's Hymn (*See* Nun freut euch)
Lux benigna 215
Lynne 491
Lyons 6
Lytlington 393

Mach's mit mir, Gott 500
Magyar 377
Margaret 326
Marion 345
Martyn 210
Martyrdom 285, 390
Maryton 418
Materna 440
McKee 415
Meditation 172
Mein Leben (Vulpius) 373
Meine Hoffnung 339
Meirionydd 426
Melcombe 36, 299
Melita 429
Melrose 434
Mendelssohn (Festgesang) 120
Mendon 238, 477
Mercy (Gottschalk) 242
Merrial 51
Miles Lane 196
Mit Freuden zart (Bohemian Brethren) 20, 325
Mon Dieu, prête-moi l'oreille 519
Monkland 463
Monsell 31
More love to thee 400
Morecambe 232
Morning Hymn 32, 406
Morning Light (*See* Webb)
Morning Song 34, 420
Morning Star 126
Mornington 401
Moscow (*See* Italian Hymn)
Munich 252

National Hymn 433
Need 342
Neumark 83
Nicaea 251

Nicht so traurig 281
Nun danket 29
Nun danket all' (Graefenberg) 241, 256, 504
Nun freut euch (Es ist gewisslich, Luther's Hymn) 271, 442
Nun ruhen alle Wälder (*See* Innsbruck)
Nunc dimittis 49
Nyland 343

O filii et filiae 191
O Gott, du frommer Gott 198
O Jesu 92
O Jesu Christe, wahres Licht 208
O Jesulein süss 135
O mensch sieh 262
O Perfect Love 465
O quanta qualia (Regnator orbis) 310
Old 22nd 259, 419, 505
Old Hundredth 4, 5, 11, 514, 515
Old 124th 451
Old 134th (*See* St. Michael)
Olive's Brow 178
Olivet 348
Omni Die 539
Onslow 479
Ora labora 293

Palestrina (*See* Victory)
Park Street 10
Passion Chorale 170
Peace 578
Peek 489
Penitence 374
Pentecost 367
Personent hodie (Theodoric) 136
Petra (*See* Redhead No. 76)
Picardy 107
Pilot 213
Pleading Savior 409
Portuguese Hymn (*See* Adeste fideles)
Potsdam 233
Praise my soul (Benedic anima mea) 16
Psalm 36 577
Psalm 42 (Freu dich sehr, O meine Seele) 104
Psalm 80 168
Puer nobis 142
Puer nobis nascitur 39, 144, 188
Purpose 298

Quebec (*See* Hesperus)

Ramwold 303
Randolph 61
Rathbun 157
Ratisbon 43
Ravenshaw 258
Redhead No. 76 (Gethsemane, Petra, St. Prisca) 158, 245, 359
Regensburg 368
Regent Square 117, 263
Regnator orbis (*See* O quanta qualia)
Remember the Poor 417
Rendez à Dieu 282, 289, 508
Rest (Whittier) 341
Rhosymedre (Lovely) 169, 466
Rhuddlan 435
Richmond 261
Ringe recht (Batty) 332
Rock of Ages 26
Rocking 482
Rockingham 357
Rockport 105
Rouen (*See* Iste Confessor)
Royal Oak 478
Russian Hymn 446

St. Agnes 225, 240
St. Andrew of Crete 364
St. Anne 1, 264, 583
St. Asaph 387
St. Bernard 347
St. Bride 338
St. Catherine 365
St. Cecilia 448
St. Christopher 160, 161
St. Clement 48
St. Columba 80
St. Crispin 320
St. Cross 164
St. Denio (Joanna) 7
St. Drostane 175
St. Dunstan's 371
St. Edith (*See* St. Hilda)
St. Edmund 318
St. Flavian 153, 280
St. George's Windsor 461, 462
St. Gertrude 382, 383
St. Hilda (St. Edith) 329
St. James 266
St. Kevin 185
St. Louis 134
St. Magnus 78, 200
St. Margaret 399
St. Mary 497
St. Matthias (*See* Song 67)
St. Michael (Old 134th) 237, 444
St. Peter 221, 414
St. Prisca (*See* Redhead No. 76)

St. Stephen   201, 321
St. Theodulph (Valet will ich dir geben)   155
St. Thomas (Williams)   269
Salzburg   69, 308
Sandon   97, 216
Sarum   307
Savannah   458, 525
Saxby   392
Schönster Herr Jesu (Crusader's Hymn)   227
Schop (*See* Ermuntre dich)
Serenity   230
Serug   265
Shepherds' Pipes   328
Sicilian Mariners   63, 277
Sine nomine   306
Slane   217, 391
Sleepers, wake (*See* Wachet auf)
Something for Jesus   331
Song 1   275, 292
Song 5   509
Song 13 (Canterbury)   162
Song 24   207, 386
Song 67 (St. Matthias)   336, 360
Southwell   314, 361
Splendor Paternae   40
Star-Spangled Banner   496
Steadfast   86
Stille Nacht (Holy Night)   138, 139
Stockport (*See* Yorkshire)
Stracathro   255
Stuttgart   100, 103
Sursum corda (Ecumenical)   286
Swedish Litany   166
Sweet Story   483

Tallis' Canon   56, 57, 91
Tallis' Ordinal   18, 94

Tana mana dhana   394
Tantum ergo (*See* Dulce carmen)
Tender Thought   576
Terra beata   485
The Agincourt Song (*See* Deo Gracias)
The First Nowell   141
The King's Majesty   176
The Staff of Faith   381
Theodoric (*See* Personent hodie)
Tidings (Angelic Songs)   302
Ton-mân   167
Ton-y-botel (*See* Ebenezer)
Toplady   358
Toulon   432, 470
Trentham   234
Trinity (*See* Italian Hymn)
Truro   82, 114, 450, 454

Uffingham   89, 452
Unser Herrscher   503
Uxbridge   257

Valet will ich dir geben (*See* St. Theodulph)
Vater unser   44
Veni, anima mea   506
Veni Creator   575
Veni Emmanuel   110
Vesper Hymn   52
Vi lofve dig, O store Gud   28
Victory (Palestrina)   181
Vienna   243, 301, 404
Vigiles et sancti (*See* Lasst uns erfreuen)
Vom Himmel hoch (Erfurt)   121, 278
Vulpius (*See* Mein Leben)

Wachet auf   24, 108
Walsall   154, 224

Waltham   296
Walton (*See* Germany)
Wareham   430, 475
Warum sollt ich (Bonn, Ebeling)   123
Was Gott tut   96
Was mein Gott will   354
Webb (Morning Light)   305, 385
Weisse Flaggen   180, 413
Wellesley   102
Wellington Square   493
Welsh Melody   526
Welwyn   411, 471
Wentworth   98
Were you there   179
What a Friend (*See* Erie)
Whitford   315
Whittier (*See* Rest)
Wie schön leuchtet (Frankfort)   145, 244
Wigtown   330, 396, 530
Wiltshire   81
Winchester New (Crasselius)   9, 115
Winchester Old   146
Windsor   226
Wir glauben all' an einen Gott   250
Wir pflügen (Dresden)   460
Woodlands   156, 352
Woodworth   319
Worgan (*See* Easter Hymn)
Wulfrun   527
Wunderbarer König (*See* Arnsberg)

Yattendon 46   535
Yigdal (*See* Leoni)
York   95, 473, 474
Yorkshire (Stockport)   127, 304

Zu meinem Herrn   173

Topical Index

ADORATION AND PRAISE 1–31

All creatures of our God 64
Ancient of Days 249
Angels holy 73
As the sun 33
Before Jehovah's 9, 10
Come, thou almighty 246
Father, we praise thee 41
Fill thou my life 396
For the beauty 66
Glory be to God 65
Heaven and earth 75
Holy God, we praise 247
Holy, holy, holy 251
I sing the mighty 68
Let the whole creation 69
Let us with a gladsome 70, 71
Lift up your hearts 189, 190
Look, ye saints 203
Morning has broken 38
O Lord, almighty God 473, 474
O my soul, bless God 100
Rejoice, the Lord 204
Rejoice, ye pure 345
The spacious firmament 72
When morning gilds 35
With songs and honors 459
Ye servants of God 206

ADVENT
(See JESUS CHRIST: Advent)

ALL SAINTS' DAY — ALL SOULS' DAY

For all the saints 306, 307
For the brave 308
O what their joy 310
Ten thousand times 311

AMERICA
(See NATION)

ANNIVERSARIES
(See CHURCH: Anniversaries and Dedications)

ANXIETY
(See PILGRIMAGE AND CONFLICT)

ARMED FORCES
(See NATION)

ARMISTICE DAY
(See NATION; PEACE: World)

ASCENSION
(See JESUS CHRIST: Ascension and Reign)

ASH WEDNESDAY
(See also LENT)

Christian, dost thou 364
Lord Jesus, think on me 314

ASPIRATION
(See FAITH AND ASPIRATION)

ASSURANCE
(See also FAITH AND ASPIRATION; HOPE, JOY, PEACE; TRUST)

A mighty fortress 363
Abide with me 209
Beneath the cross 160
Give to the winds 337, 338
God of our life 97
He leadeth me 370
How firm a foundation 372
I know not how 149
I to the hills 85
In heavenly love 343
Our God, our help 1

AUTUMN
(See SEASONS: Changing)

BAPTISM
(See CHURCH: Baptism)

BEAUTY

All beautiful the march 456
All things bright 478
Fairest Lord Jesus 227
For the beauty 66
Our God, to whom 86

BEGINNING OF WORSHIP
(See also ADORATION AND PRAISE; MORNING; EVENING; PROCESSIONAL HYMNS)

Come, let us join 346
High in the heavens 82
Jesus, where'er thy 402

Now let every tongue 24
O God, we praise thee 18
Praise thou the Lord 17
Through all the changing 81
Unto thy temple, Lord 276
We gather together 21
We praise thee, O God 22
Worship the Lord 31

BIBLE 252–259

How firm a foundation 372

BROTHERHOOD AND SERVICE 409–423
(See also PEACE: World; RACE RELATIONS; SOCIAL JUSTICE)

Awake, awake, to love 34
God is working 298
Lord, we thank thee 268
Master, no offering 405
Men, whose boast 425
Rise up, O men 300
The voice of God 426
We bear the strain 220
We would be building 494

CAROLS
(See CHRISTMAS CAROLS; EASTER CAROLS)

CHANGING SEASONS
(See SEASONS: Changing)

CHILDREN'S HYMNS 478–487

All creatures of our God 64
Fairest Lord Jesus 227
For the beauty 66
I would be true 489
Joy dawned again 188
Let us with a gladsome 70, 71
Lord, I want to be 353
O Jesu sweet 135
Savior, like a shepherd 327
We would see Jesus 152

CHRIST
(See JESUS CHRIST)

575

TOPICAL INDEX

CHRISTMAS

(See CHRISTMAS CAROLS;
JESUS CHRIST: Birth and Infancy)

CHRISTMAS CAROLS

All my heart 123
Angels we have heard 116
Away in a manger 137
Bring a torch 124
God rest you merry 122
Good Christian men 125
It came upon 129
Little Jesus, sweetly 482
On this day earth 136
Silent night 138, 139
The first Nowell 141
Unto us a boy is born 142
We three kings 143
What child is this 140

CHURCH

Anniversaries and Dedications 472-477

Built on the Rock 270
Christ is made 263
City of God 261
God of grace 366
God of our fathers, whose
433
God of our life 97
Jesus, where'er thy 402
Jesus, with thy 301
O God, above the 297
O God, beneath thy 438
O God of Bethel 389
O where are kings 264
Our God, our help 1
Spirit divine, attend 241
The Church's one 260
We come unto 271

Baptism 277-279

I think when I read 483
Now thank we all 29

Communion of Saints
306-312

Ecumenical

Christ is made 263
Forgive, O Lord 262
Hope of the world 398
O God, within whose 265
The Church's one 260

Fellowship 271-276

Forward through 383
I love thy kingdom 269
Spirit divine 241

Lord's Supper 280-292

Blest be the tie 272, 273
Break thou the bread 254
Breathe on me 233, 234
Let all mortal flesh 107
The King of love 79, 80

Mission in the World
293-305

Christ is the world's 198
Forward through 383
God of grace 366
Hills of the North 106
In Christ there is 414, 415
Jesus shall reign 202
Lord God of hosts 411
Lord of, our life 378, 379
O Word of God incarnate 252
One holy Church of God 266
Onward, Christian soldiers
382
Remember all the people 484
Soldiers of Christ 384

Nature and Unity
260-270

Christ is the world's 198
Come, let us join 346
Father, we thank thee 289
Rejoice, O people 304
We all believe 250

Worship and Prayer

Again, as evening's 46
All people that 4, 5
As the sun 33
Blessed Jesus, at thy 212
Built on the Rock 270
Father, we praise thee 41
From all that dwell 11, 12
Praise to the Lord 15
The day thou gavest 47, 48
Unto thy temple, Lord 276
We worship thee 28
Worship the Lord 31
Ye holy angels bright 23

CITY

The voice of God 426
When through the whirl 422
Where cross the crowded 423

CITY OF GOD

Hail the glorious 424
O holy city, seen 420

CLOSE OF WORSHIP
60-63

(See also RECESSIONAL
HYMNS)

Blest be the tie 272, 273
Father almighty, bless 333

COMFORT

I look to thee 92
In the cross of Christ 157
Lift thy head, O Zion 377
Rock of ages 358, 359
Still, still with thee 37

COMMENCEMENT

(See TRUTH; YOUTH)

COMMISSIONING

(See INSTALLATIONS)

COMMITMENT

(See CONSECRATION; DI-
SCIPLESHIP)

COMMUNION, HOLY

(See CHURCH: Lord's Supper)

COMMUNION OF
SAINTS

(See CHURCH: Communion
of Saints)

CONFESSION

(See PENITENCE)

CONFIDENCE

(See ASSURANCE; HOPE, JOY,
PEACE; TRUST)

CONFIRMATION

(See also YOUTH)

God be in my head 393
Gracious Spirit, dwell 245
He who would valiant 371
O God of youth 491
O Jesus, I have promised 218
O Master Workman 412

CONFLICT

(See PILGRIMAGE AND CON-
FLICT)

CONSECRATION 394-408

(See also STEWARDSHIP)

Christian, rise 416
Dear Lord and Father 341
Eternal God 294
Eternal Ruler 275
Faith of our fathers 365
I sing a song 481
I would be true 489
Jesus, Friend, so kind 277
Just as I am 319, 320
Lead, kindly Light 215, 216
Lift up your heads 114
Now in the days 490
O thou by whom we come
336

576

We are living 427
When I survey 177
When Stephen, full 493

CONSOLATION
(See COMFORT)

CONSTANCY
He who would valiant 371
How firm a foundation 372

CONTRITION
(See PENITENCE)

COURAGE
A mighty fortress 363
Christian, dost thou 364
Father, hear 368
Fight the good fight 367
Give to the winds 337, 338
God is my strong 373
God moves in a 87, 88
God of grace 366
God's glory is 369
He who would valiant 371
Lead on, O King 375
Lord God of hosts 411
March on, O soul 380
Men, whose boast 425
My faith, it is 381
Soldiers of Christ 384
Stand up, stand up 385
The day of the Lord 417
When Stephen, full 493

CREATION
(See GOD: Works in Creation)

CROSS
(See JESUS CHRIST: Passion and Cross)

DEDICATION
(See CHURCH: Anniversaries and Dedications)

DEDICATION OF LIFE
(See CONSECRATION; DISCIPLESHIP)

DEMOCRACY
(See NATION)

DISCIPLESHIP
Come, labor on 293
O Lord and Master 224

DUTIES, COMMON
Awake, my soul, and with 32
Behold us, Lord 395
Forth in thy name 406
Jesus, thou divine 409
Lord of all hopefulness 217
New every morning 36
Teach me, my God 401

EASTER
(See JESUS CHRIST: Resurrection)

EASTER CAROLS
Good Christian men rejoice 184
Joy dawned again 188
The whole bright world 194

ECUMENICAL
(See CHURCH: Ecumenical)

EDUCATION
(See TRUTH; YOUTH)

EPIPHANY
(See JESUS CHRIST: Epiphany)

ETERNAL LIFE
(See also CHURCH: Communion of Saints; FUNERAL SERVICES; JESUS CHRIST: Resurrection)
Be still, my soul 77
God of the living 468
Jerusalem the golden 309
O Lord of life, where'er 469
O Love that wilt not 399
Still, still with thee 37
Through the night 387
Within the maddening maze 360

EVANGELISM
(See CHURCH: Mission in the World; GOSPEL CALL AND RESPONSE)

EVENING 44–59
Abide with me 209
God be with you 61, 62
Savior, again to thy 60

FAITH AND ASPIRATION 346–361
(See also ASSURANCE; TRUST)
As pants the hart 390
Awake, my soul, stretch 362

Before the cross 161
Blest are the pure 214
Breathe on me 233, 234
Come down, O Love 239
Come, gracious Spirit 238
Come, Holy Spirit 235
Dear Master, in whose 208
Draw thou my soul 318
Faith of our fathers 365
Fill thou my life 396
Holy Spirit, Truth 242, 243
I need thee every hour 342
Lead us, O Father 376
Lighten the darkness 386
Lord Jesus, think on me 314
Lord of all being 89, 90
My faith, it is 381
O Holy Spirit, enter in 244
O how glorious 74
O Light that knew 407
O Morning Star 145
Our God, to whom 86
Spirit of God, descend 232
Thou God of all 419
We limit not the truth 259

FAITHFULNESS
(See CONSTANCY)

FAMILY
(See MARRIAGE AND THE FAMILY)

FELLOWSHIP
(See CHURCH: Fellowship)

FOREFATHERS' DAY
Faith of our fathers 365
For the brave 308
God of our fathers, whose 433
Life of ages, richly 236
My country, 'tis 437
Not alone for mighty 439
Now praise we great 476
O beautiful for spacious 440
O God, above the 297
O God, beneath thy 438
Rejoice, O people 304
We come unto 271

FOREIGN MISSIONS
(See CHURCH: Mission in the World)

FORGIVENESS
(See also GOD: Love of; JESUS CHRIST: Friend; Love of)
Lord, as to thy 347
O word of pity 173

FREEDOM, SPIRITUAL

Make me a captive 356
Men, whose boast 425

FUNERAL SERVICES
467–469
(*See also* CHURCH: Communion of Saints; ETERNAL LIFE)

Abide with me 209
For all the saints 306, 307
God of our life 97
In heavenly love 343
Jesus, lover of my 210, 211
Lead, kindly Light 215, 216
O what their joy 310
Ten thousand times 311
The King of love 79, 80

GOD

Creator
(*See* GOD: Works in Creation)

Eternity and Power
Before Jehovah's 9, 10
Glorious things 267
God is working 298
I sing the mighty 68
Immortal, invisible 7
O God, thou art 248
O worship the King 6
Our God, to whom 86
The God of Abraham 14

Fatherhood of
(*See* GOD: Love of)

Glory of
God is working 298
Lord of all being 89, 90
O how glorious 74
O worship the King 6

Goodness of
All glory be to God 2
All my hope on God 339
All people that 4, 5
Give to the winds 337, 338
God of earth and sea 316
Great God, we sing 454
High in the heavens 82
How gentle God's 76
My God, I thank thee 98
Now thank we all 29
O be joyful 26, 27
Praise, O praise our 463
The Lord is rich 328

Grace of 98–102
God of grace 366
High in the heavens 82
Life of ages, richly 236

Guidance of
Come, gracious Spirit 238
Eternal Ruler 275
Father eternal 445
Father, hear 368
Father in heaven 392
God of our fathers, whose 433
God of our life 97
God of the nations 432
Guide me, O thou 93
He leadeth me 370
If thou but suffer 83
Lead, kindly Light 215, 216
Lead on, O King 375
Lead us, heavenly Father 344
Lead us, O Father 376
Lighten the darkness 386
The Lord's my shepherd 84
We gather together 21
We praise thee, O God 22

Judge
God of our fathers, known 431
Judge eternal, throned 435
Mine eyes have seen 443
O Day of God, draw 444
The day of the Lord 417
Thou Judge by whom 442

Justice of
(*See* GOD: Righteousness of)

King
(*See* GOD: Majesty of)

Kingdom of
Ah! think not 112
Creation's Lord 303
Father eternal 445
Rejoice, O people 304
The Lord will come 95
Thou God of all 419
Thy kingdom come 448

Light of
(*See* GOD: Guidance of)

Love of
Father almighty, bless 333
If thou but suffer 83
Let us with a gladsome 70, 71
O God, thou art 248
O Love of God, how 99
O Love that wilt not 399
O my soul, bless God 100
Praise, my soul 16
Praise to God, immortal 464
Praise to the Lord 15
There's a wideness 101, 102
When all thy mercies 94

Love to
My God, I love thee 313
Sing praise to God 20
Take my life 404

Majesty of
Ancient of Days 249
Before Jehovah's 9, 10
Come, thou almighty 246
Holy, holy, holy 251
Immortal, invisible 7
Let the whole creation 69
O God we praise thee 18
O worship the King 6
Praise, my soul 16
Praise the Lord, his 19
Praise thou the Lord 17
Praise to the Lord 15
Stand up and bless 25
The God of Abraham 14

Mercy of
(*See* GOD: Love of)

Peace of
(*See* PEACE: Inner)

Power of
(*See* GOD: Eternity and Power)

Presence of
God be with you 61, 62
God himself is with us 3
God of the earth 67
I look to thee 92
Nearer, my God 351
Still, still with thee 37
We thank thee, Lord 421

Providence of 76–97
Give to the winds 337, 338
God is working 298
Have faith in God 361
O God of Bethel 389
Our God, our help 1
Sing praise to God 20
This is my Father's 485
We plow the fields 460

Refuge of
(*See* GOD: Strength and Refuge)

Reign of
(*See* GOD: Kingdom of)

Righteousness of
God the Omnipotent 446
God's glory is 369
O God of earth 436
O Lord, almighty God 473, 474
The Lord will come 95

Strength and Refuge

A mighty fortress 363
As pants the hart 390
Eternal Father 429
Father, hear 368
Father, in thy 334
God is my strong 373
Hast thou not known 78
I look to thee 92
I to the hills 85
In heavenly love 343
Lift thy head, O Zion 377
Now God be with us 59
O Lord of life, where'er 469
Our God, our help 1
The Lord's my shepherd 84
The man who once 91
Through all the changing 81
We come unto 271
Whate'er my God ordains 96
Who trusts in God 354, 355

Works in Creation
64–75

All beautiful the march 456
All things bright 478
Creation's Lord 303
God of earth and sea 316
Joyful, joyful 8
Morning has broken 38
O Lord, almighty God 473, 474
Praise, O praise 463
Praise the Lord, ye 13
Praise thou the Lord 17
Praise to God, your 458
The heavens declare 257
This is my Father's 485
We plow the fields 460
With songs and honors 459

GOOD FRIDAY
(See also JESUS CHRIST: Passion and Cross; LENT)

Go to dark 158
Jesus, in thy dying 166, 167
My song is love 169
O come and mourn 164
Sunset to sunrise 165
There is a green hill 171, 172
Throned upon the 174
'Tis midnight, and 178
When I survey 177
When my love to God 162

GOSPEL CALL AND RESPONSE 313–331

Before the cross 161
Christ for the world 295
Christian, rise 416
Come, labor on 293

Fill thou my life 396
Go, tell it 488
I sought the Lord 408
Lord, speak to me 397
My faith looks up 348
O Jesus, I have promised 218
O Lord and Master 224
O Master, let me walk 418
Son of God, eternal 413
Spirit of God, descend 232
Take my life 404
The Son of God goes 388
The voice of God 426
We bear the strain 220
What a friend 335
Where cross the crowded 423

GRACE
(See GOD: Grace of)

GRATITUDE
(See also SEASONS: Thanksgiving)

For the beauty 66
My God, I thank thee 98
O be joyful 26, 27
O gracious God, whose 492
When all thy mercies 94

GRIEF
(See ASSURANCE; COMFORT)

GUIDANCE
(See GOD: Guidance of; HOLY SPIRIT; JESUS CHRIST: Guide and Leader; Presence and Guidance)

HARVEST
(See SEASONS: Thanksgiving)

HEALING

At even, ere the sun 55
Immortal Love 230
My song is love 169
The Lord is rich 328

HERITAGE
(See FOREFATHERS' DAY)

HOLY SCRIPTURES
(See BIBLE)

HOLY SPIRIT 231–245

O Spirit of the living 299
O Splendor of God's 39, 40

HOME
(See MARRIAGE AND THE FAMILY)

HOME MISSIONS
(See CHURCH: Mission in the World)

HOPE, JOY, PEACE
337–345
(See also ASSURANCE; FAITH AND ASPIRATION; TRUST)

Hope of the world 398
Joyful, joyful 8
Lord of all hopefulness 217
Lord of our life 378, 379

HOSPITALS
(See HEALING)

HUMILITY

Blest are the pure 214
God of our fathers 431
Lord Christ, when first 325
Lord, enthroned in 291
Lord, thy mercy 332
O Light that knew 407
O thou by whom we come 336

IMMORTALITY
(See CHURCH: Communion of Saints; ETERNAL LIFE; FUNERAL SERVICES)

INDUSTRY
(See CITY; LABOR OR LABOR DAY)

INFANT BAPTISM
(See CHURCH: Baptism)

INSTALLATIONS

Gracious Spirit 245
Lord, speak to me 397
My God, accept my heart 321
O Master, let me walk 418

INTERCESSION
(See PRAYER)

INTERFAITH
(See also BROTHERHOOD AND SERVICE)

All people that 4, 5
Let the whole creation 69
O be joyful 26, 27

Our God, our help 1
The God of Abraham 14
Turn back, O man 451
We gather together 21

JESUS CHRIST

Advent 103–115

Christ is the world's 198
Christ, whose glory fills 43

Ascension and Reign
195–206

(*See also* JESUS CHRIST:
King)

Birth and Infancy
116–146

Go, tell it 488

Boyhood

I love to think 480
O Master Workman 412

Character and Glory
221–230

All praise to thee 147
I know not how 149
O love, how deep 150, 151
O Morning Star 145
Thou didst leave 326

Crucifixion

(*See* JESUS CHRIST: Passion
and Cross)

Epiphany

As with gladness 119
Brightest and best 126
Christ is the world's 198
Christ, whose glory 43
We three kings 143
What star is this 144

Example of

Jesus, thou divine 409
Lord, as to thy 347
O brother man, fold 410
O Lord and Master 224

Friend

Jesus, Friend, so kind 277
My song is love 169
O Jesus, I have promised 218
O thou great Friend 219

Guide and Leader

(*See also* JESUS CHRIST:
Presence and Guidance)

Be thou my vision 391
Dear Master, in whose 208
O Master Workman 412
Savior, like a shepherd 327

King

All hail the power 195, 196
At the name of Jesus 197
Crown him 199
Hail the day 205
Hail to the Lord's 105
Jesus shall reign 202
Joy to the world 130
Let all mortal flesh 107
Lift up your heads 114
Look, ye saints 203
On Jordan's bank 115
Rejoice, the Lord 204
The head that once 200

Life and Ministry
147–153

At even, ere the sun 55
I think when I read 483
Thou didst leave 326

Light

Christ is the world's 198
Christ, whose glory 43

Love of

I sought the Lord 408
Immortal Love 230
Lord Christ, when first 325
Love divine 228
My song is love 169
O love, how deep 150, 151
O sacred Head 170
Strong Son of God 357
When I survey 177

Love to

Heart and mind 394
Jesus, the very thought 225,
226
Master, no offering 405
More love to thee 400
Savior, thy dying love 331

Name of

At the name of Jesus 197
Creator of the stars 113
How sweet the name 221
Ye servants of God 206

Passion and Cross
154–179

In the hour of trial 374
Lord, as to thy 347
Lord Christ, when first 325

Praise to

All glory, laud 155
All hail the power 195, 196
All praise to thee 147
Angels, from the realms 117
Crown him 199
How sweet the name 221

Jesus shall reign 202
Join all the glorious 229
Joy to the world 130
Let all mortal flesh 107
Lord, enthroned in 291
Love divine 228
O for a thousand 223
O thou great Friend 219
Of the Father's love 111
When morning gilds 35
Ye servants of God 206

Presence and Guidance
207–220

Fight the good fight 367
For all the saints 306, 307
Immortal Love 230
Jesus, the very thought 225,
226
Jesus, thou joy 290
My faith looks up 348
Now cheer our hearts 54
O Master, let me walk 418
Sun of my soul 50
Those who love 403

Reign of

(*See* JESUS CHRIST: King)

Resurrection 180–194

Crown him 199
O love, how deep 150, 151

Savior

Come, thou long 103
Creator of the stars 113
Hail to the Lord's 105
Hope of the world 398
I greet thee, who 207
I know not how 149
I sought the Lord 408
Join all the glorious 229
Just as I am 319, 320
Lord, save thy world 452
My faith looks up 348
My song is love 169
O love of God, how 99
O thou to whose 324
On Jordan's bank 115
Rejoice, the Lord 204
Son of God, eternal 413
Sunset to sunrise 165

Second Coming

Ah! think not 112
Come, thou long 103
Come, ye thankful 461
The King shall come 201
When through the whirl 422

Shepherd

In heavenly love 343
The King of love 79, 80

TOPICAL INDEX

Strength and Refuge

Be still, my soul 77
Come unto me 315
Fight the good fight 367
He who would valiant 371
How firm a foundation 372
I greet thee, who 207
Jesus, lover of my 210, 211
Jesus, priceless treasure 222
Make me a captive 356
Rock of ages 358, 359
What a friend 335

Teacher

O Master, let me walk 418
O thou by whom we come 336

Triumphal Entry

All glory, laud 155
Draw nigh 156
Ride on, ride on 175, 176

JOY

(*See* HOPE, JOY, PEACE)

JUSTICE 424-428

(*See* GOD: Righteousness of; SOCIAL JUSTICE)

KINDNESS

(*See* GOD: Love of; JESUS CHRIST: Friend; Love of

KINGDOM OF GOD

(*See* GOD: Kingdom of)

LABOR OR LABOR DAY

Behold us, Lord 395
Creation's Lord 303
Forth in thy name 406
Jesus, thou divine 409
Those who love 403
When through the whirl 422

LAW

(*See* NATION)

LENT

(*See also* ASH WEDNESDAY; GOOD FRIDAY; JESUS CHRIST: Passion and Cross; PENITENCE)

Forty days 148
Lord, who throughout 153

LIBERTY

(*See* FREEDOM, SPIRITUAL)

LORD'S SUPPER

(*See* CHURCH: Lord's Supper)

LOVE

(*See* GOD: Love of; Love to; JESUS CHRIST: Love of; Love to)

LOYALTY

(*See* CONSTANCY; COURAGE)

MARRIAGE AND THE FAMILY 465-466

MEMORIAL DAY

(*See also* FOREFATHERS' DAY; NATION)

For the brave 308
O Lord of life, where'er 469

MINISTRY

(*See* ORDINATIONS)

MISSIONS

(*See* CHURCH: Mission in the World)

MORNING 32-43

Blessed Jesus, at thy 212
Holy, holy, holy 251

MOTHER'S DAY

(*See* MARRIAGE AND THE FAMILY)

NATION 429-443

Father in heaven 392
God the Omnipotent 446
O say can you see 496
Turn back, O man 451

NATIVITY

(*See* JESUS CHRIST: Birth and Infancy)

NATURE

(*See* GOD: Works in Creation)

NEW YEAR

(*See* SEASONS: New Year)

ORDINATIONS 470-471

God send us men 434
Life of ages, richly 236
Lift up your hearts 189, 190

PALM SUNDAY

(*See* JESUS CHRIST: Triumphal Entry)

PATRIOTISM

(*See* NATION)

PEACE

Inner

(*See also* HOPE, JOY, PEACE)

Dear Lord and Father 341
Father, in thy 334
God is my strong 373
Jesus, priceless treasure 222
O for a closer walk 349, 350
Savior, again to thy 60
They cast their nets 340

World 444-452

Christ is the world's 198
God of grace 366
God of our fathers, known 431
God of our fathers, whose 433
Lord Christ, when first 325
O brother man, fold 410
Send down thy truth 237
Thou God of all 419

PENITENCE

Ah, holy Jesus 163
Beneath the cross 160
Dear Lord and Father 341
Father eternal 445
Lord, thy mercy 332
O for a closer walk 349, 350
O God of earth 436
O Jesus, thou art 329
O thou to whose 324
Thou Judge by whom 442
When I survey 177

PENTECOST

(*See* CHURCH: Nature and Unity; HOLY SPIRIT)

PILGRIMAGE AND CONFLICT 362-389

Guide me, O thou 93
Lead us, heavenly Father 344
Lord, as to thy 347
Lord, save thy world 452
O Jesus, I have promised 218

PRAISE

(*See* ADORATION AND PRAISE)

PRAYER 332-336

(*See also* CHURCH: Worship and Prayer)

Behold us, Lord 395
Dear Lord and Father 341

Father, hear 368
Father in heaven 392
God be in my head 393
God, that madest earth 58
I need thee every hour 342
In the hour of trial 374
Lord, I want to be 353
Lord of our life 378, 379
Lord, speak to me 397
More love to thee 400
My faith looks up 348
Spirit of God, descend 232

**PROCESSIONAL
HYMNS**
A mighty fortress 363
All beautiful the march 456
All creatures of our God 64
All glory, laud 155
All hail the power 195, 196
All people that 4, 5
Ancient of Days 249
Angels, from the realms 117
Angels holy 73
As the sun 33
As with gladness 119
At the name of Jesus 197
Awake, my soul, and with 32
Awake, my soul, stretch 362
Christ is made 263
Christ, whose glory 43
Crown him 199
For the beauty 66
From all that dwell 11, 12
Glorious things 267
Glory be to God 65
God himself is with us 3
God of grace 366
God of our fathers, whose 433
Holy, holy, holy 251
How firm a foundation 372
I sing the mighty 68
Immortal, invisible 7
Jesus shall reign 202
Joyful, joyful 8
Let the whole creation 69
Look, ye saints 203
Love divine 228
Now thank we all 29
O be joyful 26, 27
O God, beneath thy 438
O how glorious 74
O worship the King 6
Onward, Christian soldiers
382
Our God, our help 1
Praise, my soul 16
Praise the Lord, his 19
Praise the Lord, ye 13
Praise to God, immortal 464
Praise to God, your 458
Praise to the Lord 15

Rejoice, O people 304
Rejoice, the Lord 204
Rejoice, ye pure 345
The Church's one 260
The God of Abraham 14
When morning gilds 35
Ye holy angels bright 23
Ye servants of God 206
Ye watchers and ye 30

PROPHETS
God of the prophets 470
Life of ages, richly 236

PROVIDENCE
(*See* GOD: Providence of)

PSALMS
(*See Authors, Translators
and Sources*, p. 559, for
hymns based on psalms)

RACE RELATIONS
(*See also* BROTHERHOOD AND
SERVICE; SOCIAL JUSTICE)
In Christ there is 414, 415
Not alone for mighty 439
O brother man, fold 410

RECESSIONAL HYMNS
Crown him 199
For all the saints 306, 307
Forth in thy name 406
Glorious things 267
God of grace 366
Guide me, O thou 93
How firm a foundation 372
I sing the mighty 68
In Christ there is 414, 415
Jesus shall reign 202
Lead on, O King 375
Lord, dismiss us 63
Love divine 228
March on, O soul 380
Now thank we all 29
Onward, Christian soldiers
382
Rejoice, the Lord 204
Rejoice, ye pure 345
Rise up, O men 300
Soldiers of Christ 384
The Church's one 260
Through the night 387
Turn back, O man 451

REFORMATION DAY
A mighty fortress 363
Book of books 253
I greet thee, who 207
Now thank we all 29
We come unto 271

RESIGNATION
Be still, my soul 77
O love that wilt not 399
Whate'er my God ordains 96

RESURRECTION
(*See* JESUS CHRIST: Resurrection)

RURAL
(*See also* GOD: Works in Crea-
tion; SEASONS: Changing;
Thanksgiving)
Awake, awake to love 34
Morning has broken 38

SACRAMENTS
(*See* CHURCH: Baptism;
Lord's Supper)

SAINTS
(*See also* CHURCH: Com-
munion of Saints)
I sing a song 481
When Stephen, full 493

**SCHOOLS AND
COLLEGES**
(*See* TRUTH; YOUTH)

SCIENCE
Eternal God 294

SCRIPTURES
(*See* BIBLE)

SEASONS
Changing 455–459
All things bright 478
Praise to God, immortal 464
We plow the fields 460

New Year 453–454
Awake, my soul, stretch 362
God is working 298
God of our life 97
Our God, our help 1
Rejoice, O people 304
Turn back, O man 451

Thanksgiving 460–464
(*See also* GRATITUDE)
Let us with a gladsome 70,
71
Not alone for mighty 439
Now thank we all 29
We gather together 21
We praise thee, O God 22

TOPICAL INDEX

SECURITY
(*See* GOD: Strength and Refuge; JESUS CHRIST: Strength and Refuge)

SERENITY
(*See* PEACE: Inner)

SERVICE
(*See* BROTHERHOOD AND SERVICE)

SIN
(*See* PENITENCE)

SOCIAL ACTION
(*See also* SOCIAL JUSTICE)
Creation's Lord   303
Men whose boast   425

SOCIAL JUSTICE
(*See also* BROTHERHOOD AND SERVICE; RACE RELATIONS; SOCIAL ACTION)
Father eternal   445
God send us men   434
Judge eternal, throned   435
Let there be light   449
Life of ages, richly   236
O beautiful for spacious   440
O Day of God, draw   444
O God of earth   436
O holy city, seen   420
Once to every man   441
Ring out, wild bells   453
The day of the Lord   417
Where cross the crowded   423

SORROW
(*See* COMFORT)

SPIRITUALS
Go, tell it   488
Let us break bread   288
Lord, I want to be   353
We are climbing Jacob's   495
Were you there   179
When Israel was   428

SPRING
(*See* SEASONS: Changing)

STEWARDSHIP
Awake, awake, to love   34
Forth in thy name   406
God of earth and sea   316
Master, no offering   405
Savior, thy dying love   331
Son of God, eternal   413
Take my life   404

SUFFERING
(*See* JESUS CHRIST: Passion and Cross; PILGRIMAGE AND CONFLICT)

SUMMER
(*See* SEASONS: Changing)

TEACHERS
(*See* CONSECRATION; TRUTH; YOUTH)

TEMPTATION
(*See* PILGRIMAGE AND CONFLICT)

THANKSGIVING
(*See* SEASONS: Thanksgiving)

TRAVELERS
Eternal Father   429
God be with you   61, 62
Jesus, Savior, pilot   213
My faith, it is   381

TRIALS
(*See* PILGRIMAGE AND CONFLICT)

TRINITY, THE   246–251
All glory be to God   2
Lead us, heavenly Father   344

TRUST
(*See also* ASSURANCE; FAITH AND ASPIRATION; HOPE, JOY, PEACE)
All glory be to God   2
Be still, my soul   77
Father, in thy   334
Give to the winds   337, 338
God of our life   97
How gentle God's   76
How lovely are thy   274
If thou but suffer   83
Lift thy head, O Zion   377
Through all the changing   81
Whate'er my God ordains   96
Who trusts in God   354, 355
Within the maddening maze   360

TRUTH
Book of books   253
Once to every man   441
Our God, to whom   86
We limit not the truth   259

UNITY
(*See* CHURCH: Nature and Unity)

VETERANS' DAY
(*See* NATION; PEACE: World)

VISION
Be thou my vision   391
Creation's Lord   303
These things shall be   450

VOCATION
(*See* CONSECRATION; LABOR OR LABOR DAY)

WATCHNIGHT
(*See* SEASONS: New Year)

WHITSUNDAY
(*See* CHURCH: Nature and Unity; HOLY SPIRIT)

WINTER
(*See* SEASONS: Changing)

WORLD–WIDE COMMUNION
(*See* CHURCH: Lord's Supper)

WORSHIP
(*See* CHURCH: Worship and Prayer)

YOUTH   488–495
(*See also* CONFIRMATION)
Be thou my vision   391
Father in heaven   392
God send us men   434
My faith it is   381
O how glorious   74
O Master Workman   412
Rejoice, ye pure   345
Take my life   404

ZEAL
Awake, awake to love   34
Awake, my soul, and with   32
Awake, my soul, stretch   362
Christ for the world   295
Christian, rise   416
Come, labor on   293
Faith of our fathers   365
Fight the good fight   367
Lead on, O King   375
March on, O soul   380
Onward, Christian soldiers   382
Rise up, O men   300
Soldiers of Christ   384
Stand up, stand up   385
We are living   427

Index of First Lines

	Number	Tune
A mighty fortress is our God	363	Ein' feste Burg
Abide with me; fast falls the eventide	209	Eventide
According to thy gracious word	284	Bangor
According to thy gracious word	285	Martyrdom
Adeste fideles	133	Adeste fideles
Again, as evening's shadow falls	46	Canonbury
Again, as evening's shadow falls	509	Song 5
Ah, holy Jesus, how hast thou offended	163	Herzliebster Jesu
Ah! think not the Lord delayeth	112	Alles ist an Gottes Segen
All beautiful the march of days	456	Forest Green
All creatures of our God and King	64	Lasst uns erfreuen
All glory be to God on high	2	Allein Gott in der Höh'
All glory, laud, and honor	155	St. Theodulph
All hail the power of Jesus' name	195	Coronation
All hail the power of Jesus' name	196	Miles Lane
All hail the power of Jesus' name	581	Coronation (*Descant*)
All my heart this night rejoices	123	Warum sollt ich
All my hope on God is founded	339	Meine Hoffnung
All people that on earth do dwell	4	Old Hundredth
All people that on earth do dwell	5	Old Hundredth (*Faux-bourdon*)
All praise to thee, for thou, O King divine	147	Engelberg
All praise to thee, my God, this night	57	Tallis' Canon
All praise to thee, my God, this night	56	Tallis' Canon (*Canonic form*)
All things are thine; no gift have we	537	Herr Jesu Christ
All things bright and beautiful	478	Royal Oak
All things come of thee, O Lord	536	
Alleluia! Alleluia! Hearts to heaven and voices raise	180	Weisse Flaggen
Alleluia! The strife is o'er, the battle done	181	Victory
Almighty Father, hear our prayer	520	*Response*
Alone thou goest forth, O Lord	159	Bangor
Amens	585–594	
Ancient of Days, who sittest throned in glory	249	Ancient of Days
And now, O Father, mindful of the love	292	Song 1
Angels, from the realms of glory	117	Regent Square
Angels holy, high and lowly	73	Llanherne
Angels we have heard on high	116	Gloria
As pants the hart for cooling streams	390	Martyrdom
As the sun doth daily rise	33	Innocents
As with gladness men of old	119	Dix
At even, ere the sun was set	55	Angelus
At the name of Jesus	197	King's Weston

Awake, awake to love and work!	34	Morning Song
Awake, my soul, and with the sun	32	Morning Hymn
Awake, my soul, stretch every nerve	362	Christmas
Away in a manger, no crib for his bed	137	Away in a manger
Battle Hymn of the Republic (*See* Mine eyes have seen the glory)		
Be known to us in breaking bread	280	St. Flavian
Be still, my soul: the Lord is on thy side	77	Finlandia
Be thou my vision, O Lord of my heart	391	Slane
Before Jehovah's aweful throne	9	Winchester New
Before Jehovah's aweful throne	10	Park Street
Before the cross of Jesus	161	St. Christopher
Before the day draws near its ending	508	Rendez à Dieu
Behold us, Lord, a little space	395	Dunfermline
Beneath the cross of Jesus	160	St. Christopher
Bless thou the gifts our hands have brought	538	Breslau
Blessed art thou, O Lord (Benedictus es, Domine)	569	*Chant*
Blessed be the Lord God of Israel (Benedictus)	568	*Chant*
Blessed Jesus, at thy word	212	Liebster Jesu
Blessed Jesus, here are we	279	Liebster Jesu
Blest are the pure in heart	214	Franconia
Blest be the tie that binds	272	Dennis
Blest be the tie that binds	273	Boylston
Book of books, our people's strength	253	Liebster Jesu
Bread of heaven, on thee we feed	281	Nicht so traurig
Bread of the world, in mercy broken	282	Rendez à Dieu
Bread of the world, in mercy broken	283	Eucharistic Hymn
Break forth, O beauteous heavenly light	118	Ermuntre dich
Break thou the bread of life	254	Bread of Life
Breathe on me, Breath of God	233	Potsdam
Breathe on me, Breath of God	234	Trentham
Brightest and best of the sons of the morning	126	Morning Star
Bring a torch, Jeannette, Isabella	124	Bring a torch
Built on the Rock the Church doth stand	270	Kirken den er et
Christ for the world we sing!	295	Italian Hymn
Christ is made the sure foundation	263	Regent Square
Christ is the world's true light	198	O Gott, du frommer Gott
Christ the Lord is risen again	183	Christ ist erstanden
Christ the Lord is risen today	182	Easter Hymn
Christ the Lord is risen today	582	Easter Hymn (*Descant*)
Christ, whose glory fills the skies	43	Ratisbon
Christian, dost thou see them	364	St. Andrew of Crete
Christian, rise and act thy creed	416	Innocents
Christians, awake, salute the happy morn	127	Yorkshire
City of God, how broad and far	261	Richmond
Come, and let us sweetly join	525	Savannah

Come down, O Love divine	239	Down Ampney
Come gracious Spirit, heavenly Dove	238	Mendon
Come, Holy Ghost, our souls inspire	231	Das walt' Gott vater
Come, Holy Ghost, our souls inspire	575	Veni Creator
Come, Holy Spirit, God and Lord!	235	Das neugeborne Kindelein
Come, Holy Spirit, heavenly Dove	240	St. Agnes
Come, labor on	293	Ora labora
Come, let us join with faithful souls	346	Azmon
Come, my soul, thou must be waking	506	Veni, anima mea
Come, risen Lord, and deign to be our guest	286	Sursum corda
Come, thou almighty King	246	Italian Hymn
Come, thou long-expected Jesus	103	Stuttgart
"Come unto me, ye weary"	315	Whitford
Come, ye faithful, raise the strain	185	St. Kevin
Come, ye faithful, raise the strain	186	Ave virgo virginum
Come, ye thankful people, come	461	St. George's Windsor
Come, ye thankful people, come (Thanksgiving Version)	462	
Comfort, comfort ye my people	104	Psalm 42
Create in me a clean heart, O God	528	*Chant*
Creation's Lord, we give thee thanks	303	Ramwold
Creator of the stars of night	113	Conditor alme
Crown him with many crowns	199	Diademata
Day is dying in the west	45	Chautauqua
Dear Lord and Father of mankind	341	Rest
Dear Master, in whose life I see	208	O Jesu Christe, wahres Licht
Doxology	514, 515	Old Hundredth
Draw nigh to thy Jerusalem, O Lord	156	Woodlands
Draw thou my soul, O Christ	318	St. Edmund
Each morning brings us fresh out-poured	498	All morgen ist
Enrich, Lord, heart, mouth, hands in me	527	Wulfrun
Eternal Father, strong to save	429	Melita
Eternal God, whose power upholds	294	Halifax
Eternal Ruler of the ceaseless round	275	Song 1
Fairest Lord Jesus	227	Schönster Herr Jesu
Faith of our fathers, living still	365	St. Catherine
Father almighty, bless us with thy blessing	333	Integer vitae
Father eternal, Ruler of creation	445	Langham
Father, give thy benediction	540	Alta Trinita beata
Father, hear the prayer we offer	368	Regensburg
Father in heaven, who lovest all	392	Saxby
Father, in thy mysterious presence kneeling	334	Donne secours
Father, to thee we look in all our sorrow	467	L'Omnipotent
Father, we praise thee, now the night is over	41	Christe sanctorum
Father, we thank thee for the night	479	Onslow
Father, we thank thee who hast planted	289	Rendez à Dieu
Fight the good fight with all thy might!	367	Pentecost
Fill thou my life, O Lord my God	396	Wigtown

Fling out the banner!	296	Waltham
For all the saints who from their labors rest	306	Sine nomine
For all the saints who from their labors rest	307	Sarum
For the beauty of the earth	66	Dix
For the brave of every race	308	Salzburg
Forgive, O Lord, our severing ways	262	O mensch sieh
Forth in thy name, O Lord, I go	406	Morning Hymn
Forty days and forty nights	148	Heinlein
Forward through the ages	383	St. Gertrude
Founded on thee, our only Lord	477	Mendon
From all that dwell below the skies	11	Old Hundredth
From all that dwell below the skies	12	Lasst uns erfreuen
From heaven above to earth I come	121	Vom Himmel hoch
Give to the winds thy fears	337	Ich halte treulich still
Give to the winds thy fears	338	St. Bride
Gloria Patri	511–513	
Glorious things of thee are spoken	267	Austrian Hymn
Glory be to God on high, Alleluia	65	Gwalchmai
Glory be to God on high (Gloria in Excelsis)	554	*Old Scottish chant*
Glory be to the Father (Gloria Patri)	511–513	
Glory be to thee, O Lord (Gloria tibi)	546, 547	
Go down Moses (*See* When Israel was in Egypt's land)	428	
Go, tell it on the mountain	488	Go tell it on the mountain
Go to dark Gethsemane	158	Redhead No. 76
God be in my head	393	Lytlington
God be in my head	543	God be in my head
God be with you till we meet again	61	Randolph
God be with you till we meet again	62	God be with you
God himself is with us	3	Arnsberg
God is my strong salvation	373	Mein Leben
God is working his purpose out	298	Purpose
God moves in a mysterious way	87	Dundee
God moves in a mysterious way	88	Dundee (*Faux-bourdon*)
God of earth and sea and heaven	316	Llansannan
God of grace and God of glory	366	Cwm Rhondda
God of our fathers, known of old	431	Folkingham
God of our fathers, whose almighty hand	433	National Hymn
God of our life, through all the circling years	97	Sandon
God of the earth, the sky, the sea	67	Herr Jesu Christ, mein's Lebens Licht
God of the living, in whose eyes	468	Gottlob, es geht
God of the nations, who from dawn of days	432	Toulon
God of the prophets, bless the prophets' sons	470	Toulon
God rest you merry, gentlemen	122	God rest you merry
God send us men whose aim 'twill be	434	Melrose
God, that madest earth and heaven	58	Ar hyd y nos
God the Omnipotent! King who ordainest	446	Russian Hymn
God's glory is a wondrous thing	369	Hummel

Golden breaks the dawn	486	Le p'ing
Good Christian men, rejoice	125	In dulci jubilo
Good Christian men rejoice and sing	184	Gelobt sei Gott
Gracious Spirit, dwell with me	245	Redhead No. 76
Great God, we sing that mighty hand	454	Truro
Great God who hast delivered us	577	Psalm 36
Guide me, O thou great Jehovah	93	Cwm Rhondda
Hail the day that sees him rise	205	Gwalchmai
Hail the glorious golden city	424	Llansannan
Hail to the Lord's anointed	105	Rockport
Hark! the herald angels sing	120	Mendelssohn
Hast thou not known, hast thou not heard	78	St. Magnus
Have faith in God, my heart	361	Southwell
Have mercy upon us	532	*Response*
He leadeth me, O blessed thought!	370	He leadeth me
He who would valiant be	371	St. Dunstan's
Heart and mind, possessions, Lord	394	Tana mana dhana
Heaven and earth, and sea, and air	75	Gott sei Dank
Here, O my Lord, I see thee face to face	287	Langran
Here, O my Lord, I see thee face to face	557	Adoro te
High in the heavens, eternal God	82	Truro
High o'er the lonely hills	42	Dawn
Hills of the North, rejoice	106	Little Cornard
Holy God, we praise thy name	247	Grosser Gott, wir loben dich
Holy, holy, holy, Lord God almighty	251	Nicaea
Holy, holy, holy, Lord God of hosts (Sanctus)	550, 551, 553	
Holy Spirit, Truth divine	242	Mercy
Holy Spirit, Truth divine	243	Vienna
Hope of the world, thou Christ of great compassion	398	Donne secours
How brightly shines the Morning Star (*See* O Morning Star, how fair)		
How firm a foundation, ye saints of the Lord	372	Adeste fideles
How gentle God's commands	76	Dennis
How lovely are thy dwellings fair	274	Bishopthorpe
How sweet the name of Jesus sounds	221	St. Peter
I greet thee, who my sure Redeemer art	207	Song 24
I know not how that Bethlehem's babe	149	Bangor
I look to thee in every need	92	O Jesu
I love thy kingdom, Lord	269	St. Thomas
I love to tell the story	317	Hankey
I love to think that Jesus saw	480	Childhood
I need thee every hour	342	Need
I sing a song of the saints of God	481	Grand Isle
I sing the mighty power of God	68	Ellacombe
I sought the Lord, and afterward I knew	408	Genevan Psalm 22
I sought the Lord, and afterward I knew	578	Peace
I think when I read that sweet story of old	483	Sweet Story

I to the hills will lift mine eyes	85	Dundee
I would be true, for there are those who trust me	489	Peek
If thou but suffer God to guide thee	83	Neumark
Immortal, invisible, God only wise	7	St. Denio
Immortal Love, forever full	230	Serenity
In Christ there is no East or West	414	St. Peter
In Christ there is no East or West	415	McKee
In heavenly love abiding	343	Nyland
In the bleak midwinter	128	Cranham
In the cross of Christ I glory	157	Rathbun
In the hour of trial	374	Penitence
It came upon the midnight clear	129	Carol
Jerusalem, my happy home	312	Land of Rest
Jerusalem the golden	309	Ewing
Jesus calls us, o'er the tumult	322	Galilee
Jesus calls us, o'er the tumult	323	Gott des Himmels
Jesus Christ is risen today, Alleluia	187	Llanfair
Jesus, Friend, so kind and gentle	277	Sicilian Mariners
Jesus, in thy dying woes	166	Swedish Litany
Jesus, in thy dying woes	167	Ton-Mân
Jesus, lover of my soul	210	Martyn
Jesus, lover of my soul	211	Aberystwyth
Jesus, priceless treasure	222	Jesu, meine Freude
Jesus, Savior, pilot me	213	Pilot
Jesus shall reign where'er the sun	202	Duke Street
Jesus, the very thought of thee	225	St. Agnes
Jesus, the very thought of thee	226	Windsor
Jesus, thou divine companion	409	Pleading Savior
Jesus, thou joy of loving hearts	290	Federal Street
Jesus, where'er thy people meet	402	Federal Street
Jesus, with thy Church abide	301	Vienna
Join all the glorious names	229	Croft's 136th
Joy dawned again on Easter Day	188	Puer nobis nascitur
Joy to the world! the Lord is come	130	Antioch
Joyful, joyful, we adore thee	8	Hymn to Joy
Judge eternal, throned in splendor	435	Rhuddlan
Just as I am, without one plea	319	Woodworth
Just as I am, without one plea	320	St. Crispin
Lamp of our feet, whereby we trace	256	Nun danket all'
Land of our birth (*See* Father in heaven, who lovest all)		
Lead, kindly Light, amid the encircling gloom	215	Lux benigna
Lead, kindly Light, amid the encircling gloom	216	Sandon
Lead me, Lord, lead me in thy righteousness	524	*Response*

Lead on, O King eternal	375	Lancashire
Lead us, heavenly Father, lead us	344	Dulce carmen
Lead us, O Father, in the paths of peace	376	Langran
Let all mortal flesh keep silence	107	Picardy
Let the whole creation cry	69	Salzburg
Let the words of my mouth	522	*Response*
Let there be light, Lord God of hosts	449	Elton
Let thy word abide in us, O Lord	518	*Response*
Let us break bread together	288	Let us break bread
Let us with a gladsome mind	70	Innocents
Let us with a gladsome mind	71	Chinese Melody
Life of ages, richly poured	236	Buckland
Lift thy head, O Zion, weeping	377	Magyar
Lift up your heads, ye mighty gates	114	Truro
"Lift up your hearts!"	352	Woodlands
Lift up your hearts (Sursum Corda)	552	
Lift up your hearts, ye people	189	Du meine Seele, singe
Lift up your hearts, ye people	190	Greenland
Lighten the darkness of our life's long night	386	Song 24
Little Jesus, sweetly sleep, do not stir	482	Rocking
Lo, God is here!	499	Aus Gnaden soll ich
Lo, how a Rose e'er blooming	131	Es ist ein' Ros'
Look, ye saints, the sight is glorious	203	Coronae
Lord, as to thy dear cross we flee	347	St. Bernard
Lord Christ, when first thou cam'st to men	325	Mit Freuden zart
Lord, dismiss us with thy blessing	63	Sicilian Mariners
Lord, enthroned in heavenly splendor	291	Bryn Calfaria
Lord, for the mercies of the night	501	Farrant
Lord God of hosts, how lovely (*See* How lovely are thy dwellings fair)		
Lord God of hosts, whose purpose, never swerving	411	Welwyn
Lord God of morning and of night	500	Mach's mit mir, Gott
Lord, have mercy upon us	544	*Response*
Lord, have mercy upon us (Kyrie)	545	
Lord, I want to be a Christian	353	I want to be a Christian
Lord Jesus Christ, be present now	521	Herr Jesu Christ
Lord Jesus Christ, our Lord most dear	278	Vom Himmel hoch
Lord Jesus, in the days of old	44	Vater unser
Lord Jesus, think on me	314	Southwell
Lord, now lettest thou thy servant depart in peace (Nunc dimittis)	572–574	*Chants*
Lord of all being, throned afar	89	Uffingham
Lord of all being, throned afar	90	Louvan
Lord of all hopefulness	217	Slane
Lord of our life, and God of our salvation	378	Iste Confessor (Rouen)
Lord of our life, and God of our salvation	379	Cloisters
Lord of true light, we gratefully adore thee	471	Welwyn
Lord, save thy world: in bitter need	452	Uffingham
Lord, speak to me, that I may speak	397	Canonbury

Lord, teach us how to pray aright (*See* O thou by whom we come to God)		
Lord, thou hast known our joy	472	Italian Hymn
Lord, thou hast searched me and dost know	576	Tender Thought
Lord, through this holy week of our salvation	168	Psalm 80
Lord, thy mercy now entreating	332	Ringe recht
Lord, thy word abideth	258	Ravenshaw
Lord, we thank thee for our brothers	268	Austrian Hymn
Lord, who throughout these forty days	153	St. Flavian
Love divine, all loves excelling	228	Beecher
Make me a captive, Lord	356	Llanllyfni
March on, O soul, with strength	380	Arthur's Seat
Master, no offering	405	Love's Offering
May the grace of Christ our Savior	539	Omni Die
May the words of our mouths	523	*Response*
Men, whose boast it is that ye	425	Ives
Mine eyes have seen the glory of the coming of the Lord	443	Battle Hymn of the Republic
More love to thee, O Christ	400	More love to thee
Morning has broken	38	Bunessan
Most perfect is the law of God	255	Stracathro
My country, 'tis of thee	437	America
My faith, it is an oaken staff	381	The Staff of Faith
My faith looks up to thee	348	Olivet
My God, accept my heart this day	321	St. Stephen
My God, I love thee: not because	313	Abbey
My God, I thank thee, who hast made	98	Wentworth
My song is love unknown	169	Rhosymedre
My soul doth magnify the Lord (Magnificat)	570, 571	*Chants*
Nearer, my God, to thee	351	Bethany
New every morning is the love	36	Melcombe
Not alone for mighty empire	439	Austrian Hymn
Now cheer our hearts this eventide	54	Ach bleib bei uns
Now God be with us, for the night is closing	59	Diva servatrix
Now in the days of youth	490	Diademata
Now let every tongue adore thee!	24	Wachet auf
Now, on land and sea descending	52	Vesper Hymn
Now praise we great and famous men	476	Ach Gott und Herr
Now thank we all our God	29	Nun danket
Now the day is over	51	Merrial
Now the day is over	510	Eudoxia
O be joyful in the Lord!	26	Rock of Ages
O be joyful in the Lord!	27	Finlay
O be joyful in the Lord (Jubilate Deo)	565–567	*Chants*
O beautiful for spacious skies	440	Materna
O brother man, fold to thy heart thy brother	410	Intercessor

O Christ, thou Lamb of God	556	
O come, all ye faithful, joyful and triumphant	132	Adeste fideles
O come and mourn with me awhile!	164	St. Cross
O come, let us sing unto the Lord (Venite)	562–564	*Chants*
O come, O come, Emmanuel	110	Veni Emmanuel
O Day of God, draw nigh	444	St. Michael
O for a closer walk with God	349	Caithness
O for a closer walk with God	350	Beatitudo
O for a thousand tongues to sing	223	Azmon
O gladsome light, O grace	49	Nunc dimittis
O God, above the drifting years	297	Duke Street
O God, beneath thy guiding hand	438	Duke Street
O God of Bethel, by whose hand	389	Dundee
O God of earth and altar	436	Llangloffan
O God of love, O King of peace	447	Hesperus
O God of youth, whose Spirit in our hearts is stirring	491	Lynne
O God, thou art the Father	248	Durrow
O God, we praise thee, and confess	18	Tallis' Ordinal
O God, within whose sight	265	Serug
O gracious God, whose constant care	492	Lobt Gott ihr Christen
O holy city, seen of John	420	Morning Song
O Holy Spirit, enter in	244	Wie schön leuchtet
O how glorious, full of wonder	74	In Babilone
O Jesu sweet, O Jesu mild	135	O Jesulein süss
O Jesus, I have promised	218	Angel's Story
O Jesus, thou art standing	329	St. Hilda
O Lamb of God (Agnus Dei)	555	
O Light that knew no dawn	407	Harewood
O little town of Bethlehem	134	St. Louis
O Lord, almighty God, thy works	473	York
O Lord, almighty God, thy works	474	York (*Faux-bourdon*)
O Lord and Master of us all	224	Walsall
O Lord of hosts, whose glory fills	475	Wareham
O Lord of life, where'er they be	469	Gelobt sei Gott
O Lord, open thou our lips	534	*Versicle*
O Lord, turn not thy face from them	580	Contrition
O love, how deep, how broad, how high	150	Deus tuorum militum
O love, how deep, how broad, how high	151	Deo Gracias
O love of God, how strong and true	99	Eisenach
O Love that wilt not let me go	399	St. Margaret
O Master, let me walk with thee	418	Maryton
O Master Workman of the race	412	Kingsfold
O Morning Star, how fair and bright	145	Wie schön leuchtet
O my soul, bless God, the Father	100	Stuttgart
O perfect Love, all human thought transcending	465	O Perfect Love
O sacred Head, now wounded	170	Passion Chorale
O say can you see by the dawn's early light	496	Star-Spangled Banner

INDEX OF FIRST LINES

O sons and daughters, let us sing!	191	O filii et filiae
O Spirit of the living God	299	Melcombe
O Splendor of God's glory bright	39	Puer nobis nascitur
O Splendor of God's glory bright	40	Splendor Paternae
O thou by whom we come to God	336	Song 67
O thou by whom we come to God	530	Wigtown
O thou great friend to all the sons of men	219	Ffigysbren
O thou to whose all-searching sight	324	Grace Church
O thou who hearest prayer	526	*Response*
O thou who through this holy week	154	Walsall
O what their joy and their glory must be	310	O quanta qualia
O where are kings and empires now	264	St. Anne
O Word of God incarnate	252	Munich
O word of pity, for our pardon pleading	173	Zu meinem Herrn
O worship the King, all glorious above	6	Lyons
O Zion, haste, thy mission high fulfilling	302	Tidings
Of the Father's love begotten	111	Divinum mysterium
On Jordan's bank the Baptist's cry	115	Winchester New
On this day earth shall ring	136	Personent hodie
Once to every man and nation	441	Ebenezer
One holy Church of God appears	266	St. James
One who is all unfit to count	330	Wigtown
Onward, Christian soldiers	382	St. Gertrude
Open now thy gates of beauty	503	Unser Herrscher
Our Father, by whose name	466	Rhosymedre
Our God, our help in ages past	1	St. Anne
Our God, our help in ages past	583	St. Anne (*Descant*)
Our God, to whom we turn	86	Steadfast
Praise be to thee (Laus tibi)	549	
Praise God from whom all blessings flow	514	Old Hundredth (Original)
Praise God from whom all blessings flow	515	Old Hundredth (Altered)
Praise, my soul, the King of heaven	16	Praise my soul
Praise, O praise our God and King	463	Monkland
Praise our God above	487	Hsuan p'ing
Praise the Lord, his glories show	19	Llanfair
Praise the Lord! ye heavens, adore him	13	Hyfrydol
Praise thou the Lord, O my soul, sing praises	17	Lobe den Herren, O meine Seele
Praise to God, immortal praise	464	Dix
Praise to God, your praises bring	458	Savannah
Praise to the Holiest in the height	497	St. Mary
Praise to the Lord, the Almighty	15	Lobe den Herren
Rejoice, O land, in God thy might	430	Wareham
Rejoice, O people, in the mounting years	304	Yorkshire
Rejoice, the Lord is King!	204	Darwall's 148th
Rejoice, ye pure in heart	345	Marion
Remember all the people	484	Far-Off Lands
Ride on, ride on in majesty	175	St. Drostane
Ride on, ride on in majesty	176	The King's Majesty

Ring out, wild bells, to the wild sky	453	Deus tuorum militum
Rise up, O men of God!	300	Festal Song
Rock of ages, cleft for me	358	Toplady
Rock of ages, cleft for me	359	Redhead No. 76
Savior, again to thy dear name we raise	60	Ellers
Savior, like a shepherd lead us	327	Bradbury
Savior, thy dying love	331	Something for Jesus
Send down thy truth, O God	237	St. Michael
Silent night, holy night	138	Stille Nacht
Sing praise to God who reigns above	20	Mit Freuden zart
Soldiers of Christ, arise	384	Diademata
Son of God, eternal Savior	413	Weisse Flaggen
Spirit divine, attend our prayers	241	Nun danket all'
Spirit of God, descend upon my heart	232	Morecambe
Stand up and bless the Lord	25	Carlisle
Stand up, stand up for Jesus	385	Webb
Still, still with thee, when purple morning breaketh	37	Consolation
Stille Nacht, heilige Nacht	139	Stille Nacht
Strong Son of God, immortal Love	357	Rockingham
Summer ended, harvest o'er	579	Freuen wir uns all in ein
Sun of my soul, thou Savior dear	50	Hursley
Sunset to sunrise changes now	165	Kedron
Sweet Savior, bless us ere we go	542	Gottlob, es geht
Take my life, and let it be	404	Vienna
Teach me, my God and King	401	Mornington
Teach me, O Lord, the way of thy statutes	517	
Ten thousand times ten thousand	311	Alford
Thanks be to thee, O Christ (Gratia tibi)	548	
The Church's one foundation	260	Aurelia
The day of resurrection!	192	Lancashire
The day of the Lord is at hand	417	Remember the Poor
The day thou gavest, Lord, is ended	47	Les Commandemens de Dieu
The day thou gavest, Lord, is ended	48	St. Clement
The duteous day now closeth	53	Innsbruck
The first Nowell the angel did say	141	The First Nowell
The God of Abraham praise	14	Leoni
The head that once was crowned with thorns	200	St. Magnus
The heavens declare thy glory, Lord	257	Uxbridge
The King of love my shepherd is	79	Dominus regit me
The King of love my shepherd is	80	St. Columba
The King shall come when morning dawns	201	St. Stephen
The Lord be with you	531, 533	*Versicles*
The Lord is rich and merciful	328	Shepherds' Pipes
The Lord will come and not be slow	95	York
The Lord's my shepherd, I'll not want	84	Crimond
The man who once has found abode	91	Tallis' Canon
The morning light is breaking	305	Webb

The sacrifices of God	529	*Chant*
The Son of God goes forth to war	388	All Saints New
The spacious firmament on high	72	Creation
The strife is o'er (*See* Alleluia! The strife is o'er, the battle done)		
The summer days are come again	457	Forest Green
The voice of God is calling	426	Meirionydd
The whole bright world rejoices now	194	Hilariter
There is a green hill far away	171	Horsley
There is a green hill far away	172	Meditation
There's a wideness in God's mercy	101	In Babilone
There's a wideness in God's mercy	102	Wellesley
These things shall be: a loftier race	450	Truro
They cast their nets in Galilee	340	Georgetown
Thine is the glory	193	Judas Maccabeus
This is my Father's world	485	Terra beata
This is the day the Lord hath made	504	Nun danket all'
Those who love and those who labor follow in the way of Christ	403	Alta Trinita beata
Thou didst leave thy throne and thy kingly crown	326	Margaret
Thou God of all, whose spirit moves	419	Old 22nd
Thou Judge by whom each empire fell	442	Nun freut euch
Thou wilt keep him in perfect peace	541	Duke's Tune
Throned upon the awful tree	174	Arfon
Through all the changing scenes of life	81	Wiltshire
Through the night of doubt and sorrow	387	St. Asaph
Thy kingdom come, O Lord	448	St. Cecilia
Thy Word is a lamp unto my feet	516	
'Tis midnight, and on Olive's brow	178	Olive's Brow
'Tis winter now; the fallen snow	455	Danby
To my humble supplication	519	Mon Dieu, prête-moi l'oreille
To thee before the close of day	507	Jam lucis
Turn back, O man, forswear thy foolish ways	451	Old 124th
'Twas on that dark and doleful night	558	Bourbon
Unto thy temple, Lord, we come	276	Eisenach
Unto us a boy is born!	142	Puer nobis
Wake, awake, for night is flying	108	Wachet auf
Watchman, tell us of the night	109	Aberystwyth
We all believe in one true God	250	Wir glauben all' an einen Gott
We are climbing Jacob's ladder	495	Jacob's Ladder
We are living, we are dwelling	427	Blaenhafren
We bear the strain of earthly care	220	Hermon
We come unto our fathers' God	271	Nun freut euch
We gather together to ask the Lord's blessing	21	Kremser
We give thee but thine own	535	Yattendon 46
We limit not the truth of God	259	Old 22nd
We may not climb the heavenly steeps (*See* Immortal Love, forever full)		

We plow the fields and scatter	460	Wir pflügen
We praise thee, Lord, with earliest morning ray	502	Ainsworth 97
We praise thee, O God, our Redeemer, Creator	22	Kremser
We praise thee, O God (Te Deum laudamus)	559–561	*Chants*
We thank thee, Lord, thy paths of service lead	421	Field
We three kings of Orient are	143	Kings of Orient
We worship thee, almighty Lord	28	Vi lofve dig, O store Gud
We would·be building; temples still undone	494	Finlandia
We would see Jesus; lo! his star is shining	152	Cushman
Were you there when they crucified my Lord	179	Were you there
What a friend we have in Jesus	335	Erie
What child is this, who, laid to rest	140	Greensleeves
What star is this, with beams so bright	144	Puer nobis nascitur
Whate'er my God ordains is right	96	Was Gott tut
When all thy mercies, O my God	94	Tallis' Ordinal
When I survey the wondrous cross	177	Hamburg
When Israel was in Egypt's land	428	Go down Moses
When morning gilds the skies	35	Laudes Domini
When my love to God grows weak	162	Song 13
When Stephen, full of power and grace	493	Wellington Square
When the sun had sunk to rest (*See* Angels we have heard on high)		
When through the whirl of wheels, and engines humming	422	Lombard Street
Where cross the crowded ways of life	423	Germany
While shepherds watched their flocks by night	146	Winchester Old
Who trusts in God, a strong abode	354	Was mein Gott will
Who trusts in God, a strong abode	355	Bishopgarth
With songs and honors sounding loud	459	Ellacombe
Within the maddening maze of things	360	Song 67
Worship the Lord in the beauty of holiness	31	Monsell
Ye holy angels bright	23	Darwall's 148th
Ye servants of God, your Master proclaim	206	Hanover
Ye servants of God, your Master proclaim	584	Hanover (*Descant*)
Ye watchers and ye holy ones	30	Lasst uns erfreuen
You that have spent the silent night	505	Old 22nd